LINDSAY ANDERSON

The Diaries

with selected letters

LINDSAY ANDERSON

The Diaries

Edited by Paul Sutton

A gentle questioning look that cannot hide
A soul incapable of remorse or rest;
A revolutionary soldier kneeling to be blessed.

W. B. Yeats

Methuen

Published by Methuen 2005

First published by Methuen in hardback in 2004

This paperback published in 2005
by Methuen Publishing Limited,
11–12 Buckingham Gate, London SW1E 6LB

Methuen Publishing Limited Reg. No. 3543167

Typeset by Country Setting, Kingsdown, Kent
Printed and bound in Great Britain
by Bookmarque Ltd, Croydon, Surrey

A CIP catalogue record for this book is available
from the British Library

ISBN 0 413 77398 1

Contents

Lindsay Anderson in John Ford country.
Monument Valley Navajo Tribal Park, USA, 1979.

Preface

by Malcolm McDowell

I remember an evening in 1991, on an incredible yacht in the Cannes harbour, singing show-tunes with Lindsay and with Ernest Lehman, who wrote *North by Northwest* and who was going to write a film for us. We were singing 'Bye, Bye Birdie'. Lindsay was in full voice, and we were in dinner jackets. We had a most magnificent night. I was there because my Russian film, *Assassin of the Tsar*, had been entered in competition in the Festival.

When I was making the film, I got Lindsay to come out to Russia, supposedly for a retrospective of mine in Moscow, Leningrad and Kiev. Any retrospective of mine had to include Lindsay because the three films I made with him are the cornerstone of my career. So I suggested that the organisers invite him as well, which they happily and readily did. Lindsay came out to the set on the day when the Tsar and the Tsarina and the children were being shot. He was quite taken by it. And then we had this amazing trip across Russia.

He wrote to me after seeing the film and was complimentary about my perform-ance; when Lindsay went to see a friend's performance he would be as supportive as he could be and as truthful as he dare. After praising my performance he wrote: 'But the film doesn't work.' And he explained why it didn't work. And every time he said that he was absolutely right. He wrote: 'It's awfully dangerous, I think, for directors to write their own scripts. Your fellow has great ability in creating his own reality: but perhaps lacks the intellectual clarity you need to be able to combine fantasy or imagination and reality in the way that this conception demands . . .'

Lindsay was forty-seven when I met him; a young, virile director with boundless energy. And it was a privilege for me to have been around him in my formative years. He trusted my instincts as an actor – his direction bascially was, 'Go on then. Do it' – but he'd step in quickly when he saw something wrong:

'What *on earth* are you doing? Let's do that again. Now do it right.'

And you'd know what he meant.

'I know, I know, okay. I'll do it again. How's about this?'

'That's better, Malcolm.'

It was an incredible experience making *If* . . . . for a kid who really didn't know how to work in film. Lindsay passed on his knowledge to me in many ways, often subtle, but sometimes not. He taught me that, as an actor, you must be believable before you can do anything else. Only when you've established reality can the performance move on. He hated falsity.

When he was working, Lindsay was always very precise, and always seemed to have a very great confidence in what he was doing; but Lindsay the man (as opposed to Lindsay the artist) was full of doubts, and he was quite depressed for a while. After making *O Lucky Man!* he kept saying, 'That's my last film. That's it. I'm done.'

O Lucky Man! was a difficult shoot. It seemed to go on for ever. It was a much more ambitious project than *If* . . . ., which was set in a public school, something that Lindsay knew intimately having been there, and even having been to the public school where we shot it. *O Lucky Man!* was a bigger challenge: a tapestry on film that took on everything from big business, music and science, to politics and Third World countries. And when we came to make the film, my relationship to Lindsay had changed. On *If* . . . ., I was the absolute pupil ready to learn everything, but by the time we came to make *O Lucky Man!* I'd acted in *A Clockwork Orange* and a few other films. Lindsay was still the Master, but our relationship now was more comrades together than master and pupil. It was a delicate thing to move from one thing to the other. But we got on very well.

The test bed for *O Lucky Man!* was *The White Bus*, an incredible film that stands alone as a great work of art, but which served as a master's sketch before he did the big painting on canvas. It has got every element that goes into *O Lucky Man!*, even down to the changes to and from black and white. It was his sketch for the big canvas and it is brilliant. And it is quite unlike any British film that had been made before it. Lindsay loved old Hollywood films; he would show me the films of John Ford and the films that starred his favourite actresses – Jean Arthur, Norma Shearer, Mary Astor – and he would say: 'Did you see how she said that line? Wonderful!' and he would go into raptures. He had a fantasy about being a Hollywood director, but, of course it was only a fantasy. He would not have been able to make his kind of films within the Hollywood system. He was not a director for hire. He turned his back on Hollywood to make *Britannia Hospital*. A Lindsay Anderson Film. I think it's a great film; an incredible piece of work.

What comes through brilliantly in the diaries is Lindsay's love of his friends. He hardly talked about Richard Harris to me but it's clear from the diaries that Lindsay loved him and that he wanted to help Richard to become a truly great actor. I think that Richard's performance in *This Sporting Life* is one of the greatest performances by a British actor on film, and it always will be. It will always stand the test of time. But Richard was into fame and fortune. He was inundated with offers, jetting all over the place, and he wanted it all. I suppose, to him, Lindsay had served a purpose. It's amazing to read that Lindsay felt like a whipped dog around him – which, of course, would probably have goaded Richard into treating him a lot worse, because he picked up on that weakness and he exploited it. But things change. And people move on. On the set, or on the stage, if I was getting a bit uppity, Lindsay would say to me: 'Be careful, Malcolm. You're getting like Richard Harris.' A stern rebuke.

I was very moved that Richard came to the memorial evening for Lindsay at the Royal Court. Richard knew. He knew how extraordinarily talented Lindsay was.

Rachel Roberts, Richard's co-star in *This Sporting Life*, was a great talent, unique but also very insecure; and she often hid her insecurity in alcohol. Lindsay was the only person who knew how to treat her. The time he put into Rachel was beyond belief. Most people would say to her, 'Rachel, I've heard all this before. It's the same old song.' But Lindsay really listened to her. He tried so hard, really. He was angry with her when she died, when she committed suicide. He was angry that she had given up, and that she had pissed it all away. But he loved her and he would remember too the fun he had with her. We had so much fun shooting *O Lucky Man!* with Rachel. I remember vividly the scene with Ralph Richardson at a dinner table, where she is playing a Lady and Lindsay is saying to her:

'Now Rachel, for God's sake, what are you doing? You're supposed to be a Lady.'

'Linds. I am a Lady, for fuck's sake!'

'Yes, really ladylike.'

He'd tease her and she would go crazy. Then he'd say: 'Show me your look.' And she would do a sort of ridiculous Lady-look and he would laugh. And we'd all laugh.

I loved Rachel too. When Lindsay came out to LA, we'd go out to dinner with Rachel. And, of course, she would get drunk and we would have to get her home.

Over the years, the friendship is what I come back to. I think about it more than the great work that we did together. He was such a loyal friend. And God, it pained me so much, in the last few years of his life, when he couldn't get his projects going. A very great man was passed over for being too old, too this or too that. It was painful. I felt bad for him. But there you are. That's the business.

Introduction

Lindsay Anderson's 1968 film, *If. . . .* , a film about England and Englishness, was the first with a British setting and a British cast, made by a British film-maker, to win the Palme d'Or for the Best Film at the Cannes Film Festival. It was the culmination of twenty years of work making truthfully human 'Free Cinema' films that challenged the mediocrity of the middle-class British film industry, and was the fruit of Anderson's first-hand experience of the Czech, Polish and Indian New Waves led by Milos Forman, Andrzej Wajda and Satyajit Ray.

An important spur to Anderson's desire to make socially relevant films was seeing the much praised 1946 feature, *The Way to the Stars*, made by the ex-prime minister's son, Anthony Asquith. Asquith's film about life on a British air base at war was, to Anderson, an 'obviously contrived piece of artifice'. He had lived that life and he knew that the film was false. RAF officers didn't have stiff upper lips, at least not the ones he had seen as an undergraduate in a gay bar in Oxford. Officers, in Anderson's army experience, swore, got drunk, played cards, and took a perverse pride in bullying. The whips and torturers of *If. . . .* are drawn, at least in part, from Anderson's experience of the British army at war. He was himself a soldier's son, a child of the Empire. His father, Alexander Vass Anderson, was a Scot, born in North India, who rose to the rank of Major-General. His mother, Estelle Bell Gasson, was born in Queenstown, South Africa. On 17 April 1923 Lindsay Anderson was born in Bangalore, South India; he came to England in 1926 when his parents separated. Ten years later his mother married Major Cuthbert Sleigh, with whom she bought a mansion, 'Cringletie', in Camberley, and Anderson was packed off to public school. During the Second World War he spent a short spell in India when stationed there with the British army Intelligence Corps.

His abhorrence of the falsities of the Asquith film, and of a great many British films he had seen, played a fundamental role in shaping his core ideas as a director. But to describe Anderson simply as cantankerous or negative would be wrong: only a man who loved his country could make the films that he made. The key to an understanding of Anderson's art and personality lies not so much in reading his diary criticisms of people and products he found wanting, as in studying the things that inspired him. In the early years of the diaries, one finds the moments of epiphany, such as his seeing

Herbert Farjeon's *Light and Shade* revue which, in sketches and song, successfully fused poetry with satire in a manner that he himself would perfect with *O Lucky Man!* Of great interest to him were the films of John Ford, in particular the western *My Darling Clementine* and the contemporary war film *They Were Expendable*. In these two films, Anderson saw a vision of a life of patriotic and public duty, lived within a moral framework of manly togetherness that, for a young man raised in the often coarse and sometimes brutal male worlds of prep and public schools and the British army, seemed to be the very model of reason.

From 1957 to 1975, Anderson worked as a director at the Royal Court Theatre, both bastion and cannon of the anti-conservative New Wave, to take on the theatre of the 'liberal bourgeoisie' which had reduced the art to a parade of West End drawing-room dramas that knew of and cared little for life. Here he introduced London audiences to the work of Max Frisch, Alun Owen and David Storey, and to the actors Albert Finney and Brian Cox. He directed Ben Kingsley's professional stage debut at Chichester, ended his Court career with the first successful production of Joe Orton's *What The Butler Saw*, and set up a West End repertory company that alternated his own translation of Chekhov's *The Seagull* with a new play by Ben Travers. The Travers play – *The Bed Before Yesterday* – was so successful it took Anderson on a world tour from Pittsburgh to Sydney. He directed Ralph Richardson and Celia Johnson in *The Kingfisher*; Rex Harrison and Claudette Colbert in a new production of the play on Broadway; Malcolm McDowell and Mary Steenburgen in *Holiday* at the Old Vic; and Joan Plowright, Frank Finlay and Leslie Phillips in *The Cherry Orchard*. And for every revival there were masterful productions of challenging new plays by David Storey. Between 1969 and 1992, Lindsay Anderson directed the world's first productions of nine Storey plays, including three which won the New York Drama Critics' Prize: *Home*, *The Changing Room* and *The Contractor*.

His watchword was 'truthfulness'. His goal in both the theatre and the cinema was not the 'naturalistic' but the 'true'. Success was to be judged not in terms of the box-office but in the artistic authenticity of the project and the performances. There could be no falsity. His seminal 1959 production of *Serjeant Musgrave's Dance*, John Arden's play sparked by a British military atrocity in Cyprus, which opened to a cacophony of complaint from the critics and often played to a house less than a quarter full, was to him a triumph. His 'sold out' shows of *The Kingfisher* he regarded as artistic failures:

> The show is a hit, but I have not succeeded in effecting the crowd-pleasing performances of the two stars – including gross 'takes' to the audience, stylised gestures, etc. But people love it. Each laugh is like a sword in my side. So I am reduced to crying all the way to my accountant.

He spent a working lifetime rejecting 'box-office' offers from the National Theatre, from impresarios in the West End and on Broadway, and from film companies in England and in Hollywood. At a low point in his career, in the mid-1980s, in a rare rude spirit of 'let's take the money and run', he took on commissions to film George Michael in China and a three-part American mini-series, *Glory! Glory!* (the latter undertaken in part to gain an insight into how John Ford made personal work within the studio system); but once the work was under way, these films became personal to him.

In 1965, when making *The White Bus*, a blueprint for the trilogy of epic comic satires comprising *If. . . .*, *O Lucky Man!* and *Britannia Hospital* (three films co-written with David Sherwin), Anderson toured industrial Manchester, looking for locations. He saw sights that almost beggared belief: 'Everywhere we go one thinks – why has none of this been on film?' The low-point in his career in the mid-80s can be traced to the lack of public response to *Britannia Hospital*, his film about the nation state being torn apart by Margaret Thatcher's private enterprise culture. In 1981, when rioters were on the streets of Liverpool and London, and strike action and terrorist bombings had almost become a way of life, Anderson turned his back on development deals with three American studios to make the kind of film he *had* to make. Yet the lack of response to the film came as a severe blow to him, as he records in his diary in January 1985:

> When we did *Britannia Hospital* I could really believe there was an audience out there . . . who would receive my work with friendly comprehension, with complicity! I'm afraid the rejection of that work has hit me hard, shaken my confidence.

In his work as a film-maker, England and its Empire were his inspiration. But it needed something else actually to get him to work. As he himself observes, he was born innately lazy and functioned best in collaboration. He needed writers whom he could goad and lean on; he needed a wholly sympathetic technical crew, and he needed actors who could inspire him. The inspirational actors included Serge Reggiani, Albert Finney, Richard Harris and Malcolm McDowell. But the person who pushed him into making films was Lois Smith (then Sutcliffe), a subscriber to the film journal, *Sequence*, which he had founded as an undergraduate at Oxford. Deciding that he was the right man to make a film about engineering innovations in her husband's factory in Wakefield, Smith arrived unannounced at Cringletie, and persuaded Anderson to follow forth into the mines and engineering sheds of West Yorkshire. Forty-six years later she was with him, at a lakeside in France, when he died.

Serge Reggiani came to notice in films by Marcel Carné, Jean-Pierre Melville and Henri-Georges Clouzot. Anderson befriended him on the set of the British film *The Secret People*, which he was chronicling for publication. Reggiani hired Anderson to assist him with a production of *Hamlet* in Paris three years before Anderson's first professional theatre work in London. In 1960 in London, Anderson directed Albert Finney on stage in *The Lily White Boys* and, later, in the world premiere of *Billy Liar*. He wanted to film Finney in an adaptation of David Storey's novel *This Sporting Life*, but the partnership faltered because Finney was so successful in his other projects (Reisz and Richardson's *Saturday Night and Sunday Morning* had made him a star) that he wouldn't succumb to Anderson's need for an on-tap collaborator and muse. The role fell to Richard Harris, an Irishman whose magnificent lust for life, emotional generosity, and animalistic vigour put Anderson in such a spin that for four years he trailed Harris across half the world, from London, New York, Ravenna and Rome to Mexico and Leningrad, mapping out an ambitious plan of work. This adventure began in Tahiti, where Harris was filming *Mutiny On the Bounty*, and Anderson came a-calling with a copy of a script.

When the appeal of working with Harris waned, Anderson took inspiration not so much from a man but from a movement. In the films of the Czech New Wave, he saw the goals of his own Free Cinema films made concrete: truthful poetic features realised with an artistry that seemed beyond the imagination and comprehension of his fellow Britons, particularly those who controlled film distribution and wrote the press. On 8 April 1965, he travelled to Zrouch, in Czechoslovakia, and saw a scene so profound it stayed with him all his life. Milos Forman was shooting the final scenes of *A Blonde in Love*, with the young star, Vladimir Pucholt. The harmony of the cast and crew, with two writers in attendance should Forman feel the need to call on them, was, to Anderson, a vision of paradise.

Later that year, he hired Forman's cameraman, Miroslav Ondricek, to shoot *The White Bus*. The two men would work together again on *If....* and *O Lucky Man!* and planned to work together on the feature films of *The Old Crowd* and *The Cherry Orchard*, unrealised projects that fell at the feet of their ineffective producers. When, in 1990, Anderson was the president of the jury of the Karlovy Vary festival, and the first real manifestation of critical ill health befell him, Ondricek was not only on his jury but by his side.

In the same year as his famous springtime in Zrouch, a brotherhood of international film-makers seemed to be emerging. It was born, perhaps, at the Cannes Film Festival in 1960, when the festival audience booed Michelangelo Antonioni's *L'Avventura*, only to be silenced by Anderson's friend, the *Variety* correspondent, Gene Moskowitz, getting to his feet and shouting at them. That day, an international group of film-makers petitioned the press to champion Antonioni's film. In 1965, the festival at Cannes was followed by a film-makers' conference at Pesaro on the banner theme of 'Criticism and New Cinema' – the new national cinema movements that were dominating national box-offices to the chagrin of the old establishment critics. Anderson, sacked from a film reviewing job at the *New Statesman* for choosing to write about a film by Andrzej

Wajda instead of joining in the press praise for *The Bridge on the River Kwai*, was one of the speakers. He left the conference fuelled and ambitious in a way that he could never be in Britain, where the industry goal was (and remains) to make something that the most undiscerning American might like. The fruit of this new-found determination can be seen in the films that followed: after making *The Singing Lesson*, a delicious little film, in Poland, and fired by a first script by David Sherwin, Anderson made *If . . . .* , the British film that conquered Cannes and established at a stroke his world reputation.

But Hollywood 'product' has become more inane and more pervasive (the films of the British Establishment are long gone), as Anderson highlighted in his Edinburgh Film Festival lecture in 1993. Stepping in at the last minute when an American film-maker dropped out, he apologised for not being American:

> I'm sorry I haven't time to deplore the present triumph of the media – and the surrender of the media to the values of Hollywood; the Oscars; the American faces on the cover of the *Radio Times*; the vital importance of American names. Let me remind you that not a single one of those British renaissance films [made by Tony Richardson, Karel Reisz and myself] featured an American. Today *Tom Jones* would have to be played by Tom Cruise.

Despite the predominance of Hollywood films today, one doesn't have to look hard to see the Anderson influence in the films of men with whom he worked or corresponded, or whom he befriended: film-makers such as Stephen Frears, Michael Winterbottom, Stephen Daldry, Robert Benton, Richard Linklater and the cine-literate directors of the American Independents.

Anderson started writing his diary in 1942, when he was eighteen years old, preparing for active service in the Second World War and about to study Classics at Oxford. For much of the rest of his life, he used the diary as a means to organise his thoughts, to spur himself into action, and to pass the time on long international flights. As with any diary, there are omissions. For example, there are no diary records from August 1955 until January 1960 (thus missing out his first theatrical triumphs); only four diary days of 1960 have survived; only three days in 1961 have any record; and no diary has yet surfaced for 1968 (the year he made *If . . . .*). In his last years, the diary took the form of notebook jottings and copies of letters dictated to his secretary. Some of the gaps in the narrative have been filled using extracts from these letters, letters from friends, and transcripts from my conversations with his colleagues.

In the most poignant passages, the diary becomes a self-analytical tract, or poem, that reaches into the heart of light and shade within himself. In the diary we can trace, too, the genesis and the growth of a body of films and plays with a clarity and a thoroughness that is rarely possible. For example, in 1987, in Maine, he closed his feature film career, making good a promise to a friend by directing Bette Davis in *The Whales of August*. In the diaries, many years earlier, we read of boyhood visits to the cinema to see films starring Bette Davis; in the Second World War, stationed, like his father before him, in India, we read of a bicycle trip into New Delhi to see Davis in *Mr Skeffington*, and in the busy year of 1965, he was a guest of Bette Davis in New England, coaxing her into a new play on Broadway that was never to be. This is all a part of the fabric of life, an artist's life, a half-century of weavings of work-thoughts and meetings that coheres into a portrait not just of an artist, but his art, and his time.

So that the diaries could be published in one volume, they have been edited down from perhaps a million words into the current form. The unused material consists mostly of day-to-day accounts from 1965, his 1985 production of *Hamlet* in Washington, and the filming of *Glory! Glory!* in Toronto. Any selection is bound to leave out material that would be valued by some. I've included what I feel to be the essential Anderson: the entries that give the clearest picture of a remarkable man, the society in which lived, and a body of work that up till now has never been given the attention it deserves.

Paul Sutton
Cambridge, 2004

1

The Early Years

Cheltenham College – Oxford University
Army – India – Reorientation

'I find events shaping themselves more and more:
sickness and impatience with the army, rebelliousness
and unwise self-assertion, tiredness and slackness.'

1 January 1942
One of my principal New Year's resolutions is to keep a journal. In this journal I shall write only when I have something to say; its purpose is both to remind me in after years of how I felt and what I did at this time and also – quite unashamedly – to give me literary exercise. It should help improve my style and my ability to express myself and many of the incidents it records will no doubt prove excellent copy. I will however not tell lies in order to improve a story.

I am not sure whether or not it will be absolutely frank: I am not used to writing solely to myself – and that perhaps is why I am so quick to mistrust published diaries. So at first at any rate I will probably be fairly reserved. And yet this is absurd: either I am writing for myself, or for a friend or friends or for publication. I can cross out the last – though, of course, I can easily expurgate it if necessary. Nor am I writing for my friends. I will therefore resolve to be utterly frank – a resolution which I do not think I can possibly keep! So here we go.

5 January 1942
I went today for my medical exam at Aldershot [for entry into the armed forces]. It was held in a fairly large hall in which various cubicles and compartments had been erected. After filling up forms etc. in an office outside, I went into the hall and was instructed to remove all clothing save trousers and coat. My first duty was to pass water into a glass jar, which I managed without much difficulty. Whether it was due to the large plate of oxtail soup which Mum gave me for lunch, or the bout of flu, my urine was

unfortunately 'cloudy'. I then passed down the row of cubicles in each of which was a doctor. In the passageway stood five Valor stoves round which I warmed my toes while waiting my turn. I had to wait a very long time since unfortunately preceded by a complete moron. On being asked what grade of education he had reached he said he couldn't remember and didn't seem to know even what school he had been to. The incredulous doctor then asked him where Singapore was? Answer: 'In China.' Q: 'And where is China?' A: 'In Europe.' Oh dear!

The actual examination was all the routine stuff; the only thing I really did *not* like was the prodding and prigging of my genitals. I also resented – though to a lesser degree – the tickling of the soles of my feet.

After the medical I went to see *Rage in Harlem* with Robert Montgomery, Ingrid Bergman, George Sanders. Adapted from a novel by James Hilton. Montgomery's character – a paranoiac, violently and unreasonably jealous of his wife and his best friend – was interesting enough.

7 January 1942

Two events of interest today. First I had to return to Aldershot with an Eno's bottle full of urine. It is odd how any contact with military authority reduces me to a nervous wreck, and this occasion was no exception. I thought I was going to get off quickly, after having my specimen reported 'C and N' ('clear and normal' – sounds a good revue title!), but unfortunately I was told to wait for the 'army officer'. The little front office was full of boys waiting for interviews and their medical and I stood there, nervous and impatient for hours. I felt such a 'fish out of water' and in some odd way a useless member of society, a drone – for all these were working boys with a working knowledge of some 'useful' trade. And yet I am – this is not conceit – many times the intellectual superior of any of them. Why then the feeling of inferiority? Instinct perhaps. I suppose the intellectual must always feel at a tremendous disadvantage amongst the purely physical.

The second event was the dress rehearsal of this play the Frimley Home Guard are giving tomorrow; Father was asked to take part in one scene (just sitting at a table), but took me along to do it for him. I was prepared to be amused but from the start it was awful ... quite, quite, unbelievably *awful*. Very depressing as such a complete waste of time; incredibly enough they all seemed quite pleased with it.

19 January 1942

Monday: Since the past few days will doubtless occupy a very important place in my autobiography I feel a little guilty of having postponed writing about them. Not that I haven't had time; but after writing in detail about Oxford to Mum, GMP and PB I haven't terribly wanted to do it all again ...

20 January 1942

Well, anyway, I arrived at Oxford last Friday; leaving my boxes at the station I took a bus up to Carfax, then walked to Wadham [College]. There was little snow about (there had been a lot at Camberley). My rooms I was told were 9, 5. I walked up and found to my chagrin that I had to share them. I came in and a tall, dark-haired, spectacled creature with a shifty grammar school expression and a North Country accent got up. 'I'm Parkinson,' he said. 'The second scholar.' I unpacked my bag, talking trivialites as I did so; then I looked out of the window and saw A. J. Neame coming up the path – his rooms are just above mine. I said hello to him. Parkinson, rudely interrupted in his task of showing me some postcards, retired again to the fireplace and started reading Rabelais. Neame asked me to come out to tea, saying he'd wait in the rooms of some friend of his – Hancock (to whom I did not take an instantaneous liking).

   Saturday: went to see Bowra[1] in the morning. He seemed cheerful, good humoured and quite unhelpful.

22 January 1942

I will get up to date.

   Tuesday: I found Incubus, Neame's appellation for dear Parkinson, ensconced in menacing silence in front of the fire. I sit down at the desk and the fun begins.

   Incubus: 'Er . . . Anderson . . . Since we don't get on very well together I asked (lit. 'usked', but I can't write phonetically) Neame if he'd share rooms with you.'

   I: 'Oh, did you?'

   Oh, and then we got into a long argument – or at least I forced him into one – in which all the old grammar school–public school arguments were brought up and I was accused of 'superiority' (not denied!) and 'patronisation' (which I *do* deny), etc. Finally I crushed him by sheer volubility.

   Wednesday: Quite a full day. In the morning I received my call-up papers! I have been summoned to the Royal Corps of Signals, Oxley, Yorkshire. And at eleven I have my first tutorial with Bowra, who had to help me with my gown! Contrary to expectation we went through the stuff thoroughly – the first chorus of the Agamemnon – with many a 'How do you take that?' and 'Now how does that translate?' In the evening went to hear Dr Robert Eisler speaking on 'Astrology – Science or Superstition' at the Cosmos Society. He talked too much, in a delightful Austrian accent, but was so erudite, so charming and had such an interesting subject that it didn't really matter. I almost introduced myself afterwards, but finally thought better of it.

   Thursday: Too cold to work and not enough coal for a fire in the morning. Matriculation, 12.15. I hung around the lodge hoping my suit would come; as it didn't

---

1. (Cecil) Maurice Bowra (1898–1971), educated at Cheltenham College. Warden at Wadham College, Professor of Poetry (1946-51), Vice-Chancellor of Oxford University (1951–54).

I hopped into Neame's room and purloined his, and a mortar board and a white tie. I changed but, frightened to attempt tying the tie, dashed out and bought a ready-made one which the man obligingly clipped on for me in the shop. After assembling in Keeley's room and waiting ten minutes for him, we filed out and across to the Sheldonian, terrified that Neame would see me and spot the suit, for he is the sort of person who'd be angry about such an incident and not like lending it in any case. Funnily enough my suit arrived for me just about at 12.15! I was also a little embarrassed at having, with my usual lack of clothes sense, not put on my waistcoat (or rather Neame's) and left my grey sweater on instead. On arrival at the Sheldonian we were presented with excerpts from the statutes, then ushered in.

31 January 1942

I came up to the room (I can't even say my rooms!) but couldn't light the fire, then went out and had my hair cut. Wandered about a bit, crowds awful. I managed to get Parkinson out of the room by whistling!

2 February 1942

On Saturday night quite a large party of the JCR got 'pissed' – the current expression – and dashed around shouting, etc. One section of it came stamping up the stairs here and stopped outside. 'Here's Anderson,' I heard one say. I felt very nervous and not quite sure what to do. However, they were apparently only looking for Neame and Barsley; I treacherously directed them to Neame's room and went on teaching myself German. They didn't find Neame there but made an awful row and kicked over two fire buckets which made them happy; then they disappeared. Neame and Barsley were apparently dragged from Hancock's room and debagged. I heard all about it when writing letters next morning in the JCR; the details were recounted over and over again; how Spencer-Cooper had also been visited; how the door had been barricaded; how a table and wireless had been broken; how the Dean had sent for some of the offenders. All very exciting and uproarious fun; it doesn't amuse me, probably because I feel so helpless and hopeless when faced with a large menacing 'crowd' – how to behave if the same happens to me I don't know. Yet I'm quite prepared to find it funny if Parkinson is debagged!

In the evening went to my first Ballet Club meeting. A dancer named Joan Lawson spoke – very interestingly – with a vivacious squeak and very bad grammar – on 'Tchaikovsky'. After the talk a boy came up and asked if I wasn't Anderson and had been at Coll. [Cheltenham College]; he said his name was Hanson, had been at Dean Close, was a local Cheltenham vicar's son, had seen me in *Twelfth Night*[1] and *Richard*. My fame grows apace!

---

1. L.A. played Feste.

12 February 1942

Ballet in the evening again – Robert Helpmann's *brilliant* gigolo. What a dancer! What an actor! I'd adore to be a ballet dancer – or is it just the glamour of it all that attracts me? I don't think so entirely. It must be a very *satisfying* occupation. I'd love to meet Robert Helpmann.[1]

20 February 1942

My longest pause; I shan't try and cover everything, but just pick out a few incidents that come to my mind.

I have read *Jane Eyre* and been much impressed; at times the language is stilted and the conversation impossibly 'bookish', but one soon gets used to it (e.g. St John's proposal to Jane, concluding, 'As a conductress of Indian schools . . . your assistance will be to me invaluable'!), Jane's return to Rochester and indeed all that last episode is touching and pathetic. The characters are all well drawn; the story not too impossible. For sheer power it does not come anywhere near *Wuthering Heights* but in its own way it is great. Rochester reminds me of Duff [a College friend], though a bit romanticised I'm afraid.

I occasionally wonder whether I am outgrowing all that business. It doesn't trouble me as much as it used to, though, which seems a good sign. I would like very much to know what he thinks of me – if anything! I think he likes me but probably thinks me too self-assertive and, to a certain extent, looks down on me rather. My feelings about him are also interesting and (I suppose) I like thinking about them because they afford stimulation. (What a horrid word and horrid thought! I don't actually think it's altogether true anyway.) I suppose it was in the Easter term 1941 at Cheltenham that I first became really conscious of my feelings – I was fire-watching up at Coll. at the time and I remember still the smell of the masters' lavatories when I used to get up early and wash in there, then go up to the form room and sit in his chair (Oh, shameful admission! Oh degrading conduct!) and work – I managed not unsuccessfully to sub-liminate them. I think the last form picnic we had that term was, from this point of view, the happiest day I spent. (It shows I can't be very far gone, for I wouldn't say it was the happiest day I'd spent.) Then when he used to come down I used to know the meaning of the expression 'turned my bosom to water'. And that's the feeling I still get; I suppose – in fact I know – it's the feeling at any rate the woman gets when she's in love. The bottom of your stomach falls out and leaves there a gaping, miserable void – that at any rate is when he takes no notice of you. When he does, the missing organ comes back with a jerk that sets your inside spinning and your legs shaking. By the

---

1. Dancer, awarded CBE and KBE. Appeared in the lead role in Sartre's *Nekrassov* at the Royal Court Theatre in November 1957, a few months after L.A. directed his first play there.

time you've recovered he's gone and you're wishing you weren't made quite as you are! I wonder if he even suspects anything? Horrible thought! And anyway I'd bet my bottom dollar neither he nor anyone else does. This is the most candid page yet; I don't know exactly why I wrote it, but it'll be quite fun to read in twenty years time!

(P.S. I almost feel like asking him to tea – in fact I do feel like asking him to tea! – and am only restrained a) by not wanting to seem forward, i.e. shyness, and b) by the feeling that I might not find it easy to carry on a tête-à-tête conversation and that would be embarrassing!)

To revert to the other side of my split personality, I think it's rather unfortunate that there are no – or seem to be no – intelligent toughs (using 'tough' merely as opposed to 'wet') whom I can get to know. Clarke is all right and very nice but I'm afraid his Anglo-Indian, upper middle-class consciousness does rather get in the way. He keeps trying to drag one out to dinner and swears too much. Besides, he eats too much jam! Second thought: perhaps there are no intelligent toughs!

This leads me on to another thing I've been thinking: the number of first-rate people is very, very small. I'm always on the look-out for someone who'd make a really satisfactory friend. I haven't found one yet. McNeile – too inclined to desert and go over to the unintelligent toughs. I think he's the nearest I've got, though his faults are many. John Anderson – nice but also many faults and not really terribly intelligent. Neame – a 'wet' of course but we get on well. [Gavin] Lambert – too dishonest and 'wet'. Of my new acquaintances Harrison isn't very promising; Barsley, though quite a dear, is also quite a bore; John Goodall's too 'wet' – though of course very nice; his critical faculty needs developing. Perhaps I'm laying too much stress on the 'wet' and 'tough' business, but it isn't solely a matter of games prowess; it's definitely part of an attitude towards life.

28 February 1942

I am rather tired today as I have been staying up too late recently; tonight I will go to bed at ten (perhaps!) I went to a lecture on Scott, this morning, by Lord David Cecil, a very charming man and, I think, a good lecturer. As one of the infatuated undergraduates gushed afterwards, 'He's so beautifully *fresh*!' I think I shall read *Guy Mannering* and re-read *Wuthering Heights* before his next lecture.

Afterwards I met Duff and had some coffee with him; oddly enough I appear quite to have mellowed now or something and regard him merely as a very nice person and good to have as a friend. (He strays a *little* near the 'tough' but is remarkably near the 'happy medium'.) He is probably going into the Sudan Civil Service. I envy him exceedingly from the point of view of the immediate future, but as a career – no. I am coming more and more to the conclusion that I am cut out for some stage or film job, which will lead to trouble – if I survive the war! *Oh* the war! It is very depressing.

I have just been sitting in the JCR, and am quite appalled by the narrow-minded bigotry of most of its members – or rather of those of its members who talk politics. The Conservatives among them are merely stupid, and the Socialists bitter, prejudiced and intolerant – besides being just silly. They have no idea of moderation, of the 'happy medium' which is essential in life; a world run by such people will be absolutely *Hellish*.

6 March 1942

I am now a member of His Majesty's army, having today been formally attested to the Queen's Royal Regiment and presented with 5/-, 1/6 of which I spent straight away on [Walt Disney's] *Fantasia*. After seeing it a second time I am struck by its brilliance and yet by its persistent veering towards the second-rate. The *Pastoral Symphony* is a complete artistic blunder. The film is really a cartoon ballet, though ballet on the cinema is different from that on the stage; it relies either on large-scale patterns and grouping, or subtleties of the dance, not on a combination of the two.

I had a long argument with a communist girl. I am convinced she's wrong but didn't manage to convert her.

16 April 1942

I have been inspired to take up my pencil again chiefly by the thought that I shall be nineteen tomorrow. This is unimportant except as a warning that I shall soon be In It. And about time.

I seem to be getting very disillusioned with the stage and screen just now; partly as a result of my visit to Denham [Studios]. Then one keeps hearing things like – Walter Crisham is a nasty bit of work, Tommy Trinder is an unpleasant nuisance, Diana Wynyard is a bitch, Vivien Leigh and Laurence Olivier are unpleasant. These are people I hope sincerely and believe are nice (a word I use intentionally) – V. S. Pritchett, Hermione Gingold, Beatrice Lillie, Betty Ann Davies . . . It is really depressingly difficult to think of people one is *sure* must be nice. So many of my illusions have been shattered.

9 May 1942

Tonight I said grace for the first time in Hall; I was fairly nervous but got through it all right and felt fairly pleased on taking my place. Barsley then informed me I had missed out one word, 'nostris' – I blithely laugh and say it doesn't matter. A few moments later, a slip of paper is passed down the table ordering, in my name, a two-and-a-half pint sconse for 'deformed grace'. Now this made an impression on me; Barsley urged me to appeal but I refused and it was duly drunk.

16 May 1942

Pride and Honour are merely two excuses grown-ups are accustomed to make when they have behaved like children. Today I went for a picnic on the river, the occasion being Sylvia's birthday; a very enjoyable, slightly silly afternoon – I love fooling about, of course, but think it sometimes gets a little on the other people's nerves! I am very bad at punting.

On Tuesday evening (12th), I went to see *Macbeth* at the New Theatre. John Gielgud, Gwen Frangçon-Davies. On the whole I found it a most impressive and stirring performance. Gielgud's Macbeth is very fine; he carries it off better than one would have thought possible. His last great exit, with the lines 'Come wind, come rack . . .' was extremely moving.

9 June 1942

I stayed up till 2.45 writing my essay (Plato's attitude to art) so naturally feel rather debilitated. I went to Cheltenham last Saturday for the afternoon and quite enjoyed it . . . The thought that Fryer can now be a prefect rather shocks me. On Coll. field I talked to Wurm and Guggenheim. Wurm has grown tremendously and his voice is beginning to break. Also spoke to nice matron. Had a long conflab with Paul[1] on the Gym balcony about Coll. Then a chat with Eliott-S chiefly on call-up matters. Still, he was quite charming and offered me tea. Went to see Patos, whom I found sitting up out of bed and evidently much better, though one could see he'd been ill ('I've been through Hell!')

27 June 1942

So 'Continuous Training' has started, or at any rate we're on the fringe of it: a mobile column exercise tomorrow, but as it's scheduled to finish by 12.30 perhaps it won't be too bad. I am in Sgt Brown's platoon and am his 'servant' – this will probably entail dashing frantically all over the place, but at any rate I shall not have to carry a Bren gun. At present I am attempting to land a job in the Intelligence [Corp] (Japanese or Cryptograms!), spurred on by a sudden – though understandable – distaste for the infantry and by a letter which Boris received from the Corps saying that they had written to the War Office advising them that Alan, Neame, I and Robin B. are unfit to go to an OCTU without a period of training in the ranks; why exactly I in particular should be singled out for such notice I can't image – although I did make rather a bloomer the other day attempting to assemble a Bren gun.

---

1. Paul Bloomfield arrived in 1940 as a replacement for some of the staff who'd gone off to war. 'A marvellously civilising and humanising influence on a number of us at that time.' (Letter to Tim Pearce, 7 June 1983)

The ethics of the whole problem are rather difficult; of course I am to a certain extent influenced by selfish motives. The physical exertions and the mental strain of life in the infantry are things I naturally wish to escape. I am perfectly aware that it is necessary for everyone to help with the War Effort, intellectual and tough alike, but surely if there are jobs which can be performed only by the intellectual, he is justified in taking them. I am as a matter of fact not at all sure of my capability to command, though this may be the result of an inferiority complex. The question of danger is there too; I don't want to shirk danger by sitting in Whitehall and never going near the firing line. On summing up I think I will be morally justified in taking an Intelligence job if a) it is really an important one, and b) I am more capable of discharging it efficiently than I am my duties in an infantry regiment – and, if it is doubtful whether I would ever reach commissioned rank in the Infantry, I would certainly be right to take the more responsible post. Of course the Intelligence job may not materialise – but I hope to heaven it does!

Mum was up here on Tuesday when it was very hot; I showed her Trinity and New College, Blackwells and Parkers! We had a very nice lunch at the George and I gave her tea in my room. A very nice afternoon on the whole – Mum was quite carried away by the bookshops.

I took my two sections this week. One on the four Greek plays and one on the *Republic*. On the first I am fairly confident of success, on the second not so confident – though I hope to heaven I haven't failed it. Time will tell. I feel creative and wish I could think of something to create!

2 July 1942

We have been training continuously now for the last five and a half days – Weapon Training every day since Monday and it's beginning to get on my nerves. Today we had a most awful instructor – named Morgan and a Welshman at that. His normal squad, onto which I, Mitchell and Whewell were grafted in the morning, were a frightful lot of stooges; some of them even called him 'sir' which infuriated me. He looks pretty nauseous too, with shirt cuffs tied together with string.

I saw *The Little Foxes* for the second time yesterday and enjoyed it very much; Bette Davis and Patricia Collinge both superb of course. Gregg Toland at the camera.[1]

I passed both my sections by the way and even got a distinction on the Greek plays!

I write this as I listen to the wireless report of Churchill's speech in the 'Censure of the Government' debate: he seems to be completely impatient of criticism and quite determined not to pay any attention to it. Apparently he only entered the House during the speech before his. His gesture of giving the V-sign at the end of his speech strikes me as being in the worst of taste.

---

1 Douglas Slocombe contributed an eight-page feature on Toland's work in *Sequence* 8.

18 July 1942

On the whole I enjoyed camp, though that does not necessarily mean that I would wish
to repeat the experience. The strenuous side of the training was, I think, more enjoyable
than any slack moments we had (and they were not many); the march out to the night
exercise was the most arduous physical experience I have had to undergo – which
shows what a soft life I've had – but it *was* pretty tough going, at a most tremendous
pace and with a pretty long stride. Sweat literally poured down or at any rate ran down
my face, which hasn't often happened before.

Memories that stand out are the extraordinarily poor and tuneless singing of our
platoon, poor Robin's deafness, the frightful rush to get tidy in the morning, the horror
of hearing reveille at 6.30 (is there any sound more unpleasant?), shaving in cold water
and the command 'Prepare to double!' The YMCA car with its scarlet cakes, its large
cups of sweet army tea and its charmer behind the counter was a real delight.

The night exercise was a pretty complete flop largely through the puerile leadership
of the platoon. I distinguished myself chiefly by having a violent scuffle with my own
section whom I mistook for an enemy patrol and vice versa, during which I fired a
blank straight into Section Leader Taylor's face,[1] tripped backwards over a hillock, was
wrapped up in my WP cape, interrogated vainly and at last released. I also mistook
Platoon HQ for another enemy patrol and dashed madly past them in a valiant effort
to save the situation by getting through with the warning. The attack – very badly
carried out – gave rise to an absurd but amusing argument, or rather verbal fight
between Brown and Wilson in which Brown, who was almost certainly wrong, won the
victory by virtue of his undoubted superiority of rank!

The camp concert was a pretty dim affair. I tried to sing 'Miss Otis' but was effectively drowned by the carousing at the bar and Athie's ham-fisted accompaniment.
Merkin's impersonations were pretty good – especially Churchill. Chamberlain was
good but in bad taste – now that he's dead and we're in the war. In the end it degener-
ated inevitably into a selection of dirty songs, which suited the mentality of most of
the audience admirably.

30 August 1942

In London I saw *Light and Shade*. I rate it the best revue I have ever seen. Herbert
Farjeon's experiment in fusing poetry with satire in intimate revue seems to me to have
succeeded brilliantly. Of course it had been considerably adjusted since the first night:
'The Nativity Play' and 'Come Commando Come' having been cut – probably all to the
good. The atmosphere throughout is intimate to a degree never achieved even by the
little revues – though production is no less slick. The only item I really did consider

---

1. An action repeated by Mick Travis in *If* . . . .

unnecessary was 'Portsmouth–London' which consisted of three French sailors singing mournful and, to me at any rate and I suspect to most of the rest of the audience, incomprehensible French songs. The company is a talented and charming one: Betty Ann Davies – who is going to be four times as good as Hermione Baddeley and one and a half times as good as Hermione Gingold – Max Adrian, Frith Banbury, Vida Hope – superb in 'The Beasts of the Jungle' – Joan Sterndale-Bennet, Megs Jenkins, Geoffrey Dunn. Music and set-ups uniformly delightful.

18 October 1942

Things are now getting under way for the term; and it looks as though I am going to be rather busy. I have got the part of Pasqualino[1] – it is an exceedingly poor one. The Experimental Theatre Club have apparently got the idea that my rooms are now their property. I somewhat rashly offered to allow it to be used for rehearsals to help them out. Anyway, it's being used on Monday, Tuesday and Wednesday evenings, Friday afternoon and Saturday afternoon and evening. Next week, Miss Hazel Collingwood will have to find other quarters! As she has something to do with the *Oxford Mag*, I will try to use her – especially now she's under an obligation to me for my room! – to get an opportunity to write some criticisms.

Corps is becoming alarmingly demanding on time. Parades go on till 6.30 now, and Wednesday afternoon is taken up by 'Toughening Training', which is horrible.

I have an idea for a film about three coming up to Oxford and going in the army etc.

22 November 1942

In just over a month I seem to have grown at least three years older; certainly a lot of things have happened and I feel I've only just begun to take advantage of what Oxford has to offer. *The Impresario* is over – it was a definite success, though its triviality prevented it from being a Sensation. I think I acted well and made the most of my rather limited opportunities: Nevill [Coghill][2] is writing the review for the magazine (he probably won't mention me).

I see now clearly what a fool I have been not to get into the ETC [Experimental Theatre Club] before; not only would I have got some good parts, but I would have made the contacts and the friends I have been so self-pityingly and uselessly whining for. As it is I have got to know Gerard Irvine quite well – and to quite like him. My eyes have been firmly opened to the smuttier side of life by Gerard who, an open homosexual himself, is extremely fond of discussing the subject with others. His attitude is, I think, wrong; not only is he tolerant and broad-minded, but he even encourages

---

1. In *The Impresario from Smyrna* by Carlo Goldoni.
2. English tutor at Exeter College, also founded the Oxford Experimental Theatre Club in 1936.

conversation about and thus acceptance of it. His revelations about Walter Crisham, Robert Helpmann, John Gielgud have aroused in me strong distaste for the stage – or certain parts of it. He took me one night to the Endeavour snack bar in George Street, which is, apparently, the most sinful dive in Oxford. Actually there was nothing particularly sinful going on when we were there, but we were fortunate enough to encounter Frau Brunner (who was in the *Dream* last term) who is apparently an arch-bitch – and I can well imagine it. We then started talking to two RAF men, one an officer and one a Sergeant Pilot, who were very 'interesting' – slightly class-conscious and therefore bumptious at first. On the exit past him of Frau Brunner, the Sergeant-P exclaimed: 'That's what you'd call a gilded Lily, what?' – I was prepared to cut him, and keep to myself, but the influence of Gerard and the stage was strong enough to make me open a conversation. As we were leaving, a very decadent young man swayed in and greeted Gerard – 'My dee-ah!' (literally the stage-effeminate at its worst). 'We're giving a party for the Hermiones tonight. Won't you come?' Gerard said he couldn't, but naturally I was 'rarin' to go – until he explained it would probably be a sex party.

Another person I'm getting to know is David Vaughan.[1] He is more intelligent than I gave him credit for, and decidedly nice in a rather selfish way – I listen to him with enormous patience (and a certain amount of enjoyment!) but am hardly repaid in kind. But still . . . I wonder whether he will ever *be* anything: I shouldn't be surprised.

31 December 1942

It has been a good year for me. I am, I think, more worldly-wise that I was twelve months ago, and I know far more clearly what I want to do with my life. I hope that I am going to be able to get rid of my dilettante tendencies when I'm engaged in work that is really congenial to me. At present, as far as I can see, I excel chiefly in talking, gossiping, being generally charming, and writing good letters. My problems are still there and still as assertive as ever, but the busy life that undoubtedly lies ahead will probably solve them at least temporarily. Of the future it is difficult to speak. It will probably be hard and often unpleasant; still I may find it possible to enjoy it and must always remember it's 'good for me' – as an artist as well as as a man!

2 January 1943

Gavin[2] is here, and we've started on *Madame B*. Going is very slow and we've only done nineteen pages. On Friday night we gave up in disgust after about five pages, Gavin proclaiming a desire to do a thriller; today it doesn't seem too bad, the wedding sequences are beautiful and ingenious. I am inclined to think that I contribute slightly

---

1. Archivist of the Merce Cunningham company. Contributor to *Sequence*.
2. Gavin Lambert, a fellow Cheltonian. They were working on a screenplay of Flaubert's *Madame Bovary*.

more than he does – perhaps he works better on his own. Anyway, speculation on the subject is fruitless as without him I'd be incapable of producing any sort of full script and he is very good typing the whole time.

19 January 1943
At last the fatal day, which has been so much discussed, plotted, evaded and feared, has come to daunt me. Tomorrow I proceed to Wrotham, Kent, by orders of the War Office. In 1940, the Rifle Brigade, represented by Captain Cave, paid a visit to Cheltenham trying to scoop likely officers after the heavy losses suffered by the regiment at Calais. Several people were interviewed. When asked, I said I would appreciate an interview. So I went and was interviewed by these altogether charming gentlemen and by displaying an enthusiasm for the motor battalions which I was far from feeling, was 'provisionally' accepted.

I almost went into the RB in January 1942, but just managed to get to Oxford by the skin of my teeth (I had registered in December '41 while taking my school exam). I made a great fool of myself here, being medically examined at Aldershot and saying nothing of the RB, and so actually getting my call-up papers into the Signals at Oxford. These were withdrawn by the Joint Recruiting Board.

Towards the end of last term I attended with extreme distaste a tea party for RB candidates, the guest of honour being Cave (himself); at this our fates were sealed. So tomorrow to Wrotham. My real desire is now (believe it or not) to go into the Navy as an ordinary rating! I wonder how much I have been influenced by films such as *In Which They Serve*?[1]

24 May 1943
I am perhaps lacking in moral fibre; at any rate I am conscious of very little except an intense longing for the war to be over soon. I hate my training in the army, physically because I find it so exhausting, mentally because it is so repugnant to me. My mind is occupied with films more than anything else, though I have done nothing creative since *Madame Bovary* – now with Korda.[2] The commonsense thing of course is to reconcile myself as well as I can to what I am forced to do; but somehow I cannot – or will not – even bring myself to try.

27 November 1943
The mess is as usual full of little parties gambling at poker, vingt-et-un, etc. Is it mere prudishness, puritanism that makes me disapprove so? I think not. There is something, to my mind, repulsive about the atmosphere of such games. Something reminiscent of

---

1. Stiff-upper-lip British naval film, written by and starring Noël Coward. David Lean directed.
2. Sent unsolicited to Alexander Korda.

third-class railway carriages, stale cigarette smoke, 'virile' sex talk and beer slopping over the tables in Betty's Bar. A Canadian party was rather more obstreperous, because drunker, than the rest, and started singing: to anyone trying to write letters this was intolerable. I remonstrated but Tommy Braithwaite, drunk, merely said fuck off, adding that they didn't give a fuck who fucking well wanted to write letters. In the white heat of anger I wrote a complaint on the suggestions book and resumed my seat – any more immediate action would have ended in a fight or ignominy, probably both. However, Sam Holloway read out the complaint to his table, causing great indignation and a cry of 'split-arse' from Jimmy Brown.

How wrong was I when I wrote deploring the philistinism of college? I have lately conceived a distaste for the senior public school type who too often lack the bluff (if stupid) good nature of the hearty, and substitute only a shallow, smart cynicism and a habit of talking as if all their verbs and nouns began with a capital letter.

The education of character is *not* enough and even in my present mood I cannot deny that academically a Cheltenham education left a lot to be desired. Would I rather have been educated elsewhere? I doubt it. There was scope enough for individuality at Cheltenham.

How was it then that I wasted my year at Oxford so? Two reasons: shyness and laziness. Fortunately I have had the edges rubbed off the former in the army, but I still don't make friends easily except through introductions.

9 December 1943

We've just finished a rather lazy drill parade, half in 'B' lecture room and half on the square: 31 and 32 platoons combined, so we had three NCOs, all vying with each other to make the most – and the most unpleasant – noise. We started off with a long spell on 'Present Arms' – 'One, two, three, *four*. Cut off. Close it. Bolt. Close it. Trigger. Squeeze it. One stop, two stop. *Small!*' This always makes me smile. The repulsive Corporal Collins was there, hatchet-faced, shrill, harsh-voiced, with the deportment of a broad-backed dowager, only without her natural dignity.

12 December 1943

Yesterday, the morning ended with a CO's drill parade: for this I had blanco'ed gaiters and sling and pressed my trousers. My web belt I had to leave because I was on guard the night before: I could have polished the brass but didn't because I was lazy and not having to seemed sufficient excuse. But, of course, we weren't given time to change properly before the parade and on dismantling my equipment, I found the belt was far too loose; there was no time to alter it and I prayed for the best.

We were paraded on the asphalt outside the block; the sun shining fiercely in our eyes; the Colonel, accompanied by a huddle of terser officers, began, slowly and method-ically, to inspect us. I felt I was in for trouble.

When the Colonel arrived before me his basilisk eyes flew to my belt. He pulled at it distastefully. 'You must fit your belt properly – and it's in a disgusting state anyway.' I had aroused suspicion and was now subjected to minute examination. My cap badge was also disgusting (not black) 'and your boots are pretty filthy – altogether a pretty damn bad turn out'. The sun was glaring into my eyes as I gazed, with flickering eyelids across the square. I felt myself blushing. I felt rather wretched. The Colonel turned sternly to Sergeant Mace. 'Sergeant, see this cadet is chased, get his turnout smartened up,' and with another mutter of 'appalling' or 'quite disgusting' he moved to the next unfortunate.

At first I was highly embarrassed, self-conscious and, as I say, wretched: angry too with an impotent anger at the intolerable position one is in, against unkindness, insensibility, against the army. What right has a man like that to humiliate me? (for I was humiliated). We were marched onto the square and, as we drilled, anger gave place to scorn: my ego reasserted itself, not that I could pretend not to be affected by an incident like that, but I could see that it *was* largely unimportant and that my offence and hurt was not to be worried over. Throughout the parade I was checked by Sergeant Lewis. Evidently I am a marked man.

13 December 1943

I find events shaping themselves more and more: sickness and impatience with the army, rebelliousness and unwise self-assertion, tiredness and slackness.

2 January 1944

Sitting in the Cadet's mess at a quarter to eleven, before a dying fire, I lay down my copy of *To the Lighthouse*, for I have been interrupted by Teddy Vaughan. I lay down my book and I look at him; he is young and yet he is becoming old. He is still a boy and yet there is about him an air of age, of becoming a father, of having responsibilities, of earning money and settling down. In all this there is something sad: why must youth so perish, freshness so stale, virility so harden and become coarse? He will marry and have children: it is in the nature of things. And he will become coventional and stiff. And his beauty will fade and his skin grow hard. And I am not to be persuaded that this is not a tragedy.

18 January 1944

The RSM talks so fast that I find it almost impossible to understand or follow what he is saying. My mind seems clogged and tired, and my eyelids want to shut. This is a tolerable existence I suppose – certainly the food is very good.

But I cannot say I have taken very kindly to the mess. It is not really at all like a university – much more like a public school common room into which the prefects have been admitted.

1944 (undated)
Victoria Barracks, Beverley, Yorkshire. 1.30 a.m.

I read in the *Cheltonian* yesterday of the deaths of Cochrane and Markland,[1] both late of Cheltondale.[2] As a person I know I didn't like Cochrane – he had lots of faults of the loud-mouthed kind – but I was strongly attracted to him (even now my heart beats a little faster), and that makes any rational judgement of his character quite impossible for me. So when I say I feel grieved and shocked to hear of his death (in action in Italy) I'm afraid it must be pain at the loss of anyone so strong, handsome and physically splendid – though in fact he was never anything but lost to me – rather than sadness at the loss of him as a person. For Markland, whom I liked personally at least as much, I feel no real *emotion* – only intellectual regret and sympathy.

But these are mere words, and while the writing of them offers something with which to occupy the mind, they can bring no real comfort.

But to you, Robin Markland – have I even got your name wrong? – and you, Palmer Cochrane, I offer my blessing for what it is worth. Do you remember the last incident you shared together in my mind? When, Cochrane, you took advantage of your physical strength to smear you, Markland, with black boot-polish – the act of a bully, and I deplored it; the act of a strong man using and glorying in his strength, and what could I do but admire and repress my admiration? Can you see what my pen is writing? Can you feel what is in my heart, can you understand what is in my mind? To you, Markland, I offer my sympathy if not my friendship – for I never knew you well enough for that; to you, Cochrane, I offer you my love for your body and grief for its loss – which you cannot quite refuse because I think you loved and gloried in it too.

It is morning now; the window is open and I look out onto frosty fields; the crisp air is lively with the song of the birds. A mile away, the Minster rises calm and grave from the morning mist. The bells are sounding in the distance. Along the road, people are bicycling to work. Another day has begun.

23 January 1944
I am twenty years old, left Oxford to join the army a year ago, and am now, after the usual alarms and excursions, an officer. What then is my dilemma? It is the dilemma of the spirit hating the material conditions under which it is forced to live, yet forced to resign itself, or to attempt to resign itself, to those conditions.

The discomforts of army life are felt by all. Nobody, I am sure, enjoys getting up at half past six on a November morning, but that is a discomfort that can be overcome without disproportionate suffering. It is the mental discomforts, the irrationalities and

---

1. The name of the first boy who speaks in *If . . . .*
2. L.A.'s house when a pupil at Cheltenham College; used as a location in *If . . . .*

petty tyrannies of army life, and above all its dreary waste which constitute the real obstacle to the happiness, or at least the content, of the civilised soldier.

The civilised man must be alive; alive mentally as well as physically. Most people go through life like owls in sunlight; they do not realise the possibilities of life – indeed, it is only by a polite fiction that we call them alive at all. The civilised man believes that the mind or the soul is more important than the body, and the arts of mankind are the tangible evidence of great minds, of our own and past ages, and therefore worthy of some attention. He is therefore acutely aware of the spiritual deprivation, as well as the suffering, that war inflicts on the world and, especially if he is young, hungers more for knowledge and culture than for lemons and bananas. The discomfort is accentuated by the abortion of any creative urge which may possess him.

Sensibilty will, almost inevitably, accompany such interests; and sensibility I define in this context, as the power, or the misfortune, to feel continually the tragedies and blasphemies of army life; of the ATS parade on the barrack square and of the voluntary (compulsory) church parade.

Civilisation also tends to produce individuality, presumably intelligence, to think for himself. Certainly the more individual a man becomes, the less likely he is to be happy in any but a guerrilla army, if there: for consider the definition of Military Discipline: 'The habit of unquestioning obedience to the orders of your superior.' Unquestioning obedience? The very words are enough to arouse my most stubborn resistance: other things I may vow to my country, but never 'the love that asks no questions'.

To this catalogue of the attributes of the civilised man, I should like to add an instinctive mistrust and loathing of weapons and machinery of any kind. It remains a mystery to me that any man who can contemplate a 25-pdr gun without distaste can claim to be civilised.

Now what is there to pull the other way? In other words, why are all those to whom these considerations apply (supposing there to be any in the armed forces beside myself)? It is difficult to answer concisely without relapsing into cliché. We are resisting tyranny, fighting for freedom, for a chance to build a (much belated) new and better world. These are clichés it is true, yet each expresses the truth shortly and conveniently. One is encouraged also by example; by friends who have contrived to face their problems apparently with more resolution, certainly with greater success than oneself. And not friends only. As one's disgust with the army grows, and one hears and reads of deeds of physical suffering and courage so much greater than anything one has been called upon to face oneself, all doubts and dissatisfactions seem, whether rightly or wrongly, weak, cowardly and shameful.

And so the mental conflict is engendered. The stage is set for thrust and counter-thrusts.

It will be obvious by now to any reader that I have not yet seen action on the battle-field – do I hear whispers from the Officers' Mess of 'That's what's wrong with the young puppy'?

1 February 1944

At this moment I feel more dispirited than I have for some time: dispirited in that complex way that refuses to accept any comforts common sense has to offer. For on Thursday, I have to take over a platoon of my own, and for many and various reasons I don't want to at all. I almost wish I had never taken a commission and incurred res-ponsibilites which I cannot fulfil. Cannot or will not, or will, loathing it, or tolerating it? I don't know; let God judge – my powers of self-analysis are insufficent.

Christ! If only I could get out and away from all this: from the pressure of Mess society, and saluting the men, and having to worry about weapons and kit and training programmes and to be able to wake up in the morning and think with pleasure (at any rate without pain) of the day before me and of what I can and will do with it. I feel I am going to sleep.

I am sitting alone now in the billiards room; feeling like a schoolboy who has played hooky and is frightened of being spotted by his form master – Company Commander.

It is no use writing any more.

13 March 1944

Ah! An hour by myself to write in . . . I am at Morpeth, posted with fifteen hours notice to the King's Royal Rifle Corps. Will I be here till the end of the war? Michael is here also. He greeted me without surprise or fuss as I stumbled into the pitch-black room at 11.30 last night. It's good to have a connecting link to soften up newnesses, and Michael (though, as I told him last night, must be accounted 'one of my failures') is a very pleasant link to have.

Didn't really want to leave Strensall, even if it is five feet below sea level: I was just getting dug in there, getting to know my platoon, not to care much what anyone thought about me, waking up on the way to contentment.

To turn for a little to introspection: I often feel there is something lacking in me. Am I emotionally starved? In fact I think I am. I am I think starved of love: sexually – and that leaves an emptiness. Yet I will never be loved as I wish to be, for myself.

15 April 1944

I shall go mad if I don't get something to do. Yesterday I went and sat in the pine wood all day and read *Modern Reading* No 9, which is a good little collection.

Would God I had appeared more enthusiastic at the Intelligence interview – any-thing is better than this, and almost anybody better than these people whom I can neither like nor despise. I seem unable to write anything creative. There's my anti-war film, which I tried to work on yesterday, several short story ideas, articles, etc. – and I've got plenty of time to do them really. Why not try?

We had a cocktail party in the mess yesterday for the Local Gentry. Worthy they may be, but utterly uninteresting.

Anderson transferred to the Intelligence Corps and from November 1944 was stationed at the Wireless Experimental Centre in Delhi.

6 November 1944

We left our berth at two o'clock this afternoon and now are standing at the mouth of the Clyde with the rest of the convoy – some dozen ships. Our journey from Wentworth to King George Street Dock, Glasgow, was a long and annoying one. The journey was uneventful and quite comfortable, for we had a first-class carriage to ourselves and the seats were soft and deep. Excitement was aroused, naturally enough I suppose, by our passage through Kilmarnock: the country before it was very beautiful – reminiscent of Northern Yorkshire with its wooded dales, stone walls and houses. At Glasgow, we arrived at a large, dirty, dead station with no one to greet us – but I am forgetting the excitement of the journey: almost as soon as we left Glasgow, comfortably spread out in our first-class carriage with our Sunday newspapers, cranes and funnels and masts began to appear among the houses. And soon there came the Clyde, with the sun out and white clouds in the sky and grey-painted ships riding at anchor; it was impressive and exciting. We passed a seaplane, some aircraft carriers, then more merchant ships.

And as we sat there, comfortable and rather tired, I wished that the journey could go on for ever; that we should never have to 'get there' and start the whole weary battle all over again.

10 November 1944

The men's accommodation is – literally, not emotionally – beastly. They are herded together on the lower decks in great droves of a hundred or so. Granted that they can be accommodated in no other way; I suppose all possible is done for them, they are treated in fact like intelligent animals. Their life differs radically from ours, in *kind* not in degree of comfort. And when the IC addresses them he addresses them as children: 'Finding plenty to do in the evenings?' 'Find things aren't too bad, eh?' Of course the whole thing is a blasphemy: but it's fortunate that no one recognises it, or the war could not be fought.

And the other dispiriting, perplexing thing is that, continually, the men behave like animals, like children. But what else can one expect?

We have quickened pace and left Ireland behind. This morning we developed a roll which has slightly disconcerted my stomach, together with the unpleasant, thick cold that clutters up my head.

3 December 1944

This is the last day; and before us, I suppose, lies a hot and dusty journey.

But I have forgotten about Lalkaka on Kipling. On the morning after our argument, I arrived on deck before breakfast to find him writing on a bench. Feeling something of the sort to be due from me I, in some pleasantry, referred to the argument, and hoped he hadn't 'minded'.

'Ah no, my dear fellow.' A long pause while the horizon is scanned, then a quotation is rolled heavily, mystically forth '. . . To dream but not to make dreams your master. To think but not make thoughts your –' something.

Feeling weak I nodded wisely and murmured, 'Yes'. I then made my first mistake. 'Who wrote it?'

'Kipling.'

And 'If' was produced, and Kipling designated one of our three greatest poetic geniuses (third to Shakespeare and Tennyson). And I made my second mistake. I said I did not like Kipling and, inevitably, mentioned with disfavour his jingoistic imperialism. Lalkaka nodded sagely, smiling a little. 'I thought,' he said, 'we'd come to that.' The upshot of it was that I was invited to a Kipling session in the lounge after breakfast, so that the Captain might have an opportunity to enlighten me as to Kipling's true worth. The luckless Bernard who approached us on B Deck Square was also roped in.

After breakfast, there was Lal. in the lounge with his two volumes of Kipling before him on the card table. He began with 'The Ballad of East and West' – a silly piece of rubbish about the Colonel's son and the ever-so-sporting Indian brigand. This was read, not as a narrative poem, but as a weighty serious [poem] of profound philosophic truths. Now and then, as we came to a particularly odious line, Lalkaka would beam slightly and wink one of his black glistening eyes in a manner that made one want to shudder and scream. It was during this reading that I realised how physically repulsive Lalkaka really is – and how intellectually rubbishy. He seems to have grown much fatter, much grosser in these past weeks. The flesh round his eyes is black and shining. He is fat with a bloated, piglike chin and dark bull neck. I can no longer bear to speak to him or listen to his pompous, conventional, glib opinions.

The reading was exhausting. The continual strain of keeping up an expression of interest and surprise at this revelation of Kipling's greatness of mind, of continually smiling appreciatively at these nauseating sentiments and vulgar, blatant, superficial versification, and of murmuring from time to time 'Yes, that's very good' or 'Yes, I hadn't realised he was like that', seriously depleted my store of nervous energy, and after our merciful release (having to go to the Orderly Room) clasping one volume of Kipling each, I had to take two tablets of Aspirin.

Last night I had a conversation on deck with the Irish Fusilier Lieutenant Thompson, who opened the conversation by referring to the size of the moon – or its rapidity in rising. It was difficult to keep it going at first for, after all, there is comparatively little to say about the moon, though it's all very interesting. Anyway we progressed through religion, Napoleon, Hitler, war, to the army. I was charmed by his frank, tolerant, disciplined and moral personality – really the best type of non-intellectual and indeed the type that always makes the intellectual seem (to me anyway) desiccated and unhappy, despite the consolations of art. And to meet someone naive enough to have principles and actually stand by them is a blessed experience. Of course his type of army discipline is wholly abhorrent to me, but I no longer feel quite so certain as I did that one should try to persuade others, who accept it, that it is a blasphemy, and not meet to be endured.

But one is conscious of 'the unplumbed, salt, estranging sea', and that one is alone, cut off.

Tomorrow morning or tonight we arrive at Bombay and the voyage will be over. I have not established any ties to be severed, or friendships to be continued, as I might have done were we to go on to Australia. And all that remains to do again, in a new station, is a new job. I wish I were quicker at making friends – and yet, does it pay?

I have just had my first piece of dramatic tuition from Capt. Barron who dragged me, in full rant, through the 'What a piece of work is man'[1] and 'Rogue and peasant slave' speeches. This, separated from the Orderly Room by only a thin partition, which must have caused them considerable amusement for the first two minutes, and subsequently considerable annoyance. I was marked 13/20 which seemed very reasonable. I felt hideously bad about the acting part of it, movement of legs and hands hideously stiff. I let myself go without much difficulty but naturally was not wholly able to do myself justice. My stance is bad. One foot forward, shoulders up, arms balancing. Pause more; emphasise important words more. Establish preliminary link with the audience, and hold on to it.

What an exhausting life an actor's must be.

6 December 1944

I did not enjoy Bombay ... The city itself: in my mental state I could hardly be expected to take a very favourable view of it, which indeed I did not. I was not very well taken with the Western stores and the Western people shopping there with their calmly superior air (tattered, emaciated beggars lie in the street outside). Prices seem phenomenal and fabulously high by English standards – of course one treated oneself to

1. From *Hamlet.* Spoken by the Living Brain at the end of *Britannia Hospital.*

some chocolates. Since our party was composed of uninteresting and unintelligent people, myself of course excepted, we did nothing but drift along the baking streets and stare indecisively about us. Curiously enough, I remember at once the smell of India. I cannot describe or analyse it. It is hot and somewhat spicy and it took me back ten years at one whiff. The squalor and general debility are very depressing. One remembers continually, if subconsciously, that we are masters here, conquerors, imperialists. And whether our subjects acquiesce in it or not, it is not a pleasant feeling.

4 April 1945

Solitary, I swam. Eric Copson was on the roof sunning himself, and after a bathe we had lunch together, which I enjoyed. Then I cycled into New Delhi, to Bette Davis in *Mr Skeffington*. It was an interesting experience to see a film about which I knew next to nothing . . . Certainly an artistic advance on *Now Voyager* and *Old Acquaintance*, and with some good, relatively adult things in it – George Coulouris as the psychoanalyst; Claude Rains in the early, less sentimental part of the picture, and of course, Bette throughout.

7 April 1945

An increase of staff from Bulbul coincides with a very dull and stagnant period in the office. And not only in the office: though I am on far more friendly terms with Patrick,[1] I am still 'Anderson' or 'Er . . .', which rather sickens. In fact, it gives me a terrible feeling of constraint and self-consciousness, which is just what I've been wanting to break down.

I have a ticket for Edith Evans[2] on Monday. And so has Patrick. It will be interesting to see how the evening works out – but I at least have the satisfaction of knowing that nothing in the world can stop me revelling in Edith's performance – and it is a *nice*, if not a great play.

Last night was awful, with creaking doors and windows, crickets, and extreme heat. I could not sleep and almost went mad with the creaking of the doors in the wind. I have become capable of swearing most profanely at the slightest material irritation.

9 May 1945

Fuck him! then, that's what I say. Let Patrick go to Hell. Let my emotions run dry. Let me become unconcerned whether he goes or stays, lives or dies. And indeed at this moment I feel that I can. 'O Lord!' he says as I put my head through his curtain, sipping my lemonade, as Leonard asks him where he was last night (for I want to know too). ('Oh staying with some people in Delhi.') In his pyjamas, his feet on his bed, reading

---

1. A Trinity College undergraduate, assigned to the same regiment.
2. The play was *The Late Christopher Breen* by Emlyn Williams.

Scarlet and Black. Well, I am no longer to be intimidated, and three months of Hell have at least brought me this measure of independence.

And another friendship (potential) starts to slide down the drain of disillusion.

I will not be so hypocritical with myself as to pretend that even at this moment I am not rather wishing, hoping that he will shuffle down to say goodnight – extremely unlikely in view of both his refrigerated heart and his pyjamas – and that I do not imagine (the indignity of it!) him at some future date turning to me for friendship. But it will not be solicited any more. And as he is unlikely to solicit anything himself, it will have to be left to GOD.

(Why the bloody hell when ever I hear a slipper shuffle, or a door open, do I have to wonder whose it is?)

14 May 1945

It is V Day and rather dull – which is not surprising in my case, I suppose, [for one] who pitches his ambitions so unreasonably, unrealistically high. Anyway, I have almost got to the stage of perpetual discontent now, not knowing what I want and frightened to question myself too closely in case I find out.

I went to the swimming gala this morning with Pat and Leonard and quite enjoyed it, suffering of course the usual jealousy of seeing indifferent performers win races I had been too lazy to enter for.

George Wood thinks that Patrick is 'nasty', a 'yes-man'. It is terrible to feel that an emotion which one had rated pretty high may have been founded on a complete misjudgement, on wilful self-deception. (This does not affect the worth of the *emotion* perhaps, but makes it sentimental rather than spiritual.) What have I to show for Patrick's acquaintance – what has he *given*? Little interest, little consideration for me as a person. Even now, for instance, when I went to see him I received only such a welcome as to make me say 'Goodness it's hot,' and come away with artificial nonchalance.

But to all this we may reply – you knew from the first what sort of a person he was, and you set yourself deliberately to make yourself known to him. To a certain extent you may regard wounds to your sensibility as self-inflicted then. If you choose to dig, you have no right to grumble at what you uncover. Also, you knew the process was going to be a slow one and there are many signs that it is progressing. In other words, your attitude must be changed from that of a passive admirer to a positive *friend*. You are, to a certain extent, taking upon yourself the reformation or humanising of a man's character, which is a very delicate and presumptious care. If you think he's worth it, you must be prepared to endure rebuffs and humiliations. If you don't think it worth it, you'd better cut your losses, which have not anyway been heavy.

It is only now that I am becoming fully and satisfactorily self-confident. And to this extent the experience has been valuable, if only I can turn it to good account. Consider, for instance, the wild dislike I took to James Harvey on first meeting him. I find it difficult to believe that I would behave like that again. Nor would I fall quite so readily for notions of Pat's intellectual superiority, nor allow Patrick's personality so to dominate me. Of course the trouble is that being, as I consider I am, a completely frank, open and unpretentious personality puts one under a disadvantage with the vast majority of people who affect a pose or erect barriers between themselves and the rest of the world. And I am afraid that I am too ready to judge them by my standards and assume their poses to be genuine. That is why it takes time, amongst new people, to get myself properly placed and [be] justly sure of myself.

4 June 1945

Ah sex! How obvious it is that without a satisfactorily adjusted sex life, a full and happy life is impossible: and I am chiefly frightened now that the repressions and introversion inevitable for me may end in twisting me, incapacitating me somehow as a person or as an artist (if I am an artist). I feel an increasing need to come out into the open – I have no more to be ashamed of than anybody else – though this of course is impossible.

And the deeper in I get, the further I am from spontaneity and simplicity, and the more difficult relations will become. Besides there is a very positive need for physical intercourse which, if continually repressed, may seep in and poison all my friendships.

I need the help probably of a technician in this sort of thing, a psycho-analyst. I need to find out whether I am irredeemably homosexual. Whether my instincts can or should be repressed or allowed scope or subliminated. How? All very simple really. The only danger seems to be a tendency to treat sex as a mere physical act like excreting. That must be guarded against.

I shall certainly do this when I get back to England.

31 August 1945

I do not much like this book[1] and think that I shall get out of it when I have finished this entry. It has been too full of emotion repressed and seething under high pressure – is that, I wonder, all I am capable of writing about in my journal? It's clear that whenever I get on paper I am immediately tempted to indulge my introversion and my egocentricity to such an extent that there is no energy left to deal more objectively with my surroundings, my contemporaries, or indeed any of my problems except the sexual ones – if indeed I have any.

But it might be worth (and I admit it will be pleasurable) to sum up the situation as I now see it . . .

---

1. L.A.'s diaries exist in numerous books and collections of loose pages. The book to which he refers runs from March to August 1945.

I am attracted by shapeliness, strength and manliness. There is accordingly a masochistic element in my character which is excited by thoughts of ill-treatment, brutality, etc. (probably quite falsely, romanticising what is in fact sordid and ugly). But this attraction is by no means purely sensual: it is accompanied by love – that is by a feeling of great affection and tenderness – when it is felt at its full strength. This of course makes the sufferings of repression all the more acute, since apart from mere physical strain and anguish I am tormented by the thought of the waste of so much potentially good, potentially beautiful – 'there's the torment, there's the hell'.

But I am also endowed, it seems, with a certain measure of virility. That is to say that while I can giggle and 'camp' with the best, I most certainly cannot do it seriously; and when I need, I can change my attitude to an almost purely masculine one, which indeed, superficially, is what I have had to do all through my life. I am not sure how fundamental this split is, how far I could consign myself to one or the other if I wished to, how far I could even marry a woman and lead a normal sex life if I forced myself to. I am conscious of course of a reluctance to try.

23 October 1945

Today I flew to Bhopal, to 'escort' twelve I[ndian] N[ationalist] A[rmy] prisoners back to Delhi, to be called, presumably, as witnesses at next month's INA trials. This promised to be an interesting excursion – just the sort of thing to be written up in the *New Statesman* – but of course proved to be nothing of the sort, extremely dull in fact, and rather irritating, though (as with any excursion outside these monastic walls) stimulating enough to nostalgic and speculative thought.

We were at the Willingdon Airport quite early – about eight, I suppose. Americans lay about on benches and I and Brammer sat down while the others (who were of course captains) strode efficiently to and fro. Finally, on receipt I suppose of some intelligence from somebody, we all got into the truck again and drove out to a runway. On the way we picked up two Raj officers going the same way and, we found out, on the same mission. Both were superbly dressed, with Sam Brownes, silver-knobbed canes, dress hats, and one with shorts, green stockings and red flashes. The trousered one was young, with a small head and a moustache, fairly tall and stupid: shorts was small, a captain, with thick lips and many and prominent teeth. He more or less took charge. I did not like him.

No credentials of course were asked for or given. We just stood about for a bit by our Dakota, then entered and seated ourselves. The journey down was very calm and quite uneventful. The only sights of the slightest interest were indeed Delhi and its environs and Bhopal. Not that there was much of Bhopal to see – a small, uninteresting town with a magnificent (from the air) military hospital, a temple on a rocky hill, a POW. camp and an aerodrome. We circled once and landed.

By truck then to the RAF officers' mess: RAF officers stood about, some going off in a truck, some reading the papers, one phoning. There was obviously nothing to do. We were promised some eggs and chips. I looked at the flowers outside and played Brammer a rather wearisome game of darts. Lunch opposite jovial RAF Types – very few 'gentlemen', if any .

Returning to our aircraft we found it being loaded by our charges with their baggage. One watched them curiously. They were not of course imposing, not in the least smart. But they were quiet, perfectly self-possessed and dignified in a natural and civilised way. I thought them well-mannered and pleasant. One wanted to ask them all sorts of questions of course. And could not. What had they done? Why? The one in the seat next to me was fish-faced and quite affable, giving me biscuits. We could not talk because the engines made too much noise.

The landscape was almost featureless, of a uniform red-brown covered spasmodically with shrub. Here and there a ridge burst out of the plain or a river wound with an almost lacquered appearance through the dry earth. I read Trollope's *Autobiography* most of the time – an interesting, forthright, dogmatic book, without pretension. He was far too much of an English gentleman to be able to talk comfortably about his personal life, so he did not try. His views on art generally and that of novel writing in particular are almost valueless, but the details he gives (very fully) of his own methods of composition are very interesting.

Things are, at the moment, in quite a state of flux and uncertainty. I wrote to Bowra [at Oxford] about Class B, and until I get a reply cannot feel at all settled, or able to make any positive step about the future. With all this spare time one naturally has the leisure to brood upon the prospect before us, and the more one broods, the less satisfactory does it become.

———————

He returned to England in February 1946 and took up his studies at Oxford, switching from Classical Studies to English Literature.

23 February 1946

I cannot help feeling, as I settle down to covering these delightfully virginal pages with my hopes, ideas, frustrations and activities, that I am indulging in what may easily develop into a rather pernicious habit. It is so much easier to introspect than it is to write creatively, to write critically or even to read . . . and I certainly have not been doing enough lately of any of those. It is comfortable of course to be able to ascribe these hesitations and delays to the war, and to think of this as a period of reorientation; but I am aware nonetheless that I would have found precisely the same difficulties had it not been for the war, and that in fact I have never been purposefully orientated.

This morning, for instance: called at ten to eight. Feel incredibly drowsy and [too] impotent to crawl from bed: it is blowing and raining outside. Finally look at my watch, under my clothes on the chair beside my bed, see it is almost twenty to nine, pull on my clothes and fur-lined boots and dash for Hall. Scrambled eggs on toast. Sit on the Junior Scholars' table at the end; a nuisance because one has to ask for everything. As a result I have to – or prefer to – eat eggs without salt and pepper. After breakfast return to room, clean shoes. Say good morning to new Scout. With Sweet's *Anglo Saxon Primer* in hand go to lavatory. Complete translation of first section of sentences on my favourite seat – end one on right (dropped in at JCR on the way to see the morning's film reviews). After lavatory return to room, begown myself, plus Old Cheltonian scarf (wondering vaguely if I look too 'undergraduate' in it) and yellow string gloves, and set out for Jesus. Discuss the merits and demerits of Sweet's and Bright's *Grammars* with Angus Mackintosh. He alternatively puffs at and refills his pipe.

25 February 1946

REORIENTATION
A sonnet

What was it, far away, we thought we'd find
In this strange city? Now, returned at last
Out of the present to a youthful past,
Do we find comfort here, and calm of mind?
We have, it's true, grown older as we've ranged,
Yet hopes and doubts and fears are with us still
(Hope something weakened); but for good or ill
　this proud and lovely city has not changed.
And from its many steeples there still chime
　those same importunate bells, now near now far,
Each quarter telling off the wasting time
　through the long day and through the longer night:
But how and where we may achieve the light
　they tell us not, nor what, nor why we are.

5 March 1946

Tea with Peter Currie and Curtis and the Cheltonian Society Commitee. Afterwards get onto the subject of Coll. and stumble on the track of a rather exciting anti-headmaster conspiracy, but unfortunately not operating from the humane but the reactionary standpoint. Must go over and find out more about this. Curtis was very secretive, but let quite enough out of the bag to be going on with. He is a rather unfortunate type, who had a most awful time during the war but can't keep it out of his conversation ('I've been beaten up several times by Japanese guards, and I can tell you it isn't pretty').

Saw Terence Rattigan's new play tonight *The Winslow Boy*,[1] elder son Dickie is reprimanded for his failure in Mods, and his addiction to ragtime, while poor Ronnie stands outside in the rain, frightened to face his father, a man whose tongue is as ironic as his heart is golden. The boy, it appears, has been unjustly accused of theft and dismissed. Usual competent West End comedy drama type, expert, entertaining and unoriginal. Next to me was a terrible woman who would insist on attempting fully to appreciate every detail of performance and production ('a superb piece of work' – everything was a piece of work. 'Of course he's not just a popular dramatist; he's a craftsman.') A lovely little sketch by Mona Washbourne.[2]

10 March 1946

Whether it is just the turn in the weather, or I am really improving I don't know, but I do seem to be settling down a bit – not working much harder admittedly, but more content as horizons unfold. Not that they are unfolding with any great speed. Film Society is being breached, and I'm reviewing *The Stork Club* tomorrow for the *Isis* [Oxford University student newspaper], and contemplating (with trepidation) launching or attempting to launch a magazine . . .

28 April 1946

Yesterday I did nothing except see my tutor – Bamborough, Mackintosh is fortunately ill – and go in the afternoon to see *The Way to the Stars*[3] . . .

The Way to the Stars I found not very impressive: perhaps I was prejudiced, perhaps I had been told too often how 'good' it was. Anyway it seemed to me a pretty obviously contrived piece of artifice: the appalling 'upper-middle' atmosphere; the complacency of the 'typically English' type; the inhibitions, the smugness, the goodness of it all! Judging by fairly low standards, I suppose this sort of stuff is an enormous advance on callow nonsense like *Flying Fortress*, *A Yank in the RAF*, *Winged Victory*, etc. But elevate your standards a little and you soon begin to feel a little less satisfied with the present state of the British film industry. Technically, and to a certain extent intelligently, our films have advanced, but in between essentially synthetic stories like *The Way to the Stars* and works of true art like *Strange Incident*,[4] *Fires Were Started*[5] and *Hostages*[6] is a great gulf fixed. And the Gulf is called BOX OFFICE.

---

1. At the Lyric Theatre, Shaftesbury Avenue.
2. British actress (1903–1988) who would play the matron in L.A.'s own production about troubled schoolboys and an endangered headmaster, *If* . . . . (1968).
3. Rattigan-scripted film by Anthony Asquith, with Trevor Howard as a British officer on a bomber base in Britain.

I want to write something about British Films – the time is ripe for constructive *criticism*. There is too much adulation flying about at the moment.

Then later this morning I went to see Michael and unburdened to him my soul on the subject of *The Way to the Stars*, which we discussed – I becoming more and more vehement in my condemnation as the nauseatingly smug sanctification of English inhibition and class prejudice appeared to me more and more distinctly in its true form.

Wash, change corduroy to flannel trousers, then round to the Warden's lodgings (as punctually as I could manage) for tea at 4.30. At first, as he ushered me in to his little sub-drawing room, I was dismayed to see only two cups on the little table by the gas fire. Thus intimidated, words stuck and subjects of conversation fled from the mind – weather (a terrible necessity, but it saved the day, as so often).

1 May 1946

Morris – the porter – woke me at five this morning, thinking I was Wiseman who wanted to hear the May morning carols. As a result I slept late and didn't get up till nine, with a muzzy head.

Out to coffee at Miss Brown's – far too crowded – and read my review of *Anchors Aweigh* in the *Isis*. As usual it looked 'smart', slick and badly-written. After lunch the weather was so lovely that I began to feel depressed. Carried my tarts up to my room and ate a chocolate-date one sitting desparingly in my chair. Eventually I lay down with *Crime and Punishment*.

13 May 1946

I made for Blackwell's [bookshop] . . . When I got back, I found a note on my bookcase from Patrick, asking me to tea. I was not sure whether I would go or not, but after spending the afternoon in the garden, watching the rehearsal [of *The Alchemist* by Ben Jonson, in which he played Lovewit] and trying to formulate some ideas for a script, there seemed no valid reason why I should not. So I idled round to Trinity, chatted with Tom in the quad for a few minutes, then went up.

When I knocked and entered Patrick's room he was lying on his couch reading *These Foolish Things*. Tables and window sills were pleasantly littered with books; the atmosphere a little close. Partly because of this, partly to cloak my usual embarrassment with him, I went over to open the other window. Patrick got up with his usual air of polite discomfort and started to prepare tea. I sat down on the window seat.

When tea was ready I sat, legs up, in the window-seat, he in a chair opposite, the table between us. We talked vociferously enough – the Film Society, Bowra's inaugural,

---

4. American lynching film, aka *The Ox-Bow Incident*. Directed by William Wellman.
5. Humphrey Jennings's film about the Fire Service during the Blitz.
6. From Stefan Heym's novel about Nazi executions in occupied Prague. Directed by Frank Tuttle.

work . . . We drifted, naturally, onto personal topics; typically enough onto *him*. He says he is maladjusted, feels the need to kick over the traces, to go abroad so that he can do it without shaming friends and family.

29 May 1946

A bad period just now, on the whole; predominant characteristics – a sort of heavy emptiness inside.

The Alchemist is over and done with, successfully though exhaustingly. The *Isis* review today has provoked much inter-cast comment: I am not of course mentioned – not that I had much right to expect it, since Lovewit is a small enough part, however important structurally and dramatically. Anyway I am beginning to tire of all this tittle-tattle and to feel I must get my teeth into something solid. Whether writing or acting or editing. *The Alchemist* was not a happy production – too much backbiting, wrangling, conceit amongst the cast. Alan Major has just come round with the photographs. Ugh! One more inducement to retire into a monastery.

The 'emptiness' comes of course, at least in part, from other things. My extraordinary passionate crisis about Patrick was followed by an equally passionate revulsion from the whole idea, and I have made no attempt to follow it up. In general my attitude towards personal relationships has become one of hopeless sterility: I find myself shrinking from almost any human intercourse – it seems all stale, flat and improfitable. And all, I suppose, because Love has to be renounced.

There seems indeed no more to be said.

24 June 1946

Term ended last week, but as usual I linger on indecisively, waiting to trip over to Cheltenham on Friday for the usual Speech Day celebrations.

And what has the term been like? Not good, I'm afraid. I haven't been well – heavy and depressed, unable to concentrate, unable even to waste time profitably. What's the answer – sex chiefly quiescent . . . With regard to girls so strong an inhibition has been set up that I feel powerless to attempt its destruction. So I am retiring more and more into a solitary world, apathetic and defeatist now about all personal relationships.

4 August 1946

Returned yesterday from Barnstaple after three weeks with *The Castle of Perseverance*.[1] My joining the cast at all was a piece of quite fortuitous luck. I went round to John Colley's rooms in New College after seeing once again *The Maltese Falcon*[2] at the Electra, to find him drinking with Richard Falkener, whom I'd met a few days before at

---

1. Anon, medieval.
2. American thriller starring Humphrey Bogart and Mary Astor. Directed by John Huston.

dinner at the Taj. It was Dicky who suggested our going with *The Castle* – because they happened to be short of two men. My assent was somehow more politic than spontaneously enthusiastic. I was to play Sloth and John Gluttony.

Next day there was a meeting of the cast in Dicky's rooms, to be told about arrangements etc. I didn't know many people: Tim, of course, was not forthcoming since I was not in a particularly important position; there was Kenneth Tynan[1] – to be viewed at that time with something approaching suspicion – Peter Symcox; no one else really, oh – Guy Brenton.[2] Guy I'd noticed before in Oxford; quite why I don't know, except that I had the feeling that I'd like him before I'd met him. Small, pointed features, bad complexion, with something of a look about him of Claude Rains, very piercing voice (his most unfortunate feature, this).

At first I was self-conscious and rather aloof. Getting to know people is always difficult especially when they already know each other, and you are quite in the dark as regards their relationships.

After the first rehearsal in Exeter we moved to Wadham Chapel, where we went through the play time after time without seeming to get much better (I remember Dicky's incapacity, and the adornment of one of the sepulchral effigies with cigarettes, flowers, dark glasses and cider bottles, and crawling about slothfully on the antechapel floor).

On the Sunday before the London opening we had our first experience of the sort of communal production which was to be the method adapted more or less throughout the tour. Dicky, feeling no doubt his incapacity, agreed without hesitation to any suggestions that were offered to him, and the rehearsal proceeded in stages, with everyone not 'on' sitting in front and criticising at the conclusion of each scene.

The London run. During this I stayed with Gavin, did a certain amount of work (not very much) at the BFI for *Movie Parade*, and wasted an incredible amount of time. One of the most awkward and unenjoyable features of the tour was the nightly trek to some café to eat – great crocodiles roaming uneasily through the streets of Soho, ill-sorted and un-gay – the sediment of unconnected girls (Mary Scott, Heather Ogilvie); the tendency also to be cliquey – a pity.

Audiences in London were not good. Insufficient attempts had been made to entice reviewers. Indeed our only press notice was a story in the *Evening Standard*, which only lasted for one brief edition in the early afternoon. St Thomas, by the way, was an excellent playing ground. Broad, carpeted steps, dark wooden background. We had to wait in a tiny little room backstage left, the air thick with cigarette smoke (since Ken couldn't

---

1. Later the theatre critic for the *Observer*, the literary manager at the National Theatre and the creator of the nude musical revue, *Oh! Calcutta!* (1969).
2. (1927–). With whom L.A. would write and direct the Oscar-winning documentary film *Thursday's Children* (1953).

exist without cigarettes), the atmosphere pregnant with suppressed laughter – especially after the 'whipping scene' when Pride, Wrath and Envy usually joined in to swell the shrieking of the Fleshy Sins.

We only did two performances at Bath, without a matinee (in itself a mistake), and did not do too badly. At Bath I shared a billet with Joan Radford, the plump, come-hitherish wench who got more success with Eric Wetherall than with me. There was a parrot in the hall which said 'Hullo Polly' very realistically.

I journeyed to Exeter with Jeremy Gentilli, quietly working out publicity details on the way. We arrived with posters and cards ready-prepared, though of course with the cathedral as our theatre we were assured of a certain degree of success. When we arrived at St Luke's Theological College [our billet] we found it a long, ivy-covered building almost completely gutted by fire. Finally, Dicky found a side entrance to that part of the college which hadn't been blown up and we all trooped in. Dicky vanished in search of the principal. It began to drizzle. Since nothing seemed to be happening we took refuge in a garage opening onto the yard. Here, amongst some loose papers on the floor, were a number of Church Army leaflets. We started to sing hymns – 'O God our help', 'Glorious things of Thee are spoken', 'Abide with me' (a trumpet solo from Eric). Our heartfelt appeals soared to God. They were answered. We were given somewhere to sleep.

Production in the Cathedral did not entail very much difficulty, except that they had erected the stage too far back and it had to be moved further forward. However I did not take part in the fuss. It was of course the most impressive setting we'd had, and rather a thrill to play in. The first night we drew about 300 people, which was exciting, and we looked for big money in the collection – and excitement mounted even higher when we heard there was £5 for programmes. However when the collection amounted to £13, a certain anti-climax was experienced.

On the day of the matinee I accompanied Ken in the wireless wagon: 'Hello Exeter! The Oxford University Players calling Exeter! Today is your last chance to see *The Castle of Perseverance*. This lovely old play . . .'

Growing enterprising, we even gave a scene from the play – Mankind is tempted by Covetous to descend from the Castle of Virtue – and fictitious blurbs: 'Your Dean has said of this production, "This is the most exciting thing that has ever happened to me!" '

After all this, Ken got waylaid in the Clarence bar, with the result that he arrived quarter seas over for the matinee and gave a gloriously rollicking performance, riding his throne as though it were a dolphin and indulging throughout in the most delicious extravagances. Anyway the matinee produced £30-odd.

At St Luke's I made a threesome, for sleeping purposes, with Paul and Guy. On two of the evenings we played games – Adverbs and Adjectives. How acute Liz turned out to be – how, indeed, I had underestimated her!

10 January 1947

Friday . . . Last Friday was a busy, and tiring day. Up in town by about 10.30, I went to *My Darling Clementine*[1] at the Odeon, and thoroughly enjoyed it. On the slow side even taking into account its purposely leisurely rhythm, but beautiful to look at throughout, and with [Henry] Fonda giving his usual magnetic performance. The film as a whole has a sense of doing exactly what it set out to do, which makes it the most satisfying entertainment I've had for some time.

19 April 1947

The new Alan Ladd film, *Wild Harvest*, is about to appear in the West End. The advertisement consists of a clenched fist round which is wound a leather belt, the buckle outwards just waiting it seems to make contact with someone's jaw – or even, with its sharp point, to put out someone's eye. Round the wrist of this fist is hung a chain with an identification bracelet on it. It is hard enough to control my masochistic imagination as it is without having this sort of thing thrust at me in my daily paper – even to write about it gives me a rise. How many people are similarly affected? Women, of course, are proverbially fond of being dominated – is it merely an appeal to that, no more? Where does one draw the line between that and masochism? Presumably the answer is that our emotions have become coarsened, crude; now all sensations have to be violent to be felt at all.

20 April 1947

I went to Aldershot – to see *Four Men and a Prayer*, because it was directed by John Ford. You really would not know it: at first I thought it was going to be a delightful piece of romantic hokum, but it turned out to be strictly dreary. If I write to him again (as I probably will after *The Fugitive*), I shall tar him with it and ask him if he really directed it – only one tiny sequence showed any interest at all; the massacre of an unarmed mob.

As I walked up from the Cambridge, I found myself repeating not the Wordsworth which I had attempted unsuccessfully to learn on the way, but Alan's lines: 'Paradise is for the Blessed / Not for the sex-obsessed'.[2]

4 May 1947

The Czech Film Festival – *our* Czech Film Festival – took place today. A thoroughly exhausting business, though managed, on the whole quite well.

---

1. By John Ford, with Henry Fonda as Wyatt Earp.
2. These lines are spoken at the closing of the opening chapter of *If . . . .*

The Oxford Film Society gave a grant for Anderson and Peter Ericsson to re-launch Sequence, *a magazine previously backed by the Society which had closed after one issue. The first Anderson issue featured a cover still of Henry Fonda in* My Darling Clementine. *Lois Sutcliffe, who ran the Wakefield Film Society, met Anderson on a visit to Oxford. Sutcliffe: 'I saw the new* Sequence Two *and immediately ordered twenty copies. To his surprise I was confident I could sell them to members of the film society I ran in Wakefield.'*

10 July 1947

This draws to a close. Tonight I rang home, and arranged to be carted away to the womb on Sunday. What I need now is to be rescued. I have copied down Matthew Arnold's lines about 'Who, I swear, learns to await / No gifts from chance, has conquered Fate', but what I go through the streets searching for is – a gift from chance.

2

Onwards!

First Films – Serge Reggiani – Thursday's Children
Free Cinema – Serjeant Musgrave's Dance
The Lily White Boys

'As regards behaviour, I keep imagining that I have "got better",
but I am far from perfectly in control; and it was interesting
that my unbridled tongue created deeper resentment
during shooting than I was quite aware of at the time.'

———————

*After graduating, with an MA in English, and on the invitation of Lois Sutcliffe,
he travelled North, to Wakefield, to make his first film.*

21 May 1948

A new chapter all right: I am twenty-five now, and feel forty – but at least something
has been achieved. 3,000 feet of advertising film in fact.

I don't know if *Meet the Pioneers* is any good; by intuition I feel that it is quite
interesting, rather scrappy and also rather too conventional in approach. Certain
sequences – the Drawing Office for instance – are right out of the stock book; and
generally the treatment is on the obvious side. Nevertheless, it will be interesting to see
how it will be received by the many different kinds of people who will be at the
premiere.

Oddly enough, I feel that as regards a career in films this experience has left me
pretty much where I was. I never seriously doubted my ability to produce something,
once my feet were set on the track and I was given a shove. I suppose I have gained in
self-confidence. Apart from the photography, after all, I did the whole thing myself –
editing, writing and speaking the commentary, arranging the music. Yet all this has not
exactly convinced me that I can or even want to get a job in a studio – or even make
another film for Sutcliffes. Although I suppose I *shall* do the latter.

Between 1948 and 1954, Anderson made four films for the Yorkshire industrial firm, Richard Sutcliffe Ltd: Meet the Pioneers *(1948),* Idlers that Work *(1949),* Three Installations *(1952) and* Trunk Conveyor *(1954). After graduation, and with the Film Society declining to finance further issues of* Sequence, *he took it with him to London, where he rented a room in a flat owned by Gavin Lambert. From December 1947 to December 1950, with money willed to him by an aunt, he published* Sequence *as a quarterly.*

31 August 1948

This would be the time to start a new journal; but I am always doing that – leaving books half-finished – which is a bad habit, besides taking up so much room in my cupboard. So I continue in the same one, despite the huge gap between now and my last row of entries.

A great deal has happened, though I have no real sense of achievement. It is something, after all, to have made a film 3,000 feet long, whatever it is like; to be co-editor of Britain's most highly-esteemed film magazine; to be holding down a job (practically a sinecure) at £10 a week. To a certain extent, perhaps, this dissatisfaction is due to expecting to get on too fast. Some people sky-rocket to fame and accomplishment, but I know I am not one of these. I am not the sort of person to achieve celebrity much before forty (is fifteen years a long or a short time?)

In the last weeks I have attended the premiere of my film at the Savoy Cinema, Lupset; played Horatio for a week at the Civic Playhouse, Cheltenham;[1] and sunbathed at Eastbourne. At the moment I am at home, minding the dogs and the hens for three days while Father has a holiday at the Hydro. A week or ten days will see the appearance of *Sequence Five* – then another film made, called (or at any rate *about*) *Two Installations*.

19 December 1948

So it goes on . . . or doesn't. I mean to keep this journal going, but only very occasionally find myself with the energy to write it.

Things develop fairly satisfactorily; on the surface anyway. The fundamental dissatisfactions remain. The great thing that has transpired is the possibility of working for [John] Ford. I wrote to him about a month ago – after seeing *They Were Expendable* for the second time in Bradford, with Lois and Eunice. Then, ten days or so later, I asked Jack Beddington [former Head of the Films Division of the Ministry of Information] if he'd support me. In London, on Thursday morning, there arrived a letter from Beddington enclosing a note to him from Ford. At first reading, the note seemed almost embarrassingly sentimental – gushy. But it included the assurance that, *if* he comes to England, he'll certainly use me.

---

1. In Kenneth Tynan's flamboyant undergraduate production of the rarely performed First Quarto *Hamlet* (1603), in which the most famous soliloquy begins 'To be or not to be, aye there's the point.'

It is rather strange how reverential I have come to feel about Ford – in spite of not really liking his past two pictures. I think perhaps that this latest stage has been reached through *They Were Expendable*, a film which has taken its place beside *The Grapes of Wrath* for its heroic size, its subtle simplicity, its intimacy and its poetry.

Gavin's reaction was merely to remark that the letter sounded 'drunken'.

I somehow couldn't even bring myself to show it to Peter [Ericsson], when he staggered in to breakfast, coughing and bleary-eyed. In spite of all attempts at candour during the past few weeks, it is now evident that in order to find support and encouragement for my determination (slowly crystallising) to become a film-maker, I shall have to look elsewhere than to *Sequence* . . . Both Gavin and Peter make tentative efforts now and then to express polite interest [in my film-making], but they are pitifully transparent. I can't possibly regard as intimate *friends* two people who share my interest in the cinema, but who have no regard or curiosity whatever for my work in it.

Since I have now reached the stage where I should attempt to draw some positive conclusion, my spirits naturally start to flag. Problems which rouse themselves, arising naturally from these reflections are: How serious am I about becoming a film director? Am I satisfied to muddle along as I do now? Am I to stay with Sutcliffes? For how long? Should I try and get a job in the industry? Can I keep on with *Sequence*?

If I carry on this year as I did last, I shall make progress, but not spectacularly. Looking back over 1948, there is no doubt that I now know more, feel more about the cinema than I did then. I am about ripe in fact for another attempt at making – having perhaps digested *Meet the Pioneers* by this time, seen some errors and got some rather clearer ideas.

2 January 1949

In view of experience so far on *The Assembly and Dissembly of the Goliath Gearhead*,[1] perhaps it only goes to prove what I already know – that I am not good at work 'off the cuff', that I need to observe and to study what I have to film before I can, with any confidence, envisage a completed film. And I am not experienced enough to just shoot away, and rely on editing and commentary to pull me through. At a stage such as this I feel my inexperience keenly. I haven't really the slightest idea for instance how to set about filming the assembly tomorrow. Not that I am too seriously worried: something will come out of it.

Being alone in Wakefield affords plenty of opportunity for morbid introspection. I have reached a stage now of an almost complete incapacity to use my spare time, to concentrate and to organise. This is the only sort of writing I find easy to do, and an occasional letter when the spirit happens to move me.

I sleep rather badly, with continuous, restless dreams. Last night I was appearing as Caliban in Act V of a play whose name I forget (not *The Tempest* – *A Midsummer Night's*

---

1. Sutcliffe film, released as *Idlers That Work* (1949).

Dream, perhaps, under a different title). I was acting with Mary Astor, and didn't know my part, so I used a large text, which kept shutting and I kept losing my place. I was waiting expectantly for the passage 'The isle is full of strange noises . . .', but I woke before we got so far.

From October 1950 to 1 June 1951, Anderson observed and, in the book Making a Film, *chronicled the making of Thorold Dickinson's* Secret People: *'I knew that* Secret People *didn't stand a chance the moment I read the script. But of course I was merely an "apprentice" in those days, and no one was going to listen to any criticisms from me. The book I wrote is not exactly dishonest, but I had to suppress all the critical thoughts I had, because of the nature of the book and the fact that Thorold was my patron.' (Letter to Broderick Miller, 1 October 1990) One of the cast members was Serge Reggiani, whom Anderson befriended and worked with in Paris on a production of* Hamlet.

10 October 1951

Oh! to whom? Perhaps that is the first question. For when, over the past year or two, I have thought of starting a journal again, the question has always presented itself – unanswerably. Who am I to write for? The answer 'for myself' has always seemed insufficient . . . It is Serge in some extraordinary way who has quickened my desire for expression – the impulse to share, to give; and not merely material things, but experiences, emotions and ideas. But I cannot write letters – there seems to be nothing at the other end. Serge's own letters are staccato, factual; he ventures on no thoughts. One accepts that. But there is no sense in letting the impulse generated in myself run to waste on that account. A note-book may be the answer.

13 October 1951

One wants to share, to give . . . I write on impulse, at about 7.15 in the morning, before I force myself out of bed. I have just been reading Joyce Cary – *To Be a Pilgrim*[1] – a book [imbued] with life, with the pains and waste and aspiration and fruition of life all jumbled up together. Somehow this connects itself with the idea of Serge, and I am conscious of this indefinable urge welling up inside me. I cannot look beyond it, and it easily turns away into fear, the acknowledgement of impossibility, the awareness of essential isolation. But perhaps (I can only hope) it is the beginning of something.

14 October 1951

Still reading *To Be a Pilgrim*. Cary's writing is amazing in its rigour, its grasp of life. The way he conjures up whole lines out of the void, and weaves them into a texture so close and rich and true.

---

1. Also the refrain of the hymn – 'He who would valiant be' – sung by the whole school in *If . . .* .

To someone as intimidated by life, as unsure of himself as I, there is something formidable in this intensely male drive onward. 'Are you coming or aren't you?'[1] No reassurance, not much patience for the timid, the lingering with one foot in the womb. It is
something like this that I feel with Serge. Again the ruthlessness, the hardness of the
very male. Serge represents to me a way of living, of organising life and work and personal relations.

When I have finished editing *Three Installations*,[2] I shall visit Serge and Janine in
Paris, forcing myself not to write again until I am ready to go, and not to expect any
such nonsense as an invitation from friends who will be very glad to have me – if they
possibly can.

20 October 1951

Back in Wakefield my old habits of escape, indolence, discouragement have reasserted
themselves. I returned slowly on Wednesday, stopping off at York, where I walked
about a little, bought a rather handsome yellow scarf, had a drink at Betty's Bar, and
looked at the Minster. Characteristically, I responded with more lively interest in a
stocky workman, one of three hauling scaffolding up the West Front, than to the
interior grandeurs.

At the works I have started, slowly and without enthusiasm, to assemble the film. It
is a depressing as well as a laborious business, for the whole thing seems to me stale,
timid, an indication that film-writing is not my vocation. Strengthened by a viewing
on Thursday of *Idlers That Work* – shown at the Savoy to the proprietor of the
Wakefield Gazette, who is considering the celebration of his paper's centenary with the
production of a film.[3] Naturally, I did not see the film through, but observed bits of it
from the projection box (with the awful 'pi' voice dinning round the walls); it seemed
slow, pedestrian and – yes – *afraid*. To this extent, the films are truly personal. I refuse
to indulge in the flashy for its own sake, and try to avoid the more notorious clichés;
but in their place can be found only an utterly conventional conception, proceeding in
a number of unadventurous, if tastefully arranged, set-ups. I suppose it's still possible
that *Three Installations* will constitute an advance; but I feel that any progression in it
is comparative – no liberation.

Which is not surprising, since I am not liberated in any, any sense.

It is impossible to avoid quoting Amiel:

'In the name of Heaven, who art thou? – what wilt thou? – wavering inconstant
creature. What future lies before thee? What duty or what hope appeals to thee?

'My longing, my search is for love, for peace, for something to fill my heart; an idea
to defend; a work to which I might devote the rest of my strength; an affection which

---

1. Echoes of Alan Price's 'Are you coming or staying?' in *O Lucky Man!*

2. The first of twelve L.A. films photographed by Walter Lassally.

3. *Wakefield Express* , which L.A. made in August 1952.

might quench this inner thirst; a cause for which I might die with joy. But shall I ever find them? I long for all that is impossible . . . What I really want is to die and to be born again, transform myself, and in a different world . . .'

1951 (undated):
I fled to Paris in a state of physical and mental exhaustion. Derek York's[1] method of editing *Three Installations* had driven me almost mad – the interminable delays, the infantile slogans and Ford-worship, not to speak of the utter inadequacy of the film itself. I had to get away. To what I hardly knew; it was very much a case of throwing myself onto the mercy of providence. At least it would be an experience. On the last afternoon I bought a camera – the one I had been on the verge of buying for weeks, and a white shirt. Then Miriam and I went to Hector's for a cup of tea, and I charged Miriam with the care of my film, kissed her on the cheek and sent her off. I left from Waterloo at ten o'clock, with a loaded bag and a round cardboard container which enclosed a poster for *Secret People*, together with the BFI file of press cuttings.

So I arrived at the Gare St Lazare at a quarter to eleven next morning. Serge was leaning somewhat moodily over the barrier, in that well-remembered black overcoat and that white woollen scarf. He did not see me, and I did not call or wave, but walked round behind him and tapped him on the shoulder with the container.

In the final months of 1951, Anderson consolidated his reputation as one of Britain's foremost film critics, contributing articles to Sight and Sound, New Statesman, The Times *and the* Observer. *The fourteenth and final edition of* Sequence *featured a poem by James Broughton, whose next film,* The Pleasure Garden, *was produced by Anderson.*

10 August 1952
It is interesting to note that *The Pleasure Garden*[2] now over (the shooting of it, that is), angst has returned with intensity. Is this the result of being brought once more face to face with the necessity to control life? I have at least one project between myself and nullity – the *Wakefield Express* film. For this I go north tomorrow.

Largely using their own money, and with equipment from James Carr's World Wide Films, Anderson and Guy Brenton made a film about deaf and dumb children. It won the 1955 Academy Award for Documentary Short.

---

1. Who would edit the 1968 film of John Osborne's *Inadmissible Evidence*, in which L.A. played a barrister.

2. L.A. appears, in a cowboy suit, as the male love interest.

4 November 1953

This evening we showed 'the film' [*Thursday's Children*] (no title seems to have stuck to it) to Jimmy Carr for the second time, cut by twelve or thirteen minutes from the version we showed him last week. It is still not down to twenty minutes: probably it can be, though with a certain loss. Certainly as entertainment it has benefited: it fairly rattles along now, every shot sharp and tingling with life. Full of charm and personality – the children and Miss Taylor and Miss Massey. I think it is a success. Jimmy Carr will certainly 'buy' it now . . . after that, goodness knows.

We have worked hard at it, and I am tired. Exhausted too by nervous strain. Working with Guy is not exactly a holiday: no doubt I plague him as he plagues me. Also fatal is his terrible conviction of moral superiority, past which nothing can get. Humourless too. The film is his creation of course, as a project completely his. After that – I suppose pretty well 50–50 his and mine. On his own he'd almost certainly have made a mess of it – buggered it up with his 'theoretical' ideas. And on my own, I'd never even have begun.

18 January 1954

Paris –[for *Hamlet*] finishing off that piece on Stroheim for the *Observer* in the bus on the way to the airport. When I arrived I phoned Serge: he was working so I joined him. Questions of movements – coordinating exits and entrances: he went through his ideas, I contributing suggestions, sometimes valuable in themselves, sometimes combining or conflicting with Serge's own ideas to produce something new. This went well.

'This will be the *best Hamlet*, don't you think so?'

'I hope so: I've never seen a good one.'

The combination of pride, of sheer enjoyment, and of humorous self-caricature, is of course utterly sympathetic . . . He is going at it with characteristic impetuosity; he has read most of the French texts and come out for Pagnol, as being at least clear, unpretentious, *speakable* French. No poeticising, and yet more theatrical and less cold than Gide. He denies any conception or theory behind his production. He wants to work from the play . . . An example of exactly the kind of presentation Serge has no sympathy with was provided by the Stratford *Antony and Cleopatra*, of which he saw the first two-thirds. 'Thumbs down' was the first decisive comment he made (by gesture), when we met in the first interval. 'It's terrible – isn't it?' All the comments one has so often made on the artificiality of contemporary theatrical (particularly Shakespearean) production would be accepted by him completely – the mannerisms of technique and delivery. 'They try to make everything look beautiful – beautiful like a shop window. Shakespeare isn't beautiful, not like that. He is violent and cruel and ugly too.'

He is very influenced by Trauner, and by Trauner's ideas of rhythm in decor – decor not merely as decoration, but as a dynamic contribution to the theatrical presentation.

But, as indeed he admitted, he is very reluctant to make criticisms of the work of people to whom he has committed himself. This results occasionally I think in an almost wilful self-deception; one must accept the slight falsity that can result.

I am very aware of how, in a sense, undignified my attachment to Serge may seem; my acceptance of his payment – for every single meal and drink I've had in his company in Paris, and 6,000 francs beside – at a time when money is short and a worry for him. At times I feel like a moth, fascinated by the intensity of this light, returning to it again and again to singe its wings. That is one way of looking at it. Another is to regard this place – this relationship – as a source of energy, or inspiration even. Not that there is anything perfect in it: but this is how I conceive people – artists – should live: generously, emotionally, selfishly, with struggle. And this seems to be focused in Serge, its intensest luminary, the most perplexed, tortured and sensitive of its talents.

6 June 1954
Paris. Flew back from London last night after a week spent recording (and writing!) commentary for *Trunk Conveyor*, and starting work on the music. It is pleasant, and healthy to return with a sense of achievement behind one. However minor one's efforts. And I find that I am really quite proud of and even affectionate towards this film (though the pretentious ambitions I had for it are hardly realised. Humanity . . . poetry, etc.).

13 June 1954
A few words must be written, demand to be written, at this point of time. The enterprise is over. That is to say *Hamlet* has been played, has succeeded – at least for the world, and all but the most intimate critics – brilliantly. Today, the hotel has been full of the *copains* of Serge.

22 July 1954
Writing these notes is not a bad way, perhaps of setting the mind going. If there is no one else to talk to, talk to yourself. It is all a little worrying, however. This time last year, I was forced into action by Guy [Brenton]: it is a slightly disturbing thought that the only *valid* film I have been concerned with had to be made in collaboration – and with him . . . That collaboration, at least will never be resumed. Another fierce exchange with him over the showing to Republic of *Thursday's Children*, at which I connived with World Wide that he should not be present. Yes, certainly I felt guilty to have rounded and completely sided with his 'enemies'. But, of course, if you insist in so truthfully condemning another's conduct, you leave him with no alternative but to ring off. As I did.

23 July 1954

Gravitated to the British Film Institute towards the end of the morning, to misbehave myself in typical fashion, hectoring Penelope[1] for her neglect of 'documentary'. First Penelope angered me of course by her transparent indifference to these noble workers in documentary, then even more (!) by her suggestion that she might give a page to the Australian *Back of Beyond* . . . No use, her attitude to *Thursday's Children* reduces me to blind fury.

Christmas 1954

Review of the year. It has been a pretty eventful one; and an important one too I think – surprisingly, in a way, and unconsciously just by taking things as they came, 'plugging on', gaining much in self-confidence by a simple process of doing things. There has been a striking development in my 'career' – entry into the [film-makers'] union, etc.

I went to Paris in January. *Trunk Conveyor*: I had started preparing this before January, of course; but now came shooting time . . . It went well. I had started with fancy ideas, wanting the whole thing to be as realistic as possible, with a sense of work and sweat and swearing about it, and perhaps visually chiaroscuro . . . But the latter ideas went straight away – probably rightly for, after all, the film was intended to be instructional, and there would have been no point in artying it up until one was left with nothing but atmosphere. The whole operation does come out a little too easy as it is filmed – very concentrated and explicit and unmuddled. Partly time was to blame for this: partly also my not having clarified in my mind just where such a sequence should go, and what it should consist of. Another thing: although the human side of it is *not* left out, I think perhaps it could have been a little stronger. Time and again the influence of orthodox documentary filming, as represented by John [Reid, photographer], who for all his talk, didn't really grasp what I was after in this direction. Hence, at important junctures, one or two very slick, meaningless, big-head-in-foreground compositions, where what we wanted was something not *composed* but *felt* (the first of the two snap-time shots, for instance).

As regards behaviour, I keep imagining that I have 'got better', but I am far from perfectly in control; and it was interesting that my unbridled tongue created deeper resentment during shooting than I was quite unaware of at the time. When I called Len Jackson 'a silly cunt' for instance. Sadism? Not quite that; but certainly tortured nerves hitting out where they felt reasonably confident they would not get hit back – or didn't care if they did. I wouldn't have said that, for example, to any of the fitters. And poor Peter Woodward, to whom I hissed out: 'If you say that again, I'll kick your fucking

---

1. Penelope Houston, assistant to the editor of the BFI journal *Sight and Sound*; she became its editor in 1956. Co-editor of *Sequence Three*.

teeth in.' At which he walked off the picture – or did his best to ... etc., etc. But we got the picture shot. On schedule.

When it ended, there was an amusing scene: lunch with the directors, at which I produced, as a *pièce de résistance*, *O Dreamland*.[1] And after it no one said a word. Not a word.

Cannes. There was James [Broughton] of course, and *The Pleasure Garden*[2] ... Looking back, it all seems rather remote, and hardly worth remarking on the greater quality of life that I found in the Eastern films: my discovery of the festival being *Five Boys from Barska Street*.[3] Quite fun with Gene[4] over all this; and the brief flirtation he had with [Aleksandra] Slaska, its female star.

I remember hesitating at Cannes about the return journey, and thinking I should break the trip at Arles: just to see the place while passing through. I had remained in Cannes a day longer, and gone up to St Paul. There was a fete on, and I strolled around somewhat aimlessly, not enjoying it very much. Prévert[5] wasn't there; and I wrote a postcard and slid it under his front door.

April in Paris. One day I spent on a visit to studios, conducted by a boy from Unifrance. An open-air location where Marcel Carné was directing *L'Air de Paris*; then Christian-Jacque on *Madame Dubarry*; and Autant-Lara on *Le Rouge et le Noir*. A congenial Yugoslav girl accompanied me – staying behind when the escort returned to Paris. With Serge I remember little. I remember only one day when we joined Janine and the children in the Luxembourg Gardens. I returned to finish *Trunk Conveyor*.

May saw that performance of *The Changeling*, produced by Tony Richardson[6] at Wyndham's for some Sunday society or other, in which I extra-ed as a madman with half-a-dozen lines. This wasn't very rewarding, let's admit, Tony is not an actor's director – that is to say he gives nothing to his company; nor does he supply the alternative gratification of making one feel that one is working for an egoist of remarkable talent. Endless gossip precipitated by the presence of Harold Lang and Derek Prouse in the cast; both of whom professing such scorn of Tony and detestation of his methods after three or four days of rehearsal that vibrations soon spread excitedly round the *cercle*. The

---

1. The first real L.A. film, in that he chose the subject and had a completely free hand. A mocking look at the pleasure gardens at Margate.

2. It won the Prix de Fantaisie Poetique.

3. *Piatka z ulicy Barskiej*, featuring Tadeusz Lomnicki. Directed by Aleksander Ford.

4. Gene Moskowitz, film critic, the legendary Mosk of *Variety*.

5. Jacques Prévert, (1900–1977), who wrote the Marcel Carné films, *Les Portes de la Nuit* (1946) and *Les Amants de Vérone* (1947), which starred Serge Reggiani.

6. (1928–1991). A fellow-graduate of Wadham College, Oxford, whose first film, *Momma Don't Allow* (co-directed with Karel Reisz), would be invited into L.A.'s 1956 Free Cinema programme at the National Film Theatre (February 1956), and whose Royal Court Theatre production of John Osborne's *Look Back in Anger* (May 1956) would usher in a new 'golden age' in British theatre. See also p. 507.

principals were appalling, but there were one or two pleasant people in the cast. Diane Cilento[1] seemed promising, and did a little part with great humour and personality.

A flying visit [to Paris] over Whitsun. I remember stopping at a café by a river to drink a Cinzano and write a little – tentatively sketching an idea for a reply to Grierson,[2] whose second article had just appeared in *Sight and Sound*, with its implicit and explicit attacks on 'us' – and more particularly *me*.

Well, I can't go through all those days in detail: rehearsals [of *Hamlet*], crises, and all the rest of it. Fortunately, from the first, I was able to make comments entirely in the spirit of the thing – *inside* it already, so to speak. I suppose this is rather remarkable.

We are now at least into June. Serge and Annie were coming to London. He was playing in [Sacha] Guitry's *Napoleon*. Then the correspondence failed. To condense things a little: I was working, making the NSPCC trailers[3] and also preparing the *Foot and Mouth* script [film for the Ministry of Agriculture]... the misunderstanding was that his visit would take place before September ... it didn't ... various messages went unanswered. Perhaps that is where I should have let things stand; but my devotion – or my need, if that is more honest – was not yet exhausted. After finishing shooting on the NSPCC, I went to Limoges – the tour of *Tresor* had started. Limoges – Pau. I shan't forget that venture. Exhaustion: and about an hour's talk, late on Sunday night, after a performance at Pau, before the bus left to carry the company through the night to Bordeaux. I returned from Pau with a promise renewed that we would continue to write. My specific task, to send Serge a digest and a copy of *Where Angels Fear to Tread*. I did both these things, but the E. M. Forster idea received no encouragement. I also suggested the idea of making a short film about the tour, to be filmed in January. This also was vetoed – on practical grounds, if for no other reason.

How strange all this is: in a sense it is as though certain scales had fallen from my eyes. Has this seriously diminished Serge to me, lessened the importance of our friendship? I remember that Serge has *never* wished me luck on starting a picture. This is petty, I suppose. But ...

1955 (undated)
Finished my review of the two Beckers (*Falbalas* and *Rendezvous de Juillet*) at the BFI in the afternoon. Penelope there, fussily laying out her stills, debating whether to include the new Kazan in *In the Picture*, etc. General atmosphere as usual of gossip and trivia which drives me to my usual nervous outbursts of 'And why the fucking Hell *can't* you ...' find room for a still of the Henning Jensen's ballet film, for instance.

---

1. Australian actress who married Sean Connery. She made her Royal Court debut in Richardson's production of Tennessee Williams' *Orpheus Descending* (May 1959).

2. John Grierson (1898–1972), British leader of the documentary movement.

3. L.A. made four short films for the National Society for the Prevention of Cruelty to Children.

In the spring of 1955, Anderson directed the first of his five episodes of The Adventures of Robin Hood, *a TV series starring Richard Greene; failed to collect his Oscar for* Thursday's Children, *and made the first of more than one hundred TV commercials – Geraldine Chaplin in 'Lux Toilet Soap'. Other commercials from this period include James Robertson Justice in 'Cracker Barrel Cheese'; John Sharp trying to wrap a turkey in tin foil, and Bernard Miles in 'Mackeson's Stout' ('It looks good. It tastes good. And by golly it does you good'). Later in the year, he made the film about foot and mouth disease for the Ministry of Agriculture, and he wrote and directed the four films for the NSPCC:* Green and Pleasant Land, Henry, The Children Upstairs, *and* A Hundred Thousand Children.

16 August 1955

I am a great one for looking for symbols that may mark the beginning of new periods: new leaves turned, abandonment of old ways . . . Of course, life isn't like this. But can't it be? The cardinal rule is surely that anything can happen; and not only the unpleasant things. The traditional things, the clichés can happen too. Those NSPCC inspectors: upstanding, enlightened Christians . . . Not embittered, and certainly not doing the job only for some sort of morbid fascination. Well, why shouldn't I turn over a new leaf?

The diary breaks off for more than four years. During this period, the first of what would become six programmes of Free Cinema films was shown at the National Film Theatre in February 1956. More than 350 people were turned away from the sell-out screening. The programme comprised Anderson's O Dreamland, *Richardson and Reisz's* Momma Don't Allow, *and Lorenza Mazzetti's film* Together, *which starred Eduardo Palazzo.*

Sponsored by the Ford Motor Company, and produced by Karel Reisz and Leon Clore, Anderson made a forty-minute film about the Covent Garden market – Every Day Except Christmas. *It won the Grand Prix for Documentary at the 1957 Venice Film Festival.*

On 30 June, 1957 he made his professional debut as a theatre director in a Sunday production without decor of Kathleen Sully's The Waiting of Lester Abbs *at the Royal Court Theatre. He supervised the filming of* March to Aldermaston *(on which George Devine carried the Royal Court banner) and in December 1958 was invited by Tony Richardson and the English Stage Company to direct a main show at the Royal Court. The proposed play by Willis Hall had been performed as* The Disciplines of War *by an amateur company at the 1957 Edinburgh Festival. At the Nottingham Playhouse, it was revived as* Boys It's All Hell. *For its first London performance, Anderson changed the title to* The Long and the Short and the Tall, *cast Robert Shaw and a regional repertory actor, Albert Finney, in the lead roles, and replaced Finney with Peter O'Toole when, during the first week of rehearsal, Finney was forced to leave because of acute appendicitis. The play was a major success, grossing twice as much money as the second most successful Court production of the season (a double-bill of Ionesco's* The Chairs *and* The Lesson). *It transferred to the West End in April 1959.*

In October of that year, he directed the world premiere of John Arden's Serjeant Musgrave's Dance, *a play inspired by a British military atrocity in Cyprus. Starring Ian Bannen, Freda Jackson and Alan Dobie, and with music by Dudley Moore, the play was the first project on which he worked with production designer Jocelyn Herbert.*

JOHN ARDEN (*from a letter read at Anderson's memorial evening*)

It was Lindsay, more than anyone, who taught me the precision of my trade . . . As a playwright one could be on the receiving end of his acerbity. He . . . quite frankly gave me hell, until the script was rewritten – I was going to say into the shape that he wanted, but that's quite wrong – let me phrase it again: until the script was rewritten into the shape that he knew that I wanted it to be; into the shape that the play itself was demanding for itself. I had, I remember, sent him a rewrite of one of the scenes which we agreed that as it stood was a considerable muddle. He rang me up quite late at night. 'I've read your new scene,' he said. His voice was flat and dry. 'It doesn't work', he said, 'does it?'

'Doesn't it?' I feebly answered, 'I thought it did. I'm sure it does.' I went on to explain just why I was sure. I had all sorts of good reasons.

He cut me short. 'I see. So this in my hand is the definitive Act 1, Scene 3? Yes?'

'I didn't say *definitive*, Lindsay. Definitive is too strong a way of putting it.'

'Either it is or it isn't. If it isn't I don't know why you sent it to me. If it is, it doesn't work. There's really no more to say.'

There was of course, and he said it.

An uncompromising analysis of what the scene was supposed to do, what I had allowed it to do, the exact order of dialogue and action for it to be able to express its utmost dramatic potential – all in ten minutes. And a new rewrite then took me no more than half an hour. And it did work.

―――――――――

His next production at the Court saw Albert Finney in The Lily White Boys.

1 January 1960

Rehearsing *The Lily White Boy*s.[1] We have a fortnight more to go before Brighton; and I find myself fighting the temptation to feel that things aren't going *too* badly . . . Periods of agony on this have been intense; the whole sense of chaos, fragmentation, inefficiency and neurotic inability to cope. A scrappy day yesterday: mostly 'numbers', with a *Vogue* photographer in the morning shooting routines. Then the two finales . . . and total exhaustion. Alun Owen[2] appeared during the afternoon, wandering in typically . . . Success has not, I'm afraid, helped him. In the brief moments during which I chatted with him, he talked exclusively about his own affairs, the film script he has written and which Joseph Losey is directing, how he is getting a solo screen credit,[3] etc.

I said: 'What are you writing for the theatre now?'

'Nothing.'

'Nothing?'

'No – they're the media for my talent – television and the cinema – I'm tremendously excited by the cinema . . .'

Maybe unreasonably, an intense irritation took hold of me as I moved away and didn't talk to him again, resisting the temptation to say, 'Well what the fucking hell are you doing here then – slumming?' Of course Alun is talented . . . but his egotism is so dreadful and grating, his manner so pretentious, and his self-absorption so ruthless, that it requires a great deal of effort to deal with him. The thought strikes me that, instead of being affronted, one should say as much to him. Honesty and directness. These things are also difficult to achieve.

Albie [Albert Finney] is a joy to work with, and without a talent as outstanding as his, this show would be impossible. He is young though, and in certain ways crystallised, too apt to 'turn in' and get away with it by brilliant naturalism. But he knows this – he is very intelligent about himself, and about theatre – and he learns astonishingly fast. Whether to sing, or to dance, or to play 'objectively' – Brechtianly!

Talked until quite late last night with Fiz.[4] She is the sweetest person. 'Of course I'm not committed, you know: I don't know anything about it!' But her instincts are fine.

2 January 1960

Pressing on with numbers; the Quartet – Albie is getting it, though this is the most difficult one for him and gives rise to interesting speculations as to whether one *needs*

---

1. Brechtian satire by Harry Cookson with (at Oscar Lewenstein's suggestion) integrated songs by Christopher Logue. It opened at the Royal Court Theatre on 27 January 1960 after previewing in Brighton.

2. L.A. had directed a Sunday production of Owen's *Progress to the Park* (February 1959). Owen had acted in L.A.'s production of *The Waiting of Lester Abbs*.

3. *The Criminal*. He shared the credit with Jimmy Sangster.

4. Eleanor Fazan; actress, choreographer.

to be a socialist in order to play this kind of satire satisfactorily. Certainly Albie is coming on tremendously – I mean developing his ideas and his self-confidence. He is so charming and pleasant to work with too. Never a trace of egotism or refractoriness. Eager and pliant and marvellously sensitive with all his toughness and vitality.

6 January 1960

8.20 am. Writing in bed before getting up and facing fatigue and a new day's slog at *The Lily White Boys*.

Didn't get to bed till about three this morning either – having conscientiously forced myself to the actors' group at Cheyne Walk. A frankly disappointing session, consisting of improvisations in an atmosphere lacking from the start in concentration and seriousness. Donal[1] – who had been going to prepare – didn't turn up at all, 'having gone out with Dicky [Richard] Harris': Dan Massey didn't turn up (to my personal and secret annoyance, which provided me with a self-gratifying imaginary conversation on my way home in the taxi): Colin Blakely[2] didn't turn up . . . And those who did seemed particularly half-hearted. Great resistance to the idea of starting with a song, which continued as we attempted to make Ann Beach[3] sing 'She had to go and lose it at the Astor' as a song of social protest . . . The two longer improvisations attempted were utter failures. First Maggie [Smith] and David Andrews:[4] David employing far too much speech in a mannered style that made the whole thing sound like a play by John McGrath . . . and then Ian [Bannen] and Ann Beach – where Ian seemed to be imprisoned completely in the 'story' and to shut himself off completely from playing with or off Ann.

After previewing in Brighton, The Lily White Boys *opened at the Royal Court Theatre on 27 January 1960. The forty-five performances played to a 69 per cent capacity but Anderson was sufficiently enthused by Finney to give him the lead role in* Billy Liar *by Willis Hall and Keith Waterhouse. Presented by Oscar Lewenstein at the Cambridge Theatre, London, the play opened on 13 September and was an immediate critical and box-office success. Mona Washbourne played Billy's mother. Ann Beach played Barbara.*

---

1. Donal Donnelly (1931–). Acted in L.A.'s productions of *Progress to the Park* and *Serjeant Musgrave's Dance.*
2. Appeared in *Serjeant Musgrave's Dance* and in L.A.'s productions of Max Frisch's *The Fire Raisers* and John Maddison Morton's curtain-raiser, *Box and Cox* (21 December 1961).
3. Acted in *The Fire Raisers* and *Billy Liar.*
4. Played Whitaker in *The Long and the Short and the Tall.*

24 July 1960
LEEDS—LONDON

A disappointing, tiring, disturbing weekend prompts me to put pen to paper. This was my visit to Leeds, at Willis Hall's suggestion, undertaken with particular reference to *Billy Liar*. And Albie would like to come too, Willis said. Fine.

We set off on Friday, missing the 3.40 through the utter impossibility of getting a taxi. The game was to blame this on me (Willis's game that is), since I'd said there was plenty of time ... only a joke, you understand – but a significant one. For, as it quickly turned out, we weren't three, but two-and-one. Two Northerners, no-nonsense and colloquially rough spoken; and one upper-class Southerner, intellectual-type. In the train Albert read newspapers or dozed; Willis read a yellow-jacketed novel about prostitution, *The Pavement My Boudoir*, or some such title; and I read *The Optimistic Tragedy* in French – until Willis presented me with his new book of children's stories, *The Royal Astrologer*, which I skimmed lightly and speedily, finding it agreeable, thinnish stuff.

The first consideration when we got to Leeds was to get a television set – since Zoe[1] was making her first appearance on *The Herries Chronicles* at 8.30 (we arrived at 8.20). So we bundled into a car, a taxi driven by a fat, jovial Yorkshireman, and set off for Willis's father's off the Dewsbury Road. A typical, dreary, grimy, advertisement-hoardinged West Riding main road. And off it these mean streets, little red-bricked, back-to-back houses, small and grimy. The front door opened straight into the living room – tiny enough – with just room for a settee, a table by the window and a pram – and a TV set. Off, to the right, a scullery. Willis's father had been sitting reading the papers. We shook hands and within a couple of minutes we were watching *Rogue Herries*. Afterwards we went for a drink; first one pub, then another. Mr Hall, fiftyish, round-faced, spectacled, was about as chatty as his son – pleasant enough, but not exactly forthcoming. Willis and Albert talked Yorkshire. The second pub was a small, ugly little room, crammed with tired-looking, pale, ugly men swilling beer. I drank light ale. Willis bought half a dozen bottles and borrowed a pack of cards. When we got back Willis and Albert went off to buy fish and chips, while Mr Hall brewed tea. We ate. Then the cards came out. Did I play pontoon? I said no. No effort was made of course to initiate me. They started to play. It was about eleven o'clock I suppose.

I could have forecast the rest of the night ... They just played. 'Stick – twist – 2/-.' A joke was incessantly repeated. And I sat and read *The Optimistic Tragedy*. And finished it. The game went on. Occasionally one of the players would leave to go to the lavatory two doors down the street. At twenty past twelve (by then Willis' sister, also a taciturn girl, had come in, scarcely remarked), I went out and walked for a bit up the Dewsbury

---

1. Zoe Caldwell (1933–), who was living with Finney at the time. Bianca to Albert Finney's Cassio in Tony Richardson's Stratford *Othello* in 1959. Acted in L.A.'s Sunday production of Logue's *The Trial of Cob and Leach* (26 April 1959).

Road, past the boring little shops selling food and clothing and television sets, past the cinema showing – what? Something nondescript, American, and suitable. Then back. Willis's sister made a cup of Nescafé, and started playing Tom Lehrer records. She produced some long-players and asked me to choose one: I opted for *Expresso Bongo* and listened to a whole side before I said to her – how do I get a taxi? It was about 1.40. We went out to a box and phoned for one.

Of course fate would plan exactly the kind of situation for me that I am least able to cope with. A situation of exclusion. Stranded in a world I had no relationship with, rather aggressively male . . . with no time to spare for the sentimentalisms of relationships, for the arts of speculation or conversation, or for politeness, hospitality or charm.

Anderson's Free Cinema colleague Karel Reisz had enjoyed a considerable success in 1960 with Saturday Night and Sunday Morning, *which topped the annual box-office charts and won BAFTA awards for Best Film, Actress (Rachel Roberts) and Newcomer (Albert Finney). Reisz agreed to produce a film of David Storey's novel,* This Sporting Life, *about a professional rugby player's relationship with his landlady. Thinking it a perfect star vehicle for Albert Finney, Anderson agreed to direct.*

1 January 1961

Well . . . it's with remarkably little special feeling that I find myself slipping into a New Year. I suppose atmosphere is only created on such occasions when one is among friends one cares for – but at Shirley Ann's[1] party I was swamped by the horde of unknown, not seemingly very interesting merrymakers in their fancy dresses – dear, preposterous Shirley in her white-feathered bra and tufted panties, so simple and naive. Other than that I knew only Karel, and Norman Rossington[2] jiving like fun ('You only have to look at Norman's movements to see what a generous person he is,' said Karel) and Ken Haigh's[3] girl friend, Jean Marsh[4] – a nice girl I think, and pretty. They all did 'Auld Lang Syne' at midnight, but I really felt it would be too forced to join in, so remained in that well-known corner position decreed by destiny. I was reminded of that Officers' Mess dance so many years ago in Morpeth, and how I went to bed early and listened to a Mozart concerto and read some book and felt cosy rather than happy . . .

---

1. Shirley Anne Field (1938–). Co-starred with Finney in *The Lily White Boys* and *Saturday Night and Sunday Morning*.

2. Actor (1928–1999). Appeared in *Saturday Night and Sunday Morning*.

3. Actor (1929–). Played Jimmy Porter in the seminal Royal Court production of *Look Back in Anger* (1956).

4. Actress (1935–).

Karel drove me back about half past twelve, and we talked about *L'Avventura*[1] – about which I was unable to be as enthusiastic as he. But what was surprising was the depth to which the film has touched him, and the relevance it seems to have to his own problems and relationship with life so that a discussion of it led somehow naturally and imperceptibly into a discussion of his relationship and problem with Tony [Richardson] – which also at the moment is something that occupies and troubles him deeply . . . There has been unpleasantness about his percentage from *Saturday Night and Sunday Morning* – which he has been for some time insisting has been somehow fiddled (by Saltzman[2] primarily, but with Tony and John Osborne at least cognisant and therefore responsible) – so that he would get nothing until the debts on *The Entertainer*[3] have been paid . . . And even to me, who perhaps am too ready to accept Karel's perfect balance and judgement in such matters, it seemed that he was complaining rather than trying to get a legitimate grievance redressed. And these complaints have come back on him, to make him feel guilty, and get involved in acrimonious correspondence with John and shouting matches with Tony. In the car outside as we talked, there was moisture round the rims of his eyes, and he was shivering, so we came inside and had some hot whisky and coffee and went on talking.

As Bob says in his novel review for the *Sunday Times* this week: 'We are all very bound up with each other, are we not?'

Which leads me briefly to an intuition of the kind of film I really would like to make – a film about all this, all of us, and the problems and meaning of our lives now – of Karel and Albie and Zoe and Jill[4] and Willis and Oscar [Lewenstein] and where we are going, and the aspirations and the egoism and unhappiness . . . This was obviously the way *L'Avventura* affected Karel – what the *Cahiers* people call *film d'auteur*, a first-hand work, not a dramatic construction well directed by somebody – which is what *Sporting Life* could be, unless I can get really inside it and make it a personal allegory. But the other kind of film of course can only be written – or at least conceived by its director. And it is here that so far my intuitions and aspirations have been all too swift and all too glancing and quickly dimmed.

I had a date to tell Albie about the latest developments on *This Sporting Life*. When I went round I thought at first all was well. Zoe met me at the head of the stairs and shunted me into the bedroom and from the living room Albie started to play his tape of *The Lily White Boys*. Delightful, and all seemed relaxed, and after he played a tape

---

1. Michelangelo Antonioni's film about two lonely people coming together whilst searching for a missing woman.
2. Harry Saltzman (1915–1994). Canadian producer. Formed Woodfall Films with Richardson and Osborne to film *Look Back in Anger*.
3. Richardson's film of the play by John Osborne.
4. Jill Bennett, actress (1930–1990), wife of Willis Hall. Married John Osborne in 1970.

from *The Music Man*. But when he went downstairs to make a phone call, Zoe turned to me and said: 'You know we're splitting don't you?' . . . It was with some difficulty that I stifled a groan and a 'What again?' . . . But there it is: and it does seem a shame (the superficial thought) now that the room is so nice, and they seem so domesticated and comfortable – but this time, it appears, it is Zoe who has decided that she can't be sufficiently herself in the shadow of Albert . . . Which is no doubt true. Will he really find somewhere else to live this time? Or will they continue as things are for a bit? To be continued . . .

Billy Liar, directed by Anderson, was a huge success, enjoying a run of nearly 600 performances. With its West End run extended and Finney under contract to play the title role in John Osborne's Luther *at the Royal Court, a replacement was found in Tom Courtenay.*

14 May 1961
What is this peculiar quality that seems always to reveal itself in English Shakespearean production? Especially in comedy . . . A kind of persistent facetiousness: a childish over-emphasis that reminds one of schoolboy humour – 'trying to be funny'. Is this another aspect of the adolescence (emotional and artistic) of the English? Particularly middle-class. The two schoolboys next to me at the Old Vic yesterday obviously didn't think much of it [*Twelfth Night*] – from a secondary modern I should think. They aped the heavy, forced laughter of the characters on the stage – and with reason. The idiotic 'Love thoughts lie rich, when canopied with bowers . . .' ('Ha-ha-ha-ha' – exit chortling.)

I popped down feeling I ought to see Tom Courtenay as Feste – the gesture, really, rather than anticipating anything very notable. And in fact the part is not at the moment within his range: I don't really think Feste can be played as a gawky boy, and in addition there is that whole ironic, detached, sophisticated side of the part ('cool'?) that does not come naturally to him. Maturity, in fact, of thought as well as of feeling. Something of the same problem as Albie's with parts of *The Lily White Boys* – to that 'Sirs, human brothers . . .' was always straight, rather than ironic.

Of course the direction didn't give Tom much help. It was the work of Colin Graham – an opera director, I believe. Eighteenth-century Arcadian, and not altogether despicable – superior by far for instance to *The Dream* by Michael Langham. But much too much 'interpretation' – an 'idea' for everything, the lines all 'worked', no consistency of style . . . What Tom did get were one or two moments of truly poetic feeling, a wistful melancholy that was not just conventional posing. 'O Mistress Mine' beautifully sung. And during the recognition scene he seemed genuinely moved. What he does, in fact, has truth, of a very rare and unmistakeable kind. At the moment it is his range that is limited. When uncertain, he falls back on being awkward, gawky, the lost little boy. It will be fascinating to see what he does with Billy. I am slightly worried lest he finds difficulty with the extrovert side of the character.

3

With Richard Harris

This Sporting Life – Diary of a Madman

'The mixture of tenderness and sympathy with violence and even cruelty is astonishing, painful and of course endlessly fascinating.'

In 1959, producer Michael Balcon presided over the making of a film version of The Long and the Short and the Tall. *He rejected Anderson and Peter O'Toole, and hired instead Leslie Norman and Laurence Harvey. Norman replaced Edward Judd with Richard Harris.*

Two years later, Anderson was preparing to direct the film version of Billy Liar. *A postponement by its producer, Joe Janni, saw Anderson take off to Tahiti to discuss David Storey's script of* This Sporting Life *with Richard Harris. Harris was filming* The Mutiny on the Bounty, *third-billed in a troubled production that starred Marlon Brando and Trevor Howard.*

21 August 1961

Three months since I wrote . . . What was happening then? Albie was still in *Billy Liar*: the film was set for September:[1] I was just preparing to put Tom into the play. Since then we've had Albert's departure – Tom's debut – the film's postponement – *Luther* – my visit to Tahiti – and meeting Richard Harris.

I suppose most important was my meeting with Richard. It's really rather frightening – particularly since I have no idea what I can do about it – to find myself so dependent on relationships. As David [Storey], with his extraordinary perception, has pointed out – I really do exist, or at least only *act*, by relationship with others. Whereas he, I suppose, though genuinely friendly as far as he can be, is essentially a solitary.

---

1. Filmed instead by John Schlesinger, with Tom Courtenay as Billy.

Anyway, my meeting with Richard, under those strange circumstances, was a great success. Thrown by the peculiar conditions of the *Bounty* into the closest companionship, like schoolfellows or fellow soldiers, we got to know each other in a way that normal life hardly permits. And I realised quickly how much I had been missing contact with lively, emotional, extravagant and poetic responses. He is the antithesis, of course, of the cautious, defensive, emotionally ungenerous Northerners with whom I seem to have worked so much in the past year or so. Albert – Willis – David (though in every way their superior, and I am truly fond of him) – and even in his own way Karel, with his reserve and detachment. By contrast Richard is all warmth and ardour. I responded to him with a whole-heartedness that made me also tremble: for I hardly believe any more in the possibility of such relationships.

Also I am getting too old to be continuing to react like a schoolboy. It's all very well to preserve certain youthful qualities: but there is a certain lack of dignity in this attraction towards the immature. Perpetually, too, to be finding myself a perpetual 'Cliff' in relation to a succession of Jimmy Porters and their wives.[1] It feels such a false position. Would it be possible ever to be understood and accepted? I am beginning to think this is mere fantasy: in fact I dare not hope otherwise, except under my breath so to speak. Certainly this whole emotional problem might lead to my having to abandon directing actors; for the strain it repeatedly involves is too great to tolerate for ever, and one really begins to find oneself dreading each new experience for the frustration it apparently is bound finally to involve.

He ended the year directing Colin Blakely, James Booth, Ann Beach and John Thaw in Max Frisch's The Fire Raisers *at the Royal Court. Frisch wrote to thank him for an 'excellent production . . . The London critics . . . all realised the high quality of your staging.' With finance from the Rank Organisation,* This Sporting Life *went into production in March 1962, shooting at the Beaconsfield studios and on location in Wakefield. Rachel Roberts, who married Rex Harrison during a break in the shooting, played the landlady. Richard Harris played the rugby player, Frank Machin.*

23 April 1962

Five weeks (only *five?*) into *This Sporting Life* – and I should of course have been keeping a record of it, the most alarming experience of my life, in so many different ways.

People say now that the work is good – that is to say the scare of ten days ago, when my removal from the picture seemed imminent, is at least temporarily past. We have shot the rugby football scenes for a long fortnight in Wakefield, and most of the Mrs

---

1. From *Look Back in Anger*; Cliff is a bachelor friend lodging with Porter and his wife.

Hammond scenes for an even longer three weeks in the studio . . . Hold it – it is SIX weeks, for before the Mrs Hammond scenes came our two days rehearsal and three days in the Dentist's and the Metropole Bar – with which our studio shooting opened. So we *should* be half way through the schedule – instead of, as I guess, about a fortnight behind . . . No wonder the Rank Organisation is alarmed.

It really is a nightmare, and the Easter recess has only made it worse, giving one time to break the rhythm, to become fully conscious of my absolutely lost, sticky, all-at-sea feeling on the floor, and my absolute lack of confidence at being able to do any better for the latter half of the picture.

The most striking feature of it all, I suppose, has been the splendour and the misery of my work and relationship with Richard. I *think* that his performance is marvellous . . . Certainly he is acting with a strength and a simplicity that I have never seen from him before on the screen. I have grown to love him dearly – too dearly of course – with the result that I lack absolutely the detachment that would allow me to weather the storms of his temperament without suffering . . . These have been fierce and shattering. First in Wakefield – the night he insisted on getting drunk with Colin [Blakely]; and the awful finale when he went mad after the Wigan match and announced that he would not come back to London with us . . . Then the first terrible day of rehearsals with Rachel – which I suppose was his last fling of resistance against playing the part without the protection of his mannerisms. Then there was the disgraceful scene a fortnight later, occasioned by his disapproval of the way I shot the 'Why don't we go for a walk' scene, which led to him fooling about, being told by me he could leave the floor, refusing to rehearse over the weekend, being pacified by Albert – then, on the Sunday morning making himself unavailable . . . all climaxed by the evening meeting in his flat with Karel [Reisz], myself and Jimmy Fraser[1] . . . The next one was when he shouted 'Cunt' at me because I wouldn't argue any further about the cheque scene in his bedroom – and then, my special birthday present, his refusal to shoot the close shot with the fur coat because he had been accused (unjustly as he estimated) of holding us up by being late . . .

For from a certain point of view, this is a personality too big by far for me to cope with. Emotionally his warmth and wilfulness can sabotage me in a moment. And of course instinctively he knows this and exploits it. I ought to be calm and detached with him. Instead I am impulsive, affectionate, infinitely susceptible. We embrace and fight like lovers: but in Richard I sense the ruthlessness that would drop me or destroy me without compunction if I seemed to fail him.

The mixture of tenderness and sympathy with violence and even cruelty is aston- ishing, painful and of course endlessly fascinating. The familiar combination, I suppose

---

1. Agent. In 1958 signed Harris to a seven-year contract with Associated British Films.

of pride and insecurity, of sensibility and egoism: the inescapable formula for a star. All my reason tells me that this is a fatal temperament for me to become in any way involved with. Yet I am completely helpless. This mixture of power and sensitivity, of virility and immaturity, of insinuating charm and aggressive domination – how can I be expected to resist? Whether he is embracing me physically, like some big warm dog, or ordering me to 'heel' – I am at his service completely. Which of course means that I am unable at times to serve him as I really should, conniving at his self-indulgence where I should be be calmly, coolly resisting it. Like Karel.

I'll say this – and in a year we shall see if it I am too sceptical. I cannot really believe that our paths lie together. This would imply a good fortune that I can't any longer believe in. Certainly if I fail him in the weeks that lie ahead, then all will be over. God preserve us all.

April 1962
We should be thinking creatively about the subject – not devoting our time and wasting our energy on this kind of neurotic wrangling. How far are Richard's complaints justified? How far is he using *justified* complaints to destroy himself and everyone else – at the same time acting with absolute wilfulness and capriciousness. But this wilfulness and capriciousness is not to be stopped by appeals to reason and loyalty. It needs a guiding personality of great firmness and authority. This is where I *know* I am fatally lacking. Richard can destroy me. I cannot control him. I am at his mercy: and he is at the mercy of his neuroses.

He is also making the Rachel situation [her marriage to Rex Harrison and the ensuing press attention]an excuse to prevent his concentration on the film – chiefly I suppose because he is frightened of it. But again – my method of seeing the psychological truth in a situation or an action, and pointing it out is *valueless.* Richard wants a father figure. So do I. He tends to make one of me – and I of him. It *cannot* work. I cannot change. *Nor he.*

4 July 1962
The situation has not simplified, though we have got the film shot – just. We finished shooting a fortnight ago, really in a state of collapse, after a final location period that went from nightmare to nightmare, with Richard's storms of temperament and egoism reaching the very verge of impossibility not once nor twice but often. And of course finally leaving their mark on the picture and on his performance.

Richard continues to dominate my life in a familiar yet extraordinary, frightening, fascinating way. The knowledge that I now have of him, after these months of intimate contact, has certainly changed the simple image of him that I gained in Tahiti – the result, as I now realise, of a simplified situation, in which I was unmistakeably, and unreservedly *on his side, against* 'them' – in this case *Mutiny on the Bounty*; or even *This Sporting Life* – for I really capitulated completely and pretty well instantly to all his criticisms and demands. It was not till I had to assume the role of director that I experienced the other side of Richard: his intense, absolutely neurotic, sometimes quite insane resentment of authority, suspicion of 'disloyalty', fear of being manipulated or exploited . . . coupled with a kind of monstrous wilfulness – a demand for an absolute acceptance or indulgence of his moods or whims, as a condition of continuing to know him or to work with him – which is self-indulgent to an appalling degree.

The friends I suspect he values most – Robert Mitchum or Laurence Harvey – are fond of him, I'm sure, but with a degree of detachment that must cut his nonsense at the root. It is to be emotionally dependent on Richard that puts one in an impossible position; because it means one has to accept his moods and his whims absolutely – or else, as he puts it, 'Fuck off'. And as I write this, and evoke that tyrannical, bullying temperament, I am conscious of the excitement, the perverse gratification it affords, as well as the anger and the sense of inferiority and loss of dignity . . . That there is a strange sado-masochistic element in my relationship with Richard is undeniable – on his side the obverse of the kindly, generous, sensitive self which is also there, which welcomes, embraces, declares its affection and thanks. It is almost as if this personality has grown with Frank Machin: the narcissistic looks in the mirror, the admiration and enjoyment of his body, the relish of power, the sudden humorous, yet very vital expressions of savagery – as he turns to me, and with clenched teeth and clenched fist threateningly jerks out 'Cunt!' or 'Stop smiling!' – 'I'll smile if I wish to.' 'You'll smile when I tell you – *Cunt!*' (these yesterday in the Albany travel agency).

And what is the precise significance of the blows which, towards the end of the picture, landed more and more frequently, and more and more heavily on my arms? It certainly became something more than a game, or a game with more to it than horseplay – the yellow bruises are there yet. I can't remember exactly when this began. I suppose when he lost any fear he may have had of me at the start, and realised – as he came to do more and more, presumably – that the ascendancy was his. I remember him well, sitting in the Hammond kitchen between takes and suddenly calling, pointing at the ground by his feet: 'Lindsay! *HEEL!*'

August 1962 (*Rome*)

I have been here two days now, nearly three: probably a mistaken idea since I can't think of much but Richard, puzzling endlessly over the events of last week, and the weeks before . . . trying to understand the course that events have taken, to distinguish what has been inevitable from what was avoidable, endlessly pursuing the truth of this extraordinary relationship – and generally falling back on a sheer sense of absence and loss, that kind of emotional absolutism which denies life of *any* sense of enjoyment or purpose, if one is deprived of the company of the one person to whom, for good or ill, one has given one's heart.

It is such a see-saw, such a jumble of memories. If I go back to that fortnight a year ago, how vivid is the simple, brotherly companionship of those days in Tahiti! Kindness, respect and generosity were the keynotes of Richard's attitude towards me, with only as much violence as we both understood – violent rejection chiefly of the script that I'd brought him – but no conflict of loyalties: in everything, against MGM, against his fellow actors, against the world which undervalued him, I was his ally – with still the advantage, at that stage, of a certain prestige, a certain unknown quantity, a certain superiority.

What a fantastic contrast to the Richard of our last meeting: that nerve-wracked Tuesday afternoon which started so ominously at the Britannia, with myself late for lunch (having sat through one and a half hours of the film being screened that morning), and finding Richard and Elizabeth[1] with his bar-fly friend Peter – myself reacting badly to this – and reacting even worse (or badly enough for Richard to fly into a defensive anger) at the news that they had to return to Peter Jones, then to the travel agency, before we could go to the opticians, the fatal object of my visit . . . the slightest word from me and Richard defended himself with the utmost intolerance and savagery – 'Don't you give me an ultimatum . . . Don't try to dictate my movements to me . . . if you don't like it you can fuck off . . .' Anyone else would have, of course, and standing there on the pavement of Kensington High Street I had half a mind to, then resolved: if all this was a manoeuvre to avoid in the end being fitted for reading glasses, if, that is to say, *whatever* I did, he would not come to Wigmore Street . . . then I would give up. But how would I ever know this except by suffering through the afternoon, eating whatever shit Richard pushed my way, and just seeing what happened in the end; an exercise in self-discipline, to betray no impatience, no anxiety, no resentment at the indignities heaped upon me.

So I went to Peter Jones, and bided while Richard behaved abominably in the glass department, the ash tray department, the bag department, fussing neurotically about his receipts, shouting at Elizabeth, all the time the wild animal who at any moment might go berserk and smash everything in sight . . . Pausing for a moment by a selection of women's belts and murmuring in his American accent – 'I'll take a dozen of those' (thick leather belts) . . . 'Yeah . . . and half a dozen of the chains . . .' (I remember still in his dressing room how he would pick up his belt and play it, not hard, but sharply, across my thighs). And in the travel agency – out of the blue at me, the snarl 'You cunt!' and the clenched fist an eighth of an inch from my face . . .

Yet, after all this, as we walked away, for a few moments, the warm, caressing friend again, as he put his arms round Elizabeth and myself, and chatted amusingly, amused

---

1. Elizabeth Harris (née Rees-Williams), repertory actress. Married Harris on 9 February 1957.

about going to Italy and not being able to speak the language . . . And amazingly, with only the smallest flicker of hesitation ('Do I really need glasses?'), we did get to Wigmore Street, and – with much palaver over frames – did order his glasses.

Over tea afterwards – and on the corner of Wigmore Street, swinging his leg round to kick me – back to infantalism and aggression. And foolishly, I suppose, I let the subject of the post-synching come up, and again provoked Richard's guilty rage – even if only by a smile which showed I saw through his pretence. For why was he refusing to work? Really just because his brother Jimmy was arriving from Ireland, and that would have to take priority.

'Ring me tomorrow,' he said, as I left the cab. But was it any more than the compulsive invitation he issues to anybody?

I didn't see him again.

It does all seem to add up to a strange pattern of rejection. Yet it was only two days before, at Jared [Harris's son]'s christening that he had put his arms around me (drunk with champagne laced with brandy) and kissed me and called me dear to him: and standing together in the wine shop, said he wanted to work with me again – that I'd given him what no one else had – if I was prepared to go through the same ordeal again . . .

My problem of course is to evaluate the situation, our relationship, without sentimentalism. It is always my temptation to endow those moments of relaxation and friendship with more 'reality' than the moments of suspicion and cruelty and rejection. Is this the case? Or is it like the tiger, who is being just as true to himself when he is being wary and destructive and alone? Of course, the *whole* is the reality. But this is a severe and terrible test of my own nature. For to be able to accept the black as well as the white – instead of always striving to make the black white – goes profoundly against my instincts. I don't indeed know if I can. I don't even know if it's right. It seems to imply a kind of objectivity that is fearfully hard in relation to someone one loves. For the dark side of Richard is his neurotic, destructive, self-destructive side, which, if it gets on top of him, will prevent him fulfilling himself either as a person or as an artist.

It is dangerous too because it has its fascination. Richard has never really used me with violence – except for the strange game of fists which developed through the film [*This Sporting Life*], a safety-valve I suppose for his resentment against me – the director, the potential betrayer – yet in the thought, or the fantasy, there is certainly an excitement, that portion of me which delights to serve him, to cosset him, to bring him shaving lotion, and to write to John Sturges[1] for him – it is deep in me, and no doubt bad for him. How much, I wonder, was it responsible for the increasing narcissism, the increasing megalomania which undoubtedly marked his last weeks on the picture. And none of us were strong enough for him: and this could be his ruin as well as ours – or mine.

---

1. Director (1911–1992) of *The Magnificent Seven* (1960).

Yet even as I write this, I perceive that it is *the* challenge which he offers to me. For I need to mature just as much as he does; and this is where, in a strange way, our natures, our problems coincide. In both there is an immaturity, an insecurity [that] reflects a childhood rejection: in my own case the lack of a father, which results, when I meet a personality of strength, and of a certain inaccessibility, in my wanting that personality to love me and to father me . . . While Richard wants the same, though with the addition of a violent suspicion of betrayal, a readiness to resent, an incapacity really and truly to give himself to anyone.

1962 (undated)

. . . Considered from another point of view, though, the challenge of Richard's conception of 'loyalty' is a healthy one, for all its difficult and frequent injustice, for I can see, from his point of view, that I am sometimes disloyal: that I speak to others about him as I suppose I should not. That old constitutional inability to lie (at least in this way) which stems I am sure as much from weakness as from any moral strength. Where it comes to trust I am sure Richard would never let me down in this way: as I would and do him. In this respect his attitude is far more realistic, and *manly* than mine. 'Accept me as I am – or don't accept me . . .' But don't whine because he's not different, or use weak threats like 'I won't direct the picture . . .' (Though here, in self-defence, I must query whether Richard, in his own way, didn't do exactly the same thing when he shrieked 'Get out of my life . . . I don't give a fuck, I don't give a fuck, I don't give a fuck . . .')

1962 (undated)

. . . Over the Alps, on the way to Rome. I slept badly last night. I had several dreams, waking up between. I dreamed I went to a restaurant with Richard and Elizabeth. They went off (to wash?) saying they'd be back. After a long interval, I went to look in the restaurant: there they were at a table. Elizabeth was mixing the salad.

If friendship isn't there – and almost certainly Richard doesn't want friendship – nothing I do or say can create it. Do I really feel love for him – as opposed to just need? Can I be strong enough to feel sorry for this wild spirit, imprisoned as it is in egotism, to *love* him as an egotist, a monster, ungrateful and disloyal? For that is what he is.

1962 (undated)

ROME – FONDI – SPERLONGA. A sign of improvement? As I washed this morning, I found myself considering the letter I might or should write to Richard after our relationship, partnership, whatever you will, has been definitely concluded . . . a letter of wise analysis which presumably would do nobody any good and which I would regret having written twenty-four hours after putting it in the post. Still, other sights, sounds, faces are beginning to have an effect. What I rather dread, of course, is returning to the film, so heavily impregnated with the pregnant image and personality of Richard – [as] Frank [Machin]. When we were doing that post-synching last week I'm afraid I fairly revelled in the shots of Frank – God knows if this is wholly personal, but the dynamism, fascination and mysterious power of the man seem to me quite over-whelming . . . I certainly have no eyes for anyone else on the screen (or is this no more than what Cocteau felt for Marais, or Carné for Roland Lesaffre, or Asquith for Paul Massie ?!) . . . I think particularly of the bus scene – where we disputed the playing – but I can see how Richard's way with the lines raises the intensity and *size* of the character, above the circumstantial and the naturalistic. Part of the fascination of the character is of course its inaccessibility; its refusal to make concessions; he won't come to us, so *we* have to go to *him* . . . In the taxi on the way to the station I was thinking, 'Whatever else, we must do *Hamlet*' – because I know that Richard's temperament and problems equip him to be quite fantastic and unique in this part. I only hope he won't run away from it.

Last night a really rather strange dinner with Daniel and Lorenza.[1] We drove and drove and drove, down the Via Appia, then over to the left and up a hill, stopped briefly by a lake where there were two unhopeful-looking restaurants, both seeming dead – then back furiously to Rome, where we finally settled at the restaurant we had first sighted!

This Sporting Life *opened in Britain to an enthusiastic press in January 1963.*

20 March 1963
Notices for Richard Harris in *This Sporting Life*, suitable for poster quotation:
RICHARD HARRIS –
  A screen giant – a towering talent (*Daily Graphic*)
  A magnificent performance . . . one of the half-dozen finest screen actors
    anywhere in the world (*Sunday Express*)
  Strides through it like a giant (*Sunday Graphic*)
  Splendid, fierce (*Sunday Times*)
  I'm cheering wildly for RICHARD HARRIS (*Sunday Citizen*)
  Gale force . . . More than a touch of greatness (*Sunday Telegraph*)

---

1. Lorenza Mazzetti, novelist and, later, puppeteer. L.A. edited her Free Cinema film *Together* (1956).

In the Spring of 1963, Anderson directed Richard Harris in The Diary of a Madman, *a one-man show they adapted from Gogol. The twenty-eight performances played at the Royal Court from 7 March.*

2 April 1963

Now, with *The Diary of a Madman* in the past, I am in something of a quandary. I can't pretend it went exactly as I hoped. In fact I often have to remind myself that to have got it on at all was something of a triumph. Through that abominable winter: then Richard in his nursing home, nose bandaged and eyes bruised, 'working' on the *Madman*, writing letters behind my back to Christopher Mann [Anderson's agent] demanding first billing for the adaptation; the nightmarish opening of *This Sporting Life* – climaxing with that dreadful party, Richard shrieking at me and insulting me ('Liz – change his nappies for him will you?') from the steps of the Troubadour,[1] then disappearing on the piss for three days . . . The chaotic rehearsals, the bottles of wine, the endless delays and chatter, and then that final weekend of drink and panic which followed the explosion of tantrum which blew poor George Devine[2] to the sky and almost laid me low in desperation . . .

The truth is, I suppose, that so crowded and exhausting have these weeks been, that I am left with almost nothing . . . it's somehow impossible to chronicle them, and whatever I pretend to myself, or would like to pretend, I certainly feel disappointment under it all . . . Contact with Richard was not really achieved; from the time the play opened we did no rehearsal, nor was he ever interested to hear anything I had to say about the performance. My notes were unread, and any comments I had to make were countered practically before my mouth was open . . . I went to the theatre for every performance; but towards the end I felt this was as much because I wanted to see him – and this was my only opportunity – as because he needed it, or it would help to keep the performance going. The end, of course, was characteristic anti-climax, with Richard loading himself with silly, boring people, evading the creative and the intelligent. After the show his dressing room was crammed with Philomena and her brothers, Elizabeth, and various faces recognised from the Britannia. As Richard was setting off with Elizabeth and Morgan[3] for their supper date, he tried to make me go with them, but I was exhausted and determined not to get caught up in a night of drinking and idiotic conversation. 'Alright then – fuck off!' he shouted savagely.

---

1. Actors' haven and café where Richard Harris and Elizabeth first met in January 1955, while he was casting for a self-financed two-week run at the Irving Theatre of Clifford Odets' *Winter Journey.*
2. Artistic Director of the Royal Court Theatre.
3. Morgan Rees-Williams, Elizabeth's brother.

Richard wants everything totally his own way. And as long as he retains his fascination, I suppose I am ready to give it to him. And of course he still is fascinating. Physically overpowering in a way that reduces me to subservience – with that kind of frank, outrageous self-love, that draws me mysteriously. (Why should narcissism be attractive?) Richard is a tremendous self-admirer – and has become so even more since his hair was trimmed and his nose altered and his body developed for *This Sporting Life*. But his *sloppy* self-indulgence of course I don't admire: his boring drinking, his endless dishonesty in evasiveness, and his use of high-pitched shouting to quell opposition, or the threat of an opinion or a judgement that questions a position he holds . . . I used to feel this attitude of his as a sort of challenge to my maturity . . . I don't feel this any more; at least not to the same degree. Perhaps because I *did* get through *The Diary of a Madman*. I *did* get it on the stage: but the result disappointed me. My influence just was not strong enough. Nor did I ever really get to share the basis of Richard's performance. It was developed in private: his consultations with his psychiatrist-lady were in private and I was not permitted to meet her when she came to see the play . . . Much of what he said about his performance (the growing insistence on the *sanity* of the character for instance) seemed to me to be *wrong* – but I was never able to discuss this with him, if only because there was never any time to do so (he would not come to the theatre to rehearse). Finally, there was a growing accent on self-display at the expense of truth of feeling that took away my pleasure in the performance, however much it apparently increased its effectiveness. *Coriolanus* is undoubtedly the part!

But I'm not sure I could do this for long – stifle my opinions – pretend to an admiration I don't feel. And does Richard give me quite enough to justify it? My strength is not in cynicism. But there is a certain pleasure in playing with these ideas: it's the nearest I've come to a love affair, ever: to sacrificing principle for love in the way that most people do at one time or another. And to feel one's soul in danger – it's something of a novelty. If I really am a masochist I might as well go as far as I can – if only, my black side sometimes sighs, he would go a little further. One of my most cherished memories is of Richard planting his booted foot heavily on mine, and grabbing me by the throat.

4 April 1963
Is he on the piss? Is he avoiding me? . . . I suppose he'll be drunk, and still sleeping it off at midday.

14 April 1963
Richard has been sulking over my announcement that I was going to do *Andorra*:[1] at least that is probably the excuse he is giving himself – it may also be merely another of

---

1. By Max Frisch, at the National Theatre.

those spells of cutting himself adrift from those who threaten to come too close to him . . . He did have lunch with Oscar [Lewenstein] on the Friday – which he started apparently by remarking with a smile that he was 'avoiding Lindsay'.

'Why?'

'I don't know.'

19 June 1963

The pages are a challenge, and though often people think that writing a diary is unhealthy – as it certainly can be, when it confirms a tendency to turn in on oneself – it can also be the reverse, forcing one to objectify, to pursue one's thoughts, to marshal them and use them. And although, at the age of forty it is a little chilling to think one is starting again, it is still possible one may yet improve.

I think of Richard, of that side of him which has a somewhat insidious appeal to me: the dark, powerful and sadistic side, proud and narcissistic, to which I play the servant while he plays the king . . . He has just read the proof copy of *Radcliffe*,[1] and rang me up to say it's marvellous: where did David [Storey] get it from? I wonder for an instant if *he* is wondering if there's anything in it of him and me . . . is there? Not too much I imagine. When did he start the book? I told him David had spoken of it before we met . . . He talked of the idea of filming it and, momentarily, I wonder also if *he* would like to direct it.

Knowing Richard, and experiencing these extremes of warmth and cold, the gentleness and the violence, the reason and the hysteria, has certainly been an education for me . . . making real and comprehensible much that before was only theoretical. It *is* a battle of wills, and it is something of an experience to find myself in a relationship where my will is the weaker, where, intermittently, I am made to accept domination, and made to accept behaviour – treatment – I would accept from none other, through fear of losing favour. It's interesting that for all my masochism in fantasy, I am not able (so far) to enjoy *consciously* the treatment in practice. When on the stage of the Royal Court, Richard grasps me by the throat – I am conscious only of the will to stand firm, to survive . . . In little, I suppose this does crystalise the *Radcliffe* relationship . . . But how far from (for instance) the relationship we had at Cannes[2] where he was all kisses and appreciation: 'I don't know how you put up with me.'

Of course it is precisely this duality of nature, this comprehension of evil and goodness, that gives Richard a quality of genius as an actor. So that to wish that he were always 'nice' *is* to wish him other than he is – an impossibility anyway. And since it is what he *is* that attracts me so: why should I wish him otherwise?

---

1. Novel by David Storey; at its heart is a sado-masochistic relationship between sensitive, artistic Radcliffe and Tolson, a charismatic working-class married man.

2. Where Richard Harris won the Best Actor prize for *This Sporting Life*, and the film won the International Critics' Prize.

Easy to say, of course: but such a perpetually shifting personality *is* hard to live with – and I must admit the thought occurs that maybe too continual a repetition of those silences, those refusals to speak, may in the end sap devotion and break one through fatigue, even boredom. That last weekend of *Diary of a Madman* rehearsals: could I go through that again? There must be an improvement, or it really will collapse.

'Quarrelsome friendship' – so Fiz described it (thinking also of herself and Stanley) when we had supper in the Black Angus last night. So she is going to leave Stanley and go and live with Nigel Davenport: and I listen; and speak calmly and sympathetically, and think abstractedly that if things had been different, she would be coming to live with me . . .

23 June 1963

On Friday, Richard and I went down to Pinewood to have lunch with Julian Wintle[1] . . . When we reached Pinewood we went in and, being a trifle early, strolled down the garden and back, speculating on the Profumo case, whether Macmillan is lying, whether Edinburgh is involved. Seeing the bar there, Richard wanted to go across for a preliminary bloody mary – but I said we'd better go up.

In Julian's office, Richard somewhat nervy at first, Julian gauche, not inviting us to sit, Richard tending to look at me while talking . . . We went down to the bar for a drink first, and had only just begun chatting when Robert Shaw[2] appeared, hair dyed white for his role in the new James Bond film . . . Bob talked volubly, about Pedro Armendariz (who had been on the film, had known he had cancer, and had just shot himself in a Los Angeles hospital), about *The Caretaker*,[3] did not scruple to reveal his attitude towards *This Sporting Life* (making no comment to Richard); and reported how Harry Saltzman had remarked: 'Well you can't deny – Lindsay has talent' – to which he subscribed . . . talked about his new daughter – the fact he now has five daughters and one son – his new book . . . certainly an exclusive sort of conversation, with no great concern to involve either Julian or Richard . . . Dear Bob – likeable, but he is certainly his own kind of monster.

Lunch with Julian was of course ridiculous. He started off with his boxing film idea . . . except there appears to be no more to the idea than that, no story – nothing . . . Richard countered with 'a story about a bandit' . . . Salvatore Giuliano[4] in fact, with one seeing Giuliano's face . . . This was as nebulous as Julian's boxing film – so *that* got no

1. (1913–1980) Rank Studio executive in charge of production.
2. Actor, writer (1927–1978), whom L.A. had directed in *The Long and the Short and the Tall*. He was acting in *From Russia with Love*.
3. Play by Harold Pinter, filmed by Clive Donner. Shaw starred with Alan Bates and Donald Pleasence.
4. Francesco Rosi's film of *Salvatore Giuliano* was released in London in June 1963. In the film you do not see Giuliano's face.

further. *Wuthering Heights*[1] was again mentioned – no *practical* response from Julian, but 'interest' . . . then we got on to *This Sporting Life* – its disappointing commercial career, Julian's naive disillusion that it should make so much less than *The Fast Lady*[2] . . . We go into aspects of the publicity, the Rank handling, etc. – none of which Julian is prepared to concede.

But what am I trying to set down? My most pregnant image of the day is Richard's left fist and forearm, against the window of the car during the drive back – the red-golden hairs on his arm lit by the sunshine. An image of power that is infused at the moment with the peculiar warmth, that uniqueness that belongs to love – but from which, I suppose, this warmth, this particularity, will fade, until the memory of such obsessive feeling becomes merely odd, and somewhat embarrassing – like thoughts of Serge.

24 June 1963

Richard was given what sounded like an absurd script by Wintle called *The Magnificent Leonardi* – and on the stairs at Pinewood we ran into Harry Saltzman, who started talking about *The Ipcress File* – mentioning it for Richard – though it was at present planned for Harry Corbett – and saying he would send it. And send it he did: it was there, with the sequel, *House Under Water*, delivered by hand through my letterbox when I got home that night.

16 July 1963

Tonight *This Sporting Life* opens in New York. Of course I haven't heard a whisper from Richard since he left. Is it just petty of me to resent this – to feel that he has gone there primarily to advertise himself – and to have a good piss-up with Malachy McCourt? I seem to have a vision of a 'me' who might accept this – of course, that is Richard . . . yet that 'me' does not really exist, except in fragmentary moments. I go to clear up the study: and there is the still of him, huge arms crossed, brooding in the chair beside his bed . . .

21 July 1963

State of extreme vacillation – depression – absolute inability to think concretely of any project – except in terms of Richard Harris. He has been gone a fortnight. The film has opened in New York to a splendid press[1] – all the dailies excellent to superb . . . a few notes and phone calls have conveyed what Richard has been up to – indiscriminate

---

1. From a script by David Storey.
2. Comedy in glowing Eastmancolor starring Stanley Baxter, Leslie Phillips and Julie Christie.
3. Harris and Roberts both won Oscar nominations.

fucking, with Malachy McCourt in constant attendance – actually living, it seems, at the Sherry-Netherland . . . My morale has disintegrated lamentably.

That greedy puckering of the lips as he mimes the sucking of a cunt – that extraordinary, animal sensuality which is with Richard almost all of the time – in the street or in a coffee bar, so that he will at any moment almost break into a mime of masturbation, of sucking or of fucking . . . This, no doubt, is part of the continual magnestism, the continual excitement of his presence – the sense that at any moment he may follow his instinct to almost any sexual end.

But of course this is only an element in Richard: as it is only an element of myself; one to which I, through years of frustration, and perhaps also just by temperament, am peculiarly vulnerable.

The hope was of a relationship that *balanced*. But the balance has not been achieved, I needing love and security too much – therefore lacking the strength that Richard needs, if only to fight against. This dominant, brutal man of power is only a fantasy, of *his* also – a game to play – but a dangerous one, self-indulgent, and weakening to my moral authority.

Of course the answer is not to make moralistic judgements and accusations of Richard, but to discover and stick to my own truth . . . to accuse an animal of ingratitude is silly – however touching it is when one finds it grateful! Even if it were possible to realise the fantasy of subjection, it wouldn't work for more than a fortnight: for Richard doesn't *want* me in his 'family'. Strength is the only resolution.

Only – and here's the rub – I am continually sabotaged by my own weakness, emotional and pervading. The resolution to be strong only goes so far, when one works emotionally – needs the emotional stimulus to give one something to be strong *about*. Here is a theme indeed!

14 August 1963
Fat – in the barber's mirror, the flesh under the chin is undeniable – greying – balding – with the marks of emotional fatigue clearly showing under the eyes . . . no wonder discontent, a mild despair is my dominant mood.

For my fantasies with Richard have become more and more masochistic, more and more centred on that game of master and servant: 'Lindsay – heel!'

At Max Frisch's urging, Anderson agreed to Laurence Olivier's request to become the National Theatre's first guest director. His production of Frisch's Andorra *opened at the Old Vic on 28 January 1964. Tom Courtenay starred with Lynn Redgrave, Colin Blakely, Diana Wynyard, Robert Stephens, Cyril Cusack and Derek Jacobi.*

2 February 1964

Andorra over: the effective notices out – mixed, but by no means disastrous. The production a success as far as I'm concerned, and now for a certain relaxation, a feeling of thankfulness that another achievement can be registered. A mild day, like yesterday, with even a touch of spring: one looks around.

Richard came through London from Ravenna[1] nine days ago, when we were dress-rehearsing in the theatre. I knew he was coming, because together with Anthony Page I had phoned him the night before. We had spoken to Elizabeth who had told us that they were leaving the next morning – and that Richard had to fly straight on to the US with only a half-hour between planes. I was rehearsing *Andorra* the next day, and there was no hope of my getting to the airport; but Anthony decided to go, hoping to talk about plans for the Court season.

We had a run-through the next day – a somewhat painful one as it happened, since it was the first one for some days, and in addition there was the presence of Max Frisch to make everyone additionally nervous. As the last scene started I got a message that Richard Harris would be staying overnight in London, and would I phone him . . . Eventually I managed to contact him at the Brit (my heart acknowledged the inevitability of it). He was excited, friendly, racing (later Elizabeth told me he'd had seven brandies on the plane). He talked with his usual obsessiveness about his last days at Ravenna – which seemed genuinely fantastic, all the tricks and connivances which Antonioni had used against him – how Antonioni had played him utterly false, had never believed that he would leave, had refused to sign his contract, how he had refused to shoot, the scenes of hysterics and tears, how he (Richard) had implacably preserved his dignity, and won through. How the sound man, who had worked with Antonioni on several pictures, had shaken him by the hand, and told him he was the only one who ever defeated Antonioni . . . But he wasn't staying the night – he had to catch a plane at 6.30 – couldn't I come over? I explained I couldn't, and suggested that he drop in at the Vic at 4.15, and go straight on to the airport. I would lay on a car to be there and take him on. He agreed: and with warmth rang off. *Wuthering Heights*, of course, had never been mentioned. He never turned up of course.

31 March 1964

Well today I did it [persuaded United Artists to finance the Anderson–Harris production of *Wuthering Heights*]– like taking sweets away from children – sitting in that office talking sweet to Arthur Krim and Robert Benjamin and David Picker, somewhat pale between them, hoping no doubt that I would make a good show of it and justify him.

---

1. Where he had been filming *Il Deserto Rosso* (*The Red Desert*) for Michelangelo Antonioni.

And with charm and seriousness and fluency – I did it. Perhaps because it really doesn't mean much to me really. I did it for Richard. Because that is the way that my heart and my instincts have led me. Because that is the way destiny seems to lead.

I shall see him tomorrow: shall I? I spoke to him this evening, in Cuernavaca, Mexico[1] . . . It is over three months since I saw him last, on Ravenna station. Richard has been, amongst other things, a whole education for me – without him I should certainly never have been able to do what I have done for *Wuthering Heights* – come to New York and talked with the authority and confidence that I have . . . I really long to see Richard again, and enjoy the presence of my handsome, powerful friend: the sensitive, the poetic, the generous, the egotistical – the most exciting actor in the world. The creative to my receptive: the strong to my weak. And having got this far, I really do begin to feel that my confidence is greater than my doubts.

3 April 1964
Yesterday I met Richard again, to be greeted with as much affection as ever before – as much excitement and delight and warmth as I could have hoped for. I had arrived at Mexico City on Wednesday night – anxious, wondering whether there'd be anyone there . . . Standing in the plane, waiting to disembark, I glimpsed a crowd through the windows, standing by the first-class gangway, and I thought for a moment it contained them . . . but as I descended self-consciously into the warm Mexican evening, there were no welcoming calls.

After I got through customs – feeling the altitude this time, with shortness of breath and fatigue – I caught the eye of a young, pleasant-looking Scottish chap in shirt sleeves, and he stepped forward. This, though I didn't realise it immediately, was *the* Bob Wild – devoted follower and driver – of whom I'd heard so much.

We started off in the little green car with a dash, Bob Wild thrusting a map into my hand, missing the entry onto the freeway we needed . . . a long drive up into the hills, then steadily down, hugging the contours of the mountainside, till we arrived at the Posada Jacarando . . . a lawned and spacious refuge set in its own gardens, with chalet-type bedrooms around. The air tranquil and balmy. It was past one and Richard had gone to bed. On my pillow in my room were two pieces of paper: on one (on which also lay a red rose) was written 'Bien Venido a Mexico – Elizabeth.' The other said simply (and magnificently) 'I am Heathcliff.'

8 May 1964
London. Images are there, the visit over, feeling alone now and very empty, after that last three weeks alone with Richard . . . very close, up to those final five days in New

---

1. Where Harris was filming Sam Peckinpah's *Major Dundee*.

York, surrendered completely to his influence, emotionally dependent, admiring and so gratified to serve. To hand him his orange juice; and ask him if he wants a cup of tea, pour it and hand it to him still in bed: 'Well done, Lindsay!'

Looking in the window of the whip shop, and discussing the cat o'nine tails, the leather bat, the black leather thong: 'I'd put my hand up her skirt, and pull down her knickers, and put my finger up her arse.'

'I suppose you could write my biography ...'

Should I offer myself to Richard as his personal assistant?

One aspect of Richard that was revealed to me was his interest in the subtleties and varieties of sexual experience ... It was at the Maria Isabella that he suddenly noticed and pounced on (as I had intuitively known he would) the paperback I had bought at New York airport, *The Velvet Underground*, a journalistic account of a sexual 'movement' which the author purported to have uncovered of couples joining up to share each other in various forms of sexual activity; with strong emphasis on sadistic and masochistic practices – and a cover adorned with whips and a tall leather (female) boot. This book he digested avidly.

In New York the fascination became most insistent. Up the street there was showing a horror film, *Blood Feast*: that of course drew his attention at once. 'Let's go and see that – just for a giggle ...' and we stood outside and watched the slides of blood, knives, whips and disembowelling ... It took us some days to fit it in; and before that we had come upon the umbrella shop, Uncle Sam's, just off Times Square, in the small side window of which were displayed an intriguing assortment of instruments of punishment – none too huge or elaborate: handy little whips; instruments reminiscent of the sole of a shoe – a ferocious tawse of black leather, reminiscent of the Jesuit *pandy bat*. These fascinated Richard. 'We'll get three – which do you like best? – that, that and that ...' That was on the Saturday. On the Sunday we returned to study the collection again through the window. And on the Monday, together with a couple of umbrellas for Elizabeth, we actually bought them. 'The Secret Life of Richard St John Harris ...' But nothing would make him admit to anything beyond curiosity.

26 May 1964

Much of the violence on *Sporting Life* was connected with getting his own way; and too obscured by that motivation to strike me as 'sadistic' ... the punching ... How or when this started I can't well remember: it may well have been me that encouraged it – or in response to a threatened raised fist of his. Anyway, by the end of the picture, the bruises were marked; and sometimes the interchanges of blows quite painful. Certainly undignified. I remember one of the last shots – an insert of Richard lying on the doss-house bed – and how we got involved, like two schoolboys, in a suddenly quite violent interchange of blows (and I with my front tooth embarrassingly loose).

I remember Richard saying that it was *Sporting Life* that had made him conscious of his appearance – that before it he never looked in a mirror and didn't bother with photographs. Certainly during the picture, and with all the concern over makeup and the nose, narcissism had every chance to intensify.

Boots first entered the picture that memorable day when Richard arrived down in Beaconsfield after a riding lesson – magnificent in riding boots, white breeches and scarlet sweater . . . We lay on the floor and consulted I-Ching . . . then afterwards, when the others had gone, I remember kneeling by Richard, booted Richard, as he sat on the chair by the door, consciously enjoying the position of subservience (like kneeling by the bed on the film set: the still which appeared in *Films and Filming*).[1] Then pulling his boots off for him . . .

With *Diary of a Madman* things took a further step – a sense of romantic self-display; and further explorations of love-hate between us. Rehearsals for *The Diary* varied between friendship and creativity on the one hand, and resentment, fear, compulsive talking and nervous bullying on the other. Of that sort of 'playing' with one that I'd call sadistic I can only recall one or two examples. Once, when he was jibbing at going up to Leeds for the opening of *Sporting Life*, I had written a note to Karel – asking him, I think, to lend a hand . . . I hadn't sent the note and, as we were listening to music played over by Carl Davis,[2] it fell out of my script. Richard pounced on it, saw a phrase like 'Richard is no easier now than he ever was . . .' and with great glee scented betrayal. I went white.

The next incident between us must have been that protracted, drunken, violent row after Percy Herbert[3] and his wife had been to dinner . . . that went on late and late into the night . . . into the morning . . . with Richard, alcohol now freely running through his veins, after me again like a hound after a hare . . . I remember coming round the table, trying to get him to stop, and Richard – the ruthless inflicter of pain now – saying 'You love it – tomorrow you'll be able to say – Richard was so cruel to me last night – You love it, of course you do . . .' Eventually, at some shaft, I rose from my chair and flew out of the house, out of the gate, and I was half way across the road when I saw that Richard had followed to the front steps. He called me back. I did not allow myself to be drawn back ineluctably, the helpless, mesmerised victim . . . Instead I think I said: 'Well you might meet me halfway . . .' And Richard did not. 'I can't. I've got no shoes on . . .' I returned anyway, and cat-and-mouse continued. I remember only Richard copying my incensed run across the street – from which *he* returned and we stood in the doorway, the early summer morning bright around us, continuing to

---

1. February 1963.

2. Composed the music for *The Diary of a Madman*.

3. Actor (1920–1992), appeared with Harris in *The Guns of Navarone* and *Mutiny on the Bounty*.

squabble (fragments come to mind of my mocking Richard's idea that he could be called 'professional') until I burst again, and tore off, this time not pursued . . .

4 June 1964

Now the truth is that Richard *had* told me of the Sophia Loren picture;[1] and I do seem to remember him once saying that it was planned to follow straight after *The Bible*[2] . . . But equally, he had never – from the moment he joyfully heard of *Radcliffe* – himself mentioned the fact that it was dependent on other things. As so often in these situations, I was wrong through a tendency to react emotionally and get confused and count too much on a personal commitment . . . while the situation was aggravated through Richard's vagueness, and his underlying *reluctance* ever to be really clear or specific. I suggested on the phone that if he didn't want the meeting with Sandy Lieberson[3] 'to clear things up' – if he felt it would commit him to being represented by Sandy – then we should cancel it. But he wanted to have it all the same . . .

I had been seeing Oscar about my idea for the trilogy.[4] And we went on talking till eight – the time of the meeting. But I would need to eat something. And I reflected with some satisfaction on being late. Why should I rush? Let me arrive and find Richard and Sandy waiting for me for a change . . . so I went to a pub in Shepherd's Market (the same where Richard and I had eaten when we went to Curzon instead of the premiere of *Mutiny on the Bounty*) and had cold pie and salad . . . Then I caught a taxi . . . Alas for fantasy. My taxi drew up just as Richard was letting Sandy in through the front door.

When I got in the hall I saw, through the open door into the drawing room, that all were settled, watching television. *Gunsmoke*. Elizabeth on the couch, clad in some dark, spangled, trousered boudoir garment. Damian on the floor. Richard in a chair behind him. Sandy in another chair. Some joke about putting my coat on the hooks half way down the stairs. ('Well trained . . .')My attitude already frosty. Then silence, except for *Gunsmoke* and comments by Damian and Richard.

After about ten minutes of this farcical situation I think Elizabeth, who had not moved from my entrance, said: 'Would you like a drink?' I refused. Richard went down on the floor with 'Dides'. I exchanged a look with Sandy, plainly nonplussed. My tension grew. The absolute unreality of the whole thing oppressed me . . . Again one was plunged in that familiar situation – Richard playing a part: of non-communicative dumb insolence, trying to manufacture a reason for blowing up, for evading whatever issues might be raised . . . Myself not wanting to precipitate a rupture, my sense of rightness, of dignity, of the simple laws of hospitality outraged, emitting (whatever my reason

---

1. *The Fall of the Roman Empire.* Harris had been offered the part of Commodus.
2. Directed by John Huston. Harris played Cain.
3. L.A.'s new agent; later the head of production at Twentieth Century Fox.
4. Oscar Lewenstein had proposed a three-part film based on stories by Shelagh Delaney.

dictated) *waves* of resentment . . . If I were Karel, I thought, I would simply say: 'Shall we talk?' And because the detachment would be real it would probably be effective. But I would be quite unable to say it without emotion . . . I could of course just leave. But then I fear that Richard would accept *that* action as an excuse to let the whole thing go by default. Perhaps this would be best . . .

I went upstairs to the 'study' – as neat and tidied-away as after a death. I picked Breughel out of the shelves and tried to look at it. Tried hard, but only felt worse at my lack of response. A shout from Richard downstairs. 'Lindsay!' In different circumstances acceptable. But not like this. I didn't answer.

After about ten minutes I went downstairs. The same scene. Now the TV was on sport. Elizabeth said: 'Where've you been?' I said 'Upstairs.'

Damian: 'Did you rob our money?'

L: 'What?'

D: 'Did you rob our money?'

L: 'Yes.'

D: 'Dad – he robbed our money . . .'

After some minutes of – what was it? Horses maybe . . . Sandy said nervously: 'Shall we go upstairs?'

Richard replied: 'I want to see the end of this.'

I went upstairs again, took up Breughel again, and waited. Sounds of Elizabeth's carping tones, the child being chased to bed . . . Eventually Sandy and Richard appeared. Tension. 'Well?' said Richard. I forget the word pattern: but I must have said something about the discussion. 'You arrived half an hour late,' said Richard. 'So you've nothing to complain about.'

'Don't be ridiculous.'

'Come on – ' says Sandy: but the required spark had been found. Richard breaks out into an hysterical attack on me because – according to Sandy (according to Richard) – by phoning to create this meeting, I was 'hurt and confused at hearing that Richard was still considering other projects which would clash with the Woodfall trilogy and the Royal Court . . .' It was impossible of course to discuss the situation rationally.

'Liar!' he shouted. 'You're a liar.'

'Alright Richard – I heard you . . .'

'Liar! Liar!'

Useless to attempt to argue: 'You can call me a fool – but not a liar.'

'LIAR – LIAR!!'

In the midst of this absurd, destructive, hysterical, abortive meeting, the phone rang. It was Wilk O'Connor. Verbally it seemed Richard had agreed to finance him in coming to London to write a draft script of *Michael Collins* . . . After the call was over, when I tried to reason the whole thing out – to suggest that this wasn't worth going on with, I was met with a flood of infantile arguments: 'Lean and Spiegel couldn't get the money for *Lawrence of Arabia* at first. It took them years.'

'But that's quite a different kind of subject.'

'Why? No one had ever heard of Lawrence – in America he was quite unknown.'

'But *Lawrence of Arabia* has the appeal of an exotic pictorial film.'

'It's a war film – so is this. Look at all that marvellous material we saw in that film about the Civil War.'

Etc., etc. All unreal. Playing at it.

On Monday, I went round, and did in fact work with him for an hour or so, talking about Cain while his tape recorder was switched on, giving him the benefit of my ideas. To nothing did he respond with any enthusiasm, any spirit, any suggestion that plans were good and hopeful. Everything whittled down to his personal whim, his egotistical gratification and – even without that relish – almost a resented intrusion between him and his family, or his television set. And never have I felt so strongly the awful pressure of domesticity, of the managing, absorbing female. The only quality I have found in Elizabeth before has been the feeling for Richard, her desire to do what's best for him, to shield him from those destructive influences. And in this context we had something in common, a sort of alliance. Now, however, what was there to shield him from? And *I* became an intruder. Like an Osborne-image of femininity, she coiled round Richard, drawing him apart . . .

4 August 1964

Of course I don't *know* that Richard flew to Rome to discuss an alternative propostion. And it is a clear indication that one is dealing with a neurotic personality that one knows that his behaviour does not even necessarily postulate motives so clear and rational. Any more 'rational', that is, than his refusal to return from Wakefield to London when we were on location with *This Sporting Life*, because he imagined he had been 'insulted' by the assistant director: which involved a night of agonised phone calls, and a day's rescheduling. Or than his refusal to rehearse one afternoon on *The Diary of a Madman*, because he had seen an advert for the film, in which he felt his notices were not featured sufficiently prominently. The pressures, of family and finance and professional status are mounting on him. Agents are pursuing him. He can trust no one. He wants everything. And he wants to pay for nothing. The pattern is, literally, 'infantile'.

18 October 1964

Returning from Moscow . . . Strangely, though everything in this book has been written this year, I had almost forgotten its existence: things with Richard having been patched up again – two weeks spent in Italy, at the Villa and at the Grand; and now this week in Moscow and Leningrad.

What stretches out front now is a daunting propect of work: *Julius Caesar* – David's play – *Wuthering Heights* – then the possibility of *Hamlet*. How to accomplish these things in my present state?

I have not continued my visits to the psychiatrist. I suppose it is significant that I can't remember his name. What amounted from our talks – at £5-5-0 a time? The probability that I had suffered traumatically from some early prohibition against masturbation; that I wasn't really ('couldn't really be') homosexual; that an early emotional deprivation, which he located in the departure of Nanny Bullen, had cut off my capacity for emotional commitment and expression . . . There was something interesting in his pointing out my inability (reluctance) to talk absolutely *personally*. That I tended to give 'the facts', but probably this was at least partly defensive. It seems I need something different from a psychiatrist – something (yes) more fatherly, more able to pull me along, or at least *prod* where necessary.

Anderson's production of Julius Caesar, *designed by Jocelyn Herbert, and scored by Marc Wilkinson, who would write the music for* If . . . . , *opened at the Royal Court on 26 November 1964. Caesar was played by Paul Curran, Casca by Graham Crowden, Ian Bannen played Brutus. Anthony Hopkins made his Royal Court debut as Metellus Cimber. Mark Antony was played by Daniel Massey. Richard Harris had quit two weeks into rehearsals.*

11 *January 1965*

I dreamed: a school or institution somewhere – Richard and I estranged: Albie showing me his drawings – very accomplished – standing outside – going to a ceremony – wedding? Funeral? As we walk out to the bushes I am walking near Richard, close up I inspect him, louche, his reddish hair growing untidily, messy sideburns, face pale (how much less healthy than Albie, I reflect). Outside I stand by Richard, neither of us saying anything, then as I move away, he starts to speak – it is film-making now, and I am going to do the part of somebody's father? – we establish contact, and talk. I am wearing no clothes and I say I'd better put some on. As I walk back to the building I'm not too ashamed of my figure. Make my way to room 125 – in the corridor a servant is cleaning. I open the door and find the room in a terrible mess – a great pile of rubbish at the door, on which is my typewriter. I send for 'the manager'. Climb out of the window to look over towards the gate and roadway, wandering if Richard has waited for me? Yes – he's still there. He wanders back, with a companion, on the gravel down there below me. I call: he doesn't hear, they move on round. I call, he looks up, doesn't see me. I call – he sees me . . .

4

Towards an International Brotherhood

India – Miniatures – Czechoslovakia
Madrid – Cannes – Pesaro – Warsaw
Bette Davis – The Berliner Ensemble – George Devine

'The last two weeks have reawakened my interest
in the cinema – given me a context, if you like'

Anderson accepted an invitation to serve on the jury of India's first competitive
international film festival. The jury president was Satyajit Ray.

19 January 1965 (Delhi)
In the morning the jury went to a special show of *Mahanagar*[1] – all highly respected it,
seemingly . . . was I wrong? I don't think so . . . I rose late. Strolled out taking a few
pictures. Felt rested . . . Evening invited with Satyajit to dinner with Mrs Gandhi.
Discover this not ideal for my 'interview' as Benjamin Britten[2] and Peter Pears, on
Indian vacation, also there. The unmistakable musty old-maidish aroma of English
liberal good taste. God! How dreary a country it is . . . Unable to get any sensation of
enthusiasm or effective interest in the Festival from Mrs Gandhi, who seemed
nervously looking round at the servants dishing out curry most of the time, though
unpretentious and direct enough . . . Not really 'with it'.

---

1. *The Big City*, by Satyajit Ray.
2. British composer (1913–1976). Britten was a member of the first governing council of the English
Stage Company.

Return to the hotel for first jury meeting . . . Interested to spot Wajda[1] votes for Turkish sensation: *Heroes of Golden City*. I partly understand.

20 January 1965

Jury deliberates and all is solved by 1.30, including *The Tiger of Bengal* for Sukh Dev – proposed in the end by Kalatozov[2] (because I had proposed the Soviet actor for *his* prize?!) . . . A perfectly pleasant and amicable meeting. We were in a minority who would've preferred not to give a Grand Prix: and I really can't grudge it to Lester James Piries for *Gam Perpalya*[3] . . . Brusil statesmanlike and pleasant: I translate for him: we are quite buddies. *Guns at Batasi* and Richard Attenborough[4] never mentioned! Afternoon work out wordings of prizes with Satyajit. The only prolonged stalemate turns out to be the wording of Gam Peralaya's award! But no acerbity. In the evening I dined alone and strolled to Safter Jang's rosy-lit tomb. Disappointing.

22 January 1965

Departed Claridge's at 11.15, bidding farewell to Kalatozov with an EP of The Rolling Stones . . . Heavy delays at the airport. Drive through golden evening sunshine rather intoxicated (idiotically) with our first welcome, garlanding, etc. to Madras. To cinema for usual futile opening ceremony. Meet Manvell,[5] who makes speech on our behalf. ('What eloquence, what a command of language! . . . You can see he speaks from the heart,' says Narayanan.) . . . Return to the hotel and appalling dining room, where we insist on a curry instead of Boeuf Napolitaine on the 'Western Menu'. My imperialistic intransigence impresses Sadoul:[6] rather shocks Guy Glover[7] I fear. Evening write my piece for *Sunday Times* with difficulty.[8]

24 January 1965

Started from hotel about 9.30, on tourist expedition. First stop at Thirukazhug-Kundram. We climbed hundreds of steps to see the sacred eagles fed. But they did not come. On to Mahabalipuram, where first we bathed, lunching at the guest house, then

---

1. Andrzej Wajda, Polish film-maker (1927–).

2. Mikhail Kalatozov (1903–1973), Russian director of *The Cranes are Flying* (1957).

3. *Changes in the Village*. L.A. noted that it 'astonished the Slavs with its elegiac, near Chekovian grace.' (*Sunday Times*, 31 January 1965)

4. John Guillermin directed Richard Attenborough in a tale of a British regiment under siege in Africa.

5. Roger Manvell, film historian. Director of the British Film Academy from 1947.

6. Georges Sadoul, French film historian, author of *Dictionary of Films* (1965).

7. Canadian documentary film-maker.

8. 'It Makes One Think', subtitled 'Film Director Lindsay Anderson draws some lessons from India's first real film festival.'

saw the sights: the temples and statues carved out of the rocks, the sea-shore temple . . .
Sadoul bathed in his underpants: he appeared to have a tremendous cock . . .

25 January 1965

Awoke from a dream of running, running freely and effortlessly . . . Two interviews,
first a girl from *Indian Express* – whom I at first frightened and antagonised by
irritation at her total ignorance – then charmed by sympathetic outspokenness; then
lively fellow from *Film-Advance* – delighted by my frankness. Went out with Sadoul,
strolled around, he is catching on to the necessity for Raj-like intransigence.

26 January 1965

CALCUTTA: huge, sprawling, dirty, begin to feel overcome by India, ever-present squalor
and this strange remoteness behind the effusiveness, the lack of real contact, the platitudes of respect and affection whose truth one cannot gauge.

Afternoon driven miles by Mr Sen Gupta of Cine-Advance to see a 'neglected'
independent film made four years ago by an ex-student . . . Tyaro Nadir Parey – *On the
River Bank* turns out a pretentious and I'm afraid quite untalented piece. Director
doesn't really want to know. Return for Governor's Garden Party – elite of Calcutta on
green sward, band and meatballs, curry paste, and Indian sweets. But the Lady
Governor is splendid – remarked that if she had to stay her full second term of five
years in Calcutta she'd die and there'd have to be a State Funeral . . .

27 January 1965

Morning tour with Satyajit Ray: the image and religious decoration-makers' quarter,
then two superb decaying nabob mansions: classical displays of marble and columns
and statuary; heavy mahogany and teak; art nouveau decoration; formal gardens running wild . . . Stimulated to ideas of thriller set in Calcutta with these marvellous back-
grounds. Afternoon visit hideous Jain temple with Guy Glover. Evening: India Studios:
picnic supper in canteen with Satyajit, wife and son: then see *Postmaster*[1] and *Charu-
lata*.[2] He's a fine, developed film-maker, though I do have to fight sleep and push
enthusiasm a bit. Sorry.

31 January 1965

Morning I try to write to Sandy Lieberson, which brings me disturbingly close to
reality and I discover how far I am from any firm assurance about myself or my
capacities. I consult I-Ching: which is not too clearly indicative. After lunch, see the
first three or four reels of Satyajit's taxi-driver film,[3] and newsreels of our reception at

---

1. First part of Ray's *Teen Kanya* (*Three Daughters*), a three-part film of stories by Tagore.
2. Ray's *The Lonely Wife* (1964).
3. *Abhijaan* (*The Expedition*).

Technician's Studio. We go to the Rays for tea: I feel tired: and Satyajit doesn't – I have to admit it – relax or warm me. We discuss methods slightly: but I sense his firm and closed mind. Lucky fellow. But no 'anima', I suspect. He draws his setups. Is it possible to say there is something cold about Satyajit? The films are so sensitive. But not empathetic? Does one need to be?

3 February 1965

It is the morning: the awakening hour that is most dangerous. The hard-on; the idle thoughts that so easily stray to masochistic dreams; hotel bedrooms in Mexico City, New York or Rome . . . Best to get up, but laziness to conquer in the limbs, and inertia in the mind. No emotional objective. I need to find a closely sublimated activity to spring into at 7.30 each morning!

Spend the first half of morning tying up visa arrangements, including forged vaccination certificates . . . then to Shantaram's[1] studio – where I imagined my lateness would enable me to evade his retrospective of past triumphs: however the Siva dance routine we blundered in to proved only the fourth of seven extracts: the most notable being his remake of *Shakuntala*, with splendid sequences of the heroine subduing a posse of ravening lions by her yogi-detachment. Luncheon served on vast stage dominated by plaster lady-Buddha figure. Took so long that Guy Glover and I absented ourselves to go to All-India radio for talk . . . 50 Rupees.

Bathed at All-European Candy Pool, with glimpses of white youth that took me right home.

9 February 1965

Back home – much should be changed though of course one knows it's not. Except that I feel really cut off from many of the things that have made up my life in the past . . . the Court particularly. Oscar – in Tony [Richardson]'s pocket – though he wants me to do things, he jars on me. Richard – the deceptive romantic glow has certainly gone. By chance Rachel [Roberts] rings, and we have lunch. She sends her car for me – most luxurious. She is leaving *Maggie May*[2] this week, happy and even less obsessive.

10 February 1965

Meet Bud Ornstein.[3] All is set for me to go Norway [where Harris was filming *The Heroes of Telemark*] Friday morning – Bud to fly over to Oslo a few days later, on his way to Jamaica for the new Beatles picture . . . He is obviously far from the producer of

---

1. Vankudre Shantaram (1901–1990), who made the first Indian children's film (*Ranisahiba*, 1930) and the first Indian colour film (*Sairandhri*, 1933).
2. Lionel Bart musical, at the Adelphi Theatre.
3. George Ornstein. British production head at United Artists, who were financing *Wuthering Heights*.

my dreams, with no creative apprehension at all, and no sense of *taking* the subject. I go with the stream.

Go to Karel and Betsy[1] for lunch, rather Spartan with salami; Betsy pale and sweet in her white nightie but now better after her operation. We go to see Karel's rushes.[2] Colin [Blakely] and David Warner. Colin wrong. I feel David Warner also wrong. A good actor; an intelligent face, intelligent and sensitive. But no empathy. I mention Richard – Karel shuts up like a clam! 'I couldn't work with him.'

11 February 1965

Richard has informed John McMichael [his agent] that he is now working so hard that it isn't worth my coming. I phone Richard. First I am told he is 'unavailable' till tomorrow. Then John McM. phones to say he has been with Kirk [Douglas] and now awaits my call. Finally I contact him. Within five minutes we are quarrelling – Richard outraged when I insist I am not 'committed' to *Wuthering Heights* – demanding that the date be changed to *June*. As usual totally unamenable to reason. Phone breaks down. I phone John McM., furious.

Letter from Anthony Hopkins

12 February 1965

It was so good to hear from you; also many thanks for those photographs. I need not say as much but it was a wonderful experience working for you in *Julius Caesar*. It was unfortunate and sad things went the way they did. [Richard Harris resigned and the 28 performances played to a 53 per cent capacity.] But in the general scheme of everything one could say: 'No matter.' It was still an exciting, 'gutsy' and very truthful production; and I'm sure you must have felt, from the whole company of actors involved, the disappointment we all felt. Perhaps I'm saying too much. But thank you very much for everything, Lindsay. Have just finished *Out of Africa* – a beautiful book.

I hope to see you sometime. Good luck and kind regards.

15 February 1965

Read script for *De Sade*. Makes me laugh. Lunch with Peter Brook,[3] arranged before I went to India. A pleasant chat. Why does he like me? He seems to. Not attracted – *surely*?! Then I see Bud Ornstein: the pressure on Richard to jettison or postpone *Wuthering Heights* for *Hawaii*[4] – $250,000. I almost wish he does.

---

1. Betsy Blair (1923–), American actress, Oscar-nominated for *Marty* (1955). Married to Karel Reisz.
2. Tests for the lead in his film *Morgan – An Unsuitable Case for Treatment*, written by David Mercer.
3. Theatre director. Had a cinema success with *Lord of the Flies* (1963) after L.A. turned it down.
4. Film by George Roy Hill.

With the trip to see Harris in Norway cancelled, he caught a train to Bradford,
hired a car, and went scouting for locations for Wuthering Heights.

19 February 1965

The Midland Hotel is a morgue – but the water is hot, the rooms are clean, and what does it matter really? Make for Haworth,[1] take pictures in the church yard, then inspect the parsonage. It is strange how pregnant it is with the atmosphere of that family – is it because of their peculiarly tragic circumstance; the peculiar romance of their lives? Because they were a family? There is a falling of snow. Lunch on meat pie and chips at a hospitable café with a fire. In the afternoon make our way, by car and foot, to the Brontë waterfall. Not spectacular, but attractive; you can see the sisters there.

20 February 1965

Set off earlier and we make for Ponder Hall – the original Thrushcross Grange – which we had looked at yesterday after the Brontë Falls. We set out on Walk No 3 – Penniston Crag and *Wuthering Heights* – with the weather veering from grey to sudden squalls of snow. The valley, the waterfall, up the steps, to the Crag. It is not huge and Wagnerian, but humanly scaled. Snow and wind beat fiercely in the crag.

On to the stones: then across heath and snow-covered hillocks to Top Withens, the poor dilapidated Heights. In afternoon drive to Wycoller (Jane Eyre's ruined mansion) – then across the moor to Halifax.

21 February 1965

A less early start, with the familiar irritation of the Sundays – the vulgarity of Philip Oakes, Tynan and Gilliatt; the soppy self-caricature of Hobson . . . We make towards Ilkley, exploring the edge of the moor, which is flat and featureless – quite good for roadway, pathway shots – then cross the moor by bumpy track down into Ilkley – the cow and calf rocks daubed with *up the mods* in green paint, and spattered with humans. They are melodramatic but without the poetry of Haworth. Lunch at the Devonshire Arms, quite pleasant. Then on up the valley, beyond Appletreewick, and recklessly we take the right fork for another venture on a grassy track across the moors . . . we crest the hill, through a gate, Simon's Seat on our left – and stick. All to no avail. We walk down to the village – and blessedly encounter a farmer on a tractor. So we are saved.

22 February 1965

Back to a few bills at an empty Greencroft, then to Sloane Square, where I have a drink with George Devine and the Brazilian British Council rep. Nice of George to offer me

---

1. Yorkshire village famous for its associations with the Brontë Sisters.

as a visitor for Brazil. Interesting to note he does not urge my *theatrical* claims – indeed, agrees with me when I say I am more a professional of cinema than theatre! Oh well . . . Birthday party for Jocelyn, given by Sandra and Brian in their nice, modern, tasteful, lived-in flat. Architects do make things nice . . .

23 February 1965

Richard Harris arrived home yesterday: meeting tentatively arranged for 4 p.m. this afternoon. I ring John McMichael. Will I be free to see Richard tomorrow? I say what about this meeting today? John embarrassed, feigns surprise and pleasure at the idea.

Admitted by the brisk, over-chirpy Sylvia – Richard in bed, a transistor playing by his bedside: fine if I were a stranger. As if a new 'policy' is in operation. As we talk I go to the window. A huge Rolls drives up: chauffeur lets out Elizabeth, she brings flowers in: very cool – 'Hullo Lindsay.' Richard suggests we meet Sunday – I get huffy – McM. cringingly says, 'I've not looked at the schedule in detail'. I leave in a huff.

24 February 1965

Worry remains. What to do? Consult I-Ching – DELIVERANCE. I write to John McM. and call the whole thing off. Apparently Richard was shocked that I left the room so abruptly on Tuesday – and has even proposed sacrificing some of his percentage for another producer. Anyway, John agrees that Richard must phone me about Sunday – if the meeting is to happen – otherwise we abandon ship. Then to NFT – see *Queen Kelly*[1] with Anthony Page and Diane Cilento. Afterwards supper with Sean Connery (what a pleasant fellow!) and Ronnie Carrol at the Australia Club. Sean tells stories. Anthony *laughs*.

25 February 1965

Lunch with Oscar [Lewenstein] – the White Elephant. Decide we should try to see Serge [Reggiani] about the French version of *Inadmissible Evidence* . . . Oscar on at me again about [the] Shelagh Delaney story. Why not? Suddenly feel the itch – go off to see *Young Cassidy*[2] – which is no good, might have been worse. Of course I should have done it. AGENTS again. And my infernal weakness.

28 February 1965

Fatalistically wait for Richard's call – today is the day . . . Each time the phone rings, nerves jolt. Eventually there's a call about 2.45: very quick, abrupt. 'Lindsay? Richard . . . You in? I'll be round in half an hour.'

---

1. Newly discovered 'African' footage had been incorporated into this 'lost' silent film by Erich von Stroheim.
2. Jack Cardiff's film of Sean O'Casey's autobiographical *Mirror in My House*, with scenes directed by John Ford.

I eat a tin of mince, for strength.

Richard arrives: in white Norwegian sweater, with metal clasps and embroidery ('I had it made for me'). Nervous, prowling, picking up letters, books – noting with a laugh *The Divided Self: the Neurotic Personality of Our Time*.[1] We started jaggedly, with nervous defensive-aggressive sallies. Richard impatiently looking through my slides ... A cup of coffee ... We talked for about five and a half hours: Richard unable to make a single concession or admission or hold his hand out an inch. ('I'm glad you're in an up phase of schizoid cycle,' I remarked nicely.) I *tried* not to posture and moralise. But it was difficult. It seemed unreal – we were sympathetic as ever, but some screen has come down on Richard. This sort of thing – 'Richard, the demands you make are too great.'

'I don't make any demands.'

'Well the demands made by working with you.'

'I don't understand. What do you mean?'

Morgan was summoned to fetch him home – and had to wait outside for about an hour and a half! We parted amicably. They gave me a lift to Kensington. 'Ring me – come and have dinner.' He waved from the back window of the car.

3 March 1965

Get a call from Robin Fox[2] who would like a word with me ... since this is the day I've fixed for *My Fair Lady*, arrange to see him at 6 p.m. ... It proves to be occasioned by Robin having received a cable from Martin Poll[3] asking him to send the script of *Wuthering Heights* to Julie Christie – saying this course has the approval of R.H. and L.A. ...! I tell Robin the whole background. He says suddenly – 'Would you like me to look after things for you?' I say 'YES'!

Why not? Robin's smoothness is familiar and at least the Court etc. is not unknown territory.

My Fair Lady – after about three minutes I look at Daphne and she at me ... The luxury is authentic, but Cecil Beaton ostentatious to the point of vulgarity. Rex [Harrison] pulls it off at the end.

5 March 1965

Letter from Peggy Ramsay:[4] Michel Saint-Denis[5] would like to use [*Diary of a*] *Madman* in Stratford Studio. This gives me the excuse to call Richard Harris ... boisterously

---

1. By R. D. Laing.
2. Theatrical agent. Father of actors, Edward and James.
3. New York film producer (1922–) who reopened the long-abandoned NY Biograph Studio made famous by D. W. Griffith.
4. Literary agent who discovered Joe Orton, and who was representing David Sherwin.
5. Co-founder with George Devine of the 1930s' London Theatre Studio.

'friendly' . . . Alludes to Robin's call, saying I would still be ready to do *Wuthering Heights* with a producer. Also learned they've cabled Cliff Owen[1] to ask if he'd like to do it. And Poll raring to go ahead! Richard talks of Kirk Douglas[2] and how he's mentioned *One Flew over the Cuckoo's Nest*[3] . . . small world. He has been having fainting spells and heart-pounding. I tell him its inner tension. But he'd never believe it.

6 March 1965

First the builders . . . the rather bright ginger-haired boy had seen *Sporting Life* four times: when he left he said: 'Go carefully with those films you're making . . .' Then John Dunn Hill[4] picks me up: to Stratford East. *Zoo Story*, with his protégé (or confrère) Steven Berkoff.[5] Good-looking, dark lad – bad production, but plays with presence and power. See Berkoff in the dressing room – he calls me 'Lindsay' as I leave and I sense the dangerously attractive monster in him. Muscular arms.

7 March 1965

Went to David [Storey] and Barbara for lunch: took a bottle of champagne . . . Noisy, nice children. Walked out for sweets, then David walked back with me. Took notes about *Wuthering Heights*, Richard, etc. with his habitual understanding. We discussed the problem (my problem) of finding the resources within one to transcend what one feels to be one's limitations . . . David is serious and perceptive: and showed more concern than anyone.

9 March 1965

In the afternoon Ian Rakoff,[6] the South African boy who was Victor's assistant showed me his amateur film about South Africa – pieced together out of odds and bobs – but a real job . . . afterwards had coffee with him: really touching in his respect and aspiration. I fear for his honesty and simplicity. He would have been a *real* Free Cinema chap. Buy Dylan Thomas books in Charing Cross Road! There is no doubt the chord is stronger than reason! [Harris had proposed a film about Dylan Thomas.]

12 March 1965

Breakfast with Fiz[7] – say goodbye to Anthony [Page] with usual platitudes. Suddenly decide Fiz should come up to town and we rehearse for an hour on the train: find a

---

1. British B-movie director (1919–1993).
2. With whom he acted in *The Heroes of Telemark*.
3. Later produced by Douglas's son, Michael, and directed by Milos Forman.
4. Played Strato in L.A.'s production of *Julius Caesar*.
5. Berkoff made his film debut as the police 'heavy' who assaults Malcolm McDowell in *A Clockwork Orange* (1971).
6. L.A. hired him to be an assistant editor on *If . . . .*

good pattern for the scene, and set plentiful lines looking out front. It is a good scene . . .
Have a final encouraging drink at Victoria, then she returns to Brighton. Lunch with
Jimmy Booth at Escargot . . . Jimmy very decent and generous: describes how he once
punched Richard for slamming into Morgan when pissed. Richard then (of course)
blubbing repentance.

13 March 1965

Shelagh [Delaney] arrives with a bad cold – so has to be given grog: we talk about the
project [*The White Bus*].[1] She is sympathetic, direct, and I feel creative. Wish something could happen to make it more real for me. We agree to do it – I am encouraged
by her liking the 'Songs of the Tyne', and even suggesting 'Blaydon Races' for the
picture.

21 March 1965

Thoughts come over me as I turn my bed down: the elaboration of that scene –
springing from Richard swinging at me with that knife he used in *Sporting Life* the last
time he was here. Of course it's fantasy: Richard would never commit himself to such
violence, unless drunk – and he doesn't drink much now. But why didn't I grasp his
fist, and fight?

Back home, waste time writing letter to *Sunday Times* trying to boost *Tokyo Story*
against vapidity of Dilys Powell. 'Respectful but dry-eyed.' Jesus!

22 March 1965

Read *People Are Living There* [by Athol Fugard] which hardly seems to me the stuff of
which great successes are made but I send a telegram to NY saying I find it interesting
and sympathetic . . . Must do something and I will plainly not get through a film.

27 March 1965

I phone Donald Howarth,[2] catching him finally at the Court, and discuss my part in
his Sunday production . . . Agree to audition on Monday [for the part of Reg Parson,
the Deputy Headmaster in *Miniatures* by David Cregan]. . . . Could be fun – a bit
frightening – half of me thinks I'd be very good – imagines notices – offers – an easier
fame!

7. Eleanor Fazan was playing alongside Nicol Williamson and Arthur Lowe in the Wyndham's transfer of John Osborne's *Inadmissible Evidence*, then previewing in Brighton.

1. In which a young woman leaves her job in a London typing pool and travels up to her home town
in the North. She boards a tour bus, hosted by the Mayor and filled with foreign dignitaries, and is
shown the town's industrial, social, educational and recreational facilities.
2. Dramatist and director whose first play, *Lady on the Barometer*, was staged at the Court in 1958.

Anderson successfully auditioned for the part in Miniatures, *and joined a cast that included Nicol Williamson, George Devine, Graham Crowden and Mary McLeod. In the same week Bette Davis came to London to make a British film,* The Nanny. *Her director was Seth Holt, who was in possession of a script by David Sherwin about a rebellious schoolboy –* Crusaders. *Before starting rehearsals, he met the star of Andrzej's Wajda's* A Generation *(1954), the film that ushered in Poland's post-war film boom, then he went to Prague for two weeks to meet the men behind the Czech New Wave.*

29 March 1965

Tadeusz[1] beaming as we sat together on his bed at the Crofton Hotel, while Miriam[2] took our photograph. Funny world . . . He'd tested for Tony today – it had gone well apparently – and there he was, radiant in his scruffy cords and denim shirt and un-shaven when I arrived about five – after lunching with Anna Massey[3] and then shopping, sweltering in my heavy coat and scarf and Kashmir pullover on this lovely fresh spring day. It rather took my breath away when I *realised* that he was proposing I should go to Warsaw next year and do *Hamlet*. I feel indeed Fate may well have planned it this way.

1 April 1965

PRAGUE: I'm afraid I started early and badly – which probably exacerbated my bad temper at not being brought my breakfast with reasonable promptitude . . . row in the dining room downstairs.

Projection of *The Golden Rennet* – new film by antique director [Otakar] Vavra . . . Poetic explanation of decay of no-account Stalinist and ex-drunk. Over-tricky, but well done. Lunch at film artists' club, then return to hotel at three to find Jaromil [Jires] waiting. He talks in detail of his projected films – he is now engaged in working on a story of a young girl fantasist[4] – which he's writing with the girl from *Cry* (also in *The Golden Rennet*), Eva Limanova . . . She arrives, a rather mousey blonde with dark eyebrows.

2 April 1965

Pearls of the Deep[5] – the portmanteau film of the avant-garde. Struck again by the BRILLIANCE of the camerawork, and the amazing free sophistication of the style. The first episode[6] – of the eccentrics at the motor-bike meeting – the most wholly successful.

---

1. Tadeusz Lomnicki (1927–1992), Polish actor.
2. Miriam Brickman, the casting director.
3. Actress (1937–). Took the role of Renee de Montreuil in *De Sade* (1969).
4. *Valerie a Tyden Divu / Valerie and Her Week of Wonders* (1970).
5. *Perlicky na Dne*. Five-part film from stories by Bohumil Hrabal, directed by Jiri Menzel, Jan Nemec, Ewald Schorm, Vera Chytilova, Jaromil Jires.

6 April 1965

Morning – with Jan Kadar to his show of *A Shop in the Square* at Barrandov Studios. Solidity, craft, decency and sincerity. Nicholas Ray[1] arrives (late of course) to see it for the work of cameraman Novotny. He is going to make *The Doctor and the Devils* in Yugoslavia!

Afternoon – discover [Humphrey] Jennings's[2] films for tonight have not arrived: am very offensive with the man at the Embassy; hope the Czechs are impressed. See *Konkurs* (Milos Forman): most poetic, original and sensitive. *Excellent.*

8 April 1965

Accompanied by Mme Tarantova and another pleasant French-speaking gent from Film Export, make for Zrouch where Forman is on location for his new film.[3] Rackety car and bad roads, but plentiful chat and a refreshing stop at Kvyna Hera to inspect the simple and beautiful Gothic Abbey.

Arrive Zrouch, at the Bata shoe factory, about 12.30, just as the unit breaks after morning shooting. The usual situation doesn't faze me – only one more shot to make this afternoon: but Milos Forman, a dark, genial and handsome young man is very pleasant and welcoming and speaks good French. His cameraman, Ondricek,[4] is the nice-looking young chap I've seen in the film club: and a fine cameraman. I'm very envious – seriously, and consider the problem of trying to invite him, or all of them, to London. Forman remarkably welcoming: one feels immediately accepted, to watch shooting, rushes, etc. Atmosphere, with two writers in attendance, marvellously relaxed and collaborative. Play billiards with Forman.

13 April 1965

To Barrandov to see the cut of Forman's film *Loves of a Blonde*. Full of superb and delicate poetic things: the reminiscence of Free Cinema is extraordinary: the drinkers, the National Anthem – but with of course a great 'something more'. He behaves with astonishing courtesy and calm, even in the face of idiotic Italians.

---

6. *Balthazar's Death* by Jiri Menzel, who would win the Best Foreign Film Oscar with his debut feature, *Closely Watched Trains* (1966).

---

1. Who made *Rebel Without a Cause* (1955). In 1962, David Sherwin sent him a copy of *Crusaders*. Ray turned it down.

2. British maker of 'poetic' documentaries (1907–1950).

3. *Loves of a Blonde*, aka *A Blonde in Love*, starring Vladimir Pucholt (1942–).

4. Miroslav (Mirek) Ondricek. L.A. hired him for *The White Bus*, *If ....* and *O Lucky Man!*

14 April 1965

Certainly when Jaromil pointed out today in the club that Britain was represented at Cannes this year by films directed by a Pole and an American,[1] I felt that I'd been fooling about in a ridiculous way . . . I would like to feel that this is a turning point – while at the same time knowing that I remain so dependent on ambience, on mutual support or atmosphere. And that won't change.

16 April 1965

As arranged with Donald last night, make for the Court for rehearsal at 10.30. Nice to lose oneself in rehearsal. Seems to go quite well: feel reasonably effective – and what else, in such a context, can one be? Immediately start being sceptical about Donald's set ideas – rostra etc. We will see. Stay on and run lines in the afternoon. Return home via underground: cook myself a tin of stuffed cabbage and peppers – and watch TV.

19 April 1965

I wake early: 6.30, a prey to tensions, I suppose my thoughts returning again and again to Richard aren't really returning to *him* – but merely betraying my frustrated *need* of someone, somewhere, something . . . my incapacity to achieve self-sufficiency, self-dynamic. Call Jill [Bennett]: she doesn't want to do *De Sade*. My impetus checked.

24 April 1965

In my dream – I seemed to be on a visit to a country – returning for dinner – in the dining hall sat Richard with Martine Carol. Not intimate – politely talking. (M. Carol's picture in the *Express* two days ago). Formal politeness observed all round. I note that Martine's stupidity is very like Elizabeth's. I tell Richard I've re-seen a film he likes very much – *Earth*.[2] (George remarks to Anthony yesterday – however humorously – 'I think Lindsay is going to get all the notices!'). Obviously I'm 'not really an actor' – which I know. Though little bits are quite good.

25 April 1965

The play [*Miniatures*] performed: nervous certainly – though not exactly *sick* with nerves; that intense self-consciousness, which in the first scene caught up with me so that, when the scene was going *well*, I started being aware, and more than aware, and thinking as I spoke – this can't go on – until I, so to speak, deliberately dried myself. Otherwise pretty fluent and forceful: though not really easy and relaxedly in the skin of it. Only one telegram – from Jill Bennett . . . Interesting how one notices.

---

1. Polanski's *Repulsion* and Richard Lester's *The Knack*.
2. Alexander Dovzhenko's lyrical film on the theme of collectivisation.

26 April 1965
Returned to life – after that pleasant interlude of isolation (notice in *The Times* irritatingly describes the occasion as a 'charade' – not even wishing to insult! Levin facetious – naturally).

The pattern as usual – start with quite a bounce, the reaction from completion of a 'job' – then after a day of talk and movement a feeling of total exhaustion and the vanity of effort and the need of reassurance – which *isn't* there.

27 April 1965
It's not after all that one *enjoys* being out of step, alienated from one's own, etc. . . . But, however good the intentions with which one goes to the National Theatre,[1] how can one help being sickened and infuriated by that frightful middle-class, bourgeois audience, philistine to a man, and the production of *The Crucible* that matches exactly – Larry [Laurence Olivier]'s great theatricality and effectiveness that betrays a basically vulgar, heartless, vacuous imagination and sense of values. One is a freak, with one or two others – Miriam [Brickman] reacted similarly: but the audience loved it without experiencing a jot. Colin Blakely greatly enlarged in authority and skill: badly attired and bewigged; much over-Larryed in emotion . . . Joyce Redman interesting: but . . . falsity . . . anyway what a *bore* the play is. I've never liked it: now less than ever.

Sold the idea of the Czech article[2] to old John Lawrence in the morning, which initiated a one-and-a-quarter hour conversation with all the necessary falsity: for if I said what I really thought of John Russell Taylor and Irving Wardle – how could I write for them?

29 April 1965
A letter from Tadeusz [about directing him in *Hamlet* in Warsaw]. It seems serious – dates of his movements, etc. Can this be my salvation? I am a little scared of my personal proclivities – but what can I do? Try to work without emotion? or suffer and eventually fuck up sentimental relationships? Met Adrienne Corri[3] about *De Sade*. Yes will do it if it all works.

4 May 1965
Called wearily to St John's Wood Studio at 8.30 for Ronson Shaver commercial . . . camera operator Alex Thomson, focus puller the plump Kevin (Nic Roeg's team),[4]

---

1. Formed in 1963, but still playing in its temporary home at the Old Vic Theatre, London.
2. Published in *The Times* as 'Nothing Illusory about the Young Czech Film-makers', 19 May 1965: 'In spite of an outstanding harvest of international awards, they have largely passed us by. Hardly a single Czech picture has won commercial release here . . .'
3. Played Mrs Alexander in *A Clockwork Orange*.
4. Nic Roeg. Cinematographer turned film director.

Larry lighting.[1] Definitely a cut above the usual. Not camp or bored. Pleasant use of 'Sir'. Helpful and good.

Fred Stone turns out [to be] excellent casting: the (only slightly) camp father from *The Boy Friend*[2] – has just closed in Sandy's *Divorce Me Darling*. A trouper, and good. On hearing me sing 'Spread a Little Happiness' remarks – 'I was in that show – Mr Anderson'!

All goes well enough, though depressing. Feel a little queasy through smoking and general idiocy, and retch a bit in the lav – but nothing too dramatic.

5 May 1965
Have to retake first shot of commercial – hectic disputes about wording – what the ITCA won't allow – 'Can we say "shaves as *clean* as a cut-throat"?' In the end the artist improvises a line which eliminates the word 'cut-throat' – and we reshoot without taking the extra hour. Make the usual mistake of getting caught in the pub afterwards: futile argument with Kevin (focus-puller) – about *Angry Silence*.[3] Overwhelmed again by hopelessness of trying to communicate with English people stuffed to the ears with philistinism.

7 May 1965
Hooked up with St Martin's student Fernandez: gathering material for his thesis on the influence of the Polish School on British film-makers. Told him there wasn't any, and attempted to sell him on the Czechs. On the loose and with that 'work completed' feeling bought a pair of exciting, sexy denim hipsters in Shaftesbury Avenue – then brown leather belt in posh leather shop in Piccadilly – discover *gum* gives one the feeling of casual assurance ... Also Bob Dylan record – 'Times-a-Changing' (EXCELLENT).

Having been approached about a number of projects, Anderson spent the next few months travelling, to see which, if any, inspired him. Rex Harrison and Rachel Roberts asked him to direct them in an as yet untitled film for French television. He accepted an offer from producer Irving Schneider to direct a Broadway production of Athol Fugard's new play, People Are Living There. *Serge Reggiani had contacted him to discuss working together again, and he attended the Cannes Film Festival followed by a film-makers' conference at Pesaro at which he was one of the speakers. This busy period began with a visit to Serge Reggiani in Paris, from where he flew to visit Robert Shaw in Spain.*

---

1. Larry Pizer, later photographed Reisz's *Isadora* (1968).
2. Sandy Wilson musical, later filmed by Ken Russell.
3. Film produced by and starring Richard Attenborough.

14 May 1965

Lunch with Robin – given a script (*Love Revue*) by Willie Donaldson – as far as I can make out because he is living with Sarah Miles, who is Robin's protégé, and his son's ex-mistress! Lunched at some celebrated oyster bar – Robin fairly spasmodically 'covering the ground' in familiar agent's style – that's to say with that basic lack of concentration that I suppose is inevitable from anyone but a personal manager. It is agreed I go to Spain to 'discuss' *The Mayor of Casterbridge* with Robert Shaw. I go to party thrown by Mike Medwin,[1] and Albie – jokes about my performance. Moody reflections on the childishness and silly camp of the English.

17 May 1965

[PARIS:] Is this, I ask myself, 'growing up' – at the age of 42 – accepting a destiny of comparative solitariness – a realisation that the desired relationship of mutual love – shared intimacy – of someone to whom I can submit, and at the same time support and cherish – is not feasible? It is a strain always to be in the lead; so many of my instincts lead me rather to a childlike subordination. But to whom? . . .

Serge phoned me at the hotel, and we make a rendezvous at the Flores. Serge fatter in the face, tired under the eyes, sitting at the Flores . . . No use denying that what I used to find in Serge I find no longer: the confidence, the youthful dynamic – the poetry of intuition . . . He talked of his decision to remount *Sequestres d'Altona*, of his singing the Boris Vian[2] songs - a number of which he sang over the table - against the noise of the party to celebrate Noel Howard's[3] return from Switzerland – and at least I shamed him into agreeing to go to London to see *Inadmissible Evidence.*

19 May 1965

Fly to Madrid: am pleased with myself for eschewing all carbohydrates in the plane meal. Of such minutiae are our lives composed! Bob [Robert Shaw] and Mary [Ure] at the airport with little blond Colin. We drive back to the house they have rented seven or eight miles out of Madrid. I am reminded of another film star's house I have visited – outside Ravenna, outside Rome . . . Bob talks about *The Mayor of Casterbridge.* It has everything to recommend it as a project except that certain, compulsive emotional commitment. But perhaps I am better off without? We dine pleasantly in Madrid.

20 May 1965

Yes, it was strange above all to find myself in this situation so exactly reminiscent of visits to Richard – except another country, another family, another actor-friend . . .

---

1. Actor turned producer, whom Albert Finney had employed to run his film company – Memorial Pictures – and through whom L.A. would make *If . . . .*

2. Anti-establishment guru who wrote popular songs and surrealist novels such as *L'Herbe Rouge.*

3. Director and writer of *Marco the Magnificent* (1965).

And to see also (with all the variations of personality) exactly similar reactions from Robert as from Richard: films 'we' will make in the future – we'll get a few friends together and show films – comments on other actors, precisely similar giant egoism.

Unfortunately I have to declare that while Robert is I'm sure infinitely more reliable, he is also infinitely less attractive: I don't mean physically, for all his good looks and decent build, but temperamentally. Is it that dry, reserved anti-emotional manner? In Robert's egoism there seems to be an arrogance that I don't in truth find sympathetic. And a lack of at least emotional generosity. Impossible not to note how, when *The Times* came with my article on the Czech cinema, he merely grunted when I showed it to him, and never made any comment at all. Nor can I pretend to have been particularly enthusiastic about his work: didn't see *The Caretaker* or *From Russia with Love*, missed *Hamlet*,[1] and I didn't I'm afraid mention *The Flag*[2] until he asked me about it . . . I don't really believe in Bob's work. It seems to me deficient in real sensibility, to be studiously worked, and somehow over-conscious of *effect*. This point I certainly made to him about *The Flag* and to be fair he accepted it. It is the basic lack of course I can't be honest about. I can't even be altogether clear about it. Is it a superficial talent, or is there some temperamental clash? Certainly I do have to find myself continually making reserves with Bob – and concealing them – in a way that I don't find very enjoyable – and I don't have the personal engagement there to remonstrate, or at least show my feelings as I suppose I would with Richard.

So I feel oddly detached, uncommitted, *unfuelled* about this whole idea in a way I don't like, and sense that the experiment of adopting a 'professional' attitude is not likely to succeed. I must go to see *Ginger Coffey*[3] (which I see is showing at Cannes) and see what that does for me. I have to admit I'm doubtful.

On my last afternoon – after a visit to that Spanish Civil War battle field (Robert quoting 'Death stalked the olive trees, picking his men . . .') which I'm afraid didn't really move me – there was that curiously violent and contemptuous attack on *Viridiana*[4] – and then at lunch broadening it to include Bergman, Buñuel and Truffaut. Well, it's obvious nonsense of course. But in a certain way disturbing. I don't feel a great personal affinity there, that's all. And I am confronted again with my own impossible nature.

Which really does seem disturbing: I didn't ever get down to Shelagh's script [of *The White Bus*]. Nor have I re-read the Fugard play. Laziness and neurosis inextricably confused. The sun's appeal is too strong . . .

---

1. Shaw acted in a 1951 production with Alec Guinness. L.A. is probably referring to the 1964 TV film starring Christopher Plummer and directed by Philip Saville.
2. Novel by Shaw published in January 1965.
3. *The Luck of Ginger Coffey*, directed by Irvin Kershner.
4. Film by Luis Buñuel (1961).

El Cordobes[1] was quite an experience when I went with Mary (the seats cost £20 each – which Bob obviously felt as a tribute to his status: and anyway in that atmosphere everything became unreal): a genuine talent of our time – anti-classical, daring but without polish like Godard – physically like Nureyev, or Albie, or James Dean – or a Kennedy brother!

Just time to mention the party given by Mary's dreary camp friends: and the tussle between Robert Ryan[2] and the Southern USAF major who used the word – 'Nigger!'

23 May 1965

This week I learned, in a letter from Frank Granat, that Richard had written saying that in view of *Wuthering Heights*, he would 'as soon' I didn't direct *Dylan* [proposed film about the poet Dylan Thomas]. It is probably for the best: and I can't rationally express surprise. Richard is also a creature of pride, and in the end pride is petty and mean, lacking the broad gesture of generosity. But my heart (nobody seems to guess or to care) regrets it. I still fantasise – consciously – taking most often those two moments of failure. When in our hotel room in Mexico, Richard revealed that coiled black belt in his suitcase, and when he invited (or laid the way open to) me to watch him fucking the arse of that big blonde in the Grand Hotel, Rome. Why didn't I suggest I stand by, as his mute manservant, and serve him champagne between strokes?

24 May 1965

CANNES: Back on the old Waldorf Terrace . . . then to the Palais and receive my accreditation form . . . Bump into some wacky American friend of Gene [Moskowitz]'s (working for Harry Saltzman) who is going to pick up the Polish girls. We pick up Beata, Wajda's fiancée last met in Bombay – then go downstairs and knock up Tadeusz. 'Leensay . . . !' with that charming beam. How it brings out the best in me: it really does. I expand, am happy, not pinched, my juices flow. No tension.

Strolled to Palais and back – diverted at the start by [Roman] Polanski – then on Carlton Beach had a small glass of wine with Michael Caine[3] at the Saltzman table: scrounged Gene's meat course at his Spanish lunch – went with Tadeusz to his Alex Ford picture *First Day of Liberty*: impossibly old-fashioned and melodramatic, but Tadeusz splendid; Rosi['s] *Moment of Truth*[4] – followed by noisy Polish reception.

25 May 1965

Tadeusz' weakness is obviously and undoubtedly for the girls – with whom I'd say he makes a fool of himself at the drop of a hat. The rather spiky German he was devoting

---

1. Manuel Benitez. Famous bullfighter. Survived a spectacular goring in May 1964.
2. American actor, best known for his role in *The Wild Bunch*.
3. Who took the lead role in *The Ipcress File* after Harris turned it down.
4. Francesco Rosi's film about a bullfighter.

himself to was presumably responsible for him not turning up to our appointment at lunchtime today . . . Finally ran him down about 3.15: somewhat confusing explanations which I couldn't follow. I imagine my suspicions correct. (This came after seeing French dubbed version of *Ginger Coffey* first thing. Unfair of course, but humour lacking, and fantasy, in both Bob's performance and direction.)

Drink with Nemec at four – in the ordinaire bar where he insisted he'd be happy. Cheerfully agreed when I called him neurotic. An intelligent, absolutely original fellow – loathed *Red Desert*. Spent the evening with Tadeusz and two nice Germans drinking tea in a port café.

26 May 1965
I spent ten or so minutes chatting with that fool Hollis Alpert[1] . . . and in the evening saw the rather sympathetic, naive and (*I* think) promising *Stranded* by the kooky American girl Juleen Compton.[2] Ed Harrison next to me snorted and made foolish cracks: and afterwards Agnès Varda[3] explained how the lack of titles made appreciation impossible (!). 'I feel so ashamed' said Juleen Compton (to me) sympathetically.

27 May 1965
Of course it is ridiculous to expect Rachel [Roberts] to operate with simple, mature 'poise' (why do I always construct these images of what people 'ought' to be like?): she erupted into the Waldorf dining room in a frilly, flowered creation, with a feather boa and Homer on the lead – like Blanche du Bois . . . Within two minutes she was showing me her pictures (taken by the photographer-acquaintance of Picasso) and even able to produce a magnifying glass with which to inspect the contacts! This could be quite touching I suppose, except that the raging, egotistical insecurity inside her makes her equally impatient (unconcerned almost) with one's reaction. It is just necessary for her to *show*, not to hear what one has to say. And of course the result is extremely boring. At the Carlton yesterday evening, in that large group, of Carroll Baker,[4] Horst Buchholz[5] all sitting around drinking, she could only accuse me of being uninterested in shooting this TV film with her and Rex Harrison in Paris . . . It is all unreal, over-heated. But I suppose it is Rachel – and another instance of one of these temperaments just succumbing to the pressures of the climate. Rex [who was serving on the jury] also came on Monday and was charming.

---

1. American critic.
2. New York film-maker.
3. French film-maker (1928–).
4. American actress (1931–). Oscar-winner for *Baby Doll* (1956).
5. German actor (1933–2003). One of T*he Magnificent Seven.*

28 May 1965

I finally contacted Serge and he drove down to pick me up, after I had spent an hour with Rachel, uselessly trying to get her to change her image! (She can't.) Serge a bit tense, rather brusquely dictatorial to my suggestion that we spend ten minutes with Rachel . . . There really is something rather pedantic and self-important about Serge's manner (a bit French), his analysis of his feelings, his bossy superiority. The house charming, rather over-designed, in its dusty Provençal country setting. Annie really seeming well . . . The little girl, Maria, beautiful. Serge talks about *Inadmissible Evidence*. He has seen the performance at which Nicol temporarily passed out. Still says he wants to see the translation but still unconvinced by the play: thinks he would make it heavy. I see no point in trying to convince him. Anyway he gives a strong impression of (habitually) not listening . . . The other children, Simon and Celia, returned from school . . . In the garden Annie watering with a hose. Suddenly Serge starts shouting irritatedly at the children, within five minutes comes down into the garden with my cap and coat, says he's in a hurry as he wants to buy some bandages (?) in the town: and away we go. Annie laughs. So would I: but underneath it all is a chill. It just seems completely immaterial whether we meet or not. Is it in me? I don't honestly think so. Would it feel like this with Richard now? I suppose so.

Went for a spin with Rex and Rachel in a speedboat after hearing the awards . . . not too pleased about *The Knack*,[1] extremely displeased about Stamp and Eggar[2] . . . Bed too late after Rachel insisting on a last croisette drink.

31 May 1965

Pesaro [Conference on 'Criticism and New Cinema'] opened with *Table Ronde* held in a United Nations atmosphere of formality and microphones, making anything but speechmaking impossible – the Czechs in full strength at their table: Schorm, Forman, Jaromil. At the next table Skolimowsky, the athletic firework, the Douglas Fairbanks of the avant-garde: very very clever, rather cold, as in person he is oddly attractive. Polanski-ish I'd say, but in the end I could be fonder of Polanski I think . . . Bertolucci: young, a bit naive in his committed way, but open and sensitive I'm sure. I must see *Prima della Revoluzione* . . . the gallant Juleen Compton, thrusting but shy, whose film I after all like . . . and Ben Amotz[3] – whose *Hole in the Moon* I missed at Cannes, but whose wry, common sense honesty appealed to me greatly. Philip Saville quite a pill: and I loathed his film of course (*The Logic Game*). Lotte[4] in magnificent form: at least

---

1. Richard Lester's film adapted from Ann Jellicoe's Royal Court play (March 1962). It won the Palme d'Or for Best Film.

2. Terence Stamp and Samantha Eggar, Best Actor and Best Actress for *The Collector*, which L.A. had been offered as a project for Richard Harris.

3. Dahn Ben Amotz, Polish actor.

4. Lotte Eisner (1896–1983). German film historian.

I am not silly enough any longer to resent her vagaries! . . . First contribution by Pasolini[1] – an hour-and-a-quarter paper dealing largely with semantics – definitions – attempting to formulate his own aesthetic – resulting in a torrent of abstractions quite impossible to follow . . . one or two interesting remarks on Antonioni, Godard, Bertolucci . . . Followed by Castello[2] and a film-maker – both I found in varying degrees formless and boring. Spoke a little dreary nonsense[3] after Tullio Kezich.[4]

5 June 1965

The return has to be faced. Alas, I don't want to. Don't want to read *People Are Living There*. Don't want to face *The White Bus*. Don't want to write about Pesaro for *The Times*. In bed formulate paragraphs: neurotic blocks prevent me getting them on paper . . . The last two weeks have reawakened my interest in the cinema – given me a context, if you like – but return to London brings those rapid sensations of negativism, fatigue, irony, being *against* and knowing oneself in an out-of-step minority. It is infinitely disagreeable. I wonder vaguely about Richard, and just to imbide emotionally, spend an hour or so pasting cuttings into my bizarre (alarming?) scrapbook of his activities. I am honestly more pleased than sad when his notices are bad.

To Karel and Betsy's about teatime. Karel incidentally pouring cold water on both *The Mayor of Casterbridge* and Warsaw *Hamlet*.[5] I feel it's all wearing thin: I am nearer the Czechs! M. and Mme. Kadar drop in for a drink.

7 June 1965

Excellent joint and potatoes and veg lunch at Fuschia[6] largely spoiled by my inability quietly to take Mum's complaining (yet emerging from the station, and seeing the blue Daimler parked down the road, and Mum there, I thought – a few years and she won't be there . . .).

Went for a drive with Mum after tea – the levelled waste of St Ronans,[7] on which the little houses are now already beginning to rise . . . there were our gardens: where John Anderson and I played tennis when we had chickenpox; where there was the chapel,

---

1. Pier Paolo Pasolini (1922–1975), poet, novelist, film-maker.

2. Giulio Cesare Castello, who attacked the poor critical reception in Italy for Bertolucci's *Prima della Rivoluzione*.

3. He referred to his difficulties with the 'Socialist' publication, the *New Statesman*, when he dedicated his column to Wajda's *A Generation* (not then showing in London) instead of *The Bridge on the River Kwai*.

4. Writer associated with the films of Ermanno Olmi.

5. The *Hamlet* production was to evolve instead into a production of Osborne's *Inadmissible Evidence*. See February and October 1966.

6. Fuschia Cottage in Rustington, Sussex. His mother's home.

7. The preparatory school L.A. attended, and where he wrote and published his first film reviews.

Class III, Class II, the Reading Room, Harry's study, the cricket pitch: the smoke shed . . . what pathos if we could allow our hearts to feel it. Alas, that all this saps – not supports – me.

9 June 1965

To the Academy – catch *Red Desert* on its last day. Find film boring: i.e. visually monotonous – full of brilliant colour-supplement still photography. Characters psychologically underdeveloped: [Monica] Vitti static and exhibitionist. Richard attempts a performance: bricks without straw. Some uneasy moments – but he certainly learned from *Sporting Life*!

Dreadful evening at Marie Seton's[1] – little party thrown for Ed Harrison (boring and gaga) . . . Feel utter vanity and stupidity and provincialism of it all. Behave badly: violently rude to John Gillett[2] – quite ineffective – he personifies arrogant English provincialism.

10 June 1965

In town meet Alain Tanner[3] for a drink at the Arts.[4] He is a nice, sad, sympathetic fellow – joined by Derek York, with whom I go on to the world premiere of Polanski's *Repulsion*. There he is in the foyer – with beautiful girls and smart young men: quite merry though – I mean to say something, but a shout of 'Polanski!' from Lionel Stander[5] scares me off. Film clever but rather thin, really quite boring.

12 June 1965

As Nicol [Williamson] sat there, manically detailing how Peter [O'Toole] and Richard [Burton] had made the wrong decisions; how Tom [Courtenay] was infinitely limited; how Alfie[6] wasn't good in *Godot*; how he saw through Anthony [Page] – saw through Tony Richardson . . . with sinking heart I felt myself again falling victim to these monstrous egoisms, these more-or-less charming children, these cracking bores . . . Nicol had phoned to ask for help on the T. S. Eliot poem ('The Hollow Men') which he was to read at tomorrow's memorial performance . . . I felt myself again responding – the empathy and warmth which comes from me – but knowing now the vanity – the expense of warmth and the relationship doomed.

---

1. Assembled the feature *Time in the Sun* from footage Eisenstein shot for *Que Viva Mexico!* (1932).
2. Appeared in Kevin Brownlow and David Gill's documentary *Buster Keaton, a Hard Act to Follow* (1987), narrated by L.A.
3. Swiss film-maker, whose short *Nice Time* (1957) played in the third Free Cinema programme.
4. Club theatre in Great Newport Street.
5. American actor (1908–1994). Played the Guru Brahmin in Tony Richardson's 1965 film *The Loved One*.
6. Alfred Lynch (1933–2004), acted in *The Long and the Short and the Tall*.

A dreadful double-dose: dined with Rex and Rachel and their poised photographer friend Nancy – dinner at the Mirabelle – at the next table Liza Minnelli,[1] Leslie Caron, Laurence Harvey, Honor Blackman . . . Rachel pissed . . . though not as bad as usual . . . over-insistent about my singing – I must say Rex took it very well – until she wanted me to sing 'I've grown accustomed to her face!' . . . Rex separated to go and see the Reverend Roberts, dying of cancer in the London Clinic, while Rachel, Wendy [Toye][2] and I went to Annabel's, a long, dark, drinkery-cum-discotheque in Berkeley Square. We discussed our zodiac signs – analysed Rachel's masochism and inferiority complex ad nauseam – 'Rex is always thinking of Kay [Kendall, Rex Harrison's second wife] . . .' etc., and Rachel ended by declaring that she loved me and would leave Rex flat at the drop of a hat – and similar absolutely baseless fantasies! Great rudeness to the waiters who hesitated over admitting us . . . Then taxi (about 3.30 a.m.) to the Clinic – and I accompanying Rachel to her father's room where he lies gaunt, skeletal, open-toothless-mouthed against the pillows. Rachel introduces me and I grasp the thin hand: when she speaks he seems to apprehend, can slightly nod or shake the head . . . Rachel speaks kindly, firmly, gently and arranges for him to have another injection for sleep . . . Downstairs in the taxi Nancy is now asleep, spread out on the back seat. We drive her back to Chester Square: then at the Connaught I am impressed in for a cup of coffee – Rachel with her vile manners demanding . . . and maundering on about her ambition – her knowledge that she is better than Maggie Smith – Joan Plowright!

Bed at five. Wake at nine. EXHAUSTION. And in my four hours sleep – my first wet dream for years.

15 June 1965
New York [to cast the Fugard play]. I find the place amusing; preposterous; interesting; certainly not intimidating . . . I feel liberated (which I suppose I am, for my other *four* spells in NY have all been under the spell of Richard. Now no one mentions his name.) . . . Quick drink and hash with Charlie Baker[3] in the Oak Room at the Plaza – then dash back for a full afternoon of auditions . . . reasonably exhausting . . . no absolute 'hits' – afterwards I begin to think of Ronald Pickup?[4] . . . after Charlie and I go to indifferent performance of *The Glass Menagerie*. Ten minutes or so in the dressing room of the frank, engaging, plump Miss Stapleton[5] ('You can't win every time', she remarked truthfully about the poor performance).

---

1. Who would make her film debut in Shelagh Delaney's *Charlie Bubbles* (1967), directed by and starring Albert Finney.
2. British choreographer and theatre director (1917–).
3. Charles Adams Baker of the William Morris agency.
4. He played Octavius Caesar in L.A.'s 1964 *Julius Caesar*.
5. Maureen Stapleton, American actress (1925–).

21 June 1965

Half-dozen more auditions included John Carradine's son, David[1] – who refused to read . . . not right for the part: but returned to say he's been chiefly interested in the idea of me! Most interested and frustrated by Barry Primus.[2] Talked to him in the dressing room after lunch – found him quite nervy – shy – awkward – exposed – jokey . . . very admiring about [Elia] Kazan . . . Didn't let me get much of an oar in, but I liked him, and saw traces of Don. Then, on stage, all gone – in place either a monotonous downbeat – or a 'straight' authority. Puzzling. *Old Acquaintance*[3] on TV. *Cried* at the end!

24 June 1965

Does it seem just intellectually snobbish to say Rosemary Harris[4] (charming though she is) is limited because she likes (thinks good) *Lawrence of Arabia*?

Exhaust myself further by compulsive viewing of *Big Shot* movie: Steve Cochran[5] as victimised good-fellow worker, kidnapped, beaten-up, child kidnapped by crooked union boss Mickey Rooney. Steve Cochran still vastly handsome: now alas he too is ageing, thinning hair, powerful figure going. Too late – too late . . . Move thankfully from TV-dominated hotel to Juleen Compton's grand two storey flat, 131 E 66th Street. Not air-conditioned, but fine. Big 'baronial' living room. Realise she *is* moneyed and knows how to make it with stocks, real estate. We have brunch and talk about her script: *All the world wants to sleep with America.*

25 June 1965

Cilfford Odets' son drops in early to breakfast and takes pictures of Juleen. We talk a lot. Juleen is a woman of much energy, shrewdness and intuition. 'A little horse,' she says . . . I go down to the office, where Irving cannot get through to Maureen. No answer . . . engaged . . . no answer. Shades of R.H. After lunch: back to Irving. Maureen at last rings. I speak to her – and she says 'I'm not enough in love with the part!' I arrange at least to meet her for an iced coffee tomorrow. Discuss other possibilities with Irving. Not many. Bette Davis? Thora Hird? The project wavers . . . Meet Charlie Baker for dinner. We chat away: $25,000 for Paris TV assignment with Rex and Rachel. Why not? – and $70 a day expenses in Paris and NY – of course it's corruption. But what alternative?

---

1. John Carradine appeared in many John Ford classics. David found stardom as Kane in *Kung Fu* (TV, 1972).

2. A member of Kazan's Lincoln Center Company.

3. Vincent Sherman's 1943 film of the play by John van Druten, with Bette Davis and Miriam Hopkins.

4. British actress (1930–), played Aunt May in *Spiderman* (2002). No relation to Richard.

5. American leading man (1917–1965), starred in Antonioni's *Il Grido* (1957).

He returned to London until an alternative 'star' actress on whom to build the
production of Fugard's play could be found. His first choice was Bette Davis.

28 June 1965

In the *Daily Express*: 'THREE FRIGHTENED GIRLS WATCH AS FILM STAR DIES ON YACHT.'
Farewell, Steve Cochran! I think back: and wish I'd met him. To the Court. *A Patriot
For Me.*[1] Well . . . *is* it worth all that? I think [Maximilian] Schell lacks size, majestic star
quality. Production a bit 'sensitive': needs to start every scene with a line.

30 June 1965

Energy, alas, soon goes in London. Even holding in my stomach is more of an effort:
while touching my toes forty times morning and evening . . . it can't be done. At four
pick up Max Wilk's notes [for the proposed television film starring Rex Harrison and
Rachel Roberts] at Fox and peruse them over a cheese salad at that Compton Street
Coffee Bar where they shred the cheese nicely . . . They seem mostly perfunctory bullshit. Have arranged to meet Ian Rakoff for a drink at 5.30. He shows me notes for a
script, which I tell him to reconsider.

Dinner with Bob Bolt,[2] at that Trattoria, the slightly swanky one. We obviously talk
a lot, and at least he has got over all that rubbish about success which he was spouting
last time. He now feels 'You can't have it both ways'. He would like me to direct a play
he's writing – for the Aldwych. My interest flags a little when he reveals it's a children's
play. He's a nice man: but unfortunately not really my wavelength.

1 July 1965

Down to Alan Cooke's to have my ritual haircut from John. Feel smart and confident
in my blue rinse. Lunch with Stephen Frears.[3] He brings out with (very decent) shyness
his idea to do a production of *Musgrave* at Stratford. Of course I give him my blessing.
Then to the Court; where I try to phone Tadeusz: but after the usual delays – no answer.

3 July 1965

Tadeusz's number never replies – so in the end I try for [Erwin] Axer and get him . . . on
a miserable line . . . He will be away at the end of next week! None the less – decide to
go, from Portofino. Because I want to! Spent most of the day trying to fix my air ticket

---

1. Written by John Osborne; directed by Anthony Page; designed by Jocelyn Herbert. The cast of
thirty-seven included George Devine, Jill Bennett and Edward Fox. At £12,506, it was more than
twice as expensive as any previous production by the English Stage Company.
2. Robert Bolt, playwright; wrote Lean's *Lawrence of Arabia*.
3. Whom L.A. employed as an assistant director on *If . . . .*

– Genoa – Milan – Prague – Warsaw – A series of experiences unhappily symbolic of
Britain vanishing beneath the waves of the twentieth century. First one lady extracts
herself from business to search through endless files for lost tickets; maddeningly
(nervously I suppose) announcing 'I can't attend to anyone' – I explode and quit the
shop. Discover that *all* travel agencies are closed in London from 1 p.m. Saturday. What
contrast with New York! Just sluggish, unimaginative, complacent RUNNING DOWN ...

5 July 1965
Well – we are off. On Saturday evening Karel said, 'It's ridiculous – you ought to be
working seriously – the Shelagh Delaney script – we all know you're rich.' I said, 'You're
a fine one to be talking. It'll be my *Night Must Fall*.'[1] Karel pours cold water on my Rex
and Rachel TV idea. I am suspicious of Karel's immediate scorn – even of Rock
Hudson and George Peppard in *Tobruk* (script never arrived!). But Karel is fantastically far from understanding my motives: or even my needs. I need a setup within
which to work, a dynamic that carries me forward – it's difficult to put it more clearly.
Oscar doesn't provide it. Shelagh is very sympathetic, but doesn't really fuel me. Karel
– of all people – should know how much Richard counted on *This Sporting Life*. But of
course they never mention Richard – maybe through finesse – maybe (I suspect)
through not wanting that kind of involvement. Betsy in all this more encouraging. But
possessive of Karel. These possessive wives are the Devil!

6 July 1965
Villa San Genesio:[2] – beautiful, in an impossible, luxurious, tasteful, MONEY way:
swathed in red and purple – flowering creeper. Tiled floors, spotless. Notepaper and
envelopes and pen laid ready on the desk in the guests' bedroom ... a rooftop view
made for 20th Century Fox and De Luxe Color. Leatherbound books (Carlyle, the
poets). The garden impeccably tended and lit throughout from switches attached to
trees and shrubs. The tiered circular pool which needs a fountain: the new Japanese-
style music room where I suggested the old table should have its legs sawn short ...
Rachel's influence excellent in the Welsh dresser, the lemon and blue cushions – and
the panelled studio for Rex.
    Rex generally charming, veering occasionally into drunken sharpness, irritation,
explosiveness – as when, at twelve on the Monday night, he suddenly got up, with some
remark such as 'I'm on my feet now, so you'd bloody well get up too' – and expelled
poor Norman Baer and Sabrina into the night ... His temperament fluctuates extraordinarily: 'I must shut up,' he's capable of saying. Rachel by comparison is impossible.

---

1. Reisz's 1964 flop starring Albert Finney, Susan Hampshire and Michael Medwin.
2. At Portofino, near Rapallo, on the Italian Riviera.

Mad. Everything, everyone, becomes drawn into her push-pull, love-hate relationship with Rex: and so absorbed is she with him there isn't really room for anyone else. And with herself, when she talks about 'hating' Nicol Williamson – Albie – Maggie Smith, a kind of wilfully possessed glint is in her eye. But it's all somehow unreal. Wednesday night, when we had dinner in the Port, she did talk more or less quietly – after a lot of appalling rubbish about Albert – about the 'generosity' of Richard Harris – about her insecurities etc. But that didn't last, and in the end she marched off to drink in the Port – I kissed her goodbye, but she didn't notice. And I never saw her again. Rex drove me back and we went to bed – he insisting on getting up in the morning to drive me down the hill in the jeep. In the event, of course, Pina's knocking didn't wake him, and I had to walk down with Giuseppe carrying my bag. I don't like money.

The 'conference' on Tuesday was almost disastrous. Going out in the boat for lunch – taking a dip – Rachel then walking off to the church – we had kept Norman and Max Wilk waiting for two and a half hours! (Rex apologises, sets things right – has *some* basis in reality.) Max Wilk is revealed as a boring, tactless, talentless, uninventive, lazy, bullshitting buffoon. The ponderous way of talking may be neurotic – I think it covers awful unsureness, or intuition of his real incapacity – but it's also maddening. A great argument Tuesday evening as we discussed his 'outline' – he's done no WORK – over his story of the blowing up of Paris – to which Rex took blurred and irascible exception . . . Rachel joined in, with fierce and lunatic ideas about churches, Georges Charpentier, and 'students'. But eventually we shook hands.

9 July 1965

Leaving chronology aside – and looking back on Warsaw – why this sense of apprehension, this fear, when all seemingly went well? Recognition, of course: the sense of a pattern repeating itself, and a knowledge of what the end of that pattern has been in the end. I feel essentially no less affection, warmth, personal commitment towards Tadeusz than I did towards Serge or Richard in the early days. He has great charm, poetry, gentleness, and powerful talent. He is another (as I came to realise) who through mixed pride and insecurity hasn't quite made the progress he should . . . I hate to ask it: but will his warmth persist? Is the charm, the generosity real? Or am I offering myself again to the fire? At every turn I am haunted by the past – for who could have been more respectful, more affectionate, more poetic, *nicer* than Richard in Tahiti? When Tadeusz went off to record his poems for the short film on Friday he was careful to leave me full instructions on how to get to the hotel . . . to say he'd phone: to receive me back with anxious care . . . He would gently take my arm in moments of contact. We talked with rare ardour and communion of sensibility: he occupied himself (as Richard certainly would *not*) with fixing my return.

20 July 1965

Lunch with Rex and Rachel with Laurie Evans at the Connaught – elucidating Rex's position – he wouldn't have time to do the Paris project before the Mankiewicz film [*The Honey Pot*], since he's called a week earlier. Also heard how Max Wilk was reported as referring to me as 'that ARROGANT COMMUNISTIC BASTARD'. True? False? Misinterpreted? A good joke anyway. Saw *The Knack* – gloomy thoughts.

23 July 1965

Lunched with David Storey – who has another little boy: born this morning. Over our Chinese meal we talked rather extensively of Karel – David raising the question of my presenting a 'disturbance' to Karel – as I had experienced the other evening . . . The pattern is clear, we've talked about it enough, of Karel trying to be, wanting to be either something he isn't, or something the accidents of his life have prevented him being – the man who can live emotionally, making those connections, statements, relationships . . . As David says: *Sporting Life* was a traumatic experience for him . . . And I confront *him* with some sort of challenge – by my nature, not by any design or specific action. David also said he'd had a letter from Poll, saying they hope to shoot *Wuthering Heights* next spring – and will have a decision on a director within two weeks. (Can you imagine what sort of a dance Richard is leading all those poor Hollywood producers?!) David remarked engagingly that it's a terrible script: not personally involved. And I suddenly said that if any other director in the world did it – it'd be a DISASTER. Anyway, I don't believe it'll be made.

25 July 1965

Really NADIR land – succumbing to sudden waves of angst for Richard [Harris] – contact I-Ching – but interestingly *that* consultation no longer seems to work. I keep getting THE ARMY: and anyway no longer really wish to hear about the self-cultivation of the SUPERIOR MAN . . .

26 July 1965

Went to see three-quarters of *Lord Jim*. Did me good: silly, shallow – poor Richard Brooks spouting nonsense about Conrad. A poor, disjointed performance by Peter O'Toole. Felt *much* better! Robert Shaw rang – must see him next week: full of offers – [Fred] Zinnemann wants him to play Henry VIII:[1] or the sub commander in a comedy – fortunately feel *Casterbridge* likely to be set back!

29 July 1965

It is being left alone that's dangerous: when the dynamic to make an effort, an act, to 'lay hold of life' simply seems non-existent, and there is nothing, no one to respond

---

1. In the film adaptation of Robert Bolt's *A Man for All Seasons*.

to – unless I create it myself. And the only dynamic that continues to have that instinctive emotional power continues to be Richard. However, in my rational moments I can diminish him by reflecting on his cowardice, his irresolution, his treachery, the cheapness and emptiness of so much of his taste: on the Richard that goes with Elizabeth in her purple pyjamas and dyed hair and mink. The other Richard, the King, the brutal arrogant sensualist, the narcissist with the powerful, graceful limbs, the self-admirer in the mirror, the one who will *use* another person without scruple, with a sort of magnificent disregard of anything but his own pleasure or whim, and a magnificent confidence in his own power of attraction and domination – this Richard, with the aid of a photograph or two, is always there to be summoned up. I can't believe Richard never thinks of me. Or are these just shop girls' dreams – as my reason would tell me?

30 July 1965
Spent the morning – well – 11.30 to 3.30 with Shelagh Delaney discussing the script of *The White Bus*. Before she came I typed out dialogue from a series of interviews in *The Queen* with young titled Englishman, which fitted marvellously into the character invented (apparently by her brother!) for the station scene . . . Discussion went well, sympathetic, though the structure remains vague and the central problem of the introduction of the White Bus difficult. We seem to get bogged down in TIME and attendant REALISM. (We may have to sacrifice that night arrival?) I showed her *The Wakefield Express*: which she understood: and we chatted about the style – the beginning – the end – the crucial mid-point where the bus arrives and a sort of realism (however personal) changes into a sort of fantasy (however concrete). I long just 'to do it'. No use discussing scripts really. I have confidence that something concrete and individual and poetic will emerge.

2 August 1965
A peculiar state of mind – I write in the early hours on my way to New York. Warsaw a peculiarly half-completed situation – and the Dick Daring Paris fantasy falling through like that, leaving me at sea and sorry for myself. The illusion of effectiveness rapidly disappears. Neurosis returns. When I speak on the phone to anyone I sound fine – decisive – on top of things – I am conscious of this 'rising to it' – and consequently giving a totally false impression – or at least of completely concealing (or failing to convey) the real split in myself, my real difficulty: the recessive, adolescent, *impuissant* self which wastes so much of his life. To Tadeusz just now I must be sage and 'effective' (as I was to Richard when we first met), to Karel self-indulgent and difficult, David Storey would formulate the truth more or less rightly I guess. But there is also the fact that human beings haven't very much time for each other. Except when they are in love. And then their concern is tainted with self-indulgence.

3 August 1965
Checked in at the Meurice – a very pleasant, modest suite (no TV – but I'm afraid I remedied that!). Slept fairly briefly. Irving picked me up, and we drove to Bette [Davis]'s out-of-town lodging; a small bungalow in the garden of a house about one hour out. We are greeted by a vibrant, fast-talking, haggard, late-middle-aged Bette – nervy and emotional and self-willed, but not clipped or dry or smart in the manner of her movie image. Present also: Jack Hulto, small, courteous, seemingly a bit diffident, from William Morris – and Violla Rubber, Bette's friend, confidante, sidekick, victim, leech, boss – whathaveyou? Bette starts violently, forcefully, uncompromisingly, demand-ingly – I see this as a TRAGEDY – the image, from some aged play she had seen, of the actress left alone on the stage, screaming . . . change locale, change title, change name of character. My intuitive reaction is to play cool; practically to *become* the detached, wise, authoritative, strong personality the situation calls for – and which is hard for me to be or to sustain when I am not required to play that role.

That first meeting was long and exhausting – though I always find those person-alities exciting – exhaustion only setting in afterwards. Anyway Bette's kick-off was so intransigently demanding that it would have been impossible to say immediately – 'You're right, you're marvellous, we want you.' Impossible that is for anyone but David Merrick.[1]

4 August 1965
Lunch with Violla Rubber at the Plaza – seemingly a quite engaging old trollope, whose position vis-à-vis Bette remains somewhat mysterious, a potential easer of relation-ships I suppose, but equally one determined to establish her importance and necessity. I appear to have made a very good, strong impression – 'You'll stand no nonsense,' etc. Equally I am remarkable for having said how *bad* much of *Old Acquaintance* is. Can I *really* be the first to have said such things?

Next morning I go to Juleen Compton for breakfast and we discuss the play: she likes it, but is very vehement about a *happening* in the second act – that Milly should maybe throw Ahlers out, that something should change – a positive dynamic be intro-duced. I allow myself to be fired and go to Irving full of such conviction. But no sparks are struck. I realise Irving is no more anxious than I to plunge into the script again. Dinner with Charlie Baker – 'ugly pills again' – and this time he says – 'You *must* come and spend a weekend with me . . .'

6 August 1965
We have to make off for Quog – my next meeting with Bette being booked for Long Island. Realising this is my last opportunity, I take a taxi at about 9.15 down to Times

---

1. American impresario who brought *Look Back in Anger* to Broadway.

Square to buy myself what I find is called an Ivy League belt! Finally locate one in 42nd Street. Return in triumph to breakfast in Coffee House. Driven by Ann Schneider to Quog. Here we are again. All that slightly acid, feline, NY-type conversation I don't much like, and fall into too readily.

Bette comes over in the afternoon: another talk, mostly alone with me – she volunteers that her identification with the play had been impulsive (I don't believe she'd read it that carefully). It is not exactly a *concrete* conversation – nothing like Richard's carefully annotated scripts – and I have a sense of her wildly flying kites – and not minding if they are hauled in, so long as the hand is firm and inspiring of confidence. We discuss the character of Milly – what do we know of her – and I sense the unsureness, the erratic, grasping, rejecting nature of her temperament – to be hauled with great care: not too great honesty, dangerous to admit weakness.

That evening we eat lamb: very well cooked by Ann – there having arrived Dudley – son of the famous lawyer I believe, Dudley Field Malone – tall, queer agent friend of the Schneiders, who would be very handsome if he were not so unmistakably camp.

7 August 1965

In the morning we got through to Fugard in South Africa – amazing – he sounded precise, small, bearded! Ready to concede Davis's relatively unimportant points. In the afternoon Irving and I drive down to the sea and look at the boats in choppy water while the foghorn blares, then ate a hamburger; then to the modest, rather homely ugly little beach house where Bette was staying with her old friend, ex-Warner publicity. A tense, long and wearing, over-heated four hour confab, starting very uneasily – Bette playing it friendly but evasive – calling out for her friend every time it looked as though the conversation might become practical. Large drinks: I stuck to orange juice. Boring and protracted 'joke' by friend simulating Ahers' footsteps – part genuine square, part to relieve tension I suppose.

Bette stimulating but fearsomely over-emotional – particularly when she started discussing the possibility of falling in love with her director – 'Yes, when I look back on it all my best performances I've been in love with my director'; how she had been investigated by the FBI – and their verdict: 'hyperthyroid but with a kind heart'; how she had prepared for suicide in her Warner two-storey dressing room, but surrounded by pills – and in her smartest rig out – had laughed herself out of it . . . She never (significantly) actually said – yes I'll do it – but somehow contrived to do it in parenthesis – 'and I know I ought to – I must do it . . .' Endless repetitions of the *Iguana* story (a bit pissed I think, or warmed up), of how she wiped the floor with Margaret Leighton, and how the show collapsed when she left.

I no longer have (if I ever had) the conviction and the persistence to take on the responsibility for these emotional vagaries. Anyway you can't forestall the inevitable.

We parted very amicably. Bette said she would write to me and say all the things her New England temperament stopped her saying face to face. It was superficially all fixed: she had said there was nothing that could or should take priority. Yet I couldn't rid myself of this intuition of fantasy, and not sure whether it was correct or too coloured by my own hesitation – I left it to facts.

In New York had an unimpressive hour or so with Gabe Katska – amateurish as a producer – superficial – talking really on 'package' and financing level – intermittently occupied with ringing girls about some party he was going to . . . I left in no way fuelled.

10 August 1965

Woodfall: this is getting to feel like the Institute – i.e. a place where one is resented, made to feel like an angry young man. Meeting with Oscar takes place with Mike Deeley[1] – Oscar nervous, unprepared really. Myself edgy, in mood of resentment against unperforming Papa. Shelagh has not delivered script: and of course no one has been in touch with her. Oscar rings her, and we agree to meet in the evening to look through what she has done before delivering to Oscar. I was visibly annoyed with Oscar. Mike Deeley hadn't read the story – didn't even know its title. When I (out of spite laughing!) threatened to start shooting late September or October – he blanched . . . I quit the meeting 'obviously' angry . . . I went onto Miriam's office and wrote him note, saying I didn't want Michael Deeley as producer.

14 August 1965

CHICHESTER: I stayed with Albie [Albert Finney]: an unfortunate thing really, but he was in the room when Pauline[2] phoned, and invited me – and it seemed impossible to refuse. We got on well – would appear to doubtless to the world – but to me Albie is boringly constricted in taste and conversation – completely closed. The acting also: closed; technical; uninteresting (compare with Hilmar Thate for charm and *intelligence*). I was bored with *Armstrong*,[3] which anyway I find tiresomely affected – all this ridiculous Scots accent and vocabulary – and atrocious construction. *Trelawney*[4] charming play: don't like Louise Purnell much. Paul Curran *superb*, really. I pretended to like *Miss Julie*[5] though in reality I found it boring: just not really naked or passionate. *Black Comedy*[6] – well . . . overlong and facile and showy. Very superficial direction (John Dexter).

---

1. Associate producer on *The White Bus*, who later produced *The Italian Job* (1969), *The Deer Hunter* (1978) and *Blade Runner* (1981).
2. Pauline Melville, novelist, then the casting director of the National Theatre.
3. *Armstrong's Last Goodnight* by John Arden. Directed by John Dexter and Bill Gaskill.
4. *Trelawney of the 'Wells'* by Pinero.
5. By Strindberg.
6. By Peter Shaffer.

All in all a depressing visit. Of course I feel a spare prick around the National: and it's not enjoyable thinking things are bad. Nice of Robert Stephens to suggest reviving *Andorra* with Ronald Pickup! Ron and I spoke after *Armstrong*. He belongs to 'them' in a funny way: find myself resentful that he acknowledged neither my card about *Sporting Life* nor my good wishes for the season. It's sad. Well, let him go to the Court to play Shelley for Bill Gaskill! Expressed myself freely to Pauline – but I wish I'd spent more time with her and less in Albert's beach house – his refuge. Rowed with Oscar.

28 August 1965

It was ten days ago that George [Devine] had another heart attack, a bad one, that landed him in St George's Hospital. Touch and go at the time; then better; then another attack about now which paralysed him . . . oh dear, oh God . . . such is the price of the Court: and how impossible not to reflect on the irony of George, abandoned and finished really, with his disciple [Tony Richardson] now a rich and famous director, and his theatre drained to provide Larry [Olivier] with a step to the peerage. Of course his deficiencies have played their part: but what matter. When I suggested to John Gale, in search of a subject, that he should do something about George's end at the Court, the *Observer*'s reaction was that it wasn't newsworthy – compared of course with David Warner's *Hamlet*, or whatever.

I had planned to follow my first visit to the Ensemble[1] with *The Threepenny Opera* on Tuesday – tickets provided by Miriam [Clore], whom I escorted with due pomp (and orchid) to *Arturo Ui* on Friday: having (Good God!) slipped in *The Commune*[2] on Friday – and then *Coriolanus* on Saturday . . . Was it really as high pressure as that?

Well: *Arturo* somewhat disappointed me the first time, having had such expectations of electricity built up over the years. Partly it is a play that *demands* knowledge of the text, and theatrically it did seem to have settled into somewhat mechanical vitality. Ekkehard Schall, a great tour de force, etc. but didn't make me feel it was the performance of the greatest actor in the world. Hilmar Thate, an excellent and more appealing Goebbels . . . It was after the *Commune* that I met the two young directors, Manfred Karge and Matthias Langhof, whom Anthony Page arranged to have supper with, with Felicitas Rich and Annemone Haase – the first rather gaunt, humorous, direct (who played Jenny and sung 'Solomon's Song' wonderfully); and the second less dynamic and unconventional, but sweet and ordinary . . . It became apparent that these, with Hilmar, constitute a group of friends – and very sympathetic, though in an interesting way – not enormously forthcoming, tremendously secure in their own

---

1. The Berliner Ensemble, founded by Bertolt Brecht, paid its second visit to London in 1965, playing at the Old Vic.
2. *Threepenny Opera, Resistible Rise of Arturo Ui* and *Days of the Commune* by Bertolt Brecht.

values and tradition, not hugely interested in one's own – so that it came as quite a surprise to be enveloped by Manfred's bear-like hug as we said goodbye last night: 'Mein erste Scottishe Freund!' Manfred has this marvellous dozy fat-boy's face, with a shock of dark hair and great attachment to 'Auld Lang Syne': keen at least for one to see his work (I hope not merely ambitious!), since he urged Anthony, Arnold Wesker *and* myself to come to Berlin for his new production which he and Matthias start rehearsing with Hilmar next week . . . Matthias sharper faced, short hair, very serious and sensitive, not communicating a great deal. Hilmar I quite fell in love with from *The Commune*: humorous, great plastic authority and a splendid voice – a great 'player-out'; the second time I saw *The Commune* I thought a bit too much so, and too much face pulling . . . maybe a bit because he's so short . . . *Why do* I find myself effectively engaged in this way? Is it vitality that attracts me? authority? sensibility? God knows. Felicitas I also very much like: somewhat mannish – somewhat eccentric – with her own mystery; her own off-beat humour.

The first supper was with Sean Connery and Diane Cilento. Pleasant enough: though Diane really is wacky and a bit boring. Sean is attractive – in more than one way; but I'm afraid doesn't much like me – thinks me a show-off, in some way seems to resent me . . . But his relationship with Diane is always what matters most, so I don't imagine he's spared me many thoughts (also the dear fellow isn't very bright). Second encounter was at Sean and Diane's after *Coriolanus*: the Clores, the Reiszes and Vanessa Redgrave in attendance. You don't really discuss things too seriously on these occasions: they get enough of that I imagine from the Peter Brooks and the Ken Tynans – and really our worlds are very far apart. I had a conversation with Hilmar about *Coriolanus* – which Diane's interventions didn't really help. I think it does in the end come down to the dialectic conception – *Hamlet* would have to be the drama of the man of new, humanistic ideas in conflict with reaction, etc . . . But the trouble is they aren't really *interested* in discussion – in understanding, for instance, one's own point of view. Probably so much the better.

I took Victor Henry to *Coriolanus* and Anthony Hopkins to my second visit to *The Commune*. These young, ardent, serious spirits do me good. I *like* them. And there really is much of the teacher in me. All part of the total psychological fuckup I suspect, but at least a positive emanation. I *ought* to be a more consistently and dignified father-figure with some reserve. I despise myself afterwards for the degree I've been frank, open, revealing with such youngsters – telling Anthony Hopkins much of the truth about Richard for instance. Probably because I know that behind this eager frank-ness is too much wish-to-be-loved. But objectively it's not heinous. It's unfortunate that amongst my contemporaries friendship seems to have failed me. Anthony H. res-ponded with the understanding and sensitive appreciation of *Days of the Commune* that I'd expected.

Afterwards to a party in Blackheath given by volatile progressive Peggy Middleton[1] – wine and folk songs: but humorous and kind-hearted . . . Saying goodnight, Manfred obviously wanted to meet the next day, so I invited our group to the Escargot and got Jocelyn to come also . . . in the event only Manfred turned up – the others were working in *The Threepenny Opera*, and Hilmar was resting. (How marvellous to have an actor who really would rest rather than enjoy himself – like our old school!) We had a nice lunch anyway then picked up Matthias outside the London Pavilion, and went to the Portobello Road for Jocelyn to buy a Tiger's Eye for Helene Weigel.[2] There in a stationers was a long-player of a Scots evening: Manfred had told us at lunch how the actors at Chichester had given them a meal when they went down – and had sung 'Auld Lang Syne' . . . so I bought the record and we went back to the studio and played it – and 'My Love is Like a Red Red Rose' and 'Will Ye No Come Back Again' in waltz time . . . I took Manfred and Matthias back to the theatre – where Hilmar was by the stage door, in his red shirt (British) and quite smart mod suit (German) . . .

After the show – whose purity and vigour was stunning as ever – there was this ridiculous and awful muddle and graceless anti-climax – which ended fortunately in a smashing little party of our own. Ken Tynan's secretary had told me going into the theatre – 'There's a do in the Dress Circle bar afterwards' – and so, clutching my bottle of whiskey, I told Manfred and Matthias . . . but they didn't know anything about it, and wouldn't go anyway as they'd not been invited – 'Let's go back to the studio' – so I went to see Hilmar – found him in his dressing room with Schall – all around actors lugging their things from the theatre – then over the tannoy came the belated announcement – drinks in the Circle bar. Fuck that – we were leaving: but Wolf Kaiser caught hold of Hilmar and said politeness demanded . . . so he went up, and I went out, sent the others off and promised to come on . . . In the Dress Circle bar were sandwiches, champagne, drinks: practically no actors – Gaskill and Dexter – back from holiday and as camply brittle as ever. I got immediately involved in acid recriminations with a smooth girl handing round sandwiches – so superior in her Englishness she drives me nuts. I stuffed my brief-case and pockets full of crab and smoked salmon sandwiches – then we beat it to the studio in a taxi. And what a nice party we had! Egg and bacon; and *The Trial of Lucullus* which (BLESS them) they had given me; then singing and waltzing to our Scots record, and then we all sang 'Auld Lang Syne'.

I felt so at ease: amongst fellow artists. 'It's good for us you are here on our last night' Hilmar had said in the taxi – I am irredeemably sentimental, of course. Manfred waltzing with Anne-Marie ('Lindsay – sing!') and Hilmar with Jocelyn . . . straight and proud and cheesy. Happily the taxi we phoned for went away before we came down –

---

1. Labour councillor who become Mayor.
2. (1900–1971) Brecht's wife. Co-founder and first director of the Berliner Ensemble.

so Jocelyn drove all back to their Carlyle Hotel. They invited us in for a drink – others were still sitting around in the bar. And we sang *Mother Courage* songs, and Hilmar sang his *Commune* song – and 'Auld Lang Syne' again. Then out on the pavement and we all embraced with *genuine emotion*. I really miss them!

And George . . . George had this repeat heart attack when I was in New York: it was the last-but-one Saturday of *Patriot*. My last meeting with him had been when visiting Jill Bennett a previous Saturday – and he had sailed in in his drag,[1] looking certainly rather splendid, very caustic, complaining that his dresser had drenched him in scent . . . When I came back he was in St George's – a public ward – since he'd been a casualty, and Dr Henderson wasn't available . . . It had been bad, then better; then, after nearly two weeks, he had a stroke, which paralysed his left side, and partly his face . . . Jocelyn was splendid. She arranged for me to see him – a rather scarring visit to that public ward – with a man choking, being sick in the next bed – George terribly thin, terribly old – gone the old luxuriance of that white hair – that sturdiness – which to tell the truth went really a year ago. He had been eating fruit, and fragments still seemed to clutter his mouth. Prepared for the worst, I suffered no shock – what *could* shock one? But I had been primed to be cheerful, and to amuse, and that was hard, with George from the start seeming removed and bitter . . . He started saying something like 'It's not worth it . . . it's not worth it . . .', then (it was difficult to understand – and more difficult because one mustn't show the difficulty) 'I'm going to ask you something you may feel an imposition,' said George, and asked me, if there was a farewell reception to the Ensemble, to represent him. Like a fool, I tried to tell him the Ensemble had gone – but he didn't understand. It was awfully hard but I forced myself on – telling him about the *Trial of Lucullus* and *Coriolanus* and all – how much he took in I don't know. I didn't feel very good at it. Then Jocelyn came, and I kissed George's hand – I had been holding it, pale and cold and weak – and embraced him.

29 August 1965

One bumps into people – disastrously.

I taxied to the Embassy and arrived at the end of the first scene of *The World's Baby*, Michael Hastings' play at last put on by the English Stage Company with Vanessa [Redgrave] playing inaudibly; tentative and *wrong* (it turned out afterwards that she had decided to play this obsessive feminist and fighter as a schizophrenic, with nervous laugh and dislocated movements). Nerveless, tasteless production by Patrick Dromgoole (Jessie Matthews and projection of a detail of Guernica for the late 30s). It was really dreadful, only Alan Dobie[2] acted like a real intelligent actor . . . In the second interval I *unfortunately* caught the eye of Jack [J. W.] Lambert who had that morning

---

1. As Baron von Epp, hostess in the drag-ball scene in *A Patriot for Me*.
2. (1932–) Rachel Roberts' first husband, acted in *Serjeant Musgrave's Dance*.

been represented in the *Sunday Times* by a sweeping farewell to the Ensemble – disposing of all enthusiasts as ideology-prone hysterics. Unfortunately, so needled was I by his mock-apprehensive, nervous no doubt, look across the entrance hall – that I called out rudely: 'Have you brought that intelligent, sophisticated friend with you?' Then, because *that* seemed merely rude – I went up to talk with him – and of course became much ruder . . .

Anyway, Jocelyn hadn't turned up – I phoned her and found she'd imagined the play was at the Court! So I left in the second interval to go and have supper with her: passed Bill Gaskill returning late for the play, and in a sudden access of weakness, sentimentalism and need of sympathy (*partly* brought on by my row with Lambert I suppose) invited him to have a drink – then I was lumbered. He wanted to know if I was eating. I said I was going to see Jocelyn – could I give him a lift? so he accepted one, said he'd come in 'just to say goodnight' – stayed on and on until invited to eat – ate – stayed on . . . until finally some allusion to Oscar and Tony by me receiving defending comment from Bill – I snapped – and as he was in the loo next door I said loudly 'I know more about the cinema than fucking Bill Gaskill . . .' plus something, no doubt, which had the effect of driving him out. My fault though, really, because I know Bill well enough, and I should stifle this desire for friendship. *Queers are bad security risks.* This thought often occurs to me, when I find myself (as so frequently) drawn into 'sincere', heart-revealing conversations – just through loneliness, or lack of a central relationship in my own life.

5

The White Bus

Dylan – The Cherry Orchard
Venice Film Festival – Inadmissible Evidence

> 'I note I am much better. More in control.
> But still my fundamental need is to be protected,
> set and kept on rails – so that I can work on creation
> not on shouting at assistants . . .'

4 September 1965

I feel a mood of listless rather than intense defeat. However unreasonable my needs, they are not likely to be satisfied: I see clearly that my demands are hopelessly high. People just don't want to 'father' an ageing adolescent anarchist, however talented. My job should be to father: but I seem neurotically incapable of 'laying hold on life'. In this opportunist society no organisation of the kind that could support and enclose me – and withstand or absorb my tetchy demands – is likely to exist. Whatever I accomplish is likely to be at the expense of endless irritability and threshing around and weak-violent reaction to the goads. Consider the problem of getting a sympathetic unit for *The White Bus* – or *don't*!

I met Mike Deeley, and decided that in fact there's no reason why we shouldn't get on together – provided I don't hanker after what he can't give me. He seems quite dynamic; quite efficient; some of his opinions chime with my own – his attitude towards *The Knack*, for instance, though I have no great trust in his intuitions. Anyway he plainly wants to do the picture, and has got on with the organising – Kevin Brownlow,[1] for instance, to edit – I'm toying with the idea of Peter Suschitzky[2] to light it . . . I just

---

1. Film historian, director, editor. Made a feature film about the Nazi occupation of Britain, *It Happened Here* (1965). L.A. saw it on 6 September: 'awfully good: fine atmosphere'.
2. British cinematographer (1941–), who lit *It Happened Here*.

feel Ondricek is swinging it a bit – I mean it would be bloody-minded of me: and the difficulties of communication are so great . . . I occasionally get brief spells of thinking creatively and freshly about the subject: but most of the time I am bogged down in familiar fashion. I really begin to wonder what, if any, my talent really is – and yet I have done some good things, haven't I? But too few . . . not enough . . .

6 September 1965
To London Airport: plane to Manchester; met by nice driver Stan; driven to horrible new 'international style' Piccadilly Hotel . . . Shelagh comes and we sally out. Usual stimulating awful marvellous Northern urban landscape. Feel *The White Bus* in these surrounding can be funny and poetic. Dine in awful grill room (minimum charge 25/–) all money and pretentiousness and poor food.

7 September 1965
Extensive drive round this morning: the Central Library (excellent),[1] back to Hulme, with its isolated cinema, and magnificent burned-out church – housing estate – the hide and fat yard, floor covered in blood, too much for Shelagh and Miriam [Brickman, casting director]. Shelagh's schools. Mike Deeley arrives and he and I recap our tour: end up outside Strangeways Jail – grim and impressive. Everywhere we go one thinks – why has none of this been on film? Search for a restaurant in the evening, in the pouring rain. Then back to the City of the Future.

8 September 1965
The Piccadilly Hotel appears more and more an image of the affluent, tasteless, expense-account society – with its impersonal 'modern' decor, its air-conditioning that doesn't work, its tapes of continuous musak relayed even into the bathroom. Breakfast, we discover is 10/- extra on top of the 90/- for a room, with 2/- charge for serving in the room *and* another 2/- if the orange juice is fresh . . . Such display is made of everything, of decor, service, etc . . . that one is positively incited to rebel!

Anyway, in the evening, sitting in the coffee shop, so shocked was I at the discovery of fresh orange juice being 2/- extra (*though* – NB – only 1/- more than tinned on the à la carte menu) that I complained bitterly to the Irish woman in charge – rather pleasant, though infuriating me by repeating 'Yes I think the charge is fair' – who sent for the Assistant Manager, who arrived young, sallow, bespectacled and with a limp, who enquired with mock concern – and attempted to defend 'the price structure' (fixed by

---

1. Around the library's central dome is written: 'Wisdom is the principal thing: therefore get wisdom: and with thy getting get understanding.' Read out in the film by the Mayor, played by Arthur Lowe, this creed was used as the preface to *If . . . .*

management) as best he could – poor fellow. After this blow-off, Miriam and I went to *Say Who You Are* – the latest Keith–Willis farce:[1] middle-class sexy stuff now, with Ian Carmichael . . . 'Are you queer or something?' We only saw the first half.

17 September 1965

A note about that inner world . . . It has continued to exist of course, to exercise a pull on my imagination however friendly or momentarily affecting. And in a few days it will be pulled into the forefront again by a call attempting to summon me (invite if you like) to John Heyman's office: 'about *Dylan* . . .'

On the phone, in the box in Manchester, in the middle of quite other preoccupations, I typically (like Richard himself) say okay – Tuesday – fix a time . . . Then later – together with a churning of the feelings, the old insecurity, excitement, slight sickness – a reaction of indignation, of affront. A feeling that too readily *again* I am not standing on dignity – AVAILABLE – and that, not just on principle but actually in practice, makes me too small beer, easy pickings. At Richard's disposition, to pick up when he feels like it . . . Of course (and here is the paradox) this position is in fact absolutely the fantasy vis-à-vis Richard that I enjoy . . . that he should say – 'I've only to call him, and he'll come running' ('You know you love it . . .', 'Heel, Lindsay!') . . . And perhaps the *real* reason for our break is not that Richard wanted to dominate me but that he refused to dominate me consistently enough. Where the domination-fantasy in him ran into just the drinker – the family man – the careerist . . . where I had no place.

At times I feel I am capable of playing the part of detached, objective 'director' – but is *this* anything more than fantasy? Or would it start all over again? Richard sniffing the scent under his armpits – kissing his image in the mirror – speculating on whips and leather belts and boots – recounting to me how he near-raped that girl in John McMichael's Rome hotel bedroom – how he'd like to get his rod up some blonde bitch's arse . . . of course part of me longs for this – and in such a mood I can imagine, in spite of all, dashing to John Heyman's office tomorrow, and playing it cool, but making myself *most* available.

But think then of all that is boring in Richard. As he stands surrounded by those phoney nonentities – hiding behind his wife's magenta lounging-trousers; boasting about his fights; making an idiot of himself with the *Evening Standard* and the *Daily Express*. And his meanness – to me at least. The result of my sensed demands? Could I conquer my susceptibility, and actually *run* him? Or would I suffer and row again? If I could hold off from Richard would it actually tame him? Have *I* the strength?

---

1. Keith Waterhouse and Willis Hall.

21 September 1965

Mike Deeley and Jake Wright [the production manager] return from ACTT with news that the union will permit Ondricek [to be the director of photography on *The White Bus*]. This is as exciting as it is intimidating. In the evening, Miriam and I go to Hornchurch to see Anthony Hopkins in *The Devil's Disciple*.[1] Sad little theatre – and think an abominable production really. But Anthony has real distinction – if playing a bit too soberly and enjoying too much the sensitive side. No doubt we *did* see a 'down' performance. Felt rather awful in the pub after when unable to say a good word about the production. Does one do good – or is one resented? I do lack generosity – then am over-warm to those I feel strongly for.

24 September 1965

A Good Day. In the morning two excellent industrial visits – to Proctor and Gamble, where tangled machinery produces soap, and these three girls sit packing three tablets into a carton with lightning, automatic movements of the hands . . . Some good vistas . . . Then to Turner's, who make train wheels . . . with marvellous scrap-steel yards, and furnaces, and men shovelling in the sand like fiery circles of the damned . . .[2] Afternoon another good visit took us to Reverend Warner, whom we had been recommended to yesterday by that maddening old man at the estate agency – 'It will avail you nothing . . . Only the Queen herself could give you permission . . . It is an Englishman's inalienable right to have a service every Sunday . . .' Amazingly the Rev. Warner turned out to be young, bright-eyed and incredibly commonsensible: 'The place has been desecrated so much in the last eighteen months, I doubt if you could do anything to make it worse.'

Mike Deeley and I investigated the Town Hall – the most superb neo-Gothic building you can imagine. Started on the search for permission [to film there] – first the assistant town clerk's office, with smart lads drinking tea and eating chocolate bars, then the poor Civil Defence authorities – sitting there with the butter melting in our mouths, lying like dogs, and feeling like assassins with knives under our cloaks.

26 September 1965

The Hotel Flora in Prague: after breakfast come Jaromil [Jires, film director] and Mirek [Ondricek] and we go through the script [of *The White Bus*]. Milos [Forman] gentle, unassuming. These are his qualities. He brought me a very charming oil lamp. They leave on Mirek's bike, about 12.45. Jiri [Menzel] arrives two-and-a-half hours late – at 2.30. We go out and eat . . . then to the theatre where we arrive too late for even the end of Jalka in *The Insect Play* . . . I'm afraid I scotch Jiri's idea to go to the wine-tasting (an hour's drive). Instead we take tea in the bourgeois flat where he and Jalka live with her

1. By George Bernard Shaw.
2. These locations were used in the finished film, which bursts into colour during the furnace scene.

parents (a Czech children's programme about racial discrimination on the telly). Then to Kacher's Theatre to see *Boarding House for Bachelors* from an O'Casey story, directed by Krecik, with Josef Abraham and [Vladimir] Pucholt. Pucholt *is* a brilliant *true* and splendid actor. Abraham most charming, but better as a movie actor perhaps – romantic naturalism. Beautiful eyes.

27 September 1965
I begin to feel a) Prague is pleasantly small, and b) I know quite a lot of people here. Visit to Barrandov Studios, with a bottle of whiskey for Harnach.[1] Jolly and friendly conversation – the official photographer takes an official group photograph. Stroll through studio and glimpse Helmut Käutner[2] shooting his *Robin Hood* feature and inspect new cutting-room block. Discuss terms with Bedrich – who does seem genuinely friendly, and sorry to be dissatisfied with £50 a week which I offered for Mirek. Sufferingly I up it to £65. All agreed . . . so, bearing my lamp . . . I make for the airport.

28 September 1965
As arranged, Oscar comes to pick me up. We go into the office and start talking about the script: he rightly feels some good portions of dialogue have been lost, but alternatively fails to understand the beginning or the extended significance. His big argument is that the start fails to make sense because if the girl couldn't stand the 'Shell Building' she wouldn't try to escape to another industrial area!!

Evening: went round to Wendy Toye's flat to pick up Milos Forman – found him battling in an attempt to get back to Prague tomorrow and not be put into prison – his reserve call-up having been delayed only so long, to enable him to attend *Cerny Petr*[3] press show. Milos is nice, sympathetic and charming – apart from being bloody talented. Anyway, always enthusiastic to help, I warmly offer, if he sends a treatment for a film in London with Pucholt, to push it. I can't help wondering if (knowing he didn't) he gave that copy of *Billy Liar* to Pucholt? Another possessive director?! It's a pity it has (apparently) been done in Prague. Pucholt would certainly be superb.

1 October 1965
John Fletcher has started his work filming our processes [for the documentary *About the White Bus*].[4] He is not inspired in his search for material: takes what comes in fairly

---

1. Vlastimil Harnach, the studio director. Sacked in 1969 for allowing Milota to make a documentary about Jan Pallach, who torched himself on Wenceslas Square in protest against the Soviet occupation of Czechoslovakia.
2. German film director (1908–1980).
3. *Peter and Pavla*. Pucholt had a supporting role.
4. Fletcher had also photographed *O Dreamland* (1953).

pedestrian-seeming manner: but no doubt the taste is good. Tony [Richardson] of course has refused co-operation. Do tape recording of 'Song of Resolution'[1] on piano in Tony's office: realise when I hear the tape that my voice is not as good as it sounds within my head. Miriam quite intoxicated playing accompaniment.

3 October 1965
Spent the afternoon rehearsing the 'Song of Resolution' with nice Anthony Hopkins – he is a shy and a bit screwed-up lad: but I was very shocked to hear of this Joan [Mills] – new director at the Royal Court – who had said to him: 'You're a working-class actor, aren't you? A yobbo . . . Do you know anything about style?'

Evening – see George (Devine) – of course he is still bad: but better than when I saw him last. He said: 'Who do you think would play Lear best in the world? I suppose you think Richard Harris?' I said no – some Russian.

5 October 1965
Catch 8.20 from Paddington to Birmingham – look at city centre. It isn't what I'd hoped. Though glutted with Consumer Goods. Then on to Manchester. Met by egregious Jake Wright. Realise he is useless – weak, procrastinating, one of those neurotics who only too willingly and understandingly accepts all the reasons for NOT DOING. Michael Deeley should have come North – kick myself for being an indecisive idiot, let him get away with specious behaviour behind his desk. And of course when I ring at 8.15, his home number is reported out of order. Speak to him at about 12.00: he rather surprisingly agrees to come tomorrow. (I would have prefered this afternoon).

7 October 1965
The Rubber Regeneration Co. turns out to be rather smashing – excellent symbol-rich stockyard – troglodytes at work in the murk-dark machine shops – and white, dust-covered shops . . . We all traipsed round the Trafford Park Cold Stores – through chilly rooms full of cheeses and turkey – one or two bits fun but not great dividends. Lunch with Mr Neath of the Auxiliary fire brigade.

P. M. Geigy chemicals – rather un-gargantuan labs, then the egregious Mr Unger with his collection of sea-shells ('To remind, me in the middle of this commercial world, that some of the most beautiful things in life are free . . . !). Then his awful back-attic where forlorn girls were packing frozen meat stew, spraying in gravy with a plastic hose.

---

1. By Brecht. Anthony Hopkins makes his film debut singing the song in a blink-and-you'll-miss-it scene in *The White Bus*.

10 October 1965

Driving back in our smart hired Austin – white with black leather upholstery – I suddenly felt, as I haven't for a long time, happy – even that I could get down on my knees before I got to bed, in a symbolic prayer of thanksgiving. Why?

Mirek arrived, and his manner and personality is truly all that one could wish. He arrived at 4.30 at London Airport, came through the door looking a bit pale, but was glad and excited and responsive in such an open and unaffected way. John there, filming away, very jolly and sympathetic; and Raoul shows every sign of being a first-class, most helpful assistant.

Back to Curzon Street – after a little excursion round Trafalgar Square, Whitehall and Buckingham Palace – and it was marvellous how, tired as he was, Mirek wanted immediately to discuss primary technical details. Dinner at Luigi's – and happily bumped into Jill. *And* I spoke this morning with Richard Harris in Hawaii – who wants me to do the play and film of *Dylan* come what may. To speak to a courteous and friendly Richard *was* a pleasure. Sleep on that.

16 October 1965

A fraught and hectic week, impossible to chronicle day by day or hour by hour. Mirek shines through and over it, with his ardent, warm, sensitive, humorous, vigorous, professional personality. He has an extraordinary capacity to move from the boyish to the calmly authoritative with no effect or self-consciousness. If ever there was a justification of intuition, a confirmation of I-Ching, he is it. From the first, I can't think of a moment when his attitude has not been what I would call correct – i.e. 'perfect'! A sensitive, humorous, *artist's* response to everything he sees and experiences – 'Fantastish!' From a wander round King's Road, Luigi's, Soho from the first evening; then the trip to Manchester, with stopover at Birmingham Shopping Centre, where Mirek complained of a headache in the middle of the Fine Fare Supermarket (the plenty, and the shouting colouring proving too much for him!) yet went off happily to shoot in Woolworth's (colour tests), speaking loudly in Czech to anyone who accosted him.

Mirek has a kind of response that I crave – sympathetic, dynamic, one that puts the project first, with the authority of a genuine sensibility. Perhaps at first (searching for weaknesses) I am inclined to give too much credence to it, but I feel he is an artist – something God-given. And what a clean, sensitive, healthy fellow. I think sometimes even a sort of Billy Budd – very boyish and amused – but, as on that occasion when confronting the man from Denham – imbued with great, real authority – the sort of authority of a man who just really knows his business. I am sure he will develop into an absolutely top artist.

It is a triumphant vindication of intuition – just as is the case of Jake Wright or Michael Deeley in the opposite direction. The organisational side of the film absolutely predictably lacks grasp, dynamic, efficiency. Michael Deeley is an expert stonewaller and bullshitter. He has spent *two* days in Manchester over this period of preparation: no wonder we are starting to shoot with permission from only *one* factory.

19 October 1965

First real day's shooting – and bad luck strikes. Sunlight. We get down to the York cinema, and get set up, and the sun streams over the buildings and spoils the shot. What to do? Of course I had started off by saying to Oscar that we shoot whatever the weather was like – it was going to be that kind of film, etc . . . But Mirek very properly thought differently. And what could I do but go with him – such is the intuitive confidence I have in his judgement. Anyway, it was a rather sad morning beating around in the bus – shooting interiors – which went pretty well: a Lollipop Lady in the afternoon . . . Further unsuccessful attempts to get the close-ups on Patsy [Patricia Healey] done . . . Oscar buzzing around fatuously: he is incapable somehow of supporting and encouraging – combines ignorance both professional and aesthetic.

20 October 1965

Too strenuous, too varied, too tiring, too frustrating to note in full . . . the familiar agony in fact – though a bit less agonising than before . . . I note that I am much better. More in control. But still my fundamental *need* is to be protected, set and kept on rails – so that I can work on creation, on relationships, *not* on shouting at assistants etc . . . It isn't *just* neurosis that makes me feel let down – the production team generally are weak, lacking leadership and decision. The familiar loathing of these smug, phoney 'professionals', who spend all their time bullshitting each other – and themselves. I really, honestly feel I don't want to make any more films in this country – it is too frustrating, too exhausting, too ruthlessly abrasive to my own sore-est, most exposed points. And I hate the falsity of the whole business. How they are shown up by the extraordinary enthusiasm and professionalism of someone like Mirek – 'there is a daily beauty in his life which makes them ugly . . .' I have never met anyone who corresponded so closely to my ideal of what a collaborator should be.

23 October 1965

The school – well, we get away with it – Miss Pearson, once the magic word 'documentary' was brandished to make all things nice and 'uncommercial', couldn't have been more heartfelt, or indeed have enjoyed it more . . . A tricky moment when I had to take a shot of Patsy singing among the children – and explained this to Miss Pearson, who cavilled a bit – but given the word 'memory' to bite on accepted it gratefully – and greeted the visitors like a Trojan.

6 November 1965

Saturday – exhausted and a bit sulky – Marjorie, the constipated-voiced continuity girl, refused to go on working after 3 p.m. . . . A hell of a day. The difficulties defeating me really, and resulting in my allowing the scene between Patsy and Stephen Moore[1] to go much too hectically; and over-shooting the tracking shot. Glad when it ended – Patsy just walked off when told shooting was over: numb rather than rude I suppose . . . Dined with the Reisz's and Milos Forman and Pucholt. He is really a charming boy.

9 November 1965

At Westminster Pier by 9 a.m. Instead of the three-man unit I've looked forward to – there are Mike Deeley, Jake Wright, Patrick, Ray (second assistant and nincompoop), Anthony (stills), Miriam, Raoul, David Wimbury – the pale and hopeless assistant-assisting. Two interesting boys from Miriam: I choose the younger and slightly prettier – but really because he handles pigeons[2] . . . which he does very well for hours as we pick setups and shoot . . . Mirek goes a bit mad on the misty Thames, the Houses of Parliament certainly looking grand – 'Hodmy Anglie' – actually when I said it I meant 'Poor old England' – but it means 'Dear England – *nice* England' . . . which is what Mirek feels, I'm glad to say! Nice easy day. Milos proposes my participation in film to be made by him in Prague and London.

25 November 1965

Farewell to Mirek. I write a week later and it is strange how – I'm reluctant to say – he's *faded* . . . I think it must have something to do with the language problem: I mean that our communication was really through looks, inflections, laughs, shared experiences – not through shared thoughts, reflections, discussions, confessions . . . Like all airport farewells, it was unsatisfactory – rushed. We were lucky with the excess baggage, since he'd booked first-class to Paris – and I kept his hand baggage back till we got upstairs. Mirek was moist-eyed as we all quickly said farewell, and I would certainly have cried, and Patsy said she would have too . . . and so Mirek vanished past passport control . . . waving . . . I drove back to the cutting room where we started the painful job of assembly – usual initial difficulties. It is definitely a push with Kevin, all of whose instincts are in quite a different, mechanistic direction . . . he has no fantasy at all and is not old enough for ambiguity

---

1. At the train station, a bowler-hatted man follows her, spouting autobiographical nonsense and wild propositions and finally bursting into song.
2. This is the opening shot of the film. A boy on a moving barge.

1 December 1965

It may be of interest to record – and how extraordinary one's compulsive behaviour is!
– that in preparation for lunch with Richard Harris today, I decided to wash my hair –
went out early, having turned on the bath – and collected my trousers from the
cleaners, bought some pine bath tablets and lemon shampoo – came back, bathed, put
on clean clothes, decided on my grey hipster trousers, grey (dark) polo-necked sweater,
and leather windcheater jacket . . . Truly I should wash my hair more often: it is better
when not flat and oily.

All this made me lateish in the cutting room. Only as I walked up the tunnel leading
out of Piccadilly Tube station did I think – probably after all that Richard won't turn
up . . . and smile . . . Outside, hesitating about buying some chewing gum, I bumped
into Thorold [Dickinson]: how strange! I noted too that in some funny way he made
me feel youthful – I mean *dependent* etc. Neither of us suggested meeting. Just as well
really – but he was jolly. I was glad to find, editing during the morning, that I *wasn't*
consumed with anxiety about the arrival of one o'clock. Would he come etc. – as in the
old days I would have been.

'Does Mr Lindsay Anderson live here?' – with that Richard breezed in as I was
talking to Kevin: Kevin quite shy and pink, I noticed. And indeed after a long gap I see
it somewhat freshly – what vitality and presence and vibrancy, however outrageous –
the fellow has! I suppose we were both a bit awkward: it would make me cool, as it
would make Richard thresh about, be loud, etc. But then he really *is* that too – practically sniffing the girls in the street, going to the door of the coffee bar to spit on the
pavement. But thank goodness – I have got quite beyond now wishing he were otherwise – pussy reformism etc. I think our relationship was much healthier.

We talked a great deal of course – perhaps Richard is like that with everyone, but he
certainly unlocks my tongue – but I stuck to my guns about Warsaw and the autumn.
The talk of *Dylan* – theatre and film – and even *The Ginger Man*[1] (Carl Foreman[2]
thinks it could be cheap, 'modern' in style, hand-held and shot in any weather) – what
will become of it all?! . . . But I really must write better than that: though I get fatigued
after two pages, and end up just saying, 'We talked a lot.' How will it shape in my
autobiography? Or my *Life of Richard Harris*?!

Seeing him again after all these months – after a year really – I had a certain objectivity. I was telling myself – he *is* like this, really like it, and how ridiculous to try to
change it . . . He was talking excitedly, egotistically, extrovert, loud, irresistible. Within
a couple of minutes how the doctor had examined him – for he's had two 'collapses',

---

1. Harris had played Sebastian Dangerfield in J. P. Donleavy's own adaptation, which opened at the
Fortune Theatre, Covent Garden (15 September 1959), and which was famously closed 'on moral
grounds' after three days at the Gaiety Theatre in Dublin (26–29 October).
2. Who wrote and produced *The Guns of Navarone*, which featured Harris in one 'bloody' scene.

one in Ireland, the other just the other day, been in the clinic, had his heart examined (perfect) and now been told he's got uric acid in his bloodstream, and must stop drinking and eating fatty foods . . . Before we left the cutting room I showed him the section of 'pictures' on the movieola . . . He chortled over the nude in the Manet[1] . . . As we walked down the street he said a few words in a deep American drawl, then 'Have I seen you since I did that picture with Huston?' I said yes – marvelling that he should seem to have forgotten so much – but it was probably just excitement. 'I must just have a plain steak – I'll stand you lunch.' I said I'd consider the offer.

We walked along, chattering away, and I can't remember what about, down Wardour Street, and past *The Heroes of Telemark* without remark, then we stopped in front of the window full of stills from *The Battle of the Bulge* . . . Bob Shaw – 'They say he's very good' . . . As we came into Soho Square we bumped into Tom Priestley, strangely enough, with a couple of reels of Karel's film under his arm . . . We lunched eventually at the Escargot – Richard talked about *Hawaii*, etc. It took him some time to get around to business – which was chiefly the elaboration of a quite impossible plan to do the play and film of *Dylan* straight off – to start rehearsing *Dylan* (play) in January! then prepare the picture. Really it is too ridiculous, and one would think *someone* by now would have made it clear. But they all go down like ninepins: it's the percentages of course . . . Richard is well aware of the 'two worlds', and quite eloquent in his condemnation of the trivial, shallow, 'industry' one. But it still dazzles and flatters him, and he still thinks he can use it, and still thinks he *really* gets that Rolls Royce for nothing!

5 December 1965

Dinner at Bedford Gardens – just Elizabeth and Richard. Everyone on their best behaviour. Elizabeth met me at the door: I realised as I shook hands that she was ready to kiss on greeting – which is not her normal natural style – but I had resolved not to! Anyway I was welcomed, came into the hall, and Richard came down the stairs . . . He offered me a drink . . . I inspected the layout: the same 'dentist waiting room' – with the dining room now full of Mexican purchases – chairs, wrought-iron candelabra, an antique wooden sideboard. This prompted me to ask if my coat (of my suit) had ever come back: 'Oh yes,' says Elizabeth – 'We wondered whose it was.' (So much for one's presence in the thoughts of those about whom *we* think.) . . . Richard takes me up to his study to show me his record player-cum-tape machine – expensively fitted into an antique Mexican chest (he shows me Jamie and Jared in their beds on the way upstairs: yes – pretty children . . . he puts on three records – a Mass – Richard Strauss . . . Downstairs I show him the Berliner Ensemble programmes: he is struck by *Coriolanus*, but does not listen when I start to mention Brecht's version of it; he shows no interest in *Days of*

1. Manet's 'Dejeuner sur l'herbe' is re-created in a fantasy scene in *The White Bus*.

the Commune. He starts saying how the only way to work is to do shit, then do something like *Richard III* – how he had suggested to United Artists that they might finance a production, and he'd give them a picture for a lower fee . . . of course the check is only momentary when I (idiotically) point out that you didn't do work like the Ensemble by sandwiching it between a couple of bad films . . . We chatter really through dinner; then Elizabeth went out; came in later and said she was going to bed: 'You must come more often.' How can he if you never invite him? . . . ! (We had had our embrace earlier, when I presented her with a box of Victorian peppermints.)

On a practical level I explained that I thought the *Ginger Man* script was poor – but (predictably) Richard's mind is so confused between *Dylan* play and film and *The Ginger Man* and I am so totally un-pushy that I can't believe anything will come of it.

8 December 1965
Great disinclination to get up and to face a day's shooting on Whitbread Tankard commercial – 'Rugger' at Rosslyn Park . . . The car drove me down there to inspect players and pick one . . . The ground frosty – cold – David Gifford an affable assistant. Push it through with detached confidence. I pick a young chap who seemed sparky at first: though I soon found he was sensitive and a bit self-conscious; but nice looking, a good head, short hair. Then shooting in the bath-house – interesting talking to two or three of the lads after shooting: they remembered *This Sporting Life* with vividness – and more understanding than you'd think.

9 December 1965
Richard rings in the afternoon – in irritation at first: why wasn't I at the meeting with Francovitch? It turns out there *was* a meeting yesterday – attended by Robin and John Heyman . . . all very mysterious when you consider I heard nothing whatever after saying I couldn't manage the afternoon[1] . . . Richard shows all signs of getting confused in his habitual way – talking also about an offer for him to play Cromwell . . . I find my ardour much cooled.

12 December 1965
With Miriam to the Court: *Serjeant Musgrave's Dance.*[2] Really – am I being hasty and uncharitable? – an awful evening. 'Another dreadful experience!' Well, a half-cock production, not worked physically or psychologically, presumably all in the cause of anti-naturalism. The soldiers in Berman's fresh tunics – no greatcoats – no atmospherics – nor any plastic or formal invention. Rotten music and appalling sets. We only stayed an act. Got unfortunately trapped in the bar with rather shamed Desmond O'Donovan and paling Peter Gill. Last act in the pub with Victor Henry. Indiscreet.

1. He was filming at Rosslyn Park.
2. Revival directed by Jane Howell; designed by Paul Mayo; scored by Robert Long.

22 *December 1965*

THE WOODFALL MESS: Oscar returned yesterday afternoon – his arrival heralded by Michael Deeley, who had rung the cutting room to book a viewing [of *The White Bus*] for today at 4 p.m. Of course my immediate reaction on coming in to finish off going through the picture with John (Fletcher) was to cancel the booking – but after more temperate words on the phone with Deeley (of all people) – I came to the conclusion there was no point in starting with gratuitous affronts.

I met Mischa Donat [composer] about 2.15 at Woodfall, and we played a little on the mini-piano in Tony's office: he is shy, not facile, but sympathetic. I liked the theme he'd done for *The White Bus* – rather Tati-ish, but *not* the 'lyrical' (sentimental) piece for the boy and river at the start . . . still . . . frankly I can't be bothered to search further in this alien climate.

Oscar was sitting, pale and diminutive and a bit nervous, in the editorial theatre when we arrived . . . All polite, a bit self-conscious . . . The showing . . . okay . . . I realise that the film *is* deeply 'alienated' . . . too deep for tears, I'm afraid . . . It's strange that it has come out like this: not rationally chosen: but a true reflection of my attitude – and Patsy's character. An interesting film.

Well, at the end of the projection the usual silence of the uncomprehending, and to fill in the gap I say to Mischa, 'Any ideas?' – facetiously I'm afraid. He is startled, and I have to explain I'm joking. Then Deeley weighs in with the helpful observation that undoubtedly Miss Pearson will sue – even Oscar is prompted to suggest such points can be left till later. Oscar appears impressed: his points are really not bad – though his suggestions are not feasible – i.e. although the arrival of the bus is rather weak, it is *not* possible for the first sight of it to be the Lollipop Lady, nor should it be in colour . . . However, I wouldn't call his attitude disrespectful – and the exchange of comments is perfectly friendly.

We return in the limousine to the office 'for a cup of tea' – my having confirmed to Mischa that I do want him to do the music (What the hell?) . . . When we are alone, I take the bull by the horns and say – let's try and get things cleared up. Immediately Oscar is evasive. He is tired. He's only been back in the country twenty-four hours. He wants to think things over . . . But I override these objections ruthlessly, and indeed just force him to talk . . . myself heated, standing, walking up and down, ruthlessly logical; Oscar small and tense and white-faced behind his desk, logical up to a point, then implacably stone-walling. The most remarkable thing was his complete refusal to make even the most obvious steps towards compromise. Comically, I had actually to put the words in his mouth: 'Oscar, you are supposed to be the overall producer of this picture. It's up to you to help resolve this difficulty – Well you've seen the picture – how long would *you* estimate it should be?' I suppose that he really wanted to leave the whole question until Tony returned: either so that he could consult Tony, or at least have his support – for I imagine that in Africa Tony had refused even to discuss the question with him.

Forced to parley, Oscar stuck absolutely to his demand that the film should be finished, put away, and then in six or nine or however many month's time projected together with the others, with himself, Peter [Brook], Tony and myself sitting harmoniously in some projection theatre, agreeing to our mutual satisfaction what should be done with them – including cuts. I tried to point out the manifest absurdity of this fantasy – to no avail. Anything else would of course throw Oscar back on his own responsibility, his own utter insecurity, which is even greater than I could have imagined.

'Because of the nature of your story, it does lend itself particularly easily to cutting . . .' Of course I pitched in strong, remarked that Woodfall proved themselves in practice no different from the most commercially minded Hollywood company (a bit unfair I suppose) and tried to explain to Oscar the *reason* for my feeling as I do about my work. To no avail. For the poor man really *is* a philistine – to the extent that the sacredness of a work – or the idea that an artist may feel this – is totally foreign to him. He just has no comprehension of it, and this makes him feel even more insecure.'It isn't as though you needed the money . . . It would be different if you were poor' (!) Really, what an apology from a 'producer'.

I forced him eventually to re-state his thirty, then thirty-five minute offer, then:

'Well, go on – ask me what length I propose?'

'I don't want to turn this into a Dutch auction.'

'It isn't a Dutch auction, Oscar – this is called negotiation.'

'Well, what length would you say?'

'Fifty minutes.'

'That's impossible.'

'Well, what would you suggest?' . . . etc.

Eventually he was forced to concede an offer of forty minutes. Which of course I rejected.[1]

26 December 1965

Saturday December 11th was surely my last direct communication with Richard . . . *Except* that, about ten days later came a message from Arthur Lewis – via Robin: was I still ready to start rehearsing the *play Dylan* at the beginning of February? 'He says he's got a contract with Richard's name on it lying on his desk at the moment . . . No, it isn't signed, but he's confident it will be . . . unfortunately he has to go off to New York tomorrow and won't be back till January 2nd.'

---

1. The film was released at 46-minutes. It was the only film in the trilogy, completed by Tony Richardson's *The Red and the Blue* and Peter Brook's *Ride of the Valkyries*, to be given a British theatrical release. The trilogy was screened in New York in 1979.

I laughed and said maybe *mid*-February – if it could be cast.

It's all sad, of course, in a way, but probably healthy too, for increasingly I can only see Richard as a greatly diminished, preposterous, rather foolish fellow . . . Also extraordinarily ungenerous or rather only generous when the whim takes him, so that the generosity is never personal in relation to oneself – merely gratifying to *him*self.

As I say – silence . . . A Christmas card, signed (by Elizabeth) *Richard and Elizabeth.* Is it just 'falling out of love' – out of that period when one was inclined to credit the loved one with all potential or desired excellences? Or *is* there a coarsening, a cheapening, as a result of the inferior influences to which he has surrendered in the past two years – joyfully surrendered, of course? And of course – no false humility – the loss of *my* influence.

So Richard falls into place with Albert (Finney), and to a lesser degree with Tom [Courtenay] – from whom I haven't heard either this Christmas, or indeed since he made *Zhivago* and moved house, and dedicated himself even more frankly towards success.

And it *is* as it should be, though lonely: because after all they are impossible and shallow creatures . . . and love from them of anything approaching the love I've given *to* them is something of which they are all totally incapable. A challenge certainly to my own maturity. Certainly better for me to move *on.*

31 December 1965
Let me end with an account of my last meeting with Ken Tynan, after many, many months. It was at the BFI party, which I had dropped into chiefly because I had an 8 p.m. booking to screen *Walkover* – Skolimowski's pic – for James Mason (that quite nice, quite stupid, quite sensitive, quite boring fellow) and an hour to fill in after work . . . First embarrassment, there was Ken queuing up to leave his coat – we greeted each other, myself a bit tense, Ken a bit nervy.

Inside – Penelope [Houston]! How long is it since we met? The last contact was surely when she was 'too busy with the proofs' to talk to me . . . I looked but did not approach. (Later Sylvia tried to bring us together – but Penelope would not approach me, and as I got up – to leave actually – she did evasive action to the other side of the room.) But Ken came up and made contact and invited me to an evening with Arthur Miller. With misgiving, I said 'Okay'. Then Ken asked me what I was doing.

I said a film and story by Shelagh Delaney – the trilogy.

Ken: 'Oh – she's making a come-back through the movies then?'

And note – not said bitchily or smartly – but 'straight', a sincere revelation of values . . .

The Arthur Miller evening – which I did go to – was ridiculous, preposterous, boring, and totally confirming my feeling that 'This country's impossible.'

Ken launched into a vehement attack on Beckett as 'negative, defeatist, leaving his audiences with only the sensation that life is pointless, that there is no sense or use to social improvement or progress ...'[1] In fact the familiar middlebrow shit. Then Ken in defence of 'REASON' – and attacking the moderns for wishing to throw away this marvellous weapon for forging human happiness and prosperity. How shallow, glib and second-rate he is now revealed, once the youth, explosive freshness, iconoclasm has gone!

I formulated something quite well I thought: 'I would have more confidence in a social legislator who perceived the relevance of Beckett than in one who denied the importance of his vision.'

Bamber Gascoigne[2] – what a drip! with a pretty girl or wife.

Arthur Miller – let's face it, a bore – says some quite interesting things, but at such length that one can't be bothered to listen.

Miller – 'A lot of these destructive leather-jacket motorcyclist gang members were encouraged I'm sure by a film like *The Wild One*.'[3]

Ken – 'But you know, that film was banned in Britain yet we have the same sort of trouble ...' (I arsk yer!)

1 January 1966

As the New Year came in, I was between St John's Wood Station and Daphne [Hunter]'s – not knowing quite where Cunningham Place was, and content to let midnight pass anonymously – I had been in the cutting-room with John till 9.15, wrestling with the Social Centre sequence [of *The White Bus*] – the Brecht – and those maddening panning shots.

Daphne's party – quite nice. Alan Tagg,[4] of whom I am really fond, and Rosemary, Karel and Betsy, Jack Clayton,[5] Derek Prouse drunk and over-excited, introducing me to Umberto Orsini[6] in therefore an impossible manner; Albie, with a silent blonde, observing him devouringly ... Albie right about so many things: his attitude to Larry and Ken, his respect and fondness for Shelagh, his scornful dismissal of the Royal Court productions ... But with me he remains defensive: as to the rest of the world, I suppose. (Incidentally he reports that Larry, when my name was brought up in connection with *Arturo*, shook his head, puckered, and said, 'He gives his technical staff a terrible time, you know.') ... Home with Catherine Willmer.[7] Spent most of the day in bed. Supper with Rex and Rachel at the Connaught. Rachel different but thank God it

---

1. In April 1958, Beckett's *Fin de Partie* was given its world premiere at the Court; other premieres followed including the English version of *Endgame* (1958), *Krapp's Last Tape* (1958) and *Happy Days* (1962).
2. Theatre critic for the *Observer*; television personality.
3. 1953 film starring Marlon Brando.
4. Production designer for *The Long and the Short and the Tall*, *Billy Liar* and *The Fire Raisers*.
5. English film director (1921–1995).
6. Italian actor (1934–).
7. Actress, first worked with L.A. on *The Waiting of Lester Abbs*.

ended on an even keel . . . But I have to note the Christmas card Rachel showed me
from Richard – 'Why, oh why won't you play Caitlin?[1] Longing to see you . . .' In his
handwriting – and signed by them individually. A large card! – SHIT.

4 January 1966

I have crystallised my decision to drop projects with Richard – from whom I have heard
nothing for about three weeks. Richard really is, I'm afraid, a lost cause and a waste of
time.

To George and Jocelyn in the evening. George is now back at the studio; he is better
since the water was drained out of him; 'better' meaning more edgy, more lively, not
spongy . . . but there seems only left the residue of bitterness, resentment, that escape
into looking on the dark side which has always been part of him. And he has no
mentor any more, with the loss of Tony. 'What do you think of *Musgrave*?' was his first
question . . . Talk late with Jocelyn after supper: astonishing courage and resolution.

8 January 1966

Was it reading a paragraph in *Sight and Sound* last night that brought on that surprising dream of Marlon Brando 'after me' . . . sitting together on a bench: the strong,
comfortable, quite unacknowledged warmth of bodily contact – the dream was curiously chaste.

Late afternoon visit with Rachel, and do an hour and a quarter with her on her TV
Nelson script by Rattigan . . . It is rather astonishing that I really can, with a sort of
shorthand, say some quite fundamental things. I sometimes am led to feel I am quite
an exceptional director! Then supper with Patsy – at the Golden Carp . . . and we
discuss her Lady Macbeth problems.

10 January 1966

Kevin Brownlow returns to work, and we go through the picture . . . of course *he*
discovers a number of points – many quite valid – all the same I do have this rather
pleasant internal feeling – the picture is *cut*.

The sales are on, and I feel I should be going round buying some clothes – but I
don't . . . It is certainly true, I wonder where I read it, that clothes, and the buying of
clothes, represent a sexual urge, a sexual satisfaction . . . Equally significant, I suppose,
must be the way I tend to stop short of actually *buying* anything. I really do need some
more trousers. I often think of having two pairs made. But I don't.

Eat kippers and beans at home and watch a second rehearsal programme conducted
by John Fernald. What a square nit! How could *anyone* have protested against his
removal from RADA?!

---

1. Caitlin MacNamara, Dylan Thomas's wife.

12 January 1966

One really shouldn't be disturbed by the intrusions of theorists and publicity merchants . . . A phone call in the cutting room today from an American compiling an issue
for *Drama Review* – inarticulate, taking hours to say nothing. Afternoon – worse . . .
Tony Snowdon in the cutting room to photograph Shelagh and myself, with an affable
ignoramus from *Life* . . . We played the game – crouching low and absurdly close to the
Moviola; Tony keeping going with a brittle succession of with-it comments, but he
is too busy to be really interested, and only made me feel how *un*-with-it is *The White
Bus* . . . I was as usual pushed into being controversial and 'outrageous'. (Angry – also
unfashionable!) Afterwards one feels somehow ashamed.

13 January 1966

I think of phoning Robin about *Dylan* – the I-Ching was quite positive – yet I do
nothing. Karel drops round: we have a cup of tea; he asks my advice about getting Long
Distance Films to put up money for his partial re-dub (of *Morgan*) . . . Poor Karel . . .
He is friendly, nice, intelligent . . . yet . . . I show him a cut on the Moviola; I say, 'Isn't
that splendid?' He can only say, 'It will be . . .' He talks about the possibility of doing
Ned Kelly – and asks my opinion of JOHN HURT! Karel is mad to consider John Hurt
for *Ned Kelly*.[1] With Fiz to *Life at the Top*[2] premiere. Really awful. *England!*

14 January 1966

I can only smile, I suppose, when I look back on Jan. 4th's entry, where I see 'I have crystallised my decision to drop projects with Richard' – and today I phone Robin and say I'll
do *Dylan* . . . Personally I *don't* believe in it coming off: I feel sure Richard will wriggle
out once his bluff is called, and I will be nothing if not relieved! . . . A surprise – a postcard this week from Richard in Leningrad: it's characteristic that such communications should arrive when they are no longer prayed for. I really don't rationally *believe*
in anything about Richard any more, except the instant truth of what he feels at any
instant. Another echo of past obsession: a letter from Serge, mostly about his progress as
a *chanteur*. I *think* actors have lost their appeal – I mean basic romantic appeal – for me.

16 January 1966

Arthur Lewis [impresario] has a very pleasant first-floor flat in Eaton Square. I drink
vodka: he excuses himself, having just returned from New York and acquired a belly.
He is businesslike, keen, obviously hasn't thought too much about the play [*Dylan*]:
would just like to get the enterprise going. Our talk is interrupted by a call from

---

1. The role of the Australian outlaw was eventually taken by Mick Jagger. Tony Richardson directed;
Jocelyn Herbert designed.
2. Film sequel to *Room at the Top*, starring Laurence Harvey. Directed by Ted Kotcheff.

Herbert Kretzmer[1] – writing a piece on failures for tomorrow's *Express* – casting is
discussed, and I realise again there is no exactly marvellous Caitlin. He wants it done
'simple' – with 'lighting'. I point out that the play poses certain physical problems . . . I
am quite frank – admitting my doubts and fears . . . saying the time is really too short
. . . it's just a case of 'have a bash'. He agrees, and finally I say okay. Lewis rings John
Heyman – I had restrained him once, earlier in our conversation – and says 'I'm here
with Lindsay Anderson, and he's ready to go ahead . . .' We chat a bit, and I rather like
him. A pro. His dinner guests start arriving: the first are Mr and Mrs Jerry Bresler![2]
We greet each other warmly: we must meet. I stand in the dark snowy square outside
and piss through the wire fence.

17 January 1966
The [*Dylan*] contract has *not* been signed, as Richard was taking his children to the
pantomime. It will be delivered in the morning . . . I speak to Robin, and we agree on
a time limit – by midday. He communicates this to Lewis.

18 January 1966
There has been no call. Am I free? I am free! – for I won't pretend not to have been
scared: both by the project itself and by the familiar pattern of evasion which signals
NO CHANGE from a year and more ago . . . I go off having asked Robin to ring Arthur
Lewis and tell him I am carrying on with other plans. Then I hasten away in case Lewis
turns out to have the signed contract in his hand.

19 January 1966
Well – of course it happened. That's to say a phone call from Robin to say Arthur Lewis
had phoned him to say Richard's contract was in his possession – *signed*. I said 'No' . . .
Robin did not dispute my decision, though I could tell he was a bit reluctant about it.
Lewis expressed his bitter disappointment, couldn't he persuade me, went on to admit
his partial responsibility for the delay in the contract's arrival . . . I made my first
concession – if the date for starting rehearsals could be postponed . . . YES – it could –
Richard's contract being 'on or about' the 14th – it could go up to a fortnight later. I said
I would think. I was lost, of course.

Fiz rang me. I asked her what she thought. 'You must do it' – she was persuasive.
'Good work must be done.' And thinking of the existence of Larry, of the Aldwych, of
the Court – I felt these were the strongest arguments. Plus of course fatal sentimentalism, fatal sense of Fair Play. Wouldn't it be petty to turn the play down now, on the
quibbling excuse that Richard's contract was twenty-four hours late?

---

1. Theatre critic of the *Daily Express*, later, the librettist of *Les Miserables*.
2. Producer of *Major Dundee*.

20 January 1966

Last night Jocelyn, not immediately putting the idea [of designing *Dylan*] out of court, asked me to ring again this morning. I do so, and we talk it over: she is a bit tempted, but feels the time is not yet come when she can leave George for work. In the background his voice is calling out, sharp and vigorous: 'Tell him to send the play ...'

I meet Miriam [Clore] at Hatchards, and we make for Simpsons. I buy a £25 grey suit: plain and straightforward, though I feel I should really have something a bit more dash, of a refined kind ... But Miriam vouches for it ... She is useful – why is it I *cannot* do this kind of thing myself? – and I grab a pair of hip-fitting black trousers and a beige jersey shirt. I lunch Miriam at the Escargot ... as usual the talk centres on Betsy and Karel: how Betsy is spending £20,000 on doing up their new house, ordering tiles from France, driving Karel nutty with the need to earn big money ... Before the run of *The White Bus* Miriam says: 'George is dead.' A heart attack. It was over in about five minutes. It is shocking and sad and just beastly. Poor Jocelyn.

22 January 1966

Call in on Jocelyn, who is drawn and shattered but in control. Peggy [Ashcroft][1] there: we greet with warmth. What is there to say, beyond that expression of sympathy which so exhausts, making one feel the emptiness of one's heart. Am rather touched when she asks me to escort her to the funeral – and also by the pages which George left of the start of his autobiography. 'For me the theatre is a temple of ideas ...'

24 January 1966

I rewrite my piece about George – which looks more soppy in the light of day – which I have promised *Tribune* ... What a difficult thing to do! He *was* remarkable: he was in his way a heroic figure, though not of heroic size ... Perhaps in his last days most heroic of all ... A strange mixture of disciple and father-figure ... None of the cowardices and snobberies and inadequacies of which I accused him were untrue exactly, but if only I could have been bigger, they would have mattered less ... He only partly liked me – respected me certainly – but partly was intimidated by me, even was somehow jealous of me ... I find myself thinking of Jocelyn mostly when I write.

25 January 1966

GEORGE'S FUNERAL: Peggy had asked me to escort her ... I get to her house in Frognal Lane about 11.30 ... A cup of coffee first ... I like Peggy, but there is a sort of mannered constraint about her ... As we drove she said how she's thought about George – and been impelled to write it all down: she had been in twenty-five productions with

---

1. Actress (1907–1991). Played in Brecht's *The Good Woman of Setzuan* in the 1956 season at the Royal Court, and joined the ESC Council the following year.

him . . . The funeral: all woeful and treading on emotional glass. We are shepherded by a pale Julian Lousada[1] round to a sort of porch at the side of the chapel, where we wait in a hush. It is sort of awkward because we find it difficult to be spontaneous about such solemnity.

28 January 1966

We recorded music for *The White Bus* with Ken Cameron at Anvil today. Back to Beaconsfield. I strolled round the deserted studio before we began: Rachel's dressing room; Richard's dressing room; I didn't even notice where 'our' (Karel's and mine) office had been . . . On the cutting-room door was still a notice, THIS SPORTING LIFE: PETER TAYLOR[2] . . . I wondered if Mrs Hammond's staircase was amongst the junk on the lot? . . . The recording went quite well: Marcus Dodds an efficient hack, who went down in my estimation when he arrived (plus the parts) at 9 a.m. precisely.

I got a message to ask if I would be interested to direct *The Cherry Orchard* at Chichester with Celia Johnson[3] and Tom Courtenay . . . 'Fuck!' I think I said on the phone – or at least 'Damn' – seeing my summer months of leisure disappearing . . . For just the name of the play, and those actors, was an immediate spur. That's to say, why not?

1 February 1966

It's impossible for me not to wonder a little, considering the understanding and liking that *appears* at least to exist between Richard and myself, at the apparent complete lack on his part of wanting any normal, friendly relationship . . . to work together – perhaps – but not to share experiences . . . When he says he saw Peter Hall's *Hamlet* (from the front row) I can't help remembering saying, when we last met, 'Shall we go and see it?', and noting the infinitesimal but quite real hesitation when he said 'Yes'.

Now so much more objective, I note his fantastic, childlike egoism, his continual chattering in whispers during the auditions this morning – 'Do I look well? I've never been fitter, at least during the last three years. I've reduced from sixteen stone to fourteen stone three' . . . In the taxi I said I'd been asked to do *The Cherry Orchard* at Chichester. 'Have you . . . marvellous . . . I've just turned that down in New York, with Cacoyannis.'[4] 'I've spent the last two days in bed, pulling the old wire.'

4 February 1966

I put the knife which Richard had used to clean his boots in *Sporting Life* as a paperweight over some letters on my desk, in fact with Manfred Karge's underneath, think-

---

1. Jocelyn Herbert's son.
2. The editor of *This Sporting Life*.
3. Actress (1909–1982), remembered for *Brief Encounter* (1946).
4. Michael Cacoyannis (1922–). Greek director, who later directed a film version of the play.

ing Richard might read Manfred's – sure that Richard's eye would fall on the knife, and he would pick it up, and open it, and stab the air, and maybe threaten me . . . He did all that except the threatening.

I called off *Dylan* readings today: I just can't manage them and the film at the same time. Took some delicious time off, and went to Better Books: bought *Last Exit to Brooklyn*, a 'frank' (but I think good) novel of degradation, with much explicit sexual description, interesting as well as fascinating: also Auden's latest. Took a bus up the Tottenham Court Road to see if that surplus store had leather jackets. Carry on with John, working late, and do a lay for the Industry sequence.

10 February 1966

Back to *Dylan* auditions: I don't honestly remember them too well . . . At seven was the showing of *Morgan, a Suitable Case for Treatment*, to which I was at last invited! . . . The result alas too familiar and expected. As always with Karel one senses the colossal *effort* in the whole thing: the labour to make the thing fit together, the papering over the cracks, the lack of spontaneity or rhythm. There is *no* sense of dramatic growth, nothing is organic, it is all painfully thought out, rationalised . . . Is the film enjoyed? I didn't really feel a wave of empathy, though this may be subjective: of course people were murmuring compliments, and I was driven to lying drivel about it being very disturbing and the last part really frightening, etc. David Warner incidentally, now hailed as being marvellous, seems to me as unattractive, and as hollow as ever. I can't accept his performance at all: at least Jimmy Booth has balls.

After the premiere we drift across to the pub – incidentally Columbia 'are mad about it – they think Vanessa is the new Garbo,' etc. So I suppose that will quieten the Rocking Horse Winner in the Reisz household for a bit . . . In the pub, David Storey, unimpeachable for seriousness, intelligence and sensitivity of response, can't help saying: 'It's awful.'

17 February 1966

More auditions in the afternoon: enlivened by my very irascible insistence on someone getting us tea – having been informed by some office-girl voice on the phone that it is impossible . . . Eventually two sulky schoolgirls appear with a tray and 'Can we take the pot back?' . . . Further row with the Polish Cultural attaché, who says that complications over my visa are my fault for not applying sooner . . . then a call from Bob Shaw, who says when could I meet him and Phil Yordan[1] – I say that evening, and make for the Savoy – one of those tall drink, expensive food evenings in which I am pressed to make the first artistically great Cinerama-(type) picture (*When Worlds Collide* dept.).

---

1. American writer/producer (1914–2003).

18 February 1966

A real day: the two main scheduled events being George Devine's Memorial, and Oscar's, Tony's and Peter Brook's viewing of *The White Bus* . . . It started off in true style, with my abortive attempt to get my vitamin injection, so efficiently arranged by Miriam, who can't help fulfilling herself by *doing* things for people – except that she gave me the wrong address . . . so vitamin-less to the Court, where Robin and Bill, then Peggy, Jocelyn, Albie, Joan Plowright joining . . . I had the tapes to supervise, and the sound and light levels to set – which brought back old days, five minutes before the first-night audience was due to enter . . . Albie studying the Galileo speech which Bob Stephens was to have read (Bob having to 'be at the studio') . . . And down below was Jackie MacGowran,[1] whom I'd only phoned that morning, ready and courteous and willing to do Clov's speech from *Endgame* – which he did pretty beautifully, not moving from his chair . . . A last-minute panic (which I was able to note myself somewhat relishing – making something of rather than dismissing) gave rise to the possibility that John Osborne would not appear if Tony took part . . . However such appeared not to be the case . . . A sudden diversion provided by Edith Evans, suddenly announced by Bill as having arrived and wanting to speak . . . I went down and greeted the dapperly-dressed *dame* and welcomed her in.

It went very well. The theatre wasn't full, as I had sensed it would not be, and the speakers drifted on to the stage without being led, as Thelonius Monk played *April in Paris* . . . I kicked off without too much difficulty, with gravity, but humanly (I hope), then Peggy read the notes from Helene Weigel and Sam B[eckett], and spoke herself . . . followed by Jackie reading *Endgame*, Joan Plowright, then – but I forgot to say that as we settled on to our chairs – there was Tony, murmuring something about his plane being delayed, and sitting down next to John . . . This made a problem, who to speak when . . . but I decided not to rattle John by letting Tony precede him . . . so John followed Tony, then Edith Evans, then Albert, then Robin, then Bill Green, then Tony, [then] Bill; and I concluded with George's last credo about the theatre. As I say, it did go well: a very British friendly informality – without any camp – and a seriousness that didn't exclude humour. Really the best kind of British-ness. John was really remarkable – particularly remarkable – in preserving that personal and honest tone, and conveying quietly and firmly the depth and quality of his feeling for George . . . Alas for my irrepressible spirit of judgement, which no doubt cut me off from the same friendship. I was struck by John's revealing that George, just before he died, was thinking of starting another theatre, and asking John to write a play for it.

---

1. Jack MacGowran, who played Clov to Devine's Hamm in the seminal 1958 Court production.

20 February 1966

EN ROUTE — WARSAW: At this moment I regret *Dylan* . . . I don't need the money . . . and it isn't a really good play . . . and Richard seems to have disappeared – presumably gone to Wales, or Ireland . . . of course the celebrated NOTES (which last week were still being typed by his secretary!) have never materialised . . . and though I'm pleased to note that I don't agonise *at all*, I naturally miss the collaborative inspiration which I *always* need – I suppose that Richard will exercise the magic of his personality once contact is forced by the actual start of work . . . I suppose exactly the same sort of thing might have occurred in the past, if I had then been too busy, and too cool, to chase around after him from the pub to the lavatory . . . yet I'm not sure this is so: I mean, he used genuinely to be anxious to gruel his directors through his notes . . . Now life has caught up with us all.

Tadeusz and Teresa at the airport. I am changing: I can no longer indulge in warm waves of sentimental friendship; I tend to see egotism in everything . . . We drive in Tadeusz's tiny car to the Bristol: he looks tired in his fur hat; he has lost weight a bit; then they pick me up and we drive to their new flat – they've just moved in, and I am their first visitor! T.'s son there, a slight, shy, nice boy.

23 February 1966

Yesterday had a brief look at a bit of *Inadmissible Evidence* with Tadeusz – this morning we were to have worked from eleven, but it turns out he has a commission meeting to attend. After dinner, Tadeusz sets off to rehearse for *Diary of a Scoundrel* and Teresa tells me the outline . . . then we make for the theatre. We sit far too close: the second row, which is uncomfortably near. I don't enjoy the evening much. Tadeusz is brilliant, plastically and verbally, but it doesn't spring enough from character – what I feel *Arturo Ui* must have been like, but it doesn't seem at all right for Ostrovsky. I am not alarmed though. I feel he wants to escape – and needs to – but can't find the means. A contemporary role is probably best for him now.

24 February 1966

Tadeusz came to pick me up: we went to the Czech embassy and I got my visa – a little look at *Inadmissible*, them Tadeusz and Tereza drove me to the airport. Direct to Prague. The first I saw of Mirek was when I was passing passport control: there he was down beyond customs, waving in the doorway, in his blue anorak. We embraced with pure friendly warmth – how marvellous to be able to be absolutely without self-consciousness or inhibition. Surely Mirek is the purest, best spirit on Earth! . . . Mirek rather shattered and incredulous when I tell him *White Bus* is not widescreen – I feel a beast. Excellent dinner at Chinese restaurant, then to Film Club, where Jiri Pitterman, Milos,

Ivan[1] and Pucholt emerge from a meeting. We go to a very nice wine cellar and eat
sausages (Moravian).

25 February 1966
Mirek comes to ride down to the airport with me; so does Ivan Passer. Words really
can't express the fantastically simple and relaxed atmosphere of cordiality and respect
among this group. It contrasts so basically and so utterly with the bitchery and com-
petitiveness of London.

At London I was met by Stephen [Frears] – looking a bit green, and feeling sick. We
went to have a coffee at the Forte's snack bar. 'Sorry, only lunches!' said the girl. '*Christ*
– back in this *bloody* country!' I said with impetuous venom. We went on sitting there,
and in the end the girl brought us coffee.

Bought a paperback, *Image of Kate* by Mary Astor. We drive back to town, to the
Saville and a handful of auditions. Then Stephen and I make for Richmond. Tim
[Timothy O'Brien] has it all [set designs for *Dylan*] spread out on a side-table: beautiful doll's house furniture, a real job. I feel guilty that it doesn't mean more to me. But
it doesn't. We go through it scene by scene. During this meeting I get a call to inform
me that Richard's agent has rung, and if *I* do not ring him within half an hour, the play
is off!! So I get Stephen to ring. The usual mysterious responses. At first the housekeeper. Then Morgan dithering: 'Richard's just gone for a crap.'

Me: 'Gone for a *crap*?!'

Then Morgan, tumbling over himself, 'No, hang on, here he comes – hang on a
moment . . .' Then finally Richard: tense and cagey. Making no direct attack on me,
volunteering nothing as usual.

I give him the lead: I hear he's worried about something, etc. So Richard begins to
divulge: there isn't enough time to rehearse – only twenty days – and he hasn't worked
out his makeup yet – and maybe he should have two wigs . . . and he doesn't know the
cast, or the sets . . . he had been promised things in his contract. I reason a bit with him,
but without a great deal of enthusiasm – that he's allowing himself to make the worst
of the details, only nourishing his worry, etc. Then Richard says he is going to insist to
Arthur Lewis that the play should open later . . . I tell him Lewis is to be found at the
Imperial Hotel, Torquay.

27 February 1966
Let us go into the last chapter of this saga: not merely the saga of *Dylan*: but the saga
of Richard Harris . . . I know this may sound ridiculous, when I only have to look back
in this book to see absolutely firm decisions to have no more to do with him – followed
by apparently inevitable collapses . . . But the difference of *really* giving Richard rope

---

1. Ivan Passer (1933–), film director.

enough to hang himself, and really standing by and watching him do it – rather than (as earlier this year) cutting off on intuition, or even just umbrage at delays, phone calls not made, etc. . . . In this sense, under everything, I was aware of going through a ritual – in which my chief fear indeed was of the ritual *not* working itself out.

In the morning Stephen phoned me. I had no news, so he asked me if I'd like him to call Richard and make a date. I said yes with relief . . . and after this I think I must have spoken to Tim, who suggested we might come and see the model. But he had to go out at 7.30.

Stephen called me back: Richard could not manage to meet before 6 p.m. . . . A typical pronouncement – from anyone else absurd, of course, but absolutely characteristic of Richard, who will always want to make a situation *worse* – i.e. he wants to meet, but on the other hand is not going to be pushed into altering his life-routine or commitments a single jot, thus, by his Irish logic, all the delays for which he has been responsible become the responsibility of someone else . . . Otherwise Richard sounded, Stephen said, quite okay – though as if *hunted* – *pursued* . . . I thought I'd call him direct. I did so, and it was all confirmed – a tight manner, not offensive though, and seemingly reasonable, beyond the fact that he could not see me before six. I explained about Tim . . . and he said yes it was a pity: he would like to see the model. I phoned Tim. Tim had to go (to work) at 7.30. But Tazeena [Firth, co-production designer] would be there. And we agreed that to run through the designs etc. might be a good way of edging our neurotic star into action . . . At this stage, I certainly hadn't accepted that the project could never be . . . Back to Richard, and I said that if we could leave for Richmond at six we'd still have an hour with Tim before he had to go. Why couldn't Tim change his appointment, Richard wanted to know? I allowed myself, consciously, a flash of the kind of reproof I knew Richard would bite on – 'Other people have lives to lead too, you know . . .'

He bit, of course; for even as Richard makes these outrageous demands, he cannot bear any insinuation that he is going beyond what is normally and naturally his right.

The Dylan *projects were finally to be abandoned when Richard Harris walked out.*

11 March 1966

O Blessed Leisure! But now to see if I have the relaxation and the discipline to use it with enjoyment. Long chatty lunch with Jill Bennett at the Escargot: run through the Harris saga . . . she had observed him in dreadful behaviour at the Garden Restaurant recently. (An interview with R.H. giving his account of *Dylan* in the *Standard* yesterday . . . must get!) . . . Jill repeats again that George said we should get married the last time she saw him.

12 March 1966

The new Reisz residence: a handsome Victorian residence, tastefully and extravagantly altered . . . I am shown round the house by Karel and Betsy. It really is simple and nice, and doesn't look showy, but the structural alterations – the open dining room, necessitating steel construction, putting a pillar down to the basement to take the weight of the house – must have been hugely costly. No wonder Karel feels tense under his plumping exterior . . . We end up lunching at the White Tower, with Sophia Loren symbolically lunching in the same room . . . A little interchange takes place towards the end of the meal which spotlit the intolerably smug and pretentious aspect of Karel now – he suddenly remarks that Anthony [Page]'s agent has written asking if he can be put on Film Contract's list of directors: Karel asks my opinion but comments, in a summing up, *exclusive* tone, 'I think we'll try him . . .'.[1] Intolerable, stuck up bastard, I thought. Betsy's reaction to hearing of my Cinerama offer is predictably to say – you see, you both could be famous and secure. Karel, on the other hand, makes little dismissive facetious jokes. Back home: phone calls from Anthony Page, spinning on about his involved ups and downs with John Osborne and David Merrick – and from Irving Schneider, [for] whom I promise to contact Fugard. Trapped, trapped . . . Evening with Jocelyn: what is there to say about this good woman?

14 March 1966

Rex and Rachel press me to go to the Connaught to see *Nelson* with a select gathering. Secretly my most pressing inducement to go (would you credit it?) is the news that Warren Beatty (with Leslie Caron) will be there . . . Go into town, then drop into the first two-thirds of *Jules et Jim*. Once more I am astonished at the flair and originality of the shooting and editing . . . there are deeper levels Truffaut doesn't explore, but what style! Oskar Werner so good I am inclined sentimentally to regret not speaking to him in Foyles on Saturday.

The Connaught: preposterous, phoney . . . Naturally Warren Beatty doesn't appear. A glib, poor play: badly directed. Actors really aren't any good without a good director.

10 April 1966

The total collapse of many days, dating I suppose from the reaction after intense work on *The White Bus*; the anti-climax of *Dylan*; the growing sense of alienation; awareness of conflict with all around – without quite the compensating sense of real or lasting adequacy in myself. How intensely autobiographical *The White Bus* has turned

---

1. L.A. played a barrister in Page's *Inadmissible Evidence* (1967), and a Gestapo lawyer in Page's television production of David Mercer's *The Parachute* (1969). The cast also included Osborne and Jill Bennett.

out to be! In fact when I think about it, I wish vaguely I had been able to make it personally expressive in a more complete way – including particularly that consumer-goods section, which suffered from weakness in the shooting, then exhaustion and weakness at a particular editing stage . . . My chief creative problem undoubtedly remains this one of *being* essentially a reactor: unable to function fully alone, or at script stage, therefore dependent on collaboration to a huge degree . . . unable to read scripts even without that detailed and creative collaboration they need. Considering the comparatively little I have achieved, it is remarkable in fact that I should have the reputation or regard that I have – to be in a position for instance of having offers, or at least enquiries, from both Cinerama and Mosfilm!

30 April 1966
A week in Prague: staying rather unsatisfactorily since Monday with Milos – unsatisfactory because it's far out, his study (where I am sleeping on the usual hard couch) is full of his things, and no room for me to unpack, spread out, feel at ease, to write, order breakfast, lie down, etc. Milos is a late-hour man, and a late-riser, whereas I am the opposite. Everybody couldn't be nicer, couldn't be kinder: if it all makes me somehow aware of my own impoverishment, that can't be helped.

The White Bus was shown at the Film Club yesterday. It wasn't (of course) the ordered, rather ceremonious, friendly occasion I had imagined, but a late, untidy, hot, crammed occasion, with a humourless lady translator fighting to make herself heard over the English dialogue, in a way that completely destroyed the atmosphere. Mirek and I watched from the side: just as the Civil Defence sequence was coming up, a figure detached itself from its seat and was making for the exit, when it came up against Mirek and myself – it was poor Nemec,[1] who then had to stand through the rest of the film in unease and discomfort! I'm pleased that I don't take umbrage or get upset by these kind of misadventures – chiefly perhaps from people I respect (the bad manners of Peter Brook and Tony Richardson are something different).

Anyway, reactions seemed favourable.

21 June 1966
I've lost heart in recent weeks and let this diary fall – part of a general, neurotic recession from life – ever since *Dylan*, ever since the definitive exit of Richard from my life. It's a melancholy period, of wasted time and squandered opportunites.

---

1. Whose *Diamonds of the Night* (1965) was photographed by Ondricek.

*Not quite 'wasted', as he was in Chichester directing Tom Courtenay and Celia
Johnson in a Festival production of Chekhov's* The Cherry Orchard *that opened on
19 July. Making his professional debut was Ben Kingsley who, to work with Anderson,
had turned down a recording contract with the Beatles manager, Brian Epstein:
'I had auditioned for a festival theatre in the south of England. There was a Chekhov
play and a Shakespeare play . . . One of the directors was Lindsay Anderson. He's a
genius. A colossus. He had made all sorts of amazing things. You could say Lindsay
Anderson tipped the balance.' (Atlanta Journal, 26 December 2003)*

22 June 1966

NAG'S HEAD, CHICHESTER: Ten days into *The Cherry Orchard*. It isn't working . . .
nothing is working as a matter of fact – who am I and what am I here for? *Beastly*
rehearsal room and IMPOSSIBLE FRAGMENTED CONDITIONS – rehearse bits, then
run; the actors unable to consolidate; and the whole thing taking place within an alien
tradition, and alien, un-SERIOUS atmosphere.

I've landed myself right in the middle-class middlebrow area of English theatre,
where people work exclusively in the realm of effect, of technique . . . It is all thin and
meaningless; a sort of conjuring trick. Perhaps I'm just (also?) fed up with theatre.
I begin to understand how the extreme subjectivity of my approach (to everything)
makes cinema a better medium. Also the prime fact: never to do a play I haven't cast
myself, or at least only with a thoroughly congenial company. Here Hugh Williams,
John Standing – every fibre in me shrieks 'false', 'non-actor' – the moment they open
their mouths . . . Celia is 'divine' as they say – genuinely charming and witty and with
a most sensitive intuition . . . But it will remain on a home-counties level. And Tom
[Courtenay]? Well he *is* a nice lad, but he doesn't develop imaginatively, isn't too con-
vincing talking in terms of *ideas* – intellectual terms, that is. Is he really a character
actor? I feel Victor Henry would have done it better . . . And oh dear – Catherine
Willmer! Well that is *my* mistake.

26 June 1966

Afternoon went with Fiz to talk *Cherry Orchard* music with Mischa. Somehow inevitably he had done no work, found no pieces, didn't know the text, and was totally, dep-
ressively lacking in vitality . . . I become more than ever aware of my own need for vital,
stimulating collaborators . . . I had hard thoughts about Mischa: including not working
with him again.

6 July 1966

Dine with Anthony and Fiz to drinks at Alec Guinness's[1] at Petersfield ... A beautiful house, one of those impeccably ordered, every square inch telling of a refined and cultivated taste. On the way, Anthony recounts his rebuff by Bill and Desmond,[2] after long consultations about what he might do at the Court. Life plays a splendid trick of irony when Guinness tells us he is going to Paris tomorrow to try to persuade Simone Signoret[3] to play Lady Macbeth with him – at the Royal Court! under Bill's direction[4] ... Guinness couldn't be more charming, though always with a rather tense, guarded, defensive *politesse* that makes relaxation difficult. It's hard to know whether he *really* wants to listen to anything one has got to say. Certainly his attention soon wanders.

Alec pressed us to a barbecue dinner, during which it rained and we all fled indoors, then pressed me to stay the night so that Fiz and Anthony could drive straight back to town. I couldn't refuse – and wasn't too averse anyway. Slept in the exhibition guest's room, with two early Lownes, fitted carpet in own bathroom and lavatory, and impeccable toilet articles down to the new American toothbrush ... How do people *live* like this?

Boiled eggs for breakfast and driven back to the Minerva by Alec's affable young chauffeur from Stoke-on-Trent, who never goes to the theatre but prefers a good film.

8 July 1966

A run-through in the afternoon. Tom driven to despair by sudden attack after the morning run-through of *Macbeth,* by Michael Benthall, accusing him of not 'thinking' – 'Why are you so modern?' Well he *is* of course, and peculiarly un-technical, one would almost say un-*imaginative*? I don't honestly feel we have got far with Trofimov, and certainly Tom has made no great attempt to create the tight, somewhat inhibited character I had suggested – perhaps he is really only able to play characters fairly closely through his own personality.

9 July 1966

I had a good go with Tom this afternoon, now recovered from his go with Benthall, and we took the end of Act II to pieces, and found an overall dynamic for it ... A temporary illusion of progress?

---

1. Guinness made his Royal Court debut in September 1963 in Ionesco's *Exit the King.*
2. Desmond O'Donovan, then and briefly co-associate director of the Royal Court.
3. French actress (1921–1985). Oscar winner for *Room at the Top.*
4. This had 32 sell-out performances from 20 October 1966. A bright-lights, bare-sets production that infuriated the critics.

23 July 1966

Today the *Daily Express*, lying open on Mum's bed when I went in after a good, pill-assisted sleep – announced STAR'S WIFE AFRAID OF HIM, or some such . . . Elizabeth, suing Richard for divorce, has applied to the court for an injunction, forbidding him to molest her, forbidding him to remove the children from England . . . blaming drink, which drives him berserk, and irresponsibility . . . the housekeeper also testifying that Richard's behaviour has on occasion terrified the children . . . I wonder mildly how the balloon went up? . . . The injunction served on him in Paris: 'This is the unhappiest day of my life,' he says . . . 'I treated her like a flower . . .'

Went over to Chichester this afternoon, then took the train to Hove, and spent the evening with Oscar. Usual skimpy meal from Eileen [Oscar's wife].

25 August 1966

To pick up again . . . ? In Rome: once again at Bruno and Lorenza's but in no state of abso-lute fatigue, near desperation as I was in 1962 when I limped here after the shooting of *This Sporting Life* . . . *The Cherry Orchard* and *The White Bus* have been good, con-firming experiences. In a strange way, *The Cherry Orchard* most of all . . . I find it hard to say why . . . A difficult assignment – in terms of casting, in terms of staging, in terms of rehearsal time; but in my assessment, all limitations duly considered, successfully carried out . . . The *personality* – rhythm, feel of the production – I like: the grace and elegance of Alan [Tagg]'s designs (which nobody noticed), the wit and style of Celia's playing – in general, a directness, clarity, truthlessness in the style which has led me, more consciously than ever before, to a sense of my own personality and *gift* as an artist – making no great claims – but with a satisfying sense that this is something I *can* do, and also that this is at least the basis of what I believe in in the theatre – without which it is just a waste of time and money and trouble.

Before going down to Chichester for the last weekend, I took Tereza to see *A Bond Honoured*[1] at the Queens' National Theatre season. Note to start with that our front row Dress Circle seats cost 35/-: an immediate indication of the type of show we were about to be given. As was the case. The *pretence* of a direct, unnaturalistic production, which in fact substituted its own kind of theatrical gloss, on a sort of fake-Brechtian presentation. Nothing was really true or violent: Bob Stephens quite miscast as the ruthless egoism-preserving hero, and very false, as was Maggie Smith . . . But basically I fault John Dexter, obsessed with manner, and never really confronting the problems of the play – much more concerned with 'getting away with them' . . . And overall, the sense of a now-developed 'National Theatre style', deriving strongly I suppose from John himself – a style of effect and decoration, a certain intellectual pretentiousness,

---

1. John Osborne's version of a play by Lope de Vega.

a lack of truth. Of course it's Bourgeois Theatre again. I made yet another 'never again' decision. Never again, that is, just hoping against hope, or for 'interest', *not* to see *Royal Hunt* or *A Flea in Her Ear* or *Othello* . . . it just costs too much, and isn't worth it.

Yes, well, Chichester was rich, not just in the sense of accomplishment, but in the sense also of self-fulfilment through a kind of gift for leadership, for inspiring, out of my own genuine feeling for '*ensemble*'. Youngsters: *Charles Bowden*. He was the lad who stumbled downstairs when I arrived – in his pyjamas – then offered me a cup of coffee while deploring the fact that Macbeth was not being played by Jack Palance. *David Sterne* the fugitive from Sandhurst: he did talk a lot, but amused me with a certain shrewdness – and cried on my shoulder as we said goodbye . . . Not that I think any worse of him for that! *Gordon Reid*: a *good* little actor, which sounds patronising, but isn't meant to be, and I mean good. *Ben Kingsley* and his wife *Angela Morant*: a sweet couple and serious at their jobs.

27 August 1966

Lorenza having discovered that this is the last Saturday of the month, and that on this day entrance to the Vatican is free – we decided to go . . . *The Vatican*: It did assert itself, though as usual the crowds and the world and my own obsessive and trivial subjectivity made it difficult for the greatness really to work on me. But we saw the Raphaels and the Sistine Chapel (which I had imagined smaller and darker) and the Borgia apartments . . . and something of the magnitude and the vitality of the Renaissance imagination and spirit came alive to me. But how ignorant and trivial it is easy to be!

To the airport after lunch: Dado, Bruno's 'difficult' son, standing by, with all his self-contained sensitivity, as we cleared the plates and humped my valise down the stairs. He will receive no record of the Animals[1] from me! A delayed and slow flight via Florence: marvellous approach to this fantastic city by air. Naturally no festival people there or enquiry desk, etc. By bus to Venice [where he was serving on the jury of the Venice Film Festival]. To the Lido. The Grand Canal, yes, superb: though gnawing hunger and irritation tended to mar the aesthetic and historic thrill.

28 August 1966

I can't see the sea from the room, only tennis courts, and the poached eggs I order for breakfast are little round balls . . . Out on the beach, the Loperts[2] re-encountered . . . torn away from Ilya Lopert's repeated description of how he was indirectly instrumental in getting *Tom Jones* made, and how Tony has insulted him ever since, etc. . . .

---

1. Rhythm and Blues rock band powered by singer-songwriter Alan Price.
2. Ilya Lopert, produced David Lean's Venetian romance, *Summer Madness* (1955).

To grisly jury meeting where I seem to be surrounded by smooth (*Bassani*[1]) or nervous conformists, *Lewis Jacobs*[2] simple, and old *Lev Kuleshev*[3] courteous and gaga ... feel very despondent ... Evening opening performance: Beckett's *Play*, which is made incomprehensible by noise of late-comers, usherettes' torches, then storm of whistling, booing and slow hand clapping – which gave a certain avant-garde dignity to the occasion! Then Roger Corman's[4] *Wild Angels*, a shallow, melodramatic certainly vital piece of work, but preposterous ... its chief virtue I suppose was at least a kind of realistic dirt and scruffiness.

31 August 1966

See again *Courage Every Day*, this time with French titles: the film seems clearer, also in a way less specific than I had first thought ... The idealist revolutionary who wants/ needs to live in a revolutionary situation, and finds himself bugged by 'The long littleness of life'. What remains so touching and good is the fine, moral integrity of style.

Evening: *Battle of Algiers*.[5] An *impressive* film: fine reconstructions, not great and epic but quality.

1 September 1966

I walk up and down the beach with Ilya Lopert, who is pleased to use me as a sounding board for his admissions of whoredom, his denunciations of Tony Richardson and Albert Finney (who has a budget of $450,000 for *Charlie Bubbles*, having started negotiations with United Artists, then dropped them without communication ... 'I told Michael Medwin, whom I adore, you're a stupid cunt to produce this picture without being paid a penny,' etc.) – but when a minion interrupts our 'conversation' with news of a call from Paris, Ilya is off without a look or a word in my direction ... Everyone, here more than in most places, is locked in his own obsession, his own concerns. How can real relations, or art impinge in the slightest? It would be odious if one took it seriously. But hey for the sun and the crisp water.

In the evening Conrad [Rook]'s *Chappaqua*,[6] which does not set afire, and I find very hard to assess: a brilliance of handling – particularly Robert Frank's camera; an uneven quality of visions, perhaps insufficiently *presented*, but what the hell, one must

---

1. Georgio Bassani (1916–2000), writer; credits include Antonioni's *I Vinti* (1953) and Visconti's *Senso* (1954).
2. American film historian.
3. Russian film-maker (1899–1970).
4. American poet, film-maker (1934–).
5. *La Battaglia di Algeri*, Gillo Pontecorvo's film about Algerian terrorists bombing for independence.
6. Drug-addiction film named after the town near where Rooks was born.

be on its side. Lewis Jacobs: 'He's a fake, an imposter: I've made Hallucination films myself . . .'

5 September 1966

Jury meeting got more support for *Chappaqua* (self, Butor and Bantesek) than I thought . . . Strangely (and rather sadly) we were all against *Au Hasard Balthazar*;[1] this let us in for an interminable, hectoring interpretation by Bassani, including a long dissertation on Bresson's affinity with Morandi. . . . This jury service is really unpleasant if one doesn't respect one's colleagues.

10 September 1966

Took off by motor boat at 8.30 to the Isle of St Giorgic, where we were closeted till 5 on jury discussions. A happy end to the Festival provided by a list which corresponded *exactly* to the list I had sketched in three days ago.[2] Not achieved without some queasy moments of course, though in fact the discussions were confused, the results achieved by talk and agreement and vote-juggling.

30 September 1966

Pick up my visa finally at the ungracious Polish Embassy – though the wretched man behind the desk does his best to be pleasant . . . No, that was Thursday . . . start again . . . Tube to Piccadilly Circus, my sudden yen for a pair of brown Chelsea boots must go unsatisfied: none at Simpsons, and in Bond Street am told the firm has gone out of business. Hatchards, and buy Bill Brandt's book, and an historical-gossip book, *The Mistresses*, which I send to Mum at the Old Hall . . . In the Brighton Arcade, an Anderson tartan scarf and a Kashmir pullover for Tereza . . . Via Carnaby Street, and various union-jack pop-articles for presents . . . Pick up framed Conrad's photo . . . then to Anglo Preview Theatre where Oscar and I view *Ride of the Valkyries*.[3] I could rejoice I suppose at the utterly disastrous amateurism of this: it is impossible to say anything good about it . . . I tell him the only hope for it is to give it to a good professional editor, and devise a consistent, blanket music-track. But God knows really what the ultimate fate of the trilogy will be.

---

1. Bresson's film of Morandi's tale of the work-life and death of a donkey.
2. *The Battle for Algiers* won the Golden Bear for Best Film. A Jury Prize to *Chappaqua*.
3. Peter Brook's contribution to the Shelagh Delaney trilogy.

Taking with him David Sherwin's re-drafted script of Crusaders, *Anderson travelled to Warsaw to direct Poland's most celebrated actor in a production, in Polish, of John Osborne's* Inadmissible Evidence, *designed by Jocelyn Herbert. Despite the bureaucratic red-tape and his being arrested outside the Communist Party Headquarters, the play opened successfully at the Theatre Wspolczesny on 13 December 1966.*

3 October 1966

First day's rehearsal today: only four hours a day possible – 10 till 2. Everyone is paid so little for everything, that they all seem to be doing about three jobs (theatre, radio, TV) at the same time. No hanging around for friendly chats: the moment they sense they're finished – they're off like whippets. I am appalled.

5 October 1966

Arrested this afternoon, taking pictures of the exterior of the Communist Party Headquarters – a heavy lumpish building, rows and rows of windows set in a heavy concrete framework, in the middle of Warsaw. No doubt my behaviour was suspicious – for who would ordinarily spend five minutes training a camera on such a negative, ugly piece of architecture? (And in a way their suspicions were correct, for my impulse was antagonistic; I couldn't think of anything else to photograph in the featureless streets, and I only waited so long in the hope of getting an interesting group of passers-by on the pavement dominated by that implacable facade.)

Even this far after Stalinism one is still apt to be self-conscious using a camera on the streets of an Eastern European country, and I wasn't really surprised when two policemen materialised (in their military-type uniforms) and motioned me kindly to step off the street, into an alley that led to a courtyard. I looked around, and noticed, standing off with a kind of shifty aggressiveness, a rat-like civilian whom I surmised had emerged from Party Headquarters to report my suspicious actions to the police. The policemen of course didn't speak English, nor did the dark-suited individual who appeared from nowhere and attempted to question me. My name? Was I tourist? I told him, no, I was working at the Wspolczesny Theatre. Documents? I told them my passport was at the Grand Hotel. Why was I photographing that building? Did I know what it was? I did, but thought it better to say merely that it was an interesting example of Warsaw architecture. This rather stumped them. There seemed nothing to say except to ask again for my documents.

It went on for some time: I began to realise that my interrogators were at more of a loss than I was. What were they to do? The trouble-maker from Party Headquarters was demanding some action, but perhaps they didn't have the right to arrest me.

If they marched me round to the hotel they might get into trouble, and if they just let me go they might get into trouble. There was only one thing to do. They asked me for my documents again.

After ten minutes or so of this, a new plan was formulated. I was asked to take a stroll with one of the policemen, while the dark-suited bureacrat crossed the road to Party Headquaters, presumably to telephone. My custodian offered me a cigarette; we walked down to the street corner; he chatted away in Polish. Round us, on the opposite side of the street, little groups of policemen now stood and observed us. We strolled back, my policeman anxiously preserving a relaxed, friendly pace (when I stepped out briskly, he asked me not to hurry). We got back to the scene of my arrest, and he offered me another cigarette, my camera still round my neck. A car drew up with two more policemen. Still no one could speak English and no one knew what to do. I was again asked for my documents.

It was really a question of responsibility. At last the two new arrivals decided to act. I was asked (instructed?) to get into the car. We drove to the hotel. I got out and went straight to the desk. Behind me I heard one of the policemen anxiously asking the porter: 'Does this man live here?'

The comedy didn't quite end when I got my key. 'I'm going to my room to get my passport.' The manager (cropped grey hair like a Prussian) clucked officiously. 'No, no, you cannot. You are in custody. Follow me please.' We trooped up the stairs to his office. He sat down at his desk, picked up the telephone, and put in a call to the reception desk we had just left. Meticulously, relishing his little moment of authority, he jotted down the details I had been giving everyone for the last half-hour. 'Anderson, Lindsay. Room 613. Theatre Wspolczesny.' He looked up at me. 'You are a British subject?'

'Of course I'm a British subject.'

The play opened on 13 December 1966, with Tadeusz Lomnicki as Bill Maitland, Mieczyslaw Pawlikowski as Hudson, Mieczyslaw Gajda as Jones and Zofia Saretok as Shirley. At the 7th National Congress of the Polish Communist Party in 1975, Lomnicki was elected a member of the Central Committee and took the position of artistic and managing director of the Wola Theatre. Anderson declined further invitations to work with him.

6

If . . . .

Stand up! Stand Up! For College,
    Each manly voice upraise;
Clasp each the hand of brotherhood,
    And raise the roof with praise.

And when these days of school are past,
    Though near we be or far,
We'll stand again for College
    Who made us what we are.

('The College Song' by Anderson and Sherwin)

From letter to David Sherwin
(*on* The Crusaders, *the screenplay that became* If . . . .)

6 *November 1966*

Dear David – Thanks for the phone call: and also for the new selection of notes.
As I think we agreed, the problem with them seems to be the lack of an organising
principle: and also a somewhat *literary* style, which makes them excellent often
on the page, genuinely poetic and suggestive, but sometimes in a way that doesn't
translate into images or drama: I will try to be more specific about this later . . . But
I do think that writing them has been valuable if only because they do suggest the
opening of a more poetic, less axe-grinding and I think less sentimental attitude to
the subject. But plainly the time has come to consider *form* a bit, i.e. who are the
characters in this story; how do they relate; what is happening at the beginning,
middle and end; what are the main incidents?

    I have read again the two scripts I've got. Interestingly, the first (dated 1960) is
understandably a bit . . . shall we say immature: bad on construction, and very

romantic-sentimental in a touching, adolescent sort of way. But some of its scenes are good material – funnily enough I prefer the scene with Mr Lord and Garibaldi, to Mr Stewart and Carlyle (that Carlyle prose is incomprehensible to me).

– A little bit about Fisher and his 'Holy-Holy' stunt (a good character?).
– Wallace and the talk about death – transformed later to Mick and Johnny: but I quite like Wallace; perhaps there should be all three of them in this conversation . . . Maybe it's a pity to lose this Wallace altogether? I had an idea it might be he who was after Bobby Phillips and ends up being expelled.
– Willis and his punishment shower: I know this becomes Mick, maybe usefully, I don't know. It could be Peanuts, who remains to me an interesting character, largely because of that telescope scene.
– The cross-country run is good: particularly that workman on the railway embankment (an instance of a kind of invention that *is* visual and economic and somehow says a lot about the peculiar world of school, momentarily related to commonsense everyday reality: with pregnant class overtones).
– That scene late on in the pub with the lager glasses, and the following smashing of glass is rather good: I don't know if any use to us, but rather good . . .

In the most recent script there is obvious improvement in construction; but I think we're agreed that too much has been lost in order to achieve a tight narrative involving really only Mick and Johnny; and of course there remains the basic flaw of Glenda, still entirely sentimental in conception – and having become the basic subject of the whole story.

Apropos Glenda: it seemed to me that perhaps the best introduction to her might be on the afternoon when Mick and Johnny cut loose from the football match and go into town, using maybe the new motor-cycle idea: Johnny and the salesman chase after him; Johnny runs one way and finds him; Mick yells, 'Get on the back' – and they ride off – they both get carried away by the excitement – drive out of town and stop at a transport caff – where Mick makes mock-passes at the girl dishing out the egg and chips; they hitch a ride back to town maybe in a truck, leaving the bike behind . . . and maybe later *this* is the misdemeanour that catches up with Mick when the salesman and a policeman arrive to interview his housemaster . . .

Maybe Mick returns to the caff later: it could be when he's left alone on the visiting day; and maybe Glenda seduces him . . . anyway it's having sex, probably for the first time, but not Romeo and Juliet.

It seems to me that the film should start at the school, and in the school; because that is the world of the film; not coming into it with scenes in the 'real' world first. For instance, the titles could be over shots of the empty school, details of chapel, desks, gym, dormitories, passages, etc., with at the end a jump cut (for instance) from a deserted corridor to it suddenly full of boys, shouts, trunks being dragged, etc. . . .

'Peanuts Observatory' is a nice scene, well written. 'Mick's Dream' goes on a bit, doesn't it? (How do you film: 'Mick loved him, wished to blow his nose and cut it off for an organ pipe'?) Where the hell is that dream about becoming an enormous leg – or have I imagined it?! It seemed to me better: but again was it susceptible to being shown on film? (' . . . At the bottom of a mile-high cliff filled with Nazi soldiers all pointing rifles at tiny figures at the top. Grey skyscrapers on the top of the cliff. Mick was in Russia.' Oh yes?)

Now what about this Warden. Actually I prefer the suggestion of the Headmaster in the first script: younger and specious, I imagine. Modern and 'enlightened': glib. Probably because he relates more to my headmaster at Cheltenham. But this Warden could be interesting somewhere. Maybe he is the Chaplain? You have got a bit carried away by him: but the book-polishing idea could be good.

How can you possibly follow the explosion of the tree with a shot of the Warden's wife passing the chapel in which is being sung 'The Day Thou Gavest'? This doesn't make sense to me.

Karl Reinhof – an interesting cranky member of the staff. For a classroom scene I should think rather than in his home doing the pools.

Notes on the Changing-Room Bullying Scene. The names of the characters change so often I can't identify them with definite personalities. Who is *Hopkins*?

Dormitory scene with Fat Boy: good, worth fitting in if possible.

Mick's clean teeth: looks to me like another red herring.

Narrow country lanes: first part good, including hair twisting. I don't know about country lanes. How do you visualise showing that he wants to be a Bedouin?

The penknife: this becomes quite David Storey in its 'poetic violence'.

Electric machine: funny.

After Mick's expulsion (much better consider exactly *how* he is expelled: and *if*). What on earth is Glenda doing here? She is very persistent. What a peculiar end to the film: *is* it the end? Seems to me nonsense: the point of the wall of death – if indeed we use it – but the *idea* was the sudden violence, the explosiveness of image and sound.

You have (excuse me writing like a school report) a fecundity of imagination, but it seems to operate rather without organic sense, like a series of prose poems: or jottings for a script. Sometimes a whole idea is valuable, sometimes a couple of lines, sometimes nothing.

What is really wanted, if not a tidy 'skeleton', is some idea of the progression: and some key scenes – instead of a plethora of peripheral imaginings . . . For instance, do Stewart and Mick ever talk together? How is the whole idea of blowing up the tree invented, organised, executed; and what follows? Any structural ideas? You remember you thought of using songs as some kind of linking device: I expressed scepticism: have you still a place for the school song? What about the speech, or Founder's Day celebrations, with the visit of the Corporation members who provide an opportunity to demonstrate the social foundation and implication of the school?

Who are the principal characters? Warden; Housemaster; wife; Chaplain; what masters? Stewart – who else? Mick; Johnnie; Wallace; Peanuts; Stephans; Bobby Phillips; Barnes; Denson, etc., The Girl.

I think the houses should be separate: I suppose because they were at Cheltenham, but it seems to make it clearer.

I mentioned the idea of a Wallace who was after Bobby Phillips: I imagined Mick hearing a noise at night – going to see what it was, and finding Wallace with Bobby – (I don't know what Bobby feels about all this) – maybe telling him not to be a fool – sending him back to his own bed. Maybe he (Mick) would kiss Bobby before going . . . The Under-Housemaster playing Mozart on his gramophone.

I haven't mentioned, and I'm not sure if I should – what is the *theme* of this film . . . Maybe it can't be put down on a postcard . . . the image of a world: a strange sub-world, with its own peculiar laws, distortions, brutalities, loves . . . with its special relationship to a perhaps outdated conception of British society . . . its subjection of young minds to disciplines hardly related to the contemporary world; and to the domination of often freakish or deformed or simply inadequate 'Masters'.

From the two scripts, and from the notes, I find it difficult to get an absolutely consistent picture of Mick, whom I take to be the principal character. I suppose I see him as a lively, independent, anarchic character; who arrives at the end at an act of violent, poetic protest . . . But what precipitates this act? Has it something to do with the expulsion of Wallace (if you accept this idea)?

I am not quite sure where we are now with the Johnny-Mick relationship . . . the device in the most recent script whereby Johnny let Mick down because he was playing in a racquets match was shakey . . . after that there is the division because Johnny is made a prefect: is this still a basic feature? It may be: but then be careful the story doesn't get diminished into a conventional, 'personal' struggle between Mick and Johnny.

An early scene, first waking day maybe, should show the music master teaching the new boys the school song. 'The New Boy' should be a character. What is his name?

I don't very much like the juxtaposition of the naked H.M.'s wife with the military footsteps: isn't this a rather heavy symbol? (Maybe it depends 'how it's done'.)

'Field Day': some misdemeanour here might precipitate a beating for Mick. Anyway a funny and significant sequence is possible with this material.

I don't know if all this is much use. What is necessary now is to be CONCRETE. The truth is always interesting. And an overall conception, integrating detail with 'theme', 'story' or 'pattern', whatever you like to call it.

No word from Seth. The really universal problem in the world now is *time*: no one has time any more to do anything; let alone achieve the sustained concentration necessary to achieve something in terms of art.

I won't start about Poland: which is not a vital, exciting temperamental place, but a sluggish, drab, egocentric place, strangled in bureaucratic red-tape, with personal initiative and responsibility practically unknown . . . Everything takes an age, no one is paid enough: in other words what is known as an 'interesting experience'.

1 January 1967
Saw the New Year in without ceremony – at Sandra's party, to which I went with Jocelyn – surrounded by rather boring architects and their women stubbing their cigarettes on to balloons.

David Sherwin and John Howlett came at 3.00 or 3.30 to talk about *Crusaders* . . . Outline, characters, relationships of this remain appallingly fluid. I'm afraid I am too subjective to be a writer; and I don't trust myself: their problem is opposing me with enough confidence. Now it ends with close-up of Johnny's hand transfixed with Mick's knife . . .

2 January 1967
Evening: dinner with Albert Finney and Michael Medwin[1] in the restaurant of Albert's apartment – or self-service flat-block – in Mayfair . . . At the pub at the bottom of Park Lane where I met Michael, there was some smart young functionary from Universal, talking about the music and album rights for the *Charlie Bubbles* score – which is being written by Mischa Donat! I experience familiar nausea at the jargon and calculations.

Albert, now in his eleventh or twelfth week of shooting on *Charlie Bubbles*, is remarkably spry, on top of it, un-neurotic, though *sensibly doubtful* – talking a lot about movements, cuts and reverses. I am interested, and in a way quite pleased to hear his dissatisfaction with Peter Suschitzky – not with the work, but with the coldness that I suspected . . . According to Michael he drives a hard bargain too – at £200 a week!

4 January 1967
Lunched with Tony Richardson: fetched and transported luxuriously to St Peter's Square by Tony's limousine . . . Arrived to find lights and cables outside: in Tony's drawing room tests in progress – I look in and catch a glimpse of those cocky British

---

1. When Seth Holt dropped out of the *Crusaders* project, it was taken up by Finney and Medwin.

technicians – feel immediate nausea . . . Tony downstairs in his aviary, feeding his birds. We have a drink: Tony in his wholly alienated form, everything discussed in that bored, flat tone that drains every subject of significance or feeling. 'Nobody wants to be in this film' (*The Charge of the Light Brigade*): 'What are you doing now?' I mention the projects for the Polish and British documentaries – 'Why don't you make a classic?' – 'What kind of classic?' *Middlemarch*. I suppose he was thinking of Vanessa . . . Over lunch I started talking of the trilogy, and ideas of packaging, billing obligations – all dismissed by Tony as uninteresting, boring, etc. A passage which became quite nasty . . . He said Hollywood (from which he's just returned) was horrible: 'I saw your hero' – but he said no more of Richard, and of course I wasn't going to ask him . . . Tony is certainly impressive: the impressiveness of star personality, potent in its self-absorption, its continual exercise of power. But sterile and exhausting: and conversation is impossible when one becomes so overwhelmingly conscious that nothing is discussed for what it *is*: when everything becomes an issue of personal domination.

5 January 1967

Spent the day – twelve to six – with David Sherwin and John Howlett on *Crusaders*: working confusedly towards an outline at least and fixed characters . . . Seth Holt has never been in touch, in fact no communication whatever since I said goodbye to him in September outside Jaeger's – apart from a telegram to Warsaw 'writing soon' . . . I don't think Seth anyway would be much use to us . . . I feel the story, the style even, *is* shaping, but I find myself very confused, between epic, fantasist, liberal protest (an initial danger), etc. . . . I used to throw myself against reality, out of which I can create something – but to create that reality is very hard for me. I only seem able to work through some kind of dialectic.

28 March 1967

Somewhat exhausted after work on script [of *Crusaders*]. Final adjustments – David typing out – dictated hurried beginning to Speech Day sequence . . . also desperately copying titles for *Thérèse Desqueyroux*.[1]

Phoned by Liz Kustow, in a flap about her Donovan-Logue programme – involved in BBC bureaucratic complaints because she wasn't fulfilling her brief to do a programme on the sonnet. Liz came round, can't make out if she is slightly mad, just a bit clueless – or even (it struck me) fancies me. Then Oscar, with his typical edgy, nervy, irritating – *something*. We went to the Bistro in Finchley Road. I broached the subject of the trilogy, Brook, etc. And soon we were in the middle of a vexing row. 'You're like Pontius Pilate' . . . '*The White Bus* isn't Jesus Christ'.

---

1. L.A. wrote the English subtitles for Georges Franju's film of François Mauriac's novel.

In April, Anderson went to Warsaw to make Raz Dwa Trzy (The Singing Lesson),
*a twenty-minute film of drama students singing Polish folk songs intercut with
shots of everyday Polish life.*

2 May 1967

Sudden spasm of self-indulgence as I retired to bed last night prompted me to order
two boiled eggs and *café complet* . . . Do I get any closer to happiness these days? We
start shooting at the Contemporary Art Exhibition: tracking shot calls for six takes,
much to Sigmund's[1] disgust. I don't think Stasek is much of an assistant, which seems
borne out by delays when we go to shoot alienation close-ups of shop assistants (back
to *O Dreamland*: the figure in the carpet?). Lady manager of glass shop – catching on
– 'Is this positive or negative'? Rushes at the studio: the rain material: good, but actually a bit too 'abstract' in conception.

Distressed call from David Sherwin saying that Seth was refusing to sign the legalis-
tic document prepared by the lawyers and brilliant Robin Fox . . .

4 May 1967

Shooting: Pierre sings 'The Coat', which I find very poetic and suggestive the more I hear
it, and the enchanting Andrzej Nardelli sings 'Groszki' ['Sweet Peas'] . . . unit discipline
and communication become impossible, climaxing in the disappearance of the entire
unit after the first song – which has involved endless delays and unnecessary retakes. I
blow my top, and hate doing so, since it has to be at Sigmund. But the working atmosphere gets noticeably better – and 'Groszki' restores our sweet harmony. We shoot
'Groszki' with great care and concentration . . . Andrzej performs with splendid professionalism and breathtaking charm . . . This and 'Plaszcz' alone would make the film
remarkable I think. The students – our students – overall fantastically correspond,
poetically, to my ideal of charm, seriousness, sensitivity – young humanity at its sweet
best. I can't see how this film can be other than beautiful, and very poetic: really no
boring narrative or informational elements.

7 May 1967

A long, packed day at the school: Professor Sempolinsky arrives, fortunately a bit late:
also students . . . We have a second cameraman, a broad-faced, likeable young Pole. We
shoot a lot: a bit grabby; the Professor is impatient; the lights are terribly hot; we waltz
and waltz . . . raz, dva, tze . . . of course I can't direct it as I'd like. Everything takes too
long, and so the shooting has to go quickly. No food, Andrzej Nardelli brought a box of
cakes: Sigmund, Tony and I repair upstairs for a slug of whisky.

---

1. Zygmunt Samosiuk, cinematographer.

The students are really charming, excellent, good-mannered; hard-working. They are, like the young Czechs, the best possible advertisement for socialism. What will become of them? Nardelli has the most winning charm, Pierre unobtrusive, but splendid and strong on the screen; the simple Marian heroic in his handsome face and powerful build. End the day exhausted but feeling good work has been done.

14 May 1967
Tereza joins my lunch party. She has been crying, and wants to speak with me: I know what about . . . Later, while the others listen to records in my room, drinking champagne ordered by Sigmund, I walk outside with Tereza in the park and she tells me that she and Tadeusz will part: hints at his monstrous and cruel behaviour, though extraordinarily without rancour . . . She loves him but knows it is impossible . . . Well, I have really grown up or changed and to some extent hardened: I can only congratulate her: Tadeusz is so recognisably a monster – a hypocrite too. It *is* Sophie apparently. All part of the real sadness of life . . . Was the Tadeusz of *Pokolenie* just my own sentimental illusion: or the Richard I first knew? or Serge? Do they change? or did I lose my illusions?

15 May 1967
BACK – to no joy: but a world in some ways more alienating in its commercialism and self-imposed corruptions . . . In London even the film seems to lose substance. Too thin and 'humane': what would *Sight and Sound* or John Russell Taylor have to say about it? Nothing. It is too simple, too plain.

16 May 1967
Dramatic sudden immersion in the shit of Kellogg's, Universal-Seth-Memorial, Robin Fox, Royal Court and all the rest of it . . . the feeling growing of my inability to *cope* . . . to choose . . . to conduct a career which in any way satisfies me.

Morning inspecting [the] Kellogg's houses at Hatch End with Derek Banham and Larry Pizer. Can we shoot the Kellogg's [commercials] in nine days? I ought to write something about Poland, naturally people are just bored by it in conversations . . . but what desperate contrasts!

Lunch with David Sherwin, then joined by Michael Medwin and Albert Finney, at Escargot . . . Hear more about the Seth situation . . . He plainly is some very weird kind of neurotic – as I say to David later – with a sort of obsessive, paranoid quality . . . all the emphasis on one-way 'friendship' etc. . . . and no capacity to imagine the needs and complexes of others. Another grotesque failure.

Meeting with Memorial and Jay Kanter of Universal: respectful but of course not convinced or optimistic of *Crusaders'* capacity to attract exhibitors. How can I blame them? Albert Finney really impressive – generous, intelligent, dynamic and confident.

Whirl back to interview Kellogg's artists. WHAT A DAY. No wonder I collapse – David spending the night – to TV and records.

19 May 1967

David Sherwin arrives early morning – well 10.00: but I am not up . . . the idea of getting down to discussing *Crusaders*, rewrites etc. is really alarming and distasteful. Call from Albert to say that Universal are referring it to the Coast . . . to gauge possible TV returns . . .

Rush to Warners to meet David a quarter of an hour late for *Privilege*. A sad, compulsive, weird film. Sad because – can Britain not produce a new, thirty-one-year-old director who is not an adolescent? Peter Watkins plainly paranoid, with only the most tenuous connections with reality . . . Paul Jones a good-looking narcissist. It is an *auteur* film: i.e. compulsively personal. That is all.

Back to Dateline and work for four hours on *Valkyrie* music, splitting, trying, relaying. Let's face it: I *have* a gift for it . . . Was to have dined with Elizabeth Harris, but her uncle has died. For all my feelings about Richard, a good deal of my immediate acceptance of her invitations seems to be the sense of, the possibility of, renewed connection with him. 'We have scotched the snake: not killed it.'

20 May 1967

Lunch with David Sherwin – who stayed the night . . . We discuss Milton and Mozart (whom David likens to Gilbert and Sullivan!) . . . Finally get down to talk about the script. But full vitality is absent. There will be time.

22 May 1967

Start shooting Kellogg's. All seems slow and very British in padded comfortable way. Larry lights meticulously. But he is a nice, boring, at least quite unstimulating fellow. But I feel trapped – doing it for money – and quite incapable of pushing it on quickly. It has somehow to take its course. Fully resolve – am no good at commercials. Never was . . . Derek Banham says: 'We don't want these to be like commercials . . . that's why we ask people like you and Karel to do them . . . This is a family that ribs each other . . . a real family . . .' etc. I feel the shooting lacks Karel's conviction – and expertise . . . He 'believes' in the family, and he 'believes' in commercials in a way I can't.

It is peculiar about Larry – his total suburbanism . . . His responses to things are conventional – I mean even the idea of boys riding bikes with fishing-rods in their hands . . . and his rhythm rather constipated. Doesn't read the scripts or really think about what set-ups need to be done – which is boring for me! Camera operator is Frank – whose other name I forget – quite affable, but also suburban in approach and values. The *work* has no spark anywhere.

I was to have seen the Goldini production at the Aldwych with Jocelyn. But we were both so exhausted and fed up with theatre that we went to the Star Steak House, where we compared wounds.

24 May 1967

Shooting moves to Worthing . . . A hard day in that peculiar little hotel – no view of the sea – and the usual wild variations of light outside, from rain to sun, and incessant delays.

I stay at Warne's, the spacious, empty, ugly hotel just round the corner on the front – not without its reposeful, vacuumatic appeal. Clumps of old ladies, moneyed and upper-class, who sit together in the lounge and gossip animatedly about each other and nothing. That English world where all stern realities are dismissed: but under it the grim reaper neareth . . .

25 May 1967

The weather not favourable – nice very early, but by the time we get the camera on the beach, and Peter and Raymond, it is blowing hard – the sun has gone – and by the time we get the shots of them throwing stones, they are almost in the sea. I feel very impatient with the unit – but of course don't *drive* them correctly, being still infuriatingly dependent, as ever, on suggestions, co-operation, etc.

Slog it out in the hotel dining room: little Rupert 'difficult' – the American scriptwriter arrives just before lunch, with his glib, camp quips that make me more and more despondent.

Out on the beach I overshoot those set-ups – the kids finally running down onto a dark strip of sand. Raymond (a cheery little boy after all) sprinting out after his ball – as a result of which I miss the train I want up to town – and go in to Brighton in the bus with women and kids; very bad-tempered.

Anderson's Kellogg's commercials swept the board at the annual advertising awards. In 1968, his 'Fat Chef' (commercial for Alcan foil) won the Gold Award at the American Commercial TV Festival.

27 May 1967

Robbe De Hert,[1] the Antwerp Terror, came to breakfast – though that's an unkind reference, since I find him strangely touching, and for all his compulsive, obsessional egomania, somehow sympathetic. Undeniably attractive also, particularly in pictures – he is astonishingly photogenic . . . I don't know why, but I even found his advert mildly

---

1. British-born Belgian film-maker (1942–).

stimulating . . . We talked of his project, *The Bomb*,[1] and I tried to suggest a more satirical or ironic approach – but he is incapable of it. I can really only encourage – and leave it to Betsy (she has expressed her readiness to act in it).

Phone call from producer Michael Laughlin about his script *Skinner*, which turns out to be the work of Mike Sarne.[2] To tell me basically that the part has been offered to – naturally – Richard . . . I made noises of reservation – interestingly Richard had apparently reacted favourably to the mention of *my* name (and indeed why not?).

Anyway, after seeing Robbe off at Victoria – I let this jog me into sneaking into the New Victoria to see three-quarters of *Caprice* – the leaden Tashlin comedy Richard fled into after the *Dylan* debacle . . . Most curious . . . that familiar sensation of being unable to judge the performance of an actor one knows so well. Very uneasy performance really – curious, mock-posh voice, depriving the character of *any* reality, stiff. I notice he gets his shirt off four times – rather disgusting since he was in fine bodily shape. I reflect that this was while he was fucking right and left.

I read *Skinner* and amazingly – alarmingly enough – it is the story of a sadistic homicidal maniac . . . but thinly scripted – really only on a *Z-Cars* level . . . Should I not really have the firmness, on every level, to say an absolute NO? Yet I can't bring myself to wholly; I continue to flirt . . .

2 June 1967

Press on reasonably successfully with Cornflakes Complete Anglers, with two little boys looking through windows, coming in – Earl is charming, a really attractive little boy – Bobby Phillips?[3] a bit young . . .

Meet Milos, Ivan [Passer, film director] with Miriam [Brickman] and Betsy in Soho – Miriam immediately puts Milos in touch with Alan Arkin[4] – whom John Heyman, agent, had sworn was impossible to locate. We dine at the Escargot – the bill is £12.10 – no one says thank you. We are joined by Karel, who is friendly, affable . . . and adjourn to England's Lane . . . to which Alan Arkin is fetched. (After all the talk about affability etc. I find him rather 'close'; not particularly warm on impact. Maybe a bit somehow suspicious?) . . . Milos talks with him mostly; I with Ivan – about whom I realise we don't talk enough. After all, *his* film[5] was enormously praised; and *he* wants to make another! . . . They are all here on a weird invitation to see the Russian play *The Promise*,[6] which Frank Hauser directed so badly and so successfully – to be shot as an

---

1. *De Bom* (1969).
2. British film-maker (1934–).
3. The 'pretty boy' character in *If . . . .* , who would be played by Rupert Webster.
4. American actor (1934–).
5. *Intimni Osvetleni* (*Intimate Lighting*).
6. By Aleksei Arbuzov. The production starred Ian McKellen and Judi Dench.

English-language production in LENINGRAD! Of course it will never happen! . . . Karel, as I say, affable, unpretentious and nice . . . No one would know, and he would probably not acknowledge, that we are not really friends any more. But I feel it *absolutely*. The fact that he could take and read *Crusaders*, and make no comment, and have it returned in a plain envelope with no note, isn't merely inexcusable – it's a comment on the emptiness and basic unreality of all our 'friendships'.

5 June 1967
WAR STARTS IN THE MIDDLE EAST. Leon [Clore at Kellogg's] rushes plays his usual grunting approval, which always annoys me by its laziness – its absolute refusal to take the trouble even to think about what's been done – and its acceptance of 'We'll get away with it' as the highest standard required. The idea of making a film with him as producer – *All Neat in Black Stockings*[1] – is really unreal.

After rushes, to Memorial, and I am given a batch of letters from headmasters – my feelings about *Crusaders* compound of lazy fear now – but pressures have been generated.

Anderson flew to Poland to serve on the jury of the Cracow Film Festival and to work on the editing of The Singing Lesson.

8 June 1967
CRACOW: not fun quite like the luxury festivals – nor with the freshness of that first year at Pesaro . . . And of course the boring faces outnumber the friends . . . Slept in – or rather lazed in – since I can't manage to sleep late, till 12 or so – missing the Auschwitz excursion, but I really couldn't get up at 7 for it . . . Then Louis [Marcorelles, film critic]called and we strolled out . . . why do I get so irritated with the poor preposterous fellow? Chiefly I think because I don't want to be reduced to simply treating him like a child . . . 'You know Juleen says you think she's a goddess.' 'You should change your ideas and be prepared to make a cheap film.' 'You know Karel is very successful these days; why don't you ask him to help you . . .' etc., etc. Dine with Gene [Moskowitz] at excellent restaurant.

10 June 1967
I kick off by proposing [Walerian] Borowyck's *Rosalie* for the Grand Prix; and the US *Napalm* as runner-up: this, to be honest slightly against my better judgement, as I found *Rosalie* in fact rather theoretical; great refinement and sensitivity of style, but somehow unconvincing: anyway, *Napalm* took the majority, and the rival move to put

---

1. Susan George and Victor Henry starred in this tale of an amorous window cleaner, directed by Christopher Morahan after Lindsay turned it down.

the Russian whimsy *The Umbrella* into second place was defeated. No difficulty with Zygmund's *Byc*, the cartoon *Noah's Ark* and *Plaisir d'Amour* – that charming Czech sketch written by [Jiri] Trnka, of the passage and transience of love and life itself. We (Gene and I chiefly) managed to carry a Diploma for the Russian *Physicists* and also the exuberant Danish cartoon *Slambert*. Where is Britain? Poor and provincial with its sentimental, amateurish *Jemima and Jenny*, and typical Shell Film Unit tripe about River Pollution.

14 June 1967

To the studio where I press on with breaking down all school material. We discover the art gallery material is just *missing* – and another reel of shop material has been sitting in the projection box for God knows how long.

Make off to the airport at 11.15 – only to discover the plane is late by two hours – so I return to the studios. After my talking about the school films, Sigmund actually presents me to Marek Piwowski, the young fellow whose *Knaipa* film we much admired. He is agreeable, speaks English, but remains mysteriously 'closed' like so many of those Poles – it appears Sigmund may be working on a film about youth he is just going to start. Assure all that I will be returning at the start of July: and I think I must . . . otherwise in the end no doubt they'll do it themselves.

Back to Greencroft: dull post – Stanley Kauffmann offering me tutorial job in Yale or Harvard. Vladimir [Pucholt] is in town.

15 June 1967

Alas, how short-lived is the sensation of return; of that change of scene, of that slight sense of accomplishment, rather than of *rest* . . . Immediately I switch on the phone I am deluged. One of the first Pauline [Melville]: her Foreign Legionnaire lover had turned up again – had suddenly walked into a pub where she was sitting before going to a party . . . *coup de foudre encore* . . . he demanded that she should go off with him: she demurred, resisted, felt the irresistible impulse – but resisted it – or was she also playing a game – anyway she went off from him, caught a bus – and felt she had done the wrong thing . . . She had a phone number, but went to Southend for three days, then rang him up. He had left the day before. Wretchedness. She described how she felt she had made the wrong decision, even in the name of some kind of snobbery – what would her friends think? . . . A party she was at – Robert Stephens, and Maggie [Smith] and Joanie [Plowright], and Albie, where she has been wretched (was this the glamorous world for which she was turning down her feckless, impossible, crude lover?) – and had to go upstairs to howl till finally Maggie had come up to show her a back way out – to spare whom embarrassment? I hoped Albie would be better: she said he was worse – she had heard him say, 'I hope she hasn't slit her wrists yet.'

Welcome back to London camp . . . I told her to go off to Paris and not to wait for the boat train . . .[1]

I got to the London Pavilion a bit late . . . My taxi stopped by the railings, just where Vladimir was leaning against them, his back to me. He greeted me anxiously, with relief – he had been ten minutes late and was frightened I had left already – not his usual wide-smiling self. 'Lindsay, I have escaped . . .' I hadn't consciously formulated this thought, but it didn't surprise me. We walked up Shaftesbury Avenue, past the clothes shops and the record shops and the glossy eateries . . . My first comment was to tell him – 'Don't say escape: say *leave* . . .' It poured out from him as we walked . . . An impossible life, making not just comfortable life impossible, but even proper work, proper artistic development. He had read an essay by Capek on communism, which had been copied out and passed round from person to person (the artist, the thinker *can* directly influence: the responsibility *can* be a real one): 'What the communists want is not to make happiness: it is power.'

We ended up in the Shaftesbury Hotel: I suddenly remembered the Buttery where we used to go six years ago, when *Billy Liar* was on. It was still there. Vladimir wanted nothing – well, a fruit juice . . . He talked on . . . of course there was nothing to argue about. I put it to him that things were not perfect here – nowhere – but that was not the point.

He had thought it over; however practicable, he had a plan. He would get a job in a hospital, start to earn money, then train to be a doctor. Perhaps he would not act again. He'd be sorry, but then he can no longer act in Czechoslovakia – not creatively . . . We must have talked for a couple of hours: then we went to Better Books, and maybe more sympathetically than wisely I bought him two George Orwell Penguins: *Animal Farm* and *England Your England*. Then to Film Contracts where we saw the two Kellogg's I had not seen completed; then walked through Soho and Carnaby Street and Mayfair to London International, where we shook hands. He took off to catch his bus to Victoria, boyish in his check shirt: 'Lindsay, I feel strong because I can make this decision.' How can one argue with someone who, for good or ill, *must* be his own master – even if it means leaving mother, father, sister . . . There is an essential, direct purity about Vladimir (his quality with the camera of course) which carries a conviction beyond that of logic or intellect.

I went in to London International; and there they were: Robin Fox and Brian Maller with the Fox script of *Tree Frog*, vehicle for Robert Shaw . . . and a script of the French thriller which I've already turned down, *Praying Mantis*. Expensive dust.

This full day continued: taxi to Bedford Gardens, where I was met by Elizabeth [Harris], anxious to promote her scheme for getting a short film made about the Commonwealth expedition over the Asian highway . . . Elizabeth is good-hearted.

---

1. She did go after him, and she married him.

To bring Thursday to an end – no wonder I find London exhausting – on to the Court to see the Joe Orton double-bill with Jocelyn. Anthony and Miriam [Brickman] also there with two camp young men. I found the evening utterly horrible: interestingly the second play – *The Erpingham Camp* – was what remained of my idea for the 'holiday camp *Bacchae*' idea: not good: but both that and *The Ruffian on the Stair* badly directed by Peter Gill. Really awful, camp, done for the most superficial laughs, thin and self-satisfied. Michael Standing taking part: but not quite good enough, despite a certain attractive assurance. Certainly returning from Europe to this, and the encounter with Vladimir during the day, made the evening all the more mediocre, distasteful – in a word, crumby.

Finished off with dinner with Jocelyn at Nico's. Funny story from Jocelyn about Larry asking her advice about taking a lordship! He received a stone, of course!

16 June 1967
David Sherwin and I went to Dulwich [scouting for locations for *Crusaders*], where we saw the headmaster – name forgotten of course, but like his school not quite a top-drawer man – then were shown round by Mr Cook was it? An ex-advertising teacher, and their dramatic enthusiast: suitably struck by my name etc. . . . pleasant enough fellow; but the school not better than B+. A mixture of styles: the Victorian–Italianate Renaissance style of the main buildings striking: interiors without much atmosphere: boys a bit sloppy. Not really good.

Evening: viewing of *O Dreamland, Every Day Except Christmas, White Bus* (Stephen, Albert, David). I am impressed and rather moved by *Every Day*: it is a bit over-long; but so concentrated and tenderly aspiring in its lyric style – almost wanting to create a one-man revolution of love – one feels it.

Afterwards straggle indecisively, then make for the Kebab House. I crunch down on a stone, I suppose, and sickeningly break a tooth; decayed remnants in my left upper-jaw.

Incidentally, I've been maliciously pleased that Danny Kaye had deserted J. Clements at Chicester!

19 June 1967
Michael Medwin and I set off for our 12 p.m. meeting with John van Eyssen at Columbia. Smoothly, with a few tepid criticisms, *Crusaders* is accepted – but Van Eyssen is concerned obviously to cut an influential figure, and I am raising no premature cheers. It all seems very unreal – our expensive lunch: GULLS' EGGS AND LOBSTER – and discussion about the Royal Box, costumes for the Derby, etc. Albert, also at the meeting, smokes a cigar, and puts another in his pocket. He enjoys it.

(I pulled my tooth out over the kitchen sink on Saturday: it gives no trouble.)

I rush to Holborn and the Home Office address: but Vladimir is late – I discover, a bit to my surprise, that this is obviously the routine office for visa extensions: we take our position in a queue of sixty or seventy people . . . but the queue moves swiftly, and it can't be more than twenty minutes before we are there in front of one of the capable women . . . I must admit from then on the thing is done with dispatch . . . When I say, 'He doesn't want to go back,' the girl immediately makes a phone call, and we are put at a table by a window at the side of the room; after five minutes an old courier arrives and leads us into the bowels of the building, institutional corridors, to a windowless box of a room, walled with faun-coloured, plastic tiles, with three chairs and a utility table, where we sit for half an hour until Mr Grey appears . . . As we sit, we chat, we speculate whether the room is wired, whether the waiting is engineered to set up nervous tension – though when Grey appears, he explains that the discreet waiting place is to prevent Vladimir being spotted by other Czechs on normal visa business . . . Grey suggests he should speak to Vladimir alone, but he lets me first introduce him and give the background, then I go off: it will take two hours – and they hope to give an answer on Wednesday . . . I make sure Vladimir has the Memorial phone number; and I go out in the world.

It is like a death, or some intense personal or public event that for a moment breaks through the comfortable norms of routine, the safe cocoons in which we spend most of our lives; and like the Israeli war, there is some kind of melodramatic tonic in it – I am reminded of the end of *Heartbreak House* – 'I hope they come again'. Inevitably, the third eye operates, and one thinks of it all in a film – and why films never achieve this kind of suspense and shock: chiefly I suppose because they don't start by achieving the right kind of normality.

I wait in the Memorial office: Michael is in a great flap, verging on real annoyance, because he has to go to Ascot tomorrow, and Dallas, who was sent to Moss Bros to pick up his tails, appears to have gone off leaving only a grey topper sitting on his chair . . . At last the suit is found hanging up behind the door, and I get a call from Vladimir and Daphne can't give me a lift because she has to visit a sick friend in hospital . . .

I meet Vladimir just on the way out of the staff entrance with Grey who is friendly – but warns me that his job is only to collate the facts. I go with V. and we have a bite – he still won't take anything stronger than orange juice – the tension still persists, and even when he goes down to the gents, I wonder if he'll return, or if we are under observation, and imagine scenes of suspense and violence.

After all this, I go off to Chalcot Gardens, to get in on the end of a Greek resistance meeting, where I am alarmingly depended on to write some letter to *The Times*.

20 June 1967

Well, Vladimir, leaving the Home Office yesterday, was told to report again on Wednesday . . . This put the affair beyond my reach, because I am scheduled to leave at

12.25 for, or all places, Prague, on that very day, to attend some preposterous UNESCO meeting – or some international body of film and TV people. Karel did his best to imply my visit wasn't really necessary. He only inspired me however to phone Mr Grey at the Home Office to say I was going . . . This from the Westbury Hotel, where I had just done one of those TV interviews for Belgian TV – like water coming out of a tap.

Next stop – Universal – trapped into an actual meeting about this rather absurd *I'm Not Stiller* project. Jay Kanter and Cecil Tennant again. Once again I feel myself being charming, intelligent, lucid and forthright: how are they to know I also feel quite unreal? I propose giving the script to David Sherwin and meeting next week to see if he has positive and acceptable reactions. Of course I don't mention that David has already read *Stiller* and made criticisms that matched my own nebulous feelings of lack of interest: interestingly, he is rather like David Storey in his liking to use theoretical and philosophic terms like 'existential' to describe perfectly concrete reactions. Is *Stiller* real or fantasy? I become interested in it when forced to – largely thinking of the set-up – working in Prague, Mirek as cameraman etc. I do think it's a case where Max Frisch's writing overbalances on the theoretical, philosophic side: i.e. what the hell *is* it all about? and do I care? The 'favourable' attitude of John Van Eyssen at least has enabled me to turn down *All Neat in Black Stockings*.

Tuesday afternoon: David and I at last – and at least – get away to Charterhouse. When we arrive I am momentarily struck by the compactness of its Victorian Gothic: an isolated fantasy world set amid rich green expanses on which white-flannelled figures are playing cricket. Momentarily I am again swamped by a tide of nostalgia for that youthful celibate fantasy . . . but it doesn't last long. The Headmaster, Dr Van Ost by name (or similar), is a breezy eccentric, impatient and rather over-quick to demon-strate he knows exactly what it's all about, etc. – 'You want to shoot in winter? – The *Wuthering Heights* atmosphere I suppose . . .' – seemingly quite ready to co-operate, pleased to suggest he could let us have four hundred boys when we wanted them . . . The school itself – we were shown round by one of the Heads of Houses, a cool, complacent scientist, a confidently superior type without charm. The Houses are un-fortunately being renovated – but even the old one we saw lacked the spacious ugliness of Cheltenham. Much better than Dulwich, A or B+ . . .

As we left, David announced himself as feeling quite ill and intimidated by the whole experience . . . we recovered a bit with teas and a Kit-Kat and records on the juke box in a chara caff on the road home . . .

Back to Greencroft: Vladimir arrives after 8 p.m., meanwhile we nourish James Bond fantasies at the gate – really it is easy to do so, to wonder if one is being watched, and by whom. Anyway Vladimir, refusing everything except a glass of water and a digestive biscuit, produces his little gifts and letters for his father, mother and Milos, and continues to be hopeful. I give him £30, and arrange for him to collect the key to the flat from Murray if and when he wants it . . . As we part, he draws a map for me of his special bathing place, where the water is clear and warm: 'I am sorry, Lindsay, I can't take you there myself, but Mr Forman will know the place . . .'[1]

Pucholt's application was unsuccessful, and he was given a week to leave the country. Anderson telephoned the private office of the Home Secretary, Roy Jenkins, 'objecting in courteous terms' to the decision, and wrote him a letter suggesting that Pucholt's case was analogous to that of Nureyev. He arranged for Pucholt to be interviewed by Mark Arnold-Foster of the Guardian, *and agreed with Arnold-Foster to 'put Pucholt on television' the following day if the decision to expel him wasn't reversed. Arnold-Foster contacted the Irish and Norwegian Embassies to establish which country would have Pucholt. Leave was granted to appeal against the decision.*

28 June 1967

It takes me some time to get up: the telephone is ringing. Vladimir goes off to the Alexa Hotel to pick up his letter from the Home Office. Pepsy calls to say that Mr Grey would like to see him. I speak to Grey, who says that no letter has been sent. I speak to Betsy, to Oscar (bumbling away at his usual length) from Paris. Murray calls in. Leon rings, finally, Ian Rakoff with one of his frankly extraordinary progress reports [on *Crusaders*] – why should he – anyone – imagine I *care*?

Then I phone Grosvenor House: 'Mr Richard Harris, please' – the nervous excitement less overwhelming than it used to be – in fact I resolve to enjoy it . . . because the whole thing is a self-indulgence. Naturally anyway he was either out or 'not answering', so I had to be content with leaving a message. Delicious suspense?

[Visitors.] – They go: and I fall prey to the emotional tension and excitement interesting to observe – because I ring for my messages and Mr Harris wants me to ring him at 7.30. Fantasies crowd in: what shall I wear? What belt? What trousers? I try to iron my slimfit greys (perhaps that new brown belt) but the iron doesn't work. Leather jacket certainly. White shirt, dark blue tie and my Swedish black hipsters. Shall I take my tape-recorder?

At the start of July Anderson was in Poland to supervise the editing of The Singing Lesson.

---

1. The bathing spot was used as the main location for *Cerny Petr*.

12 July 1967

WARSAW: a catastrophic day, overshadowed and dominated by the loss in the lobby of the Europejski Hotel of my Pentax and my Phillips tape recorder . . . My own fault: I suppose a just punishment for the self-indulgent way I lost my temper because that blonde bureaucrat informed us we couldn't check in at the hotel because the receptionist was at lunch. If one loses one's temper and starts kicking the manager's door – naturally one forgets that one has IDIOTICALLY left two valuable pieces of equipment lying on one of the tables – CONSCIOUSLY TOO . . . I actually remember noting the fact when walking from the table to the receptionist . . . Lines of communication overstrained. It has all been too much. My affective, reassurance-needing temperament won't stand it. I forgot my linen coat. I left my briefcase in the chemist at the airport – fortunately picked it up again. I left my dark glasses on the plane . . . more harsh words at Warsaw airport . . . My big affecting welcome to the cutting room consisted mainly of being asked if we were going to get through the work quickly so that the assistant could implement her holiday plans.

Read *Justine* – Ivan Moffatt's screenplay. I really can't cope: feel it all slipping away.

22 July 1967

Karel. It's a long time since I visited Chalcot Gardens – good heavens, it must be nine or ten months – probably the last time was when he asked me to discuss the script of *Isadora* . . . As we got out of Ivan's car, I looked up at the imposing, expensive, good-taste, solid bourgeois front – and felt myself even then resenting it . . . Greeted by Betsy in long brocade housecoat – stroll on into the huge, recently white-painted living-room with its huge Japanese paper globe lampshade . . . the bookcases now climbing down from the ceiling . . . proliferating plants and huge sofa – all colour and clean good taste . . . Karel on the balcony playing bridge with the children.

Why on earth am I struck, from the moment I enter this gracious, informal, apparently unpretentious atmosphere, with a feeling of strain, falsity, edginess – a desire to get the hell out of there? Everything is somehow an 'act', a substitution for real feelings. I feel no warmth, but it is impossible to analyse this feeling.

Karel seems all pretence now. Of course it is his kind of truth, so the word is probably unfair. But when he puts on that serious look, that frown of interest, while he questions Ivan about his film – or about the Czechs – I want to call out – 'You don't really give a fuck, do you? Towards myself everything seems edged (however unconsciously) with resentment.

On 17 August 1967, in possession of the script of Crusaders, *now entitled* If . . . . ,
Anderson was granted permission to film on location at Cheltenham College.
With filming on If. . . . *not due to start until January, he made a series of television*
commercials for Kellogg's and Alcan Foil and, after an abortive attempt to set up
a film with ballet star Dame Margot Fonteyn, he went on holiday to Africa.

16 September 1967

Invited myself to the Clores in the evening, don't quite know why – maybe I felt like a
meal, and strong enough to support Miriam [Clore] . . . After shooting Alcan Foil
yesterday I have that comfortable, relaxed feeling of job just finished which is about as
near as I ever get to happiness.

15 November 1967

TANIT HOTEL, DJERBA. Two specific impulses led me to buy this book in Djerba – I
think a general one, rather reinforced by reading Angus Wilson's gloomy new novel,
No Laughing Matter, of time passing, life frittering away unrecorded and made nothing
of, Death coming over the horizon, and somehow a journal always seems to me one
way of making something of experience – of developing thoughts, and even of organising myself (routine for the day: rise at 7.00 . . .). This may be mere superstition, but
it's better than nothing. And the other impulse was the result of realising – on arriving
in Djerba – how little I remember of my previous North African visit, to Marrakesh, in
January or February of 1963 . . . I don't even remember the name of the hotel, only
vaguely my room . . . yes, and walking the long roads round the hotel area after dinner
– and I did follow, or was I followed by some Arab? Nothing very Paul Bowles anyway.
And walking in the morning in a gentle, softly showering, truly balmy atmosphere. It
probably did give me the rest I wanted: yet I'm afraid I remember most vividly
endlessly consulting the I-Ching about the prospects of my relationship with Richard.

Of course it's true that I didn't really make any contact with Marrakesh and I came
to Djerba on much the same impulse. Having got back from Warsaw late in August –
and somehow by the end of it, Poland had proved fairly exhausting – and plunged into
two weeks of Kellogg's, then Alcan Foil, and hanging round for the editing, and two
increasingly nerve-racking visits to Fuschia with David (Sherwin), rewriting the
Crusaders script, and then Memorial, and just somehow feeling myself being torn to
shreds in London – Robin Fox: his script and that script . . . I'm glad I did that one day
on *Inadmissible Evidence*[1] – if only because it gave me a sense of something *done*,
something registered on celluloid – something of myself, as opposed to time just lost,
or generously thrown away helping others.

------

1. Anthony Page's film of Osborne's play.

Another episode of waste: Adrian Gay's Margot Fonteyn enterprise with that composer fellow, quite intelligent but an exhausting, clever talker, who lives round the corner from me, but whose name I never caught, and the photographer-protégé of Fonteyn's, whom I think of as Keith Moon, intelligent, spoiled, neurotically baby-ish . . . The climax of that little episode – a Saturday tea-time in Keith's flat off the King's Road: Dame Margot tensely unbent, to me so strongly reminiscent of Princess Margaret, with that chilly, hard English upper-class manner so difficult to define, an apparently (extremely *conscious*) informal manner concealing strong defences, the bourgeois 'sophistication' (or camp) implicit in every line. Two strange, Renaissance-haired, King's Road young men (who had been there with proofs?) whose presence remained unexplained till they finally left, Keith begging them to return if they needed a TV set on which to see *The Innocents* – 'It's such a marvellous film. I can't bear to think of anyone missing it' . . . sitting on the sofa: and Dame Margot putting jam and Devonshire cream on Keith's scones, in just the right way.

She had been to see the all-male *As You Like It*[1] at the National ('The play came through so beautifully . . .'): when I testingly remarked that I was 'off' the National and could never bring myself to go. Margot scented some kind of scandal (she *hasn't* got breadth): 'Oh I'm sorry – ought I to know?' . . . Or maybe she hasn't got what I call humour – her intuition is largely devoted, I should imagine, to defending her own position – and, of course, like most middle-class Royalty, she is continually aware of her position.

DJERBA. I felt, quite suddenly really, that London was too much. I wanted nothing but sun, water, quiet – nothing to see, no tourism or social intercourse. Jocelyn [Herbert] wanted me to go to Opatija, where they are shooting *Isadora*:[2] and on the phone, Betsy had urged it too. I felt tempted, and a bit of duty to Jocelyn, but self-preservation won. Djerba was David Sherwin's idea, from the Wright's travel brochure. Wright's proved full – so Daphne arranged it through Memorial's agency. Albany, £90 for two weeks, and £8 extra for the single room.

I must say it lived up to the brochures. The transit stop at Tunis was alarming: grey, cloudy and puddled. As we took off again for Djerba, rain came down in thin sheets. But in the late afternoon sun, Djerba was warm and faded-golden. I drove alone in the tourist bus, through an astonishingly clean, white-walled town, in which every shutter, balcony, gate and paling was painted the same pale blue; through a dusty landscape, palms and scrub a faded green, along the sea-shore, to the Tanit Hotel, and my chalet-room with its two beds, clean linen, hot water when wanted, its doors opening directly on to the beach, with the sea a hundred yards across the sand.

---

1. Directed by Clifford Williams, with Robert Stephens and Derek Jacobi. Anthony Hopkins played 'Audrey, a country girl'.
2. Karel Reisz directing Vanessa Redgrave in a script by Melvyn Bragg.

Has it been a hard year? A disappointing year? I'm not quite sure why – my Polish experience, the *Crusaders* script, the possibility of shooting – whatever the disappointments on the way, surely these are positive achievements . . . Is it just loneliness, middle-aged *cafard*, which makes for so much angst, which makes the moments when I feel appreciative of, take comfort from the positive factors in my life, so fleeting and so rare? Partially, no doubt, but certainly also there is the fact that professionally as well as emotionally, or personally, I do find myself more than ever isolated: alliances of the past ten years (Free Cinema; the Royal Court) have come to an end; friends and contemporaries (the ever-recurring name of Karel in the forefront) have passed on to working out their life-patterns, more or less ruthlessly, in terms of compromise, or adjustment to the established order. And let me not be self-righteous: my need, as well as my gift, is an independent, uncomforming one, at odds with the tradition of my class and my country. The discomfort I feel is to a great extent due to the disparity between my subjective, non-conforming impulse – and my strength to battle and survive in a position of such isolation.

To come to some positive resolve: it is clear (rationally) that in order to survive, I need to formulate and adopt a much more ordered way of living – one tailored to my necessities and possibilities, and not to fantasies or discredited aspirations of the past. So many of my relationships exist in terms of the past only – and seem to oblige me to fall back on an image (*enfant terrible*) that I should prefer to escape. To grow a new personality in such a context is exceedingly difficult. I know that I need to 'lay hold on life'; somehow to shed the habit of dependence, the need for support and fatherly shelter, that has always been a tiresome half of my ambiguous personality. I know that only by achieving this kind of confidence will I ever be able to play the part I would like to play – and which perhaps only I can play.

In practical terms: a car; a secretary; a house – a flat for Mum (take it easy, Anderson: step by step); 7.00 a.m. rising: exercises; fresh lemon juice in warm water; answer my mail. At least waste less time chattering in other people's offices in London. Live alone and like it. Plant bulbs; make collages; write those essays; finish that monograph on [John] Ford. I will soon be forty-five. However strange and conscious the effort, if I wish my image to change – only I can change it.

23 November 1967

However little I want to admit it – it is indisputable: that emotionally isolated, adrift, as I am – however good my spasmodic resolutions – the idea of Richard still – however bitter and dismissive my thoughts – yes and my words – excites, colours, supplies a dynamic . . . Not that it dominates or upsets me . . . I was genuinely annoyed that I have to contact him, with all the attendant hazards . . . Nor did I dash to call his number. In fact I didn't do so till the next day . . . A secretary answered: Richard was out, and would be returning only briefly before a lunch appointment . . . where could he contact me this afternoon? He had tried to contact me before, but it seemed I had been away. He had wanted to invite me to the premiere of *Camelot*[1] as his personal guest . . . I gave her Memorial's number saying I would be there between four and six.

Leaving the house at about 3.20, going out of the front door, I thought I heard the phone ring. Yes, it was. Suddenly, hurrying, I turned back, fumbled for my keys, got the door open . . . the phone must have gone dead as I lifted it.

I get into the office about 4.00. I wasn't thinking, wondering or hoping as I certainly would have *three* years ago. Then a call came: Roy was saying 'I'll see if he's here,' and putting his hand over the phone and saying 'Richard Harris' . . . I said 'Oh yes – I might as well . . .'. I took over the phone; was handed by the secretary to – Richard's husky and warm tones . . . 'How are you? What are you doing?' He wanted to take me to see *Camelot*, with him – uttering some feeble clichés about it being well reviewed . . . How did he feel? He felt he had done some things marvellously: some things not so well . . . It had been cut, so some of his scenes lacked their preparation, looked like just playing results . . . 'You'll see . . .' When was I free? I told him the weekend was bad. Well when? I thought quickly: Tuesday was already booked for Oscar and David; casting starting soon . . . and I was conscious of wanting it to be a good clear space . . . Monday? When? 'When you like,' said Richard. 'All day . . .' And I put the phone down, already excited.

And it is later, during my exquisite boredom watching Godard at the NFT, that I permit myself to savour the fantasy of renewing my relationship with one of the most potent sexual animals in the world.

With If . . . . ready to go into production, Anderson negotiated with the British unions and the Czech authorities for Miroslav Ondricek to return to England as his director of photography.

3 January 1968

To 'Check Land'. Lufthansa to Frankfurt; forty-five minutes to wait in the terminal, bulging with cameras, clothes, whiskey, brandy, perfume and cigarettes, then in the Czech airline twin-engined job, with its utility fittings immediately evoking Stalinist austerity, and on to Prague. I feel rather numb most of the way: how undignified and unpleasantly hypocritical air travel has become! The hostesses with their mechanical smiles and brisk indifference, herding passengers this way and that, into buses to stand jammed up against each other for ten minutes while crew and girls gossip happily outside, waiting for a signal from some remote authority. The socialists are slightly more pleasant,

---

1. Joshua Logan's $15 million film of the Lerner and Loewe musical.

I think; at least their inefficiency is frank, there is no great glossy pretence going on, and their air terminals are decently shabby. The customs man at Prague was friendly and unofficious: he let me bring in the copy of *Raz Dwa Trzy* [*The Singing Lesson*] . . . which I thought I'd bring to show my friends.

Mirek, Milos and Ivan were waving as I crossed the tarmac; and as I emerged from the customs shed came forward to embrace.

Ivan (after dinner): 'I'm afraid we are really trying to do something hopeless. Nobody wants art in this business: not the public, not the distributors, not the critics. We are really like Don Quixote . . .' I could only agree with him. We had supper at the Slovak Restaurant in the Paris Hotel – Mirek, Ivan and I – I can't help reflecting that, if we are wiser than we were three years ago when we first met, we are also sadder.

On 5 January 1968, Malcolm McDowell, grappling with Christine Noonan, gave what David Sherwin called 'the best audition in the world' and was cast in the lead role of Mick Travis. Shooting started at Cheltenham College on 31 January, prompting McDowell's withdrawal from Jane Howell's unadmired Royal Court revival of Twelfth Night; *Jocelyn Herbert was shortly to join the production team.*

MALCOLM MCDOWELL

Lindsay didn't walk out. He just didn't stay for the second act, which was my big bit, so I thought I'd lost the part. I didn't know the man then, but he never would judge an actor by one silly production.

JOCELYN HERBERT

I was abroad doing *Isadora* [with Karel Reisz]. Lindsay kept ringing me up and saying: 'Come on. You've got to come back and do *If . . .*'

I said: 'I can't. I'm in the middle of this film.'

And this went on and on, and I used to say to him: 'Supposing I was doing your film and I left in the middle of it to do somebody else's, imagine what you'd say?'

Of course he couldn't answer that because he would have had a fit. (*Laughs.*)

But then I finished *Isadora*. I'd hardly got home and he had just got to Cheltenham and he'd seen what the designer was giving him for the hall, you know, the big hall at the end of the film, and he said: 'You've simply got to come down.'

I said: 'Well, what about –?'

'He doesn't mind. He would like you to.'

'Well, you'll have to send a car for me and bring me back.'

I must say the big hall that had been prepared was hopeless. In these big school halls they have these portraits of old generals and headmasters and things, and he had just

1. His family home, 'Cringletie', in Camberley, Surrey.

2. A fresh-faced Anderson (seated right) called up for National Service, 1943.

3. In January 1943, his studies at Oxford were interrupted when he received his call-up. He joined the 60th King's Royal Rifles and then transferred to the Intelligence Corps, serving in India from November 1944 until his return to Oxford University in February 1946.

4. The Oxford University Players' production of *The Castle of Perseverance* (1947), in which Anderson (foreground, on steps) played Sloth and John Glutton. Kenneth Tynan gave 'a gloriously rollicking performance'.

5. The cast and crew of *Billy Liar* at the Cambridge Theatre. (September 1960)

6. With Rachel Roberts on location for *This Sporting Life*. (1963)

7. With Richard Harris, *This Sporting Life.*
8. Patricia Healey in *The White Bus.* (1966)

9. In Warsaw filming *The Singing Lesson* (*Raz Dwa Trzy*). (1967)

10. 22 May 1967: 'Fully resolve - am no good at commercials. Never was.' But in 1967, Anderson's Kellogg's commercials swept the board at the annual advertising awards.

11. With Miroslav Ondricek (Mirek) during the filming of *If....* (1968)

12. On location for *If....* with screenwriter David Sherwin.

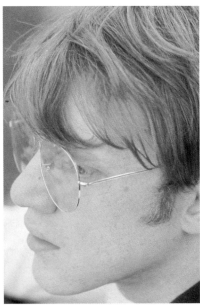

13 and 14. Malcolm McDowell, *If....*

15. Cannes 1969. Showing off the Palme d'Or for Best Film for *If....;* on his arm Vanessa Redgrave who won Best Actress for her performance in Reisz's *Isadora.*

blown up portraits of a lot of military people. They didn't look like oil paintings at all. And he'd put them in huge frames. Terrible. And they were supposed to be shooting the day after next. Luckily I knew the set-dresser, and so we went out, and sent other people out, to buy things and we repainted this and that and we did it all in a day, which was pretty good going, really. And the designer was helping, you know the one who was there before I came. He kept saying to me: 'You must explain to me about Lindsay. Why do I get on with him so badly?' I tried to explain to him. But he hadn't got a clue about design.

If . . . . opened in London on 19 December 1968. A shooting diary is not among the Anderson papers at Stirling University, but his notebooks contain this publicity 'interview' for which he wrote both the questions and the answers.

What would you say your new film is about?

That's a horrible question. I don't think one can ever say what one's work is 'about' – certainly not if one has managed to make anything of value. You see, one doesn't set out to make a film 'about' anything. One starts with an impulse and a subject and an area of experience, and whatever one makes grows out of that. It is for the critic to decide what it's 'about'. All I can say is that it's a story that takes place in an English school, a public school. It's set in the world of boys, of three boys in particular, and it uses that peculiarly hierarchic world to dramatise issues of authority, tradition and freedom, with, I hope, a sense of humour. I suppose what attracted me to the subject first of all was the sort of nostalgic feeling most people have for their schooldays. They are such an important, formative part of one's life that anything one makes on this theme must be extremely personal. The other aspect that appealed to me, I think, was the extent to which a school is a microcosm – and particularly in England, where the educational system is such an exact image of the social system. I like very much to show a little or a limited world which has implications about the big world and about life in general existence.

Did you enjoy your own schooldays?

Yes, I wasn't unhappy at school. I liked my school – it was a pleasant, friendly place. I wasn't radically critical, though I am told I have a critical, rather disputatious temperament. Certainly this film isn't at all like the public school novel of the thirties, when sensitive young middle-class writers who had suffered at school, wrote novels to tell everyone how awful it was – it's not that kind of picture at all. I think there's quite a lot of affection in this film.

It has been said your films carry a romantic point of view. Would you agree?

Yes, I think I am very romantic, idealistic by temperament, and perhaps I try to balance this with a certain irony and scepticism. I believe in ambiguity. *The White Bus*, for example, which I made from a story by Shelagh Delaney two years ago, is the kind of film I want to make and am quite proud of having made. Some people find it a very sad film and some people find it a very satirical film. I hope it is both. I wouldn't dictate to anybody how they should receive it. Probably all my work, even when it has been very realistic, has struggled for a poetic quality – for larger implications than the surface realities may suggest. It is enjoyable to work naturalistically. In fact, it's usually easier to do. But I think the most important challenge is to escape from or get beyond pure naturalism, into poetry. Some people call this fantasy. But these terms are dangerous, because words always mean different things to different people. I would call *If . . . .* a realistic film – not completely naturalistic, but trying to penetrate the reality of its particular world. I think Brecht said that realism didn't show what things really 'look like', but how they really are. Interestingly too, I think that the events which have been happening in the world around us as we shot our film[1] suggest that in working on the script more than eighteen months ago, David Sherwin and I were being, to some extent, prophetic.

What do you mean, 'prophetic'?

I mean forecasting the shape of things to come – the conflict between established tradition and youthful independence that is evidently breaking out all over the world. This seems to me one of the functions of an artist, perhaps the most important function, to prophesy. As the most important function of a critic is not to judge, but to interpret.

How exactly is If . . . . *prophesying?*

Not in any literal sense. But it ends with a particular violent episode, which relates absolutely to the kind of things we are reading about in the newspapers every day. Whether they are happening in America or Berlin or Paris, or among teenage and younger than teenage schoolchildren in Britain. The problems of young people and their relationship to traditions seem to be more and more important.

Do you think that the film's attitude towards all this could be taken as an incitement to violence?

---

1. That year saw the student revolt in Paris and demonstrations in Europe and America against the Vietnam War.

I can't see why it should. The work is not a propagandist one. It doesn't preach. It never makes any kind of explicit case. It gives you a situation and shows what happens in this particular instance when certain forces on the one side are set against certain forces on the other, without any mutual understanding. The aim of the picture is not to incite but to help people to understand the resulting conflict.

I see the film as an illustration of the consequences of people blinding themselves to reality – society pretending that the real facts of life don't exist. Is this a valid impression?

I suppose it's valid. But, again from my point of view, I would never use a word like 'illustration'. Perhaps to you the film may be an illustration. To me, it isn't. I would hope that it's an experience, not an illustration. Certainly people should be able to draw from a film like this what they like. One of the marks of a good film, or a good work of art, is that it is susceptible to being interpreted in a variety of ways. This shows it has the richness or ambiguity of a real experience, that it isn't in any way a tract. But that is one interpretation you might put on it. Somebody who has completely different values from you might say it was an illustration of the ruinous effect of irresponsibility and over-lenient treatment of the young.

Yes. This is why I asked, because I felt I might be giving it a completely personal interpretation.

I hope you are. It is a completely personal film. Of course, I wouldn't deny that my sympathies lie on one side rather than another. But I hope that the sympathy of the film is not a narrow one.

What is the relationship between your film and today's 'permissive society'?

I don't know what the permissive society is. I think you'd have to be more specific because that is rather a journalistic tag, isn't it? What does it mean?

I suppose it means a kind of casual, sexual freedom . . .

Actually, I don't think this film has anything to do with the permissive society on any level, because implicit in it throughout – implicit in my own temperament if you like – is a sense of responsibility. What I associate with the permissive society, or with that cliché, is the idea of life lived without notions of responsibility. But that isn't what *If . . . .* is about at all. It is about responsibility against irresponsibility, and consequently well within a strong puritan tradition. Its hero, Mick, is a hero in the good, honourable, old-fashioned sense of the word. He is someone who arrives at his own beliefs and stands up for those beliefs, if necessarily against the world. The film is, I think, deeply anarchistic. People persistently misunderstand the term anarchistic, and think it just means wildly chucking bombs about, but anarchy is a social and political philosophy which puts the highest possible value on responsibility. The notion of somebody who wants to change the world is not the notion of an irresponsible person.

It seemed to me that sex and violence had similar implications in the film.

Well, yes. It is traditionally a kind of anarchist tenet, I think, that the impulse of freedom naturally finds expression in emotional relationships as well as in action. Perhaps the film suggests the link between sex and anarchy, if you like – the emotional and liberating quality that there is, or should be, in sex.

Has the film got anything to do with current fashion?

Very little, I should say, either in terms of morality, i.e. the permissive society, or in terms of art and style. In fact, I was very concerned to avoid any suggestion of what is currently known as 'trendy'. We very deliberately didn't use any of the kind of contemporarily fashionable allusions or tags that would be included in a trendy film about young people, made for the permissive society.

Stylistically, how does the film fit into the contemporary picture of film-making?

As I say, it doesn't fit very closely into a contemporary picture of film-making except in so far as developments in the cinema in the last ten years or so have made it possible to work with much greater freedom and to be personal and not to be bound to the traditional and conventional ideas of narrative construction and narrative style. *If* . . . . isn't really a narrative film, although I suppose it's got a story that eventually flowers into action with a climax and an end. But much of the film is constructed not really in a narrative way but in what might be called an epic way. I mean epic in the Brechtian, not the Hollywood, sense, where one is less concerned to tell a story than to show ways of life. To take a specific instance, when the boys are beaten, which is obviously a crucial point in the film, they aren't beaten because they've been discovered doing anything specifically bad. They're beaten actually because of what they are. And the concern of the film is much more to show what people are, what things actually are, than to tie everything together in a specific cause and effect. In that way I think it can be regarded as contemporary. Where it isn't contemporary is in its technique, which I would think on the whole is extremely sober. This is both natural to me and the result of quite conscious determination on my part. The more eccentric or showy or 'trendy' technique has become in the last few years, the more I have felt I wanted to try and make films with as much simplicity and as much directness as possible. Of course, simplicity and directness are actually the most difficult things, and sometimes one fails to bring it off maybe, and is simply dull. But this is the direction in which I try to work. I'm quite out of sympathy with the modern school of criticism which says that you should just let things happen in front of the camera, and then the audience will create the film for itself. I feel that it is my job to create the film. It's my prerogative as an artist to select the things that I think are worth looking at. I don't leave it to the audience to select them. Even if we were to have a take running three minutes, for instance, I would never just let people loose in front of the camera to 'behave' for three minutes, and expect chance to dictate something interesting. I would organise those three minutes. Qualities of rhythm and balance and composition inside a very straightforward and sober technique are the problems that interest me most, and in that way I think my approach to film-making is very traditional and perhaps un-modern.

How does working in Poland, where you made The Singing Lesson, *compare with working in England?*

My work in Poland was, of course, much less ambitious than a film like *If . . . . The Singing Lesson* was a documentary film which took about two and a half weeks to shoot. It was a very pleasant, maddening and illuminating experience. The frustrations of working in Poland are different to the frustrations here: there the techniques and the resources are primitive, but their industry is not over-organised, as I think ours is, so that there is a personal quality to the work and the working relationships throughout. In Britain we have endless possibilities from a technical point of view, but a more intense time pressure. From the imaginative point of view I would say we are much more restricted. And now there is this absolute compulsion to shoot in colour (so that eventually the films can be shown on American TV), which is not so bad for the 'big budget' films, but which adds enormously to the difficulty of making pictures reasonably cheaply. On the other hand, if one were to attempt something more ambitious in Poland, one would probably be even more frustrated than one is in Britain. In our system, commercialism obviously imposes certain limitations, sometimes very great ones. But in Poland now the political pressures are so strong that it's practically impossible to make a really serious feature film at all.

In the fifties you made documentaries and from about 1957 to 1962 you made no films at all but worked in the theatre. Between This Sporting Life *and* If . . . . , *apart from making the short films we've mentioned, you were working in the theatre here and in Poland. Do you regard your film work and theatre work as complementary to each other?*

Not particularly, except in the economic sense.

You have a reputation for working very closely with actors. Can you explain your attitudes towards this?

I like to – in fact I need to work in close contact with actors. I don't think this is because I have done a lot of theatre, for I came from the cinema to the theatre: but even in documentary films I have always tried to work from a close relationship with people. Of course the theatre provides much greater opportunity for this kind of collaboration between actor and director: in the cinema one is often too pushed for time to rehearse and discuss. This is one reason why it is so difficult to achieve film performances that have the subtlety and the development of good stage acting. Often the rush to get through on schedule can mean that actors get rather a poor deal, and the film can suffer accordingly. Of course discussion 'in depth' can sometimes be irrelevant to a screen performance, particularly a brief one, but I certainly have no affinity with directors who regard actors as mere instruments and consider discussion of character and motive a waste of time. For me, the values in a story are best expressed through the personalities of actors, and for that it's necessary to have their understanding and their collaborations and to do things that, in fact, I hadn't thought of myself.

I see that your cameraman on If . . . . *is a Czechoslovakian, Miroslav Ondricek, who also worked on* The White Bus, *besides making films with Milos Forman and Jan Nemec. Did this not present a communication problem?*

Not a big one. Although he hardly spoke a word of English, we had a very happy collaboration on *The White Bus*. I first met Mirek in Prague when he was shooting *A Blonde in Love* for Milos Forman, and I found the whole atmosphere and way of working immensely sympathetic. It reminded me of the kind of atmosphere that we (i.e. myself and Karel Reisz, Walter Lassally, John Fletcher) used to have years ago when we were working on the Free Cinema films, and which it's practically impossible to get when you're working on a full-scale feature film in this country. I've always found it difficult to find people here who understand what I'm trying to do and who don't think I'm completely mad. I felt that this was somebody whose method of work and approach to work was very much my own and to whom there were an enormous number of things I wouldn't have to try and explain or teach. And so it proved. Mirek and I work with an interpreter, but our understanding has always been intuitively close, which of course is the best kind. On *The White Bus* he entirely understood the spirit of the film and brought an exceptional creative contribution to it. This is why I asked him to return to England for *If* . . . .

Finally, there has certainly never been a film that shows English public school life with such directness as If . . . . *How do you think it will strike audiences who know nothing of these places?*

I should have thought that such an intimate and authentic picture of these great and influential establishments would be appreciated by anyone interested in the way the world works (which I believe most people are). And anyway, it is not a film *about* public schools, any more than it is a film about *a* public school. It is a film about law and disorder, about freedom and responsibility, about love and the denial of the heart. Now, you see, I have answered your first question.

1 January 1969

... and in the freezing evenings the queues straggle down Lower Regent Street for *If* ....

Is it post-natal, this exhaustion and emptiness, so that I can hardly feel pleasure about the astonishing success of the film – certainly no exhilaration ... Is it reawakening to an emotionally empty life? ... A lazy and reposeful day, with no qualms of guilt or conscience: though I know that ahead of me looms *In Celebration* and attempting to read David [Storey]'s cut and (minimally) rewritten version on my bed before supper (while Mum watches TV below) – I don't get much beyond half the first act. I shall just have to make it LIVE – which means of course the most important thing is a perfect cast.

Write to Jeremy Saunders at Paramount, urging him to take action to get a good version of the optical in Reel IX – which is, in theory, our only remaining problem on the printing of *If* .... In the evening Jeremy rings me, worried about New York. And indeed if we are opening mid-February I suppose there is some urgency.

I lie down in the afternoon and drowse and read *The Wide Sargasso Sea*. At first exotic, then gripping, sad and bitter. A little walk, a cup of tea ... two chump chops for supper and nonsense on the telly.

I thought today, maybe apropos some award in the New Year's Honour List: really quite shortly I shall be fifty. How to account for my extraordinary mixture of maturity and immaturity? Do all men of fifty feel no different from small boys?

2 January 1969

Yes, this is really a Lotus Land: I can fully imagine never working again, anaesthetised by TV, happily succumbing to this quiet routine of inactivity. 'Thou art tired: best be still ...'

Stayed in bed all morning; read the papers; drowsed ... In the afternoon I shopped a little in Littlehampton, then walked home, down the promenade and the damp sands, where scattered couples, family parties, were taking the air, and common boys threw stones. I took a picture or two; but the Pentax hangs heavy round the neck.

3 January 1969

A call from Robert Shaw at 11.30 tonight ... I go in already beginning to feel the effects of my Soneryl tablet ... He thinks *If* .... is a great film, 'a masterpiece', perhaps the best he's seen ... Can it really be on this level, objectively and historically? In comparison with the great humanist-realist-poetic films? I find it difficult to believe, exhilarating and enlivening though much of it is . . . Talk to Michael on the phone. Twice. Gave me yesterday's figure: £1,600 which is well up on Boxing Day.

4 January 1969

In Celebration fills me with doubt and depression: David can write; but seems determined not to write like a dramatist. Determined *not* to clarify or progress through conflict . . . I feel the material is very intractable; but in the end I'll have to settle for it . . . Also read a lot of *Anarchists in Love*: novel given to me by Oscar. But what film is there in this rather well written yet uneconomic and in the end not important story of girl in love with young man torn between homo- and hetero-sexuality? Oscar is the strangest mixture of foolishness and (sometimes) good intuitions. He would have done better to ask me to direct Joe Orton's play; but of course he would be scared to make such a suggestion.

Malcolm McDowell phoned, just to say hullo – how are you – he is a nice, sociable chap. Thank goodness he is now working – or will be next week.

Mrs Wilson's Diary on ITV: 'pathetic' is the schoolboy word for its schoolboy facetiousness. Am I affected also by the 'pathetic' jibe against me in this week's *Private Eye*?! YES.

5 January 1969

Well, I had certainly better make a New Year Resolution *now*, and put it into action from tomorrow – to cut down on the telly drug; and seriously I ought to diet and exercise, difficult though it certainly is in this cold weather. But how am I to look good in New York? I must admit I still feel totally debilitated. Emotionally drained. It can't all be *If* . . . . – can it?

6 January 1969

So back to Life: as I pack my bag, with its usual freight of unread scripts, unanswered letters, I reflect on how habitually reality betrays those eternally hopeful fantasies of reading, study, fruitful labour and research.

From Victoria to the Royal Court: as I lug my heavy grip upstairs, I pause and go into the Circle [of the Royal Court]. On the stage (bare, except for a curving modern streetlamp) a group of women chorusing commonplace working-class woes – down in the Circle I see Peter Gill and Jocelyn; a technical rehearsal[1] . . . I go down to see Jocelyn . . . How inadequate it all seems. Was there really no more to it than this, that string of run-throughs from *The Long and the Short* . . . to *Julius Caesar*? Didn't we bring more

---

1. For *Life Price*, by Michael O'Neill and Jeremy Seabrook.

temperament, more intensity, more sense of importance to our work? Will I recapture the feeling on *In Celebration*?

To Memorial and thence with Michael Medwin to see Peter King and hear (we hope) news of Associated British's circulation offer for *If....* My chief contribution was to comment unfavourably on the idea of getting a blanket, simultaneous North and South London Release, with consequent over-ordering on prints ... But I never felt he was coming quite clean. Viewed the re-made optical in Reel IX: okay. So today sees completion of work on the print!

7 January 1969

David [Storey] comes in to talk about *In Celebration*. We go through the play: he buys the idea of quite a few more cuts, some minor adjustments, and the complete excision of Eric (Ms Burnett's son) as a character – which is no mean step ... But my attempts to simplify, clarify dramatic 'lines' don't really bear much fruit. It *is* literary, he agrees, rather than dramatic; but when he changes things for the structural reasons I suggest, even though he may appreciate why theoretically, he loses his sense of truth and reality. 'I feel like someone trying to move furniture about in a room according to instructions signalled from outside the window ..' So my arguments – which I put forward with some force – don't accomplish a transformation ... oh well: we must do what we can. (The truth, I really believe, is that David *isn't* writing for the theatre. The experiment for me will have to be: how much can I achieve by sheer realism – reality – psychological penetration? But why *did* I agree to do it? Again, I can't really even remember my first reaction.)

Interviewed in the afternoon by John Francis Lane and an Italian TV team – standing on the river bank outside the NFT. The usual nonsense. John looking prosperous and benign: no doubt emigration suits some people, particularly those who will never be quite first class at home.

Returning to Memorial: a phone message from Peter King at Paramount – to say that *If....* has got its ABC Release. I think I allow myself the first twinges of pleasure.

8 January 1969

Elizabeth Sussex[1] is really irresistibly reminiscent on the phone of Gladys George in *The Maltese Falcon*: you lift the receiver and immediately you are in the middle of an unstoppable, obsessive flow of confession, sympathy-demanding details of her life, troubles, problems. But not, as you might read it off the page, *moaningly* delivered; but rather bounced out in a sort of dreadfully jolly, over-inflected monologue. It is the strange insensitivity of the recital, the monstrous imposition of it, that enables me to be really quite ruthless in my rejection of the appeal. It's fortunate really, otherwise pity

---

1. Author of an excellent little book, *Lindsay Anderson*, published in 1969.

might trap me in the most terrible way. Of course the terrible clumsiness of her physical approaches is itself enough to scare me off.

2 February 1969

After a day of diverse strains typical of all the things with which I can hardly cope – here I am speeding Pan Am (President Special, or some such gold label) to New York, fat and fatigued, trailing loose-ends behind me.

I am fatalistic about *In Celebration*. God will have to provide. I like Fulton Mackay. And Brian Cox.[1] God will provide.

Peter Docherty comes to talk about the set for *In Celebration*. He talks about furniture, but about a ground plan he hasn't a clue. In the Austin Princess provided by Paramount, I drive to Chelsea where Michael has been in conversation with Sean [Connery]. I join them for a drink. Sean spends most of the time detailing how his investment in *Shalako* is being nibbled away by irresponsible expenditure by producers, executives etc.

17 February 1969

Malcolm has had his hair cut and it suits him. He has got the part in Bob's film.[2] I am really pleased, and please God, here's one who won't get spoiled. I truly hope so.

I get to the Court lateish – waste time as it is fatally easy to do in that building, see twenty minutes or so of the rehearsal of *Saved*[3] . . . What boring, trivial, minuscule stuff it seems, all cups of tea and bottles of sauce and *News of the World* sensationalism togged up in artistic clothes . . . The Court is appropriately devitalised.

19 February 1969

A really dreadful day: waking, exhausted, to a phone call from Mum – the phone, that instrument of torture . . . I try to ring Malcolm about his trip to New York . . . Fiz rings, and I have a long conversation about *Hamlet* – then about Robert Vaughan (*The Man from UNCLE*) . . . I phone Daphne . . . Miriam calls: will I ring Leon? Leon calls: will I see the first reels of *All Neat in Black Stockings* and advise cuts? . . . Michael calls . . . Fanny Carby calls. I call Malcolm, another longish chat. Leslie Pound calls: Paramount have been incapable of concocting a fifteen-second trailer for TV for *If* . . . .

(O, I die Horatio . . .)

Gillian [Diamond, casting director] calls from the Court: Ian Hendry and Alan Dobie have never received their scripts . . . Will I call Ian Hendry? I call Ian Hendry;

---

1. From Anthony Page's Dundee repertory company. Cox was making his London debut in the play.
2. *Figures in the Landscape*, co-starring Robert Shaw and directed by Joseph Losey.
3. By Edward Bond, directed by Bill Gaskill. The first uncut production following the removal of the Lord Chamberlain's powers of censorship under the Theatres Act of 28 September 1968.

he's left for Walton-on-Thames. I ring him at Meadway and reach Janet Munro . . . I call Tom Bell; he's out; I speak to Lois. Gerry Lewis calls. Ian Hendry calls. Ian Rakoff calls. (I am being pounded steadily into the ground.) Gillian calls.

I go out (it is six o'clock) and buy an evening paper (for the TV programmes). I return, and put on a kettle and fill a hot-water bottle. Tom Bell calls. I will get a script to him. Then, the end of a terrible day, Rachel calls from the Connaught: a low, sinking voice. Goodbye Lins; thank you; I don't want to live; I'll never see you again. Forth into the snow at 10.15.

On 28 February, If . . . . began it's national release on the ABC circuit. At a special screening for ABC managers and guests, a BSA motorbike was on show in the foyer – the first prize in a national competition. If . . . . picked up nominations for Best Director and Best Screenplay in the British Film Awards, but lost out to Midnight Cowboy, *which, together with Richard Attenborough's* Oh! What a Lovely War!, *swept the board. In March, David Sherwin won the British Writers' Guild Award for Best Original Screenplay. On 27 May If . . . . won the Palme d'Or for Best Film at the Cannes Film Festival. There were no further diary entries for 1969.*

7

Courted

Artistic Director – In Celebration – Jon Voight
The Contractor – Home – Alan Price

'The knights are just marvellous and I have nothing more to say.'

From August 1969, Anderson shared the Artistic Direction of the Royal Court
Theatre with Bill Gaskill and Anthony Page. His production of David Storey's
play, In Celebration, *starring Alan Bates, James Bolam, Constance Chapman,*
Brian Cox, Gabrielle Daye, Fulton Mackay and Bill Owen, opened at the Court
on 22 April, running for more performances than any Royal Court play since
Beckett's Waiting for Godot *in 1965. He turned down an offer from the 1969*
Cannes Festival juror, Sam Spiegel, to direct Nicholas and Alexandra (*in*
which Brian Cox would play Trotsky) to direct instead another David Storey
play, The Contractor. *Designed by John Gunter, and starring Bill Owen,*
Constance Chapman, Philip Stone and Jim Norton, The Contractor *opened*
at the Court on 20 October and transferred to the Fortune Theatre on 6 April 1970.
In the same month, he started work on David Storey's Home, *a play about decline*
and loneliness, which paired Sir John Gielgud with Sir Ralph Richardson.

1 January 1970
This year I'll be forty-seven: I don't feel middle-aged, as Karel seems – or Tony Richardson, in his quite different kind of arrogant removal into unreality. But certainly more
authoritative, both in the practice of art and in relation to fellow human beings. In
relation to self – less so. Hardly changed, in fact. That emotional immaturity – need for
dependency – wish for it – I'm afraid is as powerful a stimulus, as crippling a limitation
as ever. Is it an omen that today the phone rang as I was doing letters with the cool,
armoured, unhappy Diana, and it was Warren Beatty again making contact? I remain

as immediately and deeply affected by the contact with this kind of handsome, ambitious masculinity as ever I was. Last month's *Nova* astrology section hinted at the formation now of influential working relationships . . . It's odd: is it just the magic of January 1st? But I do feel a stirring of Hope.

Lunch with Ring Lardner Jnr[1] at the Unity to discuss his sketch of a treatment of *The Double Helix*. One of the Hollywood Ten:[2] rather hard-going. Shy? Out of his depth? Conscious of not having really worked at the thing? Anyway, hopelessly old-fashioned. There's something in that subject.

Back at the theatre: young hack from Cambridge wants to start a theatre, quite impressively determined and patronising. But another Midwich Cuckoo. When he left: 'The conversation's been helpful . . .' Piss off!

Warren Beatty, bearded and moustached and long hair and glasses – not the hoped for glamour. About a thousand subjects he wants to do.

2 January 1970

To the Court, which more and more is a trap: Marie glum in the box-office when I arrive; Helen[3] with her forced brightness; Bill this strange mixture of alternate lucidity and whim; Anthony subjective to an absolute degree; myself subject to these bursts of enthusiasm or emotion which need always a response they can't find . . . as I say to George Harewood on the phone, it's like a piece of knitting: you pull out the thread and the whole fabric disintegrates. The whole thing is breaking down – and though it will be sad to see the English Stage Company go – I am beginning to doubt whether it can be held together.

3 January 1970

Interviewed by Gordon Gow[4] at 11 – before it Malcolm dropped in, on his way to work with David Sherwin:[5] I was lying in the bath of course: bells ringing; my trousers in my room, which had to be fetched out by Malcolm so I could get dressed.

Yesterday to Twickenham with Paul Williams and his wife to see the fine cut of [his film] *The Revolutionary*. It is a very original and sincere and intelligent picture. Privately, I think less successful than *Out of It* – because of course much more ambitious. I don't think the trick of integrating idea-progression (epic) with character (bourgeois

---

1. Screenwriter, pseudonymously wrote more than forty of the 143 episodes of the Richard Greene *Robin Hood* series in the 1950s.
2. Hollywood artists blacklisted in the 1950s by the House of UnAmerican Activities Committee.
3. Helen Montagu, (1928–2004), General Manager of the Royal Court Theatre. Later plucked Catherine Zeta-Jones from the chorus line of *42nd Street* and made her a West End star.
4. Editor of *Films and Filming* magazine.
5. On *Coffee Man*, the script that would become *O Lucky Man!*

drama) is wholly brought off – but then I am so dreadfully picky – and after all was forty-four or five before I could get to *If* . . . . His sense of rhythm – of finding just the right, most economic selection of images – is also a bit faulty, so the picture lacks inevitable dynamic. But it's exceptionally intelligent and witty and (best of all) serious. Jon Voight very creative, a bit uneven, trying things all the time. In the Royal Court Hotel bar after the film, Paul Williams said how Jon Voight, speaking with him on the telephone, had said none of the scripts he'd been offered enticed him . . . and he really would like to work with me . . . It's touching to be wanted, to be respected in such a way – even if doesn't or hasn't yet resulted in Jon communicating or sending me a script . . . of course too there is a certain glamour: but chiefly I think the flattery of someone actually being interested. Anyway, I wrote him a letter: wanting chiefly to make it a human communication – just to talk – rather than to force a proposition . . . I think I'll have to have some acknowledgment from him, even if only through his agent, if I'm to persevere . . . I shouldn't be surprised, but the reaction from Paul Williams seemed quite favourable to the idea of showing *The White Bus* with *Out of It* . . . As we walked away, up Audley Street, he seemed to be talking about the film in the context of the NY drug scene. How it would appeal to the turned-on public: how the queues in New York for Fellini's *Satyricon* were all observably stoned; and therefore how the picture might have more of an appeal than I suggested.

4 January 1970

Sunday's high-spot of comedy: visit from Mr Yoo,[1] the Korean film director and his wife. Absolutely predictably Mr Yoo speaks no English – his rather nice wife speaks a little – hasn't seen *If* . . . . , really knows nothing, but has made forty feature films and is interested in documentary. I serve coffee, tinned fruit juice and scotch. They have summoned a friend, a rather socialite girl who works as an interior decorator. She arrives as the conversation has got sticky, wearing black slacks and gold-embroidered jacket. Quite unable to translate – the kind that drives me up the wall, nodding and grinning when I speak, but not translating. I get more and more irritated. Mr Yoo begs for stills, gapes and wrestles with himself behind heavy-rimmed spectacles and asks (with difficulty) absurd questions: 'What is your film about?' I have agreed to have lunch with them, but rescind the offer as I feel my temper rising – with mention of sick mother, etc.

5 January 1970

James Mossman[2] came to the office, together with one of his directors, whose name I significantly can't remember . . . slight foreign accent, superficial, culture-journalist,

---

1. Probably Hyun Mok Yoo.
2. Producer of the BBC *Review* programme.

largely ignorant, certainly knowing nothing about the Court. Mossman was more sympathetic than before – starting by proclaiming that the only thing that mattered was to get items by people who cared very much about their subjects (of course the only thing missing is his own committed cultural point of view: he twice alluded to lunching with Diana Cooper – and how Noël Coward said the Royal Court should be burned down as his birthday present) . . . I might make a film for them: I briefly mentioned the idea of starting with the morning, myself in bed, then developing into my life and view of the world[1] – about which Mossman was surprisingly enthusiastic . . . I also offered them *The Contractor* as a subject for a feature. The anonymous colleague was not so enthusiastic about this as a new production since it didn't immediately offer the stereotype of 'how a new play is born'. Really talking about art to such people is like trying to describe a jumbo jet to Hottentots.

6 January 1970

Mounting nightmare at the Court. Neville[2] gaga, the committees reduced to incapacity by their members having become absorbed in their own concerns (Harewood unable to call an artistic committee for four or five months) . . . maybe I exaggerate this, but it's fair to suggest that if people like Bill, Anthony and I are to administer a theatre, we need a bloody good manager. Helen, with her over-eager manner, her over-quick reassurances, her compulsive pasting over of cracks, hardly supplies this. And 'artistically'? The disparities – creative and temperamental – between Bill, Anthony and myself don't really make tripartite artistic direction feasible. Another sudden violent clash between Anthony and myself this evening – because I asked him to get his cast to a press reception on Friday by 12.30 . . . 'Well, I'll see . . . it's very difficult . . . it's just been sprung on me . . . I've had a very tiring day . . .' In the face of that pettish egocentric obstinacy my patience runs out almost immediately. As my tone instinctively sharpens at the sight of Simone in her wide-trimmed yellow hat and his other strange, recessive King's Road assistant, Christine – the pallid, coolly resentful publicity representative; John French – the idiotic house manager; those glum (or alcoholic) faces in the box office . . . And each evening the house five-sixths empty[3] . . . And I cannot bring myself even to visit *Music Hall* in the theatre upstairs – which closes this week. No – on expiring of contract: basta!

---

1. He eventually made the film for BBC Scotland in 1992 and called it *Is That All There Is?* It wasn't screened by the BBC until after his death.
2. Neville Blond, Manchester textile magnate; the first chairman and chief sponsor of the English Stage Company.
3. An exaggeration. Eleanor Fazan's production of Bruce Lacey's *The Three Musketeers Ride Again*, starring Rachel Roberts and Valentine Dyall, was playing to 30 per cent capacity.

9 January 1970

. . . So, last night, as I say, the telephone rings – and it is Rachel, hysterically ringing from the restaurant – one of those fashionable joints unknown to me, where Rex Harrison[1] would dine with Elizabeth Harris; where Nigel Davenport would take Fiz and Rachel, and where Jack Gold and Nicol Williamson would turn up after the first night of their film [*The Bofors Gun*] . . . well, they all paid for it . . . Standing in my pyjamas, then in bed, I hear how Rex finished his dinner, all three courses, with that bitch – how Rachel was sick of the whole business, *would* divorce, *would* sue for neglect – how Rex is a pervert, carried round obscene postcards, and needed various aids for intercourse – all this from a phone booth in the restaurant basement . . . Rachel moaning soppily: 'When they left, he didn't even look over his shoulder . . .' I was practically reduced to 'Keep a stiff upper lip . . .' 'Pride,' I think I finished with, a bit irritatedly . . .

Press reception in the Theatre Upstairs: nice atmosphere. Introduce James Mossman and Peter Adam to Brian Cox. Lunch with Malcolm and David and a little discussion about their script. Then drink with John Dunn Hill; another obsessive egocentric, talking about his experiences assisting on Polanski–Gutowski film in Denmark.[2] What energy! What unremitting flow!

Drop in to Rachel: haggard but okay. Home to poached eggs and telly: utter exhaustion.

10 January 1970

Exhaustion? . . . or a bad cold? Confined to bed. I finish *The Penguin Book of the American West* – and start on *The Penguin Book of the Civil War* . . . I suppose that, without any emotional pressure, I am allowing my fantasy-wishes to stray in the direction of the West . . . i.e. Jon Voight . . . which, from any rational point of view, is ridiculous . . . The trouble is, I really haven't anything to offer him, and I feel it's unlikely *he* will engineer anything in my direction. It's really terribly inconvenient to have this particular temperament of mine, so lacking generally in initiative, so energetic in its peculiar way, so demanding, yet also so dependent . . .

12 January 1970

The long-awaited Artistic meeting, called to fix the Artistic Directors' contracts – and also to front the problem of Neville's replacement. Neville has caused awkwardness by insisting on coming . . . also Oscar, Robin, Bill, Anthony and myself . . . and our secretary, Vivian, whom I have already noted down as a 'doormat'. She gets an interesting initiation into the affairs of the English Stage Company.

---

1. On 19 December 1969, Rex Harrison's lawyer had issued a press statement announcing: 'Rex Harrison and his wife are living separately and apart.' He married Richard Harris's ex-wife on 26 August 1971.
2. *The Fearless Vampire Killers.*

I make my position completely clear: I don't want to be an Administrative Artistic Director; Bill is prepared to commit for a year; Anthony won't commit – but wants a contract making it clear he can/will take over for one year out of three . . . but when?! Of course the thing is unworkable . . . It is agreed an Artistic Committee (working) shall be established – to meet (monthly?) under the chairmanship of Oscar (or Robin).

Most significantly: George Harewood again affirms that he has no time regularly to attend committee meetings (a statement that occasions not a raised eyebrow) – and DOES NOT raise the question of the Chairmanship of the Committee. At the end of the meeting he asks Robin if he is free for lunch with Neville . . . 'Yes,' says Robin – if Jocelyn doesn't turn up, since he was under the impression she would be at the meeting and was going to lunch with her . . . And what happened? George Harewood takes off with Neville and Robin (with 'ice round his heart' as he exclaims – or some such expression) . . . but they are saved by the arrival of Jocelyn, who, all typical innocence, joins them and effectively prevents the murder of Caesar. George Harewood takes off for India and Australia, and nothing is changed.

14 January 1970

Run-through of *Three Months Gone*.[1] Disappointing is the word, and confirming my worst intuitions of Ron Eyre's cosy company methods – not coming into the theatre, too much sitting in the author's pocket, but most damagingly this kind of intellectualising direction, full of 'ideas' *about* the characters, yet short on intuitive apprehension of them . . . Ron Eyre seems to direct in abrupt, rather flirtatious, clever-rather-than-wise, incisive *dabs*: 'That's lovely, Di darling; yes, just stand there, no need to move.' 'Perfect, Jill treasure: that's right, the sad bit, the lonely bit.' The schoolmasterly authority rings false to me: too tense, too urgent; it lacks the deeper current of true authority and therefore irritates me with its falsity. Defensive facades are amongst the supreme irritants as far as I'm concerned. [It's] direction from the outside, done with great crispness and apparent know-how, but lacking in ultimate authority . . . limitations revealed most strongly in lack of overall rhythm, lack of real acting, too much ping-pong dialogue, Ann Jellicoe-like verbal patterning.

Really disappointing – and one reason why I really couldn't be an Artistic Director . . . Not interested just to keep a theatre running with productions by Michael Blakemore, Ron Eyre, even Peter Wood or Philip Grant et al. Why bother?

15 January 1970

Just leaving the flat at 10 when the phone rings. I'm glad I answer it because – really out of the blue – it's Jon Voight . . . He wants to know if I'm free – have you had breakfast?

---

1. Donald Howarth's play, designed by Jocelyn Herbert, starring Jill Bennett, Warren Clarke and Diana Dors.

But I'm not free. At 10.30 I have to see someone from South Africa – at 11 a management meeting – at 1 lunch with Lois Sieff and Nick Wright[1] – and at 3.30 David Stone with his Royal Shakespeare friends in *The Tent* . . . so I say, 'I'll be free about 5.30.' 'I'll pick you up at 5.30 then, right?' . . . I am still amazed when Jon arrives at 5.30, comes upstairs to the offices, and I'm pleased to feel so pleased to see him, and to feel so free to express myself pleased . . . There's a forthrightness, an openness and emotional commitment that I find entirely charming . . . And a mystery also: for instance a wish that we should work together – but an ultimate evasiveness, a retirement into self, maybe into his own problems which I don't very well understand – that results in us parting with friendly warmth, but inconclusive.

I haven't talked with anyone with that kind of sympathy and interest and shared humour – well, since I was friends with Richard, I suppose. Of course there is a terrific egocentricity there, with a compulsiveness that can be boring: how he played Romeo, how he 'found' a certain scene . . . this all the way up Park Lane, halting outside the Dorchester, continuing as I summoned a taxi. We got in and proceeded to the Escargot . . . 'I found the key – I was never going to see her again – not just "Farewell" – and I thought of someone I was very fond of and I'd treated badly and I just couldn't see her again.' It's hard to keep up with that sort of thing, hard to throw in what one feels are the necessary comments . . . But there's a warmth and humour and, I don't know, is it *energy*?

The funny thing about Jon is that, though we talk away nineteen to the dozen, and spark off each other in the most sympathetic way, he never (or hasn't yet) gets to the point of specifically asking me to read anything, or to consider anything . . . He talked about a writer he admired, and a script about a boxer, which he liked . . . but, 'If I asked you to do it, I think you'd say no. You'd probably find it too American . . .' Then he talked about how the new man at – Warners was it? – wanted to set up a company and finance the development of a subject, or subjects – with his West Coast agent (whom he trusts and likes) as head of the firm. But should he? I talked about how I was suspicious of the 'industry' and the big sums . . . and he said he was too . . . I suppose the truth is he doesn't know where he is. He mentioned *Peer Gynt* as a musical and a Broadway version of *Armstrong's Last Goodnight* – and some film with the chap who directed *Cold Day in the Park*, and he also, over dinner, remarked that he might well give up acting altogether and become a pop singer like Joe Cocker.

We did laugh a lot, about my quizzing him about the Donner Pass – to show I really had read *The American West*. Then about *Hamlet*, which he said he thought was impossible and very funny, because Hamlet obviously had no sense of humour. I like

1. Nicholas Wright, director of the Royal Court Theatre Upstairs until March 1971.

him when he says he does like Alan Bates, and he was very nice when they met, but he did say some pretty mean things about me!

As we dined at the Escargot, Jon went into a fantasy – how we would set up a picture to be shot in Mexico, get all the money, go down there and shoot nothing, but send tremendously enthusiastic reports back and make a tremendous killing . . . In the helter-skelter of talk he somehow started talking of Malcolm – an undercurrent of jealousy? – maybe I mentioned the rewriting of his script, and Jon remarked how Malcolm must be pretty intelligent, with a shrewd sense of direction . . . We went from the Escargot back to his hotel – a crummy one on the Cromwell Road: he said he'd hated the Carlton Tower and asked them to book something less pretentious, but this was exaggerating a little.

24 January 1970

I met Malcolm [McDowell] at the pub up the road, where we used to lunch when we were rehearsing *In Celebration* . . . He was full of Bryan Forbes, whom he now says they have pressured into co-operating into collaboration with Shelagh Delaney, instead of just taking over her script of *The Raging Moon* . . . Of course, having the other day asked me not to cast Paul Moriarty[1] in *The Contractor* before seeing how things went on his project, he had totally forgotten the idea. I didn't raise it, and privately (wryly) smiled at my persistent regard for such pleas (since I *had* delayed giving Paul the okay) . . . Malcolm chatters most amiably, and he *is* a nice fellow, but it all seems to be *impulse* – not sustained. Good for the screen of course.

26 January 1970

Morning: screening of Barney Platts-Mills's *Bronco Bullfrog* at the trendy Trident viewing theatre . . . It steals up on you, this picture, starting simply and a bit gauchely with its genre-picture of semi-delinquent East End kids, then gradually concentrating on its principal boy and girl, a lumpen-proletariat Romeo and Juliet, sensitive and ignorant, limited irrevocably by the cultural desert into which they've been born, and everywhere, ever-present, the sense of waste . . . It reminded me of *Saved*, though without the over-aestheticism that has always made that play insupportable to me beyond the interval . . .

Michael [Medwin] came to the theatre this evening . . . Poor Michael! He spent most of our dinner unburdening himself of his disappointment and bitterness and resentment at Albert's action in taking *Scrooge* – and in choosing not to involve Memorial! Have the scales fallen? Certainly I think Michael received it as a blow. He is talking again of closing the office. I encourage him . . . Michael also informed me

---

1. Who came to notice in the Belgrade Theatre run of *Billy Liar*.

Stanley Jaffe[1] is in town: would like to see me: asked Michael about the rumour he'd heard, that I said I'd never do another picture for Paramount (where on earth did that one come from?) Michael told them I'm at the Royal Court – curious they didn't ring. I wonder if that is because Jaffe doesn't want to run the risk of a rebuff? Anyway Michael speaks of renewed protestations that they want to work with us – renewed mentions of *Galileo*[2] – and of some project Jaffe wants to mention to me which already has another producer . . . the word 'Western' seems associated . . . I pricked up my ears . . . It is really curious how, whatever our intelligent and rational objections, there *is* something magnetic, something exciting, something altogether special about the idea of the Hollywood majors. Money? Power? The dangerous challenge? I have an instinct which pulls me that way – maybe fantasy – but somehow altogether more alluring than the idea of another British film. To escape from this provincial atmosphere, where one is the freakish, unhonoured prophet.

2 February 1970

Bill [Gaskill] returns to the Court – we have our first brisk row – oil and water, according to tradition, don't mix . . . Bill is a strange character, with the kind of ambivalence and ambiguity you really seem to find only in Chekhov. He is very emotional, yet he can behave with extreme coldness. He is sensitive, but with the kind of ruthless insensibility that seems sometimes an absolute principle. He can talk with great incisiveness, logical and to the point. Yet he is essentially whimsical and erratic. His allegiances switch with a rapidity that is itself highly emotional, and I've no doubt that he himself is unaware why his feelings should be what they are. He reacted with dismissive distaste towards *The Big Romance*[3] – and permitted himself to remain totally uninvolved – to speak to no one – to indulge the famous Gaskill sniff. I could feel his defensive coldness when I said: 'It would have been nice if you could have said something to someone.'

'Well, I didn't like the play.'

'Yes, but didn't you think Roger [Williams] had done a good job?'

(*Hesitation.*) 'Y-e-e-e-s . . . And it was well performed . . . But when I saw that empty stage, I thought, oh dear, we've seen it all before . . . It seemed like every Sunday night for the last ten years. I found it a profoundly depressing evening.'

---

1. American producer (1940–).
2. By Brecht; filmed in 1975 by Joseph Losey, with Topol. L.A. was offered the role of 'the infuriated monk' in Losey's film but turned it down at the risk of 'disappointing my public, who would surely have been drawn to *Galileo* primarily in order to see my performance, and found themselves cheated by a single appearance and only two lines to speak.' (From a letter to Robert Lantz, 28 June 1974.)
3. Sunday production by Robert Thornton, with Brian Cox.

He is being carried away by a mysterious avant-garde jag (I would call it a fantasy) in which he imagines the stage – or the Theatre Upstairs – filled with some kind of weird, exhilarating, intoxicating NEW EXPERIENCES. Roger Croucher has been detailed to make a report for him of the experimental centres of activity up and down the country. In the theatre Bill is adopting a kind of 'new broom' attitude of extreme incisiveness and practicality. This is tonic in a way, but profoundly irritating when it reduces itself to parroting, 'But how much will it *cost*...' when I am trying to discuss changing our classified ads, so that they appeared at least conventionally prominent. Finally I flared up. 'Go and fucking well find out for yourself how much it will cost ...' White-faced, Bill in his leather jacket, marched brusquely out of the room.

Later we sort of made it up, but it is agony for Bill to have to make any personal concessions to anyone. He resents the idea that he should have to tell anyone what he is doing. Of course I am faulted – justifiably – because I have a fundamental evasiveness – yet when I become involved in a day-to-day administrative situation I behave with radical insistence.

I do feel a fraud just now, relapsing again into interior uncertainty – lostness – indecisiveness, behind a facade of achievement and certainty. Here is my ambiguity – I suppose this is a universal human principle? This is interesting in relation to acting ... Do we in general catch enough of the ambiguity in every human character when we do our plays? Could this be a principle of characterisation? Of course the vividness and consciousness of subjective emotions and private fantasy must vary in every human being. At times, release from the Court has seemed infinitely desirable.

4 February 1970

Went to see Monty[1] this morning, and handed him my first cheque for 22,000 dollars!

A mad visit from Desmond O'Donovan as I sit in my office with Vivian and Brian Cox, who keeps dropping in as they continue to run *The Big Romance*. Desmond says he is going to India: he wanted to meet me and got rather angry when I didn't write an appointment in my diary, 'The rich man in his castle, the poor man at his gate ...' I got a little scared, particularly when he kicked the desk, quoting Bishop Berkeley.

In the afternoon Bill starts discussing the programme: a company for the autumn: what plays do you want to do? *Home – Hamlet – What the Butler Saw* ... Really I don't know ... I find out that *Midnight Cowboy* starts at 4.39 at the Odeon King's Road ... I have been wanting to go again, and discover a strange compulsion ... Manage to break free about 4.32. (How difficult it is concisely to end a conversation with Helen!) The King's Road is wet and rainy ... there is not a bus to be seen in any direction – I walk – run a bit – I feel like one of the rats of Norway. I get into the cinema about the

---

1. Monty White, L.A.'s accountant. The money was a royalty cheque for *If* ....

second image. Interesting to see again: I feel even more acutely the *clever* nature of the talent. How John [Schlesinger], strangely, can never let an emotion play itself through – except in some of the duet scenes – gets obsessed with effects – illustration . . . I don't somehow feel any of it is *true* . . . until the end . . . somehow when Jon [Voight] changes into ordinary clothes, it was extraordinarily moving. And the end was marvellously played. I suppose this sensation I have of dissatisfaction in spite of the very evident quality of the work, is due to two things: lack of an overall, organic conception, particularly by the director – and a complementary lack of cohesiveness and organic development in the performances. Thus I don't see any real relationship between Joe Buck in the bus and in the streets of New York, and the Joe Buck who considers himself (genuinely) dangerous – and who suffered the childhood of the flashbacks and the obscure humiliations also glimpsed in those sequences . . . well, *some* relationship – vulnerability particularly – but the narcissism is too blithe . . . And Razzo's homosexuality is too disguised – his emotional isolation and need as if glimpsed from a passing train . . . Of course this all relates to the superficiality, the glitter and surface 'effect' of John's direction, always with this insistence on the laughs (as opposed to the profounder reaches of comedy).

It also highlights the enormous difficulty, in a film made under these conditions, of achieving characterisations in depth, that develop and that change. Jon achieves his end beautifully, but he doesn't manage the apparently effortless progression that the role needs. And this is because (no doubt I'm partial – but it is consistent with everything that John has ever done) the director's guiding hand, though strict, lacks the understanding and the guiding control, and the proper sensitivity, which alone could create the conditions under which such an organically conceived and developed performance could be achieved.

7 February 1970

Malcolm rang me at midnight last night, excited and overwhelmed that Stanley Kubrick wants him for *A Clockwork Orange*. (I can see this might well make a Kubrick subject). Apparently Kubrick is a great admirer of *If . . . .*, which he has seen four times. Malcolm was very sweet and generous – attributing the credit to me. It doesn't happen often.

9 February 1970

First I go to Memorial: chiefly to leave my bag. Nothing has changed: the same atmosphere of mess and unreality, friendliness, amateurish incompetence, disappointment. Albie, who had a day off from *Scrooge*. How fat in the face he looks! It's no good. It is somehow inconceivable now that I should set out to make a film of *Galileo* with him. No – really, it's over.

The Dorchester does not provide the expensive Ritzy lunch that fantasy imagines. In the Universal suite it's shirtsleeve time – the boys are leaving for New York in an hour – they have ordered sandwiches and coffee: is that all right? Dorchester sandwiches are dull and the coffee is skimpy ... It's the usual story: we're out for a new kind of film – no stars – you have complete liberty – bring you in on advertising policy etc ... They listen *a bit* ... but it's all rather as though they're calling out from an express train. It does all make me feel a bit of a cunt, though. Shouldn't I be taking advantage of all these splendid, wide-open offers? To do *something*?

I got to the theatre rather late in the afternoon – having had to return via Memorial, and again run the Medwin gauntlet ... rather nice to find on my desk a script called *The Abyss*, sent to me by a New York producer called Jon Peterson – on the recommendation of Jon Voight ... How schizophrenic I am: I don't immediately get down to reading it. I like to carry it home, and relish for a moment the sense of emotional security it gives me ...

9 April 1970

Thursday. The Council Meeting of the English Stage Company, and the inevitable collapse before the Arts Council threat of withdrawal of subsidy if Hilary Spurling[1] is not reinvited. I tried to propose a press statement first, simply making public the Arts Council's blackmailing attempt ... But only Jocelyn and Robin supported it. Interestingly, Oscar and John Osborne were both for immediate capitulation: Peggy Ashcroft's worried, charming, stupid liberal face radiated desire for the relief and calm of appeasement from the other end of the table ... Blacksell popped his eyes stupidly, and with incredibly obstinate persistence reiterated his belief that Hilary Spurling 'wasn't worth it', and his confidence (genuine or just an excuse or self-deception?) that the Arts Council would be willing to conduct the important discussions about dramatic criticism we'd asked for, *after* the tiresome difficulty had been disposed of ... Bill veered erratically, but had abandoned his radical position of the week before.

10 April 1970

Somewhat tired, somewhat deflated, somewhat depressed ... the post-coital sadness after the opening of *The Contractor* on Monday – the disappointment of the inevitable parsimonious or insensitive reviews (once again Michael Billington, repeating his misunderstanding of the play under the appetising heading of DRAMATISING WORK – I sat down immediately and wrote a complaining letter to John Higgins) – and of course the depressive effect of thin houses. Quite apart from the usual blankness now the work is over ...

---

1. Theatre critic of *The Spectator*, from whom press facilities had been withdrawn in the previous year. They were reinstated 'under duress' of the Arts Council threat.

This is the paradox of my position – of which I become the more conscious the more I am written about, interviewed, taken for granted as the epitome of the very reverse. As the epitome, I mean, of aggressive, intransigent creative independence. And I see – I must acknowledge – that I *am* 'difficult' – precisely in this confusing mixture of strength and weakness, in my need to dominate (my capacity to dominate), and yet my perpetual craving for reassurance and support. As this is not understood about me as a person, it is not understood about me as an artist.

14 April 1970

Vladimir [Pucholt] arrived back from Sheffield last night for a couple of days:[1] returning with Malcolm and Margo[2] from the reception at the Czech Embassy. Malcolm has just finished his Bryan Forbes film, and is considering now a script from Sergio Leone (co-starring Rod Steiger)[3] which perhaps he could fit in *before* his work with Kubrick!

Today I went to see Sir Ralph Richardson – at 5.30 ('Whisky time') in his elegant and civilised house in Chester Terrace. A manservant lets me in and escorts me past small landscape oils, up the beige carpeted staircase to the first-floor sitting room with its drinks table, its comfortable sofas and chairs and its aristocratic view of Regent's Park. Sir Ralph when he came in had no recollection of our having met before . . . (During our conversation I had cause to remind him, apropos his subscribing to the 'magic circle' theory – 'there's such divinity doth hedge an actor' – that actors shouldn't be *touched*: and I told him about Ian [Bannen] as Brutus not wanting to be touched – and my saying 'use it!'). He is a quite extraordinary mixture of simplicity, naivety, even simple-mindedness, combined with real acuteness, instinctive intelligence, a sort of intuitive *wiliness* . . . very direct, very honest. Which part did I think he should play, and which John? I said Jack for him and Harry for John. The idea seemed to please him. 'Johnny's more *poetic* than me . . .' He described how John Gielgud had introduced him to music. 'I had a gramophone, and I had a record . . . "Tea for Two" . . . And Johnny said – would you like me to lend you a record? And I said: I'm not so sure . . .' All the same, Johnny did lend him a record – Bach – and he thought it was absolutely spiffing . . .

17 April 1970

In the world outside – Apollo 13 is making its return (from man's twenty-fifth trip into space), and the world is supposed to be agog, hearts full of hope, fear and prayer. Yet I must admit I have seen and felt no evidence of this: not from Vladimir – not from the visiting Czechs – not from anyone at the theatre. 'We have given our hearts away – a sordid boon . . . !' Alas, except on television, I don't believe anyone cares deeply.

---

1. Where he was studying to be a doctor.
2. Malcolm McDowell's first wife.
3. *A Fistful of Dynamite*.

Had to get up this morning to get to the theatre to try to precipitate (or force) some decision on the *Home* situation with its manifold complications – Dandy Nichols's agent must be phoned by 10.10 *if* we want to get her out of her telly *if* we are going to start rehearsals early ... Sir Ralph wants to start on the 27th (!!): Sir John wants to start May 4th ... can we tour? Sir Ralph would tour for three weeks but Sir John will only tour for one week ... My feelings are very mixed. Partly through fatigue, I suppose, and not being exactly in the pink, and partly through having run out of steam somehow, lost faith in the worth of these intense efforts – I can't summon up a really dynamic personal effort ... Yet for the play – which means for David, and rationally for the Court as well, for the preservation of this current myth of creative vitality, it seems we can't let slip this fantastic cast of John Gielgud – Ralph Richardson – Mona Washbourne – Dandy Nichols *and*! Warren Clarke in David Storey's *Home*!

Oscar was supposed to be going off today with Eileen till Tuesday but he dropped in last night to pick up a script – read it – liked it – and came down to the Court to chase up Bill and Helen – and certainly helped to make it possible.

18 April 1970
I would like to have stayed in bed, but thought I'd better go in to *The Contractor* ... Business has been well up this week, and excellent publicity accruing from Prince Charles' visit on Thursday, his first night out apparently since returning from Australia. Pictures in pretty well all the papers, with the name of the play and theatre mentioned ... This being England, I'm sure the result will be helpful. Good for him, anyway.

Performance of first act at the matinee seemed to me woefully laboured: everyone seemingly laugh-conscious, pushing too hard, Bill Owen[1] monotonous and slogging at it. I went round in the interval and delivered broadside – as a result, in the course of the second act both Paul (Moriarty) *and* Connie [Constance Chapman] were 'off' ...! But the performance did improve. They thought they were not forcing it – but as a result it had got heavy. I suggested that if they wanted to save energy on a matinee, they must play *lightly*.

Also that the only attitude to laughs must be – 'If they don't get it – that's one up to us – we're not going to spell it out for them.' Dangerous advice of course, but it appealed to them. Wrote notes between the shows, then retreated back to cosy bed.

Man's Castle was on late-night TV. What innocent poetry movies had then (about 1933): and with a director like [Frank] Borzage the genuine survival of silent-film imagery. And though of course finally sentimentalised, a quite genuine, casual reality – tender-selfish – beautifully lightly presented by Spencer Tracy. The kind of thing Albert *ought* to do – or to have done. He's too old and fat now.

---

1. (1914–1993). Known nationally as 'Compo' in *Last of the Summer Wine*, made his film debut in *The Way to the Stars*.

19 April 1970
Sunday. This business of being in bed – really pleasant – and no one really wants to visit me, and I don't want to see anyone.

Well, the Clores did visit me this afternoon. And that was quite a bore and quite tiring. It is a shame that Miriam has become so preposterous, with a compulsion to indulge in a continually cutting 'wit' which, having no basis in reality, and only the most distant relation to wit (it is like some inept parody of sophistication) only manages to be totally idiotic.

I let them in in my dressing-jacket: 'Why,' drawls Miriam – 'You're in your pyjamas!'

'Of course I am – what the hell do you expect . . . ?'

Leon smokes a cigar, talks foolishly and smiles fondly at Miriam's 'outrageous' sallies . . . They are both so totally unconcerned with my state that I can't be bothered even to invite them to a cup of tea – though the kettle is boiling in the kitchen.

Before the Clores arrived – *The Last of the Mohicans*, George B. Seitz, 1935: Randolph Scott, Binnie Barnes, Heather Angel and Henry Wilcoxon. I remember how boring that seemed (I didn't see it) when I was twelve or thirteen! Now the film has an enjoyable vigour: absolutely no subtlety or 'poetry' of course. I am surprised, rather, to see that Randolph Scott *was* rather beautiful then. And at least I start reading the book.

20 April 1970
The Last of the Mohicans is enjoyable: surprisingly so . . . the writing often stiff and prosy, with quite impossible dialogue, yet the narrative gripping, and throughout the whole thing a strange poetic power, difficult to define. Is it an allegorical power? If only someone would propose *this* kind of subject. One of the maddening things about this present period of illness and fatigue is that I haven't managed to see all these films I've been promising myself: however, I did manage to squeeze in *Medium Cool* which I was expecting to disapprove of – flashy etc . . . But in fact I thought it was brilliant, nightmarish, and precisely and powerfully reflecting the kind of atmosphere Paul Williams was so obsessed by. The last part of the film is unfortunate – because the characters and the 'plot' all have to become pulled around in order to effect a junction with the Chicago material. This is what the critics chiefly wrote about, and of course it's the least poetic and eloquent part of the film. You really feel that neo-Fascism hatching.

21 April 1970
Attended a publicity meeting at the Court . . . Find myself scathing and edgy: very rude about Bill's souvenir 'brochure' . . . I don't know why, but blatantly bad layout and design work always irritates me terribly.

24 April 1970

Rachel rang from Hollywood.[1] She shot her big scene yesterday: One and a half pages in one take, and at the end all the technicians burst into applause . . . Alas that scepticism should have eaten so deep into me: my genuine reaction is, or would be, to remark *either* that their taste is so poor that very likely the performance was a bad one, or that they are so used to any kind of professionalism in acting that just the level of accomplishment you'd expect from a competent rep actress would seem to them like genius . . . Anyway, it did Rachel good, and what the assistant said, and the cameraman said, and the hairdresser and the driver and goodness knows who else. She has been invited to do a play at the Mark Taper Forum,[2] which much excites her – though she doesn't know what it is! The trouble with Rachel, of course, is that she makes one feel so totally unreal: all I am is the image of some loved, authoritative mentor, no relation to 'me' at all. I don't mean she wouldn't be generous if one demanded it.

25 April 1970

I am being pursued by a certain Charles Kasher about a script of *Edward II* – with Ian McKellen – which I shall NEVER MAKE.

At 12 I report to 1 Chester Terrace, where David [Storey] and I are to be received by Sir Ralph [Richardson] in that elegant first-floor drawing room. I arrive first: when Ralph comes in he looks intently, curiously at me – for a moment I wonder if he will remember who I am. He responds well to directness. I ask him what he imagines David will be like (he says 'Light on his toes') and am telling him about David's rugby league [career] when David arrives, having walked from Camden Town. They get on extremely well – particularly when David comments enthusiastically on Ralph's Persian and Chinese paintings. ('Nobody ever says anything about them: I feel rather hurt.') They talk of Nicholson (William), whom Ralph admires and collects. He describes how he actually started off to be a painter, but they told him he had no talent – so he got a job apprenticed to a theatre company. He was a very bad actor (he says), but he burned his boats: he *had* to learn to be good. He wished, he said, that he'd made the same determined assault on painting: he felt he really had more of a natural gift for that . . .

He took us upstairs to show us a David Cox sketch he'd bought the other day. He looked in at a drawing room on the way up, in which I intuitively sensed the impatient presence of Lady [Mu] Richardson.[3] 'Are you cross?' he murmured, as he closed the door – but carried on upstairs with us.

I was grateful for David's presence – so solid and yet so sensitive: when he looks at a Nicholson landscape and says it's good – you know it is . . . And tact. When Ralph

---

1. She was filming *Doctors' Wives*, with Richard Crenna and Gene Hackman.
2. Theatre in Los Angeles. It opened in 1967 with a production of John Whiting's *The Devils*.
3. Meriel Forbes.

asked him if he didn't admire Coldstream, he replied: 'I think I prefer some of his more decorative contemporaries ...'

The unseen presence of Mu hastened our departure: but, as David remarked, 'It might have been written for him ...' Both roles actually.

29 April 1970

Had lunch with Roger Williams and Warren Clarke: I was astounded that *neither* of them could name a play written by Maxim Gorki. And another surprising thing Roger said was that Paul [Moriarty] is homosexual. Warren said, with a certain knowledgeable firmness, 'No – he's not.' But it's strange – such a thought had never occurred to me. He is beautiful of course – beautiful eyes – but surely shy rather than 'queer'.

Trapped at the Court in that way that is so exhausting and annoyingly wasteful: Helen talking and talking, I protesting strongly at the idea of seat prices being put up to 32/6 (from 25/-) for *Home*.

4 May 1970

Just a note – for history – as, at 8.35, I finish going through the first act of *Home*, and I am on the brink of getting up, making my way to the Court, and STARTING AGAIN ... No doubt my fantasy of just doing nothing would be not much more pleasant. It will be a good thing to start. Face the challenge. Oh yes. (To my shame I have spoken to neither Mona nor Dandy Nichols since they were engaged ... the complications of life.) So one just starts.

Get down to the Court about ten – Murray lifted me down. Groans and apprehension. Feel better when Sir John and Sir Ralph arrive, spruce and dapper. Jocelyn with the set. David. Roger Williams a good, proper assistant – the first in a very long time. Julie a discreet and proper stage manager. That intelligent, respectful boy Gregory to make with the cups of tea ... Bill puts in an appearance: as he talks to John I notice the edge of slightly pushed familiarity: 'oiling up'? Warren Clarke – not very 'noticed' by the Knights. They are shy, unassuming, obstinate, slightly snobby?

The week is almost entirely spent with John and Ralph: Dandy is still televising: Mona at Guildford, on *Harvey*.[1] This means we only have the ladies on Tuesday ... Not too bad a scheme, probably, since it means a strong concentration on Act I, and perhaps even more important direct and intense and unremitting contact between the Gentlemen and myself, with David sitting down in the front row of the stalls, appealed to from time to time, often replying, 'I don't know' – sometimes commenting, sometimes enlightening, sometimes just sticking, with a kind of shy obstinacy.

We started – in my usual 'empirical' way (lazy or organic?) – with some cuts, since I was quite frightened with the idea of reading an uncut version, and reinforcing the

---

1. With James Stewart.

actors' already quite evident apprehension that they were embarking on an impossible venture.

John's dialogue runs approximately – 'I haven't the slightest idea what I'm doing . . . I don't understand a word of it . . . I am so frightened they'll just get terribly bored with me sitting here saying oh yes . . . oh . . . yes . . . I've no idea how to do it – there seem to be an infinite number of ways of saying each line and I've no idea which one to choose . . . I've no idea what it's all about . . .'

Ralph of course is much less hysterical, with much more of a method of approach (however eccentric or, at times, misguided), though even he repeats: 'I feel a complete amateur.'

9 May 1970

To recap the week, we ran the first scene this morning, and then the last bit – John apologises charmingly for being 'so useless' yesterday (which was certainly the case) and things are much better today . . . The end is quite moving: John cries; but *still* the music of 'See the church,' and Ralph's references to God, elude them both . . . However that will come.

Alan Price is there when the lights go up. We go and have a drink at the Antelope. He talks of using a Moog synthesiser – which makes a lovely bird noise . . . I am totally open-minded – empirical . . .

11 May 1970

Woke with immense weariness, aching limbs, and strong disinclination to get up. And of course, at 9.15, the phone rings and from far away there's that husky squeak – 'Hullo Linds . . .' Yes, it's the implacable Rachel. She makes me speak to her black man, Paul: a deep voice says: 'I'm going to pull her together whatever happens . . . she's one of the beautiful people' (or something like that). I grimace, and try to pull my trousers on without dropping the receiver.

Actually the day not so bad, Scene 1 is struggled through, John has got some way with the words – then on to Scene 2 – John and Ralph return cheery from lunch together at the Garrick. Scene 2 goes quite well: better placings achieved by keeping the men together more – I giggle quite a lot – plentiful cuts in the last part of the scene.

14 May 1970

Scene 1 again: John and Ralph – get some more cuts in, including that from Mrs Washington to the card tricks (goodbye to the orchard, which gives some pain to John) – harsh, but all to the good I'm sure . . . Lunch with David and Ralph at Au Père de Nico: I am rather guilty when David pays . . . but think he's getting something quite nice just now from *The Contractor*. Ralph is really charming: they talk books . . .

heavens, how little I read nowadays! Ralph is extraordinarily generous – when he says he feels privileged (or 'honoured') to be on the stage with those two ladies – he is courteously overstating of course, but the generous appreciation is certainly there.

Prospective documentary-makers from the London School of Film Technique watch the rehearsal. I am glad the pure gold of these rehearsals is not altogether wasted . . .

15 May 1970

Only half a day, which is nice . . . but at lunch – at the Antelope – catastrophe strikes. I am enjoying my lamb cutlets and salad – there appears Victor Henry in dark glasses. He is in late rehearsal stage for Arnold (Wesker)'s play at the Round House. And asks for help! I promise to join him when I've finished lunch. He isn't drunk, but there's that over-emotionalism that I don't like very much: because it doesn't seem altogether *true* . . . or rather it's true – for him – but not for anyone else . . . too much kissing: emotion demonstrated rather than felt. Downstairs are Ian Holm and Roy Marsden (the young actor who has taken over from Jimmy Bolam) and the stage manager of *The Friends*. They announce themselves in a state of desperation. Relations with Arnold appear to have broken down completely. There seems to be some doubt whether the play will go on: I'm not sure whether this is something to be feared or desired . . . Arnold doesn't speak to them after run-throughs. As far as I can make out, I am being asked to come and see the play at a run-through tonight, and really say YES or NO . . . That is to say YES – provide the authority and reassurance and confirmation that is the job of a director.

A difficult situation. Of course I am touched on a weak spot: an appeal for help – how can one leave it unanswered? But this of all plays! I don't like it (and I tell them so). Probably I can't think how they ever allowed themselves to get in such a situation: you'd think that Ian Holm at least, with all his experience, would have more sense. But they're actors – and they haven't.

(I am the more put out because Alan Price has a TV show in the evening, he's got tickets for me, and I didn't want to disappoint him . . . however: noblesse oblige.) So I set off for the Round House. When I arrive I'm pleased to see John Fletcher there: he's been doing photographs for the production. I feel protected somewhat. Arnold is there, with long thick hair and open shirt revealing black matted hairy chest. Unappetising. I go up to him. He says: 'I'm glad Victor invited you . . .' (letting me know he knows). It's a curious atmosphere. Ian Holm buys me a drink as I sit exposed in the auditorium next to John. On the stage is Sue Engel. I wave surreptitiously.

Of course there's nothing useful I can say about the play, which I like as little as when I read it. (Not exhaustively, but enough to find it pretentious and humourless and unreal in its complacent sort of way). The set (by Nicholas Georgiadis – all art nouveau and operatic) is huge – spread lengthwise in front of the auditorium. Much of it I can't hear. Enormous set speeches: acting effecty and rhetorical – but how else could you cope with the material? It's the kind of stuff I shut off from, so never begin to understand. At the end some preposterous shouted farrago about middle-class values, working-class values, snobbery, Lenin, etc.

All I can do afterwards is to assure the actors that the characters and relationships are strongly and clearly studied. The whole thing is too massive – and too set – for notes. I try to persuade Arnold to cut it: but I doubt he will.

Next morning, on an impulse, I ring Arnold. I upbraid him for not looking after his actors . . . But I've been so good to them, he wails, and they've rejected me . . . His willfulness really is Right to him. I tell him not to be self-indulgent and to cut his play. But he bobs back like a cork.

17 May 1970
Sunday – Rachel, of course rings. She just needs a father-figure, an authority-figure to talk to (or *at*), to reassure herself, to test . . . Rather an embarrassing challenge, particularly when I'm caught halfway into my clothes, one eye on the clock, as I try to go on struggling into my socks or my sweater . . . Protestations of love rather dry me up – particularly when I don't believe in them. Not that Rachel lies: it's just impossible not to feel that she's using me as a wailing wall . . . without the slightest idea or interest in what I'm doing, or indeed actually *am*. Most embarrassing is when she insists that I speak to her lover – the black gambler – or the writer of this play she wants to do at the Mark Taper Forum ('I love you because Rachel loves you and I love Rachel . . .' 'Well, thank you').

20 May 1970
We run through the first scene for hours first, then on to the girls. This is the hardest scene (Act II in the script). All moves seem wrong, and yet it's impossible to play it static. And the moves only work when the feeling is right. And Ralph's approach is so relentlessly logical: how can he be given the idea of tears which flow for some obscure, only half-perceived reason – tears finally for the woe of all the world?

Alan Price came today and watched. Then we went for lunch (David went off with the Knights for an expensive nosh-up!) to the pub. Alan has an urgent animation that I find immensely attractive: his clear eyes are very bright as he talks away – some of it nonsensical (such as his combined and urgent schemes for the Court to make films of its productions), but very sympathetic. A natural enthusiast.

Andy Gaye in great difficulties over the poster for *Home*. Alas, he has no sense of elegance, no wit, and very little style. He is quite stupid really, I suppose. His original idea today was an envelope, with emerging from it an invitation card inscribed 'John Gielgud and Ralph Richardson at *Home* . . .' the postmark on the card reading ROYAL

COURT, and the *stamp* bearing the Blake design I had presented him with. You can't win . . .

21 May 1970

Sticky wicket – the most difficult scene remains 'Act II' . . . Ralph's crying – how to produce it, how to move it, how to surmount it . . . Perhaps we have cut too much? And I make the mistake of worrying too much about *moves*. We all end up exhausted.

22 May 1970

A satisfying day: our usual 10.30 start, running the lines of the first scene – then taking the second half of it in more detail. It's continuously necessary to get them to *think* – particularly John, who learns the lines by rote (he says he can visualise them on the page!) rather than by emotional continuity . . . He can produce the most sensitive, apparently deep vibrations and apparently a minimum of *thought*: likewise he is weak at concretely imagining – creating for us the clouds, the church in the distance, the dust on the table – or rather not weak (since he can do it brilliantly, magnetically) but just *negligent* . . . such is his relationship, I suppose, with the world outside him. He isn't very humorous – his jokes are terribly weak ('No noose is good noose . . .') where Ralph's are quirky, odd, funny . . . Ralph's is a brilliantly contrasting talent: he thinks a great deal, but often tortuously, creating and sticking to an idea which is eccentric and quite wrong . . . And of course both are stars, virtuosi, therefore quite egocentric.

Lunch is always a bit embarrassing, since they like to eat well – Ralph particularly, who is very generous – but they *don't invite the ladies* . . .

We both agreed first thing: we'd got a bit hysterical yesterday. And really it's quite simple – the moment he cries, do nothing. He'd the right conclusion. We put a few lines back (I was throwing them in – say this – say this – to the utter confusion of Mona and poor deaf Dandy) – and it worked. We went through the whole play. It seemed to work.

Managed to get myself in the evening to A *Fistful of Dollars* and (half) its successor.[1] Cold, calculated – almost abstracted fantasies. But I see the power: Leone has his own, obsessive vision.

25 May 1970

Two weeks before our opening performance at Brighton. It seems to me the cast is doing very well with a difficult job – maybe I've got this strange idea about Ralph which makes me surprised and delighted that he can know *any* of it . . . Lunch at Don Luigi's: for once this brings the gentlemen and the ladies together, since I organise it (and pay for it). John chatters away in splendid form.

---

1. *For a Few Dollars More*, both directed by Sergio Leone.

Drop round to the Clores after work: Miriam opens the door, a scarf saucily, piratically knotted round her head and over her right eye. We eat toast and caviar: Marius comes in, a spoiled, cocky, rather charmless boy. He may grow out of it.

27 May 1970
In the little comedy of our lunch hours: today I attempted to say, shall we to the Antelope? But it was John's 'turn' and he bid me to our restaurant . . . Now the complication was that we were very much *ensemble*, Jocelyn having just come in and talking about costumes with the ladies . . . Then I see that Dandy, on her way out, has stopped to talk with John . . . I always get very aware of these situations, of susceptibilities and embarrassments, as opposed to Jocelyn, who is always sublimely unaware of trivialities of feeling . . . And in this case, it's not *just* the gents don't particularly want or feel the need of the presence of the ladies, but that John (though he comes each day by a Bentley driven by a lady chauffeur) is delicately *aware of the money side of the affair* . . . Anyway, whether he found himself compelled to invite his fellow-actors or not, in the end we proceed to Au Père de Nico in twos – John and Dandy, Ralph and Mona, Jocelyn and I, for a very pleasant lunch . . . I notice though that, the vibrations somehow communicating themselves, we each only order a main dish . . .

To TV Centre after rehearsal to see Robert Vas's film on Humphrey Jennings for which I did that filmed interview many months ago . . . get into a cab which promptly goes the most traffic-jammed way, gets horribly stuck in Kensington, so leave it and plunge into the underground. At last arrive in the nightmarish Television Centre. The film is revealing, quite painful – substantiating, I would say, my thesis of the twin-blooded Englishman given a miraculous transfusion of vitality by the war, then lapsing again into frustrated dilettantism when that influence was removed . . . I am slightly shocked and rather pleased by my own appearance, speaking with great deliberation and (I would say) authority – trenchant and specific in my anti-'Englishness'. Certainly I stick my neck out, and in that company, with the English un-analytical adorers all around, appear very much the disturbing, radical heavy.

28 May 1970
Booked this morning for a run-through: fairly heavy-going, though not without magic. Ralph goes through this laborious process of having to remember the line, *then* do something with it – which although always productive of 'quality', certainly slows things down . . . John somewhat underprojected – and here also a problem, because if he 'brings it up', then he starts *elocuting*. Dandy has great problems with the lines; Mona staunch, a tower of strength. The end is beautiful, very moving. I have tears in my eyes as I go downstairs. John is in the rear stalls, changing out of his suit. He says: 'It's very short, isn't it?' I can't help bursting into laughter. Alan Price has attended the

run-through. We go to the pub – Jocelyn stirred: she finds it sad and full of quality . . .
Have lunch with Roger [Williams], Alan and his girlfriend, Whiffle, a pleasant fairly
unremarkable girl who goes to spare-time acting classes at the Stanislavski Studio and
has freckles applied with make-up . . . Alan is stirred too, I'm interested to see.

29 May 1970

I go round to see Alan [Price] about six, to hear the themes and discuss them before the
recording session which he has booked for 10 p.m. He said yesterday that he doesn't
want to repeat his curtain up theme for the start of Act II, but has a new one . . . He
plays it. I am delighted. It's a slightly offbeat, slightly nursery-style descending theme.
I suggested he should play it twice an octave higher, then again in the original pitch –
then finish suddenly . . . Easy . . . then I suggest *linking* the first two phrases. It's
interesting how Alan doesn't find it easy to pick up an idea. I get the impression his
own conception, thoughts, impulses, are too strong . . . it's difficult to break in on
them. But I'm very pleased.

We walk round to Beauchamp Place and have a drink outside a rather horrid
pub where tanked-up Australians are spilling out all over the pavement, back to Alan's
flat . . . and off to the recording studio – John Haynes is there to take some pictures.
Impressive atmosphere and equipment of the young electronic era . . . I am again
impressed with Alan – the concentration and feeling he puts into it as he plays are
extraordinary, and his face becomes quite beautiful . . . each attempt at a piece is an
improvised creative venture. But he is persistent, doesn't get bad-tempered, determined
to get it right. The last piece – seventeen takes with many false starts. After, curry, tape-
editing, etc., we finish at about 1.20.

30 May 1970

RACHEL, RACHEL. The phone rings and it is a slightly pissed Rachel – twenty minutes
of that highly emotional, meaningless self-indulgence: 'Now listen to me – I love you –
more than Rex, more than my nigger, more than Christ . . . I love you, Lindsay . . . *Christ*
stop being that ascetic Major-General's son . . . You saved my life and I love you.'

I am pinned back in the chair, exhausted. She'll eat you alive given half a chance. She
wants me to go out there – 'You needn't ever see me, except when I bring you your
coffee in the morning' . . . and I suppose I might. But it's extraordinary how all her *gifts*
are really *demands*.

Exhausted: but down to the theatre for another run-through. The start has slipped
again. Ralph finds it difficult *not* to slip into the scene, and the whole style, as if into a
suit of old clothes. But some fluency is achieved, and the lines are better. I give some
notes; a few words to Warren, who is really excellent. A fine, sensitive actor, he has
caught beautifully the possibility of a certain generosity in Alfred at the end, almost

trying to 'cheer them up'. I suppose the performance will be hardly noticed – but it is a beautiful one. And also splendid in being able to *match*, in confidence and presence, these great leading actors without any sense of being shadowed or *loomed over*.

Drink at the Antelope: Robert Vas and his cameraman have been at the rehearsal ... I am a bit dubious about this – that in order to get material for the *Omnibus* film about the Royal Court we have to submit to an 'item' for *Review* – the penalty of involvement with the fucking MEDIA.

31 May 1970

I do sometimes honestly feel that, to escape from this country, to find an environment that stimulated, to find people who actually *give, respond* ... shouldn't that be tried? Or is it the same everywhere, with everyone? My relationship with David [Storey], for instance – the fine, respected writer, who wrote my first film, two of whose plays I have directed with notable success, and now a third – I suppose the world would imagine us to be communicative friends ... Yet we hardly exchange a word. I rang him this morning. He is inflexibly melancholic. Finally I say: 'What are you doing.'

'Oh – trying to work ... the same ...'

'The book?'

'Yes.'

'How's it going?'

'Oh – much the same.'

'Are you writing another play?'

'No.'

'How about the last one?'

'I'm just trying to nerve myself to read it.'

Happy days!

I've been considering Penelope's reply to my *Sight and Sound* proposals – which has meant reading them, and also bits of *Sight and Sound* AND the *Monthly Film Bulletin* ... Extremely depressing. I'm aware that it is almost impossible to directly attack a whole fashionable, accepted bourgeois cultural ethos – in an atmosphere where lack of any commitment is excused as 'impartiality', and where glibness and pretension are accepted by the ignorant as betokening expertise and authority.

1 June 1970

More Rachel Rachel this morning: less pissed than Saturday, she has spent the day alone, with her nigger's dog. He has deserted her. She doesn't think the shots were fired by Columbia Pictures, or by her lover in Las Vegas, or by any representative of Rex Harrison. 'Don't be silly' I tell her, 'I'm sure he's delighted you're living with a nigger.' I ask her if she's attended the MGM auction? 'No thanks: I'm not a necrophiliac.'

A beastly rehearsal day, exiled to the Arts: John (particularly) and Ralph a bit edgy. Great difficulty in getting Ralph to maintain any dynamic of sensitivity ('desire to please') in the first scene . . . However Ralph responds to the idea that he glances at John before he says 'Nice to be out' . . . Are there any 'star' actors who have a highly developed or acute sense of ensemble? These haven't. Even when they're acting together – John, particularly, finds it difficult to *look* at the actor he's playing with . . . it's solitary lyricism. I get nervous about the idea of doing this shooting tomorrow – the *Omnibus* material that has grown into a feature for *Review* . . . They arrive (naturally) late. Two-thirds of the way through the afternoon I suddenly decide, and tell Roger to go phone Helen to tell the BBC to call it off . . . Poor Robert Vas reacts with hurt shock when I tell him after rehearsal, but his uncomprehending protests only confirm my decision. That damned medium is anticreative, exploitative – shun it.

5 June 1970

Today fixed for our run-through in front of cast members of *The Contractor*, Café La Mama[1] and – I thought – *Three Months Gone* (but none of the latter turn up) . . . We take the morning lightly sitting and running lines. Ralph strolls round the stage during the first scene, while John sits with furrowed brow . . . Accuracy greatly improved; Ralph really quite impressive . . . The run-through goes really very well: strange how tense one becomes, just at the presence of those thirty or so people sitting in the stalls. It's quite exhausting. Lots of laughter during the first scene – some rather 'pro-ey': I detect a certain glib recognition-laughter from Ralph-addicts. And some rather boring belly-laughs from Americans? But it is all useful, I tell myself. Ralph comes up to it splendidly; John a bit more volatile. His lighter voice and style not so definitively imposing. The ladies (Dandy especially) nervous – timing in four scenes a bit shakey. Warren brilliant. The end fantastically moving. The curtain descends in stunned silence. Then some applause – but the impact unmistakable . . . How charmingly the cast sit and take notes afterwards.

6 June 1970

Wake 8.30 or so. Quite soon it is Rachel on the phone: a bit on the 'bright' side (I suppose a bit nervous of her reception): 'Hullo Linds! . . . I've grown up!' This time chiefly to say she has seen through her black lover, that he was on the make, that he took her for $9,000, which she doesn't regret, because she's learned all about how blacks want to fuck white women in a spirit of race revenge. Anyway she tried to make a meeting

---

1. Café La Mama came to notice for their pioneering production of *Hair* – later filmed by Milos Forman. Their short season at the Royal Court included *Arden of Faversham*: 'I can watch the succession of expressive *trouvailles* with interest – Arden stripped naked – a strange, Dürer-esque angular figure – his balls and prick sawn off – wrapped in a kind of cellophane – but not with much sense of enlightenment . . .' (7 June 1970).

between him and her Jewish lover from Vegas with the Mafia connections – but he walked out! So she is now back with the idea of making another go of it with Rex and turning him into a proper actor, because he is sick of Elizabeth Harris, etc., etc. 'And I've found my own friends here I love – the Mark Taper which is just like the Royal Court – and Gordon Davidson, of course he isn't a genius like you and I don't love him like you, but he's a very dear friend and of course he worships you – and they'd both seen *In Celebration* and *The Contractor* and I told them how I'd seen *In Celebration* with Rex and my ex-husband had been sitting in front and I hadn't been able to concentrate, and how angry you'd been . . .' Nonsense. Nonsense – Rachel Rachel . . .

8 June 1970

Came down yesterday to Brighton, travelling with Roger and Warren. At the station I realise I have left my camera behind, and diary! It is very hot. I am at Clarges – supposed to be a reasonably decent hotel, but in fact quite peculiarly gimcrack (while trying to maintain a 'professional' facade), and provincially hideous with its pink and green walls, and gilt beading. It is owned by Dora Bryan[1] and her husband. Which seems appropriate. A 'double' room (i.e. large single bed) filled with assorted mahogany furniture, looking out at the back, metered fire, everything somehow carrying a *feeling* of dust . . . Sunday afternoon – go into the theatre – the set on its way up: the 'neutral' cyclorama (very Jocelyn) is a lovely colour and the complementary net-and-hessian floor . . . after all these weeks on an empty stage, of course, people (including Jocelyn) immediately start talking about losing the set, but I find myself set against this kind of puritanism.

No need to have come down so early really: Tony [Richardson] wouldn't have, I moodily reflect. The Knights and ladies arrive . . . At 8.30 we start a run-through on stage – the whole shebang having come to a halt so that the WORKERS can watch the World Cup (England vs Mexico) on TV. We lose. To my puritanical satisfaction.

I keep expecting them to have forgotten the words – but they haven't.

After breakfast on Monday, which further stimulates my tendency to irritation, I decide to leave Clarges and take the empty double room (facing the sea) in the small hotel where Roger is . . . of course in the end this isn't a very good choice, as there's no telephone in the room: breakfast stops at 9.15 etc.

Monday afternoon: we run the play again – and John Haynes takes run-through pictures. And at 7.45 – world premiere!

The audience, of course, is intimidating: surely the *purest* bourgeois and petit-bourgeois public in the world. Not like a London West End theatre – because they are even more perfectly at home, confident of themselves and their values . . . Considering

---

1. British actress (1923–). Won a British Film Award for her performance in Tony Richardson's film of Delaney's *A Taste of Honey* (1961).

all this, I think it went pretty well . . . Mona, who had begun to sparkle dangerously on Sunday afternoon – both metaphorically and actually, since she appeared not only with the small brooch I'd suggested for her coat, but with swinging crystal earrings and flashing necklace – responds faithfully and fully to direction, splendidly de-sentimentalises and plays with a proper coarseness. Performances a bit underprojected, but I am going to let them find this for themselves. (In the interval the Manager tells me that some patrons are complaining of inaudibility.) Cheers at the end, in which I join, but they are only first night formalities I'm afraid. (They don't recur during the week).

After the show – Oscar appears in dressing rooms, not very volubly communicative but then this is hardly his kind of play. Bill also in evidence . . . We go off to a combined dinner at Wheelers – Alan has turned up with 'Whiffle': they got to the theatre late and missed the first music cue altogether – perhaps just as well since it comes over unaccountably bad . . .

Brighton something of a disappointment this time: I suppose I've been indulging in rosy-tinted views of the past – *The Lily White Boys*, *Billy Liar*. Then there's the curious thing of company . . . curious because although everyone is quite amiable, there's no one with whom I can warmly and wholly relax. The Knights are extremely amiable – but the gap is too great, of values and beliefs, ever really to get past *formality*. For instance, after photocall, I lunch with Ralph and John (pâté – lobster mayonnaise – Chablis), which is very pleasant, except that I am conscious all the time of having to speak rather loudly, rather simply, keeping my hand as it were on the tiller . . . afterwards I stroll with Ralph in search of some antique shop which has moved from the Lanes but of course, since we only know vaguely the direction, we never find it. The relationship is charming, touching, friendlily *formal*. Ralph laughs affectionately at John – how he can never bear to talk of anything that doesn't spring from, or impinge on THE PROFESSION – 'Sometimes I talk about diesel engines just to see the horrified look in his eyes . . . Diesel engines!' They respect each other properly and sincerely.

As I stroll with Ralph we bump into a rather sad Rank publicity functionary outside the cinema showing *Carry On up the Jungle*. He remembers me from *Sporting Life*. We talk about cinema. Ralph remarks that I don't film very often. I try to explain about the jungle, the need for a producer etc . . . but he doesn't really understand, and the imaginative leap would be too great. Ralph reminisces with affectionate warmth about Korda – 'Ralph, we are not going to make *that* picture – instead we are going to make this marvellous story about a man who can work miracles – and you will play the Col-o-nel . . .' And he chortles. A simpler era.

12 June 1970

Judith Stott and Dave Allen came on Wednesday evening: John invites me to join them for supper afterwards. He had also apparently invited David [Storey] – but David is

not in evidence at the end of the performance. Perhaps he's in the Wheatsheaf? I go in
– it's empty – apparently – but as I leave I hear a groan. I walk a few steps, collect myself
and return. There, collapsed against the bar, clutching it, head buried and groaning
('Christ – help me – help me') is the fat and wheezy publican. A heart attack? A stroke?
I run in, detach him from the bar and get him laid on the floor – what to do? As always
on such occasions I am appalled by my ignorance, and certainly not anxious to give
him the kiss of life. I run out into the street and yell to Judith to get a doctor . . . Dave
Allen runs in and is very manly and practical, wiping the recumbent publican, groaning ('Where am I? I'm upside down . . . Everything's upside down') and occasionally
drunkenly protesting. John hovers behind the bar, keeping out of the way and
worrying we're going to miss our dinner date . . . When two policemen and two ambulance men arrive, they behave like caricature bureaucrats – 'You don't want to go along
to hospital do you?' 'Course I bloody don't' 'There you are – you see he doesn't want to
come in – we can't take him against his will . . .' I am appalled by their attitude and say
so . . . 'I very much resent the implications of that remark.' 'You can resent it as much
as you like – It's what I feel.' . . . Eventually we walk away and leave them to it: I don't
think they did take him in. I found later that he was indeed drunk: but he might easily
have had a slight stroke. I go into the Wheatsheaf once more during the week, but the
incident is not mentioned.

14 June 1970

Spent Friday night/Saturday morning at Rustington. Mum was up North during the
week, for the auction of the farm. It made £12,000: anyway less than we'd dreamed, but
probably better to disembarrass ourselves of it . . . It's curious, but as regards the play
Mum seems less interested than ever . . . Indeed there is no member of the family who
takes interest or pride. Not at all what you expect from books.

I return to Brighton for the matinee, not realising that it isn't till 5.30 . . . so I buy a
towel and go on the beach. Alone in a crowd. To finish my observations on this week
in Brighton. It's been dull because there's no one here I can particularly open to . . .
Funnily enough, Warren I find almost the most congenial. The most *giving* in a strange
way. But the other artists of course are in their own category: Roger does his best but
remains a Midwich Cuckoo – there is just no emotional rapport . . . Perhaps this
isolation is bound to grow as I get older. So I end up alone on a stony beach, reading a
Penguin Special, *God Is an Englishman* [by R. F. Delderfield] – an Australian's summing up of the English psychosis that seems to me perfectly to state the question – in
much the terms indeed that I am continually using. His statement of the Northern
myth and the Southern myth is completely precise: and his description of Southern
decadence – the respect for tradition that ends as compulsive avoidance of change,
evokes exactly experiences with the Arts Council and the BFI.

17 June 1970
Home opens.

Daphne drives me to the Court: do a little work with Warren, to try to get the start of Act II back to a little *tension* (it's become rather cabbagy). Doesn't take long – though how difficult it is to keep and preserve the style, tempo and economy and simplicity of this kind of thing through five weeks' rehearsal and ten days' playing. New amplifiers have been imported, and though I've called the actors for 4.30, I have to spend the first twenty-five minutes or so readjusting the sound levels. Ralph comes and sits in the stalls and listens. It's strange that though *John* is the director, it is Ralph who seems to have much more interest, even feeling for the practical details.

This must be the first time since – well, very early in my theatre career – that I have actually sat in a seat through a first night – and I actually asked Fiz to come. I sat next to Barbara, then David, then Jocelyn. Behind David and Barbara were Alan Price and Whiffle. Alan is certainly difficult – gets atrociously moody – feeling himself left out and therefore left out. I'd made a date to meet him at 6.30 in front of the theatre: of course he was late and arrived just as I was disappearing backstage. I sent him over to the Royal Court Hotel bar, where I just managed to get across for a drink before we had to go in – juggling desperately – with Fiz having remained in the Circle Bar . . .

The performance was cracklingly good. A first night that really does justice to the work done: they came up to it like warhorses, and I'm really quite astonished by Ralph's control and smartness on the lines. Warren much better than last night. Mona I thought caught just enough of the sentiment she always wants to put into it, without spoiling it. Dandy masterly. The knights are just marvellous and I have no more to say.[1] Reception very good – though (of course) not the dead silence then the moving tornado of cheers I had imagined in my fantasy. But it was a very good performance.

Afterwards: the peculiar torrent of congratulations in which one so has to play a role that nothing seems quite real. Michael [Medwin] who is there with Sunny is sobbing and incapable, and she also in tears: Brian Cox and Malcolm genuinely moved and impressed. Malcolm, I'm rather glad to see, picks John as most 'marvellous'. Gavin plainly quite cool (nice about 'direction') . . . etc . . . etc . . . the incorrigible Alan Price doesn't like being left to wait around, and says he's going home . . . I don't let him, and send him to the Circle Bar, where he talks to Andy Gaye and then Malcolm. Although I know the Royal Court regulars don't exactly welcome him in, nor does he behave with much generosity, offer anyone congratulations I notice. I do like him, but he *is* just another sensitive, talented egomaniac!

---

1. The reviews were exceptionally good. 'A huge success after all doubts and fears. Even Martin [Hensler] lyrical about it and when we read *The Times* review we both sat holding hands and weeping.' (From John Gielgud's letter to Hugh Wheeler, 23 June 1970)

18 June 1970

Election Day: I do vote at St Mary's – and in the evening go with Oscar to his home to watch the beginning of the results. Everyone wrong. The backlash wins.

19 June 1970

Wake early (damn it) and feel uncomfortable, indigestion as well as everything else. Switch on the telly, where the marathon election tellycast is still lumbering on on both channels . . . The nonsense, the unreality, the drug-effect of the 'media' at its purest, most horrible, most spellbinding. David Frost presiding over the breakfast table, then interviewing Harold Wilson – still preserving his careful, polite 'dignity', answering those footling questions that turn everything into media-fodder – then later on the other channel, Harold Wilson being interviewed by David Dimbleby: 'I say – that was a shock . . .' – and so it is: poor Jennie Lee, poor old George Brown out on his ear: the grinning tailor's dummy 'Ted' Heath hugely pleased and fulfilled. At least they'll have the charm of novelty . . .

Don't get to the Court till about 7 p.m. Cast in good form. Watch part of the first half of the show, then the second half. John Osborne there with Jill's mother; Ian McKellen; Robert Swann[1] and the charming Nora Nicholson: Alan Bennett; Stephen Frears, who presumably didn't like it.

22 June 1970

The play now being on, and running successfully, and *The Contractor* picking up nicely too (I shall be back on percentage from last week) – now I arrive at that time when I *should* get everything organised, relax, enjoy myself, read scripts busily and efficiently, etc. Instead, I hardly need to say, I find myself in a state of EXHAUSTED INDECISION.

Stuart Burge did approach me about doing Alan (Bates)'s *Hamlet* for Nottingham. I *would* do the play with Alan – certainly after *In Celebration* I feel easy and confident enough to do so: but the idea of discussing casting now – without a spark in me – it's really just impossible.

A text and an offer from Paris – to direct the new play by Roland Dubillard . . . *Ou Boivent les Vaches.* This is via Miriam Clore – who has brought the play from Maria (David Mercer's ex-girlfriend) who lives with him . . . Miriam goes very gay on the subject – I can see her flying over and queening it preposterously at the premiere – which is exactly all it means to her (she has no idea even of the nature of the play). I find it incomprehensible, and anyway am not attracted by the idea of Paris – Paris for God's sake!

---

1. Played the cane-wielding Rowntree in *If* . . . .

As for films: there is the Gregson–Wiggan *The Delinquents* – a rather charming Australian novel which they want to do in the US.[1] This is itself attractive: perhaps the fantasy should be tried? Certainly I haven't anything at the moment that, emotionally, holds me to Britain. But, inevitably I suppose, the draft script that's arrived is coarsened-commonplace-conventional writing on TV lines. I *could* – and was momentarily tempted to – go to California to talk about it.

Ros mentioned that she'd had another enquiry from Ben – Jon Voight's agent – as to whether I was interested in *The Leatherstocking Tales*.[2] Of course this, instinctively, arouses my special interest: there is a romance about the theme – and knowing Jon is a powerful recommendation. So I endeavoured to express enthusiasm while keeping my cool. If there's any reality in it, something concrete will have to be proposed. It's quite likely it *won't*, of course.

Michael Medwin has given me a South African trial book – *A Healthy Grave* – which I hear he has commissioned John Mortimer to script . . . He'd like me to direct it but he wants it to be *his* production.

24 June 1970

Spend today rehearsing *The Contractor*. Agonising prospect – of course not so bad when one actually starts. Bill [Owen] is really extraordinarily *stupid* – there isn't really any other word for it, and if one didn't call him stupid, one would have to call him bloody-minded. Of course there *is* a Northern-ness (as Philip Stone points out!) which Bill can never really get – though funnily enough he does at the end of the play. As I watch the last act I am actually moved by the taking down of the tent. Philip is exaggerating his effects, of course, and playing the defeat of Kay like Pagliacci (or whatever) and I find Norman [Jones] now very affected – and their 'moments' just awful. But I would still proudly maintain the excellent state of the production after nearly 150 performances: It really ought to go somewhere or be recorded or something.

---

1. Criena Rohan's novel was filmed in 1989 by Chris Thomson.
2. In 1978, L.A. put Voight in touch with Robert Benton and David Newman, the Oscar-nominated writing team of *Bonnie and Clyde*. Not wanting to do *The Leatherstocking Tales*, Benton and Newman proposed instead to write L.A. and Voight a screenplay about Wild Bill Hickok. Voight was enthusiastic, but L.A. declined.

8

Coasting

Tony Richardson – New York – Jon Voight
Alan Price – The Changing Room

'In the end, what really matters is the work –
at its most pure, its most personal, its most passionately lyric.'

1 July 1970

First chore: with David, I meet Mr Meyerberg[1] at the Savoy . . . We take coffee at the breakfast table and discuss with this I am sure honourable and even tasteful doyen of the theatre the possibility of doing *The Contractor* in New York . . . He has seen it three times now, and produces a copy of the play in which he has underlined a few words – 'bloody' – I notice particularly. He says he's convinced the play will translate, with these few words changed, effortlessly to Staten Island . . . He would like to retain T.P. and Jim Norton (why?) and Billy Russell – whom he seems to think is playing the part *Irish*. He also thinks the family could be Irish.

David and I are sceptical: as so often with these American hustlers (with any hustlers I suppose), he doesn't seem anxious or even able to discuss any point in detail or in depth. When I say, perhaps if you have an American cast you should have an American director? He seems almost disposed to agree – except that he means a stage manager who would come over and take down all the moves! His film (*The Iron Law*, from Alan Paton's book) anyway he has postponed until next Spring i.e. for ever. Curious: now he isn't exactly a phoney – his record is honourable – *Lute Song, Waiting for Godot* – and his reputation ditto . . . I suppose it is age as much as anything that makes for this hardening of arteries . . . It was left that he'd try to persuade American Equity, but I don't think anything will come of this.

---

1. Michael Meyerberg, who in 1965 had invited Andy Warhol to host a nightclub and to find a band. Warhol found The Velvet Underground.

Management meeting – we will (the ESC) take *Home* into the West End ourselves. My percentage looks healthy: Helen hasn't dared put the £1,000 transfer *fee* which Robin put in my contract down in the budget!

Afterwards I talk to Oscar, who again mentions *The Hand-Reared Boy*,[1] which John Osborne has optioned. But how do you do an epic of masturbation and sexual initiation? And Oscar doesn't really attract me as producer any more. He is so ... timid? He forgets *The White Bus*!

3 July 1970

When I think ... when for instance I look around this room as I lie exhausted in bed – upstairs (12.15 a.m.), the record-player bass hammers away, and those rowdy, youthful sixth-form voices are back – and my clothes are scattered around, with dust and papers and unanswered letters, and I think – I am forty-seven, one of Britain's leading directors, too old now (and too set in my ways) to be an *enfant terrible* ... well it is an unsatisfying state of affairs, even somehow shameful ... where do I stand? What sort of a life, essentially, am I left with? However independent-seeming from the outside, however individual and intolerant – how really resourceless and isolated and at the mercy of the 'chance encounter' ... It's back to the old problem – of how to lift ourselves up by one's own straps ... To be an adult – what should I do? Get my teeth fixed, buy a car, buy a house ... only to start with. Perhaps I'll feel better after a holiday. I'm supposed to go on Tuesday to Tony Richardson's *Nest*. Actually I was going to go to the sea, to Lorenza: then had a letter saying she was having an operation and would be convalescing near Florence ...

4 July 1970

Jocelyn's party: I manage to catch the 4.13 to Winchfield, sneezing a good deal, to be met by Jocelyn in the old Avis – which has been bashed a bit in the back ... Suddenly worried about food, drink, amusements, we stop in Odiham and buy some lime juice (which is finally never drunk), some shortbread biscuits, which are not *much* eaten (I hadn't anticipated the quantity of 'pot' cookies), two tennis balls (not used) and a child's cricket bat (*very* useful for the French cricket). Then to the cottage, now extended beautifully by the addition of Jocelyn's new studio ... so beautifully, in fact, that when we first drive up I don't really notice it. We have tea, pick some spinach, and worry about whether there'll be enough wine. Jocelyn is also very worried about the POT. She has got the 'kids' at the Court to get her some – and can't decide whether it should be made into cakes, or smoked. At first she favours the cakes, then starts to worry about it 'getting into the bloodstream'. She seems very keen on the whole

---

1. Unfilmable novella by Brian Aldiss.

business – I think it has something to do with the aim – in typically serious fashion – of getting to know and understand the kids' 'scene'.

Later in the evening, Olivia arrives with her boyfriend, whom she is going to marry on Friday next. They are both teachers and are moving into a cottage near here which Jocelyn has got for them at £1 rent a week. They've been painting it. After supper we have to make the rabbit pies: I do the pastry more or less, and we don't get to bed till after two o'clock.

More cooking on Sunday: risottos – moussaka. I phone Malcolm and ask him to bring Nescafé and biscuits . . . More sneezing. What a fucking nuisance this is. Next year I really must have those injections. The party goes really very well, in spite of Jocelyn's nervousness . . . her assistant Andrew arrives with the extra wine: then Julian and his girlfriend: then Malcolm and Margo . . . Malcolm very affectionate and nice: it really is a pity there isn't much to talk about after about ten minutes. But I'm very fond of him. Then Alan and Whiffle. It's really curious this, how much I like Alan. I can't quite understand it, particularly as I seem to be the only one who feels it. I really value his work, and respect and am intrigued by the sensibility that produces it. And to me, in Alan, the very extraordinary phenomenon of the musical talent – refined and personal and poetic – that has the benefit of no background, no training, no *class advantage*. See how the English, snug in their class-cubicles, remain sublimely unaware of this. Jocelyn, for instance: with all her marvellous qualities, still the sublime example of the starry-eyed, uncomprehending, sentimental middle-class liberal. (Of course, it could be objected that *she* is the classless one, and *I* the patronising conservative!)

Bowls – or *boule* – French cricket – badminton: followed as darkness falls by dancing and sitting in the kitchen while Whiffle and Gloria baked pot cookies . . . David and Barbara came with Helen and Kate and Jake and Sean . . . Again, I can't help reflecting on the oddity of *this* relationship – that's to say that after everything, David and I have no more to pass between us than the time of day, or whatever facts need to be exchanged . . . Perhaps it isn't odd: perhaps that is all that Gilbert ever had to say to Sullivan, or Shakespeare to Burbage, or Elgar to Adrian Boult . . . Perhaps in fact there just isn't the need to say anything more. *Friendship*, in the sentimental, communicative sense, is perhaps rarer than is commonly imagined . . .

The party was chiefly memorable I suppose for the steady consumption of pot in those chocolate cookies and cakes. I had one or two drags on a hash cigarette, but that passing-around of the fag of peace isn't really my 'scene'. Alan and Whiffle were smoking their grass, but it didn't stop Alan refereeing the badminton, or Whiffle childlikely enjoying the French cricket – and afterwards in the kitchen telling their shaggy-dog funny stories, and sending Andy Gaye (who was there with Judy and tiny Sam) into paroxysms of giggling. Another rather mysterious couple: Warren, who seemed to be innocently enjoying himself very much, and his drooping, seemingly joyless and sulky wife Gail, who seemed to spend most of the time sitting on the steps in the studio, while the record player boomed out, over and over again, a lush recording of the Albinoni organ-and-string piece and 'Eine Kleine Nacht-Musik' – or slumped by the beer barrel ... A group of art-directors and set-dressers, left over from *Isadora*, kept boringly to themselves – Bill drifted around with his long hair encircled by a bandana; and his friend Frank looked quite ludicrous, I thought, in tall blackboots and a fashionable buckled *ceinture* ...

8–14 July 1970
Tony [Richardson]'s hacienda, Le Nid du Duc, to which I (and the world) have been so often invited before, isn't quite what I'd imagined. The idea of a village, for instance, had always called to mind something more widely spread than this cluster of buildings beneath a quite spacious mountainside farmhouse ... The effect is much more *con-stricted* than I'd imagined, less furnished, and much less consciously *chic* ... The pool, which Tony insists on keeping at a temperature of 40 degrees, is set into the hillside beneath the spread of outhouses with just the concrete surround to lie on.[1] Food is taken (at this season) at a long table on the terrace just outside the main farmhouse, with its beautiful view across the thickly wooded valley rising high to a skyline of trees.

We were actually in our seats in the plane before I saw that Anna O'Reilly, Tony's smart secretary, was sitting in the front row left seat chatting to someone I imagined was another guest, but in fact turned out to be just a talkative plastic surgeon ... At Nice airport we met, and I must admit I was immediately struck by her competence and matter-of-fact assumption that my well-being was in some way her concern and responsibility ... We were greeted at the barrier by Jean-Pierre [Hubert], the small, lively major-domo of Le Nid du Duc who, Tony explained later, had been imported first by Jean-François, his first advisor on rebuilding, when he (the boy) had been nothing more than a thin, starving pavement artist from Marseilles ... now a respon-sible, active man-of-all-trades, who will never take a holiday, cooks, drives and fixes, and lives on charmingly independent terms with everyone.

From Nice we drive along the autoroute, and I remember staying with Malcolm two years ago at Bargemon, then up the valley – which must be the one further than the road we used to take then – up a typically twisting, dangerous mountain road – to turn off down a rutted, winding approach road through thick chestnut woods, till finally there's a glimpse of a sky-blue pool, tile roofs, then the stone farmhouse and Tony in blue shirtsleeves and general greetings and carrying of cases and production of omelettes and a plate of condites [candied fruits] and wine ...

---

1. Tony Richardson's swimming pool at Nid du Duc was painted by David Hockney in 'Portrait of an Artist (Pool with Two Figures)', 1972.

Typically of a Tony menage, the place is full (though apparently this rates as quite empty – sometimes, he airily says, there are twenty or thirty people here), with people whose identity one is left to find out for oneself . . . There is Will, the chunky, blond American ex-Marine, very gentle and nice-mannered, apt to dress in boots and elaborate leather ceinture – is he Tony's steady 'friend'? . . . Then there is Russell, dark, solid-built and campy, also American, quite practical and good at fixing parrot-cages . . . Another blond, lithe and hippy, boyishly-haircut Frenchman is referred to as 'the *temporary Jean-Pierre*', good-looking in a feline sort of way, and he turns out to be a friend of Claude, dark, middle-aged, rather more self-contained, a public relations man from Paris. These make up the house-guests of the moment: such is the atmosphere of the place however that there are always liable to be extras, dropping in from God knows where, as on this first day there are two visitors just leaving the pool, who turn out (I find out later) to be the Jean-François who helped Tony early on, now turned restaurateur, who after two disastrous seasons with restaurants in St Tropez (where he and his friends spent more money on buying flowers than they received from customers and ended up owing millions), has now embarked with this new Vietnamese friend on a Vietnamese restaurant at a little town somewhere in the mountains. They feel it is going very well because they have already served thirteen meals in four days: if you want (Tony says) a Vietnamese dish, you have to order it fifteen days in advance . . .

It is a peculiar atmosphere – completely homosexual, in a charming, unforced well-mannered way, with Anna working efficiently away at the centre. Totally without chi-chi or camp *mannerism*. Tony is very democratic: Jean-Pierre sits down for meals, and so does the cook, the plump local lady afflicted with deafness, if there's room. Curiously, I find the atmosphere totally unsensuous, to the point where I feel I may well be *perverted* sexually – since I'm certainly not a normal homosexual. Tony's style is of course familiar, but terribly difficult to define: everything is spoken with a kind of whimsical detachment, an affectation of accent and phrasing which, whether by conscious design or now by habit, provides an effective alienation from true feeling or commitment. In fact, many of Tony's opinions and beliefs are perhaps truer, more sincere, than they appear – but so rooted and consistent is this manner of expression that it is hard to feel in them the force of genuine conviction. I've no doubt that Tony *has* had 'feeling' relationships, but in general he doesn't operate by emotion . . . There must be a void at the centre of this extraordinary energy – for the energy which has created this charming machine-for-living out of an obviously formidable wilderness is certainly phenomenal – which evidences itself in those continual invitations, the generously open house, yet still one talks as though across some chasm, or as if it is all part of some teasing game . . . The nearest Tony has got to talking about his present position is to say he feels like *Coriolanus*, and to quote some six or seven lines of bitterness.

I have tried to talk to him about *Ned Kelly*, but it isn't really possible. I doubt whether his pride will ever enable him to learn.

Wednesday: after arrival: the pool and dinner; a late-night bathe, at which I note that all are nude – except myself.

Thursday evening: dinner arranged with the Forsters: this is Peter and Pippa, who was once Philippa Hiatt: and she was in not only *The Bells Go Down*, but also *Went the Day Well?* He is this plump novelist-journalist, quite shrewd and culturally *au fait*: but not quite shrewd or *au fait* enough. I'm afraid I sound off after dinner about Ken Tynan, and also convey my scorn of Olivier (who is Peter Forster's passion). One good reason for *not* going to dinner with people. Pippa, with her greying hair swept back, and cut off short, and her intelligent, sensitive grey eyes, is a rather remarkable woman. She uses the English upper-class method of uncommitted exaggeration and facetiousness with great skill – and even charm. ('How *fearfully* exciting' – the word 'exciting' not thrown away, but given great definition and conscious gravity.) And she flatters by listening with great attention.

Friday: we went to the beach. Beautiful and more refreshing than Tony's pool. We eat, lavishly entertained as always by Tony.

Saturday: we shop in St Tropez ... vegetables and flowers, fruit and meat and fish ... the prices are astronomic: fish for one meal costs as much as meat for three. But one never has the impression that expense could ever be a reason for *not buying* anything ... During the afternoon Jocelyn arrives, having married off her last daughter (Olivia) yesterday. And another, fleeting, visitor. This is a tall, well-built, blond young man, with short hair, cut in an attractive page-boy style, and slightly pointed features.

As I looked out of my window one morning, there was Claude, sitting at the breakfast table, and (I think) Jean-Pierre – and this new arrival, standing or strolling with a bowl of coffee. Heavens, I thought: is there no end to them ... (a slight resentment). Later, when I came down, Claude introduced me – as usual the name came and went – I remember thinking idly: I wonder if life will turn that into a face that seems to me completely attractive and *right* ... something about his blond openness reminded me of Jon Voight. Claude explained that this was a young French actor, who had played 'Le Grand Meaulnes' in that film by Albicocco (which has not been very successful because the director knew all about photography, and nothing about *mise-en-scène*). Alain Fournier's sister ('qui l'aime bien') had apparently given this young man the rights to a book, not by herself, of which he would like to get a film made. He was evidently here to speak to Tony, or to give him the book, or to ask him to read it ...

I don't remember how the young man turned up again; was it at lunch? I do remember Tony leaning back in his chair and saying to me, in that drained-of-all-emotion way: 'Can't you speak to that young actor? Can't you give him some advice?' ... And down at the pool I did go up to him, standing there, suddenly getting over my habitual shyness (the incapacity to make such contacts often precisely *because* I want to – this peculiar puritanical – or is it just proud? – reluctance to admit to or betray attraction), I went up and said: 'I'm sorry I didn't see your film . . .' Strangely, he turns out to be Czech – both his mother and his father – and to speak it: his actor's name I can never remember,[1] his born name is Miroslav Brozek. When he isn't acting he works as a designer or interior decorator – and the reason why he was now dashing back to Paris was that he had to execute the decoration of a shop interior (Handbags? – not a very grand shop he said, but work) before he started a new film, which was to take him to many exciting and interesting places . . .

I came back up to the house, where the cook, and her Spanish aide were struggling to remove the extra bed from my room (I think for *another* friend of Claude's, who turned up for a couple of days). I helped them downstairs with it . . . when to my surprise Miroslav Brozek came up the stairs and held out his hand to say goodbye . . . *en plus*, he asked my address so that he could send me his book. I tore a piece of paper in half, and wrote my address – and asked him to write his . . . Anyway, I did walk up to the top to say *bon voyage*, as he went off in his sports car. I slightly surprised myself doing this – did it seem odd?

Will he in fact send me the book? It's possible . . . Tony of course (such are the ironies of life) hasn't looked at the book, and I'm sure won't . . . What I found attractive about the boy, he found quite uninteresting. As he said in the pool: 'I just don't find those Eastern Europeans at all interesting. I like the French and the Italians . . . Perhaps a little bit the Greeks . . . Then I don't like anyone till you get to Burma and Malaya. I just can't stand those Czechs and Poles and Russians.' (Perhaps a good thing he isn't making *Nijinsky*?!)

Peter and Pippa Forster . . . They are a curious couple really, like something out of Somerset Maugham, and I can't help speculating on their relationship (they are not married). Pippa quite surprised me when she diagnosed in Tony a certain desperation, a destructiveness, a death-wish . . . (*Has* he tried to kill himself? I don't know). Nor did I know – or hadn't remembered – his formative childhood: brought up by mother and aunt; weak father; sent away to horrible school and hating it . . . the need to WIN. The whole life he has constructed for himself is so extraordinary – fantastic. Spending *certainly* on a millionaire's level: the house in London – apartments in Paris and Rome – the simple paradise of Nid du Duc . . . Remarkable also for the unpretentious manner that goes with it . . . Well: is that the right word? Yes: Tony has the best of everything that he wants – chooses nothing, I am sure, for show – and lives here in the easiest, most unassuming lifestyle that you could imagine . . . So casual is it, that one could almost forget the huge scale of expenditure . . . the swimming pool that has to be

---

1. Jean Blaise.

continuously heated to 40 degrees, the champagne that is opened every morning, the cars (a new Mercedes just delivered) . . . the total hospitality of open house . . . Can really Tony's personal earnings have been so brilliantly invested as to produce this kind of an income? (Yet, as he himself says, he has mortgaged his earnings from *Tom Jones* and gets nothing now from its sales). Has he the resilience – the *realism* – to lose all this if he had to? Or would he rather put an end to himself than admit that kind of defeat? Nothing would surprise me . . .

15 July 1970

After another blazing day, as I lie on my bed reading Tony's script of *I Claudius* I am called to my window by a shout. There is a fire raging in the district, and Tony and Jocelyn are going out, driven by Jan, to look at it. I accompany them. Across the main road the hills are adrift with smoke: a line of intermittent flame sparks out. Thank God the wind is carrying it down the valley, towards the sea, away from us. We drive on the circular road – to a high point, where we park, then climb up a rocky hill, struggling against the violent wind. A certain excitement to it – something elemental at last . . . Tony and Jocelyn think how puny human beings are revealed to be when some natural cataclysm occurs. True. Yet I find myself being more stirred by the mutual aid which humans then instinctively give each other – ironically I say, 'At such times, anarchist though I am – I perceive some value in organised society.' But I don't mean it ironically. I am more stirred by the thought of all men being brothers than of all men being *ants*.

The electricity intermittently fails at Nid du Duc, and Jean-Pierre lights the oil lamps (then, rather to his disappointment, the electricity comes on again).

Later that night, as I was going to bed, I heard Tony preparing to go out with Jocelyn and Jan – a woman (Tony reported) had come down the drive in an excited condition, reporting that the wind had changed and that the fire was now heading in our direction . . . I didn't go with them, but prudently placed my passport, money and travellers' cheques together in case we needed to make a quick getaway . . . But we slept soundly.

Jocelyn left on Thursday, determined in her usual self-immolating fashion to fulfil a promise to look after Michel[1] for two days, so that Surya could go to Paris . . . Does she, as Tony suggests, *need* this maternal, self-sacrificing role? Need to be *needed* . . . ? If so, good – though plainly from any objective, rational point of view, she 'needed' her holiday a great deal more. Certainly I suspect that Michel is and always has been quite an egotistical and cold-blooded monster. We went to the beach on Friday and, at lunch, Tony talked about Michel and the early days of the Court with rather unusual eloquence and emotion . . . How in those days he had dreaded the influence of Michel, who plainly resented the Court, and George's independent venture there, and its

---

1. Michel Saint-Denis. Jocelyn Herbert had been a pupil at his London Theatre Studio, managed by George Devine.

successful application of principles rather *other* than the Compagne des Quinze . . . He (Tony) would always know when George had been to see Michel, because he would come out with tentative suggestions for old-fashioned revivals . . . Certainly I have always been struck by the fact that through all those years I was never conscious of Saint-Denis as a sympathetic presence or encouragement, and have never heard a word of praise or intelligent or constructive comment from him on *anything* to do with the Royal Court achievement. Perhaps Jocelyn is using him also partially as a kind of memorial to George?

The Aqua-Plage was, as usual, full of many young men – though never aggressively or exclusively so . . . At a long table facing me and Tony was a group with, at the head of it, a well-built, somehow not altogether sympathetic bronzed early middle-aged man who sounded in some way familiar . . . I asked Tony who it was, and to my astonishment learned it was Peter Adam – that producer sidekick of James Mossman, whom I'd taken against on *Review* – looking much fitter and more personable stripped on the beach at St.Tropez than he ever did in Television Centre. Amongst his hangers-on was a fair-haired, quite butch, *gamin* type, with wide sensual mouth . . . he had that kind of aggressive, rather insolent, absolutely not-pansy quality, yet boyish rather than manly, which I find so instantly attractive, and totally remote . . . Anyway, I was conscious that with them – and with the *gamin* – Tony was the glamorous, important, enviable attraction . . . I really can well see how lonely women can make fools of themselves over an unscrupulous, attractive gigolo – and how to certain temperaments a cynical or brutal avowal of veniality could be itself an attraction: to be treated with contempt – to be *used* . . . But I suppose from all this my pride constitutes a very effective defence. No one, I imagine, in the world could have spotted my immediate and powerful feeling for that young *voyou* . . . Nor can I readily imagine any circumstances, even in fantasy, that could bring us together . . . Something of the same hunger, though more *romantically* spiced, no doubt led [me] to read *Le Meutre de Kyralessa*, which young Miroslav Brozek had left for Tony. And actually I found the tale very sympathetic – direct and concrete – poetic in its wise understanding and acceptance of basic human truths – and in many ways a good story. But I am sufficiently sentimental to take no further action on it unless and until I receive a copy of the book from the young man for myself. It would involve after all his active participation – and I would need to feel that personal confidence and sympathy for myself – not just as a second-best to Tony.

1 August 1970

Well – no word from Miroslav Brozek – and that particular fairytale has no issue . . . Collapse in fact of diary-writing on return from the fairyland of Nid du Duc . . . A familiar collapse: London is as anticlimactic, as disappointing as ever.

Home transferred to the Apollo with a minimum of fuss. Closed at the Court on July 26th; first public preview at the Apollo on Tuesday 28th: 'first night' on 29th. We didn't do anything to the play – except to cut the 'Hendrix' lines at the end – as Ralph had suggested some weeks ago.

The Contractor continues: record-breaking now from week to week. I usually get there on a Saturday matinee – and see a bit of the end of the performance. Not at all bad these two Saturdays: Bill continues to overload with 'looks' and 'moments' which he apparently compulsively creates in absolute contravention of anything I've ever said or tried to do . . . alas . . . An impassioned plea from T. P. [McKenna], who alleges that Philip Stone is now going round the bend, indulging in paranoid boasts in the dressing room that 'with my voice' and 'with my business' – 'I could destroy any performance in the play' . . . The basic infantilism of every actor does, alas, limit severely any relationship one can ever have with any of them.

4 August 1970

Findus commercials casting: as usual, I wish I wasn't doing these three fifteen-second commercials: the usual revulsion . . . A rather mediocre parade of actors and actresses . . . A producer I've not worked with before: amiable, rather confused about casting . . . I feel uncomfortably that I am now supposed to be a miracle-working genius . . . Children, aged six to eight, appear in the afternoon, trying to enunciate: 'We got it free from Findus. What you do – you send in tokens from the special Findus packets, and choose a free gift . . .' Ye Gods!

Down to the Court. Gab-gab with two rather nice young people from *Time Out*. Old duffer speaking with witty and non-stop dynamic from the experience of middle age. Afterwards, usual reaction that I should have kept my mouth shut.

Spent the evening with Stephen Frears. who wanted to talk to me about *Gumshoe*, his thirties private eye script, which Memorial are going to make, and Albert (Finney) to star in . . . I think it *is* a clever piece of writing but, for my taste, must be hard worked on in order not to be just camp – or too much a piece of the writer's personally obsessive mythology. (i.e. not enough a real creation or recreation, but too much pastiche dialogue).

5 August 1970

Well, farewell Neville Blond: Robin phoned this morning to say that he had died during the night. I telephoned the Court and dictated a telegram to Lenore. What else? Nothing. Someone should write to *The Times*, I suppose. Everything is cracking up.

Went to give a talk to Edith Capon's American students . . . twenty dumb and unattractive boys and girls. In my present state, which I suppose is one of sexual and emotional frustration, directionless, seeking stimulation, it is interesting how notions such as 'American students' seems immediately attractive – conjuring up images, I suppose, of clean-cut campus good looks, like young Ritter of last year's visiting group. All fantasy.

All that happens is that I am forced into 'provocative' talking about myself ... being amusing and a bit shocking – and passing their time ... I shall be very annoyed if I don't get my promised £20.

6 August 1970

One of those dreadful, farcical mornings, which starts with me wondering hopelessly how I can get to Neville Blond's funeral at Golders Green, back to Hill Street for Findus commercial casting, then to Hythe [to visit his brother, Murray] by the 4 p.m. train from Charing Cross.

I lie in the bath. I am just about to get out when the phone rings, so I answer it. It is Maria Britneva ... She starts on about Tennessee [Williams]'s play, about how delighted he is to hear that I like it. (I didn't say I liked it, I try to say) ... To all this the front doorbell rings. And rings again. It is the window cleaner. I snip off the hall light and retreat through the door, try to keep my voice down ... I can't get into my suit: the trousers are too tight. A long way to go yet with the slimwheel. It is raining heavily.

In the end I get to Golders Green Crematorium by minicab. I feel some slight prickings of sentiment ... Thoughts of Mum, Father, Sandy, myself ... The tension also suddenly makes me want to go out in the world and be active. (But how? If only one could hold on to these feelings.) I also fantasise on the scene, imagining a woman (nurse) running in – 'Stop! Stop! He's not dead!' – The shock. The struggle. Would most people listen – or would they want to shut her up? Would the coffin slide into the flames with its living (?) cargo? or would it be upset? The body rolls out: everyone takes off in pursuit of the criminals – the body slowly comes to life – bewilderingly raises a hand to its head, looking around ... shoot the whole thing from one continuous high front angle ...

18 August 1970

EXHAUSTION is created these days which lack focal points of real work: in which I am set adrift in a morass of talk, of contacts which drain one without somehow giving anything. I am aware that this must be the peculiar malaise of someone like myself, with no central emotional satisfaction apart from work – nothing at home to return to. Therefore too much goes into these day-by-day encounters. Of course this makes one peculiarly (fatally) attractive – since one *gives* (always hoping, needing to receive) more than most. Far too much. And one ends up feeling *eaten.*

The Court, for instance, is far more a place of gossipy encounters than of any real creative stimulus. Bill is now planning his avant-garde 'festival' – which, rather jaundicedly, I note will eat up all the profits of *Home* – and at the same time starting to rehearse something in the Theatre Upstairs that I don't know anything about. Assisted by Bill Bryden, whom I rather feel represents the Royal Court 'at its worst' – the sweeping judgements without somehow the sensibility or humour to back them up – tendency to intellectualise and use words like 'empathy'. And, quite simply, I doubt his talent. I certainly can't use a place permeated by Bill Bryden. So I don't get correspondence done, and dictate rather bad-tempered letters to the BBC.

26 August 1970

A consistent annoyance has been auditioning for a replacement for Warren . . . How many times have I cursed Stanley Kubrick, and Malcolm, and most of all of course my impulse which led me immediately to say to Warren, when I spoke to him, that of course he should do it and I would try to make it possible for him [to play Dim, side-kick and rival to McDowell's Alex in *A Clockwork Orange*].[1] . . . And I cursed more than ever after I'd read the script – I can see *A Clockwork Orange* being another outstanding technical strike for Stanley K. – but I wouldn't mind betting that Malcolm will be the only actor to make a mark in it. And privately I wonder if he has quite the technique really to bring it off. It doesn't seem to me that the whole problem, or idea of the language has been really considered or integrated into the script: nor do I see that the whole thing amounts to much. Malcolm, of course, is a dear fellow and all that, but his idea of 'working' on the script seems to me largely fantasy – as, I suspect, is most of his work with David. He skims and chatters, has a quick, intelligent, intuitive response – but doesn't seem able to sustain an idea for more than three minutes. I am sceptical, therefore, of this idea of paying David Sherwin £1,000 for a 'treatment' – of what? And is it really a good idea to get involved in this way with something so totally unknown?

28 August 1970

Alan Price had been at the pub at lunchtime, and had been asking for me . . . I rang him. It wasn't anything particular, he said, just wondering if I was doing anything at lunchtime – but also he was about to embark on some mixing sessions for his LP – all the recording now being finished . . . Would I like to go along? I said I would.

I enjoy this very much. A small studio right at the back of the Decca building – up where Broadhurst Gardens runs into West End Lane, just by West Hampstead Tube Station. All these years, and I'd no idea the studios were there. I was escorted down passages and up a lot of stairs to the studio – a small one, full of mixing equipment and stereo speakers, with a little recording studio at the other side of a glass panel. Alan was there with the mixer – an incredibly young, gangling technician who looks like a schoolboy, but must be older, and talks with a weird, cracked voice, and is quite imperturbable. They were mixing a version of the single 'Over and Over Again', which seemed to be coming up in a new version from when I'd last heard it. Of course it was

---

1. He got the part. The part of Alex's father was played by Philip Stone, taken from the cast of *The Contractor*.

mysterious to me to know what exactly they were doing: balancing the eight tracks –
but what was the balance Alan was after? All the tracks sounded delightful played together
or singly. On some Alan puts on a vocal – moving behind plate glass into an adjoining
studio – or dubs on a second voice. I am fascinated just to see it happen, not really
familiar enough with the techniques to be able to make criticisms – played over on
omnipresent stereo at that volume *everything* sounds good!

It's a long time since I've been in this position, I suddenly realise – i.e. standing by as
a sympathetic observer while a friend is working – Serge directing *Hamlet*, or Richard
Harris in *Major Dundee* . . . I do enjoy it when the work is good and the personality
sympathetic. If only that the weight of responsibility is lifted from one's shoulders: and
I am good at sympathetic vibrations.

Alan is extraordinary – can get very nervy and impatient – yet doesn't actually blow
up. Can talk suddenly about giving up the attempt – then plunges back into it. Very
perfectionist. I sometimes wonder whether his instrumental textures are too thick to
be able to bring out all the felicities he wants . . . I admire his lyric virtuosity: drawing
only on a corona bottle containing some pink soft drink, he goes into the studio and
produces what seems to me a lovely, very personal vocal. A tremendously acute sense
of rhythm and an absolute sense of synchronisation (as he fits one voice on top of
another). Singing, or listening to the music playing back, he is rapt, feeling the rhythm
all through him. There is a fine sensibility about everything he does, also a humour
and what I can only call a continuously human scale. Yes, that's it: it is always humanistic – not orgiastic, however full of abandon or joy. His songs are about experience:
they relate always to some moral scale.

On Thursday night we ate at a French restaurant in Sloane Street – rather expensively – having returned after the session, in Alan's low-slung car lately purchased from
the Earl of Lichfield.

On Friday, the last number Alan did was called 'Country Life' – a quite fantastic
attempt at an unaccompanied piece with Alan counterpointing himself vocally on
eight tracks . . . He only did seven in the end . . . vaguely oriental in style . . . straight say;
then scatting; falsetto; the last track was not exactly his voice, but tongue-clucking to
provide a Japanese-style obligato . . . It did come out a bit of a mess, some of the
falsetto decorations did tend to go a bit off key. But he has real wit, continually
surprising, and obsessively detailed. The slightest bump in any of the tracks – quite
inaudible to me until it was isolated – had to be identified and eliminated. Very
reminiscent of film editing and dubbing – where I, for instance, will spend ages on one
split-second piece of timing, or trying to smooth a cut, which naturally no audience
anywhere is ever going to notice. And yet one has to.

After this second session we went up to Hampstead to have a meal. I didn't fancy a
crowded bistro and persuaded them into the Cresta: but I'm afraid it wasn't good.

Then Alan still felt lively – it was only midnight (!) – and we zoomed down to the Speakeasy in Margaret Street, I think, off Upper Regent Street, downstairs to this dark, rather crowded place, where music was playing – a group going: we sat down and ordered drinks, and soon there were a couple of girls and a couple of other chaps. It's a long time since I've been in one of those crimson-dark night joints . . . full of young musicians and their girls and wives . . . God knows what one talks about – except that at one stage I tried to talk to Whiffle about making oneself independent of public taste, or at least trying to lead it rather than be imprisoned by it – four hours have passed before one really knows it. About 4 or 4.15 Alan invited them all back to his place, myself included, but I made my excuses and we went outside to pick up my briefcase from his car, and I totter off home to bed . . . I'm afraid I just can't keep up. 4 a.m. is just too late for me to go to bed now: in fact it always has been.[1]

31 August 1970

'You seem to be on the side of those long-haired toughs,' says Mum, lying in bed reading *The Times*.

'These pop-groups . . . I think they're ghastly.' So much for my attempt to initiate an intelligent discussion – or rather to see if any exchange of opinion were genuinely possible – by remarking on the monotonously (and very restrictedly) carping reportage on the Isle of Wight Pop Festival by the media. The *Express* for instance today published a large picture of litter, stories about bankruptcy and young people unable to get home and troublemakers wanting to stay all summer on the island – and no mention of any *music* ever having been played at all, no names of groups, and no suggestion that anything enjoyable might have happened at all.

This would be another example of my projected piece relating the trivial, reactionary, indeed disruptive state of the 'media' at the moment with the death of documentary. For it really is ironic that the use of film (and now TV) for public comment and information – which the documentarists believed in and fought for – is now widely accepted and practised . . . Yet in a manner either purely journalistic or purely entertainment-for-profit. And the film-makers who *should* be serving the community through making poetry or genuine films of information are fully (and of course far more profitably) occupied in spreading the gospel of soap powders, breakfast foods and margarine that gullible housewives cannot distinguish from 'best butter'.

Slightly related to the documentary impulse, perhaps I really ought to do the film about the Court myself? Or a film about Alan? I can recognise in both those ideas the poetic allure out of which I could make something remarkable.[1]

---

1. This idea to make a film about Alan Price merged with the film that McDowell and Sherwin were working on to become *O Lucky Man!* (1973).

1 September 1970

Made a date last week to meet Jocelyn at the Moulin d'Or, before the council meeting of the English Stage Co. Actually I had been thinking socially when I made the date – and also when I rang Anna last week and suggested that Tony should come if he was free and would like to – the radiance of Nid du Duc persisting. I got there first . . . and Tony was first to arrive . . . looking brown and well after his yachting trip in the Mediterranean, which didn't otherwise sound an entire success, the boat being crewed by semi-hippy amateurs who seemed to resent being expected to work, and disappeared one by one till there was only the couple who owned it and one crew member. Jocelyn arrived a bit late: it was only when she said she had discouraged Robin from coming because she felt we might want to discuss ESC affairs, that I realised we stood on the threshold of (yet another) political occasion.

Tony anyway soon made this clear, launching into a great manoeuvre to discredit the (apparently) ruthless and passionate campaign of Oscar to get himself elected Chairman of the English Stage Company.[1] Oscar had been staying at Le Nid Du Duc, and (according to Tony) had immediately on arrival launched into long and excited pleas for his rightness and suitability for the position . . . Of course this involves the passing-over of Robin Fox – who has also, cancer notwithstanding, announced himself willing to stand for the position. Tony's rather spiteful comments on Oscar (with whom he is, of course, shortly to be associated again, at the Round House) I must admit rang a little bell with me – bringing to mind how Oscar had, at the last management meeting, informed me that Robin, as an agent, would not be acceptable to the Arts Council. (Just why an agent should be less acceptable than a commercial manager I'm not sure: is it true?) . . . So I must admit I was rather open to Tony's anti-Oscar manoeuvres, and between us we agreed to support Robin – whom Jocelyn was to propose in case nobody else did. (Tony, to substantiate his case against the candidature of Oscar, recounted how Oscar had urged him to get on to Paul Scofield quickly because 'Tony Page was after him for the English Stage Company'. (It was only after this lunch that I realised, yet once again, what a self-gratifying troublemaker Tony is and remains. It's truly curious that he has his knife into little Oscar in this way. And Oscar realises it, of course. Yet the relationship persists).

So we are carried poshly from Le Moulin d'Or to the lawyer's offices in Tony's limousine . . . They are all gathered – Greville [Poke] in the chair, George Harewood making one of his rare, much appreciated appearances, John Osborne, careful to sit as far as possible away from Tony (they no longer speak), Peggy [Ashcroft] in a sort of white denim trouser suit, with cap, looking quite dashing and (if you know her) rather

---

1. Following the death of Neville Blond. Blond was succeeded as Chairman jointly by Oscar Lewenstein and Robin Fox. When Fox died on 21 January 1971, Lewenstein assumed sole responsibilty.

preposterous: as if playing Helene Weigel in the Günter Grass Brecht play at the Aldwych has gone to her head). Isidore Kaplan, Robin, Oscar, Blacksell, etc . . . Oh, and of course Helen, sparking strenuously, brown back from her Italian holiday. Proceedings started extremely embarrassingly with Greville in solemn tones announcing the death of Neville and inviting comments or tributes – presumably to be taken down and sent (scripted on someone's flesh: Marie Shine's?) to Elaine . . . I think Norman Collins said something, Robin and (rather to his credit) Tony. I've no idea what. A very awkward and absurd five minutes.

6 September 1970

Sunday. I spent much of the morning on the phone, chiefly occupied with the Chris Menges–Memorial–Kestrel (Tony Garnett–Ken Loach) situation.[1] This had been reported to me by Karel, who told me that Chris had let Stephen Frears down, having been engaged, then being seduced by Garnett and Loach, who had got him to chuck *Gumshoe* in favour of *In Two Minds* . . . Certainly I immediately thought less of Chris for this – inevitably . . . Well, on Sunday morning I had a call through from Chris in Dublin. He tells me how on Thursday or Friday he had been visited by Garnett and Loach in Dublin, where he is shooting *Black Beauty*, and exposed to the most intense emotional blackmail from both of them – until, at 4 a.m., he had given in . . . He tried to phone me that night apparently, but I wasn't in . . . Anyway, plainly his conscience is troubling him, particularly since Stephen phoned him – without reproaches or blackmail – and simply asked him whom he could recommend to replace him. And Chris (honest soul) could think of nobody!! Anyway, I had little scruple against giving advice, and I gave it unequivocally, i.e. do what is right (which I verily believe). I will admit also that I was pleased enough to find the Garnett–Loach tandem (whose work I have considerable reservations about) stripped somewhat naked, and revealed as ruthlessly egotistical and unscrupulous as any caricatured capitalist outfit.

So I talked with moral inspiration to Chris, then tried to ring Stephen; but he was perpetually engaged; then Chris rang me again to say that he's been told that Albert (Finney) was very angry and maybe wouldn't want him back; so I tried to ring Albert but found that I hadn't his new number. So tried to get it from Daphne who was engaged, then from Karel who didn't have it – then I managed to get through to Stephen, who plainly *did* want Chris back, and so I rang Chris again in Dublin (he had, characteristically of all such stories, given me the wrong telephone number – Bray instead of Dublin – and I had to ring Stephen again for the right one) – and instructed him to speak to Stephen and say absolutely and definitely that he wanted the job – Chris still jittering neurotically and saying, 'They won't fire me unexpectedly will they?

---

1. Chris Menges, cinematographer (1940–), universally praised for his work on Loach's *Kes*. His first screen-credit was as the camera operator on *If* . . . . (1968).

and will they hate me at Memorial for the way they've behaved?'. . . and finally, at last, Stephen rang me to say – all was agreed. I only hope they get it signed.

1 October 1970

TV Centre, Studio 8: *Bobbie Gentry Show*. Instant antagonism: this is what I experience as I enter this huge studio – in the centre two grand pianos shoved together, Alan at one, at the other a round-faced, spectacled, short-sighted young man in a flowered shirt – Randy Newman. Between them, with tinted glasses in gold frames and tall hat, – Bobby Gentry. They are strumming through 'Happy Land'. The smooth white floor, forest of overhanging lamps, the cameras ranged in front, on pedestals and cranes, the monitors suspended in the roof, the dapper, smoothly self-assured technicians – all these speak of the triumph of expensive technology . . . The set, wooden construction with steps, large very elaborate prop tree in the centre, Punch and Judy show, fruit barrow, old clothes stall . . . the quintessence of processed 'light entertainment'.

Is it my imagination – or is there something *soulless* about the TV camera? It may also be because the conveyor-belt atmosphere is all-pervading. Even in the most routine film a shot is something special, something (hopefully) to be preserved for ever . . . Here they are just manufacturing canned goods. Randy Newman: is he completely stoned?

13 October 1970

Alan Price: 'You never want to go on these gigs. Then when you get there you enjoy them.'

Lindsay Anderson: 'You didn't want to come to Newcastle?'

Alan Price: 'And then I didn't want to leave.'

'What audiences does he like playing to most?

'You asked me that before . .'

(Perfectly true: he has very good recall). He says the tough club audiences. Because they present the most challenge. 'If I played all the time to audiences like Newcastle I'd get lazy . . .'

The strange boy, who seemed to be a part of the TV interview team, then revealed himself to be a hanger-on . . . who played the piano (he said). Alan said 'play something'. He sat down and hesitantly, yet with pluck, stumbled through a few bars of 'Puppet on a String'. Alan and Clive [Powell – Georgie Fame] watching, almost straight-faced . . . then Alan with typical brusque practicality gets up, comes to the piano, says, 'Here, I'll teach you a song. Do you know "Rose of Tralee"?'

'No'.

'My dad's favourite song . . .' He hammers out the notes. 'Do you know your chords?' The boy isn't a genius, can't follow the notes very well, tries but isn't talented. Alan doesn't give up, hammers through the tune, takes him seriously.

We drove back from Newcastle in four hours. For some miles in the Midlands there were fog patches on the road. Sometimes we could only see twenty yards ahead: then the fog would clear, and we would speed forward again . . . Alan talked of his father as we passed near the factory where he worked and was killed (the British Oxygen Company?) . . . 'He was a sort of hero.' There was a load of cylinders – of which one seemed defective – a man sent off to get a trolley – he didn't come back . . . Alan's dad took off the cyclinder and tried to wheel it out of the factory on his own . . . it blew up . . . They didn't pay any compensation because he'd clocked out . . . We got £50 from the insurance – they didn't want to pay that.'

Alan's mother only got drunk once – when he got number one in the US. (This was 'House of the Rising Sun', with The Animals). He wasn't at home. She went celebrating in the pub. Neither his mother nor his stepfather queried his actions when he decided to chuck his job and turn professional with The Animals. Just made sure he knew what he was doing, then left it to him. At work they couldn't believe it – even though he'd been warning them for six months. He more or less forced the decision on the others .
. . they were scared – particularly Eric, who after graduating from art school had gone to London and found that no one wanted him. It was Alan who finally had to say – 'Well, I'm going . . . are you coming?' It was a big risk: unknowns, with no contracts, going into the world.

The Animals. An experience about which it still upsets him to speak . . . how to describe it? Often he thought he was going to die . . . drink, drugs, success, no time for anything but work. I said 'It sounds like fighting a war.' Alan said, 'Yes, I've often thought that's the nearest.' (Of course this is the key period: I suppose an intensity of excitement – in the work – and experiences quite unimaginable . . . 'It'll be years before I can talk about it – if ever.')

Anderson's production of Home *transferred to New York, where it won the New York Drama Critics' Circle Award for Best Play, inaugurating a hat-trick of Storey wins with* The Changing Room *in 1973 and* The Contractor *in 1974.*

1 January 1971
The Hotel Royal Manhattan, preparing reluctantly to go in to the Morosco Theatre to rehearse with Jessica Tandy,[1] and Mona for this damned takeover of Dandy Nichols's role in *Home* . . . Rehearsals with Jessica Tandy are not exactly exhilarating. To begin with, the endless repetition, working over of already explored material, is just *work* – Doing it for money – And it isn't really a natural for Jessie – whose humour, I'd say, is

---

1. British-born actress (1909–1994). Oscar-winner for *Driving Miss Daisy* (1989).

not her strong point. Nor her voice, which is not powerful, inclined to small, and inclined to crack . . . Snow today, and we rehearse all day, through this public holiday. I lunch with Jessie and Hume (Cronyn) who embarrasses me by asking if I'd like to do a production with him at Stratford, Ontario . . . Happily I can use my [Alan Price] 'documentary' as an excuse, and say, quite honestly, that I want to lay off theatre for a while . . . I'm afraid that worthy, professionally talented and hard-working though I'm sure they are, Hume and Jessie really don't excite me.

Went to see *Where's Poppa*, directed by Carl Reiner – a ponderous and unfunny comedy, distinguished only by mother-fucking, cock-sucking language and jokes that exploit current attitudes with unexampled frankness. So far I've seen: *Groupies, Trash, Gimme Shelter, Five Easy Pieces, Catch–22, Investigation of a Citizen above Suspicion, Hollywood Blue, How to Succeed with Sex*. It's interesting that, of all these, the most formed and individual impression remains *Trash*.[1] The *cinema-directe* reportage films impress, at least in relation to constipated methods in Britain; but I find their form-lessness, and also their sensationalism, very unsatisfying, at least artistically. The skin-flicks, or hard-core porn, are interesting 'socially' – and rather more repugnant than exciting.

2 January 1971

Shirley Temple in *Little Miss Marker*. I see most of it before setting off for the Morosco. In these early pictures she did have astonishing charm – really because she enjoyed showing off, and it was fun to see her doing it, before 'professionalism' and vain attempts to *act* crept in.

We drag through it rather this morning: not much more I can do, since I can't give Jessie a real sense of humour or the real acting tension that either you've got or you haven't. Jon (Voight) said, as we walked back down 8th Avenue after dinner at La Gril-lade, 'Yes. Jessica Tandy and Hume Cronyn are the essence of mediocrity,' and whether it was a thought he'd just found, or whether it represented what he's always felt (but didn't suggest to me before) – it's about the truth. They fit into the Maurice Evans[2] category, of the competent provincial talents who are taken to be stars in this most provincial of pseudo-sophisticated cities.

It was a real pleasure to see Jon again . . . there must certainly be something screwy about one, to make one choose the friends one chooses – the neurotic and/or obses-sively egotistical. Jon, for instance, is certainly as obsessively egotistical as any actor – yet there is something enormously attractive about his total, enthusiastic commitment to anything that engages his attention. I suppose in a certain way he talks a lot of hot

---

1. Andy Warhol's *Trash*, directed by Paul Morrissey.
2. Welsh actor (1901–1989), who won a certain fame as Dr Zaius, the Orangutan leader in *Planet of the Apes* (1967).

air – talks experimentally, I suppose you might say – so that within fifteen minutes of our meeting he is into a long description of Iago's motivation, and why it wouldn't be a good role for him, since temperamentally he is rather an Othello . . . He has, for instance, worked out the essential quality of Iago – the tendency or habit or compulsion to *play himself down* in company, while concealing an actual intense ambition and belief in himself and sensitivity to friendship – so that when Othello (to whom he has given his friendship) passes him over, his intensity of hurt and resentment is dangerous and intense . . . My own attitude, I realise as we talk, is much more intuitive – dangerously so in a certain way, but perhaps ideally so when working with someone as liable to obscure things for himself (yet always with an attractive and creative sensitivity) as Jon.

He maintains that the kind of Fonda role in *Clementine* or *The Grapes of Wrath* he would find easy – since in anything he does there is bound to be a certain lyricism, a certain generosity and exposure. But what is endearing (and mutually attractive) is that I can say to him, 'Are you *really* as good as you say you are?' and he can say, 'No – but someone's got to say so!'

When we are going into the restaurant, a little, young, rather spotty fellow comes up, awed and enthusiastic, and asks for Jon's autograph, which he gets – then asks if he can have a drink with him. Jon refuses courteously, explaining that he's with an old friend and we want to talk . . . Later, at the table, just after I've said there was something rather endearing and pleasant about the boy – he suddenly appeared at the table next to us, smiling nervously yet intensely, and said he was going to eat. 'Not a good idea,' said Jon. 'Do you want me to go?' 'Yes,' I said. 'A Ratso[1] type,' said Jon.

3 January 1971
Breakfast up at Juleen [Compton]'s – where good old Gene [Moskowitz] is staying . . . Pancakes, bacon, and syrup and coffee, and camp snuggling up, and the slow-talking Herb Smith, scriptwriter (who, Juleen says, wrote a brilliant script on a British subject . . . from a novel by Roald Dahl . . . about poaching . . . which I don't want to read and am thankful the suggestion wasn't made). I am played some songs by Kris Kristofferson, the folk singer whom Juleen wants to film . . . they are pleasant, not very vital or original. And I'm given Juleen's script to read (written in collaboration with Derek Prouse – the fatuous story of a traumatised folk singer with the compulsion to murder any creature seeming to need release from intolerable pain. It is depressing.) As we ate our pancakes, Juleen remarked, 'I hear that one member of your cast is very disappointed in Jessica Tandy . . .' I immediately get annoyed, remarked that anyway they hadn't rehearsed together yet – and who had said it to her? Of course, Juleen wouldn't

---

1. The character played by Dustin Hoffman in *Midnight Cowboy*.

say who had been talking, but the little incident seemed to highlight Juleen's triviality and tastelessness . . . and after a time I left with Gene. I had hoped to go down to the village with my camera, but it was too late.

The second social event of the day – a sort of combined farewell to Dandy and Eric, a little dinner on Central Park West, given by George Rose's friend, Jordie Livingston. George[1] seems to have become sadly sour: ungiving – but then I suppose he always was . . . repeated his jaundiced diatribe against Mick Jagger ('Like a dreary little drag queen in an East End pub'), and moaning about the coming tour of Coco.

Eric Harrison's camp friend – Katharine Hepburn's hairdresser – tells how he used to do Constance Bennett's hair, and every hair had to be individually dyed . . . and how when she went into *Mame*, and looked about a hundred years old, she would have to be followed everywhere with a pink spot, and thirteen spotmen were fired for losing her. And finally she decided to have her face lifted, and went to Switzerland for the operation and came back radiantly youthful and was on all the talk shows and a year later she dropped dead at a dinner party with a brain haemorrhage – and wasn't it a shame, the face-lifting was guaranteed for seven years . . . ?

Another story: how Janet Gaynor and Margaret Lindsay were discovered in some passionate lesbian embrace on the Santa Monica beach . . . and the studio got it hushed up, but told them both they'd have to get married – and Janet Gaynor married Adrian and even managed to get pregnant and nearly lost the baby. When they told Adrian he said: 'Oh, don't tell me I have to go through all *that* again!' But the baby did live, and now she's got that smashing son – and married again.

Why, I wonder, do I find these narcissistic, self-powered personalities so attractive? Is it because my own passive personality (unsuspected by most people who know me) needs such contacts, as it needs specific situations, to spark it off? Of course there is also the great pleasure of a shared response – shared humour, shared values, shared intuitions – of being able to trust sufficiently to know that one can learn . . . I saw Jon Voight three times in New York: truly he is one of the vibrantly sympathetic, vibrantly attractive people who give life a savour – a really precious, almost indispensable, one to me . . .

19 January 1971
Old Parr's Head, Blythe Road. Behind the saloon bar of this Irish pub – a small white-washed passage – from behind a glass-panelled door – sounds of music. They're rehearsing off an LP, Alan in his fur coat, Clive black sweater, Tolly scarlet (crimson) sweater. Two organs – drum kit – mini piano – Alan dictating words to Clive – long takes on key angles.

---

1. British actor (1920–1988), acted alongside Rex Harrison in L.A.'s Broadway production of *The Kingfisher* (1978).

An artist like Alan Price – in view of his background, his struggle to succeed, the kind of music he has been inspired by – inevitably raises fascinating social and cultural questions. It is not this that I am most anxious to make a film about. In the end, what really matters is the work – at its most pure, its most personal, its most passionately lyric.

16 February 1971

On Saturday I went down to Alan's house in Church Gate, with my bag and my portfolio and a bunch of daffodils for Whiffle . . . I had a drink and pork pie with Brian Cox at lunchtime, and walked back with him from the Court to Victoria – he wheeling the pram containing his well-developed baby son . . . Brian is in good form, having opened in his farce, *Don't Start without Me*,[1] at the Garrick – to terrible notices – but he feels pleased to have broken through the barrier of over-scrupulosity, to be just doing a job of work, to please an audience, not always and only obsessed with the idea of playing *Hamlet*.

When I got to Steeple Close there was no sign of Alan's Lancia outside the door, and I at once knew there'd be no one at home. I rang the bell, very briefly, as if ashamed somehow, and there was a barking in the hall and Willy looked down at me from the living-room window. I strolled down the Close, and looked at the alms houses and a little bit at the churchyard. The sky was clear, the sunlight still in evidence, a fresh winter late afternoon. I was self-conscious, of course. That is my cross: to exist so wholly in terms of feeling, to be motivated exclusively in terms of relationship, the impact of another's personality.

I was standing in the little public garden alongside the main road when, looking across at the end of the King's Road, I saw the low grey car, with Alan's round, pale face behind the wheel. I moved quickly out of sight and waited for the car to go by, into the Close. Then I walked with controlled pace back to the house.

21 February 1971

Recording at Olympic. When I got there, they were listening to the take of *Rosetta*. Alan says: 'Come in: sit down and shut up.' I'm introduced to the producer. Blue shirt, shoulder-length straggly hair, glasses . . . The mixer has a red shirt, little moustache and beard. General atmosphere of cool. Alan and Clive go into the studio to record phrases to brighten up the repetitive end. 'We'll use it, if it isn't too Andrews Sisters.'

9 May 1971

CANNES: *Hotel Suisse, Friday two weeks ago:* I had arranged with Clive, and also Jocelyn, that we'd take advantage of the concert that Alan and Clive were giving in Stockport

---

1. By Joyce Rayburn.

that Saturday night to go up and see a game (of rugby) at Wigan, and also have a look at the changing room – all in preparation for David's play [*The Changing Room*]. It turned out that Wigan were in fact playing on the Friday evening, and Leigh (Clive's home town) on Saturday afternoon. So if we went up on the Friday afternoon we could catch both matches.

I got to Euston first, leaving the Royal Court general office and making a quick trip by Victoria Line. I strolled around the concourse until I spotted Jocelyn in her long embroidered Persian coat . . . (As I sit here writing in the sun a small, sunburned girl rides through the gate and up the drive on an autocycle. She stops in front of the steps, methodically puts her cycle up on its stand, unhooks the elasticated cord which retains the basket, and lifts out – still in its wrapping – a pink flower – an orchid – which she carries into the hotel . . . Relating to film: I imagine the scene – a Lubitsch picture? with the trim maid carrying the tribute in to the heroine ensconced in a lacey bed . . . *without* the establishing shot. . . . A few moments later, the girl emerges, clips back the polythene with the clothes-pegs, replaces the retaining cord, lifts the cycle off its stand, wheels it round – with a fleeting, impassive glance at me, and rides off out of the gate, disappearing behind the concrete portico) . . . and with her long hair, looking rather bemusedly at the Departures board – on which I knew there was no mention of our train, and, instead a Holyhead Express listed about six different times. So I contacted her and led her to the compartment. I had joked with Jocelyn about disguising herself as a man by wearing a moustache in the Wigan changing room. And, not joking, I had suggested she might wear one of those caps she used to wear when working, and put her hair up in it. Interestingly, this was received by her with strong resistance – as if indeed her integrity were somehow impugned. 'If they can't accept me as I am . . .' etc.

Two or three minutes before the train was due to leave, Clive came into sight and we were seated in our first-class compartment. I gave Jocelyn David [Sherwin]'s first draft of *Lucky Man* to read. Clive read a bunch of music papers. I can't remember what I looked at. Probably Edward Bond's *Lear*.

It was quite strange – in a naive way – to think of Clive, who was unshaven, as the principal figure of the current newspaper sensation involving the Duke of ———, his ex-wife and . . . really my capacity to remember the names of people who don't concern me is disappearing altogether.

12 July 1971
I've been looking at the book I bought on Saturday: *Rebels – the Rebel Hero in Films*. Nothing profound, but an attractively illustrated book about Garfield, Brando, Clift, Dean, Newman, Beatty *et al*. Two pages on Richard in *This Sporting Life*. It is an interesting phenomenon – the tough, sexy, sensitive rebel. Can I do this for Malcolm in *O Lucky Man!*? But really Alan is the character.

3 August 1971

About *The Changing Room*. Last night we went to see Jocelyn (David and I, with Colin
Cook, my new assistant) and started talking about the set. Jocelyn in an obstinate, really
bloody-minded mood. In spite of all my explanations – to have the characters entering
towards the audience, and exiting to the field also facing the audience – and despite
David's opinion that it would be more theatrical-dramatic to have a different door to
the outside and to the field – she continued to insist that we could make do with one
door. I got really quite angry. ('The really marvellous thing is when they go through the
tunnel onto the field, and we can't have that. So it doesn't really matter . . .') She also
made laborious weather over the idea of showing part of the communal bath through
the entrance to the bath house, which isn't how the play is written, either technically or
dramatically (as David pointed out). So much for Jocelyn, purist servant of the text!
She was very tired of course and rather edgy, and perhaps she resents me for not being
– in any way – like George [Devine]. Then, it was a perverse night, David took against
the idea of using that Wigan painting – the group of three from the wall of their
clubroom – as a front curtain. Frightened it will seem 'quaint', i.e. be patronised by our
London audience. I know what he means, but isn't it best to go on our own intuitions?
I *don't* like the idea of starting with the curtain up and seeing the set.

9

The Making of a Masterpiece

O Lucky Man!

'I keep wondering: will we actually finish the picture?
I still can't really see it – and wouldn't be at all surprised
if the whole thing fell to pieces beneath me.'

4 August 1971

Well, the script of *O Lucky Man!*[1] is even more of a shambles than I had expected: the lack of concrete imaginings; the attempt to pass off a string of notes (usually transcribed from a conversation we had several weeks ago) as a *scene*; lack of characterisations; lack of WORK. I read part of it on the train coming down, as David [Sherwin] bleated his incapacity to write *anything* for the scene on the roof, his incapacity to believe in Patricia or in Mick[2] . . . It isn't as if anyone else could write it.

5 August 1971

David turned up this morning with at least a draft of the roof scene with Patricia that made the thing look feasible. The end no good. We talked and he went off to write again: still the end defeated him. We went for a walk along the front after beer and sandwiches in the pub – the Hope Inn.

This evening after dinner we look at TV and see *This Week* feature on the *Oz* sentences: fifteen months for Richard Neville and recommended deportation . . . Do people care? It's hard to imagine. When Mum sees a long-haired demonstrator being

---

1. Mick (Malcolm McDowell), a happy, smiling coffee salesman, travels the length of Britain in an interlinking series of adventures involving a Northern mayor (Arthur Lowe), a nuclear research station, a mad scientist (Graham Crowden), a rock singer (Alan Price), big business (Ralph Richardson), an African dictator (Lowe again, blacked up) and a suicidal housewife (Rachel Roberts) to name but the most memorable. All ends with Mick auditioning for a film directed by L.A. himself.
2. Patricia provides the link that takes Mick away from the mad scientist, Dr Millar, via Alan Price into the world of big business.

pulled along by the hair, she laughs. More distasteful is the legal correspondent of the *Guardian*, rather smirkingly 'against' the sentences, but with a smooth attitude of dissociation that merely establishes his superior impartiality, with no suspicion of anything as vulgar or commonplace as a personal commitment. And Donald Spoor, ineffably smug, also prepared to 'disapprove' of the sentences but spend all the time stressing the trivial or vulgar or damaging 'attitude to sex' – in such a way as to remove any possibility that his audience could associate *him* with the publication – or care about the wretched fellows now in gaol. The moral of these TV discussions: either don't take part in them, or cut off ruthlessly from any of the other participants, and above all *dis*respect the laws and courtesies of polite English controversy.

A very good quote in a *TLS* piece by the Polish émigré writer Jerzy Peterkiewicz – from Simone Weil: 'Revolution is the Opium of the Intellectuals'.[1]

7 August 1971

Work on the script is naturally very slow. It is grave that David has – so to speak – lost his authority and I am *too much* in the ascendant, at least for my own comfort. I hate writing, and it tends to lose all reality for me when I get so close to it. We agreed today that a different style was necessary when working on this material than on *If . . . .*, if only because that was based on a world we both knew intimately, and this has all to be created. David admits that he really was hoping (whether consciously or not) that it would somehow be written for him by Malcolm, or by me. And then when he knew it wouldn't be, he panicked . . . I still respect his intuitions greatly – but his invention is lagging, I suppose because he is in a state of complete exhaustion.

24 August 1971

West of Suez[2] has opened, after various difficulties and excitements – including a visit from Larry on the Friday night preview, declaring how much he disliked the play, and going round to tell Ralph how false he was, and Jill Bennett that the first scene was a lift from Noël Coward . . .

Also, on Friday 13th, my violent clash with Gillian [Diamond] which led to her walking out of the theatre for a week.

The script going slowly: David [Sherwin] with his tonsillitis and now with his bronchitis: his cups of black coffee laced with Guinness which are left around the flat . . . The only way we can work is to talk; for him to write; to talk again; to write again; for me to rewrite . . . All this against the pressure of trying to cast *The Changing Room*, whose demands are really uniquely difficult, perhaps beyond anyone, but rather beyond Gillian, I suspect, who is undoubtedly fettered to her office and family. It really

---

1. This was included in *O Lucky Man!*, painted on a corrugated fence in the Derelicts scene.
2. By John Osborne. Directed by Anthony Page.

seems extraordinary that it should be so hard – impossible – to find a bulky, extrovert, bullshitting Northern cunt, between thirty-five and forty, with a sense of humour . . .

25 August 1971

Yesterday Malcolm [McDowell] was to come round in the morning to report on his conversation with Andy Mitchell . . . He got round rather late. I was annoyed at his blithe acceptance of Andy Mitchell's reluctance to attempt to work out any system of finance or distribution outside the absolutely most conventional framework:

'He thinks a major is best really, like Warners.'

'Why?'

'Well, they've got the outlets. And then it's all above board.'

'What do you mean, "above board"? Everyone knows the reputation of the majors for fiddling the books.'

'Oh well, that's true, of course. That's well known.'

'And why Warners?'

'Actually he suggested Columbia. But I said you didn't like them.'

'Who said I didn't like them?'

'Well, you don't like John Van Eyssen . . .' Etc., etc.

I went to dinner with Malcolm and Margot last night, with their pleasant American friends. A sharp brush over Malcolm's tonsils: which of course he refuses to do anything about. Shooting has to stop if and when he becomes ill . . . Almost certainly this *will* happen.

The Changing Room *opened at the Royal Court on 9 November, and was an immediate hit, grossing more money than any Court production since* Home. *Warren Clarke starred with Barry Keegan, Paul Dawkins, Edward Judd and Brian Glover.*

20 November 1971

I went out quite early and shopped: bought tapered 'brute' T-shirts and briefs, some books, some weeklies (with *Changing Room* notices), enquired about a camera. The play can only be regarded as a great success, with House Full at every performance, a transfer fixed to the Globe, and enthusiastic reviews everywhere (except *Tribune* and *Spectator* and *What's On* – both of which are written by the same critic!).

Back to the flat – before setting out for Sloane Square and the Hugo Claus[1] reception where I made rather a hit with the vivacious Madame Frey, blonde, sparky, with a

---

1. Hugo Claus, Belgian writer, whose *Friday* had been the most successful post-war play in Dutch. It was performed at the Court from 23 November 1971.

black eye concealed behind a veil fringe to her hat . . . To the Court, where there was a meeting to set on foot arrangements for Alan and Clive's benefit performance for the Theatre Upstairs. Helen [Montague] comes up to explain, in her usual breathless style, that the staff members of the theatre will in fact be away when the concert takes place – as it coincides with the out-of-town opening of *Veterans*.[1] Why this was not raised at the meeting heaven knows – except that the evasion of the real truth about anything (particularly if it involves inconvenience) seems now to have become a built-in reflex with Helen.

16 December 1971

Flying to LA to join Michael Medwin and Michael Simkin in their quest for $1.5 million. I know that I quite impress, perhaps even intimidate M. Simkin, which isn't so difficult; but it is a great bore. He raises some question about the issue of remake and sequel rights – another asset which apparently distributors are used to collaring. I pour scorn on the idea, and of course, because I am firm, Michael Medwin supports me. We are supposed to be basing our play on the *uniqueness* of our project, and I talk eloquently on the need for us to feel that the terms of the DEAL with a distributor will reflect the originality and efficiency with which this unique property will be handled – and not that it will be regarded as, and treated like, 'just another picture'. This sounds good but of course makes Michael Simkin nervous.

Malcolm drove me to the airport. He is generous in this way; likes doing it. I buy a copy of *Time* which has a review of *A Clockwork Orange* and says: 'Malcolm McDowell is sensational. His performance has the range and dynamism that signal the arrival of a new superstar!' Which can't be bad!

God! We Descend . . . What an ordeal lies before me – what an orgy of posturing and play-acting. It really does make the whole business of film-making repugnant.

18 December 1971

Gordon Stulberg, now of Fox, who at CBS was responsible for rejecting *If . . . .* , with his full and frank admission that he had been in error over *If . . . .* and he didn't want to make the same mistake again. But he queried some of the words in the script, such as 'scarper', which would be unfamiliar to an American audience and should be looked at; 'nudity' and X-rating concerns were mentioned. I rather cut off because the whole approach sounded so stale. And I was conscious of having to get to Paramout by three-ish.

———

Anderson settled on a deal from Bob Solo at Warner Brothers.

———

1. Charles Wood's play about the making of Tony Richardson's film of *Charge of the Light Brigade*.

7 January 1972

Interview six or seven candidates for Patricia. Two attractive but rather freakish dropouts are the most sparky, but not really Sir James's daughters. Michael[1] comes and sits
in, to my covered irritation ... Michael is supposed to be getting an informal note from
ACTT confirming their acceptance of my application for Mirek. I think that 'success'
has finally confirmed with Michael the idea that his job does not call for what is
generally known as 'work', i.e. in his life of hanging around and making phone calls
and dates with Sean Connery and having drinks, he is genuinely not conscious of 'not
working' ... A lot of shouting on the telephone secures my visa. The brisk Basil [Keys,
Associate Producer] stands by hopelessly.

11 January 1972

Smooth trip to the airport. Suddenly realise I should have brought a less bulky case –
in case of a tight change in Amsterdam. The girl at the BEA desk says I can't take it,
then relents, but says it may well be taken off me at the gate as the first class is full. In
fact I am the *only first-class passenger*. A four-hour wait at Amsterdam as there is fog in
Prague. An age to get through the passport barrier at Prague: one feels that the return
of Stalinism has entailed a return to bureaucracy and provincialism. Poor Mirek has
been waiting since eleven. He looks tired but also despondent. Things seem suddenly
to have become tricky. It's neither Yes nor No at the moment [whether or not Ondricek
would be allowed to leave Czechoslovakia to shoot *O Lucky Man!*].

15 January 1972

Took a pill last night: woken, very muzzy, by phone call from Malcolm: has seen Milos
and done the David Frost and Dick Cavett shows![2] Call from Oscar, with long, complicated reports about the Court – Bill (predictably) has now about-turned and decided he
would like to return as Artistic Director, with Robert Kidd as his sidekick! Peter Gill
writing to Bill to say he has come to the conclusion *he* should run the theatre.

   Go with David to Jocelyn's and talk about the script from two to nine ... Exhausted.
I cannot pretend to enthusiasm. The whole operation seems more and more lunatic.
But how can I possibly escape?

18 January 1972

Picked up by Miriam [Brickman]: we drive into her office and discuss casting. Warren
(Clarke) for Andy; Robert Swann, yes or no? I mention Robin Askwith;[3] Hugh
Thomas,[4] etc.... Miriam's sister, with cropped greying hair, who has been in prison in

---

1. Michael Medwin, who shares the producer credit with L.A.
2. US promotion for *A Clockwork Orange*.

Indonesia, is there, typing out her story . . . I have promised Brian Cox to see *Getting On*,[1] with forebodings, so I walk from Miriam's via the Queen's, buying two stalls for tonight at £2 each. To the Istanbul, where I find Warren waiting. We have a nice lunch and I cheer him by saying he can play Andy. We talk, mostly egotistical actor's talk, but I enjoy it because I like him.

To Memorial, where I am horrified by an eighteen-week schedule. Then to see *Getting On* with Miriam. Bourgeois shit. Yes, sitting in the Queen's among that dreadful middle-class audience, loving the play's fantasy-image of themselves, laughing at place names like Rickmansworth and Stanmore, chuckling at the cosy, complacent exposure of their own weaknesses, celebration of their mediocre values. It's hard to believe *The Changing Room* is going on next door.

23 January 1972

Tube to Baker Street, and walked down to the Bangladesh restaurant, where Bill and Anthony were already at a table, discussing an alternative director for *Hedda Gabler*[2] – and I brought up my suggestion, made to Anthony a couple of days ago, and which I think brilliant, of Peter Wood[3] . . . Bill was friendly and relaxed – and paid for the meal. But he reiterated his belief that Oscar was not the right person to run the theatre, our involvement with it would be necessarily less – when I reminded him that the whole situation with Oscar was his creation. We parted with the question unresolved, but friendlily.

The phone rings. 12.25 a.m. A Scots voice says, 'Is that you, Lindsay?' On enquiry, claims to be a telephone supervisor or some such title – 'A fellow was trying to ring you up today and claims he could get nothing but bleep-bleep, bleep-bleep, and we were wondering if there was something wrong with your telephone?' . . . then something about 'We don't get the chance every day to talk to a big time film-maker . . .' Finally I say, 'Piss off,' he replies, 'Now that's not the way to talk.' I put the receiver down. After, the phone rings twice, then stops.

---

3. English actor. Made his debut as a bully in *If* . . . . and found fame in the *Confessions of* . . . films.
4. Askwith and Thomas both played seniors in *If* . . . . Thomas reappears in several roles in *O Lucky Man!*, most prominently as a pickpocket in the Salvation Army scene. Askwith returned in the meaty role of Shop Steward in *Britannia Hospital*.

---

1. By Alan Bennett, with whom L.A. would work on *The Old Crowd* (1979). Kenneth More starred with a cast that included Brian Cox and Mona Washbourne.
2. John Osborne's adaptation which would open in June. Anthony Page directed; Jill Bennett starred, with Brian Cox and Denholm Elliott.
3. L.A. was being rude. He didn't like Wood's work and he didn't like the fact that Osborne's *Hedda Gabler* came as part of a package with *West of Suez* and *A Sense of Detachment*.

25 January 1972

Today we started [the production of *O Lucky Man!*] at 9 a.m. Something of an effort, but nothing for it except to plunge in. We cover much the same ground as before: I am aware of Jocelyn's propensity not really to take in (or accept) decisions she doesn't agree with. Mirek (arrived yesterday at 4.50) finding his bearings. I don't know how much of what is said actually gets through to him. We eat in the office, then sally forth in our two cars to view 1) Willesden Town Hall and 2) a Jacobean house, as a possibility for the Millar Clinic.[1] Both somewhat disappointing. Strangely, Jocelyn obviously hasn't got the epic tune. Her ideas seem consistently too small, too bitty – too naturalistic.

28 January 1972

A DREARY MORNING tramping round the Military Police Barracks in Kensington Church Street [searching for locations for *O Lucky Man!*] – cold and damp and though serviceable, totally uninspiring – then Colet Court[2] – where the front house has atmosphere but is near the road and subject to noise – then dropped in to Old Parr's Head, where at least Mirek was stimulated to enthusiastic approval of the rehearsal room . . . An abortive trip to Camden Town to look at tenements; then dropping in to Drama Centre, where a girl unknown to me called me 'Lindsay' and showed us the back hall with students doing Circus Movement to piano accompaniment.

29 January 1972

Our explorations of English society start today at the Reform Club: grand monument of nineteenth-century establishment and stability. The Lord Chief Justice is in the reading room when we intrude, and leaves indignantly. We are shown round by a charmingly disrespectful Scots young man from Ayrshire. He looked a bit like a dark weasel. To Jocelyn's: colour discussion and argument about Mirek's continuity ideas (trees changing instead of calendar). Then to Alan's, where we have Lancashire hotpot and listen to the numbers; then to gig at Isleworth. Back, dead, about 1.15 a.m.

30 January 1972

See a copy of yesterday's *Daily Express*, with Richard, absurd and scruffy, rehearsing his concert tour . . .[3] To Claridges for lunch with Charlie Baker; in his room, we drink. It's odd I like him; I say odd because his clipped, shorthand camp seems impregnated with *New Yorker* insincerity, and yet I don't think he is insincere, I think he has quite

---

1. Dr Millar, the mad scientist, played by Graham Crowden, who would take centre stage in *Britannia Hospital*.
2. An abandoned private school. L.A.'s production team converted it into a film studio.
3. Richard Harris had embarked on a profitable sideline as a singer.

genuine responses. He spoke glowingly about *The Changing Room*. Angela Lansbury[1] came in with the pipe-smoking Peter Shaw (who was it who recounted that his first assignment in Hollywood was to service Joan Crawford?), distressed because Peter Hall had, after six weeks rehearsal for the new [Edward] Albee play [*All Over*] suggested she should basically reconceive her performance. I said he was merely rationalising his own insecurity. She said she'd reached that conclusion. A forthright, pleasantly ego-maniac lady: she hated *Butley*.[2]

1 February 1972

To Columbia – and discuss the idea of filming *The Changing Room* in a desultory way. They would prefer it to cost £200,000 rather than £250,000, and John Van Eyssen seemed worried, indefinably, about the nudity. Well, they must come through with an offer.

Tried to think of some decent lines to complete some of Alan's lyrics – then down to Trafalgar Square to post lyrics to Alan.

2 February 1972

Further Patricia interviews. Impressed with Fiona Lewis, very authentically upper class, rather arrogant, yet direct and honest. Helen Mirren rather humourless (or seemingly so): prepared to think I find her RSC tradition 'absolute shit'. She may be going to work with Peter Brook in Paris – traced two different ways an actor could go: Peter Brook and Fellini or Ken Loach and me. Not *very* charming: rather *bossy* – but I seem to like that! Lunched on a kebab with Jocelyn, and then we went to look at Pana-vision tests at Samuelsons. As we set out we passed an old man collapsing to the ground, a young student trying to hold him up; we leapt out and got him into the restaurant. It took a long time for the ambulance to answer; then the police came and we left.

4 February 1972

I omitted to say yesterday that David Sherwin has returned to apparent drunken hope-lessness at Platt's Lane. I suggest perhaps a nursing home – but all seem full. Wake ex-hausted to find the prospect of a journey North to Sheffield (Alan and Clive at the Fiesta). This was Alan's suggestion. Experience tells me that he *won't* be eager to work. Arrange for David to stay a few days with Jocelyn. Catch the 11.30 from King's Cross to Leeds.

The Selbyfork Hotel sauna. Good idea this as you sauna in a bathing slip and don't have to worry about the size of your cock.

I was met at Leeds station by Alan's roadie – 'Big Alan', with long fair hair and dark glasses and a compulsive flow of chat. He did hand me a note from Alan, which

1. British actress (1925–), best known for *Murder She Wrote* (1984).
2. By Simon Gray, with Alan Bates in the title role as a university lecturer losing control.

apologised for being on the golf course – and later, as I lay exhausted on my bed, Clive rang, having returned from the course, and again excused Alan, who eventually rang me about 5.30 (I had arrived on the 2.08). I kick myself slightly for the illusion which I permitted myself that I might actually talk about the songs with Alan, or even do some 'work'. Perhaps when he suggested the visit he actually had such a fantasy himself. But really it was just social. I was feeling rather old and browned-off at dinner-time, when Alan came down to pick me up for dinner – and actually put my dinner down on his bill, which is a rarity! So, as he says, 'There you go.'

With swimming pool, restaurant, sauna, long clean corridors, just off the motorway, behind its long grey car park, this really is a marvellous setting for a train robber on the run.

We drive through rough fog to the Fiesta, Sheffield – a vast half-oval arena of pink lamps and tables rising up from the central stage, up to bars at the back. A curtain that runs round to conceal the stage. Backstage clean and simply decorated – red and blue hessian-covered walls. The club entered through one of these concrete, multi-floored car parks – again classic thriller territory. As we enter, the dinner-suited doorman says: 'Sold out.' Alan and Clive have had a very successful week. Record-breaking. They feel relaxed – though of course they continue merely to coast.

Before the performance Alan craves a taste – now he rolls his own – walks up and down – says 'I'm bored' a number of times. They decide to end with 'Rosetta'; then 'Talkin' about You' if an encore is called for, 'Ravers' if the atmosphere warrants it. (In the event they don't do any encores at all.) The Irish roadie of the comedian on the bill comes in and talks rather ambiguously about playing for a month in Kenya . . . The show goes down nicely: apparently Tony, the drummer, makes some balls-up and isn't satisfactory. I don't really notice, of course; just that it's just a working cabaret show. *No* lessons in presentation have been learned!

After the show, a party has been organised: Alan, who has completely forgotten about it, suddenly remembers that earlier in the week, drunk and trying to pull a chick, he had burst out, 'What's goin' on in this miserable town – why aren't there any parties?' Since the show has ended at 12:30, and we don't get ready to move till 1.45 or so, I am grateful for Alan and Clive's ruthlessness in suddenly deciding to split. Back through the fog, to arrive at Selby Forks at 3 a.m. – where a party is in its last stages, with bathers still in the swimming pool. We take drinks, tea and [Alan] chocolate in the billiard room and play a game of snooker: Alan and Colin vs Clive and me. We win. Bed with one and a half Sonegal at 4.30 a.m.

5 February 1971
Woke about 11.30: tea and biscuits and listened to the local radio. Round-up of local films – a different perspective from the West End all right. You can't help noting the

preponderance of X films: from 'Adult' to Horror and Sex – and realise the irrelevance of so much of what we do to the millions living quietly in the provinces.

6 February 1972

To Jocelyn's for supper, where David [Sherwin] is now staying. He seems to have done no work and to be incapable without my magic presence . . . Argue and discuss with Jocelyn, then back by minicab.

7 February 1972

Talked with Ian Rakoff and sent him off to research for Honey Conference[1] material: then David [Sherwin] arrived and we tried to work on the script – honey-bombers, club scene etc., David is in a sorry state: he is taking four kind of pills – one to counteract his depressive mania; another to stimulate; another to make *that* effective . . . We had a kebab together and I spoke to him quite roughly – irritated because, now that I've got him safely settled with Jocelyn, he decides to return to Platt's Lane. He says he can work better there. *Can* he work? Or will I just have to wring the thin bits? It begins to look like it. See Fiona Lewis in a bad film with John Osborne. She *is* striking.

To my surprise David rings tonight, to thank me for our talk.

8 February 1972

Spend a good time with Alan [Price]. We talk philosophy, which is important for the songs. In a sense the final zen-existential feeling of the film corresponds to his own feeling about life: be what you are; you are what you are; decisions won't change anything. But of course this is mixed with an instinctive, romantic radicalism . . . He is not a word-writer: except when they 'come', in a flash.

Evening we (Jocelyn, Michael, James, Alan, Whiffle and I) go to the preview of Tony [Richardson]'s *Threepenny Opera*. We all enjoy it very much. Whatever inequalities are compensated by vigorous, uncompromising handling.

10 February 1972

Power cuts started today – as we return from Berkshire location hunting, myself with Malcolm in the front, Jocelyn (asleep), Michael and Basil in the back, all down one side of Shepherd's Bush the lights are out. I have a sad foreboding that the dark evenings to come will inevitably see the end of *The Changing Room* . . . I meant to go down to the theatre tonight, but we were late back, and I dropped in with Malcolm to see Mum.

---

1. 'Honey' is the codename for chemical weapons supplied to Danda, the African dictator.

12 February 1972

David came round, unsteady on his feet and blurred in speech: he said he'd stopped taking his pills and had been sick all morning. I said: 'What have you been drinking?'

'I haven't been drinking.'

'I can smell it.'

'Barley wine.'

He talked vaguely and vehemently about how awful were Mick's scenes with Patricia in the script; how they needed to be rewritten; how she had to lead him to London and should show him 'compassion'. He crossed to his case to give me (unwillingly) the typed out sheets of the Danda–Honey nexus. I told him I thought his obsession with the Mick–Patricia relationship was only a reflection of his obsession with Gay Sherwin: that his talk about 'compassion' was a soppy, sentimental reflection of his own craving, and that all his imaginative, emotional energies were in fact going into his determination, obsession, craving, need (whatever you like) to get Gay back . . . And the day of shooting looms . . . and looms . . .

13 February 1972

Nice to have the excuse of feeling incipient flu last night to take a pill, wake reasonably late, and stay in bed till about two . . . Malcolm rings, wakes me to say he's been called a goose-stepping Fascist in the *NY Sunday Times*. Must help him reply. He comes in with the article which turns out to be much less than sensational, quite dull in fact, and not really worth answering. Stanley [Kubrick] has written a 2,000 word answer and told him he needn't bother. So of course he's determined. I write him a letter which is quite clever. He's delighted.

15 February 1972

Felt bloody awful this morning: sick and loose from the bowels – because of auditions for Patricia no doubt. The coal strike and the power cuts have not much figured in these chronicles: amazingly there seem to have been none yet at Greencroft Gardens . . . But *The Changing Room* has been [affected] . . . David rings tonight to say we can no longer heat the bathwater (too much electricity).

20 February 1972

Tonight I saw most of *Three Godfathers* [by John Ford] on TV. It *is* a disappointment – I see in Peter Bogdanovich's book that it was shot in thirty-two days, which perhaps explains much. The dramatic conception and execution very perfunctory: a dreadful studio sequence inside the wagon with Mildred Natwick as the dying mother; very badly lit; without atmosphere. Just a bit of charm at the end, with Mae Marsh and Ward Bond.

23 February 1972

Travel with Dave Allen down to Brighton, where we walk through the blacked-out town to the theatre and see *Veterans*. Ron Eyre has not been too clever. Poor set by Voytek: many of the parts miscast: Gordon Jackson as the camp dresser; John Mills boring; (Ann Bell ditto); Frank Grimes strange – is he good or bad? A somehow *attractive* narcissistic performance. John [Gielgud] delightful but unfocused. The cast have not been given CONFIDENCE. Yet the play is good – weak in the last scene – but could be a success.

25 February 1972

Started with a bang, having agreed to go to Bermans with Malcolm and then Rachel . . . The moment I get in the office I am told that Rachel is insisting that Darren[1] should design her clothes, that he should be paid £25 a sketch and a credit . . . that she put the phone down on Elsa Fennel [wardrobe] . . . I cringe immediately at the thought of star nonsense being added to everything . . . I speak to Rachel, who denies most of it, but claims that Darren 'worked five hours' last night and at the least can bring his drawings to Bermans . . . I say of course (it turned out he hadn't even read the script).

28 February 1972

Morning conference – Colin Jamison (hair), Paul Rabiger (make-up) and Elsa, also Jocelyn and Derek [Cracknell, Assistant Director]. Discussion of the principal costumes and hair. Can Rachel look like Norma Shearer? I tell Colin, who is a responsive, eager-faced, sensitive young fellow, to modify as he must. I speak rather sharply to Jocelyn when she is vague about the joins in Malcolm's artificial arms: this vagueness is part of her, but contrasts strangely with her total practicality in work. Really she is working much harder than me. How does she do it?

Catch the 6.18 to Reading, where I have promised to speak to some society at Bev Risman's College . . . I'm afraid I have neglected to note *what* society or *what* college, or to remember the name of the wretched organising secretary who has been ringing desperately to be sure I'm coming. The remembered difficulty of prising myself out of one's perhaps more sophisticated world, of being 'interested' and polite without being patronising . . . Anyway, the distinguished visitor finally descends from the London train . . .

1 March 1972

This evening I went to an Artistic Committee meeting which spent hours on the question of the Schools Scheme – with no one, it seemed, speaking clearly: Pam Brighton

---

1. Darren Ramirez, long-time companion.

muddled and chiefly concerned, it seemed, with getting herself a company. Oscar far too loose and indulgent in the Chair. Jocelyn going to sleep . . . Peter Gill embarking on those long, muddled monologues. Bill being vehement, spasmodic and flip. The best moment – and perhaps the only one that made the thing worthwhile – was Anthony's attempt to get out of *Hedda*. Oscar: 'But Anthony, you're committed to it.' . . . 'I never wanted to do it.' . . . Huge pauses.

3 March 1972

After a real tough day – conscience drove me to see *The Changing Room*. A sad, finally an awful experience. First act down, somehow lacking in nerve, edge, lightness and vivacity: Barry (Keegan) shouting . . . Second act much the same – Paul Dawkins bad – not thinking, superficial . . . Then the third act started badly with Barry apparently giggling – that kind of actor's complacency I can't stand . . . The hose completely out of hand – deliberately sprayed over the stage – then everything in pieces . . . vulgar and undistinguished . . . painful . . . At moments I only just restrained myself from calling out . . . Marched straight up to Barry's dressing room: I'm afraid I launched into a ferocious attack – leaving both Barry and Don McKillop gaping – but I was really upset. To see everything demeaned and thrown away like that. I write notes for the cast, including eight severe pages for Barry!

5 March 1972

START OF MUSIC RECORDING for *O Lucky Man*. At Olympic, down in Barnes, where Alan and Clive mixed their ill-begotten album, and their singles, and Alan first sang 'Changes' . . . Alan comes in about twenty past ten looking as usual pale and withdrawn and hating it and everybody. Frequently during the day he complains of pains round his heart, doesn't know whether he can get through it, etc. He is all nerves, of course, an incredible mixture of impulses, simultaneously autocratic yet highly sensitive. Favourite remark on the conclusion of anything: 'What's wrong with that?' Terribly difficult to put an oar in, and yet of course I must. Alan complains because I discuss the pattern of the opening song with him, saying I upset the players, intrude too early, etc. – of course I am afraid that if I leave it too long, it will all get set. I realise for instance he *doesn't* want to do a piano lead-in to *O Lucky Man* and is really proposing to do it on a guitar! In fact such is the first take . . . tense argument . . . outcries on the line of 'Don't bug me, man' . . . I pace up and down, reminded bitterly of Richard Harris. But I stick painfully. And Alan comes round after a drink at lunch. Colin Green (guitar) is a help. And the music good.

6 March 1972

MUSIC again. Alan's opening comment: 'I think I'm going to die'. Pains round his heart . . . We listen to yesterday's *Lucky Man* takes. He says they're all rubbish. Then, with vehemence he announces: 'I can't do it with a piano. It won't work. I won't do it.' This is the crunch, I feel. On a reflex of determination I simply say, 'That's impossible.' I say this with no politicking so I am quite surprised when he just gets up and tries to get it better. I honestly don't know what he's so steamed up about – apart from just being Alan Price.

In the morning I have a call from Michael Codron. *The Changing Room* must close. I am sad, and in the recording studio I near-weep a little in a corner on my own. I go to see them in the evening.

9 March 1972
First rehearsals: Rachel and Malcolm. Lecture Hall and Gloria's room. Rachel has to struggle hard and continually be checked from falling into those little placating, supplicating smiles. Malcolm's smile on the other hand – as demonstrated in the lecture hall – looks alarmingly like *A Clockwork Orange*.

Mirek at Samuelson's, testing. By lunch time the office seems to be full of people . . . we realise we don't know where to eat . . . Jocelyn has insisted we go to the horrible pub opposite, satisfying her puritanical obsessions . . . When it is discovered there is NO WORCESTER SAUCE, and I can't stand being told by Jocelyn that I don't *need* Worcester Sauce, I self-indulgently walk out to get a bottle . . . But there seem to be no shops, and the Broadway is full of vast, rather empty, dirty echoing IRISH PUBS – a sort of no man's land in burgeoning, trendy London. I order gammon and eggs and chips in one, but after fifteen sad minutes with a barley wine and total inattention I walk out.

13 March 1972
Four years ago today we started shooting *If . . . .* This morning at Colet Court we read the script. It was a splendid gathering. Too splendid. Too many people to cope with. Ralph – Dandy – Mona – Rachel – Graham Crowden – Brian Glover – Eddie Peel – Eddie Judd – Mary McLeod – Arthur Lowe . . . Malc and Alan and Ian and David.

The music got us through, otherwise it would have been dismal. Quite good – adequately dialogued – at the start – though overlong: then THIN – unless marvellous inventions are arrived at for instance in prison and thirties sequence.

Will Ralph *act* Monty?! He hasn't started to characterise him . . . After the reading I took Alan over to the pub, everyone else having disappeared. There they were: Malcolm, Fiona, Graham . . . Then we rehearsed with Ralph and Mary [McLeod]. Ralph very picky, always this sticky logic which is really against the style of it: but if one stands up to him he does accept pretty well finally. He is the strangest combination of shrewdness and intelligence and intuition – with an over-scrupulous logic and psychological naturalism.

Special FX meeting. Then home to work with David on cuts. Cook soup and bacon and egg. The X film is *Dr Sardonicus*[1] – appallingly bad, but gripping!

14 March 1972

After endless thought and calculation – trying to fit in John Gielgud as The Judge before he goes to Hollywood on the 20th – I go the Court, to propose the 13th – and, going into his dressing room in the interval, and stemming his chatter about the agony of appearing before a Jewish Charity audience – learn he is now to be in Hollywood on the 13th. Will go to NY and leave on the *8th*!! Dear John, he really is as light-headed and self-indulgent as the character he is playing in *Veterans*.

Day started with Jocelyn ... sharp clash over what I consider to be a quite irrelevant kinetic *objet* for Gloria's office. Rehearsals with Rachel, Arthur, Peter Jeffrey,[2] Malc and Hugh Thomas and Ben Aris. Feel Rachel is quite miscast. Afternoon, Majestic Hotel and sketchy look at nightspot.[3] Christine Noonan[4] still giggles self-consciously. Decide *she* is miscast. The Blue Film is unusable.

18 March 1972

Picked up at 10.30 for test rushes at De Lane Lea. As usual they don't mean all that to me: I am only too pleased to leave these decisions to Mirek. Really I don't think I *could* do another picture, certainly not *one* of 'these', without his authority and support. The strain of trying to accommodate a personal vision to a public ('commercial') context? After rushes Malcolm and Mirek and I eat fish, for health, at Manzi's. Really nice and civilised. I catch a brief glimpse of what London life surely should be like, with the red check tablecloths and white wine and friends.

Back home then to Globe for last night of *The Changing Room*. I take a blue plastic bucket on at the curtain call and distribute red and white roses.

19 March 1972

Rang David two or three times: always engaged. Then Malcolm. Suggested he come over. Really we were too impatient and too weary and scared to talk in detail. I mentioned Brian Lawson's remark about Cagney to him (not *acting* but *reacting*): Malcolm resists 'talking about' – which may be a strength, but can also be a weakness in rejecting the idea of *designing* a performance – discovering the interior dynamic ... Dined in Chinese restaurant. Rowed with Jocelyn.

---

1. By William Castle.
2. Who played the Headmaster in *If* ....
3. At the Hotel, the Mayor (Lowe) invites the new salesman, Mick (McDowell), to a nightclub show with strippers and blue films.
4. Who played The Girl in *If* ....

20 March 1972

First day of shooting *O Lucky Man.* Remarkably smooth . . . shot chiefly on Arthur and Rachel – covering the scene in (whatever you call it) main shots[1] – then close shots fairly lavishly distributed: impossible at this stage to know how it'll cut. Note that Arthur has grown quite erratic on his lines, as regards tempo, precision, etc. One or two takes sadly have a comic edge in a run-through that they never acquire in shooting . . . trust to the magic of the camera . . . We cut Malcolm's hair again: he emerges looking extraordinarily more boyish and younger and *the role.*

The chocolate sandwich is disintegrating:[2] one or two girls resign. Miriam [Brickman] only a quarter functioning. Her mother is ill.

21 March 1972

God! Only yesterday? It seems six months ago . . . Back into the Lecture Hall. We press on fast with shots of the boys listening – Malcolm's interjections – then the smiles,[3] and Gloria's attempts to instill salesmanship – then Rachel's close-ups. She is well in the character now and much better.

Everything seems to be going well. Too well, of course, and by the end of this scene we are in fact going a bit too fast – which Mick's 'Good morning, Mrs Rowe' and sincere smile pays the cost of . . . First rushes are the usual disappointing ordeal: the first shot turns out to be poorly framed (too low), and not enough light. Quality insufficient. Everybody seems rather uncertain about the whole thing, but quite prepared to accept that it 'looks marvellous'. Mirek certainly doesn't feel this. In spite of everything, Mirek thinks it's the best of our three beginnings!

23 March 1972

I have this deep and despairing intuition: that this film, if it ever could have been brought off, demanded FAR MORE THOUGHT AND PREPARATION to discover and maintain a *style*, which at the moment we are not finding. We saw the first day's factory material at rushes last night – having shot in the packing Dept. all day. I don't mind the noise, and indeed quite like the way it makes the dialogue inaudible. I realise that I should have used this MORE. Made Wallas[4] shout – dictating how we start the sequence etc.

---

1. Arthur Lowe and Rachel Roberts (as Gloria) teaching new sales recruits the fine art of selling coffee.

2. At the Mayor's 'gathering', two white women and a black man perform a 'chocolate sandwich' strip dance.

3. This image of McDowell smiling was used as the film's poster.

4. Wallas Eaton: he plays three roles, including Colonel Steiger and the Prison Warder. He later worked on L.A.'s Australian production of *The Bed Before Yesterday.*

Dropped in at Colet Court, to see the absurdity of the elements outside the office window, the rotten map, and the disappearing oil painting behind the managing director's desk – and I find them LACKING in epic size – too LITERAL and small – should have used more extras. Jocelyn deeply disappointing: she arrived at rushes with a length of commonplace 'gold' material in a transparent plastic bag, to say that *all* the gold material selected for Mick's suit[1] had by some malicious miracle been sold – to a cinema that was redecorating and to the designer of *Gone with the Wind*. Everything had been done to get hold of it and failed. 'But have *you*, Jocelyn?' 'You can't go through life disbelieving everyone . . .' etc. Where, O where is the artist's obsessiveness?

24 March 1972

Our first terrible day. I don't fully appreciate that the Managing Director's Office set is not rigged. And Mirek only then reveals that the set will take hours to light. Of course partly his fault, since he won't anticipate and gives orders like suggestions – expecting them to be taken up. Which the not over-sensitive Len Crowe isn't particularly good at. No shot by lunchtime. Bad tempers all round. Rachel's car was late: Basil gives her flowers – big deal! Arthur and Peter were called to rehearse at eight. Hung around in the office. No one there. At lunch I lay into Basil over the gold suit material: he doesn't really know, of course, and just gets tight-arsed when I'm rude. Afternoon nightmarish. The picture (on the wall in the Office set) keeps flashing where the metal is exposed. AT LAST Jocelyn – because Mirek wants it – consents to take down the sky – with a tiny paintbrush, saying it'll take her half an hour. Then she disappears and is never there. No paint. The paintshop is locked. No reverses shot. Mirek completely drunk. I try to read the Riot Act.

27 March 1972

The Dreaded Majestic Nightspot. We start at the top, with Arthur and Malcolm entering, and walking straight through into the dark hall . . . Mirek's conception probably will be striking and excellent – but one of the results is to make the shot a difficult one in terms of balance, and this immediately chokes me off the idea of shooting two ways. So immediately the question is raised: TOPLESS or COVERED? And the whole boring area of X or R rating? (I have, of course, given assurance that I will deliver a picture that is, or can be, 'R' – whatever that means). General opinion – rather supported by Mirek – is that the girls look better, also sexier – covered. And what's the point of making it if no one's going to see it? Nor do I want when the film is finished to spend ages arguing with fools about the cutting of the picture. And in our present

---

1. Mick's first port of call is Mrs Ball's [Mary McLeod] boarding house, where a mysterious tenant, Monty (Ralph Richardson), gives him a golden suit and tells him to 'Try not to die like a dog.'

climate of commercialised 'permissiveness', isn't this kind of thing going to line us up with *The Sun* and TV and popular press controversy? Or am I just rationalising? Maybe I should have shot the first set-up two ways. But of course I react with extreme violence when David Sherwin lurches onto the set, and pronounces what he sees 'APPALLING'. And then another edgy row with Jocelyn at a production meeting after shooting. We can hardly speak now without disagreeing.

28 March 1972

The last shot we set up last night was of the Screen (where the Blue Film is playing), with people framed round. On the way to Colet Court Mirek tells me he's changed his idea – better shoot the screen without people. I don't argue, because it'll be quicker . . . Arthur has been called early and now won't be used. Try to get hold of Michael to placate A, but he's late in . . . Arthur does get testy, and who can blame him. Particularly since he always is made to feel a bit patronised, i.e. no chair. No doubt: it is *not* an actor's medium. Malcolm is really angelic.

We film the Blue Film in its entirety. It really *is* good! Strange that I'm always so mean the first time I see anything – well nearly always! Then we run the song – Stephanie [Lawrence] *excellent*, and v. professional. Then the Chocolate Sandwich – which I have seen rehearsed for the first time this morning. One very good stripper, one rather charming amateur, and the black boy, Jules, totally gauche, with absolutely no sense of movement or rhythm or performance! I would have probably replaced him, but in fact his gaucherie is probably an advantage. Malcolm plays his close shots excellently: the crowd, supported by my *Changing Room* friends [and Bill Owen, James Bolam and Christine Noonan], is excellent. Then the end of the sequence proves difficult – especially because the stage can't be removed (Jocelyn's design again) in under two hours. But we struggle through.

30 March 1972

After three days' intensive, and perhaps successful work, all tends to fall to bits. Complications everywhere. Arthur [Lowe] suddenly appears in Ralph's caravan, complaining that Paul [Jamison] doesn't know what he is doing, and why hasn't Michael, as he promised, rung the BBC to find out how they make up for the *Black and White Minstrel Show*? . . . Michael, worried but professing staunchness, came up to tell me that a message had been received from Warners, that we MUST NOT SPEND MORE MONEY THAN BUDGETED. The farcical nature of our relationship with the distributors is again clear – BULLSHIT to my face, but ceaseless nagging suspicion and unbelief in everything that is done, proposed, drawn up. I keep wondering: will we actually finish the picture? I still can't really see it – and wouldn't somehow be at all surprised if the whole thing suddenly fell to pieces beneath me. The only obligation I feel, funnily enough, is to Malcolm: whose acting in the nightspot is brilliant I think.

1 April 1972

Yesterday: David Sherwin came in like a zombie. Absolutely NO REACTION. He is taking four Equanil and two Lithium a day. We drop him at New End Hospital Casualty, where a black nurse can't spell his name.

Today: David arrives – the idea that we should work on the unresolved scenes – and in the pub I lay into him – trying to stimulate him into some kind of active thought. He has spent three days looking for a first edition of *The Road to Wigan Pier* (which is supposed to contain reports of traditional children's games, or something). Frustrating and depressing to talk with David sitting there goggle-eyed and passive. The drug is supposed to be metabolising him into metal. I say that of course his psychiatrist is pleased with his state, since he's managed to turn him into a vegetable.

3 April 1972

Woke reasonably early in Jocelyn's studio. Michael was snoring, reasonably gently. He knows he snores. It was a beautiful day – early golden sun in the fields. Jocelyn was writing in the kitchen. I went and washed and had a bath. Breakfast. Everyone very *nice.* Why do I feel irritation – partly maybe when one *knows* that people's image of one in incorrect. To some degree *everyone's* image of me is incorrect. The price, penalty, cross of isolation.

We set off in cars and inspect a church near Basingstoke – the Portsmouth Family Church – but its layout, like a miniature cathedral, is not conducive. Jocelyn leads us on a wild goose chase to look for a church she remembered seeing on a walk. We lunched at the Queen's Hotel, Farnborough – which I seem to remember was where I last saw 'Dad' – of which I remember practically nothing. Curious and strange and unhappy, when I look back not just on childhood, but young manhood too.

5 April 1972

Back to the dreaded Danda Conference. The full circus in evidence when we arrive at Gerrard's Cross. Caravans for Sir Ralph; for Arthur; for Malcolm; for Michael and myself (sharing) . . . The house infested. It is slow shooting – with all those artists, and Arthur's make-up and poor old Ralph getting older and older. Had he realised from the first that he would never be able to learn those lines ('be-bom-bom of revolution') and so introduced that business with the briefcase?

9 April 1972

Bob Solo puts in a brief appearance, and I learn later he is beginning to panic at escalating costs and saying, 'You'll have to cut the script!' But I will *not* go and discuss anything with him. I grow more and more worried at the attitude revealed by Warner Bros. Would like to change distributors. I talk to Malcolm about it in the morning.

10 April 1972

Willesden Town Hall: Shooting 8 a.m. to 9.45 p.m. I keep feeling it's impossible – we'll never keep going like this. Mirek groans too, but of course it is he who is the more implacable – our last set-up he had them painting the set green where it had been left white . . . After all the hubub, the place looked good. Plenty of lamps and pictures to replace the baroque tat. I daren't think what the whole operation has cost – the gilt work, pots and hideous expensive furniture lying in crates in the storeroom. I suppose the film *will* have an overall style as a result of her contribution, but Jocelyn is strangely incapable of giving *anything* a personal, truly characterised dressing. The bedside tables of both Sir James and Lady Burgess totally denuded of any personal touches. So I take off in the Jeep to [my flat at] 57 Greencroft, and pick up a collection of books, pictures (the miniatures of Mum, Fitzy, Murray and me) with which I humanise Lady B's table. A long, long day.

12 April 1972

Go early to Denham labs to look at yesterday's rushes, all okay. Rich look, with Mirek's characteristic, delicate, *even* style . . . Of course Mirek gives the picture great distinction. Nor can he be called exactly slow. But *demanding*, often in areas that I know are hardly perceptible, and quite irrelevant to the picture as a whole. On the other hand, if I had to try to work out a shooting pattern entirely on my own, progress might be even slower. There's no doubt though that Mirek's communication problems do make things more difficult.

We attempt to crack on into the second long sequence – Mick's return, entry of the police, inspection of documents, arrest[1] – quite long rehearsal . . . slow start, probably overshooting from long front angle, but we work on hard. Ralph (who is tonight dining with the Queen) has been unusually co-operative.

13 April 1972

MICK'S BEDROOM. Back at Colet Court, to a new set on the first floor. Another white box of the kind Mirek hates. We start with Mick alone in his room, rehearsing, fantasising and then interrupted by Mrs Ball. We go into this with mistaken speed – partly because when we walk through the thing at the start, Malcolm sketches out an approach to the scene with great dash and wit – and presents a way of shooting the whole thing – including Mary's entrance and scene – in one shot. OF COURSE when we come to do it two hours or so later, the spark has gone and he never really recaptures it, even though the technicians applaud at the end of the three-minute-odd take. Maddening

---

1. Lost on a Pennine road, Mick arrives at a security fence, stands on the roof of his car to get a better look at his position, is taken away by a platoon of armed soldiers, ordered to sign a confession and then tortured.

too that we forgot to use the apple in this scene – which would have been so good being eaten as Mick rehearses his sales patter.

17 April 1972

Patsy[1] looking weak and pale: she has been unable to get up all day. No food . . . I give her soup and biscuits. She reveals that the doctor has said she probably has an ulcer. When I went in she was watching *Alfie* on TV. Poor girl.

My birthday. I don't know how, but it was known and many people on the unit (not to my great pleasure) greeted me with Many Happy Returns. Then in the afternoon a huge cake, which Michael had had baked in Chelsea, served with champagne on the set, and a hopelessly feeble attempt to sing the song . . . Only *I* can do these things!

18 April 1972

We move on the Sir James's Office complex[2] – first the secretary's office – Mick's arrival by lift, Stewart's hysterics,[3] etc . . . Black-and-white set, looks smart, but of course no one from the Art Dept. is there to hand over, and no shelf provided for Miss Hunter to reach for the Valium and the barley wine. (It spoiled the look of course: it is Mirek who suggested the proposed shelf should be inset into the wall.) Graham Crowden does splendidly. The white walls and intense overhead lighting are very taxing and by the end of the day we are all dizzy. We finish by about five. Not bad.

20 April 1972

BIG DRAMA on lighting. It is going to take ages . . . Holes have to be cut in the backing to let the arcs through, and I am told that this is more difficult than anticipated. I really am sick of British cinema, British technicians who cram themselves with bread and sausages and cakes and tea – work quite hard and accept long hours, but have absolutely no understanding of the work, think first and foremost of the money, and don't see rushes . . . Are they *all* 'intimidated' by our methods, our standards, our apparently mysterious objectives?? Can we get Mirek's [camera] operator from Prague? It *is* the last time. Malcolm told me this morning that Warner Bros are still refusing my/our billing – so I sent a nasty telegram to Bob Solo. We discuss withdrawing our labour.

21 April 1972

A really MURDEROUS DAY. We start with Malc and Ralph in Monty's Bedroom. I try to start methodically and calmly. We look through the entire sequence, *walk* through

---

1. Patricia Healey, the star of *The White Bus*. She cameos as the hotel receptionist.

2. Sir James (Richardson), an industrialist and the father of Patricia.

3. Stewart (Graham Crowden in a dual role) jumps out of the tower block window, taking with him Sir James's assistant and therefore providing a means for Mick's advancement.

it, establish what seems to be a workable pattern – and complete rehearsal by 9.15 . . . Mirek sends me off, and the actors go off to get made up. I go with Jocelyn, who refuses to admit to possibility or the feasibility of providing Monty with a *wooden* lay-figure or dummy. He just wouldn't have one – any more than he'd have his chest of drawers in front of the window. 'Well, you want me to put my ideas forward, then you always reject them.' I find her stupefying literalness as maddening as her obstinacy and her (in Mirek's charming phrase) inflexible GOOD TOAST . . . Well, what happened? It took two hours to light the set, and all I know is that we didn't get our second shot in till 1.30 . . . The nightmare of time-domination, shredding nerves and paralysed minds closes in. I get a five- or six-page page telegram of total idiocy from Robert H. Solo.

23 April 1972
Will I be – could I possibly be – tempted ever into going through this experience again? The alarming thing – and the one I feel it necessary to record – is the fact that while experiencing all the discomfort of desperation, I seem to have lost the impulse or spur of it . . . maybe this was true of *Sporting Life* when they wanted to remove me, and I couldn't bring myself to react violently . . . But there were strong emotional commitments there to sustain me . . . Now I feel the indifference of age, the fatal sense of proportion. And I am sick of conflict, and the perpetual, nagging, sickening pressure of TIME. (The covert glance at the watch by an actor or assistant which strikes like a knife in the stomach.) David Sherwin announces that he has to go for two weeks' holiday. He says his doctor says he needs it. I tell him I don't believe him.

Well – out of bed, and down at 7.30 to meet Saxon Logan[1] in the hall, and then Mirek, and off we go to the Reform Club . . . The day is not particularly kind – grey all the time – but at least it is St George's Day, so the Union Jack is flying from Big Ben, and St George's Cross from somewhere near – which makes a good approach shot for the Rolls.

24 April 1972
Are we getting – as Malcolm said today – our second wind? Today went calmly, I hope well, but somehow *calmly*, even though rather longer than we hoped: finishing Monty's room, including the presentation of the Gold Suit. Mirek invented a different method of presenting the gold suit – on a tailor's dummy – of course to Jocelyn's disapproval. (Poor old Jocelyn: she does look fearfully tired – yet she won't let go.)

26 April 1972
HA HA . . . If we have our moments of relaxed assurance, we certainly pay for them. Mirek was disgruntled all today – because his attempts to get sympathetic under-

---

1. L.A.'s assistant. He later made the cult film *Sleepwalker* (1984).

standing out of the focus-puller totally failed. Of course they just don't know what he's talking about when he speaks of 'rhythm', 'timing', etc. At the end of the day I again try to impress on him that the English are not artists . . . INTERROGATION ROOM: I would dearly have loved to do this in one day – but Mirek's demands are far too scrupulous. And of course I have to admit that good material can only be enhanced by being beautifully shot. And the playing is excellent. Quite shocking, and sadistically appealing even!

28 April 1972

HORRIBLE JOLT: The Tenement[1] . . . this is a jolt for two reasons – after an intense and successfully realised dramatic scene, on to a new area of creation, the impact of the world, all to be newly imagined and made concrete . . . Also, here we go into the dreadful last third of the film, which is so much less imagined, worked out, *real*. Disturbed start when we get down there and discover sunshine spread across half the face of the building . . . Fortunately clouds come up and we are able to start shooting. At first I am pleased, but work is somehow terribly slow. Dandy and Mona start. A poor French lady extra falls off the canteen step at lunchtime. Light goes early. More frustration.

29 April 1972

Woke early: still thinking of the SCRIPT – the Prison Governor's Office suddenly appears a key. I think: should the Governor *give* something to Mick? A closer parallel with the Managing Director's office[2] . . . Naturally *if* Mick achieves some moral revolution in prison it must be evident in this scene. At the moment he is totally passive – numb . . . I ring David's number – no answer. Thinking vicious thoughts I realise I will have to do it myself . . . this of course brings me face to face with my own most crippling weakness.

Spent a couple of hours talking to Mirek – one of those long, speculative conversations which probably mean more on an intuitive level than anything else . . . Then he goes to football (England vs Germany), and I to the Theatre Upstairs – *Within Two Shadows*:[3] Northern Irish play, rather good, nicely but over-tensely directed by Alfie Lynch . . . Afterwards, Julian Wickham – consultant architect on the air-conditioning system – hooks on to us. I take an instant dislike to his patronising amateurism, and when he asks Jocelyn how her father is, I say: 'My God – this man's an absolute dope.' He runs, thank God.

---

1. Mick tries to stop Mrs Richards (Rachel Roberts) from committing suicide.
2. Both characters are played by Peter Jeffrey. As the Managing Director, he gave Mick an apple.
3. By Wilson John Haire.

30 April 1972
Mary's Joan Crawford close-ups, followed by canteen at Olympia . . . Dandy [Nichols] is not on form: the next day she tells me she is always like that when she doesn't wear her glasses! Decide: the Prison Governor must give Mick a book. Write new scene.

3 May 1972
5.30 a.m. I wake and draw the curtain: the air is full of the chirping of birds; soft grey-pinkish glow in the already light sky; street lamps still burning. This is halfway in our seventh week . . . I reflect the curiousness of my condition. How in this hectic and exhausted period I still have emotional and sensual cravings which reveal themselves in times of solitude . . . But still condemned of course to continue in this role of responsibility and authority and creative assertion which is the other half of my persona – the one the world sees and imagines it knows . . . On the lavatory I reckon that at least now in scope and ambition, and at least partial eloquence, this is a work which incontestably sets me more *prominently* than Humphrey Jennings . . . *If* . . . . somehow, by its very circumscribed nature (part of its virtue of course), remains a minor achievement (even if a 'masterpiece'!) . . . But this is still of course unresolved, with great problems – the central passage: prison – or the necessity to *invent* an expressive passage? I just don't seem finally to work in a style that permits the disjuncture of parody. This is the penalty of my pervasive *realism* . . . I reflect also on the enormous strain imposed by this attempt to straddle the world of 'personal' (*auteur* if you like) cinema, and that of widespread acceptance as popular, and therefore commercial, entertainment. Anglo-American cinema is essentially organised for the production of pre-planned narrative cinema, and anyone who takes on the risk of personal, poetic, changing and developing film-making, exposes himself to enormous problems, strain and conflict. And this is true of Kubrick and Schlesinger and even Peckinpah as well as myself – and it is why the commercial cinema *creates* monsters of paranoia, because only they can survive within it. And it also explains why I shall *not* survive within it – whatever the success of this project – because such is not my nature, and even if I wished it to be (which I do *not*), it never could be.

Back to the studio – i.e. Colet Court. We don't get on to the Prison Governor's set till about midday, which then poses the usual agonising problems – of need for rehearsal fighting with need to work out a feasible, economic *and* properly expressive shooting pattern . . . A particular nightmare since it is my rewrite of the scene which we are having to shoot, *and* Peter Jeffrey starts very off the beam, playing the part absolutely cold, with everything technically pointed . . .

9 May 1972

An early start: 7 a.m. departure for Church location.[1] On the way Mirek says he slept badly – horrible dreams that the prologue was all terrible (it was!). It is a beautiful morning: we arrive in lyrical sunshine. My heart sinks as we draw into the three-ring circus – the tent, caravans and crowds. Mirek says how he has changed – how he is unconcerned – but when he arrived in Cheltenham (to shoot *If . . . .*) with marquee and hundreds of people all in a state of tension he felt sick. Well *I feel sick and apprehensive. Rightly.*

The church is rather beautiful and fruit and flowers nicely displayed, in a sense too nicely, with shelves around the pillars: like, as I say, the women's institute. Jocelyn's usual lack of *profusion*. And she wants to keep the altar undecorated. Then I object. Then two vases of white flowers appear. Finally I say to Derek that the altar has to be decorated, and I am not going to argue with Jocelyn about it. So for once I am grateful for his insensitive loud voice.

First trauma: Miriam's efforts to find more children have (of course) failed. I am told that the County Educational Authority have 'got wind of what we are doing' and refused permission for children to take time off school. So it is Miriam's niece and her friend Paul, looking like an Ovaltine advert from Tellyland, she in her white socks and C&A dresses, and he in little shorts . . . Jocelyn looks at their clothes but says nothing . . . With sinking heart I try to talk to them – and know I am going to get nowhere. I persuade a rather reluctant Malcolm to take them for a walk across the field. He returns despondent with the news that the little girl has no enthusiasm for green grass or sheep or lambs and complains about the 'diarrhoea' on the turf . . . so he gave up!

I realise that our preparations for a quick start, a quick set up by the church door, are impossible. I can't shoot with these children for a start. I approach a lady who has some boys to take part in the crowd and ask if they've a sister. They have. The lady will bring her at 2 p.m.

The sky begins to cloud over and we make the decision to begin shooting *in* the church, with Mick waking and seeing the children and the vicar's wife clearing the flowers away. Miriam returns with Emma and Simon. The little girl a bit awkward but looking good, and funny, sturdy little boy. Okay.

12 May 1972

COURT ANTE-ROOM[2] in two version followed at 5.06 p.m. by Mirek's departure for Cannes. NO use pretending I can approve – or rather not the simple fact these excur-

---

1. Escaping from the Nuclear Research Centre, an exhausted Mick takes refuge in a country church decked out for the Harvest Festival. He falls asleep, and wakes to be fed from the breast of the Vicar's wife (Mary McLeod). Her two happy children show him the way to the motorway, where he hitches a ride, with a mad scientist's aide . . .

sions are allowed to colour and even affect the work, i.e. before even I had definitely declared a wrap, Mirek was saying goodbye to his 'boys' . . . I do strongly resent the pressure exerted on Mirek by both Milos and George Roy Hill[1] . . . It is something I genuinely believe I would not do, and it's difficult for me not also to think that it's all part of the rather new, more pretentious, international Prima Donna Persona that Mirek *is* becoming. I really don't mind so much the ACTT caution that I can't work with Mirek again. It isn't what it was, any of it.

14 May 1972

Try to formulate some conception for the difficult, vague and doubtful Prison – Sweetshop – Slum Streets sequence. I had been thinking of doing the slum street (with Alan's *My Home Town*) on a long crane shot like the start of *Generation* . . . But absolutely no response from Jocelyn, and Roger I'm afraid has no creative spark. Then Jocelyn did mention the idea that the Governor should have given Mick a letter to the Community Centre . . . This led to sudden radical reconsideration of COMMUNITY CENTRE which we have to shoot tomorrow! Various ideas – should Mick go to the Centre and be talking to Mary when the alarm phone rings? Old people nasty? Malcolm comes round. Try to phone David: he is back but out of town. A girl is in his flat. Leave a message to phone when he returns at seven. Malcolm lifts me to supper with Stanley Donen[2] and Barbara; also present John Barry (*Clockwork Orange* art director): pleasant but middlebrow. Stanley talks about *Little Prince* (which sounds to me tosh) – and which Stanley rang me to ask about Richard Harris! I didn't falsify. Project sounds fated. Stanley is getting fat. Their house incredibly over-luxuriously fitted. Really rather boring evening, with too much talk about Stanley Kubrick: but it is an escape. Back much too late – exhausted . . . Ring David at 1.15 a.m.

15 May 1972

Wake at 6 a.m. with sudden realisation of horrific decisions. Feel – and am – sick. Mirek looks much refreshed by Cannes. Get to Colet where all is in readiness for COMMUNITY CENTRE – Announce all must be held up pending script decisions. To give camera something to do, shoot Group Corridor . . . Meanwhile send for David. The more we talk the clearer it becomes – realise solution must be to lose Slum Street – and *lose* Community Centre. Mick to wake up at night in deserted Tenement area –

2. With the jury considering their verdict on Mick's crime of illegal arms trading, the judge (Anthony Nicholls, who played the General in *If* . . . .) retires to an ante-room where he strips to his wig and scarlet briefs and is whipped by the Lady Usher (Mona Washbourne).

---

1. Hill's film *Slaughterhouse 5*, photographed by Mirek, was screening in competition at Cannes.
2. American director best remembered for *Singin' in the Rain* (1952). On the jury at Cannes when *If* . . . . won the Palme d'Or.

Policeman – 'silver lining' – meths drinkers . . . At lunch, with another flash of inspiration I realise we must cut straight from 'Changes' to Mick walking in Piccadilly gutter and seeing sandwich-boy.[1] David gets to work.

16 May 1972

Down to the dual carriageway location for Mick being picked up by the Male Nurse – now being played by Warren [Clarke]. Another pretty awful day – I really don't like location filming, with all this circus and hundreds of people drinking tea and eating sausages at the edge of the road. Also all this frustrating alternation of sunshine, grey sky, showers, etc. Lack of inspiration. We are operating a few hundred yards from Alan's new house! Get rather drunk with Mirek – provoked by seeing rushes of all the Church material – and I will say this now, unhysterically, that I am *not* sure the whole idea will work: the church not what I had wanted – bourgeois congregation – focus and operating trouble. Mirek again in agony over camera crew.

18 May 1972

We finished the Roof Top, usual redressing. Jocelyn priceless – of a hideous, huge green plastic watering can: 'But it's what she would use!' Mirek indecisive about light – lenses – how did he ever shoot *Konkurs*? Alan played his first shot ('Are you coming or staying?') . . . Fiona is very weak, and so makes it difficult – impossible – to build up Patricia into something big. I had a momentary attack of desperation this morning: surely I should have cast Helen Mirren? Then Fiona got better, but I am left with a dreadful feeling of nullity.

19 May 1972

When I talk about this being my last film I am not joking. There is no enjoyment in this. I am fed up with those around me – I don't receive the nourishment I need – and I just become more aware of my own deficiencies and limitations. At the moment a return to the theatre holds no joy. I am absolutely guilty about *The Farm*. I haven't written to David [Storey], and I haven't read it again. It seems quite good, though without the originality and poetic conception of the last three. And if I did it with Bill Owen and Connie – wouldn't it all be a bit *déjà vu* – or *déjà senti*? What is my life? What can it be now? I do feel suddenly old.

OLD BAILEY. The monstrous do-it-yourself courtroom is assembled at Colet Court. I am absolutely not sure how to tackle it – in view of the necessity of providing material for the SONG . . . Feel with panic and guilt that I should have prepared an extra

---

1. One of three roles played by Jeremy Bulloch. His board reads: 'Want to be a star?' Bulloch later played Boba Fett in *The Empire Strikes Back* (1980). (L.A. turned down the role of The Emperor in *Return of the Jedi*.)

speech for the Judge or Counsel. It takes *ages* for me to realise that the Judge's speech is too long anyway, and the first half can well be put under the end of the song . . . Despondent about the costuming of the Jury . . . lacking in personality – could be pretty well any TV series jury, further evidence of our lack of vital grasp and creative energy ALL ROUND. Exhaustion. Mirek is sleeping on the set. Get Dr Martin in to see him. Poor Malcolm has been hanging around all afternoon – his first make-up preposterously 'real' and horrific. HIGH FARCE when the Dock is wheeled out. It is like Noah's Ark – or the *QE2*. And it doesn't fit where it's supposed to. *Ridiculous*. Another triumph for the Art Dept.!

When I come down from the cutting room, everyone has disappeared except Malcolm and Jocelyn. We go round the corner for a curry. Malcolm is a fantastic *saint*.

20 May 1972
I have arranged to meet David Sherwin at Greencroft at 11. We are supposed to talk about the sketches for new scenes for the famous last quarter. But instead a basic reconsideration of Patricia is inspired by my somewhat flippant suggestion that in Mick's prison cell there should be besides pictures of Gorki, Schweitzer and Bertrand Russell – a picture of Vanessa [Redgrave]. From here it is but a moment to the suggestion – and the realisation – that Patricia should be played by Vanessa (and so *written*).

21 May 1972
ANOTHER RECCE – again the Atomic Centre escape and explosion . . . after delivering the script to Vanessa at the Shaw theatre – where she was making up in a small dressing room with Ann Beach – I got trapped with Michael Croft (who doesn't seem to *me* very enthusiastic at the idea of my directing there. Vanessa talks about *Caligula* and *The Changeling*) and then drinking with Timothy Dalton[1] – with whom Vanessa wants to act. Interestingly boring young actor: I mean personable, with magnetic eyes and good dark profile, but somehow absolutely no – is the word 'anima'? I left the script with Vanessa – shining with her usual metallic, or somehow *unreal* radiance. She seemed to be ready to accept it pretty well sight unseen – provided it 'fitted in'. Her unreality is pointed by her continuing to imagine, somehow, I might be free to direct her in a play in six weeks' time!

22 May 1972
TO DROPMORE [the location for the mad doctor's hospital] – a sensation of renewed vitality given by talking to Malcolm about new decisions (only five more weeks:

---

1. British actor (1944–), made his Court debut in David Snodin's *A Game Called Arthur* (23 February 1971). Played James Bond in *The Living Daylights* (1987).

reshoot Roof scene: recast Patricia). We get off to quite a good start. I try to disagree with Mirek's choice of angle in the entrance hall, but of course he turns out to be right: as Mick stands at the door, Mirek suggests a sinister figure should be wheeled round the corner of the terrace behind him. I have said previously I don't want any patients. But Derek has anticipated and produces Lindsay (Ralph's stand-in) in a nice dressing gown. Mirek says no good – and asks for someone grotesque. When *I* ask Derek if we've got anyone grotesque, he blows up exhibitionistically. I tell him not to be an idiot. Finally Geoff Honsliffe sits on his legs and does a legless patient. We get on well, and manage to get – by 6 p.m. when Mona must leave – the long continuous shot of Graham's entry. Catherine (Willmer) superb as Houston. David Sterne plays a porter – with admirable discretion.

Tuesday (23rd): at least, though only tentatively, we creep up in advance of our schedule.

25 May 1972

Shoot the BIKE test:[1] Graham still finds it quite hard to settle down. Then we devise the final tableau. The X-ray machine doesn't work (of course), and the 'Iron Lung' really does look too *Dr Who* – and leaks smoke anyway. Finally – Mirek's pressure – we arrange a tableau reminiscent of the *Sunday Times* picture which first inspired the sequence – but with X-ray apparatus . . . We get this shot by lunchtime.

Mirek comes up to me disturbed, and says the next set is in appalling condition. I go to Mick's bedroom. Bare boards, silver hospital bed with chain hanging above the head for self-hoist, absolutely no dressing. I am exceedingly sharp with Jocelyn – who says, 'Nobody told me you were going to be up here.' I leave in furious desperation. Then I return and say we must have some dressing, for instance chairs from the Hall.

Jocelyn – 'But it's *supposed* to be bare.'

'Well I want them.'

Jocelyn: 'I'm LEAVING' – walks out.

No doubt I *am* nasty, but that obstinacy and that refusal to take certain challenges that resulted in the Managing Director's Picture, and the PIG !! (The pig *still* lies in the room at the end of the passage: last Wednesday Brian Pettifer flew down from Glasgow to lie absurdly inside it – his head far too small for that huge, stiff body. Jocelyn of course had to say that his diminutive head made the effect 'more poetic'!!) – We go on shooting.

Evening I go with Malcolm to see all Hospital rushes. Seem okay. Back to find Mirek, having spoken to Jocelyn. Malcolm also advises me to call her. So I overcome my inhibitions (pride) and do so. No post-mortem, just apologies and tell her to rest.

---

1. Part of Dr Millar's experiments to test Mick's suitability for a bizarre experiment he is working on.

28 May 1972

I wrote a letter to David Storey this morning, saying I felt like someone tied to the railway track, and the express approaching. About 12 David (Sherwin) rang to say he was in the middle of the van scene[1] and would like to finish it – another hour, say . . . He arrived at about 2.30 – and the 'New Scene' – NOTHING. I feel ill and desperate lying on my bed, hours lying there agonising and feeling empty and trying to squeeze something out of us both . . . I don't know how we reached it, but I think it was when we got to Patricia's list of her father's iniquities, I suddenly realised that she should be *kissing* him all the way through it, and this gave a clue that she should play the whole thing as a *seduction* scene . . . so we hammered something out which at least seemed to have the merit of giving Patricia a *positive character*. But fatigue creeps over me and on a day off, after 3 p.m. I am completely fucked. What did I do on Sunday evening? – Do you know I can't remember. Maybe I tried to read John Osborne's *Coriolanus* and David's new play *Cromwell* (reading it for the second time I find it depressing – pretentious and unreal).

29 May 1972

Rendezvous at Colet Court at 11 a.m. for rehearsal with Helen Mirren. When I arrive there, at about 10.50, she is sitting on the steps, reading something. Then, as I say hullo, John Fletcher appears with a 16mm camera. God! I tell him to piss off, but as we relax, he is allowed to take some shots – certainly I shall appear a fucking idiot, but who cares. The scene reads quite well – the first time . . . well, say the second or third. I have to get rid of everyone else to feel comfortable.

3 June 1972

The devoted Saxon has decided that I should go to Rustington for the weekend – the theory that this will revive me – impossible of course. I meet Vivian Pickles[2] in the coffee shop. She is actually a bit more nervy than I imagined – but we are lucky to get her for the soup kitchen. Then I take off by car to Rustington. It is pleasant driving down. The country is lovely – and towns – and other people's houses . . . I think again: what can I do when this nightmare is over? What? For really *I have no life*. This is an extraordinary thing. But true. Incapacity to love – except where hopelessly out of reach? So what house can I live in? Doing what? Slender though our relationship is, it will be a great loss when Mum dies. I do feel fond, and wish she could be properly better, to enjoy life a little in however muted a way.

---

1. Mick hitches a lift to London with Alan Price and his band (see 13 October 1970).
2. English actress (1933–), starred in the title role of Ken Russell's *Isadora, the Biggest Dancer in the World* (1966).

6 June 1972

First reaction one of terror and apprehension. Is the scene any good? Who are these strange dropouts whom I don't know?[1] Only Adele is a familiar face, and to my horror I notice Sidney Johnstone, looking grotesque. Like Harry Welchman, with huge eyebrows and a huge bag . . . Curious effect it has on my nerves: my balls and cock shrink into a tight, tiny little bunch. I think this is because I am scared of these strange down-and-outs, and also of the scene. At least Vivian is highly professional. I take her out of the check suiting (which is too much of a caricature) and into a sheepskin jacket. Very difficult to strike the right balance between reality and caricature . . . But she does extremely well. She is a nice woman, and charmed by Malcolm.

I have a long phone talk with David [Storey] about *Cromwell*. Of course as I would expect he receives my criticisms very openly and very intelligently. In fact gives me to understand that he had felt many of these doubts himself and almost shelved the play till Oscar had pressured him to show it – and then approved of it so warmly. Apparently Jocelyn too has also written to say how much she admires it. David says it began with the idea of two actors coming on before a rehearsal of a play – but the rehearsal idea got nowhere.

10 June 1972

I will admit Mirek speaks with great tact and reassurance about Malcolm's *truth* and convincingness, and how this is a film he'd like to see . . . The lighting for the CHASE and Mick's fall takes quite a long time: somehow leisurely atmosphere. Shooting *seems* to go well, and Malcolm does his own fall: the unit does work well under Derek, even if Herbie[2] has to have his little explosion. Children's games.

16 June 1972

Today we shot the AUDITION: I played my part, for good or ill. We tried to shoot the *smile*[3] – and not surprisingly, at the end of an exhausting day, we failed . . . The sequence may be regarded as the heart of the film. The dialogue with the director is not cynical, at least it isn't intended to be so. It is intended far more to challenge Mick (and therefore the audience) with the proposition that maturity and understanding is only to be achieved when we can look the facts of life directly in the face, not obscured by materialist or by sentimental illusion. A touch of 'Zen', you might say.

---

1. Vivian Pickles is doling out soup to the down-and-outs. Mick is attacked whilst assisting.
2. Herbert Smith, camera operator.
3. At the end of the film, Mick, the happy smiling adventurer, has lost the ability to smile. The director 'coaxes' one out of him.

17 June 1972

The *whole* end of the scene won't do. Malcolm *shouldn't* have worn make-up: *should* have played much more out of desperation and the gutter – didn't play the 'smile' scene with enough *despair*. This had been Jocelyn's point apparently – but Malcolm stopped her speaking to me – and she I suppose had this attitude, 'Well, whenever I say anything you tell me I'm wrong!' I seem okay. Good? I don't know. I *think* so – but I fear the sequence insufficiently poetic. I should have checked the setups. Framing too high for my taste. Warren (Clarke) car scene actually quite good . . . The final smile remains an unsolved problem. How am I going to shoot this final sequence?? The transition?? GOD!!

18 June 1972

GRAND FINALE . . . But before this I endeavour to reshoot at least the shots of Mick with books and gun – which on rushes yesterday seemed too *constricted* . . . to this the call had to be switched from 10 a.m. to 9 a.m. When Malcolm walked on the floor I sensed something wrong – he hadn't seen the rushes and he hadn't had his new call till 7.30 – and had been to bed late after being out all afternoon playing cricket for Harold Pinter's XI.[1] Poor Malcolm; I understood. We did the reshooting. I fear it will never be what I envisage. I think we did get better setups, and did get the 'Why?' dialogue with more depth behind it. We even did a couple of hits – and smiles. I shan't soon forget the sight of Arthur [Lowe] over at the corner of the room, having to wait – while I was bashing poor Malcolm on the head with my script. At least it illuminated how the smile *has* to be achieved – i.e. by *taking time*. Ridiculous, in fact, and terribly shallow of me to have thought it adequate just for poor Malc to explode into enlightenment. But we will have to go back to this, *however* difficult Mirek says it is to match. Maybe a hypnotist? Malcolm is very game . . .

As we did those last hits – there was Arthur, with moustache and check suit, the first of our 'guests': Arthur; Rachel; Peter J; Mona; Dandy; Tony Nicholls; Mary McLeod; Helen Mirren; Bill Owen; Jimmy Bolam; Graham Crowden; Philip Stone – oh and lots more. Warren didn't come 'on principle', i.e. why shouldn't Equity members be paid if technicians are . . . this seems somehow awfully petty and weak. The crowd gathered, and while the room was being furnished and Mirek was setting the lighting, I got them all assembled in the 'rehearsal room' with Fiz, who was there to give any necessary instructions. After a slow start – things really got humming.[2]

---

1. In 1976, McDowell starred with Laurence Olivier, Alan Bates and Helen Mirren in TV film of Pinter's *The Collection*.
2. The film ends with the wrap party, with the cast dancing to *O Lucky Man!* performed by Alan Price.

19 June 1972

We sit around for much of the afternoon, until we have to set off for the QUARRY – discovered by Ted Marshall for the Explosion sequence. This is deep in the Surrey countryside – a lovely evening, and amazingly rich and verdant fields and woods. How strangely remote these places seem from the media world, where one is driven to feel that there is nowhere at all left free from violence, pollution, noise and overcrowding.

21 June 1972

THE VAN – Back in Colet Court we start with the mock-up of the van. Mirek is extremely nervous of this kind of sequence: hasn't anticipated many of the problems and gets generally 'difficult' – tumbles into it and begins to grumble and mumble instead of *asking* for things. Alan and the group FIRST RATE – really this is a relief. Alan has been a miracle of co-operation; and in front of the camera very relaxed.

Undated

Georgie Fame and Alan Price have always been my favourite pop artists (though I don't very much like using the word 'pop' in connection with them). They were my friends before I met them. When we were making *If*. . . . I carried around a lot of their music on my transistor tape recorder, and I used to play it as we drove to and from locations, to keep my courage up.

22 June 1972

From Joanna in Warsaw: Andrzej Nardelli[1] has drowned . . . I tried to write immediately to Joanne, but after about ten tries I gave up . . . I did, however, write tonight. There really isn't anything to say . . . because it isn't really as if I really *knew* or could know Andrzej. But I recognised him, and the amazing thing is that he seemed to have this friendship, this touching appreciation of *me* . . . this generosity. My withered heart.

25 June 1972

I know that I ought to spend hours today giving David [Gladwell] instructions for Assembly [editing] – but I cannot bring myself to open these huge red files that I have been carrying around for days now. There is, as they say, 'light at the end of the tunnel' – but although I feel naturally a certain relief at the thought of at least main shooting coming to an end, I feel also a sort of muted panic at the weeks of editing to come, and the certainty of being made to stand face to face with my errors and omissions. I have the strongest feeling that the Audition sequence won't 'work' – and that it was shot in the *wrong way* by Mirek – and of course by myself who let it happen. Too flat, dull, 'documentary' – and too little subjective, expressive, 'poetic'.

---

1. Who features in L.A.'s film *The Singing Lesson*.

I have been reading the start of Frank Capra's autobiography, and grimly aware of the contrast between that intensely active and ambitious professionalism – naive perhaps by 'our' standards, but wholeheartedly serious and committed – and *our* self-indulgent, weak-grasped amateurism – and my lassitude and fatigue ... But it is all too late, and I have been unable to create an alternative world.

30 June 1972
Entering the caravan on the Waterloo site this evening, Mirek, sprawled on one side of the table says: 'Very badly news.' Malcolm has seen the rushes and apparently reported that the last shot of the sequence is bad. You can't see the cheese that David Baker is carrying, and when the boot of the car is opened it is as if there's a bonfire inside[1] ... A HARD NIGHT. Mirek moody and difficult. Malcolm very tired: doing his best though.

3 July 1972
6.30 call, and we set off for CAESAR'S CAMP. Down the A30 and the well-remembered road, left at the Jolly Farmer. The little valley is reasonably burned, though in some areas the spray hasn't taken and the ferns are still green. I am tired and haven't the slightest idea how to shoot this sequence [the aftermath of a nuclear explosion] – again the script is vague. I feel that some incident should be there, some *element*, but there is none. I seem to have no option but to leave it to Mirek. I am conscious that Mirek echoes my weakness – the tendency to shoot too much in static, composed setups, without enough material for cutting. We shoot endless shots of Malcolm walking up and down burning hills. I am uneasily conscious that they are all too similar, too static ... We get on to the stream, but the light goes and we have to stop. Filthy with smoke.

4 July 1972
We return to London by the M5 and M4 – which is the way Malcolm's driver, Tommy, has found: our Jimmy Spiller, who continually takes wrong turnings, resists this, but I insist. That white hair, carefully combed, begins to irritate. Back at Colet Court in an hour ... And now the PIG BOY – at last! And Jeremy Bulloch, such a nice chap. He does the part with marvellous patience – and very well.

6 July 1972
Sitting in the car on top of CAESAR'S CAMP after the first attempt at the fabulous TRACKING SHOT. Mirek in full PRIMA DONNA mood – insisting on making a take *without* a full rehearsal, with the result that the car sticks halfway up the slope ... A pity

---

1. Driving North, Mick is overtaken by a flash young man in a sports car (Jeremy Bulloch). On entering a fog bank, the sports car crashes into a grocery van. Two policemen drive up, steal the spilled goods, and buy Mick's silence with veiled threats and a cheese.

because the take seems to be going very well: [nuclear] flashes impressive (to *us* anyway). Malcolm completely fucked: his legs given out and white with exhaustion . . . But game . . . After at the post-mortem I have the temerity to suggest to Mirek that maybe we should use two cameras. Suddenly furious, he snaps . . . I equally furious (this is not the first altercation we have had today), break away and come and sit in the car and write this . . . Now, in fact, Mirek came as I was halfway through writing – and apologised . . . and we made up (of course).

And this of course is the day that Bob Solo came to lunch! Michael good with the wine. 'Thank you, Squire.'

9 July 1972

Atomic Research Establishment at cement works. Woke and travelled with apprehension, but somehow it all worked. Derek really at his best: extras splendid; location excellent; and Malcolm ran really well.

10 July 1972

Today STANSTED: a lovely morning. I always get into the car clutching my briefcase – as if going to write something – give the cutting-room further instructions, which I should, but never do. I always fall into the trap of reading *The Times* instead. Today they have *not* printed my irritated letter about that *Manalive* film of Cannes – featuring Sam Z. Arkoff and Harold Baker and some poor pretty girl trying to rent an 'underground' picture – and about Barry Norman's cocky, vulgar, ignorant review of it. English philistinism – so *provincial* too. At Stansted there is a hold-up – the plane hasn't been towed into position . . . It later turns out that the lorry drivers who are bringing the yellow HONEY drums didn't have permits to drive loaded vehicles. Mirek and I have one of our usual tangles over tracking shot bringing Mick and Ben Aris up to the plane. At lunch, a *Time* correspondent – a gangling, humourless idiot called Fred Halpfurher interviews me about Malcolm.

11 July 1972

Today down to Dorking – now for Mick being arrested by the Military. Ted Marshall hasn't made a bad job of the location – wire fence, road, fir trees . . . The sun shines brilliantly out of a clear sky, and the unit lie around like holidaymakers – yet we manage to shoot. All goes okay, I think: quite amusing and well-timed . . . Jocelyn returns, stepping elegantly down the road with sketching block under her arm, like the Wandering Scholar.

13 July 1972

Explosions and smoke and fire at Dorking. Our luck with the weather has pretty well run out – brilliant sun in cloudless blue skies . . . We set up without haste, really because there is always *hope* that a cloud will arrive (and in fact it does): a long time is taken deciding how Mick should get down to the car. The hill is too steep for Malc. to run down. Stuntman Roy plays around with ropes: finally we settle for a descent sliding down on his arse. I honestly can't remember the progress of the day too well: sun, sun, and everybody lying around sunbathing and HAY FEVER ... I foolishly take one of Valerie's little antihistamine pills – which is yet another of those pills that are sworn not to affect one ... of course I am KNOCKED OUT – spend lunchtime sleeping on the caravan floor, alarming Mirek by my look of exhaustion and age.

14 July 1972
LAST DAY OF MAIN SHOOTING: another cloudless sky means a late start, with Malc. sliding down the last stage of the cliff-face on his bottom, running to the burning car, trying to get his case out, getting the gold suit, etc ... Very complicated procedures with smoke, explosions, fire, and this continues through the day as the car has to blow up, blaze, then sizzle and smoke under rain ... then Malc. recovering his gold suit – the rain – sheltering against the rock-face with the suit held over his head – me drenched and sneezing. And so goodbye – to those caravan lunches, wine and shredded cheese. Derek Cracknell, I will say, acquits himself well these last days – weeks even – when his big voice is a pretty good asset out of doors, and certainly he keeps things moving pretty steadily. And Malcolm, a marvellously ready and cheerful tower of strength.

17 July 1972
Impossible, for all my good intentions, to get to the cutting room before about 10.30. Start straight in on PRISON SEQUENCE ... having the idea of putting the last section of the film together first ... Oh dear – how horrid it is, starting again – the fear that the material 'won't work' – because if it doesn't there's no way out now! Actually, there does seem to be some style which works, but it is awfully like a conjuring trick. I suppose this is the trouble with satire ... No emotional yield. And I always have to remember that this is also a risk with the audience – the appeal to INTELLIGENCE – ugh! Without the music I guess we'd be sunk.

21 July 1972
The CUTTING ROOM ... sneezy and exhausted. Sinking heart. The sheer *mass* of it. And the isolation. As Jocelyn said last night: 'If you died tonight, this film could never be finished!' Ian Rakoff owlish, and David Gladwell has surely grown slower. I am absolutely sick of having this apparently paralysing effect on people. They *like* treating me as a genius – which I am *not* – because of course it relieves them of the responsibility of doing anything.

26 July 1972

Since there is no one else to talk to, this can only be a chapter of groans. Cutting room today runs into despair. The smile. Apart from the *thinness* of the audition generally, when we get to the 'smile' dialogue – Malcolm's close-up was only retaken in a two-shot, showing the hit – which absolutely doesn't match *either* of the director's shots – and the close-shot doesn't match either . . . How to do the smile? I dread this: I don't know how to do it. The cutting-room work is hard – absolutely no stimulus or contribution. David Sherwin came in and was very impressed with the PRISON-CHANGES assembly. We lunch in a pub in Cambridge Circus and I tell him that without drink and sex and violence he will never be able to write.

Looking through pix to send to an autograph collector, I find a snap of Warren and myself, filming that commercial. I am curiously saddened: made very lonely.

27 July 1972

Well, diary – my only friend! Today, during the morning, I was thinking: who could I have lunch with? . . . But there is no one I really *want* to have lunch with anyway. As the editing drags on I question myself more and more. What has happened to me? How have I lost it? Why was *If* . . . . so much more *felt*, so much more vibrant? Is it the deliberate stylistic attempt? David [Gladwell] now seems to contribute no dynamic at all . . . Everyone seems to have disintegrated, or declined since *If* . . . . Surely Ian was quite on the ball, odd, but quite clued up. Maybe those comics have softened his brain? I only know that starting to put each sequence together is torture. Today we started the finale. Actually it could be worse, I think.

29 July 1972

This is our RECCE for Northern shooting, allegedly prepared by Jocelyn. We had a meeting in the TV room last night, at which someone called Keith (to whom I was not introduced) presented smudged, unhelpful photographs, and told us that despite 'extensive touring', he could find no hotel on the North East coast suitable for an exterior.

Michael Medwin rang, with a plenitude of those dry nervous coughs. It was to say that the atmosphere had been somewhat tense in Prague and Karlovy, and that the Minister had said to Mirek at a reception that he would have to shoot some Czech pictures and not work continually in the West, and that on Thursday morning Mirek had been woken at 8 a.m. by a call summoning him to the Home Office. This visit he is to pay at noon, I think, on Monday. Of course Michael and Mirek had been speculating about the possibility of Mirek not being allowed to return – though I think it more likely that the questions will be about Milos. In any event I gave not the slightest indication of being prepared seriously to consider the possibility of Mirek not returning, let alone thinking about another cameraman – nor, sensing this, did Michael have the nerve to ask me. Instead I unleashed a torrent of complaints about the cutting room and this recce.

30 July 1972

A further mad day ranging from STEEL WORK GATES in Middlesborough, through those decaying redbrick streets – then out onto the Moors where we saw a road, looking out over a green valley, which would do well I think for the 'Pennine Road'. And so to Scarborough and the English 'enjoying themselves' at the seaside (which earns me *another* reprimand from Jocelyn's liberal guilt, for being nasty about the poor underprivileged): then hotels at Harrogate . . . then Sheffield – where in five or ten minutes it is obvious that it is impossible to situate the Coffee Factory among the grime and huge engineering sheds of heavy industry. (Jocelyn: 'Well I know, but that's what you said you wanted.')

2 August 1972

Still numbly terrified of those UNWRITTEN scenes to come (Salvation Army on Sunday!): rang David. Gay answered: 'He's out flying model aeroplanes . . .'

Got to de Lane Lea just in time for last section assembly . . . To me it all looks rubbish – badly directed, slow, unreal . . . Yet Malcolm was happy. When the lights went down, I thought David was next to me: I was delighted, then a bit amazed to hear his happy reactions. On closer inspection, alas, it turned out to be Michael.

3 August 1972

The Agony recommences . . . less than three full weeks shooting. In *The Times*, each day, reports from Prague about trials, accusations against Czech citizens with malevolent émigrés . . . Mirek was grilled about contacts with Vladimir, with Milos and Ivan, with that unpleasant bore who visited the night-shooting and who apparently turns out to be an enemy of the Republic, with an hour-length TV programme devoted to his activities. Mirek not sleeping, looks sallow and is suffering from disturbed stomach. Might they imprison him on return? At best of course he is seemingly faced by a period of Stalinist oppression, forbidden to work outside the country, and maybe even deprived of work within it. He talks of staying in Britain: of spending Monday night destroying papers, addresses, letters – posters from the Dubcek period, even Milos's telephone number in Munich . . . What to advise him?

7 August 1972

SMILE AGAIN . . . and it would be hardly possible to feel less like it: Mirek dragging his feet – every shot suggested is greeted as if an intolerable load – which makes my job even more difficult, having to drag this whole ponderous load along myself, *plus* my own not inconsiderable neurosis. We had quite nasty words as we tried to do Malcolm's smile again. At one stage – when I asked Mirek his opinion of a shot and he replied that he was technically operating the camera and unable to have an opinion of the acting – I exploded and shouted: 'Okay – break it up; we won't do any more; we'll go on to Helen's close shot.' This of course gave Mirek a good shock and in fact we carried on. But all these things add up, and add greatly to the burden. I know I should be sympathetic to Mirek's fatigue, nervous exhaustion, worry and fear . . . but I know what I am complaining about (though it may be exacerbated by all this) springs from different sources.

8 August 1972

Today takes us finally and at last to the PLANTATION Prologue.[1] The bushes (rhododendra) are neatly planted out, beans attached and eight or so extras. Brian Glover[2] replaces the disgraced Warren. Initial air of lassitude annoys me. We start the overhead shot at 10.15, which isn't too bad; and shooting goes *reasonably* well, if not exactly like lightning.

11 August 1972

Back to the Prologue: COURTROOM. Paul Dawkins[3] puts in an appearance; and Brian [Glover] is back after wrestling last night! He is really astounding in his perpetual energy and freshness. Margot with the kids . . . this time I abandon the somewhat over-ambitious reaction of the peasant's wife. Helen Mirren comes in to do the Land-owner's Mistress with Michael [Medwin] and, good sport, puts on a curly C&A wig! (She is not charging for her work this week – which is more than we deserve!) We are no longer capable of going fast: every shot is a penance . . . But gradually, gradually the blanks are being filled in.

13 August 1972

A Fucking Awful day – exhausting and frustratingly divided between Euston Tower (bodies)[4] and continuation of the Salvation Army . . . To start with, maddening dependence on the weather . . . Everyone *late* on the location and *absolute* lack of organisation. Jocelyn and Michael disappear completely. *Also* John Stears, special effects, is still trying to manoeuvre his chute up onto the roof, but it keeps getting stuck on the stairs. *Finally* Jocelyn is located helping to pile boxes on the other side of the building –

---

1. A silent movie of a coffee plantation. McDowell, dressed as a Mexican bandit, is caught stealing beans. He has his hands chopped off.
2. Who also plays the torturer.
3. From *The Changing Room*.
4. From which Professor Stewart jumps.

this isn't the side we had ever contemplated, let alone chosen. I have another shouting match with Jocelyn. Leaving Euston Tower, I have sharp and hasty words with Richard [Jenkins, Second Assistant].

15 August 1972

So we scrambled through Sunday, then Monday took the Rolls Royce out for country shots: starting and based on Black Common, near Pinewood. In these piny, fency, beech-gladed surroundings, with people (happy souls) fishing by the lake, I *feel* much nostalgia and soft regret . . . I am reminded of Camberley, family kindness and a childhood I was somehow never able to enjoy. And now fifty, and alone, and equally unable to enjoy life, almost on any level. No one to love. And every day increasingly an impatience and intolerance with those who surround me. Malcolm comes at box-lunchtime and listens to the test match on the radio: then we redo the famous Tracking Shot.

20 August 1972

No work today – because we shoot all tonight on the M1 . . . See Richard, to whom I apologise (surprising him in doing so). I wander tiredly around mournful Thornaby Centre – which is really evoked by *Clockwork Orange*: the barren, inelegant, shoddy 'clean line' architecture: the standardised building units and identical suburban shops; the hideous and ponderous sculpture called 'Thornaby' by Brian Wall; the ironic opening commemorative stone laid (suitably) by Anthony Wedgwood Benn, Minister of Technology, and now scribbled over with 'JOAN LOVES ROY' . . . Everywhere on walls 'SKINS RULE OK'. The library is closed in the centre, but two girls are playing tennis or badminton. A desert.

Starting at 9 p.m. we make our way down the M1, shooting signs. We link up with the van at Chesterfield. Then on down the motorway, with camera first in the camera car, then shooting on the van from the back of the Hillman, then shooting on the back of the van . . . I am of course wholly in Mirek's hands in all this. I don't know how far he is aware of it. To London at dawn: up and down Westway: Malcolm appears at first not in the best of tempers, and of course has to wait while we do the shot of the van: not *so* simple as we need to get it isolated *and* in the outside lane, with habitual confusions. THEN to the purgatory of the UNDERGROUND. Mirek now frightened of policemen and shooting badly.

24 August 1972

[*Morning:*] shot off an open bus which has had to come up from Southend (shades of *The White Bus*) . . . Mirek is now on valium – which seems to mean that he has developed a disposition to read the *Daily Express* between takes.

Evening: back to Leicester Square. We stage an entry for Mick. Sandwich-board boy not bad – and just manage to reshoot Jeremy's parting close-up – which Mirek had ruined on the original shoot by making him turn squarely and absolutely *unsuggestively* to the camera. Then of course it is too late to do any POV's – but Mirek knows better, and insists on fooling around in a taxi, shooting the late-night stragglers. Mirek finds interest and amusement in the *picturesque*.

26 August 1972

I had to go into town because I had promised to get Mirek's present – from both Malcolm and myself, and Michael – which meant going in to Cecil Cross to get the leather and suede coats he had admired that afternoon I was with him weeks ago . . . I got the Tube in – and noticed to my surprise the fare Finchley Road to Piccadilly Circus: 15p. Just imagine, to go into town and back by tube, six shillings. This seems an even more significantly exorbitant sign of inflation than £45,000 houses . . . Decided to drop into the Queen's as it was 5 p.m. and the Saturday matinee was just starting of *I Claudius* . . . Of course it was exactly as I'd anticipated – only somewhat worse – emptier, more purposeless. I suppose Tony [Richardson]'s refusal to work on 'scenes' (as opposed to staging) was a rationalisation of his knowledge there was nothing to work on . . . or a knowledge of his limitations in *that* direction? But the staging itself was styleless and unimpressive – and hampered by a very unfortunate design conception – with a precipitous but unimpressive staircase cutting out all depth (Bill Dudley). Acting unimpressive – including David Warner, who just did it the easy way. Warren [Clarke] overcast and under-directed. I left at the interval.

28 August 1972

We caught the 8.15 BEA flight from Glasgow last night after our day's shooting on Mick coming out of jail. Malcolm, Mirek and I travelled up overnight in the train. At first I was rather charmed by the little first-class sleeper, the pleasant Scottish attendant who gave us the Sunday newspapers before we left at 10.15, the nice little shut-away world . . . Before we sleep I have a cup of coffee in my compartment with Malcolm and we briefly talk about tomorrow's scene . . . Sleep is not easy in the rackety, rather hot sleeping car, but I think I drop off about halfway through the night. I am woken at eight with tea. I get up and look at my friends. Mirek is sitting up on his shelf by the window looking out at the grey landscape – then the ugly box-like houses which represent modern development.

At Glasgow we take breakfast at the Central Hotel, which is large and blessedly wasteful of space in its late nineteenth-century way, and at least utterly unlike the standardised new-hotel stereotype it becomes harder and harder to escape from.

The location at Belimiley Jail (this isn't the right name, but very like [it was Barlinnie]) is better than the Polaroid photos conveyed or than Jocelyn could convey either . . . a large plain gate and a splendid large wall and a good space of roadway, remote from through traffic. Scottish prison officials of great pleasantness and tolerance of our absurdity. We haven't been there long before the bus arrives from the airport, carrying actors and technicians – THANK GOD FOR THE LAST TIME. But it is nice to end, as we began, with Wallas [Eaton], Ben Aris, Brian Pettifer . . . Mirek has had one idea about the opening of this sequence, which is simply the darkness of the inside of the big door, and the noise of footsteps and the key turning, and the door opening and the light flooding in . . . This is (in his *inaccurate* imagination) to be a direct cut from the Govenor kissing Mick. Whereas in fact I anticipate the cut coming from Mick's 'Thank you, sir'; and also incline towards something *before* the opening of the door, which I fear may come too soon for its full dramatic effect. But to discuss these details, ideas, intuitions with Mirek has become harder and harder, until we have finished with a situation of virtual impossibilty and stalemate. I suppose it must be at least partly a symptom of his fatigue. So, immediately I discover Len and Lew erecting blankets, to cut off all light from the area before the gate, to create Mirek's idea of pitch darkness with the gate opening. I object, because I want an approach shot . . . then of course the thing becomes a kind of conflict. So that when Mirek tells them to take the blankets down, one can't be sure whether it is *genuinely* a new conception that he subscribes to, or just 'giving in'. The simple, sensitive, affable soul, with a belief in co-operation, becomes an arrogant, tight, secretive, absolutely humourless monster who simply wants to impose his own conceptions, and particularly his own 'photographic' and compositional fancies. Of course explanation can be provided by his 'situation', but it is hard for me to really accept all this without feeling hurt . . . And it is impossible totally to separate the personal from the professional – since that is the way the work has always gone.

In the plane on the way back, my seat was next to Mirek's. In front of me was Malcolm, with Michael next to him. Michael, of course, had ordered champagne. In front of *them*, Jocelyn; Chris, the clapper boy, behind Mirek. I was thinking about these things: I looked at Mirek, who looked at me with a complicity that I can no longer accept: he said, 'Not possible . . .' and then, 'I have been here twenty-five, twenty-six weeks . . .' I replied 'Everything is possible'. I didn't feel sympathetic to his soppy self-indulgence; artists must be made of sterner stuff, even when life, society, politics play their beastly tricks. This, after all, is our only justification for continuing to be, or to claim to be, artists.

Such are the ironies of life, first, quite unexpectedly, it was Chris, the camera boy sitting behind us, who somehow noticed my thoughts written on my face and wondered what was wrong . . . 'Tired,' I probably said. And then the rather drunk, simple-minded Herbie came across the aisle and spoke to Mirek and myself with emotion – 'I've never known, in all my professional career, two people as committed to the work, and working together so completely, as you two . . .'

(Will I think differently in months', years' time? Maybe; maybe not . . . But I don't really see us working together again. Mirek is different now. Just what will become of him I don't know. But he needs to come to terms with his ambition – and his vanity.) To Malcolm's for his little party. Very nicely done by Margot (must thank her). Jocelyn in a flowering dress given by the 'kids' – looking indecently *recovered*. Rachel looking attractive and in good form. Ralph drops in: Mirek tries on his clothes.

JOCELYN HERBERT

I don't know how I survived, actually. He behaved appallingly badly. (*Laughs.*) I can't remember where we were, Scarborough or somewhere, in a hotel, and everybody was in a rather bad mood, cross about something. We were sitting round having a drink and, for once, everybody was being rather horrid about Lindsay. I can't remember exactly what it was all about, but I thought they were being very silly. One of them said: 'I don't know why we are all doing this film,' and I exploded and said: 'We are doing this because it's going to be a wonderful film!' Which is what I felt. And they were so amazed that I should be saying that that they shut up. It *was* an amazing film. It's astonishing.

3 September 1972

Saturday. Alan phoned: he had tickets for Fulham vs Preston . . . Well, I thought it would be rather nice: we met at the Antelope for a drink – the 'chinless' clientele so fascinating and so marvellously, enviably secure (Alan remarks they are the only ones who get us Olympic medals – on horses and such!), then we drive to Fulham: the new stand 'restaurant' doesn't amount to more than a hot-pie counter and bar. We watch a poor game in which poor Fulham disintegrate to lose 3–1 . . . But Alan is very good tempered and humorous about it all . . . Thence to the BBC where Alan, Clive and the boys are recording for the *Two Ronnies* show.

7 September 1972

Go to see Ros: Jim Sharman[1] is there. Does he *actually* like me, or feel I can be useful? I wonder if he's talented? . . . He left and returned with a Kinks album he gave to me. Well, that was charming you must admit . . . Strolled home up Bond Street feeling rather like *Inadmissible Evidence.*

---

1. In 1973, the Australian director Jim Sharman directed two plays in the Theatre Upstairs. The first, Sam Shepard's *The Unseen Hand*, starred Warren Clarke. The second *The Rocky Horror Show*, became an international sensation.

'HOLIDAY': finally, weakly, succumb to Nid du Duc. Anthony, well-meaning as ever, had to tell Tony that I was exhausted and without plans. Of course Tony invited me . . .

8 September 1972

There was hazy sunshine when I arrived at Nice, to be met by talkative John-Pierre who greeted me as if I had only left a month ago. Tony is plainly *not* in good form – but only drops remarks like, 'I don't suppose I shall ever make a film again.' Neither his own work nor anyone else's, nor really *anything*, can be discussed, partly because Tony gives an impression of supreme *lack of interest* in anyone or anything. The animals flourish: but humanly the atmosphere is dreadfully sterile.

I woke up during the night, about twenty to four or so, the terrace lights shining with their multicoloured bulbs. I pissed against the garden wall. In this remoteness I couldn't help thinking of the Arab terrorists creeping murderously into the Israeli Olympic quarters, or hooligan gangs in the woods; Sharon Tate and her insane mur-derers. Only Tony, Will, Grizelda [Grimond], me and Jean-Pierre here. And I don't even know where the others are sleeping. The animals of course are good sentries, but – the world is an unsafe place.

Back asleep I have uneasy dreams – last days of shooting: close shots of Mick in the car . . . but Mirek has disappeared . . . where has he gone? and no assistant director? Shall I just pack up and go home . . . but I have to edit . . . Then on a train: we stop and I get off at the station; I think Mirek is with me; I am sitting on a bench – changing my shoes? – when a wizened old lady at my elbow speaks to me: 'Are you Mr Anderson?' I say yes. She speaks rather incomprehensibly about having run a tobacconist shop somewhere – her husband drank – she seems to have killed him – 'Were you in prison?' 'Well . . .' 'What was it like?' Trying to place my contact with this tobacconist shop. I remember going into one when on location for a commercial; and two ladies behind the counter; and me talking about Humphrey Jennings, shocked that no one has heard of him.

9 September 1972

St Tropez. The Beach. Tony, Will and Grizelda lay in the sun; just finishing off a bottle of champagne. 'Would you like a drink?' Tony's manner has become more affected, more unreal than ever, as though every remark, every question has to be the result of effort, and emanates from a profoundly detached, alienated being. Grizelda I find difficult to make out, as I always have on the occasions I have met her with Oscar. She is either shy or arrogant. I find her voice and vocabulary irritating – the voice has that brittle lack of depth to it that is typical of the 'well-bred' English. She has the habit of the same class of speaking always as if in question marks (instead of spontaneously), and the same dependence on cliché. But maybe she is a nice girl.

Grizelda, of course, is with child. All I knew when I arrived here was this fact (by Tony), and that Tony was expected by her family either to marry her or to persuade her to an abortion; neither of which course he was prepared to take . . . On the phone he said (inviting me here) that he had 'personal troubles': but he has never mentioned anything of the sort to me here. He would not countenance Grizelda going into the sea, as the cold would be bad for the child.

I didn't have a drink, but went into the water instead. It was beautifully fresh. Then we all went to eat – the kind of place where everybody remarks on how excellent the food is, though the salads seemed very ordinary to me. The ambience – 'sophisticated', i.e. dull, with a lot of svelte young Frenchmen. No families.

At lunch Tony suddenly, that's to say without any excuse that I could make out, started talking about Oscar, or rather attacking him, asking me if I trusted him . . . 'I don't think it's really wise to trust anybody' was my tactic. (Did it cross anybody's mind apart from my own that I certainly wouldn't trust Tony?) He went on about Oscar in his usual fashion – his cowardice (how he would never expose himself to any kind of risk or indignity in support of a friend or a project – familiar stuff) – and with dark hints of how he (Tony) had suffered from Oscar's ruthlessness, duplicity or treachery . . . Why was *Richard's Cork Leg*[1] being done at the Court? Here Grizelda expressed surprised surprise, saying that Oscar hadn't liked the play when he saw it in Dublin. 'Just another case of him palming off one of his options' said Tony. (I didn't ask why he had an option on the play if he didn't like it.) 'Anyway,' I said, 'these were decisions that had been taken before I had shared in the policy making.' 'When did you start?' said Tony.

'Well, roughly from Christmas on.'

'What are the Court doing then?'

I said there were new plays by Christopher Hampton, Edward Bond, David Storey. This item of news produced no reaction.

I made an attempt to introduce some element of discussion, conversation, or interest into this frankly boring occasion. 'It's very difficult,' I said, 'with a writer like John [Osborne] to know just what attitude to have towards his plays. I mean – do you think the Court ought to do them under any circumstances?' I won't say I was surprised by the violence of Tony's reaction; I would probably have been more surprised if he had been capable of a reasonable or stimulating or in any way civilised answer. In fact he bridled, with absolutely disproportionate emotion spitting out that it was a *monstrous impertinence* for anyone in 'that place' to pass a judgement on the work of a great writer like John Osborne. I did not lie down under this . . . I further pointed out that in fact Tony's point of view was shared by Oscar – and that indeed the Court *had*

---

1. By Brendan Behan and Alan Simpson.

put on all John Osborne's plays – in fact the only instance I could think of when one of John's plays had been rejected by the Court was at a time when Tony himself had been responsible – or at least involved in the decision, i.e. *The World of Paul Slickey*. 'So you must have changed your mind?'

'Yes, I have.'

In short, no discussion on this mildly interesting topic was feasible. Tony made a short, impassioned declaration of his violent emotional feelings on the subject ('That's me, that's how I am') and departed with Grizelda to lie in the sun. This left Will and Jean-Pierre and me at the table, with a bottle of cognac.

One sad result of all this is that conversation becomes on the whole exceedingly dull. Tony had put paid to that little attempt at the lunch table by saying to me, heatedly: 'It's your fault for bringing up a serious subject at a time like this. It's very frivolous of you. You can't discuss serious things at lunchtime on the beach.'

'Well, conversation becomes very boring if you can never raise serious subjects.'

'Well, it'll have to be boring then.'

Yes, boring it certainly is. The only subject that seems momentarily to tickle the jaded palate of the Panjandrum is gossip . . . Conversation must follow the dictates of his whims. And pride seems to have made his whims more arbitrary than ever: his alienation more profound. There is still a certain compulsiveness about his personality – as there is about any supreme egoist, I suppose. But he is not very charming, chiefly (to me) because so boring – so deliberately cut off. Yet my motives in coming here were not *completely* cynical: Tony is still able, by the sheer force of his demands, to exercise considerable pressure . . . And of course he holds strong cards.

But I won't deny that my own incapacity and loneliness were the strongest factors in my coming here. And with the weather disappointing (so far) and the early evenings and a certain cut-offness, it's not really perfect. It certainly makes me worry – or perhaps just sad – for the poverty of my own resources. Curiously, though, I don't feel exactly ashamed to be here: at least there is never anything in the least sentimental about Tony: he doesn't make me feel wanted on exactly personal grounds – and I don't mind being a trophy if the price is right. As I write this I see that it looks rather beastly, yet it does seem to reflect the truth of the matter.

10 September 1972

Today Tony took it into his head to make an expedition. With Will at the wheel, he, Grizelda and I packed into the car and set off on a circular village tour. A successful day: Tony was kept in a good temper, and not much traffic on the roads . . . These little towns are very lovely, with their squares and cafés and beautifully textured stucco and painted shutters. But I kept feeling the peasants could be *sinister* . . . Played chess with Tony after dinner; he won again – but I improved.

21 September 1972

Back to the cutting room, yesterday: it is very depressing, inevitably. . . . I see David's cut of the last number, which is HOPELESS AND IDIOTIC. He has actually *extended* the number, yet used all wrong material.

I get involved in this absurd scheme for film reviewing for *The Times*. Karel rings me up on my first afternoon back and says he is off to NY to 'work with' this college professor who is working on this script – so can I do this week? Principally it offers John Boorman's new pic *Deliverance* – with Jon [Voight]! Instead of waiting for next Monday's press show I do have the foresight to get Warners to put the picture on. I am intimidated by (again) the amazing surface of the pic. But after a bit I don't believe it. Jon over-working terribly.

17 October 1972

I walked along in the autumnal afternoon, and I thought I would drop in on David Storey . . . Must be the first time for years . . . I stood on the pavement and looked down into the garden, where children were playing – the girls must be ten or eleven to thirteen or so by now, and a boy of seven or eight, scampering on all-fours in the grass . . . A red plastic figure-of-eight railway lay on the grass. I hesitated. Finally I went down the steps to the front door. I hesitated. Then I pushed – the door was open. I walked in and pushed open the living-room door. Barbara was there: she got up welcomingly and said she'd fetch David. The children – or more children – were playing with clay, making pots and things at the table in the window . . . To my shame I don't know their names (except Helen, to whom *This Sporting Life* is dedicated, and Jake is the little boy. And there's a boy called Sean – is this the same?) They are exactly like the children in David's books – absolutely ordinary and nice, but remote in some way.

22 October 1972

Work with Ian Rakoff till about 6 p.m. – put in some important shots which David has omitted: tracking shot from Atomic factory – sliding down the hill – Mary feeding Malc – and do some trimming and adjustments to the end. This kind of work always makes me feel better – however falsely – just because little things suddenly *work*. The end *is* rather remarkable.

1 November 1972

Dick Lederer[1] in town this week: he had written to me in advance suggesting we meet to discuss publicity approaches for the pic – and of course it would be useful for him

---

1. Head of publicity at Warner Bros. The advertising for *O Lucky Man!* was designed by Mike Kaplan, who would produce *The Whales of August*.

to see some of the film . . . Initial response: sorry – not until finished. Then I thought again. Is there really any point in trying to confront them with a completed picture? The shock will be just as intense – and it won't look any more box-office or familiar. So I reversed my decision. We prepared our first screening to 'them': Reels 1 and 2 – the arrest, interrogation and escape – Mick in Sir James's office – then the end from the Soup Kitchen. I lunched with Malcolm at a new Greek tavern in Frith Street. I was anxious and ate too much. Then we got a cab to Audley Square. Michael arrived. The Warners contingent arrived: Dick Lederer and Bob Solo. Bob and Michael kissed. The way we live now!

I gave a short intro in my usual edgy style, and left them to it: Ian Rakoff busily supervising the projection from the box.

I was summoned from the cutting room by a call: 'The projection's over and they're going to Memorial. The atmosphere in the screening room was very favourable. They laughed a lot . . .' When I arrived at Memorial I could see Malcolm sitting talking to unseen visitors in the office. On these occasions Malcolm rises to the occasion with a slight accent of falsity – a 'sophistication' that reminds me of Gavin. Michael too. They think they're talking with 'in-style' glibness. I of course tend to go the other way. Boat-rocker.

On 20 March 1973, Anderson's mother died. O Lucky Man! *opened in London on 3 May and was screened in competition at Cannes. It did not win a prize: 'Dismal . . . really traumatic. Imagine being beaten to a prize by something called* The Hireling!' *(starring Robert Shaw and Sarah Miles). Arthur Lowe and Alan Price both won BAFTA Awards. The film was only a moderate commercial success but it remained in circulation in America throughout the decade. In June 1980, a new print was struck for Los Angeles to help clear the nine-month waiting list to book the film. Anderson hired Alan Price to compose the music for his next project, David Storey's new play,* The Farm, *which opened at the Royal Court Theatre on 26 September 1973.*

10

Sympathy and Strife

The Farm – Frank Grimes – In Celebration (film)
The Bed Before Yesterday – Lectures – Carol Channing

'How many scripts am I supposed to be reading at the moment?
And not one that there's the slightest chance I will end up directing.
But the petitioners are insatiable: and I still haven't learned that
first essential – to say "no" immediately, when it is still possible
to be polite.'

29 July 1973
I visited David [Storey]: because I had left my script [of *The Farm*] at the theatre, and felt I'd like to have a look at it over the weekend, before Hayden [Griffin] came up with his set on Monday . . . so I rang David, and he said at first he hadn't got one, then oh yes – so I walked across – fortunately David had reminded me that they had moved.

A tall, early Victorian house, a really lovely family house, quite large, but not extensive-seeming. The rooms largely bare of furniture, white-painted, sanded floors and rugs. A charming garden at the back, which David rather proudly showed me round – though everything seemed to have stopped flowering. Next door a row of three, squat, flat-roofed, red-brick modern houses with pocket handkerchief gardens – where two or three more houses like David's had stood, but had fallen into the hands of a speculator who had torn them down and built these little horrors, selling at £40,000 apiece . . . A horrible example of this mean, destructive, tasteless age. Suburban capitalism . . . One of the upstairs rooms had a lot of manuscript piles and pages in bulky heaps on tables and on the floor. I passed them over, as if something private, reflecting – 'What a gruelling capacity for work!' An advance copy of *A Singular Man* lay on the mantelpiece, but David did not mention it. I wonder if I have been forgiven for my comments on it. Is David resentful that I didn't direct *Cromwell*? I don't *think* so. We talked. It is all quite affable, even sympathetic, often wise and humorous and perceptive. But there is no real give in it – a withdrawal from a relationship rather than a development of it. A real and very firm refusal to acknowledge any kind of commitment. And with all this, a sort of growth of pride. *Arrogantly unassuming.*

4 August 1973

Things with David Storey are not the same – in a way quite difficult to define. With my usual malicious wit I say to Mary Selway: 'He's no longer a modest man who is also an important writer: he's now an important writer who is also a modest man.' For the first week of auditions of *The Farm* I worked without him – I wanted if possible to break the tradition, which I suppose (for specific reasons) we started with *The Changing Room*, and which Anthony has furthered with *Cromwell*, of over-reliance on David, putting him in a position of responsibility dangerous for an author . . . then in the second week, I thought he might like to come, and he has been to every audition since. But over three weeks there has not been a single actor or actress whom he has app-roved for casting. Except yesterday, Jiggy Bhore.

I had been very annoyed earlier in the week by his attitude to Frank Grimes. He read in our first week of readings, and I remember how strong the impression he made. Strong, but also strange: as indeed the impression I had of him in *Veterans* . . . A per-formance which was obviously not correctly on target, and yet which did have a mag-netism and an appeal to it . . . Many people, of course, didn't see it, but I remembered it, and that was why I got Mary to bring him in. At his first reading, it was uncertain, but very sensitive, and receptive. And when he read his poem to his mother, there were moments of magic. The only worries – the voice is not good – rather thin and harsh: is this an Irish characteristic? The second reading – Patsy [Patricia Healey] read with him – was sensitive again: every instinct in me recognised him as the character. I said to David, and he replied something like, 'He's got lots of the qualities, ' and maybe 'We haven't seen anyone better.' When we got back to the Court, outside, David started backtracking . . . physically he was too sturdy. I got very impatient when he started justifying his physical observation by reference to *The Changing Room* . . . conceding that I must make the final decision, yet unwilling to be positive in the collaboration.

Anyway, next morning I had to go into Warner Bros, which put me in a renewed bad temper. I called Mary from Mike Kaplan's office and said: 'Cast Frank Grimes.'

I called Frank the next morning and suggested he come in for a drink at lunchtime. Then I also called David and, in the name of harmony, asked him if he would like to come and also have a drink with Frank. He did. We talked about *Veterans*; he con-curred when I opined that one of Ron Eyre's grave weaknesses is snobbery. Then as we walked over to the Antelope, we talked about *O Lucky Man!* – which Frank, to my pleasure, was enthusiastic about – but what he hadn't understood was the blow at the end. He was surprised, he said, because I didn't seem like that as a director ('I was almost frightened to come and see you!').

10 August 1973

Last night I saw the dress rehearsal of *Cromwell*, having seen a run-through last week. The unkind thought occurred to me, recalling Bottom in *Midsummer Night's Dream* – 'It shall be called *Storey's Dream* – because it hath no story . . .' And, constructively, *Storey's Dream* is how it can best be considered – because it has the muddled confusion, the mingled insight and obscurity, the poetic impalpability of a dream, hints of David's old obsessions emerge – the fantasy of the man of power, the King, vague intimations of power, size and violence – here in a setting and style from which Romanticism has apparently been purged. But only apparently.

The economy and lucidity of the style is a sham – because the conception is not sufficiently clear or sufficiently formed to stand it. The narrative is phoney – poetic at the start, and incomprehensible towards the close. The ideas are imposed on the dramatic structure, which has no organic reality of its own. In fact – which is why I react so strongly against it – it seems to contradict everything that is best and most fundamental to David's artistic principles elsewhere. The philosophic reflections are either banal – Brian [Cox]'s line about ends and means – or impenetrable . . . in neither case do they spring out of the dramatic material.

In the chosen style I suppose it is well-executed. The actors are good, though occasionally incomprehensible as a result of an over-naturalistic approach. Albert [Finney] is the exception: I think he gives a very bad performance, selfish, with mistaken ambitions towards giving a 'great' performance, artificial and grimacing, vocally affected and, most disastrously, with no relationship at all to his buddy and sidekick, who is thereby rendered pale and insignificant. I think Brian [Cox] does extremely well, in that impossible part. There is a truthfulness to his acting which is quite absent from Albert's.

Jocelyn [Herbert]'s designs are, as usual, implacably tasteful, all grey and brown – and boring. I don't much like her cut-out elements and the whole thing looks like a tasteful pageant. But what could you do with that damned play? 'But break my heart – for I must hold my tongue . . .'

11 August 1973

I rang Frank, thinking both it would be nice to see him, and that perhaps he would like to be in contact . . . On the phone he said he'd been thinking of ringing me . . . Frank's conversation is easy, charming, lively, humorous and sensitive. It's a long, long, time since I've met anyone I like so much and so easily. There is an open warmth of response that I find very rare. He talked about his meditation – the Maharishi's method – and how it quiets his nerves. About how influenced he had been in his acting by

Montgomery Clift, whom he had at one stage imitated. He talked about Brando – as inimitable – and his disappointment in Richard when he had seen *This Sporting Life* again (for *his* imitation of Brando). We strolled round the gardens and sat down. Frank spoke of his life . . . the Abbey; then *Borstal Boy*,[1] and New York success, and a Tony nomination and various awards – then the fatal Zeffirelli manifestation.[2] 'I had to get my teeth capped . . .' and [he] was in Rome six months before Zeffirelli met a young actor he felt would serve him better, and offered Frank the part of one of his friends instead. Frank came back to Dublin, shattered, but was saved by luckily being able to plunge straight into work – *The Playboy of the Western World*,[3] and other plays I can't remember. Then *Veterans*.

Plainly Frank is a great worrier, see-sawing I would imagine between confidence and great insecurity. I like so much his quick and apparently twisting responsiveness: he attracts one's help and sympathy because he seems to deserve it and to need it and to make such immediate use of it. As we crossed the road back to the Court he turned to me and said: 'Do you think I can be a really successful actor?' I said firmly, and with conviction, 'Absolutely. I have no doubt about it at all. No problem.' And I meant it.

1973 (undated)
I was in Los Angeles to do some pre-release work for *O Lucky Man!* – largely a waste of time as it happened. I arrived on Thursday afternoon and was scheduled to leave on Monday for San Francisco. Nobody worked in LA over the weekend, I was told. I had last been in Hollywood nearly ten years before, when I had visited my friend Rachel Roberts, then married to Rex Harrison. Rex was shooting *My Fair Lady* at Warner Brothers, and one day we went to the studio for lunch. John Ford was at the studio, preparing a new western. His office was a few hundred yards up the road from Rex Harrison's bungalow-dressing room. I phoned to ask if I could drop in and see him. I was given the okay. Rachel wanted to meet the great man too, so she walked along with me.

It was not a very memorable meeting. Ford was showing his age: he had had a fall at home not long before and was a bit lame. His eyesight was worse than ever. He remembered Rachel, greatly to her surprise, from having come to see her in *O My Papa!*, a musical play she had done with Peter O'Toole in London. Ford must have come backstage after the performance; he enjoyed letting us know he had not forgotten. I asked him how things were going. He said he was looking forward to the picture.

—————

John Ford died on 31 August 1973.

—————

1. By Brendan Behan.
2. For the lead role in *Brother Sun, Sister Moon* (1970).
3. By J. M. Synge.

8 September 1973

After three weeks' rehearsals of *The Farm* we ran through this morning: I think it is maturing. Bernard[1] doesn't know his lines yet – used his book for his last appearance, but I feel it is coming all right, and certainly no use in pushing or alarming him. His experience is old-fashioned – but I feel his instinct is good, when he has confidence in it. Frank continues to be a delight. I can only talk of him in superlatives both professionally and personally. I have never worked with anyone so freely and fully appreciative: perhaps the young Malcolm came near it. Frank has such an open charm and humour, lovely taste and accomplishment. I have no great urge to do anything more – but it would always be a joy to work with him, and to help that fine, delicate talent to emerge.

Patsy got unfortunately drunk last night, and when drunk she is awfully quarrelsome, edgy, provocative. Doreen[2] is much much better, seems to be conquering her nerves. Pru[3] gauche but truthful and intelligent. Lewis[4] much better – not so neurotic.

2 October 1973

The Farm has been on for a week: the daily notices were rather constipated – somewhat patronising with their tone of 'surprisingly entertaining for a conventional, old-fashioned family play' – then Harold Hobson came up with an imaginative and *poetic* appreciation of the play, rather high-flown, but at least his lead review (I had feared that he would do a great splurge for Rattigan, whose latest play – *In Praise of Love* – opened the day after us). I wrote and thanked Harold: to be fair, he's never let us down. I also wrote a stiff correction to Irving Wardle [of *The Times*], whose piece was more than usually crass (the last scene described as 'straight out of *The Archers*').

13 October 1973

Back from Paris [and a publicity tour for *O Lucky Man!*]. A glimpse of Serge. I left for Paris on Wednesday morning, irritated because the car was late – why do Warner Brothers insist on hiring minicabs instead of hire cars? Booked on to BEA, or British Airways as they have become, which also irritates me – as it means I have to fly economy instead of first class . . . Yes, I have changed: and in the five years since *If . . . .*, so has air travel. How disagreeable it is, this being herded around, made to stand in lobbies and buses, and walk down vast corridors. I wonder if there is any subject, or product where the reality contrasts so strongly with the fantasy of advertising and

1. Bernard Lee (1908–1981), best known as 'M' in the James Bond films.
2. Doreen Mantle. Made her Court debut in Desmond O'Donovan's production of *A View to the Common* (April 1967).
3. Prunella Gee.
4. Lewis Collins. Later found TV fame in *The Professionals* (1977–83).

TV commercials. The idea occurs to me – of anti-commercials – but who would pay for them?

In Paris: the Hotel Raphael, near the Arc de Triomphe. Old-fashioned and panelled with bad oil paintings down the hall, but a Turner (*soi-disant*) next to the concierge's box. Gene [Moskowitz] has joined us for lunch, which is primarily for a pleasant lady from *France Soir*, and a cameraman and a glum girl from some TV programme. Also some publicity operator who appears to be responsible for a totally new advertising line (85 per cent *des Francais de proclament heureux . . . et ils n'ont pas encore un* LE MEILLEUR DES MONDES POSSIBLES).[1] All my critical energy has gone now: I just do what I'm asked, knowing that the effort to change or improve is vain and hopeless.

16 October 1973

My attempt to see *Discreet Charm of the Bourgeoisie*[2] is frustrated by Patsy's arrival. Next day reports that Patsy has been 'beaten up' and in a dreadful state – Patsy now incoherent, and with differing stories to the police – whom I insist have to be called. Rehearsal with Mary – I present the Lindsay Anderson Award at the Festival Hall – Jack, Bill Owen's friend, has his car stolen . . . No wonder I can never get a journal written: the inability to discover a bare, factual style – write with Proustian attention to nuance and detail, and each entry would be as long as a novel.

Where to start? The tensions and instability I have always felt within the *Farm* cast seem to be breaking out . . . Last week Pru succumbed to some stomach ailment – was this from something she ate while out with Prince Feisal? The three girls had their dinner out with him on Tuesday, so Jiggy went on when I was in Paris . . . Frank had said on the phone that he was having trouble with Doreen. Indeed she gave a strikingly bad performance – emotions strained, falsified and over-illustrated. Had she really been infatuated by the *New Statesman*'s allusion to her sitting on the sofa as if 'on the edge of an abyss'?

I couldn't spend the time between performances giving notes, because when I got round, feeling grim, I found great disturbance – 'Doreen's ill' – she had felt a sharp pain when she went out in Act III to hide the whiskey bottle . . . And no wonder, I thought, with the state of over-tension she was putting herself into. We sent for Dr Blakey, who arrived to take her blood pressure and pulse, and talk to her in that infantile way that doctors use to patients they think may be apprehensive . . . Two Valium prescribed.

---

1. Making a link to Voltaire's *Candide*.
2. Film by Luis Buñuel.

2 November 1973

5.45 a.m. After the West End opening of *The Farm* at the Mayfair. Department of anti-climax. Up aloft Frank showed me his present from David, which I too found curious – a drawing – 'Albert Finney rehearsing *Cromwell*': quite naturally Frank wondered why he had been given a drawing of Albert Finney. He didn't think David did anything without a meaning. I thought there was probably no intention there, though maybe, just maybe something a little sly?

Ascending to the crow's nest after the performance, I found David and one of his daughters up there with Frank . . . Frank very disappointed and dissatisfied, with the reception and with his performance – which I thought was excellent.[1] True, though, that the whole evening had lacked atmosphere to a rather depressing extent . . . The theatre not exactly full: not many known faces; though I was pleased Harold [Hobson] had come. Hugh Thomas arrived, looking more like *The Diary of a Madman* than ever – and now with dreadful black stubble on cheeks and chin. Then I heard that Malcolm had arrived and found no tickets at the box office (my fault). I dashed round, and found Whiffle and Margot entering together; Malcolm and Alan [Price] at the bar . . . So I put that right . . . and spoke jollily to Harold. David Vaughan sitting next to Malcolm, and not exactly a beacon of enthusiasm. And by the end of the evening, that little theatre, for all the intimacy of auditorium to stage, did seem terribly null – impersonal in some way, like its architecture, like a cinema.

The final reception okay. I was collared by Sheridan Morley and taken off for an absurd interview on London Broadcasting ('Sherry' chattering away – referring to my direction of *Cromwell* – waiting while three pages of greyhound racing results were read out . . . the whole thing surely vain and unheard), from which I returned to find Frank disappeared, Malcolm and Margot disappeared, Alan and Whiffle disappeared – the food ran out (only some horrid goulash, and cheese), the drink ran out, Patsy distraught because Trevor Howard[2] had been there, the first time they'd met since *Two Stars for Comfort*[3] – and hadn't spoken to her.

7 November 1973

After the opening, Frank really did seem to become odd – aggressively egotistical in manner, admiring himself in the mirror, in the dressing room continually dashing out on to the fire escape to look for tit undressing behind bathroom windows across the hotel roof, admiring himself continually in the mirror . . . It was a transformation for which I wasn't really prepared – it certainly had not happened at the Court. I still don't

---

1. Grimes won the London Critics Award for Best Supporting Actor.
2. British film star (1916–1988), billed above Richard Harris in *Mutiny on the Bounty* (1962).
3. By John Mortimer.

really understand it. Is there some kind of reaction against me personally (à la Finney)? Has the West End had some kind of disturbing effect?

I am reminded of nothing so much as of Albert Finney's behaviour after the opening of *Billy Liar* . . . except that Albert was more aggressively self-indulgent . . .

Monday night: another of Eddie's[1] gatherings for the ticket agencies. Hard grind, as usual. Then I found myself talking with Eddie and Frank – and, I'm not quite sure how, Frank saying, 'Would you direct my Hamlet?' I played up – as if the first time it had been suggested to me – 'Well . . . that's not a bad idea.' And I don't know whether Eddie jumped in with an 'I'll present it . . .' or maybe Frank, with light-headed effrontery, asked him. Anyway, he was interested . . . And we fixed to have lunch.

On Wednesday I did the Russell Harty Show, an impossible assignment for me really: in what terms, beyond that of a vaguely defined artistic-guru, could I possibly be significant to a public amiably philistine, habituated to think of directors in terms of Ken Russell, Hitchcock – or Joe Losey? I didn't enjoy it very much, though in fact I think it was dignified enough as these things go. I was really persuaded into doing it in the hope of helping *The Farm* – which was of course ridiculous.

8 November 1973

Coriolanus[2] was in every way dreadful. Preposterous prologue – with Nicol [Williamson] symbolically being encased in armour – his figure weedy and pallid – and Romulus and Remus lifted to suckle off a ceremonial wolf-statue . . . A reach-me-down, all-purpose Shakespearean crowd, talking stage cockney and west country – absolutely uncharacterised. Like a vigorous, boring school production. Mark Dignam doing his all-purpose, artificially inflected Shakespearean performance as Menenius. No political sense at all (the tribunes talking posh): and no class-sense – since Nicol can never get beyond the petty-bourgeois, and his notion of arrogance is only conveyed by the ill-tempered snarl. The only strength of his performance is that characteristic note of graceless, sardonic comedy. Both voice and gesture (which includes movement) undeveloped, forced, succeeding only through a harsh dynamic. We left at the interval.

On Monday afternoon we saw *Love Does Strange Things to People* in the Warner projection theatre: Mike Kaplan and Frank with Michele. A really dreadful, silly, idiotic pretentious film: [Franco] Brusati a real idiot. Frank suffered greatly – but in fact his performance had great charm I think, great potential, though completely unguided and unfocused. In fact the talent is so clear I can't imagine why everyone doesn't see it. Mike, however, apart from a nice remark or two, plainly doesn't get it – as he gets it from Malcolm . . . Yet there is a poetic presence to Frank that strikes a chord. Fonda compared to Cagney?

---

1. Eddie Kulukundis, theatrical impresario.
2. At the Aldwych Theatre. Directed by Trevor Nunn.

Michael [Medwin] came to the play on Wednesday, with Sean [Connery]. Michael at his most generous, burbling best – and very nice to Frank. Sean heavy and unable of course to pay any compliments except to Bernard.

15 November 1973
To Warners for the programme of my films – *Thursday's Children, The White Bus, The Singing Lesson*. Five or six minutes late. Mary McLeod was sitting alone in the projection theatre. The nicest person in the company.

16 November 1973
At midday was Ann Jellicoe's *rencontre* for Royal Court writers – to mark her reanimation of the Literary Department – wine and dip in the Theatre Upstairs. The old guard represented by Wally [N. F.] Simpson and Christopher Hampton – and the present generation by John Antrobus, Howard Brenton, Michael Abbensetts, [Heathcote Williams] the author of *AC/DC*, Stephen Poliakoff . . . I found myself reacting immediately in an irreverent, mocking way, noting myself doing it, and registering the fact that *this* is how I seem to function most productively, not leading or creating an establishment, but stimulating by challenge or scepticism . . . Ann made a speech, in good Girl Guide fashion: 'Anyone who's got a really good, big room . . .'

I got talking to Oscar, and somehow found myself mentioning my dissatisfaction with the theatre doctor, Blakey, who had refused to come and see Bernard the night before, and indeed seemed to me to be drunk. I was aware while talking of this, of that familiar sensation of Oscar *edging away* – not physically at first, but wanting to escape the challenge of responsibility. This reaction on his part always prompts me to push harder of course – which in turn makes him more tetchily evasive. Till he came out, inevitably with: 'I can't see what it's got to do with the Court doctor, anyway.'

'What do you mean?'

'The production is Eddie Kulukundis's responsibility now, not ours.'

This made me furious, and I said something that showed it, whereupon Oscar moved away.

'I can't discuss this now: I'm here to talk with the writers . . .'

For a moment I fumed; then, giving conscious rein to my anger, my scorn at the absolute second-rateness of the man, I chased after him. By now he was talking to someone else – I've no idea who: I grabbed his arm and swung him round.

'Don't you walk away when I'm in the middle of talking to you.'

Oscar spluttered and turned pale, and expostulated tensely – 'You're out of control – you're impossible . . .'

I can really hardly remember what I said to him, probably something about responsibility and his incapacity at measuring up to it. I talked loudly and violently. Perhaps

I was a bit drunk. Or desperate. Or both . . . I found myself later in a group with Jocelyn and Ted Whitehead:[1] everyone pretending nothing had happened. So I took to looking at Oscar and Ann very obviously, and speaking their names *very loudly*.

Perhaps all this was a preparation for the clash I know has to come. I'm damned if I will let Oscar and Albert get away with their nefarious and opportunistic schemes.[2]

29 November 1973

What I really like in Frank is the spontaneous flow of his emotion, his courtesy and generosity in social intercourse, his shyness and sensitivity and appreciation . . . and in his difficulties he is to be supported. What I have to beware of is imposing my own wants on him: for it is my strength that he needs, not my weaknesses.

26 December 1973

David Sherwin, with Gay and Luke, came round about midday: he has spoken to David Storey about the idea of doing a diary of production on *The Farm*. Which David doesn't seem to care about either way. Personally I don't mind it being done since David Sherwin is so completely sympathetic. He is going into the country – ostensibly to work on the idea he is supposed to be developing with / for Malcolm. Now this is a 'massacre of the innocents' story – the killing of children in an area of London by some undeterminedly-motivated maniac.[3] David reveals that Malcolm is also working on, or wants to work on, an idea by Mike Hodges[4] about an independent radio operator. I am very much looking forward to the New Year's Eve celebration, with the idea of linking arms with Malcolm and Margot and singing Auld Lang Syne . . . I had ordered a mini, nowadays the idea of efficiently getting anywhere seems unbelievable, to take me to Frank's; and amazingly it turned up at 1 p.m., and we drove for miles through the grey, nearly empty streets. The driver charged me £7.20, which was very steep, but it's a seller's market and I didn't care . . . It is interesting, and perhaps sad, to reflect that nothing in the world could give me as much pleasure as visiting Frank, in spite of his little suburban semi, and the suburbanism of nice Michele, and the consistent, insistent egotism which is his truth as well as his humour. We lunched off cold turkey in a salad-melange, followed by Christmas pudding which I didn't eat, producing instead a carton of yoghurt which I'd brought from home.

---

1. E. A. Whitehead, author of *Alpha Beta*.
2. For the English Stage Company to put on 'popular' plays and take over the Old Vic.
3. *Assassin of the Children*, McDowell playing the cop who tracks down a sniper.
4. McDowell didn't work with Mike Hodges until *I'll Sleep When I'm Dead* (2003), produced by Mike Kaplan.

29 December 1973

To the Court. I saw Oscar, lightly browned, back from his holiday in the Seychelles. Rather nervous, rather evasive: he told me (standing on the stairs outside the general office) that the Arts Council had, in view of the 'emergency', *not discussed* the future of the Vic. So Oscar suggested that we drop the issue ourselves – in order not to tear ourselves to pieces over what may prove to be an unreal issue. He is strangely appealing, Oscar, with his nervous vulnerability: which also makes him quite dangerous . . .

1 January 1974

Saw the New Year in at Daphne's, to which Karel and Betsy transported me. I had watched Frank in his television play, *The Illumination of Mr Shannon* – which Colin Blakely had done with him, alas, very badly directed (Brian McDuffe) and very badly designed (David Myerscough-Jones), camera consistently disfavouring Frank, concentrating on the worthy but uninteresting Patrick McAlliney . . . This was the play where Frank got himself accused of behaving like a prima donna. Then, as I spoke to Frank after the show, I watched the Variety Club Awards on TV – and saw Malcolm, rather tense, receive his hideous prize as film actor of the year (after Glenda Jackson[1]): he very sweetly and simply thanked me in his short speech. Very generous and *good*. Wendy Hiller walked with terrific poise to collect her award (for playing Queen Mary!).

I don't think I can manage parties any more. In the little room a line seemed to divide the pro from the small band of non-pro guests. Jack Clayton was there, and Wolf,[2] whom I've not seen for years, lively-looking, but walking cruelly bent, like a necromancer in a fairy tale. Malcolm and Margot arrived, Margot with a new fringe, in a sheath-like white dress, rather self-possessed. Mike Kaplan was with them. I felt real, rather sudden sympathy, comradeship for Malcolm; and we greeted each other with a rush of affection. Mike Hodges came with him: a pleasant, small man with a beard. We didn't really talk. I've never seen any of his films, and I felt too tired and out of sorts to make much effort.

7 January 1974

I went out yesterday to Hampton, to visit Frank. I set off about 1.30. The Frognal station is padlocked (ASLEF dispute) so I have to take the Tube – I am constrained by instinctive economy, and by some sense of shame, from taking a cab . . . so by Metropolitan Line to Baker Street; by Circle to Gloucester Road; by Metropolitan to Earl's Court, and so direct to Richmond . . . At Richmond a queue for taxis. After about five minutes I think I will ring for a mini, but the Yellow Pages are jammed against a corner wall,

---

1. Who made her film debut, sitting on the stairs, in a brief scene in *This Sporting Life*.
2. Wolf Mankowitz (1924–1998), wrote the screenplays for *The Long and the Short and the Tall* and *The Hireling*.

and hard to open: also I discover the print is too small for me to read *even with my glasses*: I contemplate for a moment tearing out the pages, but I am checked by the thought that such conduct is antisocial – also I might be seen, and arrested. I rejoin the taxi queue. After about ten minutes a car with a chauffeur-capped driver comes cruising, and I nab him. We drive speedily, chatting of Conservatives and Labour and what will the end of it be. I get to Frank's about 3.15.

We go for a walk with David round the field, past the burnt trees and into the playground: Frank has brought his camera but there isn't really enough light.

Back home I initiate Frank into the I Ching: suddenly how infantile he becomes when I take more than twenty seconds to explain the working of it. An embarrassing moment – I have left in the book the sheet of paper inscribed with the question, 'Am I right to continue this relationship with Frank Grimes' . . . which referred of course to *Hamlet*: but was perhaps misleadingly phrased. I rescue it – *just* . . . We consult about the Royal Court – it gives me WANDERER – then CAULDRON.

Letter to John Gielgud

9 January 1974

Dear John, I am not sure that this ends quite as well as it begins – you may think me completely crazy anyway, but the thought of doing something as eccentric as a *new* Ben Travers farce[1] does rather appeal to me! Victor also perhaps fades a bit in the second half, though he rallies at the end.

I got the play from Anthony Page, who was given it by Ben Travers – who, as I told you, was frightened of what his children would think of it . . . I think it would have to be done under his name. Not much point presenting it at Guildford as the work of an unknown writer. Anyway, as a rather unique literary curiosity, I am sure you will be interested to read it.

I hope things are going magically at the National.

As ever, Lindsay.

12 January 1974

The soap still on my face, and I am still in dressing gown and pyjamas when the bell rings at 11.30 and Ralph Bond arrives: he wants my advice as to a possible scriptwriter to succeed Alun Falconer (deceased from a heart attack at the age of fifty) on the ACTT Films project for a film about the Tolpuddle Martyrs . . . My heart sinks rather; I suggest Robert Bolt – realising from R. Bond's reaction that he has no knowledge of Bolt beyond *A Man for All Seasons*; is surprised to know that he wrote *Zhivago* and *Ryan's Daughter*. I also suggest Neville Smith, Barry Hines [*Kes*], Kevin Brownlow . . .

---

1. *The Bed Before Yesterday*. Travers hadn't written a play since *Wild Horses*, produced in 1952.

Ann Jellicoe calls: Roger Croucher doesn't want to direct *Johnny*.[1] I suggest Brian Cox. Alan Bates drops in and we take supper.

13 January 1974

Talk to Frank and tell him of the conversation I've had earlier this morning with Peter Hall, who doesn't want to be on bad terms – agrees that the possible cast for a *Hamlet* this autumn does not look very adequate – says that he'd like to do anything I would like to do as a major production in '75 – and that he wants to give Frank a 'workout' to see if he can 'speak English' and play Celia Johnson's son . . . Warners announced that there is no percentage income yet due on *O Lucky Man!*. My dynamic advisers and associates . . .

17 January 1974

North to Willesden to have my hair cut – those wisps of grey hair make me look like an old tramp. Lunch at the Baccio – a trattoria where I remember eating alone once or twice while cutting *O Lucky Man!* I am recognised, and my name frequently used – greatly to my surprise.

20 January 1974

Yesterday I left the flat at about 11.15, carrying the red leather grip that belonged to Mum: I bought a linen handkerchief at the staid, old-fashioned outfitters in Finchley Road – a small pot of African violets, and three peaches at a greengrocer – crossed the road to Mandarin Books, where I bought another copy of the Maharishi's commentary on the *Gita* – and caught a taxi to Bishopswood Road.

In daylight I see that almost all the houses here clearly belong to a school: small boys in football clothes are apparent on the pavement. I walk down to a playing field and across it to a hedge, where I sit down and start to read the *Gita* – reading the text of the poem first, rather than just the commentary. 'The solution to every problem is that there is no problem,' and 'Therefore, O son of Kanti, stand up Resolved to fight!'

At 12.30 precisely I enter No 2, and rattle the letterbox at the Campbells' flat. Mrs Campbell admits me, feeling a slightly strained, uncertain *gravitas*, into the living room, where I discover that I have made a mistake with my African violets – the flowers should be cut (to be easily handled), and so she hurries off to the village, to return with a bunch of daffs . . . On the table I see a pile of forms, one of them filled in, and a cheque for £20 in a small bowl; under the table a pair of shoes, and next to it a straw basket. Anthony Campbell ushers me into the adjoining room, consciously quiet, consciously unportentous but *hushed*. We sit in chairs in front of a sideboard on which

---

1. *Clever Elsie, Smiling John, Silent Peter*, which opened a season of *Two Jelliplays* at the Theatre Upstairs on 29 January. David Short directed.

is a dish with rice, a bowl with water, my flowers, including the violets, the peaches and the handkerchief. Some incense sticks. Over these, on the wall, a picture of the sage who formulated the technique – pudgy-faced and crudely coloured – and above him the photograph of an anonymous Indian gentleman in Western clothes. Anthony Campbell stands: he recites the words of the ceremony in a voice whisper: he sprinkles rice, takes a daffodil and dips it in water and sprinkles it, takes a stick of burning incense and puts it in a holder: after a time we kneel and he starts to speak a word. 'Join in,' he says, and I join in, not realising at first that this is my mantra. (The mantra is not to be communicated, and though it is extremely simple, I feel I don't even want to write it down.) We speak the mantra together – then, sitting down, we reduce the voice – then we whisper – then we whisper softly – then more softly – then scarcely voicing it at all – then not voicing, but thinking it . . . and I am meditating.

It is curious, because it *is* effortless, and somehow I feel no great difficulty in sustaining the quiescence, in holding the mantra, in allowing thoughts, sounds, imaginings to impinge . . . then, not resenting them or trying to repress them exactly, bringing the mantra back.

I caught a taxi and came home and tidied things up and ate something. Then I went down to the Court: I sat in my office to meditate, but after a few minutes there were footsteps in the passage, the key turned in Oscar's office, and Oscar's high-pitched, toneless, persistent voice started off . . . I found this distracting and moved off to Ann Jellicoe's script office, where I practised my new-found technique without either strain or startling results. When I got back to my office Oscar's voice was still batting away. I listened for a moment and realised he must be talking with Jane Howell: 'I'm interested in popular theatre – Lindsay and the others aren't . . . I may do something about it on my own . . . my time is up in a year and a half . .' Jane's low voice responded. I realised that Oscar wasn't plotting – seemed quite straightforward. When they came out of the office Oscar saw me – I hadn't got the door closed – and I went down with him and Jane to the bar. She seemed more friendly than usual, and asked me to read *Bingo*[1] . . . John Gielgud came and I talked with them at the bar a bit, John chattering away in his amazingly light-hearted way.

13 February 1974
Depression, or inertia, has overtaken me: which is why no record here of Stockholm or my six days in Warsaw, or of casting [for David Storey's *Life Class*]– But today lunch at TV centre, with Mamoun[2] and Norman Swallow, with the intention of soliciting

---

1. By Edward Bond. Gielgud played Shakespeare, Arthur Lowe played Ben Jonson. It opened at the Court on 14 August.
2. Mamoun Hassan, Head of the BFI Production Board (now incorporated into the Film Council).

patronage from Huw Wheldon, deserves record. I arrived first: a smooth young man – very reminiscent of Sir James's William in *O Lucky Man!* – asked me if I'd like a drink, or would I wait for the others? . . . I had a drink. Then Norman arrived: *O Lucky Man!* was *about* the BBC, he told me. Then Mamoun. Then suddenly the door burst open and Huw Wheldon burst historically into the room, eyes flashing under his picturesque eyebrows. At first I almost laughed: then it became clear that Wheldon wasn't in fact parodying the situation, but imagined he was playing it 'straight' as a dynamic, eccentric leader of genius . . . At least we prevented the occasion passing off as a mere, courteous get-together. Both Mamoun and I spoke very directly (over the bouillon, the duck and the cheese. There was even a printed menu on the table, in a frame I think) about the impossibility, as the BBC stands, of certain kinds of talent gaining employment or sponsorship. Wheldon's response to this was to become angry and to thank Mamoun not to teach him to suck eggs . . . Towards my arguing the case of the theatre – with special reference to the Court and to *Home* – he was more sympathetic. But it was difficult to take him seriously – except as a phenomenon: he has become such a self-conscious, posturing, self-caricaturing Man of Power. 'Full well they laughed, for many a joke had he . . .'

And the other point: his basic impregnable philistinism. No project, no play or film or programme to be valued for *what it is*. Only for what it represents as a fragment of culture, a piece of contemporary artwork worthy of patronage.

Anderson's production of David Storey's Life Class *opened on 9 April 1974. Alan Bates headed a cast that included Frank Grimes, Brian Glover, Rosemary Martin, Sally Watts (from the television series of* Billy Liar), *and Stuart Rayner, who was picked out from the crowd of aspirants in* O Lucky Man! *The 54 performances at the Court played to 96 per cent capacity. It transferred to the West End in June.*

25 June 1974

Lunch today with Harold Hobson – our long-delayed lunch – which came fortunately after his notice of *Life Class* on Sunday ('A blazing masterpiece . . .'). I say 'fortunately' partly because the bill came to £14, which with a tip amounted to £16 – if only because the gesture I made to the waiter suggesting that he bring me some change was interpreted to mean that he should keep the lot. Lunching with Harold does not bring out the best in me – I become instinctively Machiavellian, 'playing up', flattering, feeding, though not, I hope, ingratiating. He had requested that the BBC *Critics* review the play next week – requested, then insisted – and when this was refused (if only because they had already discussed the play at the Court), he resigned from *The Critics* – and from speaking for the BBC altogether.

1974 (undated)

I have seen Karel's *The Gambler*. It is really quite startling to see the effect of New York on Karel – very invigorating, liberating, completely different from his British films. I think the film is in many ways a very brilliant piece of work, probably his best to date, though I still always respond to the social elements in *Saturday Night and Sunday Morning*. Just how fully 'organic' this one is I am not sure, but it certainly is a tremendously effective and punchy piece of work, with much to enjoy and admire.

In the summer, Vladmir Pucholt qualified as a doctor. Anderson attended the graduation ceremony at Sheffield. Pucholt's wife, Rosemary, gave birth to a boy, whom they called Lindsay. In February 1975, Pucholt was granted British citizenship: 'I am sorry that it's taken me much too long to get around to congratulate you on becoming a Briton. I am not sure this is quite the best time in our history to have become a Briton: but I am not sure it's the best time in the history of Mankind to become anything . . . Anyway, I am sure England is better outside London – even if it is only Rotherham . . .' (26 February 1975)

Letter from Milos Forman (extract)

9 September 1974

Thank you for your letter! I wrote to Vladimir immediately. I am very happy for him. I am even proud of him . . . Your letter recalled the past for me and I realise more and more all that you did for Vladimir and Mirek and all of us. As unsentimental person as you are, I still want you to know that one day you will be declared the only English Czech Saint (to make up for King Venceslas) and a big marble statue of you will be erected on the slightly left side of Charles's Bridge.

28 July 1974

One week to go before [filming] *In Celebration*. I have been having visions – dreams – fantasies that I am going to spend this week efficiently, not wasting time, taking myself in hand, doing what needs to be done . . . In the last weeks I have become morbidly conscious of time wasted: of the degree to which one is – I am – consumed by relationships, meetings, personal demands. Rather than in any way nourished by them.

John Howlett, who had worked with David Sherwin on an early draft of
Crusaders, sent Anderson a thriller he had written called The Velvet Well. *He*
politely declined, on the grounds that the enterprising producer of the American
Film Theatre, Ely Landau, had come forward with the money for him to make
a film of In Celebration. *In his search for a 'creative' cameraman, he persuaded*
Dick Bush to leave Ken Russell's Tommy, *then filming on locations around*
Portsmouth. The collaboration did not work quite as he'd hoped.

4 September 1974

We started shooting *In Celebration* last week, and are of course already a couple of days
'behind'. Dick Bush certainly did turn out to be extremely neurotic – very insecure in
a strange way. Maybe he has been affected by a row that took place on his Ken Russell
picture, *Tommy*, which resulted in him leaving before the end. All the more extraordinary since he has worked frequently with Russell, from such television films as
Isadora and *Delius* and including *Savage Messiah* and *Mahler*. He is a quick worker, and
quite good from a lighting point of view, but doesn't like responsibility and with very
little imagination, so I have to devise the setups mostly myself. As a result we don't go
terribly fast. I long to have the assistance or the contribution of really creative technicians, but it never seems to happen.

Letter to John Osborne (extract)

23 October 1974

My dear John, I am afraid I am always terribly bad when contacted out of the blue by
transatlantic telephone. That's to say I probably gave the impression that I was nearer
to comitting myself to *The Secret Agent* than in fact I am.

I find myself very torn about this whole project. First because it is obviously a very
intriguing and challenging subject. And second because the writer is you. On the other
hand, I couldn't undertake anything unless it was a proper commitment. I think that
to start working on it with you and then to drop out later would be inexcusable.

There is also the fact that I am filming *In Celebration* before I really wanted to
undertake a film – not having yet fully recovered from the last one. And having got
through the shooting, and now embarking on the editing, I find more than ever
that I cannot face the thought of immediately entering on another film project . . .
I don't, quite honestly, really want to do anything immediately. It may seem rather
exaggerated, but I don't think I have yet really recovered from *O Lucky Man!* Please
forgive me if I seem to have been maddening and vacillating.

23 October 1974

Alan Bates is going to join Malcolm in the new Dick Lester film *Royal Flash*, which started shooting this week. He is very worried about his uniform, which is splendid but all white, which he says is bad for his figure! He is insisting on having brown piping, to relieve the effect.

22 November 1974

Malcolm is in Germany at the moment. I had a postcard from Alan Bates, who was enjoying working with him and quite enjoying (though a bit doubtful about) the breathless progress of the picture. No rehearsals really, and hardly ever a retake. I shall be getting more details from Frank Grimes, who has been out there doing a small part this week, and was rather disturbed to find that he had to do it after a quick walk-through and no rehearsal. The whole thing was over in five minutes! This is either the way to make very good or very bad films. I hear amusing rumours of Malcolm having to 'work to rule' in order to get his billing clause established in the contract. Stanley Kubrick[1] has had a disastrous influence all round, I am afraid. Anyway, I hope he wins his battles – provided he wages them decisively and firmly.

––––––––––

Anderson spent the early months of 1975 reading and rejecting film scripts, among them Christopher Logue's Modjeska, *commissioned by Sylvia Miles, who received an Oscar nomination for her role in* Midnight Cowboy *('When I met Sylvia in New York we got on fine. She certainly has phenomenal self-confidence,' but 'It is impossible for me to commit to a project unless I have committed myself to it, so to speak, within myself. And I have to say that I haven't committed myself in this way') and Melvyn Bragg's script of* Rogue Herries *('I think the most serious lack is in the relationship between Herries and his son, David. David has been reduced to a minor, and not enormously interesting character, and so the story loses one of its most powerful elements').*

1 March 1975

It is when one is not directing, not auditioning, not occupied full-time in the cutting room, that the demands become intolerable. How many scripts am I supposed to be reading at the moment? And not one that there's the slightest chance I will end up directing.[2] But the petitioners are insatiable, and I still haven't learned that first

––––––––––

1. Kubrick allowed only his own name to be used prominently on the posters of *A Clockwork Orange*.
2. Among the scripts he rejected were Glenda Jackson in *The Divine Sarah* and Donald Sutherland and Elliott Gould in *We Built the Bomb*.

essential – to say 'no' immediately, when it is still possible to be polite. The slightest weakness, the slightest hesitation, and one is doomed. 'It's very interesting . . .' Fatal word – 'interesting'. To the writer, or the producer who is on the other end of the telephone, this means – 'Yes, I'd love to do it.' And inexorable, agonising, farcical the lies, evasions, duplicities that lie ahead. I remember that wild, hysterical Greek lady, driven almost insane by her determination that I should direct her play, who arrived at my flat in huge dark glasses, with cries and tears. I fled to my kitchen and hid there in fear and shame while my secretary and my faithful Irish cleaning lady staunchly interposed themselves between me and my deserved fate.

It is to get away from all this that I am flying to the US to spend three weeks lecturing to university audiences? 'What are you lecturing on?' asked a friend, an enormously successful and capable chain-store tycoon. He was surprisingly startled and outraged when I briskly replied: 'Me.' But what else have I to lecture on? Philosophies of the cinema are not really interesting. (I see that Bela Balasz is still in print but does anyone read him?) And why should American university students know or care anything about the British cinema? This is certainly a subject I have obsessive theories about, and surely these will figure in my 'lectures'. And they relate to what is perhaps another reason for this tour: the possibility of stimulus certainly not to be found at home, and at least a temporary leave of absence from the sinking ship.

Today's *Guardian* reports a speech by Dr David Owen, Minister of State for Health, speaking in John O'Groats. 'The first prerequisite of recovery was a decisive shift of national mood towards realism, determination and idealism.' One might say the same to an assembly of representative British film producers, technicians, artists and critics. With as much (as little) hope of effect.

At Kennedy Airport I am lucky to get through customs with my little open grip crammed with films (*O Dreamland*; *Thursday's Children*) and extracts (*Wakefield Express, This Sporting Life, If . . . .*).

'You ought to have had these screened before you left England,' the lady examiner says dubiously. She opens a can at random and starts unwinding film in pursuit (I suppose) of subversive or obscene images. Leader spills down over the counter: the queue behind me stirs with slight impatience. 'What's this?' It is the *Wakefield Express* sports reporter of twenty-odd years ago walking down the street outside Wakefield Trinity ground, gathering material for his weekly column. I take the reel and spill more film over the desk. 'There's an old man sitting on the steps. And there's a footballer.'

The lady official looks at me blankly. 'Was this made for television?' Other officials accumulate behind her. She turns to them. 'What shall I do about these films? Shall I let them through?' One of them thinks of a new tack. 'How much are they worth?'

'I've no idea.' (I haven't).

'No value?'

I get the sense that this would make things even more irregular. 'Well, say a hundred and fifty dollars.' There is some more, low-pressure discussion. 'What are these?', a newcomer asks, pointing to the Film Institute's extract reels. 'These are extracts from feature films,' I say with a little more confidence. 'This one is called *This Sporting Life* and this one is called *If . . . .*'

Faces remain blank. But clearly it would be more complicated to impound the reels than to turn a blind eye. 'Oh, let them through,' one finally says. It is enough. I scrape my stuff together and cram the reels back into my grip. The tour is on.

Oscar Lewenstein's three-year contract as Artistic Director of the Royal Court came to an end in 1975. Anderson was offered the job but turned it down.

12 June 1975

Things at the Court have been rather less than pleasant. Oscar's regime has ended in a sort of decadent disintegration – and I must admit that I don't find the new generation particularly sympathetic. Really, there is nothing to do but pack one's bags and wish them luck.

In June, Anderson 'tweaked' Roger Croucher's Court production, starring Malcolm McDowell, of Joe Orton's Entertaining Mr Sloane *for its transfer to the Duke of York's. The following month, he brought his Court career to an end with a triumphant production of Orton's* What the Butler Saw. *After pencilling in Leonard Rossiter and John Cleese to star, he settled instead for a cast including Michael Medwin, Valentine Dyall, Brian Glover and Kevin Lloyd. Alan Price composed the music. Jocelyn Herbert designed the sets. In the programme it was noted that Jocelyn had 'aged ten years' as a result of working as production designer on* O Lucky Man!

1975 (*undated*)

We are halfway through the second week of rehearsals for *What the Butler Saw* now. As usual, it's been sticky to get into – to shake off the prevailing apathy, which afflicts one-self, as well as the intrinsic difficulties of the play. It is most curious stuff. Of course you can imagine that after doing nothing but David Storey plays for five or six years, the shock encounter with a totally different author is a bit hard to get over. I can't make up my mind quite how to 'place' Orton. He is certainly brilliant and outrageous, and also completely unscrupulous in his manipulation of stage characters and situations. That's to say they have an extraordinary degree of cleverness – but they *don't* quite fit together like parts of a Swiss watch. Of course they *may* fit when the audience is present. Perhaps that's the strangest thing. To be doing a play which in the end only exists in terms of audience – whereas, of course, David's plays can be performed even more satisfyingly when there is no one there to see them!

What the Butler Saw transferred to the Whitehall Theatre on 19 August 1975. Anderson ended his association with the Royal Court Theatre chiefly because the two new Artistic Directors, Robert Kidd and Nicholas Wright, turned down his proposal to stage Chekhov's The Seagull, *his own translation, a project promptly taken up by H. M. Tennent and Eddie Kulukundis, who presented it at the Lyric Theatre, Shaftesbury Avenue. Anderson's new repertory company included Joan Plowright, Frank Grimes, Helen Mirren and Eleanor Fazan.*

Letter to Rachel Roberts (extract)

27 June 1975

Dearest Rachel . . . I am delighted that you are so happy to be playing the 'Sara Allgood part' in *How Green Was My Valley*. Though, to be honest, I'm not sure I see clearly that a benevolent mother-figure of the Welsh valleys is necessarily more 'what you are about' than a self-obsessed actress, of great charm and outstanding talent, as personified by Madam Arkadina in *The Seagull*.

It was nice to say, however abruptly, that I'll probably get a better actress to play Arkadina. But speaking as your mentor as well as your friend, I must say that you show astonishing lightness in regard to a classic role in a play by one of the world's few great dramatists, under the direction of someone you have praised highly in the past, in comparison with a sentimental role in a best-seller serialised for television. It has never, as you know, been my habit or even my ability to try to persuade people to do things, and I certainly would never have tried to persuade you into playing Chekhov, when you felt that you were really more suited to playing Richard Llewellyn. But you know, when you make extravagant protestations of loyalty and regard, you do have to put a little more effort sometimes into at least appearing to live up to them.

The Seagull *opened on 28 October 1975. Anderson's production of Ben Travers's* The Bed Before Yesterday *opened on 9 December. 'The Bed Before Yesterday has been one of those extraordinary successes which come once in a lifetime . . . exactly the kind of thing the West End audience wants, which I think [is] a wonderful achievement for Ben.' (From a letter to John Dexter, 13 January 1976)*

25 March 1976

In the plane – Eastern Airlines from Washington DC to Raleigh, North Carolina, three [lecturing] engagements fulfilled. Can't remember exactly how many to go. I seem to have lost my detailed itinerary. Boston was pretty hectic: these colleges with film departments really put you through it. Tonight at 8 p.m. is the University of North Carolina at Chapel Hall. I arrive at Raleigh (wherever that is) at 3.51. Must find time to check though my contracts. I've no idea what reels anything is on, or what order they are after last night's scramble at Boston.

Before I forget. Arrived last Friday – good God, a week ago nearly.

30 March 1976

Still couldn't make the shower work: wrote rude words in the flower-covered guest book. At 10.30 the flaccid Kevin Vaughan arrived to escort me to the Hilton. He nervously said he was trying to find a student to help me with the bags. No car. And the distance wasn't long enough to interest a taxi. Another weedy student turns up, complaining with an attempt at casual humour at such activity so early in the morning. I take the heavy suitcase and march on ahead.

The Hilton is boring like all Hiltons – the second or third Hilton in the city, built for the bicentennial. (In anticipation of the guests and holidaymakers who are going to flock to Philadelphia to see the Liberty Bell. Also hopefully to accommodate visitors and relatives of patients at the University Hospital opposite.)

On the phone Ruth Perlemutter from the Philadelphia Film Fest: what a pity we clash. They have Godard flying in on Sunday. Could I slip a reminder into my speech this evening? Her colleague Stewart comes on the line. He is dealing this afternoon with the Angry Young Man movement in British cinema. Could I drop in between 3.30 and 4.30: it would give his Film History students a thrill . . . At one o'clock my phone rings. Sol . . . principal of the Annenberg School of Communications, is downstairs for our lunch together. I take my coat and cap, if only to indicate that I expect to be taken somewhere charming and picturesque, but the tall, grey, stooping, straggly-bearded professor leads me back into the lift and up to the Penthouse Hilton Restaurant. Where of course there is a queue. 'Where else is there to go?' asks the Professor, with an assumption of helplessness which I suspect is designed to put the responsibility for the whole meeting (including the bill) firmly on my shoulders.

'There's a dreadful coffee shop,' I answered bad-temperedly.

'Oh – well we'd better try that.'

The coffee shop lunch wasn't bad in fact: a salad buffet and joints of roast beef. The Professor queries the prices anxiously – is it extra for meat, or is it all-inclusive? It is all-inclusive, so he helps himself to a side order of cannelloni with his roast beef.

'I saw your last movie . . . uh . . . Now what was its name?'

'I wonder if you mean my last movie or my last-but-one movie?'

'Uh . . . about the boy and his adventures . . .'

'That wasn't my last movie, actually. It was called *O Lucky Man!* '

'I thought it had a lot of interesting things in it.'

'I'm glad,' I reply with an acidity which fails to register.

He waffles on, greyly. 'Gosh it must be twenty years since I remember seeing your documentaries . . . What was that one – about a boys' club, I think.'

'I didn't make that. It was called *We Are the Lambeth Boys*. Karel Reisz made it.'

'Of course . . . But you made something around then, didn't you? What was it called?'

'*Every Day Except Christmas*.'

'Of course! . . .'

Why is this man having lunch with me? Because, I suppose, he didn't feel he could say no when someone suggested the idea to him. I mention the Film Fest to him.

'What Film Festival? I've never heard of it. Is there a Film Festival on . . . oh yes – that affair down at the Walnut . . .'

Our conversation only livens up when I switch to the attack and he can enjoy bringing out and dusting down his liberal guilt.

'Oh yes, I oughtn't to be here . . . The only thing I enjoy is getting away and doing a bit of sailing.'

'Why don't you go West?' I say 'The East is dead – all polite culture and pretension. It reminds me of England.'

'I've been West. I loved it. I spent six months with the Navajos . . .'

'That's no good. That's just romantic escapism. You should take a job in a Western college.'

'You're right. I'd like to do that. I think it would do me a lot of good . . .'

When the lunch is over, the Principal of the Annenberg School of Communications reaches for the bill, fumbling, 'May I pay for this with a credit card?' he asks the waitress. I take the bill. 'It can go on my expenses,' I say.

The Principal's face brightens.

He shambles off to go on superintending the teaching of communications.

13 May 1976

Oscar came to see *The Bed Before Yesterday* a week or so ago – but crept out at the end (thinking himself unobserved) and didn't come round . . . He offered me a rewrite of *Billy Liar*, set in Ireland, which he calls *Liam Liar*. He wants Frank Grimes to do it in Dublin, but it would be a little like returning to one's vomit.

With the number of London performances of The Bed Before Yesterday *now*
running in the hundreds, Carol Channing invited Anderson to direct her in a
production of the play on Broadway: 'I couldn't think of leaving England without
seeing its biggest comedy hit. I didn't even know I was standing. I was in such
euphoria! Yet, I never dreamed I would have the opportunity of playing Alma.
So I was overwhelmed when Arthur Cantor, the producer, offered me the role
for Broadway. However, I wasn't so overwhelmed that I didn't ask for Lindsay
Anderson, the distinguished British stage and film director, to come here to recreate
his production.' (From the programme note)

8 August 1976

To New York, to inspect actors preselected (I hope) by Arthur Cantor's office, for the
US *Bed Before Yesterday*. For once a passable movie on the flight. Charles Bronson in
Hard Times (retitled *The Streetfighter* in Britain, probably sensibly). It is economic,
terse, with some of the qualities of a good short story, but the film is not really good.
Too bare, with no real flesh of character, no real relationships, Bronson giving too little.
And insufficient poetic power to raise it to the (implied) level of myth. Decent though.

After the film, I let the daylight in and looked out at the blue sky and the carpet of
cloud. A stewardess swooped down. 'Would you keep your blind down? Some people
want to sleep.'

'What? No.' I was outraged at the idea of spending a whole daytime flight with the
blinds drawn.

'It's our rule.'

'No. I can't accept that. No, I won't.'

The stewardess looked at me with disgust, then left. I get the impression that people
don't answer back on aeroplanes. But what an idea!

New York clammy, sunless – some rain, even. I was met by John and George from
Arthur Cantor's office. Theatre gossip came at me hot and fast . . . 'At Stratford,
Ontario, where Maggie Smith is playing Millamant, Cleopatra and Mistress Overdone
in *Measure for Measure*, she had been wonderful as Millamant – even if she and Jeremy
Brett, who was *fine* as Mirabel, weren't talking to each other off the stage. Jeremy
thought this was because of his friendship with Bob [Stephens] and he wore a hat
which Bob had given him, and Maggie didn't want the children endlessly reminded of
Bob . . . but it didn't really matter, because they worked so well together on stage, and
their working relationship was entirely unaffected . . .' Maggie 'made Cleopatra work
on her own terms,' it seemed. 'She wears her hair up at the beginning, and it makes her
look a bit matronly. But when she lets it down, she looks quite divine. And she does in
the end make it work on her own terms.'

I didn't ask what that meant exactly.

This kind of enthusiastic, infatuated, high-pressure show-business excitement is characteristic of American theatre. It has very little to do with quality or discrimination, it is gossipy and trivial – but it is at least vitally committed, energetic, compulsive. Another contrast with English weariness, marginally preferable.

Apropos Maggie and Eileen Atkins, I couldn't help reflecting that both these distinguished talents had been mentioned confidently by Joan [Plowright] as anxious to support and contribute to the Lyric Theatre Company. Who on earth would rather go back to shabby and unappreciative London?

We drove up 10th Avenue. At West 10th Street, down in the rather monumentally seedy Battery Dock area, we stopped at lights. George nodded to the right. 'One of the S&M bars.' Men mostly in jeans lined the wall drinking beer in the slight drizzle. A couple stood rather primly under an umbrella. On the edge of the pavement, his back to the road, stood a man wearing only briefs and baseball shoes and socks, quite impassive. No one taking much notice.

'There's another one,' said George as we drove up the Avenue. This looked dark and risky.

'The sidewalk is generally crowded,' said Johnny. 'It must be the rain. Have you heard of a new place called The Toilet? It's the last word in decadence. You can check your clothes in for a dollar when you arrive. So there're a lot of people running around completely naked. They've got a wall with holes in it you can stand up against. And one room that's totally blacked out. I guess *anything* happens there. And one of the specialities is a room full of baths where you can piss on people. I just must go there. I think you should experience everything.'

'It was like this in Rome, in the decline of the Empire,' said George, quite cheerfully.

9 August 1976

Arthur Cantor returned from his fund-raising trip last night. It's difficult ever to get clear and precise answers to direct questions in this particular business. (The budgets, by the way, for the two productions Arthur is engaged on now, *The Innocents* and *The Bed Before Yesterday*, are $225,000 each. This compares with costs of approximately $40,000 for the launching of *The Bed Before Yesterday* at the Lyric Theatre in London. A good week in the West End can gross anything between $17,000 and $20,000.)

We start auditions at the Billy Rose Theatre, a rather pleasant house but ill-favoured now, being a block below 42nd Street and therefore outside the charmed Broadway circle – rather as the Saville in London had the reputation of being difficult to fill because it was the wrong side of Cambridge Circus. A single, metal-shaded lamp hangs over the centre of the bare stage, unhelpful and unwelcoming. Auditions are unpleasant enough anyway, without this chilling atmosphere. At the Royal Court, or at the Lyric,

I always ask for *some* stage lighting, and generally get it. Here it would probably mean the engagement of the entire union lighting crew, and I know better than to ask.

Auditions are the same anywhere. Not hysterical, fraught and melodramatic, as represented, for instance, in *A Chorus Line*, but still occasions of tension, disguised hopes, exposed nerves and susceptibilities. Of course, it's not as bad for the auditioning director as it is for the artists who have to offer themselves and their abilities for what must usually seem a painfully cursory examination: all the same, except for the power-intoxicated and the exhibitionist, it's no joy for the director either. Sometimes one longs to hide oneself in the shadowy stalls, and leave the running of it all to one's assistants. But one cannot. The actors have to be met, greeted, shaken hands with, sometimes directed, thanked . . . And how often their hands are clammy with nerves.

10 August 1976

I wonder how any young American actor can capture the particular upper-class idiocy that must be Aubrey's . . . The style, I realise, is more likely to come from comedians, accustomed to playing directly, than from 'actors', accustomed (the young particularly) to digging around for secondary meanings, subtleties and shades that are supposed to make the characters more 'interesting'. All actors want to play every character as though it had been written by Chekhov. And why don't drama schools teach them that *no* performance can be real if it does not contain something – preferably a great deal – of the performer's own reality?

I cast Mrs Holly – a pleasant and full-blooded artist who caught the tune exactly. Of course she turns out to come from England.

Evening: I meet old friends Sylvia and Seymour Herscher and Charlie Baker and am taken to see the new sensational success of Joe Papp's New York Public Theatre, *For Colored Girls Who Have Committed Suicide When the Rainbow is Enuf.* My every instinct tells me that any entertainment with a title like this must be dreadful. Charlie, who used to be one of New York's brightest, most sophisticated and most experienced theatre actors' agents, agrees with me; but we are overruled. 'People say it's wonderful.'

Charlie and I are right. Eight coloured girls (women?) run in and out, shouting defiant poems at the tops of their voices, performing dynamic movements and indulging in a general orgy of togetherness. The respectable middle-class audience (60 per cent white) listen with enlightened attention. After about ten seconds I find I have cut off and understand almost nothing of the next hundred minutes, except a long, long account of a Harlem domestic tragedy which climaxes with the drunken husband dropping his two children out of sixth floor window while his woman stands by, voiceless and paralysed. *Cue* magazine says that the show 'culminates in a sexual political cry that unites agit-prop theatre with stage poetry'. This took the form of a free movement celebration while the actresses chanted: 'I found God in myself and loved Her – fiercely.'

Out in the foyer, the inevitable Clive Barnes 'rave' is blown up and exhibited on an easel. I note that he writes 'The words fly into the air like brown birds.'

Liberal dopes stand reading this tosh with serious faces.

12 August 1976

The *New York Times*, reviewing John Wayne's new picture,[1] describes it as one of a recent succession of 'geriatric westerns'. The kind of remark that might be made by one of our smart-ass London critics. Personally I prefer the oriental tradition of reverence, or at least respect for, the elderly.

Lunch at Macmillan's, the publishers, where Charlie and Sylvia superintend the operations of Macmillan Performing Arts. They have a musical they want me to hear. They see me shudder, and we all remember that evening when, in Sylvia's drawing room, I heard the two authors perform the songs of *Kelly* – the notorious musical which, after untold agonies on the road, ran for one night on Broadway[2] and lost over $1,000,000.

Kelly, for me, will always be the exemplar of Broadway folly, waste, compulsive and greedy activity without intelligence or the most elementary common sense. A nice idea – the legendary Bowery character who jumped off Brooklyn Bridge for a bet – an outstanding score and a *weak* book. A writer who professed himself eager to collaborate, and refused to cut or change a line. A brilliant composer blindly and inflexibly loyal to the writer. Writers' union regulations which 'protected' the author from enforced script changes. And a plethora of producers, agents, entrepreneurs devoting incredible energy, ingenuity and capacity for intrigue to the discussions of terms, fighting over billing, splitting the album rights, and squabbling over percentages. There was great excitement, I remember, about the renting of an enormous – and enormously expensive – billboard space dominating Times Square. When I tried to talk about the deficiencies of the script, I was told: 'We'll get it right on the road.'

This is the showbiz myth. Scripts have to be rewritten on the road, disaster has to threaten, shirtsleeved conferences have to take place in smoke-filled hotel bedrooms at two in the morning, directors have to be fired and artists replaced – or nobody feels that a show is really going on. When, after a week's abortive work with the author, I declined the assignment, the producer was so angry he threatened to sue me. Presumably because I was denying him the pleasure of firing me later.

Some years later I met the composer, Moose Charlap, in London. We did not talk about *Kelly*. Moose, a delightful and tremendously talented man, was working on some bizarre technique, which no one could understand, whereby *any* actor could be made to sing on a soundtrack. This was to be effected by somehow selecting and manipulating sounds or syllables from a track of his speaking voice. He explained the whole

---

1. *The Shootist*, directed by Don Siegel.
2. 6 February 1965. Herbert Ross took over the direction when L.A. resigned.

thing to me with obsessive enthusiasm, but I couldn't make head nor tail of it. He had a weak heart, and a couple of years later he died.

In the evening I go to the Duck Joint, the Czech restaurant up on 1st Avenue to have supper with Milos [Forman] and twelve or so others: some high-rankers from United Artists, a producer and his wife, Baryshnikov, the Russian dancer, Marina Vlady the French-Russian actress, and Milos's charming and talented friend, the French actress Aurore Clement. The producer's wife sparkles: 'I just love my life. I love flying. I love eating well and buying nice things. And I love movies.' How nice to be like that. Marina Vlady's husband speaks no English: we talk a bit in French, across the producer's wife.

When the party splits up, I shake hands with Baryshnikov, whom I haven't been able to speak to. He is quiet, looks rather tired – he is not dancing at the moment because of a leg injury – sensitively likable. The absolute opposite of Nureyev. He smiles and says: 'I am a great fan.' I am touched as well as amazed.

When everyone else has gone, Milos and Aurore and I sit on and drink pear brandy. I tell Milos that three weeks ago I saw a double bill in London of *Peter and Pavla* (his first full feature) and *Loves of a Blonde*: how good it was to be reminded of those early days – when we had talent! We reminisce, as we love to do, about the shoe factory at Zrouch, where in 1965 I visited the last day's shooting on *Loves of a Blonde*, and met for the first time Milos, Ivan Passer, and Mirek [Miroslav Ondricek], who was to shoot *The White Bus* for me, and *If . . . .* and *O Lucky Man!* That, if any, was a meeting made in heaven. I watched them shooting the last shot of the film, and then we went and played billiards. 'In those days,' said Milos, 'many people came from the West to look at us and talk – but you were the only one who behaved like a human being.' And for me it was the same in reverse. After the battle of *This Sporting Life* – the perpetual, nagging reluctance of the English unit (patronising at best, frankly hostile at worst), where almost the only supportive sympathy seemed to come from the stills cameraman – the feeling among those young, ardent and humorous Czechs had the warmth and familiarity of immediate comradeship. That was why, on blind and even absurd impulse, I asked Mirek (who spoke not a word of English) if he would come to Britain, always supposing I could fix it with the union, to shoot a film for me.

And how strongly, and repeatedly, and happily our paths have crossed ever since. By amazing chance, I bumped into Milos in a Paris street when I was over there with the finished version of *If . . . .*, which I had to show to Bud Ornstein, European head of Paramount, for his seal of approval. Then those harsh days, the beginning of exile, when the Russians were in Prague, the brilliant young Czech new wave was gagged or dispersed, and Milos and Ivan were struggling in a sympathetic and unhelpful Britain. And later in New York I visited Milos in his cutting room when he was wrestling with the editing of *Taking Off* – and he and Mirek came to see *Home* at the Morosco Theatre. And earlier this year I hired a dress suit and went with Ivan and Milos – now the crowned king of Hollywood after the hard-won miracle of *One Flew Over the Cuckoo's Nest*[1] – to a charity evening at the Beverly-Wiltshire, where I shook hands with Rosalind Russell[2] and was rude in a loud voice to Pauline Kael.[3]

Now, of course, not a script is written, not a production planned in the US, without it being submitted to Milos Forman. His air of wily and sceptical good humour is as fetching as ever. Of such understanding, shared experience and mutual respect is friendship made.

This morning [13th] I drop in to see Mike Medavoy at United Artists. Mike is one of those excellent, enthusiastic agents who have become film company executives – part of the revolution which has transformed the American film business over the last twenty years. It is very pleasant to be asked, with every appearance of respectful sincerity: 'When are you going to do a picture for us?'

On those occasions, I do wish I had the energy of ambition.

14 August 1976

Arriving at the theatre, Terry says: 'There's been an argument with the union about getting the furniture down to Wilmington. They want to know how it had got into the theatre – it ought to have been brought in by a union crew, but John Lee Beatty [Production Designer] fetched it along himself. So they're refusing to pick it up.'

'So what happens?'

'Jack and I will carry it out.'

'I'll give you a hand.'

'That's okay. We'll put in a bill for it. Teamsters' rates. It'll pay for my new flat to be decorated.'

There's no business like show business.

17 August 1976

Inevitably, the Huntington Hartford Theatre, where we are auditioning, is playing *Equus*.[4] This is the National tour, with Brian Bedford (an early British emigrant, now an established favourite on Broadway) and Dai Bradley, who was David Bradley when Ken Loach picked him out of his school class to play the lead in *Kes*. *Equus*, in the US as in Britain, everywhere, fulfils the middlebrow ideal of 'exciting' and 'significant' (i.e. pretentious and meaningless) theatre. It was hugely successful in Boston, where this tour started early this year, and will run until November. I have never seen the play

---

1. For which Milos Forman won his first Oscar for Best Director.
2. American actress (1908–1976).
3. Film critic for *The New Yorker*.
4. By Peter Shaffer, whose *Amadeus* won Milos Forman his second Best Director Oscar.

through, but stood at the back for the last half hour when Richard Burton was playing it in New York.

As we leave, I notice a slight, bespectacled young man in the front office, running off copies of ecstatic *Equus* reviews. Fortunately I restrain from sardonic comment: the young man, whom at first I don't recognise, is Dai Bradley, a long way now from Bolton and the pits and the pettiness of England. I greet him and he explains that he's getting evidence together to support his application to American Equity for the famous Green Card which will allow him to work freely in the US. I wish him luck.

After auditions I drove out to Rachel's taping of her third segment in the *Tony Randall Show*[1] – a new series for ABC in which, rather strangely, she plays the Scottish widow who keeps house for widower Judge Randall and 'looks after' his small son and teenage daughter.

Taping takes place somewhere called Studio City, which turns out to be a quite extensive studio layout owned by CBS. The show is produced by something called MTM, which turns out to be the Mary Tyler Moore Organisation. More interesting is the fact that this is – was – Republic Studios, the leading Poverty Row studio presided over by Herbert J. Yates, which turned out second-grade westerns with John Wayne: but late in its career the studio briefly became the home of a number of distinguished talents in search of independence. Here Orson Welles shot his *Macbeth*; Frank Borzage made his last romance, the attractively anachronistic *Moonrise*; Nicholas Ray produced his camp classic *Johnny Guitar*. And most memorably, John Ford made, for Republic release, *Rio Grande*, *The Quiet Man* and *The Sun Shines Bright*.

Now lines of gawpers form up, wait patiently and file docilely in to watch Cloris Leachman taping *The Tony Randall Show*. 1984 with a smile. The audience is ranged on long rows of seats banked up one side of the studio. One set – a judge's chambers – stands open before us. Others, on either side of it, are hidden behind yellow-wheeled screens; on a raised platform down at the end of the stage a four-man combo is playing mainstream jazz. Over the audience is suspended a row of large microphones. On the catwalk high above the set, a brown metal folding chair has REPUBLIC stenciled across the back. An electrician may have sat on that, watching John Wayne take Vera Hruba Ralston[2] in his arms . . .

Down there at the end, behind the screens, I spot Rachel, lurking in a pink dressing gown. I make my way round to the side to greet her: she looks hygienically processed, as though sprinkled with icing sugar.

'You came – I didn't think you would.'

'You asked me to.'

---

1. It ran for two years and forty-four segments.
2. Czech actress who married Herbert J. Yates.

16. Directing Ralph Richardson and John Gielgud in *Home*: 'they came up to it like warhorses and I'm really quite astonished by Ralph's control and smartness on the lines.' (17 June 1970)

17. *Home*: Dandy Nichols, John Gielgud and Mona Washbourne.

18. Directing *O Lucky Man!* (1972)

19. Graham Crowden experimenting with Malcolm McDowell in *O Lucky Man!*

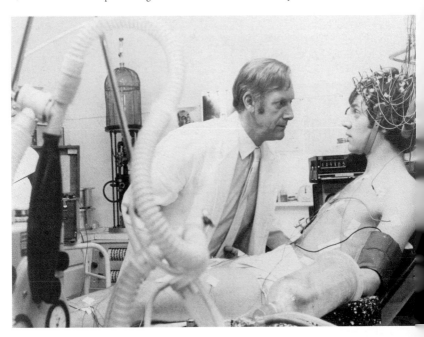

20. Malcolm McDowell in rehearsal for *In Celebration* at the Manhattan Theatre Club. (1984)

21. Rehearsing *What the Butler Saw* (1974). Michael Medwin (left),Valentine Dyall, Lindsay Anderson, Brian Glover and Jane Carr.

22. *The Kingfisher* by William Douglas Home, at the Lyric Theatre, with Ralph Richardson, Alan Webb and Celia Johnson. (1977)

23. In discussion with David Storey in the rehearsal room for *Early Days*. (1980)

24 and 25. Frank Grimes rehearsing *Hamlet*. Anderson directed Grimes in the play at the Theatre Royal, Stratford East in 1981, and at the Folger Theatre, Washington D.C., in 1985.

26. 'Rioters at the gate': directing *Britannia Hospital*. (1981)

27. 'New Experiments': Graham Crowden back as Professor Millar in *Britannia Hospital*.

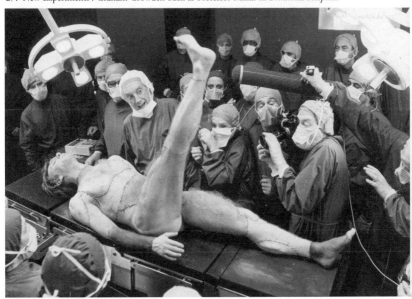

28. Lillian Gish and Bette Davis in *The Whales of August*. (1987)

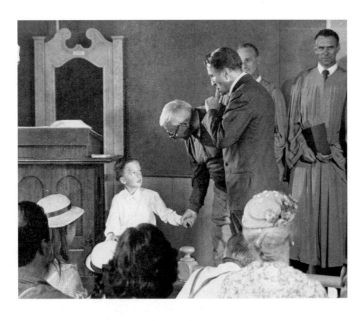

29. Directing the opening sequence of of *Glory! Glory!* (19 June 1988)

30. 'Alan Price singing 'O Lucky Man!'

18 August 1976
Visited MGM, Brian de Palma, Dino De Laurentiis, Martin Scorsese, Tony Hopkins. Plane back to New York. Dick Lederer, John Boorman.

27 September 1976
[*New York*] 10.30 at the rehearsal room. Everyone is there ... As usual I feel myself rising to the challenge: thank God for Clive Barnes (whose piece most people present haven't read), who gives me the theme for some opening remarks. I tell them who Ben Travers is, and a little about the Aldwych company, and a little about the history of this play and its first production. That it is a comedy and not a farce, and how Ben works always in terms of the reality of the characters and their situation, not in terms of 'getting laughs'. (As when he would return from National Theatre rehearsals with a long face: '*They're trying to be funny*,' he'd say).

I also firmly use the word 'serious', remembering how Ben would light up doing rehearsals at the Lyric when I talked seriously about the ideas behind *The Bed Before Yesterday*. 'We are much too ready to congratulate ourselves on our sophistication – to believe the media myths. I'm sure there are whole areas of this country, and millions of people, who still live by the old standards of puritanism, and think of sex as wicked or disgusting, or at least as something not to be talked about.' People nod. I sense myself growing bored and wind up: Ben's endless vitality and geniality: the 'innocence' of his directness: the subtleties that his simplicity can contain. 'Wisdom can often seem simple: that doesn't mean that its truths are not subtle. Cleverness is often complicated: that's why the would-be sophisticated are impressed by it. But it isn't as precious a thing as wisdom.'

16 October 1976
Not for the first time, I long for the simplicities of a team of Rugby League players or a crew of tent erectors.

19 October 1976
Waking early, as usual, I ponder the situation – which is not exactly painful, but radically unsatisfactory. How to communicate with a deeply defensive, powerfully aggressive, talented, misguided actress – compulsively working herself into a style that cannot ultimately serve either the play or herself, but which offers the security of known habits, proven 'effectiveness'? I sit up in bed and write eight pages. And this is it [short extract]:

Dear Carol – I thought this morning it might be useful if I put down in writing – so that you can look at them at your leisure, not under pressure, and then we can talk about them if you want to – some thoughts about the performance, based on our run-throughs during the past week, and my general feeling about where we've got to.

And first, let me say that I'm sorry I have found it difficult, during this last week, to say to you many of the things I have felt should be said, and to work with you in the way director and actor *ought* to work, if they are going to achieve the best possible results.

I don't know how consciously you cut yourself off from benefit (or, you may think, the distraction) of direction. But the cut-off was very specific, and very decisive. It was last Wednesday morning that I tried to say that *while continuing to work on the lines*, and while continuing to run through the play every day, I was anxious above all that we should continue to work, moment by moment, on the feeling and thought of every moment of the performance, so that these feelings and thoughts become as clear and sure and true as the lines.

This plan you rejected, chiefly because you were predominantly worried about the lines (which I fully understand), but also because you accused me of making the play 'heavy', by treating it as if it were written by Ibsen.

Well, of course, *The Bed Before Yesterday* is not like *A Doll's House* exactly – although there is a great deal of humour in Ibsen too, not always understood by actresses (and directors!). But it *is* like *A Doll's House* in that the leading role is a detailed, acute, absolutely truthful and very subtle portrait of a woman – which is something you certainly understood and relished when we started rehearsing, but which since has been lost sight of rather. But, let me repeat. The humour of Alma is essentially the humour of that character in that situation. She has not got humour about herself – that's one of the reasons she is funny. The moment the performance of this role loses truth, or appeals for laughter by stepping out of character – it may get laughs from the undiscerning, but it ceases to be funny in the way it should be.

Let me give you a few specific instances: the big, expansive gestures you are making on lines like 'All this ridiculous golf,' and 'He went away almost at once,' have nothing to do with Alma – and are completely out of character with the tight, poised, dignified, emotionally constricted woman you show us so beautifully and so accurately elsewhere (as, for instance, the passage 'I have no friends'). To be psychological about it (like Ibsen?) one may say that if Alma *could* make wide, expansive gestures of that kind, she wouldn't be forced into her 'flying up'. They break the melody like a false note.

Some of the 'out-front' playing now has too much sense of audience, and too little feeling of what is inside the woman – let alone feeling for the person you're talking to. Example: the passage following 'I'm embittered . . .' when you cross the stage to Victor. This really cannot be played out-front and on the move like that. The result is quite unreal.

*Bookings were strong in Philadelphia, where the play opened, but it closed after
its pre-Broadway tour. In London, Anderson moved into a large new flat, Stirling
Mansions. He tried and failed to get Hollywood interested in Gavin Lambert's
script of Arnold Bennett's* The Grand Babylon Hotel, *and turned down an offer
to direct Faye Dunaway in* The Eyes of Laura Mars: *'It's an absolute load of balls,
and can only make a ridiculous and pretentious movie. I must admit I'm not an
admirer of Dunaway. I'm sure she's an exceptional person, but I thought her
performance in* Network *was disastrously lacking in humour.'*

He turned down John Lahr's The Autograph Hound. *And he turned down Ray
Bradbury's* Something Wicked This Way Comes: *'Certainly an accomplished
piece of writing, but in a vein of fantasy that I think is more literary than truly
belonging to film . . . it is also surprisingly whimsical and soft-centred.'*

*For two years, his diary took the form mostly of notebook jottings and faithfully
copied letters.*

11

Edging Towards Hollywood

The Kingfisher – The Old Crowd – Dustin Hoffman
Satyajit Ray – Empire – In a Lonely Place – Richard Gere
Anthony Hopkins – Rachel Roberts

'I hope you are following now the story of the Army recruits
who were made to hang lavatory seats round their necks, and take part
in dummy executions, besides having their bottoms bitten by
jovial NCOs. It's the real stuff of which Britain is made.'

May 1977

I saw Malcolm, back in the country for a month. His *Caligula*[1] seems to be a big monster. Already a big row between the producers and the Italian director as a result of which the director has been fired and sent back to Italy. Ironically, the film is being edited by Russell Lloyd, who was my editor on *In Celebration*. An extremely nice and very competent chap, but I wouldn't like to leave him in sole charge of a feature. I rather tremble for Malcolm, who has invested so much of his time in the project. It really is a scandalous waste that he can't find anything decent to do. He really is so talented.

In May 1977, Anderson had a West End success directing Ralph Richardson and Celia Johnson in The Kingfisher *by William Douglas Home, brother of Lord Home, the former Prime Minister.*

---

1. Written by divers hands but credited to Gore Vidal.

Letter to Mitch Ericson, Arthur Cantor, Inc. (extract)

20 May 1977

When I got your subway report, I was on tour, out of London, with *The Kingfisher*. Known in some quarters as a geriatric comedy – in others as a charming, gentle comedy of Evensong. It all depends how you are disposed. A slender, bourgeois comedy, not without skill or subtlety, which I undertook after an incredibly complicated series of manoeuvres involving Peter Hall, the National Theatre, the Society of West End Theatre Managers, Ralph Richardson, the mad William Douglas Home, etc. . . . Really it's a commercial comedy, which Peter Hall tried to net for the National, first of all out of greed – he hoped I think originally to do it there and then transfer it to the West End to get his commercial percentage – and partly out of desire to keep the crowd-drawing Ralph Richardson with the National . . . In the event it became clear that Peter couldn't work the West End dodge any more, after all the criticism he got last autumn, so he said he couldn't do the play. So Ralph asked me. I said I would do the play but *not* at the National. So we ended up on tour and now in the West End.

Another defeat for me, at the hands of an intransigent star. Or rather two of them. Though this time more talented, and distinctly more successful. The show is a hit, but I have not succeeded in effecting the crowd-pleasing performances of the two stars. Ralph is a rather higher-calibre artist than Carol Channing, but adopts rather the same style – including gross 'takes' to the audience, stylised gestures, etc. But people love it. Each laugh is like a sword in my side. So I am reduced to crying all the way to my accountant.

22 June 1977

'There will *always* be an England' . . . And if we had ever been in any doubt about it, we'd certainly know it now after these endless Jubilee celebrations.[1] Every day there are pictures (on television too, of course) of the Queen walking about, being presented with flowers, driving here and there, and generally personifying the imperturbable genteel spirit of England. In fact the place gets more schizophrenic every day, with this example of unruffled and smiling traditionalism on one page, and on the other, generally facing, strikes and inflation of prices, and corruption in the police, and violent confliction on the picket lines. Which is the real Britain? I wish I knew![2]

The really extraordinary thing – and even more depressing than extraordinary – is how with all this wealth of material and stimulus, our cinema gets more run-down and

1. The twenty-fifth anniversary of the Queen's Coronation.
2. From here one can date the start of the project that became *Britannia Hospital*.

petrified each day. Certainly no evidence of contemporary reality gets on to British cinema screens. The flight of talent and now capital to the US increases every week.

Letter to Rachel Roberts (extract)

20 July 1977

My dear Rachel, yes it really is a pity that you reserve your telephone calls to me to the times when you are down, desperate, and (let's face it) usually drunk ... Everything that is Scottish in me chafes at those interminable, involved, repetitive sentences which go on and on at God-knows-what expense, particularly as I am realising at the time that the next morning you will have only the faintest recollection of what it was all about. Even the last time you called, which was when you had just 'resigned' [from *The Tony Randall Show*] and were going to see the writers the next day – it's a pity you weren't enough in control to have asked me then, quite clearly, what exactly I had written to you about the character and what advice I could give you. It might have helped you in your meeting the next day. On the other hand it might not.

I am assuming that your row has now been patched up, and that you were offered and accepted some specious assurances by the writers that your character would be strengthened and your part built-up and that there would be no more jokes about food etc., Am I wrong?

The real problem about Mrs McLellan [the part you play], and about your attitude towards the role and the whole assignment, is that you have never really obtained or demanded a full and specific account of the character and the background of the person you are supposed to be playing ... You must realise, that of all the characters, Mrs McLellan is the one about whom your writers will know the least. The others can all quite easily be adapted to the stereotypes of American TV, because they are stereotyped versions of commonplace American characters. Mrs McLellan is obviously a 'special' character, played by an actress who is 'special', not merely by virtue of her talent, but also because *she doesn't come from the same world as the other characters.* It's up to you, therefore, to force the writers to make concrete their imagining of the world from which Mrs McLellan does come.

So the first thing you ought to do, is the thing that any repectable working actress ought to do with any role that she undertakes: i.e. to ask herself and the authors certain specific questions about it. Who was her husband? Was she really married? If so, what was his profession? Did she have any children? Has she any family? Where exactly does she come from? (and you can provide the others). These are the questions to which you need answers in order to play the part. And which the writers need to be able to answer if they are actually going to write the part. I don't believe these questions have ever been really asked. This is your fault, since you never forced them into defining the character.

I know it is difficult for you, with your great lack of self-confidence, to stand up for yourself properly, and not just in fits of temperament, which don't really achieve a great deal. What you need to do is to take yourself and your talent seriously, not just as an excuse for intermittent, histrionic outbursts. You might as well face the fact that, besides being self-indulgent, you are also abominably lazy. Part of the reason why you have never really gone into the character of Mrs McLellan – and therefore you have suffered from the inadequate writing – is that you simply can't be bothered. You really are in a much stronger position than you ever give yourself credit for, or than you really wish to take advantage of. Do try to understand that your writers cannot write for Mrs McLellan because *they don't understand or know her*. It is up to you to help or to force them. Do it.

Letter to Gavin Lambert (extract)

8 August 1977

I've been having a fairly traumatic time over the last couple of weeks (my own fault of course) because the National Film Theatre has set up a mini-season of my films[1] in its two-year trudge through the British cinema. The marathon opened with John Schlesinger, followed by Nic Roeg. I came in a dubious third, at the height of the Silly Season. The programme directors at the NFT, auteurists and Losey-ites to a man, don't see what all the fuss is about, but Leslie Hardcastle (he still manages the place) insisted on my doing an exhibition of photographs, scripts, insulting journalistic affrays, etc., and we opened it last Thursday with a reception for the press (!) and a show of some extracts from my *oeuvre*, which I introduced ... My chief pleasure was in being able to deny invitations to John Coleman (*New Statesman* drunk) and, of course, to any and everybody connected with *Sight and Sound*.

I met Joe Janni[2] at Miriam's funeral.[3] He said: 'Do ring me – let's have lunch – you won't of course.' I said: 'I will, of course.' And, of course, I didn't.

15 August 1977

Saw Malcolm yesterday. He's finished his BBC film with Clive Donner[4] and seems to be moody. The *Caligula* situation continues very unsatisfactory. I can't make out whether the picture is being worked on, or whether the lawsuits are holding it up. Malcolm has some story of Dino de Laurentiis having final authority. I don't know if this is true.

---

1. The Anderson Retrospective was repeated in Chicago.
2. Producer (1916–1992), associated with the films of John Schlesinger.
3. Miriam Brickman. L.A. organised the Miriam Brickman Memorial Prize, an annual cash prize for students at RADA. The sponsors were L.A., Malcolm McDowell, Julie Christie, Richard Attenborough, Glenda Jackson, Rachel Roberts, Albert Finney and John Schlesinger.
4. *She Fell Among Thieves*, from the story by Dornford Yates.

I told Malcolm he should insist on seeing the present version, but it's impossible to get him to exercise any kind of authority.

I had an insane phone call from Boaty Boatwright's secretary yesterday, to say that she (Boaty) had met with Stanley Jaffe and Bob Benton and that everyone was very excited I wanted to do a remake of *Sullivan's Travels*.[1] In fact I had asked Boaty to set up a screening of the picture in London, *not* because I wanted to remake it – what an idea! – but because I wanted to see it again. Are they all mad out there?

12 September 1977

I have been talking in a fairly desultory way, with Michael Medwin, chiefly about that old Dornford Yates book *Blind Corner*, which I gave to Malcolm and David about two years ago. I can't pretend to be wholly committed about this at the moment. But I did go with Michael to Ireland last week, to look at Ardmore Studios, and consider the possibility of shooting there. A nice little place, completely somnolent, and completely in the pocket of John Boorman, who likes to use it as a private studio. We stayed one night and went to have supper with Boorman, who lives close by. Sean Connery was also there. A mildly interesting evening – Boorman living most luxuriously in a quite charming and unpretentious way, with his managing wife and large family.

Letter to Bessie Love (*extract*)

12 October 1977

My dear Bessie, I have enjoyed reading *From Hollywood with Love* so much – I congratulate you not only on actually getting it written, but on such a delightful and inspiring book. What a Golden Age you make it all seem! (What a shame it is to be a cinema-lover and to have been born too late . . .). I had no idea you did that stint at Ealing. It must have been a fantastic contrast. But also exciting days in British film-making. The war did something to shake the English out of their Old School Tie stiffness. And we did our best at the end of the fifties and in the early sixties, but it didn't last.

I had no idea that you were Mary Astor's sister-in-law. I have always admired her greatly – and once wrote a piece about her, when I was a film journalist, and she wrote a very nice letter back. A couple of times since, when I've been in Hollywood, I've tried to get in touch with her, but she is extremely reclusive, I know. I read that you had managed to persuade her to come out of her shell and talk to Kevin[2] – and that she said it did her good. Do you think there's any chance of my being able to meet her when I am in Los Angeles next month? Would it be very cheeky if I asked

---

1. Film of 1941 by Preston Sturges. The structure has loose similarities with *O Lucky Man!*.
2. Kevin Brownlow for his *Hollywood* TV series.

you if you could [write] her a note, asking whether it would be okay for me to get in touch? I leave this to your good judgement. I really don't want to disturb anyone who would rather be left alone. But sometimes human contact can do us good. With love and admiration to *you*.

Stephen Frears brokered a deal with London Weekend Television for Anderson to make The Old Crowd, *an enlivening, theatrical film of a bourgeois dinner party written with Alan Bennett. It was filmed in three days, and one late night, with a cast that included Rachel Roberts, Peter Jeffrey, Philip Stone, and a splendidly black-cloaked Valentine Dyall. Frank Grimes played a hired hand, a ruffian who sucks Jill Bennett's toes under the dinner table.*

Letter to Alan Bennett (extract)

21 October 1977

I'm sure Stephen [Frears] told you that he had kindly got in touch with me and asked me if I would like to direct one in the season of your plays which he's doing [for television] next year. I read *The Old Crowd*, and was intrigued by it – then found, particularly as the script developed, that it seemed to fall away from its initial disturbing and poetic quality . . . you may think it cheek if I suggest that the play could do with some rather fundamental transformation . . . It seems to me at the moment rather to fall between two stools. First of all a quite surreal, comic yet also vicious satire on bourgeois manners. And on the other hand, an amusing, but much more trivial comedy of eccentric manners, in the end *amusing* rather than *disturbing*. So many of the inventions in the script do seem to me to have a strong, poetic and bizarre quality – then it's a pity, I feel, that the use made of them sometimes lacks the corresponding strength. Perhaps in the first half it's a question of raising the style a little: so that the people are much more 'poised' and fundamentally unruffled in their 'carrying on', rather than ever fussed and apologetic in a smallish kind of way. Do you think the piano-player (whom of course I like very much) should be blind: that's to say, wearing dark glasses? And when he leaves, perhaps he has a large guide dog. The dialogue less whimsically eccentric ('furn-i-ture'), so that the bizarre effect is created more by *what* they say and the way they carry on under these circumstances, rather than the *manner* of their behaviour . . . Do you see what I mean?

In other words, that the bourgeoisie of your fable (it's impossible not to be reminded of Buñuel – but what a splendid chap to be reminded of!) should be stronger, more monumental, worthier victims of calamity.

I remember a dreadful party I once went to at the Tynans a very long time ago. They had got hold of 'the very latest thing', a brilliant young comedian from Oxford, by the name of Jonathan Miller. I remember skulking in the kitchen, while the assembled party (Princess Margaret might well have been there) were crowded into the front room shrieking their heads off at a long monologue which I was unable to find terribly funny. This would perhaps not be quite the right thing for *The Old Crowd*, but does it give some kind of a clue? (Do you think Jonathan would do it?!) Oscar, of course, should end up in bed with one of the women, preferably fucking her busily as the doorbell arrives to announce the arrival of Totty. And not stopping. Appearing later, dishevelled. Do you think Totty could have a colostomy? Perhaps she's going to die in six weeks, not six months. I'm sure there's something stronger, more threatening and undefined, to be done with Harold and Glynn. They rather remind me of the couple in *The Fire Raisers*. And that, of course, conjures up the whole *outside* world, which it seems to me should play a part in the second half of your play, in order to raise the whole thing, give it a second wind, so to speak. I know I have rather a cataclysmic imagination – but I do get a strong image of the Crowd continuing to play their parts as the world disintegrates around them. Wouldn't it be really exciting if the second half of the play could evoke the world in which we find ourselves at the moment – with hijackers, terrorists and explosions (Perhaps the television set should play a part here too). The arrival of Totty should really shift the whole thing into a much more macabre, even terrifying, gear.

December 1977
Working hard [on writing *About John Ford*] at the Museum of Modern Art (I managed to see about eighteen early John Ford films, including nine or ten silents, which I'd never seen before) ... [In New York] I saw Milos Forman and Mirek Ondricek slaving on this peculiar assignment of *Hair*. Everybody seems to be agreed that it is a real folly, but, as Mirek said to me rather wistfully, it seems that United Artists don't care whether they lose money or not. The scheduling is so ridiculous that it ended with them trying to shoot musical numbers with unclad dancers in Central Park in the December snow.

Letter to Roy Boulting (extract)
19 December 1977
I've only just got back from the States, which is why I haven't answered your letter sooner. I'm sorry to hear about [Jiri] Menzel. Of course, I know that conditions in Czechoslovakia are dreadful, but there seemed to have been some loosening up, and he has at least been able to work. I hadn't any idea that they were refusing to show his work outside Czechoslovakia.

    I think the idea of an invitation from the BFI/NFT is a good one. I only wish my relationships there were more cordial! But I'm not on bad terms with Leslie Hardcastle, who is supposed to run the National Film Theatre, and I will certainly give him a call, and see if anything can be fixed up. I am, of course, an avowed enemy of Keith Lucas, who is Director at the moment, but I'm extremely happy to learn that while I've been away he's at last been removed from his job. So some things move, ever so slowly, towards the better . . .

While in New York I visited the shooting of *Hair* two or three times – two old Czech friends of mine are chiefly responsible for it. Milos often gets congratulated, he tells me, on Menzel's film *Closely Watched Trains*. To most people in the West, one Czech is much the same as another!'

24 April 1978

I saw *Star Wars* the other day. Difficult to know what all the fuss is about. I thought it a modest (except technically), mildly entertaining picture – except for those two damned, arch robots. They nearly wrecked the whole thing in the first ten minutes.

I actually managed to see another new movie – one which has become a critical, near-cult success, something called *Assault on Precinct 13*, written and directed by one John Carpenter.[1] And I must say I found it an extremely suspenseful, exciting and entertaining picture, quite in the old style. Extremely well-crafted and performed. Infinitely preferable to rubbish like *Rocky*.

[I've been offered] a peculiar venture from the Robert Stigwood Organisation to supervise the scripting of a film about Edward II, who is famous chiefly for having died with a red-hot poker (or was it white-hot?) up his arse . . . A horrible incident of which one should not make light, except that the idea of basing a film on it does seem rather strange. Still you never can tell what they'll get up to nowadays. How about John Travolta for the lead?

Anderson turned down a request from Michael Medwin to make a film of Martin Amis's The Rachel Papers: *'There is a real danger throughout the script that the appeal is too constantly towards the snobby, initiated, "in" intelligence of the English with-it intellectual class. This makes the appeal more limited than* Annie Hall *(of which of course one is constantly reminded) which for all its comedy has a central core of seriousness and sensitivity. Woody Allen is genuinely perplexed about his emotional problems, regretful when his affair fails, and always hopeful of solutions. The central figure here hasn't anything like the same clarity or the same appeal . . .'*

---

1. Who wrote *The Eyes of Laura Mars*.

And he turned down an offer from the National to direct Albert Finney in
Brecht's Galileo: *'The trouble is I'm not at all sure that Albert is the right Galileo.*
He's shortly to undertake Macbeth *with Dorothy Tutin. His fifth production in a*
row with Peter Hall. It isn't surprising if his acting has suffered' (from a letter to
Gavin Lambert, 3 April 1978). Finney returned the favour by turning down
Anderson's proposal of David Storey's new play Phoenix, *about a provincial*
theatre director whose building is going to be torn down. Anderson then offered the
play to Peter O'Toole, with whom he hadn't worked since April 1959 and Jazzetry,
but whom Malcolm McDowell had enjoyed working with on Caligula. *O'Toole*
accepted the proposal but, according to Anderson, 'promptly vanished'.

Letter to Gene Moskowitz (extract)

16 June 1978

Haven't been up to a great deal recently: I did a peculiar salvage job on a bad play
which Ralph Richardson had insisted on doing and which I had originally turned
down. They got within two weeks of their London opening, on tour, and then I was
asked to go in and try to pull it together. A rather inadequate thriller called *Alice's*
Boys. It was an extremely bad production, and I did my best to make it shipshape,
and at least make it look as though Ralph was still able to give a commanding leading
performance. But the critics set on it like a pack of hounds, and the poor bleeding
carcass was buried after a couple of weeks in the West End. I didn't feel particularly
badly about it but it was sad for everyone concerned.

Then I went to over to New York, to meet Claudette Colbert – the candidate to
do *The Kingfisher* there, in partnership with Rex Harrison! A curious venture, which
I have agreed to do, largely because all alternatives here seem so boring. I was
charmed by Claudette, who, at seventy-two, is in a fine state of repair, very direct and
humorous. We had time, of course, to refer to *Drums Along the Mohawk*, and she
told me how Ford had made her cry. But in the nicest way! She also said that in all
her career the only director who had really given her what one would call acting-
direction was Lubitsch . . . In typical Yankee fashion, I had a phone call from the
producer (an indolent idiot called Elliot Martin) telling me that as a result of a piece
in the paper announcing Claudette's participation, there had already been a hundred
party-booking enquiries!

Letter to Alan Bates (extract)

23 June 1978

I suppose I must get used to all my friends flying to the States by Concorde . . . I went
to see Malcolm yesterday evening, and found him in a great state of nervous excitement, really revving, because he's flying over to New York by Concorde today, for

'meetings' about a new picture he's been offered – a sort of science-fiction extravaganza about H. G. Wells travelling in his time machine to contemporary San
Francisco, which has been written by the chap who wrote *The Seven-Per-Cent
Solution*.[1] Rather a windfall, and well deserved by Malc, having just finished a pretty
awful chore [in *The Passage*] with Anthony Quinn and James Mason in the South
of France (Malcolm as the traditional, sadistic Nazi Colonel pursuing Anthony
Quinn as the traditional good Basque peasant, helping James Mason as the
traditional Allied scientist over the traditional border) . . . Malcolm said he enjoyed
working with J. Lee Thompson, because *all* his suggestions were accepted and he was
able to rewrite all his dialogue and turn his character into a crazy spoof. I went down
to Dorset and spent the weekend with them . . . Malcolm was, of course, going to play
at Chichester (in *Look After Lulu*, directed by Patrick Garland) but had to cancel
because his film overran. And then the Film Finance 'pulled the plug' and he could
have done it after all.

Rachel is reaching the end of her chore in John Schlesinger's picture [*Yanks*]. I've
seen a lot of Rachel, of course, who is in excellent form and has completely given up
the bottle, believe it or not. And I've seen a bit of the young American who is playing
the Yank lead in the picture, Richard Gere, who is suffering gallantly through the
somewhat sudsy scenario. The picture is being lit by Dick Bush – remember?

I had a narrow escape from the National [Theatre]. In fact (don't despise me) after
receiving an absolute avalanche of plays from Peter Hall, I actually accepted one –
The White Guard by Bulgakov – then, for some strange reason, Peter threw the name
of *Galileo* into the ring, coupled of course with Albert's. Like a complete idiot,
I allowed myself to get momentarily interested, so the project was formulated that
I should do just that. Then I had an evening with Gillian Diamond and realised that
I was supposed to work with the NT 'company' – which in fact consists of the
accumulated casts of *The Country Wife* and *The Cherry Orchard*. I went to see *The
Cherry Orchard*. An abominable production, with everyone acting extremely badly.
Terribly depressed, I went round to see Albert and found him anxious, in a
patronising way, for me to go there, it would be 'good for the company', provided
I wasn't 'naughty' – but so smug about the whole setup and so totally committed to
the Hall-y myth, that I came away feeling I just couldn't do it. So I didn't.

Then I was offered a new (terribly exciting) play by David Mercer from the Royal
Shakespeare Company, but I thought the play was pretentious, literary and humourless. So I turned it down.

---

1. Nicholas Meyer wrote and directed.

I'm looking forward to seeing *An Unmarried Woman*,[1] which is going to be shown next week. I *did* see *The Shout*.[2] Since it has been such a success, you won't mind if I raise a sceptical eyebrow. Awful tosh really, though I did like the bit when the sheep died because you shouted.

Letter to Richard Gere (extract)

8 July 1978

I was very glad to see *Blood Brothers*, and so were Rachel and Darren. I'm sure you won't be altogether pleased if I say I enjoyed your performance more than I enjoyed the picture as a whole – but the truth must be told.

I can see that there was a good deal of commitment and a completely serious approach to the subject. But I wish the script had been less melodramatic – or that [Robert] Mulligan had been able to play against the melodrama, instead of quite so heavily with it. Of course there's a problem with these Italian characters – I know they do genuinely have that kind of extrovert dynamic, and that show-off kind of masculinity (or pseudo-masculinity) and that this was the theme, or part of the theme, of the picture. But I think the continued stridency went beyond realism, and underlined that aspect of the theme much too fiercely. It's really strange: I'm sure Mulligan is a director who is very concerned to be truthful, and yet he allows (or encourages?) playing that is terribly over-theatrical at times. I'm thinking particularly of the mother's performance: I hated the scene when she is trying to make the child eat, and found the scene where she tries to seduce the snooper absolutely ridiculous. But you provide the story with a centre that is absolutely believable and also touching. Not sentimental in any bad sense, but full of the right kind of feeling. Whether you like being told so or not, you have a tremendously strong screen presence – and also the God-given ability to convey your thoughts and inner conflicts very directly through the camera. The scenes with the children were excellent, and I wish there could have been more of that side of the story and that side of the character. (The scene with the tart too, *excellent*.)

I've been going quietly mad, ploughing through about fifty scripts which I've agreed to referee for something called the Association of Independent Producers, a bunch of 'independent' film-makers who have been invited to submit stuff to EMI and the Rank Organisation for production. Reading their scripts, one realises why – economics apart – we haven't got a film industry in this country. I haven't forgotten *The Diary of a Drug Fiend*. As soon as I've got this stuff out of the way, I'll have a proper read of it.

---

1. Film by Paul Mazursky, in which Bates starred.
2. By Skolimowski, with Tim Curry and John Hurt.

10 July 1978

Why do I find myself marvelling each day afresh at the madness of the world? Does everyone feel this? Or is this just the plaint of every generation? Rachel on the phone from L.A. Slightly drunk, enthusing about Alma[1] – 'I've got Alma, Lindsay, in my soul ... I love her, you see ... I love her so much ...'

17 July 1978

I must admit to being seduced into *The Incredible Hulk*, which has just started screening over here. A fabulous series, I must admit. I'd rather have it than *Upstairs, Downstairs* any day.

Letter to Mike Kaplan (extract)

26 July 1978

As Malcolm may have told you, I saw the first cut of *Caligula* with him just before he left London. The one made by the British editor, which has been transcended and, according to Malcolm, considerably improved on by the Italian editor. I do think Malc comes out of it with heroic forcefulness, dynamic and charge of personality. And some of the key solo scenes are extremely well played. But the director seems to have absolutely no sense of structure or dramatic rhythm, and no feeling for character at all. So the whole thing is a sprawl and a mess, and I find the flirtation with pornography simply silly. There's very little that is sensuous about the picture. If only Malcolm could have shown and exercised some of the critical sense that he's evidencing now – *but during the shooting*. But I don't think the picture will do him great harm: in fact people will probably (and rightly) admire his undaunted spirit and obvious talent.

28 November 1978

New York. Went about midday to visit the Third Avenue Advertising Agency offices where Bob Benton is shooting *Kramer Versus Kramer*. When Marion checked the floor (the 45th) with the doorman downstairs, the doorman asked, 'Want to get his autograph?' (Dustin Hoffman's).

Up in the suite was Stanley Jaffe ... broad grin ... I had meant to ask him about *Grand Babylon Hotel* (which Gavin rang me about from Los Angeles last night). Dustin Hoffman was in the passage, slighter than I had thought. 'Oh, you're small ...' he said, as we were introduced. A good, friendly smile as we shook hands. Bob cheerful, mild, welcoming as always. And Nestor Almendros[2] ... Saw a scene being shot – Dustin with

---

1. L.A. had offered her the female lead in the Australian production of *The Bed Before Yesterday*.
2. Cinematographer, noted for his work with Francois Truffaut and Terrence Malick.

the little boy – phenomenal American confidence from the five-year-old. Hoffman, who seemed to be semi-improvising, also exuding enormous (self-involved?) command and sureness. Technically very relaxed. Not at all like my rehearsed precision. (Though when we met, Dustin went on about the *specific* quality of the playing/direction in *If* . . . . 'You can't do better than that.') He introduced me to the little boy, jollying him along, as a great director. 'So we must be very good'.

Bob wanted to chat after the take, but Dustin, somewhat manic, but in a generous way, had taken over. 'What are you doing next? I'm not doing anything. I've nothing to do . . .' He wanted me to read *Scaramouche*; talked of *Cyrano* and *Arturo Ui*. 'I want to play Shakespeare . . . People tell me I should do *Richard III*.'[1]

I asked him if he'd enjoyed directing – Yes, he had, except that he was disappointed that the actors didn't want to work harder. 'Will we get Thanksgiving off . . . ? I'd offer to work with them in the evenings – but they didn't want to. We weren't like that when I started'.

Technical run at the Biltmore [where Anderson was directing Rex Harrison in *The Kingfisher*]. Elliott [Martin] trying to sound authoritative in the presence of his backer, blusters because Claudette has been having massage and treatment and isn't there at 7 p.m. 'Oh come off it Elliott,' I say, 'Rex has been at a cocktail party, and he wasn't here either.'

'Rex has been here since seven,' says Elliott, lying so as to avoid conflict with the stronger star.

'No he hasn't. He got here five minutes ago.'

No wonder they steer clear of me.

As I mount the stairs to see Claudette, I meet Rex and Mercia[2] on the landing. She extends an icy cheek. Rex bad-tempered and sulky, wanting to go off and have dinner with Mercia. 'What are you proposing to do? No one has told me anything. First it was six-thirty, then seven, and now I don't know what's going on . . . Bill called me, he was absolutely vague, except he said we *certainly* would be in costume and he didn't *think* we'd be going through the whole play . . .'

'Well, we are going through the whole play – I'm sure you wouldn't want to open tomorrow without a proper rehearsal.'

'I haven't the least desire to rehearse – I know what I'm going to do *perfectly* well – *I* haven't been off for a week – If Colbert feels she has to go through her lines I suppose we'll have to – but I'm certainly not going to do my scene with George [Rose].'

'Sounds a good idea' says good-sport Martin, nervously attempting to placate.

'I'm afraid it isn't a good idea' – I am firm – 'We have to do the cues as well, the curtain and the music and effects, and we need the artists on the stage to do the lighting.'

---

1. In 1984 L.A. turned down the offer to direct Dustin Hoffman in *Gorky Park*.
2. Mercia Tinker. Harrison's sixth and final wife.

'Haven't you done the lighting?'

'No we haven't.'

'You've been two days here.'

'Rex, I have not had two days. The technicians have had two days for an extremely difficult get in . . .' etc., etc. All this going on in the public view, on the small landing outside Claudette's dressing room. 'She's in there getting herself up,' sneers Rex, with Mercia trying to (and I must say successfully) maintain an aloof contempt for all these messy proceedings.

I break away and go in and see Claudette, sitting in front of her mirror, apparently quite unaware of – or unaffected by – the shindig outside.

'We'll go through the whole play,' I say – with concern in my voice.

'Darling we must! We have to, we open tomorrow, it's the last chance.'

Probably it never crosses my mind that she is *also* making it clear that there will be NO REHEARSAL TOMORROW. I suppose Rex's appalling behaviour was the result of nerves . . . but that didn't make it less appalling. He came and sat in the stalls and started criticising the set – and in particular the new masking executed to Alan [Tagg]'s design, to hide the obtruding roof at the back of the stage. In truth, this does rather spoil the lyrical expansiveness of the cyclorama, and it had been cut with rather too jagged an edge.

Rex: 'What's that supposed to be?'

L.A., playing the game: 'Well – I suppose it's a formalised suggestion of trees or foliage.'

Rex: 'Will anybody recognise that?'

Claudette (getting in on the act): 'It would look better if there were some leaves.' (It wouldn't of course.)

Rex's peach came just before we started when I explained that we would be lighting as we went – so if he felt underlit at any point, not to look for his light, since we'd be filling it in. At this point Claudette was all of four feet from him – we were all standing on the stage.

Rex: 'That's not the way I act. I don't look for lights. I act. I've never looked for a light in my life. That's Colbert's way of doing it. *I'm* an actor.'

It was searingly offensive. I don't know if Claudette heard: she gave no sign.

16 December 1978

Sunday: Sydney. Ten days ago *The Kingfisher* opened in NY. In the days before, I did no rehearsal, since the personalities and attitudes of the players – the stars, I suppose we should call them – made it impossible. Claudette [Colbert]'s back improved, so that she began adequately to play previews.

I never watched a preview through, since the frustrations of seeing that play inadequately performed, or rather turned into even more than a vehicle than it need to be, was too painful, and too boring. But I would see five minutes or so at the beginning, and maybe a smidgen later. I was able to ginger George Rose up a bit, who had settled into the habit of playing a Hawkins conspicuously older than Cecil, lacking edge both in involvement and speech. (Rather like Cecil's uncle, I incautiously remarked to Rex. But I had to give the impression I was still noticing things.) I did nothing about Rex, except urge him to *play* the thing, and resist the temptation or the tendency to turn it into a display of lines. And I did nothing about Claudette, except sympathise – her voice started to grow hoarse and disappear after the weekend. Probably, Elliott nastily remarked, because she'd spent all Sunday on the phone, organising her opening night tickets.

On the afternoon of my opening I went to see Henry Fonda in *The First Monday of October*.[1] The play a rather reach-me-down affair, with a lot of that clever writing the Americans manage well, but a fabricated plot and very contrived resolution. Jane Alexander[2] acting with awful glibness and complacency. Fonda as authoritative and charming as ever, playing the quirky Supreme Court elder, a mixture of the traditional and the eccentrically radical which suit him very well. But looking older, or perhaps just tired after a matinee at the end of the run. I went round to see him afterwards: he was warmly welcoming, knew who I was, and even that *The Kingfisher* was opening that evening . . . He rather floored me by asking if I thought the play would go in London. When I paused to reflect, he quickly said 'Don't try to answer on the spot.'

Henry is really rather odd: quite touchy when my humour gets too sharp or makes him feel patronised.

Of the 'opening' my sharpest memory is of the views down the staircase well from the top landing – to which I had beaten a rather ashamed, disgusted, estranged retreat – as the old, jewelled hands clawed their way up the stairs, clutching the banisters, to jostle with pathetic first-night 'excitement' at Claudette's, Rex's, George's dressing rooms . . . I cannot be sure if my absolute indifference – even repugnance – to the whole thing is really because of the quite remarkable collection of unpleasant and or uncaring people involved – the despicable business manager and the staring-eyed, obsessive company manager, the filthy theatre, William interested only in success, the slight play made trivial and worthless from any point of view except the making of money – or whether the whole business of theatre seems suddenly (or gradually) to have become stale, childish, false and insignificant. Certainly the great days are over.

The party afterwards continued the nightmare: it was made clear that it was for the 'backers' – who seemed to be a large collection of extraordinarily mediocre-looking people. I don't think any of the cast members had the grace to attend. I went on from

---

1. By Robert E. Lee.
2. American actress (1939–). She appears in *Kramer Versus Kramer*.

the party to the Rex–Marcia party, where Marcia urged me to sample her divine chocolate mousse . . . I *think* Rex hoped we would work together again . . . But I was suppressing the whole thing from my consciousness even as it happened.

I didn't spend my time in New York very profitably. I had lunch with Martin Scorsese in the middle of his auditions for the boxing picture he is making with [Robert] de Niro:[1] in attendance, de Niro and a rather too enthusiastic casting lady, who talked about Karel ('So wonderful' . . .'), and over-sold the cheesecake (made by Scorsese's mother) and the genuine Upper East Side salami and Italian bread brought in by one of the taxi-driver auditionees. Impression of vitality and egoism – Scorsese is not one to be much interested in events outside himself. Or at least not in anything *I* might be doing. He looked a great deal better than when I'd seen him before – the new girlfriend no doubt, whom he didn't mention, but I knew was the daughter of Rossellini and Bergman. He capped my allusions to Rex and Claudette, etc., with the knockout traumas he'd suffered from the adventure of Liza Minnelli's musical.[2]

De Niro a rather *glancing* presence, seeming incapable of direct communication or reception. I asked him how he had liked *Whose Life is it Anyway?* He hadn't much, nor did he admire Tom Conti's performance greatly, which he thought too quirkily charming, in a role that demanded something more violent. I told him he was right. I talked scornfully of BBC 'cultural' series – *Poldark* etc. – but neither Scorsese nor de Niro knew much about them, or were interested (the casting director loved them). I mentioned *The Deer Hunter* – which fortunately I hadn't seen. Congratulated de Niro on his British picture.[3] He appreciated the fact that I called Rex and Claudette 'performers' rather than actors. He had seen Celia [Johnson] in something in London and admired her – it took place in a drawing room, he thought, but he couldn't remember what it was called . . .

Scorsese was auditioning in his apartment on 57th Street in a new and very modish and obviously expensive block, hideously affluent in a showy way downstairs (the block has some Italian name). Predictably, the porter first thought I was auditioning, then asked if I was making a delivery.

I had dinner with Bob and Sally Benton. Bob's friendliness and indeed the enthusiasm and warmth of both of them absolutely amazes me – contrasting with and emphasising the self-absorption and heedlessness of almost everyone else I encounter in New York. So much of what seems to be affection or care is really only an extension of egoism. Perhaps indeed this is true of almost all relationships. We are only interested

---

1. Robert de Niro (1943–). His character in Scorsese's *Taxi Driver* (1976) was named Travis, after McDowell's character in *If* . . . .

2. *New York, New York* (1977).

3. By Michael Cimino, partly financed by EMI.

in, *like,* people insofar as they can fulfil a need of ours. Anyway, I am always astonished, and humbly delighted, by the warmth of Bob's appreciation and response.

23 December 1978
In London the idea of being in Australia for Christmas was appealing. In Sydney, such is our perversity, it seems, well, strange, with twinges of regret for fellowship foregone . . . I have rung no one since arriving just over two weeks ago! I've been content with work [on *The Bed Before Yesterday*] – with quite an energetic concentration – and in the evenings to have supper with Rachel, or to go out alone. Freddie, our producer, is irritating in his nervousness, gaucherie and determined pretentiousness: the cast [who include Wallas Eaton] are amiable, but hardly more.

We had our second run-through today: a vast improvement on the first, with Rachel in possession of the character, and on the way to a performance. She has been extremely nervous and worried about it – with reason, but at least it shows some healthy self-knowledge. She is not temperamentally right for it, of course, but then neither was she *right* for Mrs Hammond. Only here there is the additional barrier of *class.*

25 December 1978
I haven't called Jim Sharman, which is rude, I suppose . . . there is sort of over-insistence about his attitudes which I don't find sympathetic: over-assurance, you could say. And that lunch party was familiarly bourgeois in tone, a rather affected liberal-intelligentsia style – the humour monotonously camp . . . Perhaps I'll call this morning to wish him a happy Christmas.

Rachel and I certainly make an odd couple. She disappears 'to read the script'. Maybe that is what she is doing, in a very slow half-hour-to-a-page way . . . We probably share this disaffinity for other people – other, that is, than the handful of familiars. And we are both lazy . . . We pulled a couple of crackers, absurdly, and put on paper hats. Then Rachel cried off coming out to dinner: she wanted to dye her hair and read the script.

In the afternoon I went to the Australian Museum just up the road, and looked at the whales and sharks and the Aboriginal paintings, and the scenes of early geological periods with prehistoric animals set in their natural surroundings. I get flickers of creative thought – faint stirrings of conception (my idea of a world epic of inter-connecting stories) which perish quickly through lack of energy or encouragement . . . I strolled across the green to the Art Gallery, where I bought some more cards (my vice) and looked at some pictures: 'Sickert at the Music Hall' – 'Chaucer at the Court of Edward III' . . . Then coming back across the park I stood and watched and listened a short while to the crass speakers, shouting against systems, refugees, alien faiths . . . Always depressing in their demonstration of mindless passion, vehement logic, how easily men can rationalise their frustrations and prejudices into 'political' stances. Audiences mostly male – ugly and middle-aged . . . A voice called my name – it was Rachel, lying on the grass with her script. I went and sat by her.

The play received a cool reception and the proposed tour was cancelled. In November Anderson had signed a two-picture deal with Orion, which would see him revisit India and temporarily settle in Los Angeles. His first project was to be Empire, *a 'romantic adventure' set in nineteenth-century India.*

24 January 1979

It was late Monday night I arrived at Calcutta airport from Bangkok. The Air India functionaries adopting an air of superiority and patronage – perhaps a British inheritance? Anyway it all seemed absurdly, and wearisomely familiar when my passport was queried on arrival at Calcutta airport, and grave faces and fuss were made – because I had no visa . . . I was 'helped' by a voluble and seemingly knowledgeable member of the Air India staff who knew me (by repute), talked about [Satyajit] Ray and Mrinal Sen,[1] whom he said he knew, and gave me his number (wrong as it turned out).

A limp young travel agent was waiting outside – evidently engaged by Mr Mahaderan, the Warner representative – to meet me. We drove back into Calcutta, giving a lift to the Air India man, who chattered all the way about Kubrick, *If . . . .* , Ray, Sen, *Star Wars* and *Close Encounters*. I thought it best to humour him – though his advice had been wrong, and I never saw him again.

The Great Eastern Hotel, dank and shabby, has passed into government hands since I was last here (fourteen years ago!): it was shabby then, but with lingering style. Now cheap, seemingly dirty. Three coathangers in the cheap wardrobe, and one mothball on each shelf. One creased sheet of airmail notepaper in the writing case. But the fan worked and the water, which poured brown into the bath, was hot.

Subhas Chandra Bose.[2] Day began with breakfast in an ugly, down-at-heel, once modernistic-smart dining room, with bearers in creased whites (it is the total absence of starch which makes them look dirty) crawling around with orange juice and eggs . . . Walls pink, with 'thirties' barrel-columns emitting light halfway up: bar-area, dirty green walls and angular, red-painted, shelves . . . bearers looking sad and broken and old.

Outside I got nabbed by a shoeshine man – 'only one rupee' – who then produced 'spec-i-al powder' (which seemed to turn the shoes red) and asked hopefully for ten rupees . . . then five . . . then happy to get two. The sadly decrepit hotel guide, who wanted

---

1. Indian film-maker (1923–).
2. Independent India campaigner, fought against the British in the Second World War.

to take me to the Botanical Gardens . . . Everywhere dirt, dirt, and an unbelievable, absolutely spec-i-al kind of shabbiness. The buses looking like chipped and scratched nursery toys, to be thrown away tomorrow . . . The afternoon I spent with Mrinal Sen, voluble and obsessive and humorous and generous-spirited. We had a cup of tea at his flat, where I was met by his son – a bright intelligent young man, whose subjects were physics and computers – and who had seen *If . . . .* ten times. Mrinal is incessantly occupied by politics, though in an emotional rather than strictly rational way. A Marxist of the head, I'd say. He told me a couple of stories about my behaviour to Satyajit way back in '65 – mocking and challenging – which amused Mrinal, greatly of course – which made me shiver. Not that I'd intended to be nasty: just didn't realise the extent of the great man's pride and touchiness.

I called Satyajit, and we arranged to meet at 6.30: just time to get back to the hotel, rather exhausted, and have a bath . . . Satyajit came to my room and we talked, and after a time had a drink. He ordered a 'Thumbs Up' from Room Service – but there weren't any, so he had to make do with a cola. The bearer arrived clutching a bottle, without a glass: he had to wash out one of my used glasses in the bathroom, and after a time, at my suggestion, we went out to have something to eat.

Hard work. I had resolved to play it strictly his way – with no breaths of criticism – which wasn't particularly hard, even if it doesn't make for very lively conversation. But it's not only that with Satyajit: he is certainly arrogant, in a pompous and quite humour-less way ('Buñuel told me that *Pather Panchal* had "opened a window" for him . . .'). How he recut James Ivory's first film, *The Householder* – 'There was hardly a cut left the same' – and given advice and written the music for the second . . . etc., etc. But also he's walled up somehow, sufficient unto himself. And feeling threatened, unconsciously of course, by anything that might puncture his pride, show up his judgement or, worse, his taste as being a mite provincial, more than a mite middle-class. Myself, for instance. In much of this he reminds me of Karel – the almost visible aura of self-satisfaction, a certain touchiness that seems to betray, far inside and perhaps unacknowledged, a fundamental uncertainty. Both of them somehow contrive to suggest themselves film-makers of high repute and experience (which of course they are, Satyajit more so) – and that I am not really a film-maker at all. Which I sometimes feel I am not – but then, I think, I have surely achieved *something*! . . . To hear Satyajit lay down the law about location shooting or describe, with palpable complacency, how he seldom takes longer than two weeks to write a script ('After sometimes a long period of gestation, of course'), is somehow reminiscent of Karel making clear to me the mysteries of eco-nomics, how a professional film-maker should conduct himself.

Many of the restaurants were closed, so Satyajit and I ended up eating at The Blue Fox. One of those big, bare rooms, underlit yet cold: we had a candle to read the menu by, and across the floor, in a kind of murk, a band played from time to time and a singer performed a jazzy repetitive piece which made conversation harder – it was hard anyway, with me having to feed Satyajit tactfully, in order to keep going.

It's significant that names Satyajit mentions with respect usually turn out to be ones I would, in any other circumstances, groan at, or deride. Tom Luddy, that conceited Godard-freak who runs the programme at Berkeley; Thorold Dickinson, from whom Satyajit continues to receive cards at Christmas; his 'friend' Derek Malcolm[1] . . . Interesting too that the only signs of real animation were produced when Satyajit described with outrage the praise accorded by the British contingent of critics at Delhi to a South Indian mythological picture which was 'like a thousand others' and totally without merit. He urged me to read Orwell's *Burmese Days* – which of course immediately made me feel it would not appeal to me in the least as a film subject.

23 February 1979

I had an extraordinary trip from Kanpur to Delhi by train, when Indian Airways blandly announced that the plane on which I was booked was 'cancelled'. All the trains were full, of course, but a kindly Indian doctor managed to get me a seat on an Express leaving Kanpur at eleven that night . . . He didn't 'remain' himself, so I had to struggle through the Hindi-speaking hordes to get myself into a first-class sleeper that had no blankets and no lights – only a couple of bare electric wires that gave out terrifying sparks and crackles when I brushed against them. I thought it better to travel in the dark than to risk electrocution.

Then my trip from Delhi to Colombo, to visit Lester and Sumitra, turned into an extraordinary epic. It being quite impossible, apparently, to book from Madras to Colombo from Delhi – though you have to go Colombo via Madras *from* Delhi. I was forced to fly to Nepal by Royal Nepalese Airlines, spend the night at Kathmandu, and fly down from the shadow of Everest the next morning.

Of course India is a fantastic place, and could be a fantastic location. But I seriously wonder whether it wouldn't be absolute folly to try to shoot a picture there. I know people say it wouldn't be *my* responsibility to get the thing organised, but I would certainly be the one to suffer if they *didn't* get it organised.

I arrived back from Sri Lanka to a Britain paralysed by frost and snow and also by strikes from every quarter. Today, for instance, most of the ambulance service is on absolute strike – not even giving attention to emergencies – and an overall railway strike is promised for the near future. Britain hasn't very far to go before it reaches the general standard of India. My only advantage is that I can speak the language.

---

1. Film critic of the *Guardian*, who raised the international profile of the London Film Festival.

25 March 1979
Sunday afternoon, Beverly Hills: sunny by the pool . . . Malcolm has been lying out in the sun, trying in short spurts to get through *Dog Catcher*, which I have brought from London for him to read: Mary[1] has just returned from the airport, where she has seen her sister Nancy off back to Arkansas . . . Last night we had dinner at the beach with Marcia Nasatir [Producer], together with Bob Solo; at lunch Clive Donner and Jocelyn Rickards,[2] slow and sickly with her thyroid condition, came by and stayed till four or half past, and at 10.30 in the morning, together with Malcolm, Rachel and Gavin, I screened *The Old Crowd* cassette at ICM. To my relief, it looked good – even more ruthlessly allegorical than I had thought, and was well received – most encouragingly by the young ICM chap who came to let us in and work the viewer.

I have been here since Tuesday: I have no clear idea of what I am doing, and miserably little impulse. Certainly the atmosphere here is in no sense stimulating. I find it hard to summon up any real enthusiasm [for the Orion deal] or sense of purpose. I am only writing this, I suppose, in an attempt to get my thoughts together.

19 April 1979
Here I am in Beverly Hills, in Schuyler Road, just before midnight, and I have been here over a month . . . And I have taken a sleeping pill, because I feel exhausted. I can only put it down to the extraordinary, limbo-land quality of California. Malcolm has gone off to Vegas by the night plane: I spent the day at Burbank, saw *Shampoo*[3] and *The Hospital*,[4] disliked them both, and resented them all the more for their polish and gloss and expertise. The recognisable American film style of the moment, the camera too close to the actors, and performances of self-conscious self-absorption – the cult of personality.

Wednesday: in pursuit of a present had the sudden idea of the *O Lucky Man!* album. The way to Tower Records led through the Old World Restaurant. As I walked through, I noticed in a booth off to my left a short, grey-haired man of middle age: my brain registered something. I'm not sure what. When I returned he was still there, he rose, hailed me – it was Marek Piwowski, last met in Warsaw – when? – eighteen months ago . . . Typical absurdity . . . the irrepressibly talkative agent he was with gabbled about himself non-stop . . . asked if I had a play I wanted to film next year.

---

1. Mary Steenburgen, American actress who co-starred with McDowell in *Time After Time* (1979). They married in September 1980.
2. Costume Designer. Married to Clive Donner.
3. Warren Beatty and Julie Christie vehicle, directed by Hal Ashby.
4. Presumably Paddy Chayefsky's 1971 black comedy, with George C. Scott. David Sherwin and L.A. were at work on the script of *Britannia Hospital*.

23 April 1979

Salads with Brian Moore, who most intelligently explained why an Indian subject was not really feasible – because the end would be inevitably 'negative' – with brutality on both sides, and nothing accomplished except the cementing of British imperialist rule.

24 April 1979

In the evening Gavin [Lambert] came, picked me up and we went to a movie in Westwood – [Billy] Wilder's swansong, *Fedora* . . . a melodramatic extravaganza which is supposed to be a lament for old-style movie-making, but runs on the rocks of sheer preposterousness: a heroine who evidences insanity by writing 'long, rambling letters to Michael York'. Henry Fonda embarrassingly playing himself as President of the Academy.

25 April 1979

There's nothing down in my little book. Ah yes – I think in the morning we went to Burbank, and I called Michael Medwin – and had a reasonably long conversation. Malcolm and Mary back from Vegas. We went out for supper at the Rumanian restaurant near Paramount. Blessedly ordinary, decent and good.

26 April 1979

I modify Mike Medavoy's suggested terms: say $20,000 for the script; $20,000 for me during development; $10,000 for Michael [Medwin] during development . . . Commitment to go ahead or sell back the subject at extended treatment stage. Final cut and all approvals to me. 'A Lindsay Anderson film.'

To Burbank for a 10.30 meeting with Rudy Wurlitzer, author of *Zebulon* (a mountain-men script I read: a bit overwritten perhaps – but 'quality') and I'm interested to hear, *Pat Garrett and Billy the Kid*[1] – which Jon Voight sent me all those years ago, and I commented on in such intelligent detail . . . Wurlitzer, in his early thirties, is intelligent, voluble, and India is one of his passions. He had researched India from Madras to Kashmir for a movie he'd hoped to direct, but which had fallen through.

Drove back along the freeway, stopping off at a supermarket to buy wine . . . Pick up Marek Piwowski from the screening of his film[2] . . . Someone like him, in his position, brings suddenly home to one the close-knit provincialism of the place – the lack of interest in anyone or anything not sanctified by fashion or success. Marcia, however, showed herself to be the civilised, intelligently sensitive person she is, and spoke in an attentive and detailed way to Marek about his picture. I respected and was grateful to

---

1. Eventually made by Sam Peckinpah with James Coburn and Kris Kristofferson.
2. *Przepraszam, czy tu bija? (Foul Play?,* 1977).

her for it. Mike Kaplan dropped in. Barbara drove Marek back home, and returned to take me to Walter Hill's.[1]

The last event in a long day, and only the second private house – well, the third if we count Rachel and Darren's, and the fourth if we count Syb's – I've been entertained in in Hollywood on this visit . . . sorry *fifth*, with David Chasman's party for Maggie Smith . . . A pleasant, distinguished house in the Hollywood Hills – formerly home of Dennis Hopper . . . wood floors and plain walls . . . Walter Hill I had imagined as tall and perhaps gaunt and ascetic . . . I found him short and stocky with a beard, wearing a denim shirt and macho boots, rather aggressive and shy, with a smile of great and innocent charm when you can elicit it . . . We talked movies nearly all the time: most substantially about Ford, whom he admired in a pretty knowledgeable fashion. He described how he had met him when he was a Second Assistant on something at the Goldwyn studios (I think), where Ford was preparing something in the sixties – never made . . . The tall, bulky, irritable figure, and how he'd got a signed picture from him. We were drawn together in common discipleship.

8 May 1979

Well, yesterday Richard Gere invited me to go to *Evita* with him tonight, which I accepted: some compensation for the news that Treat Williams[2] is now in New York . . . So much for our warm friendship and his rare generosity. There was one phone call from him on Thursday, I called on Friday, left messages at his home and the studio, and never heard from him again.

Richard, whom I suppose I really should have looked up when I knew he was film-ing at Paramount, I bumped into (almost literally) when driving into the Chateau[3] garage last week. Behind me a large Land-Rover-type vehicle. From it emerged a young man in an un-chic blue suit whom I recognised as Richard. I went up behind him and muttered something in my 'American' accent, he swung round, prepared to be irrit-ated, recognised me, and we embraced . . . Happily I had invited him to the show of *The Old Crowd* on Thursday. It's curious: I like Richard, although there's so much that is mannered and self-conscious about his acting – *acting* acting . . . He's a good-looking fellow, of course, and with that vulnerable egotism that I always seem to find attractive. He is desperate to play Coriolanus, at least it makes a change from Hamlet!

I really seem to be touching bottom as far as Orion's 'development deal' is concerned. I mean nothing has any reality to me, and none of the scripts I've read touch anything deep in my imagination. The 'Indian Mutiny' subject has occasioned a succession of interviews. The only other subject that's caught my fancy has been [a remake of] *In a*

1. Director of Charles Bronson's *Hard Times*.

2. American actor (1952–). The charismatic lead in Milos Forman's film version of *Hair* (1979).

3. Chateau Marmont, the hotel on Sunset Boulevard.

Lonely Place;[1] and although I've said so, that is the one that hasn't been discussed. It would be an excellent subject for Jon Voight, and I would have suggested it to him, if he hadn't also disappeared into silence . . . I called him when I arrived, left a message, and he didn't call back. But this was a week or so before the Oscars,[2] and he made predictable excuses . . . I sent a postcard (of Churchill's statue in Parliament Square) wishing him luck . . . and an invitation to attend the New World premiere of *The Old Crowd* . . . No answer.

18 May 1979

Breakfast meeting at the Beverly Hills Hotel. I'm informed that Craig, some youthful executive from Paramount – who is Richard Gere's best friend – has got together with Jon Bradshaw and they have a new approach to the Baader-Meinhof material and Richard is mad to play Andreas Baader . . . When I got there Jan Bradshaw was already at a table, with someone called Emma Soames . . . English, would-be artsy 'liberal' upper-class, with all the English characteristics that drive me mad: assumption of superiority based on nothing but privileged social position; facetiousness instead of seriousness; essentially trivial and platitudinous response to every subject discussed. In this company Bradshaw also seems shallow and opportunistic. And foolish – why should this meeting, if it is to be in any way serious or professional, be attended by Emma Soames? (He is going to take her to Las Vegas).

Craig Baumgarten arrives, young, reasonably personable . . . conversational chat involves lengthy explanation by him of troubles with his car . . . It is I who broach the subject: otherwise the chatter – then about Britain, Mrs Thatcher, the *Daily Telegraph* – would go on forever. I take the bull by the horns: is the idea for a cast of American actors playing German characters? Where? In Germany? Some American actors? Real-life characters or invented characters? Or is it possible to invent an equivalent story in America, with American characters?

It becomes immediately clear that none of these possibilities have been really considered . . . ideas are stated which collapse immediately under the pressure of specific examination – to be replaced by others, equally flimsy, equally iridescent, equally insubstantial. Bradshaw (winging it) sees it as the territory of his *Esquire* article. Baumgarten comes up with the 'idea' that there should be some sort of prologue, perhaps factual, and that the dramatised story should start during the year's 'lay off' period of the gang – developing into the violent activity of the last burst of 'terrorism' . . . I stress my discomfort at the superimposition of an American cast on a German situation. Baumgarten says that Richard can speak German, or speak with an accent.

---

1. In 1950, Nicholas Ray filmed an adaptation of Dorothy B. Hughes's novel with Humphrey Bogart.
2. Voight had been nominated for *Coming Home*.

I try to sound them out on an American equivalent. Could such a story be imagined in an American context? 'It could easily,' says Bradshaw quickly. Baumgarten is not so sure. And anyway the American audience – they wouldn't accept it. Why not – because it isn't real, or because they wouldn't like the idea? Both . . . By the end of the conversation Craig Baumgarten has edged himself round to a you-guys position . . . 'Well it's a great subject – and if we –' ('we' is now Paramount) '– don't take it up, I'm sure you two could get a deal on it' . . . Bradshaw asked if anything needs to be written for Baumgarten to present to his Paramount colleagues – Baumgarten thinks not: our names – Anderson, Bradshaw, Gere – are enough . . . I say something must exist beyond Beverly Hills fantasy. Bradshaw grimaces his reluctance.

It occurs to me: Bradshaw is like Christopher Logue, but with more urbane pretensions, and tastes like drink and gambling . . . the same pretensions to knowledgeability – inside info mostly (or frequently) inaccurate. Jokes a bit off-centre. Essentially square, under the sophisticated assumptions. Snobby and success-oriented.

Baumgarten only really able to think in terms of packages. He had spoken to Richard yesterday. He's having a wonderful time at Cannes. He's met Fassbinder and Herzog is coming in at the weekend. He's going to do *Hamlet* with Zeffirelli – after Cannes he's going to stay two weeks with Zeffirelli at his villa . . . Shades of shades . . .

23 May 1979

Good Lord! I had a call about eight, from John Cohn in Cannes, saying that Barry Spikings had given the go-ahead on *Memorial Hospital* [by David Sherwin; this would become *Britannia Hospital*]. I didn't explode with joy – that being not my way (nor my ability) – but I did my best to work it up . . . What irony though! (I'd mentioned the idea to Barry in London – and he'd turned it down) . . . So a British director, with an idea for a film about Britain, approaching a British company [EMI], has to come to Beverly Hills to enlist the aid of the American representative of the company – in order to sell the idea.

24 May 1979

Big Day! – Yesterday, that is . . . 11 a.m. meeting with Mike Medavoy . . . since on Monday he hadn't read *In a Lonely Place* . . . and that meeting was chiefly devoted to discussion of my 'position' – 'I hear you've not been happy with the help you've been getting . . .' (Bigmouth Chesser). Bob Sherman (Mike Medavoy's co-head at Orion) puts in an appearance, all jokes and smiles. Comment on my longer hair: 'It looks great . . .' Mike in a chair, back to the window; Eric Pleskow and I on a sofa to his left; Marcia and Chris Chasser on a sofa to our left.

Usual banal and vexing start: 'Why do you want to make this picture?'

I force myself into an exposition of the story's narrative, suspenseful qualities; the excellence of the characterisation; a good thriller . . .

'Who are we rooting for?'

I am surprised – naively I suppose – but I do my best to play the game: talk about the kind of interest or fascination an audience must have with a melodrama, empathy rather than 'rooting for'. Are we exactly 'rooting for' anyone in *The Maltese Falcon*? Of course we have to share the character's suspense . . . I say, it's like watching someone cross Niagara on a high wire: he may be a murderer, we are still gripped by the possibility of his falling . . .

Mike: 'Would you start the picture in England?'

Self: 'Well maybe . . . I don't know . . . If we had flashbacks, I think they should be impressionistic – dramatic – emotional. They wouldn't involve much physical reconstruction.'

Mike: 'Do you want to keep the period?'

Self: 'I'm not absolutely sure – probably.'

Mike: 'That's expensive . . .'

Most of the discussion went on and on, round and round, the question of 'sympathy' – why should we care to what happens to him, when he murders all these innocent girls? (I forgot to mention *The Boston Strangler*). Amazingly, the question of casting, which is the one area where this kind of discussion would be legitimate, was never raised. And underneath the meeting I felt the presence, the pressure of larger issues, more oppressive preoccupations . . . Mike – was it my imagination? – seemed to be speaking with a tightening of fear in his throat. Not about *In a Lonely Place*, but from overall insecurity . . . Eric Pleskow not making his usual urbane jokes. The upshot: Mike asking Marcia about the rights . . . Eric will read the book – 'You'll enjoy it' I told him – but from no one an expression of enthusiasm.

We went to lunch at a Chinese deli: Ray Stark was eating with a girl. I remembered going to his house to be 'offered' *Robin and Marian*.[1]

I returned to the Chateau: dictated a couple of letters. Tony Kayden[2] came about 6.15 and we talked a little about the story: my feeling that Laurel must be back in Dix's apartment, in bed, when he comes back from killing the girl on the beach . . . The end of the story is certainly the weakest piece of construction . . .

Saw *Alien*, a technological tour de force: cold and really revolting.[3]

---

1. Filmed instead by Richard Lester with Sean Connery, Audrey Hepburn, Robert Shaw and Richard Harris.

2. L.A.'s first-choice screenwriter for *In a Lonely Place*. Rejected by Orion because he didn't ask for enough money!

3. Produced in London by Walter Hill in association with Gordon Carroll and David Giler. Ridley Scott directed.

25 May 1979

A mood of sombre depression. Signalling Marcia's phone call yesterday afternoon to say that Mike Medavoy had said he was prepared to go ahead with *In a Lonely Place*, provided the 'figures' were right – i.e. the cost of the subject, the writer's fee . . . (As usual, my heart, instead of leaping up, sinks . . .) Has the attitude of Mike and those about him contributed to my depression about *In a Lonely Place*? Of course if it were something I was as sure of as *If . . . .*, I would be unaffected. But it is no longer possible to be as sure of anything as I was on *If . . . .* because that confidence has gone. Amazing to think of the *esprit*, the sublime arrogance with which I went into those ventures. At home, of course, and with enough vitality around me to support my spirits.

Anthony Hopkins came about midday and we had a coffee then went to the Cock 'n' Bull – there's a room in the back which is not so deadly dark, and the buffet is fine. A whisky to Tony's Perrier – and then Perrier. Tony is the strangest mixture of intensity and simplicity, a naivety even, that enjoys very much a giggle and gossip. Strangely enough, this is a side of him I hadn't 'got' all those years back, when I remember him in *Caesar* as rather more moody and monumental. But we had an enjoyable, enlivening lunch: he says he has been working on Prospero and enjoying it more and taking more time, and we talked about John Dexter and his sadistic habits. I realise Tony, with his extreme, exposed sensitivity would be an ideal victim, as indeed he had been, and probably damagingly . . . We talked, with mutual recognition, about 'production' – working on material, moves, lines, thoughts, feelings all together – as opposed to getting the concept of the scene (as with 'teacher' directors) *distinct* from the moves or the placing. John Hersch, who did *The Tempest*, is clearly one of 'those'.

Anyway, we would like to work together. 'Do it properly,' as he says. 'No fuss.' I know what he means. How it changes the whole idea of work – that ardour – that unaffected commitment – that openness!

I drove to Burbank. Mike arrived. He talked reasonably sensibly about the subject for the first time – perhaps because we were *à deux*, and able to be informal . . . He's scared of it . . . wouldn't think of it if it wasn't me . . . The leading character – I told him it was clearly dependent on the actor – I mentioned Jon (who I said wouldn't do it) . . . A half-undressed girl walked across the studio's street – Mike made sensual, macho noises and sniffed the air like a randy hound. He asked me if I'd like to have dinner.

I gave Tony Hopkins David [Storey]'s play, *Phoenix*. And realised I've not even read this draft.

Letter to Ted Craig (extract)

25 May 1979

I don't think you should feel at all that you ever 'put your foot in it' as regards Rachel, or Rachel and Darren. In fact, I'm sure it was a temporary blessing that you arrived to

stay with them. The addition of a foreign body into that household always checks
Rachel when she is on a downward path, and at least for a bit makes her behave
better than she would otherwise. It doesn't last, of course – as you observed. After
you left, Rachel and I drifted into something she chose later to call an 'estrangement',
all fantasy of course on her part, which involved her in writing me a long letter of
explanation/complaint, which she finally came round to Schuyler Road and insisted
on *reading* to me . . . Since by that time the 'estrangement' was over as mysteriously
as it had begun, there was absolutely no point in this exercise except exhibitionism –
and to prove to me that she could write a good letter. (She also read me a couple
of pieces which she had been writing in Beverly Hills Public Library – she writes
quite well. In fact, if she ever could give it the concentration, she could probably
write very well.)

30 May 1979

I finally read Alex Cox's[1] script *Scousers*. And liked it very much. Over-dialogued and
written – too much insistence on *local* dialect and manner . . . But lively, shapely,
excellent sense of dialogue, character, incident. No end. Suddenly I think: why not do
it with Malcolm, Alan, Georgie Fame and Frank? The only problem is that one should
be black . . . I called Alex Cox (of course I should have done this weeks back). Enthusiastic – cocky – stimulating. *The Old Crowd* came up. Yes, why shouldn't he have a go
at it? Did I have a script? Why not look at the tape again . . .

I drove down to Venice. A crazy Dr Video in residence (John Hunt), who talked
complicated nonsense while a documentary played away on the jumbo screen – Blacks
in some idyllic jungle – while jazz played a bit too loudly. I broke away to let Cox in . . .
Shock-haired and buzzing comically-aggressively. We saw the piece. I was grateful for
his enthusiasm, but struck by how much he misunderstood – Oscar was a guerrilla?
Well, no matter . . . Ideas come – some good – some bad . . . He [Alex] likes the idea of
an intrusion . . . Do they *bury* Totty? Could be an extension of the 'Carry her to the
table' idea . . . Of course it's all too late: should have done it weeks ago: of course
Malcolm thought nothing much of the script. Nor Barbara . . . I said I would take
Scousers back to London. Definitely worth trying to advance. This was instead of going
to Long Beach with Mike.

31 May 1979

I picked up my phone, blinking a message from the night before – Jon Voight. I
laughed: how long has it taken him? Ten weeks? Then early I called Alex Cox. I talked
enthusiastically to him about *Scousers* – which I really enjoyed reading . . . these stories,

---

1. British film-maker (1954–). Made an impressive feature debut directing *Repo Man* (1984).

characters, themes ignite me, while American subjects remain theoretical . . . And I find Alex sparky and energetic. He says he's already started to make *Old Crowd* notes . . . I still haven't stopped the idea.

I called Jon and got Jamie, his son: I called MGM and got the horrible Kathleen, all honeyed superiority, though she did give me his number. I called his number and got the service.

Wound things up. Tony Hopkins brought back *Phoenix* – we'd talked a bit about it on the phone – he didn't respond, found it very bleak and bitter . . . really didn't enjoy reading it . . . knowing the play isn't really 'successful', I couldn't argue. First Tony seemed in a hurry, and refused a cup of coffee, but we soon tumbled into chat and before long were carried away on an impulsive tide of gossip, recollection and exchange of ideas . . . It is quite strange, to hear Tony talk, with vivid recollection, about probably the last time we met in London – which I remembered too, in the pub next to the Old Vic – he was with O'Toole and someone else, and he'd that day done his test for *Lion in Winter* – and O'Toole was saying, 'You'll just have to leave the Company – walk out – I did from Stratford . . . Do you want Oliver Reed to play the part?' In the end it was Bob Stephens who called Larry and persuaded him to release Tony.

I suppose I *did* stand for something in those days, also being intolerant and self-righteous and puritanical . . . None of it could be helped . . . The young actors had to go to the National, and it had to have the effect on them that it had. We talked a bit about *Terra Nova*:[1] strangely Tony has been approached to play it in New York, and maybe he will (if they raise the money) . . . He said he's seen it, and the second half was too long.

25 June 1979

An instinct of self-preservation drove me away from Beverly Hills, I think. I suddenly had the feeling that if I stayed any longer I would become part of the furniture, especially as far as Orion were concerned. Everything there seems so endlessly a matter of postponement – fixing a meeting for next week, which then gets put off until the week after – waiting for Mike Medavoy to read the book, which he has then passed on to his assistant, or sent to New York, or he has to go to New York, or Europe, and will be back in ten days . . . I stopped off in New York for a few days on the way back, and found to my surprise that the Californian lifestyle, and certainly its tempo, had rather spoiled me for the crowded, humid, generally bad-tempered, hyped-up tempo of New York. Perhaps part of the problem was that I was there the weekend of the Tonys – and was staying with some old friends who were emphatically a part of showbiz – Seymour Herscher has worked for years for Alex Cohen, and was up to his eyebrows in the

---

1. Play about Scott of the Antarctic by Ted Tally (1952 –), who would write *Silence of the Lambs* (1994).

struggle to save *I Remember Momma*, as well as the struggle to mount the Tony show. I think I really have outgrown all that hysterical nonsense, the huffing and puffing of the second rate and the pretence that any of it actually *matters*.

7 September 1979

At Stirling Mansions, 6.45 a.m. My review of *Public School*[1] for *Radio Times* is ready for typing . . . Two days ago I had an appointment to see Laurie Evans, prompted by the reappearance of *Early Days*[2] . . . Laurie Evans is on the phone to Ralph [Richardson] when I arrive, discussing the doggerel which Ralph is being invited to perform in a TV commercial for the *Sunday Times*, when it resumes publication.

Laurie gets out a gold or silver pencil and makes notes on a pad.

Well – what am I doing? . . . It's over six months since I went to Hollywood. What's happening? I start to explain the Orion situation – *In a Lonely Place*, etc. I am conscious that I have to speak loudly, that Laurie is rather deaf, and that he anyway isn't paying too much attention. I suggest he makes notes.

What is there? *Empire* [Indian Mutiny film]. Ted Tally's treatment has arrived. It is not very adequate. The siege section and the aftermath are extremely sketchy. Characters don't amount to much. Not too keen on Phillips pinning his medal onto a dead Indian at the end. Ted Tally's behaviour not exactly kindling. He had difficulties in getting to London – when he phoned he was unable to get the coin into the vandalised boxes at Brown's Hotel at least three times. He posted the treatment to me, didn't want to hear my reaction until he returned from the Lakes. He's soppy, no doubt about it.

The elusive Jaffe will be available from September 15th. Naturally I have had no response to my extended comments on Jim Harrison and his *Legends of the Fall*[3] which I sent as indicating a possible screenwriter.

Then there are *Memorial Hospital* and *Special Duties*. I tell him about *The Old Crowd*, to discuss which I have a date to see Jorn Donner[4] at London Airport tomorrow.

Oh! David Sherwin is writing – and I have been collaborating with him on a script . . . and I can tell him its title: *The Great Advertisement for Marriage* (not a flicker of amusement, in fact no expression of any kind crosses Laurie's face as he notes the title on his little white pad).

And Bob Solo would like to get a deal going on *Vile Bodies*.[5] Are there any others? I do remember to mention *Scousers* – and try to explain a little about it: but it is hard,

---

1. Documentary series filmed at Radley College.

2. Play by David Storey to star Richardson.

3. Anthony Hopkins starred in the 1994 film adapted from Harrison's novella.

4. Finnish film director, who had invited L.A. to make a feature version of *The Old Crowd* in Stockholm.

5. Charles Wood was writing the script, from the novel by Evelyn Waugh.

and discouraging, going. Really, Laurie feels that all these rather outlandish ideas are *not his business.* He wants film offers on recognisable projects which he can negotiate. It is an extremely limited conception of the job, and not much help to me. And of course *Early Days.*

We are reduced in the end to noting down the possibility of doing the play in December – rehearsing over Christmas and New Year and opening in January.

Letter to Derek Prouse (extract)

14 September 1979

I am really a *News of the World* chap, myself. I'm not sure how I found that copy of *The People* – I think I may have picked it up on the Underground. But of course the indispensible paper is the *Daily Telegraph.* All my liberal friends (*Guardian* readers, of course) raise their eyebrows when I mention the *Telegraph,* but really it is unrivalled in its witty and absurd relish of human folly. I hope you are following now the story of the army recruits who were made to hang lavatory seats round their necks, and take part in dummy executions, besides having their bottoms bitten by jovial NCOs. It's the real stuff of which Britain is made.

Letter to Rachel Roberts (extract)

21 September 1979

Of course all that Rex stuff is just fantasy. But not particularly extraordinary or unique, I'm afraid! Just the illusion of a stability or a support, which in the end you're going to have to find within yourself – I'm sorry, but that's the plain truth of it. And occupation is undoubtedly a help, however frustrating that occupation may be – and I don't mean the occupation of self-pity, of course. I don't like your cynical dismissive laugh when I mention your writing. Of course no doubt it's just a reaction against the over-inflation you gave it when you first started. But your writing is undoubtedly talented, and you have a real feeling for words and the expression of memories and feeling. You certainly have a great deal more talent in this direction than the majority of people who get books published. It's just a matter of sweat. God knows, I find writing terribly hard and disagreeable. You're lucky – you actually seem to enjoy it! You should keep a diary. (But not emotions please – facts!)

1 October 1979

I feel I should be dictating lots of letters. I can only manage one, to John Gielgud about the American 'acting text' of *What the Butler Saw* – a scandalously messed-about version, particularly at the end, where the descent of Sergeant Match and the final ascension of all the characters is omitted. (What was Peggy Ramsay doing to permit it?) I have already dictated letters to Alan Bennett, Jorn Donner and Ulla Ryche to accompany copies of *The Old Crowd* treatment . . . Is this really going to come to anything? Do I want it to? Is it the *right thing to do*? All my friends seem to think it is a folly. How difficult it is to get anyone to be honest. And how can I trust the enthusiasm of David Sherwin – Mike Kaplan – George Fenton?[1] I asked David Storey when I phoned him last: he could say nothing more concrete than that surrealism didn't seem to be the style best suited to my talent. But *is* it a folly?

3 October 1979

Woken at nine by Jocelyn's call. A dream: a performance at the Royal Court – or is that what it turned into? Something long and inconclusive and didactic. After it a meeting with bearded and otherwise grim-looking representatives – one looked like John Lennon. I was with Karel. They were horrible and scornful. After it Karel and I walked away. It's a good idea, he said – a film about a swimmer, Jean Taris.[2] I agreed, rather wondering if I was going to be asked to make it. 'It's already being done,' said Karel.

With his old agent and friend Sandy Lieberson now head of Twentieth Century Fox, Anderson spent a month in Hollywood during which he looked at new offers.

14 October 1979

The Beach at Malibu . . . Anthea Silbert is there, who is a vice-president in charge of production at Warner Bros: she speaks of the stimulus of intelligent, variously-minded colleagues like Jack Rosenberg (*Time After Time*): I say nothing about the great publicity dispute.[3] Frank [Grimes] and Cheryl frolic in the the big waves.

We walk down the beach – the richest piece of real estate in the country – a million dollars, a million dollars, a million dollars . . . Marcia shows me the directors' houses – to encourage me: Norman Jewison, Mark Rydell, William Wyler, Hal Ashby. All are blank-windowed, empty. I take Marcia's, Frank's, Cheryl's photograph outside Barbara Streisand's pretty house. Marcia says, won't I direct *The World's Oldest Living Bridesmaid*? Barbara will only do it with a world-eminent director – then we can all be rich . . . I feel as though all our lives are being built on sand.

As we are leaving, a tiny figure in bright yellow is walking escorted down the beach, a long way away. Merle Oberon. She is walking in the wrong direction.

---

1. Composer (1950–). Wrote the music for *The Old Crowd*.
2. Jean Vigo made a short film about Taris in 1931.
3. *Time after Time*, a love story starring Malcolm McDowell as H. G. Wells but advertised as a *Jack the Ripper* horror film.

15 October 1979

Sandy Lieberson at the Chateau. Sandy and I discuss his situation – he is leaving his post as head of Fox, which he has held for all of six weeks – and how they are quibbling over his release terms . . . how he took the job – he came out for conferences, got *caught* here by the resignations – liked the idea of the authority, and in addition, it enabled Laddy and Jay and Gareth to take another job . . . Then Alan Hirschfield is put over him – who doesn't like 'good pictures' (too much of a challenge?) so he resigned. How this affects Michael's development deal I can't be sure – but Sandy seems quite prepared to back *Report from the Sex Factory*,[1] up to treatment anyway – always bearing in mind the problems of an X certificate . . .

16 October 1979

9.30. Stanley Jaffe. Okay – what other writers? [for *In a Lonely Place*]. They mention Ernst Lehman. Good God, I say – what are his credits? Stanley fetches a typed list: *North by Northwest* – that's twenty years ago I say. Other credits – *The Sound of Music*, *Portnoy's Complaint*, *Hello, Dolly*! My heart *sinks*.

We got on somehow, I don't know why, to the subject of today's egotistical young stars: Al Pacino in *Bobby Deerfield* ('I don't feel like a Bobby'), and forty-five minutes late on set, and which side of the bed he's going to get out of; and Marlon Brando in *Apocalypse Now*, saying, 'Why do I have to be called Kurtz?' Not like the good old days of *Casablanca*, etc., etc.

When Steve McQueen was shooting *Papillon*, and they had a location a quarter-mile or so within the jungle – he refused to walk to it. 'I don't walk,' he said. They had to clear a road, cut down trees and bushes to clear a way for wheeled transport. Stanley blames the system – so do we all – the studios which give in and allow themselves to be blackmailed. Marcia throws in *The Missouri Breaks*. The days when Marlon Brando refused to emerge from his caravan, spent the whole day script-conferring with Arthur Penn. But UA wouldn't take action. They had a picture they thought, that was going to bring in $200,000,000. They should be sued for every cent lost.

17 October 1979

Invitation to *The Rose*[2] . . . packed audience – the overflow theatre. Oliver Stone[3] is in the same row – I am introduced, and later find Marcia has given him *In a Lonely Place*. The film is interminable – lush – pricey – overdominated by the star: lacklustre response. Crystallises everything that's wrong with Hollywood.

---

1. Written for L.A. by Ian Rakoff. The treatment was rejected.
2. Bette Midler stars as a singer on the road to ruin.
3. An Oscar-winner for his screenplay for Alan Parker's *Midnight Express* (1978).

19 October 1979

Evening. Dan Ford[1] joined us: he had a copy of *Pappy* for me: I am very proud to have my quote used on the back cover, thanks inside, and a marvellously warm inscription.

20 October 1979

With Ted Tally to Malibu. We have got to the end of the siege . . . I am unable to think of this work as anything but craftmanship. Ted really hasn't many ideas – he can respond reasonably and stimulate a bit, if only by his blankness. *Is* there a final battle?

Why can't Hossein save/kidnap Elizabeth from the river? Then what do they do in the forest? *I don't know.*

We decide that we must elude the final battle: the end is left unresolved. I have no ideas, and the more we talk, the less I believe in it.

We walk down the beach for a couple of miles. We pass Larry Hagman (Mary Martin's son) walking up the beach with his wife, in a red cloak, a cap with a propeller on it. He is a huge success in *Dallas*.

Marcia: 'They adore it down there'.

'They don't,' says Ted.

We drive back along Sunset. Ted likes me to wear a seat belt.

24 October 1979

3 p.m. Meeting with Stanley and Marcia. Oliver Stone not interested. Waldo Salt[2] also not available. Why don't *I* select a writer? I boggle a bit – finally Stanley says 'Who wrote *If . . . .*? I tell them David had paranoia the last time he worked in Hollywood[3] – N.B. This story is not thought as 'funny' here as in England – to which the rejoinder is – he can write in England. Marcia nods. I say I'll call him.

25 October 1979

Visit the set of *The Long Riders*. Cutting room – see sequence of hold-up – lunch – watch shooting. Dennis Quaid and James Whitmore[4] in prison-cage scene. Rehearsal was in morning: interesting that Walter [Hill] says nothing about performance to the actor after each take. They are about a million over – bad weather. Use multiple

---

1. John Ford's grandson, author of *Pappy: The Life of John Ford.* L.A.'s quote: 'John Ford was a great man (one of the few) whose personality matched his legend. Reading this book is like meeting the man again.'

2. American writer, wrote *Midnight Cowboy* and *Coming Home* (1978).

3. In 1974, when Jon Voight hired him to write a film about Robin Hood. It wasn't made.

4. Whom L.A. would use in *Glory! Glory!* (1989). Also in the cast was Harry Carey Jr., whom L.A. cast in *The Whales of August* (1987).

cameras. Ring Malcolm. Go to dinner with him and Mary at Le Petit Café. Malc gives me a copy of Tom Stoppard play, *Every Good Boy Deserves Favour* – which I must read.

26 October 1979

Phone David Sherwin, Alan Bennett in Yorkshire – no luck, George Fenton (to get Alan's address), Kathy [Burke, L.A.'s secretary], Jocelyn in NY. Read *The Silent Partner* by new white hope Curtis Hanson.[1] I'm not enormously impressed.

27 October 1979

Read *Every Good Boy Deserves Favour* by the pool: clever; not really very profound or uncomfortable. Stoppard's cleverness insulates from disturbance *I* think.

Drive to studio. Curtis Hanson turns up: a slight, somehow not very memorable, though personable fellow . . . Nor can I remember much of what Curtis Hanson said beyond that the climax should be achieved through Dix and Laurel's relationship – which I don't agree about (*In a Lonely Place*). No spark was ignited . . .

28 October 1979

Dan Ford came to pick me up – brought two files of Ford's documents – a golf score-card with Bogart (*Up the River*) – letter written to Mary on trip with Geo O'Brien – memos from Zanuck (*Tobacco Road*) – *How Green* (first casting ideas: Gene Tierney[2] as Angharad . . .)

We drive to marina north of Ventura – on the way up we stop and look at a surfing beach: Dan talks of his upbringing: sailing round the islands; Santa Cruz – the real California. He has sold his boat and regrets it. We talk about anti-Semitism and anti-Blacks among this community. Is there a boat here owned by a Black? There might be . . . Tomorrow Dan has to do the first interview of his plugging tour – at Palm Springs. He is plainly awfully nervous. We go to Santa Barbara (which is all of twenty miles) for fish and chips. Gets angry about nuclear power and the Fondas' absurdity.[3] Driving back down the freeway, as we are talking of Ben Johnson,[4] we pass one of the huge bill-boards in the valley, advertising B J homes and featuring the rugged, honest features of B J himself.

30 October 1979

To Venice, via the Holy Cross Cemetery – when we enquire for John Ford's grave they said 'What year?' Broderick [Miller, assistant] located it: ADMIRAL JOHN FORD – no sign of Mary; Francis nearby with his war record inscribed.

---

1. Later the writer-director of *LA Confidential* (1997) and *8 Mile* (2002).
2. Actress (1920–1991). Appeared in Ford's *Tobacco Road* (1941).
3. Jane Fonda had starred in *The China Syndrome* (1979), a film about nuclear power.
4. American actor (1919–1996), John Ford regular.

31 October 1979

Long, suppressed-hysterical phone call from Rachel in London, angry and distraught at the total indifference of the British press to her, John Schlesinger, Lisa Eichhorn[1] and YANKS.[2] Michael Parkinson wouldn't accept any of them – not important enough – thinking of going to Wales, getting an overdose and walking into the sea . . . I told her not to be silly: she should be grateful not to have to spend time talking about that silly film with a lot of boring journalists. But of course I praise her performance, which she laps up like MANNA. She has phoned Rex in Chicago between shows of *The Kingfisher* – and *read him* her story called 'Five Roses' – mutual affection – he is unhappy because things aren't going too well with Mercia. They love each other. The next day she calls again, at the suggestion of her lawyer. It's like Jekyll and Hyde.

Delighted at the advert for *Wild Times* – an old Paramount show – first time I've had star billing for three years. Above Cameron Mitchell and Dennis Hopper. To Fox: Sandy Lieberson: the office, panelled with faded maps of the world, *Encyclopedia Britannica*, belonged to Zanuck's legal man. Zanuck never talked deals. *Memorial Hospital* – £10,000 for script; £5,000 for development. No, £12,000 for script. DONE![3]

Evening: to relapse for a moment into self-pity . . . I feel lost, lonely, adrift, defeated in this place. And not just in this place, but in life. When I went to the studio this morning, I was ebullient, confident. It gave me a lift to meet Treat Williams again at the desk, and to feel the stimulus of his enthusiasm and readily expressed affection . . . Now it is eleven o'clock: I left a message for him – we were to have supper if he could get away – as I thought he could – from the gathering of exhibitors he had to attend this evening. But no call. I discovered when I got out of my car that I had lost my wallet. I drove back to the spot where I'd parked my car to get into Broderick's – on the way I bumped a car ahead: fortunately there seemed to be no damage.

1 November 1979

Early call – 6 a.m., from Darren Ramirez. A cry for help. Rachel symptoms of depression: drink; isolation; not caring for herself; obsession with Rex. Rachel interrupts. I tell her to go to the clinic – she goes to have her hair done . . . Who can help? I resolve to call Karel.

---

1. American actress, Gere's love interest in the film.
2. GIs in Yorkshire love story written by Colin Welland; directed by Schlesinger. Rachel Roberts won a BAFTA for her performance as a shopkeeper who gains a son (Richard Gere).
3. When Lieberson left, Fox abandoned the project. In Britain, the National Film Finance Corporation offered to contribute $1 million to the budget if another company put up the rest of the $3 million budget. The film eventually cost almost $5m.

3 November 1979

Morning call from Darren and Rachel – on her way to the clinic – Rex's 'fault'.

Drink with Treat Williams and Lisa Eichhorn.

Evening: Dinner with Malcolm and Mary – Mike Kaplan – Harry and Marilyn Carey.

4 November 1979

As I drive to the airport I see the green of the Holy Cross Cemetery away on our left; and the huge sculpture . . . En route to NY – *Monument Valley* lies in the sunshine to the left of the aircraft.

12

Britannia Hospital

Chariots of Fire – The Old Crowd Too
Rachel Roberts – Hamlet – Britannia Hospital

'The central heating engineers have been on strike at the brand new
Charing Cross Hospital protesting against the dismissal of two
of their number who had refused to change a valve (or something)
on the grounds that they would be crossing some demarcation line ...'

Letter to Malcolm McDowell (extract)

30 November 1979

Quite shortly after I got back, I caught the usual winter bug, and retired to bed for three or four days, given antibiotics, gargle, etc. by Martin, who continues to be chirpy, but distinctly fat. I have sent him a copy of John Calley's diet. Of course, I'm sure it wasn't the seasonal bug that drove me to bed, but the usual cultural, psychic, psychological jolt of getting back ... The block of splendid but old-fashioned flats on the opposite side of the road, which the builders started renovating before I left London, still stood (and stands) with gaping windows, and plastic weatherproofing flapping forlornly in the winter wind ... Occasionally a couple of workmen appear to select a plank from a huge pile down in the garden, and carry it slowly somewhere ... The central-heating engineers have been on strike at the brand new Charing Cross Hospital protesting against the dismissal of two of their number who had refused to change a valve (or something) on the grounds that they would be crossing some demarcation line ... Newspapers and television programmes have been having a fine old time with pictures of cancer patients, whose treatment has been halted by the strike, protesting to the pickets. (And being told to bugger off ...)

We have also had the Blunt Affair. Terrific excitement as the ex-spy was interviewed on television, and the English having a fine old self-righteous time with horror stories of the Spy In The Palace. In the end old Blunt seems to have come out of the affair with more dignity than anyone else – and certainly made Alec Guinness's performance in *Tinker, Tailor, Soldier, Spy*[1] seem pretty crude.

I have been finally worn down, or trapped, or however you like to put it – and will be doing David Storey's play, *Early Days*, with Ralph [Richardson] at the Cottesloe in the Spring . . . I won't go into the endless telephone calls, delays, excuses, etc., that were put up by the National. In the end I felt I *had* to do it – if only through guilt for both Ralph and David. I have given Alan Price a script, since I think it's going to need a lot of atmospheric music to get it through: Alan dropped in unexpectedly yesterday evening and stayed for five hours.

Jocelyn is back from New York – she was given a present of a pair of white roller-skates by her staff at the Met, and celebrated by going out into Central Park with her son Julian, and falling and breaking her arm.

The year finished with a festival of films by Marek Piwowski at the National Film Theatre. Anderson wrote the booklet to accompany the season.

Notebook extract (undated)
Programme One, a mixed bag of Piwowski's short and mid-length films – some of his best and most original work. *The Fly Catcher* takes its title from a low-life bar in Lodz, full of crooks, wrecks and layabouts; and *Fire! Fire!* mocks provincial smugness and inertia. The documentaries (in the old, creative sense, not like today's TV-journalistic impostures) should include *Psychodrama*, prized at Cracow and Oberhausen; *Corkscrew* about alcoholism; and *Aged Sixteen*, which I hope is the one about boys being examined for call-up. Sharp observation, wry humour, wicked satire on hypocrisy and provincialism. No wonder he was always in trouble. We are going to need film-makers like Piwowski when we're under Sapper, Scargill and Wedgwood Benn.

25 February 1980
We've had seven episodes now of Kevin Brownlow's 'Hollywood' series.[2] They are marvellously done, and absolutely spellbinding. The first time any series of TV programmes has made me adjust my life, so that I am at home, busy operating my video recorder every Tuesday evening. They are splendidly researched programmes, with wonderful material from silent pictures, and also a lot of riveting interviews from old-timers like Lillian Gish, Colleen Moore, Blanche Sweet, Paul Ivano (cameraman to

---

1. By John Le Carré.
2. Brownlow, editor of *The White Bus*, hired L.A. to narrate subsequent films about Buster Keaton and D. W. Griffith. The series inspired L.A. to make his own film tribute, *John Ford* (1992).

Stroheim), Henry King etc. What incredible vitality these old-timers still have! I was delighted to see such a charming and happy picture of Mary Astor in the *Life* magazine portfolio of stars of the past as they are today – riding a tricycle and looking quite radiant.

Letter to 'All concerned with The Old Crowd*'*

7 *March 1980*

You may have heard rumours from time to time that our celebrated venture *The Old Crowd* (which I believe is still spoken of with bated breath at London Weekend) might have a further lease of life – as a movie. These rumours have been true: but since everything in the world of cinema is so erratic and so problematical, I haven't wanted to say anything about it until I could say something for sure.

The truth has been as follows. A friend of mine, Jorn Donner, himself a film-maker and writer of European repute, was appointed Head of the Swedish Film Institute a couple of years ago. This is a remarkable organisation, extremely well funded by the Swedish government, and with a longstanding reputation as a film production unit, as well as an archive, film distributor and publisher. Their building in Stockholm has a well-appointed, decently sized studio in the basement, where they can produce their own pictures . . . Production plans are not absolutely finalised, but they will probably call for a shooting period of five or six weeks in Stockholm starting in or near the last week in July . . .

Naturally I'm anxious that everyone who made such a brilliant contribution to the original play should have the opportunity to contribute likewise to the film. So the purpose of this letter is first of all to give you the gratifying news, and then to ask you if *other things being equal* you would like to take part in the film . . . I think we've been offered a miraculous chance to do something remarkable.

Letter to Malcolm McDowell (extract)

17 *March 1980*

Just a line from beleaguered Britain to wonder how you are, and let you know how we're all doing over here . . . We're over halfway through the rehearsals for *Early Days* now. A strange enterprise. The 'play' is short – about eighty minutes playing; and I've put the word in inverted commas, because it isn't exactly a play at all – more like a dramatic monologue, or set of duologues, elegiac rather than really dramatic, with Ralph only off the scene for about four and a half minutes in the course of the whole thing, and almost everyone else reduced to one-liners, while he makes all the speeches. No one can accuse me of not accepting challenges. We started off with a big bump, Ralph arriving at rehearsals with his mind pretty well made up as to how he was going to play the part (all wrong, of course) and myself having to demonstrate disagreement and authority pretty damn quick. The result on the second day was Ralph to lose his temper, get extremely pettish, break off from rehearsal and grab his coat and hat and march out of the rehearsal room ... He returned about forty minutes later, having downed a couple of large Pernods in the Green Room.

(His initial approach to the part was cuddly and lovable, thinking he could get away with it by parading the same persona which had made him Britain's best-loved eccentric. Needless also to say, if he'd done any such thing, *he* might have got away with it, but the play would have been reduced to a potato crisp, and the whole thing would have been a disaster. He really has been dreadfully spoiled at the National – one can see why his performances are so bad, with everybody murmuring 'Magic!' as he bumbles around the stage, not really knowing what he's doing, while everyone swoons and chortles at his Ralphy mannerisms. Besides being a charming old thing, he is of course a wicked old thing. And the kind of actor whose intuitions are marvellous and whose ideas are terrible. You can imagine what his directions to the other actors are like – fortunately we've now reached a friendly understanding, and he doesn't really mind when I leap in and tell them not to take any notice.)

The National isn't exactly horrible to work in, but it's not much fun. Everything one thought it would be – hideously large, over-populated, impersonal and absolutely without creative warmth. Peter [Hall] has given up the idea of running it as an all-powerful panjandrum. He's given each of the three theatres to a different opportunist, so that he can sit back at the top, direct what productions he chooses – and take himself off to Broadway when he likes to earn fat fees from commercial transfers of his productions. There are some nice actors around, but nobody in the place seems to be interested or even aware of what is going on, apart from the bit of work they may happen to be engaged in.

Jill is at the Court – or will be shortly – where she is rehearsing Gertrude in a *Hamlet* they are putting on with Jonathan Pryce. She's not very thrilled about the whole thing, but believes in keeping working.

With his other Home *star, John Gielgud, playing alongside him as the Master of Trinity College, Cambridge, Anderson played the Master of Caius in Hugh Hudson's film of Colin Welland's* Chariots of Fire. *Later, Hudson took up Anderson's suggestion to add a narrative voice to the television version, to clarify aspects of the story, and to make it more accessible.*

Letter to Hugh Hudson

22 April 1980

Dear Hugh, I am sorry not to have written sooner: that was a great experience for me, and I do hope the results are satisfactory for you, too. Everyone was so extraordinarily friendly and helpful and it made the job so much easier than it might have been. I was delighted to get that telegram from you all on the first night at the National. I don't know why, but it really gives one a fillip to be remembered on those occasions.

Thank God it went really well, and Ralph was better on the text than he had ever been before. Of course it had to be the third performance last night, that Sir John elected to go and see, and during which Ralph suffered three tremendous dries and apparently had to be loudly prompted . . . I wasn't there, having taken my first night off to go and look at a friend's documentary (about stuffing a lion, taxidermically speaking) and advise him to bring it down to thirty minutes from nearly an hour!').

Letter to Gene Moskowitz (extract)

1 April 1980

I'm afraid I'm back in London after a fairly short, sharp visit to Hollywood, and a hectic week in New York . . . I undertook to work with the producer (Richard Roth) and the writer (Gore Vidal) on the *Dress Gray*[1] project to get the script nearer to something I felt we would be able to shoot. Since I had a producer here working to finance the project I've been trying to get going in Britain for the last couple of years, it was agreed that if *this* project achieved financing before the end of March, I would leave *Dress Gray* to do it.

Two things happened. It became apparent that Gore Vidal and I are not blood brothers: in other words, that in my judgement his script *Dress Gray* is thinly characterised and superficially imagined. If I had been going to continue with the project, we would have to have found another writer. And second, and the next-to-last minute, EMI came up with the financing of *Britannia Hospital* – the third and undoubtedly last instalment of my satirical commentary on our times. So I left Hollywood with some relief, since I could see myself being caught in the characteristic contemporary situation of a picture with a Deal, but without a satisfactory script.

I wasn't really surprised about Vidal. Of course he's a very intelligent fellow and in many ways well equipped as a writer. But essentially an essayist and a political commentator – and even in those fields his stuff is vitiated by his irresistible need to be smarter than everybody else, more knowing and of superior intelligence. (In fact his sophistication covers over a considerable naivety.) He thinks like a journalist: he certainly isn't a creative writer, and he has no feeling for character at all, and very little sensitivity towards his fellow-humans.

---

1. A film about a homosexual murder at the West Point military academy. 'Another problem with Gore Vidal is presented by his sexual obessiveness. Although West Point might seem to be a good subject for him in relation to his background, the homosexual element in the story is more dangerous. *Dress Gray* most emphatically should not be a story about homosexuality, and there is a great danger that if the balance of issues in the story is not skillfully maintained, the film might turn out to be something of a sensational mess. Gore fancies himself to be a very sophisticated cynic. I take myself to be a sceptical idealist.' (From Letter to Martin Baum, 28 January 1981)

2 May 1980

Things here continue to fall apart. Today there's a siege in the (London) Iranian Embassy, with a policeman and assorted civilians held captive by a group of Iranian dissidents who are threatening to blow the whole place up at midday. And last week poor old Lord Home was attacked by skinheads in Piccadilly underground and given a nasty jostling. We have no Tube trains after nine o'clock on Friday and Saturday nights because the underground staff are striking in protest against drivers and passengers being beaten up at Neasden and other such exciting places, and inadequate protection being provided by the police.

Letter to 'All concerned with The Old Crowd*'*

30 May 1980

This is a hard letter for me to write, and a sad one. Briefly: *The Old Crowd* film production plans have been cancelled, in a way that I can only describe as disgraceful, by the Swedish Film Institute . . . Only a couple of weeks back it suddenly became apparent that behind-the-scenes difficulties were being encountered. There were murmurs, for the first time, about 'financial problems', and a possible need to reduce the very ample schedule which had been drawn up by the Institute production manager. I flew to Stockholm, had a meeting with Jorn Donner and the production manager, and it was agreed that we would reduce the budget as far as possible and I accepted a shorter schedule. I even also accepted the large set of a late nineteenth-century house which is at the moment standing in the Institute's studio – and which would have suited *The Old Crowd* amazingly well . . .

Alan and I were told that we had to finish the script by a certain date in order that it could be translated into Swedish and presented to certain funding committees. We finished the script by the date required, it was accepted enthusiastically – but, as I only found out two weeks ago, it was *not* (for some reason I am absolutely unable to discover) submitted to the relevant committee, and so the necessary grants were never sanctioned. Now I am told that even with the severely reduced schedule and budget, there would still not be sufficient finance available for the production of the picture this year.

Letter to Harry Carey Jr (extract)

6 June 1980

The Old Man continues to cast his long shadow . . . I've very nearly completed work on my compilation – which I'm calling *About John Ford* – have only got to do a concluding chapter (the most difficult of course) and select pictures. I've had incredible difficulties trying to get pictures from Fox – for whom, of course, Jack worked almost continuously in the twenties, mostly in the thirties and for some of his greatest movies in the forties . . .

My production of the David Storey play, *Early Days*, opened at the National Theatre with Ralph Richardson . . . very successfully apart from two or three nasty notices, which made it clear how many enemies I've made by continuing to be bloody-minded and outspoken. (They don't like this kind of thing in England, you know, particularly when one is old enough to know better). We would have had a transfer into the West End, except that it was revealed that the old bugger (I mean Sir Ralph) had gone behind the backs of all of us and signed a contract to appear in a big-budgeted piece of rubbish [*Dragonslayer*] which Paramount are making at Pinewood – one of the 'Magic' pictures which are apparently the new cycle, with Ralph presumably slotted in as the equivalent of Alec Guinness in *Star Wars* . . . Of course he wants to do the play again when he's free of his film, so everyone is running around in circles to find out if and how the production can be got together again in three month's time. Well, that's the price we pay for dependency on stars, I suppose.

23 June 1980
We closed *Early Days* last Saturday – a bit sad in many ways, for the actors in support of Ralph and for David particularly. The old boy came up with a crackingly good performance on Friday night, and a very decent one on the Saturday – I think he's just about got the measure of the part!

In March 1980, on the night before she was due to start rehearsal for her role in Clive Donner's film Charlie Chan and the Dragon Queen, *Rachel Roberts took an overdose of antidepressants. She recovered sufficiently to complete the film and to take up an offer of lodging at Anderson's flat.*

17 July 1980
Yesterday, Thursday, was fraught. Rachel had decided that she would take part in a BBC television programme at Cardiff, interviewing and being interviewed by the man who has recently broken Francis Chichester's record for a solo voyage round the world. Shakey in her red dressing gown, she made an appointment to have her hair done – in Lower Sloane Street. She returned in a bad way: agitation had reached her under the hairdryer, she couldn't remain still, anxiety became intense, the agony of being among 'normal' people, 'normally' occupied in the world . . . While she was out, fortunately, I had a call from Cardiff: the Musicians' Union were picketing the studio, protesting against the disbandment of five BBC orchestras, and the inclusion on the programme of a Welsh male voice choir: the programme was cancelled. Mercifully.

New pills had arrived in the morning from Dr Colin Bell: Rachel took a couple more than prescribed: her agitation increased. We called Bell and he agrees that she should be seeing a doctor in London. He called back with the news that he has made an appointment with a psychiatrist for next Wednesday . . .

I had arranged – taking advantage of Rachel's absence in Cardiff – to go with Frank to *Hitchhiker's Guide to the Galaxy*, which has been adapted to the theatre and directed by Ken Campbell at the Rainbow. We can't go, of course. Frank alarms and offends me by a peculiar refusal to respond with any evident sympathy to Rachel's situation. He makes me so angry I find myself saying – 'And you'll talk yourself out of *Hamlet* if you're not careful . . .' We are both shocked by our inability to communicate as friends. David Vaughan, who is here until August 10th, returns and we watch *That's Entertainment!* numbers on my video. Frank goes. After eleven Dr Gerald Woolfson calls to see Rachel. He gives her sedation pills and two 'bombers' if she needs an extra one in the middle of the night . . .

18 July 1980

I resume work on the last section of *About John Ford* . . . and finish it . . . When Kathy comes, she types it out. We celebrate: I have a bourbon and she has a lager. It is finished.

Woolfson's drugs have really knocked Rachel out. Maybe it is also exhaustion after yesterday . . . She remains in bed until I run a bath for her about 2.30: our appointment is for 3.45 in Harley Street.

We go to Harley Street and sit in a traditional Harley Street dining room under a faintly glowing chandelier. I read *The Tatler* and reflect on its horrible, trendy, superficiality. I am called in after Rachel has been with Gerald Woolfson for about twenty minutes. He says she must be hospitalised. They talk about money. Rachel doesn't want to go. He says she must, and her view of reality is dictated by her mental illness – Depression is a mental illness . . . Rachel does not improve her case, of course, by continually talking of suicide and how many barbiturates she will need.

We return home, Rachel crying, in a taxi. I get her prescription made up by the chemist in Fairfax Road. A call from Gerald Woolfson announces that he has got Rachel a bed at the Royal Free. I am to take her there in an hour, or an hour and a half. (Betsy has rang: her usual sprightly, bright, tone. It is Karel's birthday celebration tomorrow. The film [*The French Lieutenant's Woman*] is going well – 'she' i.e. Meryl Streep, is wonderful. Big deal.)

Poor Rachel, condemned, packs her bag. Actually she packs David Vaughan's new suitcase by mistake. Never mind: I'll bring it back . . . We set off in yet another Belsize mini. The Royal Free is Britannia Hospital. Unconcerned functionaries operate behind the desk in an Accident Reception which is quite empty. A form has to be filled up. We are shown through, down antiseptic, cubicled corridors to a small, bare waiting room, glaringly lit. The doctor is busy: we must wait. After twenty minutes or so a dishevelled young man wanders in, with bare feet and a nightgown: he lights a cigarette in a twisted fashion. Rachel asks for a glass of milk. A willing little nurse or orderly brings her milk in a horrid polystyrene mug. Can she lie down? A willing nurse wheels a bed into a cubicle with sinister fitments on the wall. Rachel cannot lie there. We return to the waiting room. I decide to telephone Greenways, where Mr Woolfson had booked Rachel in the night before, and we cancelled this morning. I go to admissions. Have they a phone book?

'It depends what letter you want?'

'G.'

He goes to look.

'No.'

I try the porter's booth along the corridor. No books. Finally, upstairs I find one at another reception counter. A polite girl: 'Would you mind using it here . . .'

I ring the nursing home; yes, there are rooms. 'But it's too late for admission this evening . . . Do you know our terms?'

I return to Rachel, hoping against hope that the doctor will have materialised. She has not. We decide to leave. We tell the nurse as we do so – and I realise we should have exercised this threat before. She'll call the doctor . . . No, it's too late. We catch a taxi outside and return to Stirling Mansions. 'Let's go to the Cosmo and forget about it,' says Rachel. But she makes herself a tomato sandwich, drinks some milk, takes four of the antidepressants (as prescribed) *and* a bomber – and collapses into bed.

26 July 1980

So Rachel went into the Royal Free a week ago . . . We actually went in, as prearranged on the phone, at 2.30, but it still took the doctor half an hour to appear: young Dr Wilkins, who seemed pleasant and sympathetic, particularly when he revealed that he had Welsh blood . . . His attitude to Woolfon's prescribing was cautiously respectful – though he said the drugs weren't all that powerful and would take about ten days to produce an effect. (After three days Rachel was taken off them altogether: perhaps at the behest of the mysterious 'consultant' – whom she has seen *once* in a sort of conference session with Dr Wilkins.)

There is no discipline in the Nicol Ward, and one isn't sure whether this is on principle, through lack of means, or just self-deceiving slackness. So yesterday Rachel didn't see the doctor because she was out – there being apparently no schedule. She arrived pale and in a state of subdued desperation, convinced once again that she must NEVER TAKE A GLASS. The day before, the day I didn't visit, she went off the rails. She drank a glass or two, had a Devonshire cream tea and talked a great deal about Rex. She went out with another patient, the American wife of a British MP trying to get off drugs, and had another glass of wine, then a double ...

Yesterday she decided YET AGAIN that she must forswear alcohol altogether. She went to an AA meeting at lunchtime, which was dramatically disturbed by a drunken girl, violent with a bottle of whisky. She seems to have spent the afternoon discussing 'alcoholic thought' with a man who attended the meeting: then returned to the Royal Free on a 24 bus – arriving here in a state of particular perturbation because she thought she had left the large notebook in which she'd been working on the bus ... We phoned with difficulty, the Nicol Ward and finally got a nurse to look for the missing notebook in Rachel's room. It was not there. We got a minicab, to go if necessary to the 24 bus stop, stopping at the Hospital. The notebook was there. We drove to the National Theatre. Apple juice with our plates at the wine bar. Then to sit through Athol Fugard's *A Lesson from Aloes*,[1] which I liked about as much as I thought I would – maybe a little more ... Athol 'tackles' the African situation, yet always seems to obscure the issues by making them seem more complex (more 'interesting') than they really are, or need to be.

As we walked away from the Cottesloe, along the riverside, we passed a little group, a young woman with a child in a pushcart, a form (man? woman?) collapsed on the pavement, two ambulance men administering aid, an ambulance drawn up on the kerb.

'I see things like this wherever I go,' says Rachel.

'Yes, dear: they organise them especially for you.'

Letter to Darren Ramirez (*extract*)

6 August 1980

My dear Darren, I have several times been on the verge of writing, to let you know how things stand – but, to tell the truth, I've not been sure exactly *what* to write, and while Rachel has been staying here, I haven't had much time to write either (as I'm sure you'll understand).

When she arrived here from Warsaw, she was in very, very bad shape. Probably no worse than when she left Los Angeles – and certainly no worse than you will have seen her many times – so I needn't describe her condition in too much detail. The victim of severe depression, and in such a condition of neurotic anxiety that she could hardly walk out of the front door without trembling ... It has been a really difficult time. I am quite sure that Rachel is in fairly deep trouble, but I must admit to becoming doubtful whether any of these well-intentioned 'professionals' will be able

---

1. Fugard had offered Roberts the role of Gladys early in 1980 when she was lecturing at the Yale Drama School.

to do much about it. I am sceptical of psychiatry, and no one seems to have come up with any idea of a controlling drug treatment. So perhaps that was a red herring. Part of Rachel can be so sensitive and sensible and straight; and part of her seems to be absolutely compulsively devious, ego-centred and dedicated to fantasy. Drink hasn't been a great problem over the past month: a bit of backsliding, but nothing really very serious. That is what is so sad. Rachel at times can make a real effort and then one feels that she will recover her balance. But nothing is sustained: every time she sabotages herself, and I'm under no illusion that my influence can be deeper or more lasting than anyone else's.

There has been a certain amount of telephone contact with Rex – I'm never quite sure how much of what I'm told is true – or how much of the whole truth I am told. But I haven't taken any calls from Rex here – nor has she made any calls to him while she has been here. She asserts that Rex has told her that he and Mercia are splitting up. I have absolutely no way of knowing whether this is true, or how true it is . . . I wish I could be more cheerful in this letter, Darren. There have been times when Rachel has really shown improvement – and the capacity to live normally and productively.

Letter from Rachel Roberts

2 October 1980

Dearest Lindsay, The time really has come now, however clumsily I might put it, to tell you how really remarkable have been your dogged and determined and endlessly long-suffering efforts to put me right. I've kept and treasured your letters, not forgotten a word of the 'Lectures' (!) – been behoven to you for taking me to Gloucester, the Royal Free, Shrublands Clinic, here – O God Linds, you could not have done more. I know you don't want thanks, and thanks are not enough anyway, what you want is for me to get well and prove it. It seems to have been failure after failure after failure – and sometimes when I feel I'm even beyond your reach it really does seem immediately hopeless. Why I cried my way through Sunday was not anger that you should have felt it necessary to say that you 'do feel more and more strongly that there is very little one can do for her', but because it reaffirmed my own dread . . . and I don't know what else to do about the fucking hateful malaise that's taken my appetite for life away.

It all happened years ago as we both know – all the living out of expensive suit-cases and the impossibility of building a structured life.

For a moment at Frank's talking about Gertrude [in *Hamlet*] I felt like me again. I've leaned on you in lieu of a family Linds. We both know that too.

Leaving here I dread. Call it self-pity; call it cold reality – I don't know – but I listen with a shrinking courage to most of the others talking about their new attempts at a sober life with the wife and the kids, or the husband, or as in my Scottish Laird's case – his castle and his mother – when they all leave here. There will be 'emotional support' as they term it, and friendly surroundings. Is this self-pity Linds? I dread the return to LA.

In the Clinic, at least one woke up to lectures on tape, discussion groups, other people, the odd film on alcoholism, and a bit of croquet on the lawn before supper. There is isolation, loneliness and I am afraid. I need not go on about LA. You know it.

Lindsay, if I am writing without cause, forgive me. If I'm whining with cause, forgive me too. I'm still crying out for help and so deperately want my life to revert to some form of normality. It has been so unnatural for so long. I want to be Gertrude. I don't want to die. I don't want compassion and love to be so locked up inside me that I'll degenerate even further into the sick introspective negative non-giver I'm becoming.

Forgive me Lindsay, I didn't mean to repeat the litany. I meant only to thank you from the bottom of my soul for your love and care and kindness and strength.

All love to you

Rachel

3 October 1980

I find it extraordinarily difficult to remember my dreams. Coming into a pub – Lois[1] talking with someone – tells me I have left my camera again; the woman behind the bar has it; I rescue it . . . Before this was some kind of a film-dream. At the end of the film Alexander Knox is in the back of an army truck. He makes a speech with greater sensitivity and excitement than I have thought him capable of. I think it is Richard Harris beside me, shining a torch on his face. It is night. (Perhaps this is affected by seeing sequences of *A Canterbury Tale*[2] last night).

4 October 1980

Another dream fragment . . . escaping? Being searched for? . . . on a river boat, travelling up the Bristol Channel in sunny September weather . . . on the map I see that Cheltenham is some miles away to the right. I am taking photographs: will we be able to see Cheltenham? A friendly late middle-aged lady is on board: I ask her as I switch from looking through my long-focus lens at the wooded scene on the opposite shore.

(*Last night:* with a heavy-duty Rachel, Jocelyn and Jill to *Juno and the Paycock* at the Aldwych.)

---

1. Lois Sutcliffe, who commissioned L.A.'s first documentary films.
2. 1944 film, written, produced and directed by Michael Powell and Emeric Pressburger.

6 October 1980

Anxiety dreams after another devouring Rachel-day, and Frank reading the closet scene with Rachel . . . Taking part in filming – though as an actor – there is a scene which involves throwing oneself inside some sort of sewer-drain, a cylindrical tunnel running down the side of a hill into a river. It seems a long way down, but I see it isn't really. All rather macho – I feel scared. John Huston is directing – he throws himself in, amid much laughter. Then a section obviously influenced by watching newsreel of the Conservative Party Conference. Mrs Thatcher is being solicitous to some elderly lower-class lady. Then I am part of a little group of academics. Shadowy, incoherent images of surveying the college . . . safety?

9 October 1980

Dreams – or my recollections – all too fragmentary to make much sense of . . . A film is being shot, amid much laughter, of *Rebecca*: Jill [Bennett] is playing – it seems to be Rebecca, but she is also the innocent young heroine . . . and Anna Massey is Mrs Danvers (as indeed she was in the recent TV version) . . . They are chasing down a long stone corridor, out into the open air, giggling wildly.

Rachel Roberts committed suicide on 26 November. On hearing the news, Anderson phoned Jill Bennett. They met at the Waldorf Hotel and drowned their sorrows.

30 December 1980

4 a.m. Last night I made the decision – to agree to *Hamlet* at Stratford East, to start rehearsing April 13th and to open in the week of May 18th . . . to stick with *Britannia Hospital*, or rather to gamble on Clive Parsons's[1] ability to set it up, and to (seemingly inevitably) say goodbye to yet another Hollywood flirtation – *Dress Grey*.

Wisdom or folly? Courage or cowardice? I haven't the slightest idea. I've always known that I haven't the talent to plan or order a career – a life for that matter. I can see all round every question far too clearly. From one angle *Dress Grey* (*Gray* rather) would be a revitalising, challenging, freshly creative experience. From another it would be an evasion, a running away, a rash committal of myself into the hands of ruthless aliens – however seemingly friendly . . . From one angle *Britannia Hospital* is the logical, courageous development of my own style, my own thoughts and feelings. From another it is a stubborn repetition of ideas which have already proved unpopular, unwelcome, unacceptable to all except an increasingly shrinking minority.

And *Hamlet*? Of course I am doing it 'for' Frank. Yet even that is misleading. After all, I have backed Frank – not just through personal liking or attachment, but because

---

1. In charge of production at EMI, with Michael Deeley.

his quality of sensibility, of moral imagination, of emotion, is one that corresponds to my own. Who else could I do *Hamlet* with?

But do I *really* want to do *Hamlet*? Ah . . . but do I *really* want to do anything?

If Treat Williams had answered my card about *Dress Gray*, and answered it enthusiastically – would my attitude, my decision have been different?

7.15 a.m. The phone rings and I wake, drowsy from my lack of sleep in the middle of the night. My agent, Martin Baum, has spent a busy day. Bob Sherman has revealed that Albert Finney has specified *my* engagement to supervise his looping on *Wolfen*; which would mean going out to LA at the end of this week to see the picture with him next Monday and do the work next week . . . What did I think I should be paid? A standard fee, thought Martin Baum, would be $25,000 – up to $50,000, which would be exceptional . . . My mind blurry and feeling I was trapped in fantasy – abhorring the idea of *another* flight to LA, intrigued at the thought of getting away, greedy for money, flattered and revolted . . . Enmeshed even deeper in ambiguity and indecision . . . I said $30,000.

'I fall upon the thorns of life. I bleed.'

28 February 1981

Yesterday: I woke, as usual, early: 6 a.m. I couldn't do my exercises because I had left my bathing trunks over at Margot's the day before. I made some calls by the pool in the sun.

Letter to Malcolm McDowell

12 April 1981

Dear Malcolm, Someone said that the shooting on *Cat People*[1] has been delayed. So I don't know whether you're still in Hollywood or on location. I saw *Tess*[2] the other evening, and was very impressed by Nastassia [Kinski, McDowell's co-star in *Cat People*]. It's a peculiar film, very beautiful – a serious, intelligent and deeply committed work. Impressive in the end. Yet muted and somehow academic, with too much emphasis on style for my taste. The structural (and character) failures of the book are duplicated – without being redeemed by passion and poetry. But Nastassia's performance is an extraordinary tour de force, managing the language with amazing skill – yet, of course, one always pays for that consciousness of language and accent. Rosemary Martin (she was in *Life Class* and *Early Days*) played Tess's mother. I went to the premiere with her, and of course we ended up having to have supper with the producers.

---

1. Written and directed by Paul Schrader, who wrote *Taxi Driver* and *Raging Bull*.
2. Adaptation of Thomas Hardy's novel directed by Roman Polanski.

A modest affair. Not like *my* premiere, in the Presence of Her Gracious Majesty, the Queen Mother . . . When I say 'my', of course I'm referring to *Chariots of Fire* and my double act with John Gielgud. I went to the show, largely out of courtesy to Hugh Hudson who directed it, but I wasn't invited into the presentation line-up, so missed the chance of being presented to Her Majesty, together with twenty-four executives of Twentieth Century Fox, David Puttnam, Hugh Hudson, Sylvia (Emmanuelle) Kristel, Jenny Agutter and John Gielgud. It really was an incredibly and embarrass-ingly suburban affair, all too sadly characteristic of *Britannia Hospital* . . . They put on a compilation for the Big Picture, introduced by Robert Powell and Petula Clark, of previous Royal Command Performances. I suppose they thought it a happy idea to confront the Queen Mother, the moment the lights went down, with images of her dead husband and assorted now-dead film stars. A morbid kind of jollity which only the English could have thought appropriate. I've no idea what I'm like in the picture. When my first sequence arrived, I closed my eyes. Later I peeked through half-closed lids. All I can say is, I didn't seem to be much worse than Gielgud. (I don't know what he thought. He dashed for the exit at the end of the picture, having told us – Jill and me – that he had booked a bacon-and-egg supper for himself at the Garrick). The picture itself is lush, over-photographed for my taste – David Watkin in his usual pictorial form – and directed with that concentration on image that is the mark of directors who've been formed in directing commercials. Hugh is a really nice chap: but not much sense of narrative or performance.

Talking of directors formed by commercials. When I got back I had a call from Leon Clore, drawing my attention to the fact that John Schlesinger and I had both been most sneeringly insulted by Alan Parker in a BBC *Omnibus* programme on TV commercial-making. Really rather astonishing. Parker, who obviously labours under all those stupid and tiresome class resentments, had talked about the making of TV commercials before *he* and his expert mates came on the scene: ' . . . people like John Schlesinger and Lindsay Anderson, who ran around pretending to be directors, and saying things like "Turn over," and "One more time darling," then ran off home, counting their fivers.' I was furious – and instructed my lawyers to demand immediate retraction and compensation. John has done the same. We're asking for apologies in the *Radio Times* and a thousand pounds each for a charity of our choice. (I am nominating the Theatre Royal, Stratford East. A canny move, don't you think?).

The *Hamlet* casting, to which I returned, has proved incredibly protracted and hard. No doubt about it, telly and the big subsidised companies are really squeezing out this kind of dissident activity, especially if one has to maintain really high stan-dards. And professionalism is an outdated concept. Agents and actors now seem to have absolutely no hesitation in going back on an agreement if they're offered something more lucrative or otherwise enticing after they've committed. However,

I think I've got a nice cast whom it should generally be a pleasure to work with. We start tomorrow – *Hamlet* in four weeks! You can imagine what I'm feeling like today, so I won't go into it.

Yes, things are really crowding now. *Britannia Hospital* is set to start shooting at the beginning of August. I went down to Rustington with David [Sherwin] last weekend to work on the script revisions. More lunacy, which I can leave to your imagination. It's really rather sad. I think his brain must have been permanently softened by Guinness and barley wine, so that about the only function he can perform is to goad me into fury at his idiotic suggestions and his inability to put more than ten words together in as many minutes. The script has, I think, a splendid conception, some excellent invention, a few holes and dialogue that could be improved . . . Recognise the pattern? Listen, Malcolm: you must let me know if there is really the possibility that you may be able to play in it – it's not a great central role, but it has some good, outrageous stuff, and you do end up as a transplant monster, clamping your teeth into Graham Crowden's hand and having your head pulled off in the ensuing mêlée. Please let me know if there's any likelihood of your being able to be free August/ September. I should think your stuff would take three to four weeks. You know the picture – the whole experience – wouldn't be the same without you. Please say 'Yes' and I'll send you a script immediately.

Mirek won't be around, though. By chance I saw him briefly in New York. He had arrived to start work with George Roy Hill on [*The World According to*] *Garp*.[1] Moaning as usual – and I must admit that I felt myself becoming a bit impatient with him. After all he doesn't have to take these pictures . . . We talked about the possibility of him being free for August – but of course he won't be – and even if he were, he wouldn't have any time for preparation. I'm afraid that sadly we just have to admit that the tides of life have bourn us apart.

Saw Milos in New York – and even sat for half an hour in the cutting room while he was labouring at a scene.[2] (Mary came in briefly at the end of it, looking beautiful).

I had a late supper one evening with Frank and Treat Williams. Treat is a really nice, impulsively generous fellow. He took Frank and me for a trip in his plane round night-time Manhattan Island. An incredible, somehow touching sight. I wonder why. All that energy, survival-struggle, creativity and corruption magically transformed into light, defying the darkness. We passed so close to the [World] Trade Center building that we could see the diners innocently enjoying themselves in the restaurant. And in the late twentieth century, it's impossible not to see the whole great heart of the city as vulnerable, exposed to attack . . .

---

1. Adaptation of the John Irving novel, starring Robin Williams and Jessica Tandy.
2. *Ragtime*, starring James Cagney.

Anderson's production of Hamlet, *designed by Jocelyn Herbert, opened at the Stratford East on 15 May. On 10 August, filming started on* Britannia Hospital, *the third film in the Mick Travis trilogy which began with* If . . . . *and* O Lucky Man! *It continued through to 14 November, with a cast that included Malcolm McDowell, Graham Crowden, Jill Bennett, Leonard Rossiter, Joan Plowright, Robin Askwith, Vivian Pickles, Brian Pettifer, Dandy Nichols, Brian Glover, Arthur Lowe in his last film role, and a cameo from Alan Bates. It is a portrait of England as told through the events that unfold at a National Health hospital, floundering in the stranglehold of trade unions, on the day the Queen Mother arrives to mark the five-hundredth anniversary of the hospital's foundation. The highlight of HRH's visit, and the climax of the film, is the unveiling of mad Professor Millar's masterpiece, 'The Man of the Future', a living brain called Genesis.*

14 September 1981

BRITANNIA HOSPITAL MEMORANDUM

Now that we have a second opportunity to design and shoot 'Genesis' for the end of the picture, I thought a few observations might be useful.

I think we are all agreed that the present version of 'Genesis' is not completely satisfactory. However, I did find it suggestive in certain ways I had not expected. The Brain presents itself rather like the archetypal mushroom cloud, hovering over a city. There is an implication of fatality about this, which is quite appropriate. But we have to be careful that the metaphor does not become too literal, and above all it is necessary that the conception should seem an organic whole.

At the moment, the two elements – the Brain and its Electronic Support – are completely separate. There is really no sense that the Brain is dependent on the Electronic Base for life and for power. The insertion of the speechbox *into* the Brain seems to me confusing. It is certainly necessary that the speech should have some kind of localised origin, but it would seem more logical that this should be among or connected with the electronic rather than the 'fleshy' part of the construction. How are the 'electronics' to be connected with the 'Brain'? Is it simply a question of wiring (possibly incandescent) or should there be tubing, whether of glass or of plastic, carrying liquid or whatever . . . ? Is the *flat* electronic base – which emphasises the separation from the Brain – correct?

It would seem that 'Genesis' at this stage is very much an initial attempt by Professor Millar, who himself says that it will be out-of-date in a few years. Presumably this is why it represents an uneasy combination of a 'fleshy' brain area, powered by an *electronic* power-unit. However, we must still feel some unity about the whole thing, representing the new kind of dehumanised 'person', liberated from all claptrap of 'morality' and imagination, able to operate on pure Intelligence. The Brain itself seems still too firm, too rigid in outline. As a result, it doesn't seem *alive*. (Nor, perhaps, sufficiently disturbing, or even repulsive.) What we have got is still nearer to the lampshade than to the jellyfish. Can we find some more suggestive substance out of which to mould the Brain?

There needs, I think, to be a strange, difficult combination between 'mystery' and scientific precision about this creation of 'Genesis'. For this reason, I think we must consider very carefully whether it should *rise* to reveal the construction, or whether it should gradually become *translucent*, so revealing a precise construction in a mysterious way. I know that Mike [Fash, the cinematographer] favours the rise of the Pyramid, giving an opportunity for the revelation of 'Genesis' in a shaft of light. But I am not at all sure that a more *gradual* revelation may not be more effective – more dramatic, and less mercilessly demanding.

Obviously the lighting of 'Genesis' is (almost) as important as its design – or rather it is impossible to discuss its design without taking into account the eventual impression given by light. For this reason, I think it is very important we should discuss the next stage together, so that we are all agreed about what it is exactly we are aiming at.

The actual introduction of 'Genesis' will, of course, also involve Professor Millar, though no one else, and only the stage of the lecture hall. My impression was anyway that the last couple of paragraphs of Millar's speech were less successful than the main body of the speech, which I thought Graham Crowden performed brilliantly . . . It will be necessary to introduce 'Genesis' with a wider shot than the close-ups with which we ended our shooting – so that Millar can cross the stage in front of it, the camera (probably) remaining on the glowing Pyramid. This will enable us to cut back to Millar in close-up, then back to the Pyramid for 'Genesis' appearing or materialising on its own in the best way we can decide.

Letter to Christopher Isherwood (extract)

14 September 1981

I have thought of you often during the months since I was in California – strenuous, eventful and sometimes agonising months – and the agony is not yet over . . . I mean I'm in the middle (at least I hope it's the middle) of shooting *Britannia Hospital,* another foolhardy attempt to hold the mirror up to the English visage, and there to show such black and grained spots . . . With laughter too, but of that mocking kind which the English don't really like too much. The conception, which seemed to everyone to be a jolly, modest romp, has grown and grown into another attempt at epic satire – I just don't seem to be able to restrain myself in that area, although I know perfectly well that it's the hardest thing to bring off artistically, and never very popular, however well one manages to do it. Human beings have never, it seems to me, enjoyed being reminded of their idiocy, and the English are so touchy and so vulnerable in these days of decline that they react against it more fiercely than ever. (Particularly, of course, our old enemies, the Liberal bourgeoisie!)

Frank and I did our *Hamlet* down at Stratford East – *Hamlet* on a rubbish-tip, as Frank called it, not inappropriately. Since the palmy days of Joan Littlewood and her Theatre Workshop, the place has fallen into ill-organised and poverty-stricken mediocrity, still clinging to an absurd idea of 'popular' theatre, with a characteristic staff of cheerful but culturally totally blank cockneys.

Britain lurches on. Reality was swept under the red carpet for a bit in good old English style for the extraordinary fandango of the Royal Wedding. Or not a fandango, but that extraordinary dance, whose name I forget, in *Alice in Wonderland*. Which is exactly what this place now is. I hope I can reflect some of it in the film.

From here Santa Monica seems a sort of paradise of civilisation. Darren has been through London a couple of times. He deposited a bulky package with me, not large but heavy for its size. Yes – Rachel's ashes . . . I am supposed to hold on to them, until they are collected by her sister to be scattered into the sea off the Welsh coast – to which poor Rachel specifically demanded that she should *not* be returned. Not *Alice in Wonderland* but the darker absurdities of Joe Orton. What can we do but laugh?

1981 (*undated*)

I had threatening signs of weakness while shooting *Britannia Hospital*, but it [my back] never went spasmodic, thank God, and by sleeping on the floor, and carrying a stick (it can look quite impressive and certainly helps when one is directing a crowd) I managed to get through all right. One of the extras gave me some pills which he swore by. I can't remember their name – though they're quite well known – and their most noticable effect seems to be to turn one's urine blue.

Letter to David Storey (*extract*)

28 October 1981

I had the wild fantasy that when the private patients are ejected from the Hospital, we should have a glimpse of John, Ralph and Larry amongst the humiliated aristos. They nearly did it, but of course, Larry and Ralph ratted in the end. I will tell you the circumstances one day: they will amuse but not surprise you.

Letter to Malcolm McDowell (*extract*)

27 November 1981

It was hugely encouraging that you responded to what you saw of *Britannia Hospital*. As you can imagine, it's been a tremendous effort – it was made to seem a long, long shoot, largely as a result of the daily and protracted anxiety about time, schedule, expense etc. Also, as you know, the whole affair was very poorly organised, with a production department which was never able to get us on to sets that were ready for shooting, never able to provide any alternative weather cover, etc. Do you know that *every location* was found by Richard Tombleson,[1] against whose employment at first there was, of course, considerable resistance.

Ted [Craig] proved very valuable in the end, and did a splendid job casting the actors who spearheaded the crowd. We'd never have been able to manage the crowd scenes if we'd only had extras, so I got Ted to go through all the letters I'd received from struggling young actors over the last two or three years, audition them and come up with a little company of twenty-two who, together with the three splendid pickets from the beginning, led all the demonstrations and attacks. A dozen of them also appear in the kitchens – an excellent piece of doubling which I don't think anyone will notice. Not that I care if they do!

1 January 1982

New Year's Day – but we worked, having taken an extra day off on Christmas weekend: put in a different take of Barbara switching the lights on – trimmed Millar's 'Laser Needle' scene – rejigged Potter[2] and Biles[3] coming out into the Petticoat-flag – rejigged the arrival of ambulances – and ground to a halt round the Ngami's assassination.[4] Drank a bottle of champagne . . . Recorded a lot of 2001 and left *Man of Marble*[5] recording while I collapsed into bed.

———

With post-production work on Britannia Hospital *nearing an end, Anderson received an unexpected invitation to have lunch with the Queen. He described the occasion in a letter to Gavin Lambert (3 January 1982):*

It really was an extraordinary experience – extraordinary in its absolute ordinariness. All the falsely unassuming charm of the English Establishment, masking an arrogance just as stiff as the most extravagant European aristocratic *hauteur*. The Queen's modest, smiling welcome making not the slightest effort to conceal the fact that she hadn't the slightest idea who one was – and didn't care . . . In attendance, interestingly, was the Queen's Aide, one Phillip Moore . . . Captain of the College XV

---

1. Who played the 'Fat Boy' in *If* . . . .
2. The Hospital Administrator, played by Leonard Rossiter.
3. His assistant, played by Brian Pettifer, who played the same character in *If* . . . .
4. The presence in a 'private' ward of President Ngami, an African dictator, with full entourage of wives and servants, prompts a violent demonstration outside (and then inside) Britannia Hospital.
5. Film by Andrzej Wajda.

when my brother was also in the team . . . One of those stockily built, light-toed, eternally grinning Englishmen. When I reminded him of our common roots, the smile in no way lessened, but his eyes flickered to a distant corner of the room and he danced instantly away. I saw and heard no more from him. I suppose *If . . . .* has branded me forever a traitor in his mind. I left the Palace extremely glad to have made *Britannia Hospital.*

4 January 1982

6.28 a.m. Waking early, which is too much my habit nowadays unless I take a pill – which I don't like doing if I'm working – I think I really ought to leap out of bed and do some work on that Preface to *Britannia Hospital* I have *almost* promised myself to write, but David failed to deliver his specimen pages,[1] and my left leg aches a bit and I am fat again . . . I seem to have become the receptacle for people's woes, which is very fatiguing – quite apart from the sheer effort of finishing *Britannia Hospital*, there is the heavy prospect of trying to see it properly publicised and launched. Since that meeting with the agency, *nothing* has been proposed or submitted. Only an idiotic, mediocre, cover-up call from an agency director assuring me that they are giving it 'top priority' . . . *Meet Me in St Louis* [on TV]. I cried.

Worked all day on the Sammy–Red climax:[2] no, I think we must have started with the Tour, tightening, losing link shots . . . or was that before Christmas? Anyway by the end of the day the demises of Sammy and Red were hugely improved – all Frank's stuff on the top of the van, excellent crowd, etc. . . . Dennis produced a couple of bottles of red wine at lunchtime, his black (dark) eyes sparkling naughtily.

To dinner with Graham [Crowden] and Phyllida in their charming Mill Hill cottage. Sara their daughter looks eccentrically like Graham, and is gauche, lively and charming. The guests were Ben Travers's grandson Andrew and his wife: Andrew is a TV director and seems to have his grandfather's unaffected good taste and general judgement. I was my usual caustic, predictable and tiresome self.

7 January 1982

In spite of the rail strike – or go-slow – the Slough train took off practically on time at 9.31. At the station, Alan Price was waiting in his low-slung car. We drove to the cottage at Farnham, behind high walls, in a grassy garden. I feared it would be cold, but it wasn't too bad. Jill [Townsend] greeted me – and her little boy, Luke, now at a boarding school nearby, came in delicately. I suspect spoiled. She took him off to play with a

---

1. Additional 'news' dialogue was needed because the BBC and ITV networks both refused to release news footage of the 1981 terrorist bombings and inner-city riots.
2. The characters in a van, this time played by Frank Grimes and Mark Hamill. Reporter Mick Travis beams them pictures of Millar's atrocities, but they are too stoned to do anything about it.

school-friend. Alan and I went into his small chock-a-block 'studio', where he had the time-coded tape of the film. He played his melody of what he thought was the intro to 'Rule Britannia', though in fact it was the preceding piece on a record of 'Last Night of the Proms' – possibly 'Hail the Conquering Hero' – an idea which took some dislodging. Alan's idea, I soon realised, was to conceive and execute, then and there, the entire score on his synthesiser . . . once again, it was a question of 'What do you want here?' We did a good deal of work: 'Rule Britannia' over the whole Dying Man sequence was incredibly eloquent I thought. Also some good abstract sounds – drumming – and horror-sci-fi for Jill's death.[1]

8 January 1982

Into town for a farcical viewing of the film: Barry Spikings, flanked by a plumping, surly, subservient Bob Mercer, and an on-his-dignity Johas Kohn, and a quiet, amiable mouse in charge of foreign distribution. Barry, bronzed and smiling as ever . . . and David Sherwin. A great *Britannia* occasion: the soundtrack played, the picture didn't start . . . After long waits we were told we could project without the automatic changeovers – nonsense, said Barry – half an hour later, when the engineer could not be found, I said, 'For God's sake, let's see it with bad changeovers.' (This was also when an alternative booking at Columbia/Warner had to be scrubbed because the projectionist hadn't turned up) . . . So I climbed out of my boots and into my slippers again, to find that the projectionist now said the projector could in no way be started without risk to the fingers . . . Finally a booking was found at Coronet down the street, so boots on again and we stumble through snowy Wardour Street . . . A small theatre with a large screen. The film unrolled without a glimmer of response from anyone. To me it seemed scrappy, without form or grasp, unfunny, obvious, pretentious and ineffective. Awful. Afterwards, back in Barry's office, he at least prevented a too-destructive discussion by remarking cheerily – 'Well, it's really just a matter of nips and tucks, isn't it?'

17 February 1982

Worked for about four hours with Derek Wadsworth, on the 'music' which he and Alan had worked on so exhaustively yesterday – the idea that anything takes hard, sustained work strikes these people as extraordinary . . . I bash away without great confidence . . . Derek takes the attitude, 'I'm only assigned to arrange Alan's music.' But I cling to the thought that Alan usually *has*, amazingly, pulled the cat out of the bag . . . Sped back to the flat, where two BBC producers, David and Bob, are waiting to discuss Alan [Bennett]'s George Orwell programme. As usual, they want to try to fit Alan to the design of the programme – which he can't possibly do.

---

1. Jill Bennett's character in the film. She is killed by Mick Travis's reanimated and decapitated corpse.

Letter to Michael Medwin (extract)

15 March 1982

Quite unexpectedly, I had a call from Jay Cocks[1] on Friday . . . He asked if we could meet, said he had a couple of tickets for a play on Saturday evening, and could I join him? The play was *Another Country*. And, of course, I couldn't resist.

I was delighted to see the theatre was packed. The audience enjoyed the play very much and gave it a fine reception. I think it is exactly the kind of thing that will appeal hugely to the English middle-class audience. I absolutely agree about the talent of Rupert Everett. He has great, intelligent, witty skill, knows how to play the audience without ever – well, hardly ever – sacrificing the character for effect.

He really didn't show off at all, and it would have been very easy to do so, since the audience were only too happy to be eating out of his hand. The other boy, Kenneth Branagh, held his own well, too, though I wish he had been helped to play with more emotional and intellectual conviction, instead of being allowed (encouraged?) to act continually in a peppery, shouty style, which of course enabled the audience to laugh every time he used a word like 'bourgeoisie'.

There's a great deal in the play that's interesting and subjective. I only wish Julian Mitchell had a richer talent. He does write effectively for the West End audience, but he seems to me to hammer away at his thesis until it is weak and very thin. And the preoccupation with schoolboy homosexuality, though a good crowd-pleaser, got a bit monotonous.

2 April 1982

The picture moves steadily towards completion. The show with the cutting copy and the dubbed track really did go rather well. Both the Head of Distribution and the booking manager for the ABC circuit said: 'We don't like it, but it's going to make a lot of money.' I'm sure this feeling was enormously helped by the fact that we packed a good few 'human beings' into the show . . . Michael Medwin almost disgraced himself by laughing so loudly and continually. Some good horrified reactions when Malcolm's head came off.

2 April 1982

Ipswich to London in a very bad temper . . . It's partly of course because *Britannia Hospital* has continued to raise so many problems, to be so messed around and mis-handled all round. If only, I think so often, I could be like Tony Richardson, detach myself ruthlessly, not attempt to goad second-rate bullshitters into flair and effective-ness and commitment. The whole publicity and advertising and press relations side of the operation is an incompetently-handled mess – presented with the usual pretentious

---

1. Screenwriter. Ex-film reviewer for *Time* magazine.

bullshit by agency hacks – equally defensive and complacent, without the capacity to devise or execute anything original. I am infuriated by the bullshit, the pretence and by the knowledge that there's no one here with the professionalism or the concern to see through the mask of breezy competence – except myself.

A further reason for tension is that it becomes clear to me that the film is going to be badly received, sneered at, begrudged and dismissed. Once again, I realise, my idea of the 'popular' film which can also carry a charge of poetry and ideas, is going to be proved illusory. The moment of truth came after that 'magazine and multi-media' showing at BAFTA ten days ago, on Thursday 21st. A dull spiritless atmosphere, awful theatre, with sound too loud at the front and too low at the back, no compactness, like a lecture hall, reception rooms badly lit, without warmth. I had expressed doubt about the composition of the audience, which we had managed to get a lot of. Graham Crowden arrived during the show, and was met with friendly indifference. After the show, the usual desultory, unenthused reaction. Jocelyn and Julian were there, and though Jocelyn didn't waver in her enthusiasm, she didn't greatly help by insisting that the voice of Genesis was incomprehensible, and mistakenly treated.

12 May 1982

Well, now it's finished, and in about ten days time [*Britannia Hospital*] will be unveiled to the world at Cannes. If, that is, Britain doesn't suffer some appalling reverses in the South Atlantic. That destroyer which the Argies put out of action last week almost did it for us. London Transport refused to accept the poster, chiefly because it featured a headless, naked man, waving a Union Jack. (They also objected to the amount of white paper there was left blank on the poster: an invitation, or a temptation, to the graffiti merchants.) Signs of the times. EMI began to wobble – it doesn't take much – and to consider whether the picture should be withdrawn. How are the mighty fallen! The English have lost their nerve all right.

The film premiered in Cannes, in competition, on 19 May. The British delegation stormed out of the cinema shouting abuse at the screen. 'Success!' notes David Sherwin in his memoir Going Mad in Hollywood. *'We've achieved what we set out to do so blindly two years ago. An assault on Thatcher's Britain that hurts.'*

8 July 1982

Fiji – Honolulu – Los Angeles. In Hawaii, at the airport, I saw and bought a *Blade Runner* souvenir magazine: Ridley Scott, director, and Michael Deeley,[1] producer, both

---

1. Who produced *The White Bus*.

from Britain. A $20,000,000 budget (is that all?) . . . of course a technical, stylistic bravura that I could never hope to compete with, whatever my budget . . . Is there any way that a film directed by me could compete with a movie like this in the American market? So what price *Britannia Hospital*? Our limited Los Angeles experience (let alone Cannes and Britain) has made certain things clear to me – wit, satire, ambivalence: these must militate against popular success. Then further: those who take the cinema 'seriously' i.e. read and write criticism, run festivals and institutes, lecture on and pursue Film Studies – these must, almost by definition, be 'bourgeois'. That is, not primary producers, but living off other men's labour. They have a stake in the way things are. Once a considerable portion of the bourgeoisie believed in other political solutions.

Letter to Malcolm McDowell (*extract*)

3 September 1982

I'm sorry not to have been in touch sooner. I've been back in London – how long? – about three or four weeks . . . Time is rather featureless at the moment. I'm sure you'll understand when I say it's a dispiriting place to return to. The dark waters have closed over *Britannia Hospital*. I wonder if, on dark stormy nights – as in the old Cornish legend – the warning chime from its clock tower can be heard, tolling faintly beneath the waves? . . . You know how it is when people prefer not to talk about a 'failure'. And anyway, a lot of people 'didn't manage to see it'. Well, it was around for only four or five weeks. My spirits were quite lifted the other morning when I had a telephone call from Paris, from someone who wanted to discuss the dubbing of the film into French. 'Oh,' I said surprised. 'They're going to make a French version too, are they?' 'Mais naturellement,' said the chap, surprised. 'C'est un tres grand film . . .' Makes a change!

———————

More people saw Britannia Hospital *in the first two weeks of its run in Paris than in the whole of Britain. In October, supported by a glowing notice in* The Times, Britannia Hospital *returned to one West End cinema for two weeks only.*

13

Reworking

The Cherry Orchard – Joan Plowright – 'If (2) . . . .'

'I'm sorry you missed Princess Margaret in *The Archers*.
I have it on tape, not awfully well recorded I'm afraid, but you can
recognise those unbelievably plummy royal accents. What a country!'

---

*In 1954, Ralph Richardson and Celia Johnson starred in a film version of Wynyard
Browne's* The Holly and the Ivy, *a tale of secrets unfolding when an ageing vicar's
grown children come home for Christmas. In the autumn of 1982, at the
Roundhouse Theatre in New York, Anderson saw Frank Grimes in a run-through
of a revival and strongly disapproved. He took over the direction. The play opened
on 21 September and, with excellent notices, ran until March 1983. In January,
Anderson served as the chairman of the jury of the Ninth International Film
Festival of India.*

2 January 1983

At midnight I was packing and tidying. I went to bed at about 1.45, having with
difficulty managed to finish letters to Frank, and to Richard Harris. This morning I
woke about 6.30 – managed to get up and pack my hand luggage. I wrote to Ralph
[Richardson] saying I couldn't commit to *Inner Voices*.[1] Right or wrong? The truth is,
I have no confidence in being able to bring it off within the setup of the National
Theatre, using Michael Bogdanov's 'stream', an adaptation idiomatically colourless,
and a wilful, spoiled old star whose instincts and judgements I generally doubt. It's
really amazing – even if entirely predictable – that since this project was first proposed,
I've not managed to meet Peter Hall or discuss the problems with him. Which puts me

---

1. N. F. Simpson's adaptation of a play by Eduardo de Filippo.

at a considerable disadvantage since Ralph does have his ear, and they even like to lunch together every couple of weeks or so, hence the plan to visit di Filippo in Rome, which even Laurie Evans regards as extravagant, involving as it would a couple of first-class flights, a suite for Ralph at some posh hotel and a room for me, and a good deal of high-priced 'grub' no doubt . . . It all comes back – the tiresome pretensions, the obstinacy and the cunning, the wretched obsequiousness of all and sundry to 'darling Ralphie'. On *Early Days* I at least had David and Jocelyn, a play of my choice and a company of my free casting. With *Inner Voices* I would be myself in the National Theatre stream with a vengeance: a victim, not master of the situation; in a word 'used'. (I've not mentioned other factors: the fact that I would have to wait to start rehearsals till April 18th – work with actors I don't really think have the necessary vividness of personality – find myself – inevitably playing the uncomfortable role of dissident etc.).

To quote from Sir Anthony: 'Sorry, Potter – it's just not on.'[1]

At the Air India counter in Terminal 3, the rather glum receptionist said: 'The flight is delayed till twelve o'clock – okay?' (Take off was scheduled for 9.50). I cursed myself mildly and said: 'Well, it's not exactly okay . . .' Apologies were not forthcoming.

The first-class lounge: a middle-aged Indian lady introduced as co-producer of *Gandhi.* Extreme depression. Oh well . . . She talked to me over the back of her seat, then came and sat next to me. Depressing: she is lodged happily on the David Puttnam –Attenborough level.

19 January 1983
Kuwait–London. Good resolutions don't go far. Why can't I write, either diary notes or that piece about *Britannia Hospital* I think of so often? Is the habit of restraint too strong? Or laziness? Or the frustration of defeat? Or . . .

Letter to Malcolm McDowell and Mary Steenburgen (extract)

21 February 1983
I hope Little Red Riding Hood and the Big Bad Wolf[2] are proving as amusing as anticipated. Didn't I read somewhere that Mick Jagger is playing another fairy-tale character? It all sounds good, friendly, innocent fun. I envy you.

India was rather a disappointment. To begin with, and most disappointingly of all, the weather was chilly and misty, and for our jury projections we had to sit in a draughty theatre with electric heaters playing about our ankles. Fortunately, since I was Chairman, I was able to terminate the showings of at least half-a-dozen sub-standard entries from the Third World – like Malaya, Saudia Arabia, Red China etc.

---

1. Sir Anthony is the royal protocol adviser in *Britannia Hospital.* He is played by a midget.
2. For *Fairie Tale Theater*, produced for TV by Shelley Duvall.

We were all so browned off with the rotten selection of films and the terrible organisation that we refused to give any Grand Prix at all – either for feature films or for the short films. Still, I rather liked being in India again – where even the childish incompetence of the bureaucrats is amusing, as long as one isn't personally their victim.

. . . Have just heard the radio announcing Ten Oscar Nominations for *Gandhi*, followed by Sir Dickie himself spouting all that rubbish about what a great honour it is to be prized by one's 'peers' . . . I shall be furious myself if *E.T.* doesn't win the Oscar (I've actually seen it, by the way, and didn't enjoy it very much). And I am really hoping Dustin Hoffman gets the acting award.[1] If *Gandhi* (which I have *not* seen) gets prized, it will be a horrifying blow *for* smug, English middlebrow cinema. I'm seriously considering having T-shirts prepared bearing the slogan: *Britannia Hospital* for Oscar 1984.

February 1983
I had a very brief – three day – flirtation with Dino De Laurentiis (again!), when I was 'rushed' the script of *Mutiny on the Bounty*, as scripted by Robert Bolt for David Lean . . . though considerably condensed and probably re-expanded over the years. They've been thinking of turning it into a television miniseries and have now reverted to the idea of a movie, starting in April. I thought it a rotten script, and as the whole thing is already under way, I didn't feel like involving myself in another predestined disaster, on the lines of *The Hurricane*.[2] A pity – but that's movie business.

18 March 1983
Took the underground to London Airport – why? Sick of minicab drivers – expensive taxis. Don't have to play a role in the Tube.

To my surprise, there was Arnold Wesker, beaming as ever, off to a writer's conference in Budapest. He introduced me to an American girl who runs an independent theatre in Camden Town – or Kentish Town. Anyway – 'a very exciting space' . . . And to David Edgar, travelling with his wife, who seemed unfriendly or disapproving. Somehow Arnold and I were talking about prizes. I said I wouldn't accept one from the British. I would say, 'Too little and too late.' 'Who said that?' Arnold asked. I think Dryden wrote a poem which began: 'Farewell, too little and too lately known . . .' Ask David Edgar, suggested Arnold.

David Edgar: 'I don't know anything about Dryden. Except that he wrote two very bad plays.'

---

1. For *Tootsie.* He lost to Ben Kingsley in *Gandhi*.
2. Mia Farrow and Trevor Howard in a 1979 flop directed by Jan Troell, who had been brought in at the last minute after Polanksi withdrew and L.A. rejected it.

I read *Brecht in Exile* on the plane. The author didn't like Brecht, perhaps all to the good. Fascinating gossip and picture of Hollywood in the wonderful Salka Viertel[1] days. Compare with my barren LA visits.

I visited Arnold during the flight; to my relief I discovered I was travelling Club Class, Arnold and his fellows in Economy. He was going to speak about 'The Author as Director', and also to address the PEN Club on 'The Birth of *The Merchant...*' He said he'd been offered the job of scripting a TV series about the founding of the CIA. He'd queried the job offer, saying there were much better writers – Le Carré etc. – in that line: 'They'd turned it down,' I suggested humorously. A mistake. Arnold was wounded.

Letter to Jocelyn Herbert (extract)

29 April 1983

It's ironic, but just at times during the filming of *Britannia Hospital* I really began to feel that it's not so bad, and that I might even *enjoy* making another picture. I've decided – pure fantasy, of course – that if I make another film, it has to be about a WINNER. Also naturalistic and 'stunningly' photographed. (What will David Watkin be doing in eighteen months time?) And of course it must have a big dramatic role at its centre: none of this nonsense about making a film without a hero, or without, as they put it in Hollywood, 'someone to root for'.

I know you think that I subconsciously try to wreck projects, but I've been doing my best to further *The Cherry Orchard*. Against some odds ... A largely futile day of auditions yesterday, mostly of young actresses, who, irrevocably English middle class, whatever their talent or appearance, are unable to manage the unselfconscious warmth and mercurial spirit of Russian girls. What a problem it is! When I hear that they've trained at Guildford or the Bristol Old Vic my heart sinks. I know exactly what I'm going to get. However, we've a long way to go yet.

I tell you all this just to reassure you that I am *trying*. But I do find myself thinking (and saying) more and more frequently – 'We were spoiled by the Court ...' It's no good, though, thinking that those near-paradisal conditions can be recreated. It's not just a question of personality and talent, it's also a question of history. And ours were times when humanism was still possible, still understood, even if only by a minority public.

I did go to *Gandhi*. It is amazing to see so many 'intelligent', though artistically unsophisticated, people being completely taken in by this kind of specious, glossy, glib and sentimental charade – a sort of *Little Arthur's Nursery History of Indian Independence*. It's interesting too, to see how people are happy to have a political subject treated without any sense of politics or history at all. There is not even the

---

1. Writer who worked exclusively with Garbo from *Queen Christina* (1933) to *Two-Faced Woman* (1941).

slightest attempt to identify Gandhi's assassin, to explain whether he was Muslim or Hindu, what his motives were or from what political convictions they sprang. In some strange way perhaps the bourgeois audience likes to think of an inconvenient prophet like Gandhi being killed. Like Jesus. It's so much easier to admire them when the threat has been removed. I have been invited by the Indian Ambassador to a reception honouring Sir Richard Attenborough and the makers of *Gandhi*. Do you think I should go?

Lois was down last week, and insisted on organising a post-birthday party for me. Some nice old friends from Wakefield days, and a few to represent the present. I amazed myself by having rather a pleasant time.

1983 (*undated*)

I was in Prague for a couple of days, to visit Mirek and Milos during their shooting of *Amadeus*[1] at Barrandov. A pretty extraordinary venture. Milos had regarded the whole thing as a wonderful joke as well as a covenience – but I think that now he is experiencing the rigours of Barrandov bureaucracy, he is finding it not so pleasant. Really, it's a hugely ambitious project for such an arrangement, and I think they, or at least the producers, my eventually regret it.

10 July 1983

The Cherry Orchard.[2] After one week's rehearsal, familiar feelings of despondency . . . There's no magic about the enterprise . . . and inspiration is not in me. Joan [Plowright] with her boot-button eyes and admirable technique can play charm, but she hasn't got any real notion of aristocracy. And Frank Finlay, turning down in the process we are assured of dozens of Major Film Offers – can any real humour, sensitivity, feeling, be got out of that impassive visage? Is he closed – or stupid? though an effective actor. Catherine[3] looks like a disaster – nervous, affected, hysterical, clumsy, irrevocably, one would say, 'Gone.' Frank will surely be excellent. Joanna David good, but fearfully 'English'. Cora [Kinnaird] I think may be quite special, if she can be redeemed from grotesquerie. Bernadette [Shortt] perfect. Bernard Miles[4] . . . true or false? Michael Siberry – striking – still a dark horse: uncommitted in some way?

---

1. In October 1980, L.A. turned down Tadeusz Lomnicki's offer to direct the play in Warsaw.
2. Opened at the Haymarket Theatre on 12 September, after a tryout at Guildford and performances at the Edinburgh Festival.
3. Catherine Willmer, who played Houston in *O Lucky Man!* and *Britannia Hospital*. She was arthritic and having trouble with her hip.
4. Actor and producer, who built the first theatre (the Mermaid) in the City of London since Shakespeare's day.

14 July 1983

'Fun' is not the word. Joan absolutely cannot resist interfering, making suggestions for other actors' positions and actions which they – after the manner of actors – immediately adopt (about 15 per cent of them prove to be correct). She herself plays, or rehearses, purely technically, intelligently sometimes, *never* sensitively. She has absolutely no affinity with the charming, feckless, *feminine* Ranevskaya. If I attempt to talk to her about *feelings*, I get the feeling that she immediately switches off. She reminds me somewhat of Carol Channing trying to do *The Bed Before Yesterday* – though of course is more capable and plausible.

Yesterday evening she had invited Frank [Grimes], Joanna and myself to supper. Somehow Joanna got the impression, or decided, that Cora was or should be invited too.

After a gruelling rehearsal on a very, very hot day, we broke about 5.20 – to be informed that we would be expected chez Olivier at 7.15 . . . the reasons being given a) that Joan wanted to get Larry out of the house on a dinner date, so that he wouldn't take over the evening, and b) that Joan wanted to have a massage . . . So Joanna dropped Frank, Cora and me back here, then went home to her little girl and have a bath. Cora and I had baths, and Frank flew his kite from the roof.

We taxied back down to Joanna's. I was now in my dressing gown and pyjamas, which seemed sensible. We arrived about 7.30. Cora dashed off to get some cigarettes, which was just as well, since when Joan ushered us into the dining room, I noticed that only four places were laid with cellophane-covered salmon steaks . . . Joan didn't exactly light up when told Cora was of the party, vanished into the kitchen, returning with another salmon steak, saying: 'She'll have to have Laurence's.' . . .

Joan had two principal subjects. First that Leslie Phillips[1] was being allowed to develop too 'camp' a performance, and that she (Joan) was apprehensive lest I don't encourage Frank Finlay to cut loose and perform a 'wild peasant dance' at the end of Act III. She also had an interesting tendency to *justify* our commercial sponsors – even going so far as to call Duncan Weldon 'brave'.

It was all lightly nightmarish. Frank wasn't drunk – but was, I later realised, lit up by having had a smoke earlier. He got very enthusiastic about the strong actors' 'vibes' in the house, and about sitting under David Garrick's portrait.

Fortunately Larry arrived back quite early – about ten perhaps. Quite drunk. He did his pseudo-apologetic act about breaking up the party – or the serious discussion – greeted Frank with great warmth (after being told who he was), kissed Cora, told me how brilliant I was and how he wanted to work with me. Larry attempted to get a bottle of French red wine – but Joan hustled us all out. 'He's very drunk,' she explained

---

1. Playing Gayev. Popular British comedy actor (1924–), from the *Carry On* and *Doctor* films.

sotto voce, 'and I'll never be able to get him upstairs if he drinks any more. And it's a long way up.'

'God bless Larry,'[1] I breathed, when we found ourselves in the open air.

15 July 1983
Joan bad-tempered this morning – she gets terribly impatient at other actors' inaccuracy. We began with Act I – the scenes involving Leslie . . . starting with the arrival of the family, Ranevskaya's delight in the nursery, crossing the stage . . . About twenty-five seconds . . . should be easy. It took about forty minutes, with Joan fretting about the position – could Joanna cross? Upstage or downstage? Do you still want me to go up to the windows? Does she have to go so far away? Wouldn't it be easier if she went upstage to the sofa? . . .

I am told that the Musicians' Union are demanding £1,500 for the use of the Chichester tape. Can we make do with a piano? I can only suggest fighting them – and if we lose, slipping into the programme: 'Owing to demands beyond our financial means by the Musicians' Union, the orchestral music at Madame Ranevskaya's dance in Act III, will be represented by a piano.' Probably they wouldn't have the guts.

Did some work with Bernard. His principle of flattery has become a way of life: and repetition of charming stories. He is bitter – yet philosophical – about what the City never did for him. He is saved by his lack of sentimentalism. Lois [Sutcliffe] looked in and came to supper – very well and elaborately cooked by Ginette.[2]

August 1983 (undated)
Notes for meeting: From my point of view I would like to say that I think we have a production which from a performance point of view will stand comparison with anything London has seen in recent years. Audiences here [in Guildford] seem to enjoy it. But in two weeks' time we have to perform at an international festival in Edinburgh, and eventually at the Theatre Royal, Haymarket. And reactions from more sophisticated theatre people. Friends of the cast, people coming from London – have indicated what we should have known – that the look of this production, even if it gets by with provincial audiences, is simply not up to London or international standard.

---

1. Laurence Olivier agreed to play Firs when a transfer to Los Angeles was arranged for February 1984: 'He became very itchy, attending our last run-throughs and various performances of *The Cherry Orchard* and it seemed an absolutely ideal role for him to do – and he agreed. Unfortunately, he developed an infected kidney and had to go into hospital to have it removed, so the plan fell through.' (L.A. to Gwyllum Evans, 30 December 1983)

2. Frank Grimes's partner. They were temporarily living in L.A.'s flat.

Specifics. The set for Acts I and IV is badly built and horribly painted. We have not managed to get any atmosphere into it – Why should Madame Ranevskaya be so happy to get back to it? A bookcase, a table and a washstand are mentioned in the text and they're there. Otherwise there's nothing on the set with any real personality. The floor has never been glazed and is now in a shocking condition. I'm told *again* that the doors are now substantial: they've been shaking. The windows are *flimsy*, with poor, cheap fittings – and the shutters were so skimped and badly constructed that they've never been able to use them. No carpet on the upstage raised area. Not much wall space – but used in a perfunctory way. The look of the place is drab – I've suggested papering the walls: some old-attractive look. The stove looks dreadful.

Lighting – Lamps at the start need to be mellow. The handling of the upstage windows is tricky, I know – but that's the chief feature and challenge of the set. The area is not really lit at all. And – most important – what we see *through* the windows, i.e. *the cherry orchard*, is absolutely inadequate and ill-defined. We are still getting reflections from the lamps in the windows.

Two. Striking in conception, but the execution is so poor that I fear we may get laughed at. Frankly we are not far from Pantoland.The stage cloth is horrible: the bottoms of the trees show absurd and ugly gaps between the base of the trees and the cloth: they aren't properly masked at the tops. The piece of trunk and the anonymous excrescence that Lopakhin sits on really are of panto standard.

Three. The only improvement is the hanging of drapes. We still have those abominable mirrors.

2 August 1983
We start the 'technical' at Guildford today at 2.30. I've not seen a single costume and of course lighting has hardly started. I feel totally exhausted, and rendered impotent by the mediocrity and lack of quality and dynamic of the whole thing. God knows what standard one is working towards – adequacy on a provincial level I suppose . . . There is absolutely no 'magic' about the performance. But I keep telling myself that the critics and audiences who adored and prized Judi Dench as Juno will presumably accept and even enthuse over Joan Plowright as Ranevskaya. I am trying to accept the limitations philosophically: to be a Clifford Williams, in fact, if not a John Dexter. John would be cleverer, though much less sensitive. What price sensitivity, this?

Letter to Bill Douglas (extract)

29 October 1983
I needn't say how pleased I was by your response to *The Cherry Orchard*. And, by the way, you should never hesitate to come backstage after a performance – particularly if you've enjoyed it. It does the actors (not to speak of directors) *so much*

good. I know non-participants can feel shy, but if one ever mentions to an actor that a friend has been to see the show, they always say in a disappointed tone, 'He didn't come round . . .'

I agree with you about Leslie Phillips a hundred per cent. And I've been very disappointed by the ungenerous response to him – as to much of the production – by the wretched critics. Of course, you're right: they do want the sentimental treatment, they adore Stanislavskian 'texture' and emotionalism, and they care just as little as Stanislavsky did for Chekhov's protestations that he had written a *comedy.* Clarity and irony are absolutely *not* what the bourgeois audiences, or its bourgeois critics, want. They want to bathe generally in nostalgic regret. Just what Chekhov disliked!

2 January 1984

9.55 a.m. The flat is quiet. In Kathy's office, Sandy sleeps late on the camp bed. Frank, Ginette and Tilly slumber on in the guest room. In the boxroom, Lois's son, Steven is (presumably) asleep on a mattress on the floor (he arrived yesterday after spending two days in Amsterdam). And in the front room Patsy Healey will be sleeping on . . . I suppose it is a reflection of myself that all of these my guests seem to suffer from – or to evidence – the same kind of passivity or inertia in the face of the challenge of living (as I do myself). It's rather depressing. Frank of course will be agonising – understandably – over the possibility of getting a role – the role of Nathan Wise in *King David*[1] – opposite, or under Richard Gere, from Bruce Beresford, which he was told he would hear about in the New Year.

And I? 'A dull and muddy-metalled creature . . .'

Well, this diary entry implements one of my New Year resolutions.

Letter to Satyajit Ray (*extract*)

25 *January 1984*

My warmèst congratulations on becoming a Fellow of the Institute – I *think* that's what they made you. I didn't go to that BFI celebration, but I watched it on television. You won't be surprised to hear that I found it horrific – I don't think that art and worldly pomp really go together, and particularly not *that* kind of worldly pomp. Awfully dowdy, with many pasted-on smiles and the kind of snobbish conformism that always brings out the anarchic element in me. You know the kind of thing when I become rude to John Gillett and start insulting Penelope!

No one quite knew what a Royal Charter meant in relation to the Institute. Apparently it *doesn't* become the 'Royal British Film Institute'. In fact it doesn't seem to make any difference. The Prince of Wales made one of those charmingly amateurish

---

1. He failed, but Eleanor Fazan was hired to choreograph.

English speeches protesting that he really didn't know what it was all about but he was glad to be there . . . Then Dickie Attenborough, at his most effusive, introduced Orson Welles at his most would-be discursive, witty and false. Marcel Carné was introduced as the most 'influential' of French film directors. The jaunty Michael Powell and a near-senile Emeric Pressburger were wheeled out to general acclaim – and Marie accepted your fellowship with great aplomb. David Lean's Award was accepted by Alec Guinness, who, of course, had sworn after *Bridge on the River Kwai*, never to work with him again. (Though he overcame his scruples for *Lawrence of Arabia* and, of course, is flying out to Bangalore any day now to be in *Passage to India*.)

From what I hear, the dinner was a generally uncomfortable one, with longstanding enemies carefully placed together, and everybody generally questioning the validity of the whole media-orientated occasion. Forgive me if I sound crabby, but there's no question that the Institute has become just that: media-orientated. One of the great attractions of their Jubilee programme was a series of trips round Hollywood, with BFI members treated to visits to the Universal Studio Tour to Las Vegas and a conducted tour (I expect) round the Hollywood Cemetery.

Letter to Robin Askwith
(*who, announcing his role in a pantomime, had formulated that* 'Lots of back patting and good notices = no money and AUDIENCE divided by two. Trouser dropping and rubbish = XMAS in Barbados')

30 January 1984

I know I'd have enjoyed your *Aladdin*. Yes, *very* Brechtian: of course he loved all that music hall and vaudeville stuff. And quite seriously, that way of delivering, half out-front (I don't just mean the screaming to the children bit) *is* related to the way his plays have to be done. As you know.

I hope your *Milkman* series is a bit less crude than the *Adventures of . . .*[1] movies. In fact, I suppose it will have to be. I'm sure they will be a riot anyway, and so much the better: they'll make you a national institution – more like Penelope Keith[2] I hope than Warren Mitchell[3] – and then you'll be able to do anything you like. But I hope you'll be able to do your *Arturo Ui* again somewhere other than the National. I wish that horrible place and that horrible director no good fortune at all.

I hope you read that little item in the *Evening Standard* Diary about the colossal success of *Britannia Hospital* in Buenos Aires. The Argentinians have really gone for it, they tell me, both critically and commercially. And we'll be opening in Japan soon. So there's still hope.

---

1. Bums-and-breasts slapstick film series that topped the British box office charts.
2. Upper-middle-class character actress in TV sitcoms.
3. British actor, famous for playing a right-wing buffoon in *Till Death Us Do Part*.

Or is there! Reagan to stand again – and of course he'll get in. Really, the human race deserves all it gets. And after all, they wouldn't listen to *us* . . .

17 April 1984

ITV paid me a charming compliment (inadvertently, of course) by showing *Britannia Hospital* on Channel 4 on the evening of my birthday. Malcolm came to supper and was in excellent form, and also my old friend Gavin Lambert who is in London doing a script. The film looked remarkable on television, particularly coming after news shots of the siege at the Libyan Embassy in St James's Square, and scenes of confrontation between the miners and the police.

1984 (*undated*)

I hardly ever go to the cinema nowadays. I did see *This Is Spinal Tap*[1] and thought it brilliant – and also very funny. About the only American picture, in fact, I've really enjoyed since *The Texas Chainsaw Massacre*.

21 May 1984

Cross Creek . . . Martin Ritt has many uncommon and fetching skills as a director. The truth is that, with all his qualities, he isn't a poet. I thought Malcolm did his scene excellently, totally persuaded me of Perkin's sympathetic authority. I've seen and talked to Malcolm quite a few times, and he is a living, walking advertisement for his new regime. He's almost persuaded me that alcohol is the poisoner of legend – I've been doing two weeks on the Scarsdale Diet, *almost* alcohol-free, and certainly feel better for it. He's promised to get me some brown rice and show me how to cook it. I feel I'm going to need to be in good trim, since I seem to be on the verge of a new production – *The Playboy of the Western World*,[2] which I'll be doing in the weird context of a kind of summer school organised by a dubious body called the British–American Drama Academy.

Letter to Broderick Miller (*extract*)

23 May 1984

I understand only too well your feelings about LA. I do sense how much worse it's got, like New York. And like London, too, in a rather different way. Economic insecurity has bitten deep into everyone, and of course the Californian variety of opportunism is particularly stomach-turning in its materialistic vulgarity. The

---

1. Pseudo-documentary about a British rock band, directed by Rob Reiner, son of Carl.
2. L.A. first saw the play whilst an undergraduate: 'a delightful comedy adequately put over by the Playhouse' (diary, 2 March 1946). After two weeks in Oxford, and two weeks on the Fringe at Edinburgh, his own 1984 production played for six weeks at the Riverside Studios in Hammersmith.

Sunday Times here printed a contribution from Michael Caine the other week in its series *A Day in the Life of . . .* Wonderfully nauseating stuff. It reads just like the kind of thing David Sherwin would copy out slavishly and use as dialogue in one of those movies:

'I've totally accepted the American way of life . . . I thank God for the day I came here, not just because of the tax saving, but because the Americans really do know what they're doing from a business point of view.

'Life is worked out by professional business managers. I have a law firm, a business management firm and, of course, the agency all working on my behalf, with one person from each dealing specifically with me. Here you can structure your life so that you can retire.

'We have a very high standard of living, but not in a stupid way . . . We've got four cars – a Rolls-Royce Silver Wraith too, which I bought from Tony Thompson who runs Rolls-Royce of Beverly Hills and was my partner in the British Olympic Dinner for Prince Andrew (we hope what we raised will pay a few hotel bills), then there's an old American banger, a Volkswagen station wagon and the new VW saloon.'

Excellent stuff for the sequel to *If . . . .* which I idly and speculatively mentioned to David Sherwin, Malcolm and Michael Medwin.

In the autumn, Anderson flew to New York to direct Malcolm McDowell in a brilliantly reworked off-Broadway revival of In Celebration, *which opened at the Manhattan Theatre Club on 28 October.*

MALCOLM MCDOWELL

In Celebration is a very great play and a beautiful piece of writing. I remember Lindsay calling me up and saying: 'Are you doing any films?'

'Well I've got –'

'Look Malcolm, I think it's time you did some serious work. Would you like to do *In Celebration* in New York?'

'Yes, I think, probably. Why not?'

'Come over and let's talk about it.'

When I went over, Frank Grimes was there and I sat down with Frank and we read the play aloud. And I realised what a great part it was. I knew already, of course, I'd seen Alan [Bates] do it a few times. And Alan was magnificent in it. The way I did it was very different to Alan's. Alan did it more jaunty. I did it with edge. Obviously we are two very different actors. I brought my strengths to it and Alan brought his. When David saw it he was thrilled because he had no idea the part could be played like that. He said he loved it. I honestly think it was one of the best things I ever did – that performance.

And I had such a good time with Lindsay in New York. For the month of rehearsals, we lived in sort of little bed-sitting rooms, adjoining. It was hilarious. He was always looking for *The Honeymooners*. He thought that was the best show ever. He loved it. I'd come back late at night and I could hear the bloody TV blaring out and it was Ralph in *The Honeymooners*. It used to tickle me, actually. I'd say: 'Haven't you seen them all?'

'No, I don't think I have. I've seen most of them.'

30 November 1984

I've just written an introduction to *The Old Crowd*, which is being printed in a collection of Alan Bennett's TV plays – he asked me himself to write the preface, which was very sporty and generous of him. I'm afraid it's unrepentantly dissident and provocative, and will certainly annoy a lot of people.

––––––––––––––

The year ended with a commitment to direct Hamlet *at the Folger Theatre in Washington.*

16 December 1984

6.25 a.m. Should we/I be doing *Hamlet* at all? or 'What are we doing here? What am I doing here?' . . . which is what Frank asked helplessly as we walked back from the theatre last night after sitting, suffering, witness to the Folger Company performing its Christmas 'pantomime' *Crossed Words* – a witless, confused, incomprehensible concoction which is being withdrawn two weeks early – even provincial Washington apparently perceiving its poverty (how could anyone ever have accepted book, music and lyrics so absolutely rubbishy?)

Of course it is unfair – perhaps not even possible – to judge actors under such wretched circumstances. Polonius and the Ghost/First Player weren't performing – and Claudius was appearing as an ostrich. But there was enough evidence for it to be clear that John N[eville] A[ndrews] is rough and ready at the business of casting: a specious hack, 'winging' his way through everything.

And of course I should have inspected the company sooner. Frank and I should at least have come down to meet the company during *In Celebration*. I'm sick of doing these scraping-through productions – downhill from the time-wasting arguments (and the wretched salaries) on the Guildford–Triumph Apollo *Cherry Orchard*, the threadbare *Blithe Spirit*, the penny-pinching *Playboy*, the less than living wage paid by the Manhattan Theatre Club for *In Celebration* . . . to this . . . though strangely it does seem as though the Folger has the resources to do *Hamlet* – the professionals hired to design and light and dress the show are of good professional standard. It is the theatre itself, and its complement of actors, who seem wretchedly inadequate.

Is there really the slightest reason to do this production? It cannot get Frank anywhere – can it? It certainly can't get me anywhere . . . One wouldn't want anyone to see it.

18 December 1984

5.40 a.m. – no, 6.40 a.m. Yesterday in that little room up on 7th Avenue, with Ronnie, the worried, conscientious but outclassed casting director, and John Neville Andrews, the accomplished-in-evasion hack, we (Frank and I) auditioned eleven Horatios and twelve Ophelias . . . (Orphelia as the listing printed it). We are indeed the Prisoners of Circumstance. The standards of the Folger Theatre are low indeed – as of course I should have known. Yet another example of American bullshit winning out – the vague lip-service paid by everyone to the name of Folger, the fact that nobody actually goes to see the shows there, the acceptance of everyone of claims (however empty) put forward with assurance and the kind of confidence that assumes credence . . .

Possibly one Horatio; possibly a couple of Ophelias . . . But I know this isn't the way I can possibly work with success, as indeed I have not been able to do since . . . well *The Bed Before Yesterday* in Australia? I feel priced out – or out-manoeuvered: unable to work at the National, the RSC or the Royal Court, not in commercial demand, fed up with cheeseparing on the Fringe.

Yesterday evening after auditions, I talked with John Neville Andrew in his $135 [a night] room. There had been a dispute about his credit card – as a result of which we had to go off during the afternoon to get cash to take to the hotel – or as I understood. When the waiter arrived with the shrimp bowl and drinks he'd ordered, he wasn't permitted to sign for them . . . and when I had retired to my room, had a bath and got into my pyjamas, a knock on the door announced two bulky blacks who presented themselves as coming from the Credit Department of the Hotel. Perhaps my English accent reassured them, anyway, they let me be.

19 December 1984

The nightmare that is NY – and the revolving hypocrisy of 'I [heart – love] New York' – is emphasised at every moment, every time you switch on a TV set.

Two films opening this week cost over $50,000,000 – *Cotton Club* and *Dune* . . . TV news also carries, without the slightest tone of comparative irony, an appeal for contributions to a fund for New York's starving – or at least underfed. 'Take your gifts into any fire station' – and the burly firemen group behind newscaster Connie Chan . . . Let alone the continual features on Africa's famine-stricken millions, perishing before the TV cameras. Figures are quoted (and soon forgotten) on the high percentages of the US population 'below the poverty line' . . . There have been five thousand subway fires in New York this year, and an investigative body has reported to the Transport Authority that the risk level on the subway is 'unacceptable' (the level of filth and sheer ugliness goes without comment).

This overpriced hotel – I am shocked to find that we are paying $135 a night – serves awful, expensive food – and locks you out of your room on the slightest suspicion that your credit card is not in order. Hardly necessary to add that the situation is handled without the slightest grace or politeness.

Americans are without any sense, one reflects not for the first time, of nonconforming protest.

1 January 1985

I feel the reins loose in my hands, my confidence in being able to guide the course of the stagecoach less and less as the years pass. Fatalism, no doubt, comes with age. I think of death quite a lot – though in a theoretical rather than a painful way. A fatalistic way: nothing we can do about it, no way even we can prepare ourselves for it. Yes, the rope slips through one's hand, one lacks not just the strength, but even the will to grasp it. To remember those names, to make the effort to read those scripts, shape life to any desired form.

I grow more and more conscious of difference, of dissidence; of the fact that my work now, however much appreciated by a Happy Few, is quite removed from the mainstream of success and acknowledgement. *Britannia Hospital* is of course at the centre of this complex: it is impossible for me not to remark, with a sense of fated exclusion, how it is totally disregarded, not so much dismissed as unacknowledged even as a failure, as though it had never been . . . The script was only as good as we could make it; not as good as it should be. But that only means it's not quite a masterpiece – or a masterpiece *maudit* . . . The first five reels are so *uncomfortable*, but by the end, I always feel it has delivered its message.

Fame to some degree *is* the spur. I do resent lack of acknowledgement. Which I suppose I should accept, and use a motive for activity, rather than an excuse for inaction.

Snoo Wilson,[1] at that party,[2] talked about the praise of his 'peers' as a motive for work, or at least a source of gratification. I expressed astonishment, and asked him – too sharply, no doubt – *what* 'peers'. Characteristically, he had no names to deliver. I pushed on with some desperation and myself mentioned the names of Howard Brenton and David Hare . . . 'Do you care what they think of your work?' I tried to lay myself open – 'I don't care what my peers think of my work – Karel Reisz or Tony Richardson . . . I know my peers like John Dexter and Bill Gaskill don't give a damn about my work.' But all in vain. Snoo Wilson, for all his original-sounding name and his creative status, is as incapable of nourishing conversation as anyone else at such a gathering.

---

1. One of seven writers involved in the Court's 1971 experiments in collective authorship.
2. Given earlier in the week by Otto and Louise Plaschkes.

The only 'serious' (or substantial) talker I can think of encountered recently was David Hockney at Jocelyn's party. What the hell was he talking about? Something to do with the decay of Christianity, the loss of Ikon-function of art, as being the crucial factor in the discovery of perspective. I didn't really follow it, and of course while he talks with great conviction and the gift of the gab, he is in *no sense* a conversationalist. An intelligent and even humorous monologist, which in the end is boring.

I do believe [in] or I find myself stimulated by the idea of New Year, of fresh starts, of resolutions. Which is why I am writing in this diary, and resolving to make a schedule for the three weeks which remain to me in London before I set off for New York and Washington . . . to see Jocelyn at the farm; to see Mu [Richardson]; to go to Rustington; to read the scripts that await my attention. To lose weight, to tidy up the place, to start working on the idea of a book of collected pieces – to plan a film even?

To take one's life in hand – at the age of sixty-one and three-quarters?

Really, I think the resolution is a big, comprehensive simple-yet-various one: to *act* on the promptings of common sense and decision. When I know I should do some-thing – *do* it. To jettison time-wasting neurosis, which only wastes the time that is left, which may not be so much. And start today. Let's see by this evening how much has been accomplished.

2 *January 1985*

Woke at seven and started immediately to dictate letters – Kathy due in this morning – to Oscar, returning *Boadilla* and the *Romilly* script to him (I cannot see this as a serious proposition – too difficult, and too clear also that Oscar doesn't envisage himself as anything more than a packager) – to Allan Arkush, director of *Rock 'n' Roll High School*, who wrote that amazingly enthusiastic note about *If . . . .* in *American Cinema*. Spoke to Maggie Parker,[1] who in fact rang me. Would it be absurd to 'go with her'? Arranged to go to Jocelyn for a couple of nights from Friday. Arranged for David Sherwin to come down on the 12th, and we will go to Rustington. Will this be the historic start date for *Reunion*?[2] David Sterne came to lunch and stayed till four; poor chap, he needs support now his marriage seems conclusively to have come to an end.

3 *January 1985*

I went to lunch with Malcolm down at Notting Hill Gate . . . He is really in extra-ordinary good form, good-natured with the children, generously enthusiastic about *In Celebration* and his fellow-actors . . . Getting a bit fed up, no doubt, with being an adjunct to Mary and the children – yet philosophic about not being offered work of

---

1. Agent, fomerly an actress, Margaret Johnstone.

2. The sequel to *If . . . .*

any substance. We lunched at the Ark, and Mary talked about *Tender is the Night*, which she's been doing for the last five months or thereabouts, and only another three weeks to go. I passed on to her the warm praise of Jonathan Powell, the producer, whom I'd met at the Plashkers' party. Mary's next director, Philip Borsos, came to talk to her: the director of *Grey Fox*, who seemed an affable, perhaps shy, large young Canadian. I told him his film was the only good picture I'd ever seen on an aeroplane.

4 January 1985

At Jocelyn's cottage: no central heating, of course, and she had forgotten to put on the electric blanket on my bed . . . but she has given me a hot-water bottle and there are plenty of bedclothes. Julian is here, with Jo and two boys and their friend . . . Over dinner we talked long and entertainingly – first about titles – should one or shouldn't one – a discussion I've had many times with Jocelyn . . . She sticks to her convictions, but I'm happy to note that she's broadened, relaxed somewhat. She can even envisage the idea of accepting a knighthood in a spirit of pure mockery. I should have taped the political discussion with Julian – useful for *Reunion*? I find I just can't retain those conversations: my scepticism is so complete.

Before catching the train down I lunched with Nicola McAuliffe and her proposed producer for the film of *Annie Wobbler*[1] which I have allowed myself to be slated to direct . . . I can't remember his name, of course. Not at all unsympathetic, yet I experienced that uncomfortable alienated feeling as he talked. I cling to the underlying hope that it won't materialise.

(In the small hours.) Although I have (for four days) kept going on this diary, it remains a problem as yet unsolved. How does one get it all down? And at the end of the day I'm simply tired . . . Also I'm no good at *selection* . . . everything being somehow significant.

Amazing that when we did *Britannia Hospital* I could really believe there was an audience out there – in Los Angeles if not in London – who would receive my work with friendly comprehension, with complicity! I'm afraid the rejection of that work has hit me hard, shaken my confidence – rendered me resentful, or scornful, and impotent? I wonder . . .

6 January 1985

We awoke to snow. The children were excited: Tom and Ben built a snowman. Max stayed in, not feeling well. I took some photographs. Jocelyn thought she and I should leave in the late morning (she thought we might get stuck in the lane). We drove back smoothly. Riggs was up and welcomed us in: I'm sure he's not ill-natured, but the continual flow of wisecracks or of crisply formulated verdicts is tiring. He and Jocelyn

---

1. From the play by Arnold Wesker.

had a sharp-edged dispute about Tony Harrison, the poet-writer and 'translator' of the *Oresteia*, whom Jocelyn adores and Riggs strongly dislikes. My instinct is to suspect him – as I suspect anyone who has been able to get on with Peter Hall.

Poor old Mike [Kaplan] rang from LA, bubbling on about Bette Davis for *The Whales of August*. Maggie Parker asks if I want to play Samuel Beckett in the new Puttnam–Roland Joffe film . . . What a relief that might be!

9 January 1985
Lunch with Jill Bennett, with her new boyfriend, Jonathan, dropping by for coffee – and a meeting with the literary agent at Curtis Brown, in anticipation of my book of essays for Faber and Faber . . . And maybe, now I think of it, my anthology, which might well be better worth doing with them than Plexus.

Jill was in excellent form – because happy, I'd say – making some money out of Trevor Nunn's film of *Lady Jane Grey*, standing by while Nunn flies to Hollywood with his begging bowl . . . She is going to do a TV miniseries written by John Mortimer, which I have encouraged her to do. It's not a question of being *good*. It's a question of being *exposed*. Jonathan seemed very amiable, rather young, not handsome but nice-looking. I only hope Jill is not too high-powered for him.

12 January 1985
Midnight: at Fuschia Cottage. I drove down with David [Sherwin], having shopped at Waitrose in the morning; returned; put David in front of *The Devil's Playground*[1] and *The Promised Land* (BBC *Forty Minutes* documentary) . . . suggest politely to Patsy[2] that she might get a snack together for David and myself before we set out.

We talked about *Reunion* in our usual indecisive, intuitive, feeling-towards-something way. I think this was the first time I had the obvious idea that the *pretext* of the film should be the destruction of College House – from life, of course, echoing the re-possession of Cheltondale[3] by Cheltenham Council and its reported transformation into a morgue . . . We lightly and suggestively skim over possible themes and characters. No use pretending I am not conscious of every moment of the *rejection* of *Britannia Hospital* – and the necessity to find a more 'naturalistic' style. Whether we can do it or not I've no idea. David suggests Frank should be the new chaplain . . .

13 January 1985
My situation still remains one of unsatisfactory drift – assuaged a little by the acceptance that I have, as I frequently say and truly feel, 'left the building'. The remark

---

1. Feature film about an Australian Catholic boarding school, directed by Fred Schepisi.
2. Patricia Healey, who was living in L.A.'s flat.
3. L.A.'s house at Cheltenham College.

isn't wholly complacent – since there is also a sense in which I have been pushed out of the building. I may proudly choose to go from where I am not wanted, but in the not being wanted there is a real element of rejection (I am too proud to use the word 'failure') . . .

As I frequently discuss with my few sympathetic friends – the suppression of *Britannia Hospital*, and only to a slight lesser degree my other films, is remarkable as well as painful. And with it goes my own total eclipse in this era of the New British Cinema in unholy alliance with the pretentious commercialism – or the commercialism with pretensions – of the Puttnam-Goldcrest era. It really is as if one has never been – all those years of valiantly (foolishly? Quixotically?) 'standing up' for British cinema not so much disregarded as despised.

So halfway through the eighties, and into my sixties, I am more isolated than ever. Karel (now shooting his country and western pic with Jessica Lang) is in the US, and so is Tony [Richardson]. Neither has any sympathy with my work. I have no colleagues in Britain. Michael Medwin has collapsed back into acting – and anyway has long since ceased to function as a producer . . .

[But] there is *Reunion*. Well, this weekend is a proper effort, and we must attempt to crystallise something. I woke thinking about it. The balance between the 'naturalism' that one feels to be acceptable and the instinctive satirical extravagance of both my temperament and David's is not going to be easy to achieve.

Necessary: to define the occasion which brings all the old boys together. Perhaps a jubilee *combined* with the sad loss of College House. (Too near *Britannia Hospital.*) What brings them back? What is the attitude of the present generation? Entirely conformist; or do they have their rebels too? The singing of the school song – which the boys like and the authorities think is sentimental junk, or is this itself a sentimental idea?

14 January 1985

We talked a lot yesterday before we drove out to buy papers, onions and teabags. I had the impression we were making surprisingly good progress. Is our plan for *Reunion* just nonsense? I fear so: though without being quite sure that my feelings aren't essentially failures of nerve. I can't quite analyse what David's attraction for me as a collaborator is. I just find it easy to talk with him – and let myself be stimulated into invention. But then I don't really believe in my own inventions. A certain nerve has, I fear, gone.

15 January 1985

Mirek, in London, for the Premiere of *Amadeus*,[1] but also to meet Hugh Hudson with the possibility of shooting his American Revolution picture, came to supper, in good

---

1. Photographed by Ondricek; directed by Milos Forman.

characteristic form. He went on to talk about Hugh a bit, and I told him Sue was his wife. Mirek was so astonished I almost believed he'd had a fling with Sue at the time of *O Lucky Man!* . . . He also said he was being pursued by Ivan Passer to shoot a film about the Russian Revolution, being produced in Yugoslavia by a Frenchwoman . . . but I note he doesn't ask me how my work with David is going. Mirek also announces with triumph that he has arranged two tickets for me for the *Amadeus* premiere – a little odd in view of the fact that I (impulsively and probably unwisely) wrote him that long and unfavourable critique of the picture . . . quite likely he didn't really understand it, or didn't really read it. Patsy quite blossomed, as she does with visitors, was delighted to be told she had not changed since Mirek last (well, almost) saw her on *The White Bus*.

19 January 1985
The preview of *Amadeus* – the usual absurdity – Mirek and Milos, Saul Zaentz [producer] and Peter Shaffer! at the end of the line at the ABC Shaftesbury Avenue, awaiting the arrival of Prince Charles and Princess Diana[1] . . . Inside the cinema an instrumental ensemble was playing Mozart . . . they were replaced by trumpeters who played a fanfare and we rose for the royal entrance. The film had an intermission so that Charles and Diana could move from ABC 1 to ABC 2 . . . I was grateful for it, since it enabled me to relieve my bursting bladder.

Yes, it is a *handsome* film: tremendously, solidly impressive – most skilful in its manipulation of camera, editing, design, music, choreography, etc. Yet the material remains totally meretricious, and the film *soulless*. Milos is clever – brilliant if you like: but cold, unpoetic. I really don't know what 'fascinates' him . . . The picture is really finely shot, though.

20 January 1985
As I was just sitting down to my curry the phone rang. Sandy answered – 'Jill! You sound terrible!' My heart sank as I went to take it on Kathy's phone . . . Yes . . . Jonathan has left her. She had gone out to lunch with friends, from whom he'd excused himself on grounds of work, and when she returned he'd flitted, packed and cleared out, leaving a letter saying she was too much for him. Jill, of course is a powerhouse. But she was distraught.

---

1. Both attended the world premiere in Cannes of L.A.'s *The Whales of August* (1987).

14

West to East

Hamlet in Washington – Frank Grimes
WHAM! in China – George Michael

> 'I was not prepared for the incredible waste, silliness, lack of conscience,
> ignorance, lack of grace, lack of scruple, egoism, weakness, duplicity and
> hypocrisy which have characterised the whole operation. Nor did I quite
> realise that however cool I might be during the shooting, I could not resist
> total and creative involvement once it came to the editing.'

23 January 1985
On Pan Am 101 . . . with the thought of Washington, the Folger and *Hamlet* . . . Can I claim to be facing my challenges more successfully? I do feel guilty at spending rather a lot, and earning so little, and taking advantage of my relative security not to face my own problems, of what I should do with myself these next (how many?) years before I die . . . I feel lively enough temperamentally, but so, I'm sure do many elderly people . . . but my legs are not at all what they were; I am too fat, and I don't, and don't want to remember names. All of which goes to nourish this feeling I have of having dropped out of the race . . . I have insisted always on doing things on my own terms, which has won me the respect of a (very) few, but the neglect of many, of the media, of the commercial centres of power – and of the critical establishment too . . .

26 January 1985
Feel awful: last night Sylvia cooked up, invited Charlie Baker. A real penitential evening and I say to myself, it isn't worth it. Every value – emotional, artistic, moral, seems to be false . . . The vodka and tonics are large, the glasses of wine small . . . the pasta-cake rather hard and tepid. (Don't these people like their hot food *hot*?) Charlie is getting plump in the face – alcoholic bloat, I suppose. Happy or unhappy, he talks always with offensive certainty, with a complacent rejection of anything new. The most

revealing – and odious – conversation concerned Alan Bennett, starting off from Charlie's unbounded enthusiasm for *An Englishman Abroad*:[1] 'I never thought Coral [Browne] was a great actress, she's a lovely person of course and I adore her, but I thought she was quite wonderful in that . . . so clever . . . The most original thing I've ever seen on television . . . What's happened to Alan Bennett?' I tried to explain that the failure of *Enjoy* had dried up his writing. 'But he's been successful . . . I mean, *Forty Years On* was a smash, and he must have been pleased . . . When it first came on, nobody talked about the play, only Gielgud . . . This time round, the *play* was a great success.'

I tried to explain that he was sick of being stuck with a stereotype. 'Then I think much less of him than I did.'

In other words, success is the only value that signifies. Nothing else is comprehensible.

29 January 1985

As life picks up, with its stimulus, one's mood changes . . . this, after all, is the real problem. The sympathetic stimuli are so rare – one is thrown back on oneself – and the essential passivity which is so fatally at my centre, together with doubt and scepticism, takes over, reducing me to inactivity.

Well – today's stimuli . . . Frank read me his Joyce work, insisting that I lay down on the couch. I protested that I'd go to sleep – which I did. In addition, Frank swore, I snored . . .

Night – a preview of *Harrigan 'n' Hart*[2] – the musical about two vaudevillians with Mark Hamill[3] in the lead . . . We sat up in the second circle – the place full of a theatre party – all jammed and rather frowsy. The man at the box office threw my tickets at me.

Mark Hamill did well, performed energetically, danced and sort-of sang with a will . . . But the essential content of the show was just not there – whatever was the *chemistry* between the two performers, what *was* their special contribution and talent? The numbers all seemed the same, performed with that intense energy that leaves no room for charm. Whizz-bang staging by Joe Layton that reduced everything to 'getting through the show'.

30 January 1985

Washington is extremely provincial. An unreal place, really. All grand bureaucratic buildings, excellent museums and huge areas of black poverty, complete with drunks, drug-pushers and muggers. Met at the station by Kevin Kinley, after I have struggled

---

1. Directed for television by John Schlesinger, with Alan Bates.
2. Written by Michael Stewart, better known for *Hello, Dolly!* The show closed after four performances.
3. Actor (1951–). Appeared in *Britannia Hospital*, played Luke Skywalker in the *Star Wars* films.

with my two large suitcases . . . We drive to the Folger. John N. A. beams. His policy is never to talk about anything connected with the production. There is a lot of chat about the present crisis of the Folger – Senator Moynihan and Mrs Elizabeth Dole are heading a fund-raising body to save the Folger . . . I meet Valerie Hanlon, who is apparently in charge of accommodation. She seems nice. But she hasn't seen the Bristol (my hotel) and doesn't know exactly where it is. Kevin says its about four miles away, and is immediately jumped on by John N.A. (But he is right.) I get the impression of John N.A. as the seedy pasha in a very provincial harem. The female functionaries sit round in the 'drinks' session in his office at the end of the afternoon.

31 January 1985

As usual, or more than usual, it is extraordinarily disagreeable STARTING . . . Every nerve is shrieking – fool! idiot! Have I really not lived, experienced enough to recognise a shyster when I see one? To take *nothing* on trust, and to know that this little outfit here *must* be riddled with provincial pretension, incompetence, phoniness and careerism? Not to mention *amateurism*? Why oh why – *a year ago* – did I not satisfy myself about the credentials and the conditions of the Folger? Of course I can ask what I'd be doing if I wasn't doing this – Coward's *Cavalcade* at Chichester – or working on a script for a 'last film' – which of course is what I *should* be doing . . . Well, maybe I have to do this to learn *that*. At least that's all I can tell myself.

The talent is not impressive. We start with Sally de Souza's son – who is plainly untalented, though a good-looking boy. Not especially charming – a bit conceited. Then a little procession of adequate-to-untalented aspirants. I pick the favoured Fortinbras, who is at least tall and reasonably spoken.

3 February 1985

I can lecture Frank, of course, and I do, but he clings to *his* essential passivity . . . He cannot help waiting for the 'heavens to open'. And it seems they don't. Poor Frank! Who is going to come to Washington to see *Hamlet*? And who will particularly note it or him if they do? What use am I going to be to Frank, now that this run-of-three, my independent programme initiated a year ago, is drawing to an end? More and more I feel 'turned off' the theatre, repulsed by every silly, trivial, demeaning aspect of it . . . And the *inorganic* nature of work on this level . . . How can anything *form*, with Judianna Markovsky[1] doing her costumes in New York – and Jeff Beecroft God knows where – with this scratch company? I find myself turning against it all, against this situation of struggle to produce work for a non-existent audience, for critics who want something quite different to write about.

---

1. Oscar-nominated in 2002 for *Harry Potter*.

We go the Vietnam Memorial and the Lincoln Memorial. The first name on the Vietnam Memorial is 'Anderson': Frank finds a 'Grimes' . . . It is a brilliant, powerful, moving memorial . . . though it would be better without the people promenading in front of it. (And the same goes for the naturalistic statue-group of three young American combatants, tactfully and suggestively posed in the distance.)

The traditional rhetoric of the Lincoln Memorial fails to move me, I'm afraid: those traditional values have failed too decisively for such pomp. They trumpet patriotism – nationalism – too redolent of the folly of mankind.

5 February 1985

The date has arrived: rehearsals must start. I taxi up to the Folger offices early, and find Judianna and John Lee Beatty there. In the light of day Judianna's drawings look less 'professional' than I'd hoped, and with less flair. My heart sinks. Frank's costume in particular has defeated her – his 'double-breasted' idea – exaggerated by her into a demand, is partly responsible. I talk with John about the ghost appearances, which *of course* he has neglected to concern himself with. John N.A. greets me with big smiles. His lack of concern is truly amazing – it doesn't occur to him to ask me how we got on yesterday in NY. (Auditions for Horatio . . . A lot of the auditionees are really *Laertes*.) Frank's telephone is still not connected and he has had his duff TV set removed.

The rehearsal room is crammed with thousands, well hundreds of people. The actors sitting at tables set in a square, theatre workers all round the walls . . . O to escape! As usual I respond with apparent jokey, relaxed authority. What alternative have we? Everyone called on by Margaret, introduces him/herself; many of them incomprehensibly. Someone (in charge of set construction?) gives out with a comic poem about the Folger crisis. We read the play. During the reading John Lee Beatty takes off for Baltimore, where his Broadway comedy opens this evening. I realise that, having shown his set drawing, John has shown *none* of the scene settings or how they are to be achieved.

The reading? I know what Frank means when he says Hamlet disappeared and he just found himself shouting. The rehearsal room is a nightmare; so small, lacking depth. I can't feel anything when we start trying to rehearse the first scene.

Return to the hotel by taxi: driven by talkative Black, complaining loudly about Reagan. 'I never saw a soup line before this government' – but I can hardly understand anything he is saying. On the pavement outside the hotel I slipped and crashed to the ground. Fortunately only on my side. No damage.

The lift wasn't working. After five or six minutes, the man at the desk said: 'Oh – the elevator is running slow, Mr Anderson, we've sent for the engineer.' Remember *The White Bus*?[1] I climb the six flights of stairs.

---

1. In which there's a scene with a line of VIPs, an hilariously useless employee, and a broken elevator.

7 February 1985

TV: Ronald Reagan delivering his State of the Nation speech ('Eliminate Dependency and Encourage Opportunity') – calling for a Second American Revolution – and being serenaded by the Congress and Senate with 'Happy Birthday to You'. Also the Oscar nominations: eleven for *Amadeus*; seven for *Places in the Heart* . . . Milos and Bob! [Robert Benton] Good show chaps.

I still can't shake off the overwhelming sense of pointlessness about the whole oper-ation. How reality *shrinks* a project like this! In London 'I'm doing *Hamlet* at the Folgar Theatre in Washington' sounds quite grand – exciting. The reality, cut down to the size of John Neville-Andrews is nearer *Hamlet* in fortnightly rep at Frinton. I have supper with Edward [Hibbert] and Madeleine [Potter, cast as Gertrude] and her brother. We go to the Greek restaurant over in the row of shops and restaurants along the main route a few blocks from the theatre. I really love that Avgolemono soup. Madeleine reveals herself as an intelligent and talented actress, and interestingly clearly well-born. She has been with Vanessa [Redgrave] in *The Bostonians* – and they got on fine. Her brother is witty, whimsical and well-mannered: can't be sure if he's 'gay' – or just upper class.

9 February 1985

Two traumatic days, during which it becomes starkly clear that *Hamlet* at the Folger, so rashly undertaken, represents the NADIR of my career – in terms not of impoverished means, but of second-rateness of standards, and generally of acting talent. Now I realise what people mean when they talk of the American actors' lack of technique, training or stage sense. This is *amateur stuff* – college drama. Poor Tom Apple blinks in self-conscious surprise when Frank takes his hand. He looks vaguely out front most of the time when speaking to anyone. He cannot *grasp* Hamlet to restrain him following the Ghost. He cannot adjust his positions to the movements of another actor. HE CANNOT ACT. What madness overtook me in that little room? Of course one makes allowances for nervousness, but it's too painfully obvious that the poor fellow has no idea what to do.[1] It's not just the mediocrity of the company – it's the glibness, the provincial com-placency and affection with which the whole thing is run – and which makes it all-but-impossible for me to function effectively. Let alone creatively.

John Lee is, within certain bounds, a good and professional designer. But the total concentration on the work – the design as an integral, *working* part of the production is not there. The *look* of each scene, as opposed to the overall look of the stage as a whole . . . Here the work of Jocelyn stands in shining contrast: her use of a model, as opposed to John Lee's rough sketches, is significant. Really, there's been little work on the practical movement of the play from scene to scene: and the physical limitations of

---

1. He was replaced by James Maxwell.

the theatre (and the set) impose severe restrictions. I shall have to wait until we are on the stage, and improvise my way through it.

14 February 1985

Frank is beyond my and his control . . . The explosion came after rehearsal yesterday – another difficult day . . . The company had a matinee for schoolchildren. We had to rehearse Hamlet pursued by Rosencrantz after the death of Ophelia . . . this was the cruncher – Frank suddenly declaring that he did not want to play the scene with the manic 'foolery' we had keyed it formerly, not 'princely' enough, Hamlet is *grieved* at the death of Polonius – Gertrude 'says so'. But Gertrude, I counter with lame good sense, is saying this to Claudius: she wants to protect her son: Hamlet himself, at the end of the closet scene, does *not* show great constitution or compassion . . . But obsessively Frank returns to 'A weeps for what he's done . . .'

The row took place at the deli to which Frank and Edward and I had repaired after rehearsal . . . I made one big mistake . . . we reached the point somewhere, somehow, at which Frank declared – 'We'll start again tomorrow: I'll listen to you, I'll be good.' And somehow, instead of stopping there, I continued . . . wanting to screw him down too tight I suppose . . . And the result was that we lost sense and agreement completely, paranoia returned, and finally Frank, feeling himself cornered I suppose, defeated by 'logic', exploded, got up, walked out . . . I drove with Edward and Madeleine Potter to the art exhibition opening they were attending, then took the cab on to the Iowa Building. Ginette tells me he had banged out, having returned in a black mood, though controlled, then exploding at some remark of Ginette's. I sit and write Frank what I hope is a placating note.

Across the street, on the corner opposite, I see that 'Irish' pub – where Ginette has suggested Frank might be . . . I look in the window, and there, hunched at the counter I see Frank sitting . . . I go in: he is surprised, not hugely pleased . . . He is drinking Guinness with Jameson chasers – three or four large men further down the counter are laughing and calling him a 'Thespian'. Frank gets me a drink: I decide on bourbon on the rocks. The jukebox is loudly playing Irish ballads. 'My father used to sing this,' says Frank. One of the drinkers, who turns out to be a marine, shows his card and recites a goodly chunk of 'To be or not to be'. Frank asks him how he got a scar on his cheek – 'I was mugged here, outside this bar, a week ago . . .' He lives just across the street.

Somehow Frank and I start again: it's no good: 'The honeymoon is over,' quotes Frank – from where, I ask. 'Fonda said it about Ford . . . you told me.' 'But they were reconciled', I said. But Frank hugs his resolution. Our conflict becomes intense again. The marines depart.

I am reminded of Richard Harris: an intense, pulsating ego, confident only of its egoism, desperately trying to rationalise, unconfident of argument, mistaken, but fiercely, implacably resistant . . . My heart sinks . . . I can't cope with this, either personally or as a director . . . Well, I got myself into this mess: old enough to know better . . . O that I could walk away from it all – but then I reflect it's only another five weeks or so, and it's only *Hamlet* at the Folger Theatre – and who will know or care about it? So little is *expected of one* . . . But I prefer to pitch my ambitions high . . . I really need to be very, very clever.

20 February 1985

Yes, I've meant to write : but exhaustion – and laziness – inhibit. Aided and abetted by TV . . . The dreaded TV . . . Tonight, for instance, I watched a lot of a very poor, facile Agatha Christie vehicle,[1] in which poor, gallant Bette Davis appeared (one could hardly say 'performed'), still evidently affected by her stroke, moving carefully and speaking with effort . . . Great pathos, when one thinks of that vital, crisp, incisive, quick-witted talent . . . 'To what strange uses are we returned.'

22 February 1985

We go to Eddie Murphy's *Beverly Hills Cop*, which I am interested to see because it is well on the way to beating *E.T.* – and it is directed by Martin Brest, whose *Hot Tomorrows* I saw and admired years ago (with Malcolm and Margot, I think). Shot, very smartly, by Bruce Surtees. I am quite diverted by the extraordinary, show-off dynamic of Eddie Murphy and the hugely adept, confident handling of the whole thing – though essentially thin, carelessly plotted TV stuff . . . Still, it's the kind of clever, punchy style that makes me feel *I can't make movies*. Eddie Murphy is brilliant, but his anarchy is conformist really – toothless.

24 February 1985

There is a meeting at 10 a.m. in John N. A.'s office . . . Naturally nobody has told me what it's about . . . Except that Regan's note informs me that we may not be able to have pictures in the programme because of a 'space' problem. She also enclosed the *Hamlet* 'logo' which I find quite ugly – the 'L' as a dagger – boring . . .

The dolly-eyed Regan arrives, and manages not to look at me as she chats with Margaret on the sofa. Bess, of the laughs and giggles, joins us. I kick off with some observations about the rehearsal habits of Mikael Lambert and Michael Tolgado – Mikael, it appears has gone to somewhere in Virginia where there is a conference . . . I ask with uncomfortable directness just how many hours a week Michael Tolgado is allowed to miss – to be met with the usual shiftiness . . . Not that it matters really: just another instance of mess and mutual cover-up.

---

1. *Murder with Mirrors.*

The discussion proceeds to the programme. 'I don't want photographs in the programme' suddenly and categorically announces John N. A. There is obedient silence all round. I speak with controlled reasonableness. 'Why not?' John N. A. speaks without effort to be conciliatory or polite. 'We don't have pictures in the programme. I don't want to change the format' . . . I think I tried again to be met by a refusal as blank. No contribution, of course, from anyone else. Silence. Just this stupid, defensive, conceited, insecure, talentless 'director' issuing the commands which will prove his authority . . . In the end I say – 'If you don't want suggestions, please don't ask me for them . . . I'm quite happy to stay out of it.' I say I'm not going to do the radio interview set for me, and I withdraw my programme note. But even as I do these things I realise their uselessness. The women leave the meeting, but I don't. I close the door and speak – in controlled fashion – to John N.A., telling him I feel he spoke unnecessarily rudely and that we should discuss things together. He loses his temper and starts shouting that I have been a 'pain in the arse' to everyone in the theatre . . . I leave, with commendable quietness.

The amusing – though tiresome – sequel to all this is that I have already agreed to have supper with John N.A. . . . and go.

25 February 1985

We had a production meeting at which Mikael Lambert softly put forward, on behalf of the actors, a request that we should take our breaks regularly and according to schedule during rehearsal . . . and that food should not be consumed in the rehearsal room while work was in progress. At first I wonder is this is an objection to me and my tuna sandwiches, blobs of which tend to fall on the floor – but it transpires that it is an objection from Jim – the untalented fat actor, the ex-Vietnam vet – to Edward Hibbert drinking his chicken noodle soup during a rehearsal . . . O to put the whole lot in that well-known bag and chuck them off the end of the pier!

26 February 1985

Tuesday morning, 6.20 a.m. A dream from which I have just awoken: I was flicking through one of those books which have a series of photographs in the corner, which animate as one flicks the pages. This might have been about John Wayne – because in the background was John Ford – turned away from the camera, on a chair – talking to someone . . . his back moved, he gestured in a characteristic fashion . . . Then I was in a long hut with a bar in it. Ford was there: we were in conversation: he was angry with me for having directed *Wagonmaster* – and for not admitting it was an arty, pretentious mistake; a load of rubbish and a failure – yet (he accused me) of refusing to admit it . . . I could only protest that I hadn't been pretentious about it, that I honestly *liked* it . . . Ford only became angry. Someone came in, a gnarled ex-serviceman, or old prop man? They recognised each other. They were in a comradely clutch: fiercely Ford was biting the other's nose . . . I turned away.

Out of the window I saw Ford walking shirtsleeved away. He was alone. I wondered if I should go after him, join him. Then I thought it would be quite immaterial to him: he preferred to be alone.

8 March 1985

I was in my bath yesterday: the phone rang: I took it back into the bath. It was someone called Martin Lewis calling from New York. He had produced *The Secret Policeman's Ball* or *Other Ball* which had enabled him to work with Alan Bennett, his favourite . . . Had been doing a documentary about Julian Lennon with Sam Peckinpah. And now WHAM! – the new POP sensation – were visiting China and he had undertaken the job of making a documentary of their visit. Would I be interested to direct? Also he said he had loved *Britannia Hospital.*

It's a measure of my real feeling of having 'left the building' that my heart did *not* leap up. Rather sank. Oh God . . . Have I the energy? The curiosity? The conviction? On the other hand it would be an invigorator. Give me another chance? Frank got excited of course and urged me to go . . . So did all the other actors with whom I had supper.

10 March 1985

I enjoyed the chicken which Ginette cooked after our return from strolling in the pleasant gardens of Dumbarton Oaks. When I returned to the hotel I found a package waiting for me – the WHAM! videos, most strikingly featuring 'Wake Me Up Before You Go-Go'. How on earth have two (lower) middle-class boys from Watford managed to transform themselves into these vibrant figures of pop myth – top of the charts in the UK *and* the US – brilliant in their showbiz know-how, triumphantly touring the world from Japan to California to New York? It's a complete mystery.

12 March 1985

I ring George Michael of WHAM! in London . . . 'The idea of us representing the West if you see what I mean . . . Slightly corrupt . . . only slightly – slightly ambiguous, I don't know – also a few scenes slightly surrealistic not involving them – taking things involved in the tour and putting them slightly out of context'.

13 March 1985

Rehearsed with Frank, gave him notes and attempted a soliloquy or two. Encountered the usual resistance – spent *ages*, for instance, trying to explain his first two lines – 'A little more than kin . . .' and 'Not so my Lord I am too much i' the sun.' Essentially he doesn't *understand* the wit of the line, and therefore the bitter irony escapes him. He wants to say the line as he says 'O that this too too solid . . .' Of course – I suppose – we are going deeper with the role than we did at Stratford, and Frank is able to perform it very much better. Much of it he speaks beautifully – and the advantage of his approach is that it can *never* be merely 'technical'.

After rehearsal my interview with David Richards of the *Post* – brought over to my room by the unputdownable Regan – the cupie-doll of steel. I had a row with her on Friday when I realised that the date set for the interview (Monday 1 p.m. at my hotel) might be an inconvenient one . . . Without lunch?

'Isn't one o'clock an odd time?'

'It's the only time David can manage: he has a very tight schedule.'

'What about my schedule? Are we supposed to have lunch together?'

'No, David doesn't lunch with work.'

'Look – why don't I contact him direct and we can fix a time between us?'

'That's my job, Lindsay.'

'Well, you'd better bloody well do it' – and I put the phone down.

This attitude of unyielding refusal to discuss any change in custom, even to give the slightest impression for the welfare of the 'artists', is absolutely the keynote of this really unpleasant theatre.

On Monday afternoon Frank called me, having realised – and typically neither he nor I had noticed, not having bothered to read and study schedules, *as one should* – that the 'opening' comes at the end of *nine* performances of *Hamlet* – and on the *Monday* after a weekend with matinees and evening performances on Saturday *and* Sunday . . . Bureaucratic idiocy in the highest degree. Mary Ann de Barbieri: 'This is how we've done it for ten years, there's nothing I can do, the seats are sold, the *Washington Post* critic comes on Sunday night. I can't make a change simply on a whim. Well, I'll speak to John and call you back.'

Later I called John myself . . . Mary Ann de B. hadn't spoken to him – the reaction was exactly as I'd expected, tempered only when I said: 'I've been called a pain in the arse once and I think it's better if it doesn't happen again . . .'

18 March 1985

Well, we 'preview' tomorrow – having been unable to run a dress rehearsal, even of the most imperfect kind, yesterday. Work will go on, on set and lighting today – the actors' day off – but there is no doubt that we have been licked by the Folger and by US pre-tension and sloppiness . . . Since Thursday we have been labouring on the stage, continuously frustrated by the problems of a set which has been conceived in terms of visual effectiveness rather than practicability – which has not been 'thought through' from scene to scene, with staging problems unsolved or just not faced – of lighting by a designer who had *never seen a complete run-through*, and who starts with ideas (imprecise and unrelated to the text and my staging) vaguely 'pictorial' and 'conceptual' – and by a general amateurishness and lack of grasp, drive, professional rigour in management. There is no organisational impulse. People take refuge in chatty amateurishness. There seems no real concern to get the production ready for the first previews – indeed, the attitude towards the previews is essentially that they are a sort of dress rehearsal. 'We've even had previews where we have to stop,' says Margaret . . . 'Oh, the audience loves it.'

Two saving graces. Judianna is first-class – very talented, professional, committed. She has not let the Folger folly destroy her, or shake her in the least. And Frank came through with flying colours: since our last fight two weeks ago, he is transformed, controlled, considerate and thoroughly *positive* in his contribution. If anything does, surely this makes the whole experience worthwhile.

22 March 1985

Wednesday and Thursday contained much that was comic – but much, too, that was infuriating and finally destructive.

Pictures had to be taken – 'Just a few two-shots, and they want pictures of Frank' – now mark that *no* production pictures have been taken . . . and this call consisted of a photographer from the *Washington Times*, the girl who had photographed me ages ago for an interview *and* who had done our 'rehearsal shots', and a girl 'from the library' . . . By the time we got to Ophelia I noted that the *Washington Times* photographer had gone – this irritated me further – oh, I should say that Regan was in attendance, smiling her self-possessed 'smile', but of course without a clue of what was wanted or should be staged. *Indeed she'd not seen the production!*

By unfortunate coincidence, before the session, Regan herself gave me two contact sheets, first of the 'group', and second of the 'rehearsal shots' – which consisted of about twenty shots of people standing, quite static, talking. This failure ('They didn't work out too well') accounted for the non-appearance of my requested boards, pictures in the foyer – never, of course, communicated to me . . . Well, a short tale to tell, I'm told 'The *Post* want a picture of you.' Who's to take it? The infamous Folger photographer. I refuse. Why can't the *Post* send their own photographer? It's too late – there isn't time. I see orange – 'Then they won't get one.' You don't want your picture taken? No, I don't want my picture taken . . . Regan and the photographer stand insulted and nonplussed . . . I see RED, and . . . well to be honest I can't exactly remember what I approached them to say – probably just an impulse to get rid of Regan – to make her understand and even acknowledge her failure and her ineptitude . . . A foolish impulse, of course, but understandable . . . The sight of Regan's doll-like (*The Painted Doll*) unyieldingly self-justifying face was too much for me. *I grabbed her arm* – while saying, as scornfully as I could – 'Your work is third-rate' . . . She gasped. Madeleine then appeared in her green robe, for the play within the play, but the photographer (with Regan) had disa

We continued the rehearsal. Some forty minutes later John N. A. appeared – with an elderly photographer with a plate camera – and announced aggressively that I was going to have my photograph taken for the *Post*. Of course I agreed readily – and was positioned, skull in hand, on the stage, to pose for the *Washington Post* . . .

The aftermath is the most absurd. Regan had been met, white-faced and chattering with rage, on her way back to the Folger, declaring that she was *going to sue* (she called her lawyer, in fact, and was advised to 'sleep on it'. Which she did.) The next morning, arriving at John N. A.'s office to discuss 'cuts', I found myself attending a serious-faced top-level 'crisis' meeting of management to deal with the Regan Emergency . . . the story of Physical Abuse . . . It was reported that I had run down the gangway and *shaken Regan*! John N. A. added that there were twenty witnesses who would attest. 'Who are they? I'd like to see them?' I mocked the whole business. Mary Ann de Barbieri, determinedly grave, stressed how serious things became once they entered 'the physical arena' . . . I laughed.

I broke the impasse by suggesting Regan be sent for *now*. She appeared, a self-conscious, semi-smile playing on her lips, her doll-like face as impeccably made-up as ever . . . I spoke: 'I believe you think I owe you an apology.'

'Yes.'

'Could you tell me what for exactly?'

'Well, for . . . physically *touching* me.'

I spoke without hesitation. 'Then I apologise for physically touching you.'

There was a brief pause. Then, still smiling, Regan turned and left the room.

25 March 1985

Well, we opened, and the Folger got a fine performance – a great deal better than it deserved. John N. A.'s last destructive act – to post notices round the dressing rooms on the subject of alcohol, invoking the management, Equity (falsely) and threatening dismissal . . . which aroused again Frank's urgent wish to hand in his notice. But I 'entreated him to a peace'.

26 March 1985

Caught the 7 a.m. shuttle to La Guardia: met by Martin. Concorde to London. WHAM! didn't feel like meeting – thank God! Back to Stirling Mansions: Patsy and Sandy, spaghetti and meat sauce . . . Rapidly watched *Eraserhead*[1] at the end of the Oscars.

---

1. By David Lynch.

27 March 1985

By car with Martin to lunch with George Michael and Andrew Ridgeley at Langham's Brasserie . . . I have really nothing to say to them: confident, bright, uninteresting, respectable, of the eighties . . . I get the impression they will be reasonably cooperative: certainly not inspiring.

31 March 1985

Off to a new adventure (twenty-two hours to Hong Kong!) . . . My right leg has 'gone': not the knee, but the tendons behind it. Perhaps the Chinese will know how to deal with it. Rheumatism in the joints: sometimes I can't open my right hand – have to ease my fingers back with my left hand. Too fat too: I've never recovered from those insidious breakfasts at Balliol[1] . . . How I would like to be back at Stirling Mansions. I have no interest whatever, I'm sorry to say it, in China and its millions. Cynicism has closed over me: 'I do not like the human race.' I have no interest in WHAM! either . . . Essentially I am 'doing this for the money' – but without 'feeling like a whore'. If the world doesn't want (and won't pay me for) what I can do well – let them pay me for what I do badly. I am *not* a commercial film-maker. How I am going to make out on this? I've no idea . . . I'm exhausted of course. I ought to be going home for a rest. How wonderful it would be if the Chinese suddenly turned thumbs down, and we could drop the whole silly business!

1 April 1985

A long flight – but undoubtedly first class does help. A three-hour stopover at Tokyo: as usual, once one is off the plane, one's pampered first-class status disappears . . . I have to go through immigration and customs, lug my handluggage (thank God for Frank's stick) round to the elevator and up to the third floor where there is a semi-comfortable room, a TV set playing without sound – a pop programme displays WHAM! in 'Wake Me Up . . .' the moment I arrive.

On to Hong Kong, met by Lee and a couple of eager and efficient Chinese. We drive to the Regent Meridian, through neon-lit streets – incandescent skyscrapers line the harbour as we descend – the hotel is marble-paved. Before I go to bed I drop in on Martin Lewis, who is next door to me. He is his now-familiar sympathetic and compulsive self. I realise that the organisation of this whole trip has been a fantastic driven labour, yet he has a wonderful capacity to rise above things and not get put down or exacerbated.

The WHAM! concert: the huge Hong Kong Coliseum pretty full.[2]

---

1. Oxford college where L.A. stayed while directing *The Playboy of the Western World*.

2. After playing two warm up gigs at the Coliseum, the WHAM! in China tour opened on 4 April, in front of ten thousand people at the Workers' Stadium in Peking.

13 April 1985
A note from Frank that was left in his dressing room: 'To Frank Grimes – THERE IS ABSOLUTELY NO CONSUMPTION OF ALCOHOL OR ALCOHOLIC BEVERAGES PERMITTED BACKSTAGE DURING A PERFORMANCE. I HAVE CONFISCATED THE BEER FROM YOUR DRESSING ROOM. IF YOU WISH TO COMPLAIN, PLEASE SEE MARY ANN OR JOHN NEVILLE-ANDREWS ON MONDAY.

15 April 1985
Waking early in my room at the Regal Meridian Hotel, the thought was in my head: 'I was not engaged to direct a film of WHAM! in China – I was engaged to occupy the *position of director.*'

Of course this is not a distinction which would actually have occurred to any of those responsible, except perhaps for Martin Lewis, though it is a thought he would have suppressed. None of those people know what a *film* is, what a *documentary* is, what a 'director' does . . . This is the most difficult thing to do – to realise that the definitions which one takes for granted are irrelevant or unknown to Simon Napier-Bell, to Jazz Summers or to WHAM! . . . This is the exploitive world of Rock.

I didn't attempt to keep a diary through Hong Kong, Beijing, Guangzhou and Hong Kong again, chiefly I suppose because the whole thing was too crowded, too nonsensical and in a certain way too *rich*. Also too unreal. I managed to strain or rip a ligament at the base of the Great Wall of China, conscientiously searching for a decent camera position in that scruffy location (all souvenir shops and soft drinks stands) and spent half my time 'directing' from a wheelchair. Theoretically there was a feasible project there, the organisation of the 'documentary' coverage of WHAM!'s concerts in Beijing and Guangzhou, Peking and Canton – of their organised visits here and there – and whatever other phenomena of contemporary China came our way . . . It took me a little time to realise how inept – or at least mistaken – had been the preliminary arrangements, all of them designed to 'get the show on the road' (or to capture the commission), few of them based on any sensible, thought-out appreciation of the essential requirements of the undertaking. As I learned later, negotiations between Nomis (Simon's and Jazz's company) and the Chinese took a long time to finalise – so that when the visit finally was agreed on, there wasn't much time to do any organisation. Simon wanted a film made, while knowing that George Michael, effective genius of WHAM!, disliked 'being photographed', so came up with the idea that the lads from Bushey need only be seen at the film, after sequences of documentary shooting which need not include them . . . A completely specious idea, of course.

*Anderson returned to London to complete his film about the East. In the West, in
April, at Waco, Texas, the Baylor University President suspended a student film
society for showing* If . . . .

6 June 1985

Two weeks ago I swerved and contorted myself violently, while attempting to sit in a
collapsing deckchair, and my leg swelled up like a balloon again. I am limping around
and this week have to start work on editing the documentary material.

Letter to George Michael

18 June 1985

Dear George – Don't shudder – but I thought you might be interested to know how
work on the film is proceeding. I have been through all the material with our editor,
Peter West, and now he is going through it again throwing out the junk and concentrating on the sequences that have some quality. I think there will turn out to be
more interesting and even excellent stuff that one might imagine.

I know you had a look at some material last week. I don't know what you saw,
but I can well imagine it was a depressing experience. The truth is that the shooting
of the film was badly prepared and pretty badly organised. It was a pity that I was
relatively out of action for so much of the time. But to be honest I don't think that,
even if I had been able to tear around and belabour people, it would have made a
great deal of difference. The cameramen were not (in my view) particularly well
chosen – more experienced in video than in documentary-shooting – and anyway
were exposed to so many conflicting instructions that it is not surprising they came
up with a great deal of rubbish.

However, I do think that when this has all been discarded, we'll find that there is
a surprising amount of really interesting and original stuff – and three or four
sequences, I am sure, which may stimulate you to write some music. You may find
this hard to believe, but looking at rushes is a depressing business however experienced one is – and if you are not used to the business of film-making it can make
you positively suicidal. In our case, when one has discarded all the wastefully shot
material, there is a lot that will intrigue people. And certainly enough to make a film.

I think we need a couple of weeks, maybe a few days more, so that you can see the
good footage put in some kind of order. Then I am pretty confident you will feel less
horrified and annoyed about the whole project. Sometime in the first week of July.
Till then, try not to think about it too much – and don't listen to *anyone*!

I don't guarantee that *WHAM! in China!* is going to be a classic. But my guess is
that it will be more than respectable. We'll do our best to surprise you.

Letter to George Michael

2 October 1985

Dear George – I am truly sorry to disturb you, when I know you are closely and creatively involved. I would not be doing so if I didn't feel we had reached a dangerous crisis with our *WHAM! in China!* film.

As I think you know, we had a screening last Friday, attended by Jazz, Simon, Martin, and even Harvey Goldsmith. The film went very well and was well received. It isn't *completely* finished: I am still working on the finale and of course we only have a token soundtrack, chiefly using the sync sound recorded during shooting, plus a few 'specimen' effects. The music track for the concert numbers will of course need remixing and possibly adjusting – and there are sections which have been left for the addition of the specially composed score.

I was sorry you would not be writing anything yourself, but I fully understand the circumstances and I agree that it would be a mistake to take it on if you know that you won't be able to give it the concentration and time that it would call for. Richard Hartley (at Jazz's suggestion) came to see the film in the cutting room and was very responsive and encouraging. He said he would be very happy to undertake the writing of special music.

After the showing on Friday, I had supper with Jazz, Martin and Lee, at which Jazz was very enthusiastic and approving. We agreed on a schedule to complete the film – after you had seen it with Andrew this Friday.

During the weekend, unfortunately, Jazz got hold of the videotape which was made from the cutting copy of the film a couple of weeks ago (so doesn't faithfully reproduce the cut, and particularly the numbers as we have them now). As far as I can make out, after repeated viewings of the tape Jazz started forming criticisms and (offering) cutting suggestions. He didn't communicate this to me, but seems to have got into a series of more-or-less hysterical arguments with Martin – in which he has been joined by Simon. This has reached the point where Jazz and Simon are saying that the film can't be shown to you 'in its present form', or you will certainly 'can' it. I think this is nonsense, but you know that when people who don't really understand the creative process – whether it is film or music – start formulating criticisms and making demands on a work in progress, it is only too easy for the whole enterprise to founder.

Jazz and Simon both seem terrified of you – which may be useful sometimes but at other times can be dangerous. I certainly have enough respect for your creative verve and intelligence not to be scared to show you the work, and of course to be interested in your feelings about it.

I am to meet Jazz and Simon tomorrow, when presumably they will put their opinions (demands?) to me. I shall tell them I don't want to do anything more to the picture before showing it to you and discussing it with you. My personal feeling is that we have come up with an original and enjoyable film, which deserves to be shown as widely as possible. It is *not* a video piece but a genuine movie, and I think it says a lot about China and about young Chinese people, as well as giving a very engaging portrait of WHAM!

Good luck with the work

Yours, Lindsay Anderson

With WHAM! selling a million copies of their first official album release in China, Anderson continued to work on the film while making a British television documentary about Free Cinema.

Letter to Alexander Walker (extract)

13 November 1985

The BFI grows more intolerable all the time: not just because of its Marxist terror-bands, but also for the arrogance of its bureaucrats. I've been having an awful fight with them over the use of my little film *O Dreamland* in my Thames *British Film Year* programme – they insisting that the film was a BFI production, and I insisting (as is indeed the truth) that I paid for it myself all those years ago . . . But the fact that one actually *made* a film is quite irrelevant to these pedagogues of Film Culture. They make me see purple.

28 November 1985

I have meant to keep this diary going – especially as I think, often, of my autobiography – and realise how much I have forgotten in the course of these last thirty years . . . Briefly: in the last two months – we finally got to show *WHAM! in China!* to George Michael and Andrew Ridgeley, with Peter West and the editing crew, and guests Kevin Brownlow and Jocelyn and Saxon Logan . . . It went extremely well, with much amusement and applause. At the end everyone stood around and drank wine and smiled. The managers were mighty relieved.

We were to talk to George a week later. The day before the meeting it was cancelled. I heard from Maggie that Jazz had called her and told her that I was being replaced and the film would be recut.

While all this is going on – and I call the fuddy-duddy Brian Shemmings[1] at ACTT from time to time – I am working on finishing my *Free Cinema* programme for the

---

1. British union leader. Failed to act when L.A., a union director, was replaced by a non-union and non-British director.

Kevin Brownlow–David Gill *British Film Year* series. I rewrite and reshoot my to-camera stuff, having found my first attempt far too pussyfooting, allusive and academic. I take my cue from Kevin's advice to talk 'in headlines' and I speak with a directness very rare on television about Puttnam and Attenborough, which gets the thing off to an edged and dynamic start. I write explaining my attitude and my action to 'Dickie' Attenborough, but he neither acknowledges nor answered my letter.[1]

It takes ages to get the stills and inserts right and correctly shot. I finally get the operation organised, by insisting that the attractively cherubic Michael Winterbottom[2] be my assistant. But although he is conscientious in pursuit of stills he is quite happy to absent himself from crucial, if routine stages of finishing. He is wholly unsentimental and not in the least put out when bureaucracy rules that he cannot have a credit on the programme.

It looks as though *Holiday*[3] is a go-project – this sparked off by the intervention of Mary Steenbergen, who called me with Malcolm some three weeks ago to say – 'Let's do it' . . . I had the copy which Michael Winterbottom had found in a library – I don't even remember if I've read it right the way through . . . The Albery seems a possibility. Tony Sher not being the draw in *Torch Song Trilogy* that the media might make you expect.

And David Sherwin is slowly working on *If . . . . Two . . .*

November 1985

Having received a few days ago my VHS tapes of *If You Were There* – which is the title I finally gave to our WHAM! documentary film – I feel the time has come to outline, for anyone who may still be interested, the history of this enterprise since shooting finished and we all returned from China.

After an apparently very successful showing of the cutting copy of the film some three weeks ago, with a rough dub of the soundtrack, I was informed (through my agent, ten days after the showing) that I was replaced as director of the film, which was to recut in some unspecified way. I gathered that an associate of Jazz Summers was being flown in to supervise the recutting. His name is Strath Hamilton and he is Australian, apparently experienced in the making of commercials and video promos. I felt almost sorry for him, particularly since the editor, Peter West, and his assistant, together with the sound editor, Tim Arrowsmith, and *his* assistant all resigned.

---

1. In October 1983, the two exchanged letters over Attenborough's BBC film *Britain at the Pictures*. L.A. wrote expressing 'distress' and 'anger'. Attenborough replied: ' . . . although the treatment was inevitably superficial, I do believe that bearing in mind the audience who were likely to watch it, it created a worthwhile focus on British cinema, even accepting a number of distressing and infuriating omissions.'

2. Later a major film director. Winner of the Golden Bear at Berlin for *In This World* (2002).

3. Comedy by Philip Barry, first produced on Broadway in 1928.

Such was the climax of some five months work on editing. I need hardly describe the magnitude of the task, or the concentration and skill necessary to achieve a shaped, cohesive and rhythmic whole out of the miles and miles of material – some of it excellent, much of it unuseable – which was the product of those hectic days of filming in Peking and Canton.

During those months, the work in progress was seen and each time approved by WHAM!'s two managers, Jazz Summers and Simon Napier-Bell. So struck, indeed, was this dynamic duo by the punch and vividness of our first cut of about half the material, which ran just over an hour, that they asked enthusiastically whether the completed film might run ninety minutes. I replied that I thought it could, and that was the length we had in mind (I'm sure I don't need to add that we never had any inclination to stretch the material beyond what seemed to be its natural length). Several sequences, in fact, were dropped completely – including the notorious football match and the interview with George Michael on a Canton hotel massage table, in which he gave out his ideas on China, the Chinese people, their system of government, etc.

George Michael himself – 'the man who signs the cheques' – as Jazz Summers put it, did not visit the cutting room, although he was supposed to be providing additional music for the picture. After our return from China, two days' additional shooting were done at Shepperton Studios, shot by a three-camera team under Peter McKay. I was never exactly sure – since I was never consulted or given any information – of the purpose of these extra days of shooting. I *think* it was something to do with providing versions of the songs mimed to the soundtracks from the Hong Kong concerts. In any case, they did provide a number of useful inserts [although George had had his hair cut and had to wear a wig]. After this, George Michael unfortunately viewed four or five hours of rushes, preparatory to his working with a video director on the promo of 'Freedom'. Being completely ignorant of film-making, he became quickly discouraged and even despairing of the quality of the film material. Talking with his usual disarming frankness, he later gave interviews to the press in which he expressed his disappointment and scepticism about the film and said it would very likely never appear. I became alarmed at this, but was vehemently reassured by Martin Lewis.

As cutting proceeded, showings were regularly scheduled at which WHAM!, or at least George Michael, were to appear. First George was exhausted after his China experience, then he was preparing for his American tour, then he was delayed in the US to relax after his tour and to have dinner with Brooke Shields,[1] then he decided (still without having seen anything) that he would *not* after all write any music for the film, then he got the time wrong or was delayed by traffic . . . On three occasions I wrote to

---

1. American actress and model (1965–), who starred in *The Blue Lagoon*. David Sherwin wrote her 1983 TV film *Wet Gold*.

him to let him know of our progress and to hope that he would involve himself creatively with the formation of the film. I had to write because I was not allowed to know his telephone number. None of my letters were acknowledged or received an answer.

By later September, the film had acquired its final shape. It was/is constructed in episodes, each preceded by a title.[1] The concerts in Peking and Canton, which constituted the latter half of the film (with some documentary intercutting) featured four numbers, with 'Go-Go' as a finale. I would describe the tone of the film roughly as 'humorous-lyric-ironic'. Of course I am not in a position to be objective, but I can certainly say that I am proud of what was achieved in a style of pure montage – no commentary, much freshness of observation, a musical rhythm throughout. A picture that could certainly appeal to a wider audience than the familiar WHAM! teenies.

Dubbing or 'mixing' was set for late October. This had to be postponed because the composer selected by Jazz Summers to supply additional music was not free until November. Amid great apprehension, WHAM! – both George and Andrew – finally appeared at a screening in mid-October. A few friendly 'outsiders' had also been invited to provide an atmosphere of 'audience'. Everyone enjoyed the screening and applauded happily at the end. WHAM! hung around for forty-five minutes afterwards, drinking wine and smiling broadly.

Seemingly what happened was this: George, Andrew, Simon and Jazz all had dinner some nights later. Alcohol was consumed. George expressed his disapproval of the film, or at least his feeling of its unfitness for purpose. The only specific objection I heard is that the cutting of the numbers was insufficiently 'modern'. This I take to mean that they don't look like a video – but then of course documentary material can never look like video. The decision was made to 'get rid of Anderson'. George disappeared, either to finish working on his new single or to have a holiday, Andrew went to race cars on the Continent – and it was left to Jazz Summers to mastermind the transformation of *WHAM! in China!* into an acceptable piece of pop promotion. Strath Hamilton and a new editing crew were the answer. Plus, of course, the expenditure of another million dollars or so.

None of this, I suppose, is exactly astonishing. When I first took on the assignment I warned myself not to get too *involved*, since such projects so often end by conflict between creators and exploiters, and in such situations the exploiters must always win. I must admit, though, that I was not prepared for the incredible waste, silliness, lack of conscience, ignorance, lack of grace, lack of scruple, egoism, weakness, duplicity and hypocrisy which have characterised the whole operation. Nor did I quite realise that

---

1. If You Were There . . . – Honoured Guests – Honoured Guests II – Meeting People – Getting In – Afternoon Off – Before the Show – Warming Them Up – If You Were There . . . – To Give You Money! – South To Canton – Canton Concert – Encore and Farewell.

however cool I might be during the shooting, I could not resist total and creative involvement once it came to the editing. I am not going to claim that the loss of *WHAM! in China!* is a creative catastrophe on the scale of Von Stroheim's *Greed*: but I do think that between them the Whammies have destroyed, or suppressed, an enjoyable, informative, entertaining and even at times beautiful film.

1 December 1985

The invitation was announced in a letter from Laurie Evans – a four-day visit to [Argentina to] include two lectures – signed by Dr Mario O'Donnell – Minister of Culture. My immediate instinct is to go – as always when it's a question of getting out of England. But information, and travel arrangements, are difficult.[1] Communication has to be through the Brazilian Embassy – also it is important that I specify the titles of my lectures. I am just finishing my *Free Cinema* for Thames TV, so that will be one, and 'Film Criticism', as delivered in Sydney in 1982,[2] can be my other 'lecture'. No preparation necessary. I am to fly via Rome.

Maggie Parker shows her mettle by securing me first-class flights and accommodation, and a fee – either of £1,200 a lecture, or £2,000 cash. Plus of course all expenses. (My ticket is economy: so much for Maggie.)

In Rome, bored young Italian soldiers lounge about with automatic weapons. They inspect my hand language (rather heavy, by the way) idly . . . It is an atmosphere where the sudden crackle of gunfire or an explosion would somehow not astonish . . . As I mooned round the duty-free shop at Rio – the familiar names of international materialism – which we *had* to visit while the aircraft was cleaned, I saw my silhouette with despondency and regretted the solid omelette I'd eaten on the plane, and the roll and marmalade. It takes self-control to pass it up. At Buenos Aires the formalities don't take long: my bags turn up, thank God. When I emerge into the hall I face a barrage of Italian–Spanish emotionalism. Families stand in the passageway, embracing with tears in their eyes. I'm not surprised there is no one there to meet me. Perfectly happy to wait and observe. After ten or fifteen minutes a small, early middle-aged woman approaches tentatively to ask: 'Are you waiting for someone?'

'I am.'

Am I Mr Anderson?

'I am.'

---

1. On account of the Falklands War.
2. Which begins: 'Criticism is a big subject – one with many, very various aspects. Is it important? I think it is. It is important because it is – or can be – influential. It can influence audiences; it can even enlighten them. It can influence producers and distributors; it can encourage them to make certain films and it can discourage them. It can even, theoretically, influence artists. Of course there are many artists who refuse to concern themselves with criticism, and they are probably right.'

January 1986

I went down for lunch with John Gielgud, accompanying Jill and Mu Richardson. John is in extraordinary shape, lively and rather rubicund, with a fetching little white beard. He is starting a long stint in an American miniseries about the Holocaust (what else?), which takes him over a period of about eight months to locations in Yugoslavia, Rome, Switzerland and finally Dachau, where he will walk into the gas chamber. His vitality and liveliness is perfectly amazing.

15

The Whales of August

Lillian Gish – Bette Davis – Holiday – Glory! Glory!

'End of the third week of shooting – our first two-day weekend off,
and just in time . . . Bette Davis has been so destructive this week,
so fatiguing to everyone, that we desperately need a break.'

---

*In February, Jon Voight walked from a proposed film of Dr Schweitzer: 'I had calls
from the writer, tremendously excited about Jon's creative input. And I had calls
from Jon burbling on about how God wanted us to do this. Then a couple of days
later, I had a distraught call from the writer, to say that out of the blue Jon had
said "I don't want to do it – I don't want to talk about it." And that was that.'
Later in the month, Anderson served on the jury of the Berlin Film Festival: 'The
president of the jury was Gina Lollobrigida: so you can imagine how ridiculous it
all was.' And after almost a decade of trying, Mike Kaplan secured the finance and
persuaded Bette Davis and Lillian Gish to play sisters in Anderson's first and only
American feature film, an adaptation of David Berry's play* The Whales of August.

27 June 1986
Los Angeles–New York. As the TWA plane flies East, and I sit comfortably in Ambassador class, and *Young Sherlock Holmes* unfolds on the screen (with Brian Cox's son
Alan as Young Dr Watson) – I set to chronicle this visit. Will it turn out to have been a
momentous one? It's hard to feel it for I really have 'left the building' – nothing seems
exactly real – or (worse) reality doesn't seem very important. Here's the chronology:

Wednesday 11 June: left London. To the Mayflower Hotel [Manhattan]. Mike Kaplan
greets me with enthusiasm. We consult with David Berry on *Thursday* . . . I run
through my chief points – eliminate flashbacks, confirm Libby's change of heart over
the window and Sarah's resolve to stay together . . . use the material of the flashbacks

to fuel the mood and recollection of the present . . . take the action out of the house . . . Sharpen Tisha's attempt to break up Sarah's 'dependence' on Libby.

David seems to go along with everything, which of course pleases Mike. It rather worries me, since it implies a lack of firmness in his conception. However, it's certainly better than obstinate resistance to change. He reveals how tortuous the formation of the play has plainly been – ending at one time with Sarah's suicide. He talks a bit too much: he has the arrogance of the academic – not warm and certainly not humorous. I sensed this the first time we met, which is one good reason why I've always edged away from this project.

Thursday evening: Mike and Marc and I went to the universally praised *Hannah and Her Sisters* by Woody Allen. After ten minutes (at the most) I found myself groaning – 'What on earth is all this about? Why are we supposed to be interested in these people?' I have become more and more, and more and more clearly alienated from the omni-prevalent middle-class drama – the preoccupation with self and sensitivity . . . Woody Allen is of the same ilk as Frayn, Stoppard, Simon Gray and, with differences, Alan Ayckbourn. In a 'culture' that rhapsodises over Woody Allen and Michael Frayn, I cannot expect my social-satirical films to be appreciated. Or understood.

Mike and I went to see Lillian [Gish] on Friday. I was shocked – she seemed to have declined considerably since I saw her last (but that must have been some years ago). Difficult – impossible? – to have a conversation with her: she hardly followed what I was saying: Mike, of course, is too besotted to be objective. We drank lemonade provided by Jim [James Frashier, Lillian's manager] – hovering within earshot in the kitchen – and also his little canapés (a vegetarian spread for Mike). Lillian came out with her story of only drinking champagne because her father had given her a taste when she was ten days old – to celebrate the new century. Which definitely makes her eighty-six or eighty-five.[1] (When did she start with Griffith? 1912? Was she really then only twelve years old?)

She talked of Gielgud – 'The best actor in the world . . . During the run of *Hamlet*, the stagehands would watch his performance . . .' How he could pace himself, etc., etc. She seems to have an extraordinary capacity for reliving and recounting the past without boring herself. And of course, in the presence of a living legend – how could one be bored?

Leaving, I had to say to Mike that – *other things being equal* – I would say she was too old to play Sarah . . . Not just too old, but now too infirm. Mike of course fights back – she had a bad week last week, went to some award presentation (at which, a hitherto unknown occurence, she broke down); suffered the news of her dear friend Anna Neagle's death *and* it was the Anniversary of Dorothy [Gish]'s death . . . If I had

---

1. Lillian Gish was born on 4 October 1893. She was ninety-two years old.

seen her on Monday, says Mike, I would really have been shocked . . . And did I notice the firmness with which she rose to see us out and opened the door? I pointed out that we were talking about eight weeks' work . . . And what was this about going to Minneapolis at the end of August for a celebration of Dorothy's life and work? That would be quite out of the question if we are shooting at the beginning of September.

To be fair, Lillian herself was entirely reasonable and professional on the whole subject. She would definitely do it – if she felt strong enough. The only problem which is not yet really being faced is, when will that decision be made? I can only think of arranging a medical examination at the earliest opportunity . . . though a medical examination will not be exactly conclusive. It's not a question of *health* but of energy . . . Then again: does reason enter into it? Is the whole justification of *The Whales of August* not that it gives an opportunity once again to these mythic creatures? Suppose Lillian Gish is not 'up to it'? Would that *matter*?

Returning from Lillian's, we walked, my right shoe – one I hadn't worn before – rubbed against my heel painfully. And we couldn't get a taxi . . . We attempted a couple of times to buy something that would soften the leather, something like Dubbin back home, to be met with the usual New York stare of blank incomprehension.

19 June 1986
Meeting of Jocelyn [Herbert] and Bette Davis.

Well . . . we anticipated a difficult meeting, even a hostile meeting – in the sense of uncooperative, obstinate, unwilling to consider ideas . . . but none of us anticipated a meeting of such abrupt discourtesy.

Bette in black. Jocelyn went in first. I kissed Bette's cheek, and felt her guarded tension, could feel her walk was unsteady – less firm than yesterday . . . I could feel the defensively unfriendly vibes . . . I excused myself and asked to use the lavatory. When I came out I could feel the implacable, fiercely defensive-aggressive vibrations emanating from the tense little black figure in the big armchair. Jocelyn attempted to start a conversation – to no avail. 'I've been through all that, discussions and fittings, and I can't go through any more. I've got to get my strength together. Nobody told me this was a meeting about costumes. I've had Julie Weiss to do my costumes: she's very good: I think you'll like them.'

Jocelyn attempted to show her the Polaroids which she'd been sent from Los Angeles. 'What are these? They're ridiculous. I've never heard of anyone sending pictures like these.'

'I know they're ridiculous,' says Jocelyn. 'I quite agree. But these are what I was sent.'

She tries to ask Bette if this is what she wants: this belt, or collar or apron. 'I don't know why there should be an apron: she never wears an apron.'

Bette shrugs such questions away. She is determined not to discuss *anything*. 'I'm very upset. I had no idea my costumes were to be discussed. Nobody told me you were concerned with my costumes!'

I cannot tell whether this is the desperation of infirmity or of egotistical wilfulness. Whether Bette is possessed by anger or by defensive panic. Faced by this stone wall – she cannot even open her portfolio to show Bette some drawings – it is not long before Jocelyn rises, considerably vexed but courteous to the last, and departs. 'Well, there doesn't seem much point in my staying . . . I'll leave you and Lindsay to talk.' I judge that it is best for me to stay, for however short a while, rather than for both of us to leave together. (Although it is quite obvious Bette would prefer both of us to vanish together.) I attempt to deliver some placatory, even reassuring bromide, but there is no way of calming Bette. The refrain is repeated: 'Nobody told me of this. My costumes have been settled by Julie Weiss. I can't discuss them now . . . ' etc., etc.

Bette beats a retreat into the bedroom. The devoted French slave can offer nothing save blind loyalty to the distraught diva. I say, 'I am just going to write a dedication to Miss Davis.' I sit down and produce a copy of *About John Ford* from my briefcase. On the title page I write: 'FOR BETTE. WITH THE GREATEST ADMIRATION, from Lindsay, 1986' . . . Then a postscript: 'I'm sorry Mr Ford denied himself the joy' (I hesitated over the word, thinking perhaps 'pleasure' would be less fulsome – then, what the hell, write JOY) 'of working with you' . . . I pressed it into the slave's hand, who passed it to Bette in her bedroom refuge. The slave let me out, still fiercely defensive for her mistress.

I take a taxi back to the Mayflower. No sign of Jocelyn.

(She'd been down to Houston, to see if she could find something suitable for Lillian . . . no luck).

I call Mike and we have a long conversation. He makes all the excuses for Bette's 'misunderstanding' of the situation. I reply that essentially those are irrelevant. When one is dealing with a neurotic, hysterical personality one finds oneself continually held to blackmail, continually questioning whether one has failed in tact, or frankness or whatever . . . wasting energy and time and concentration trying to placate a monster . . . But what becomes of the work? And what will become of Lillian, with such a performance *hurled* at her? Not played with, but played *at* . . . It's not a responsibility I wish to take on.

Mike recounts that he has had a long conversation with Bette's agent, Robbie Lantz. (Ironic note: Lantz has been an agent of both Jocelyn *and* myself!) Bette had apparently reported that Jocelyn rejected her costumes out of hand – said they're dreadful, hopeless, useless etc . . . 'I knew she was exaggerating,' says Mike. 'It's not an exaggeration,' I reply. 'It's a lie.' Robbie is now supposedly assuring Bette of Jocelyn's great talent, reputation, etc., and Bette is anyway fully appreciative of *my* talent . . . etc.

I get as far as telling Mike I couldn't direct Bette if this is now her professional personality, and moreover that she would be incapable of playing with Lillian. And honestly

I sense that her balance is now so insecure, her desperation and fear so acute, that anything like 'acting' is beyond her – as opposed, I mean, to wilful and egocentric 'performing', for effect, effect, effect . . . with decisions not open to discussion. 'I'm playing her totally blind' – announced with a categorical abruptness that forbids discussion. And what might she get up to? 'Perhaps I should smoke?' she said to Mike on a previous call. 'My public likes to see me smoke.' Paul Henreid could light her cigarette (though not, of course, à la *Now Voyager*).

I've not even mentioned her violent disapproval and dislike of Danny Kaye. Indeed going so far, at our first meeting, as to say she couldn't do the film with him. She offered to call Paul Henreid – and apparently had done so. She mentioned Jimmy Stewart, but knew, as I said, he was 'too American'.

It's an evening of phone calls. David Berry, ploughing on through the script, has had a bad week. On Monday his agent died – from the Plague . . . He hadn't told anyone he had AIDS – went into hospital with pneumonia, showing extreme symptoms, responded apparently to treatment, had a relapse over the weekend – and on Monday he died . . . aged thirty-seven.

Call to Marc [assistant] in London. He has spoken to Oscar. Oscar said: 'I wonder if Lindsay has a little doll of me to stick pins into.'

20 June 1986

I woke this morning early – a brilliant solution to the impasse occurred to me: Anthony Page! Who else could cope with – and enjoy coping with – Bette Davis *and* beautifully look after Lillian Gish?! . . . I had my breakfast delivered to Jocelyn's room, and told her my idea.

28 June 1986

Saturday: The rewrite has been completed. *I did not read it.* I panicked: went to Jocelyn and we had our coffee and brown rolls together. We talked about the feasibility of the script . . . I saying, 'The premise of the script I can accept, and also the characters . . . and the phenomenal casting . . . It's a question of getting the dialogue right . . . I'm just not sure it's possible.'

How often has one seen films on which all the energy has gone on the organisation, the financing and the deals, while the script, with all its imperfections, has simply been taken for granted? Hence disaster. Are we one of those?

I take off for the Mayflower and our 10 a.m. meeting with David [Berry] . . . The police boundaries are up for a parade. The doorman at the Mayflower says it's for the Dominicans (monks, or nationals of the Dominican Republic?). I go up and catch Mike just getting into the shower. We talk for a few minutes. Mike is placatory. David will surely make all the changes he is asked for. He is quite conscious of having only sketched in the new scenes at the end of the script . . . My doubts of course spring from the knowledge that it's not *just* a question of executing the changes I ask for. Something 'creative' is needed – particularly in making something of the ghastly Maronov scene.[1] My confidence goes up and down like a see-saw.

The Dominican procession starts to roll by outside. Mike, Jocelyn and I take a taxi to Lillian's apartment. We are late. It takes an age to get through the procession as a large float seems to get stuck in Fifth Avenue. With great discussion and difficulty the taxi manages to reverse (we are in two-way 57th Street) and go down Broadway to take a lower cross-town street.

Lillian greets us in a long garment – would you call it a negligee? – not looking in the least groomed or as if wanting to make any kind of impression. One of the great problems, of course, is that one is so concerned to treat Lillian with extreme concern and respect that one doesn't exactly allow oneself to look at her unsparingly or judge her impartially. So one tends to overlook her extreme uncertainty of movement (or unfirmness), her deafness, the lack of clarity in her articulation. One treads delicately; one conducts the conversation as if handling a precious, delicate china object. And yet Lillian's strength, her fibre, her honesty and the firmness with which her opinions are held, all make themselves felt.

We sit as usual round the table in her [living] room, a low table with chairs and a couch round it, a little selection of cakes and in the centre a vase of huge rather exotic flowers, lilies and broad leaves – which apparently 'we' (Mike and I?) have sent. On a side table are jugs of yellow lemonade and pink lemonade. I am offered, and accept, iced tea.

Lillian seems to think it's a long time since we met, which it isn't really . . . Anyway, I am not too successful in my contributions to the conversation, since she doesn't understand much of what I say. It appears that with her deafness, she tends to anticipate – talk pursues the line she expects – if you cross her bows with something new or unexpected, she is likely to fail completely to pick it up.

We talk about the apartment, which Jocelyn of course finds charming with its timeless and unshowy elegance, its mementoes of a fully-lived life on every shelf and wall and table. Pictures of mother and sister Dorothy. Lillian explains that this was her mother's apartment; she and her sister were accustomed from earliest age not to having a home – they lived in hotels and boarding houses, as young travelling actresses – she having started at four and Dorothy at five . . . And this is where they always, later, had 'home': her mother in one bedroom and she and Dorothy in the other. Then, when Dorothy married, Lillian moved in with her mother and Dorothy and her husband took the other

---

1. Maranov, a Russian nobleman seeking a new place to live on the island.

room. Until her mother told Dorothy that the arrangement wasn't fair – the man hadn't married three women, he had married Dorothy, and she would have to go and live with him in his apartment. 'Dorothy cried . . . She said she'd never thought the day would come when she'd be thrown out by her mother . . ' Anyway, it didn't last long. In two years, Dorothy was back, and the marriage at an end . . . Later, Lillian remarked: 'My sister always used to say men and women couldn't live together, and I think she was right. They are so entirely different.'

Make-up and costumes are discussed. Lillian asks whether she needs to be made up by the film people: she has always done her own. This of course immediately sets off Jocelyn, with her scorn of all things 'false' and her conviction that movie make-up people give everyone 'yellow' complexions (of course it is true that their tendency is to standardise and exaggerate but I begin to get nervous at the thought of Lillian with *no* make-up, especially in juxtaposition with an elaborately made-up Bette Davis. Then I remind myself that Lillian is an old hand and an old fox too, and will certainly know how to make the best of herself).

Lillian explains how the huge screens in silent days showed their faces in such magnified detail that they couldn't afford anything false . . . like eyelashes, etc. This is the kind of thing which, spoken by anyone else, would certainly give rise to argument – for after all, screens are even bigger today; and make-up can emphasise and enhance as well as falsify . . . But with Lillian one lets it all pass.

We talk about hair. Lillian has never cut her hair: her mother was always bobbed, but she and Dorothy never cut their hair, they saved money that way. How much money most women waste in the course of a lifetime, having their hair cut and 'done'. Lillian unpins her hair and it falls down her back and frames her face: cries of astonishment and admiration: 'You can sit on it!' cries Jocelyn. 'I've never cut it,' repeats Lillian. She is totally – almost unbelievably – cooperative, and one senses the discipline, maintained life-long, of Mr Griffith. She'd rather not wear a wig; is quite happy to have her own hair tinted. She piles it up on her head, twisting the long strands expertly, as Jocelyn thinks she should be wearing it on the morning. We talk to her of Paul Huntley and explain he comes from England, where he used to work for us at the Royal Court. She would like him to come and do his tinting at her apartment.

Dresses, shoes, hats, are discussed and produced. I had rather imagined that Lillian would take Jocelyn through wardrobe after wardrobe of old costumes, but in the event Jim offered up a selection of possibilities, suggested by talk and Jocelyn's drawings. The dresses on the whole were too elegant – timeless, yet unmistakably well designed and made. Lillian is worried about the freckles on her arms (sleeves must be *long*) and a general urging of *simplicity*. She hates unnecessary sparkle and decoration. (Has she seen Bette Davis in her splashy red dress?) Jocelyn responded to these avowals of simplicity and honesty. I nodded agreement.

Lots of shoes – about which I'm afraid I never really care. 'I could never buy shoes in England,' Lillian said. 'I'd go to Paris and be able to buy any number.' English women have long feet, and narrow; French women small and broad – like hers.

Hats. Two delightful straws: a little boater which made her look like a Griffith heroine – a must. And a broad-brimmed one, with flowers. (Jocelyn: 'We might lose the flowers'). A charming black straw, with flowers *under* the brim: but we preferred the natural straw.

'I haven't learned any of the script,' Lillian said to me.

'No need,' I said – especially as it was being revised. I don't think she heard this: she went on talking about Griffith – how they never had a script: they improvised everything in rehearsal. Mr Griffith only once commissioned a script. 'I remember, we sat around reading it – and I wondered, why ever would Mr Griffith pay sixty thousand dollars for an old-fashioned piece of melodramatic nonsense like this? And the film was *Way Down East* and it turned out to be his biggest success since *Birth of a Nation . . .*'

Seeing us off, Lillian stood at the door while Jim waited for the lift to arrive. We told her not to wait – but she wouldn't go in until the lift had arrived. I kissed her goodbye and looked forward to the work together.

Lillian and Jocelyn hit it off beautifully, as you'd expect. She admired the blue of Jocelyn's working suit, and the twist of material she was wearing like a scarf. Again the elegance of simplicity.

Back to the Mayflower, and resume work with Mike and David. Finish through to the end of the script. David goes home about 7.30. Walk back to the Dorset. And on the Classic Channel an old silent with Richard Barthelmess. At first I thought maybe *Tol'able David*. Then, as the girl is unmasked by the gossiping scold as an unwed mother, I realised: *Way Down East*. And, yes, it was Lillian driven out into the snow and floating down towards the falls on that ice floe, rescued in the nick of time by Richard Barthelmess . . . That hair trailing in the icy water, the very hair we had seen let down that afternoon from Lillian's aged head . . .

16 August 1986

[*Hollywood.*] I am here to 'meet with' possible Maranovs. Up to yesterday Danny Kaye was favourite – in spite of Bette Davis's vehement disapproval and dislike. What was it she said to Mike? A third-rate, failed comedian – something like that. But chiefly she dislikes him for his bad taste: at some Paris award celebration he *imitated*, she says, the doddering walk of some doddering old comedian who preceded him to the platform. He would give a terrible time, she said, thinking only of himself and making a heart-warming impression

Well anyway – after our hearing that Danny Kaye liked the script and wanted to play the part – dependent on a meeting (which originated my trip here) – his manager, it seems, started upping his demands in an absurd and unacceptable fashion. So by the time I got here, Kaye was OUT.

And Paul Henreid? This was originally my idea: I kept hearing that he was returning to LA and Mike would meet him, but it never happened. Then he complained to Bette Davis that he was only being offered $8,000 (untrue). He also gave it as his opinion that his renewed partnership with Bette would be the only reason why anyone would want to see the picture. Further exorbitant demands, both money and billing. He seems crazy, and was dropped. So, a day of meetings.

11.30: David Opatoshu:[1] immediately seems a good actor; seems he's not been doing much lately – particularly with the obsessively youth-oriented policies of today . . . I mention that Gielgud was originally going to play this part – it turns out that David O. knows all about John's present commitment – in fact he was up for it himself and hoped to get it . . . He likes the script, he says, and the role.

Well, he could do it well, I'm sure. But not a 'personality' exactly. *Probably too good for our enterprise.*

I called Vincent Price: my mind stuck as I put through the call and I found myself unable to remember Coral's[2] name. Vinny *loves* the script and the part . . . More than ever I feel that this must be the effect of the rubbish which is all these actors are ever asked to do . . . He has other commitments – including a vacation voyage with Coral, which it seems he is prepared to put off. By now Broderick has come over to have lunch. We drove to Swallow Drive.

Coral opens the door of the big, pink-washed bungalow. The Prices' home is cool and elegant and spacious – but not pretentious. I remember coming there for dinner all those years ago, with Rachel and Darren and Roddy McDowall[3] . . . Just the old crowd . . . We are given white wine. Coral doesn't have anything: 'I don't drink until the evening. One glass before dinner and one after, if I can manage it.' They have no great desire to go out partying any more, or seeing things. 'We generally get to bed at 9.30. Then we watch a tape, and then the light out by 10.30.' Vinny gets up early, about seven . . . It is a picture of harmonious tranquillity, of European civilisation, infinitely relaxing.

Coral has her Bette Davis story, of course. They had been going to a dinner party and had stopped by to pick her up – Coral didn't know her . . . From the moment she got into the car she was bitchy, insulting, nasty . . . When they arrived at their hosts, she continued in the same vein. Coral made a beeline for the opposite side of the living room. 'What are you doing?' said Roddy. 'What are you hiding over here for?' 'To get away from that monster,' said Coral. Roddy crossed the room, took hold of her [Bette]

---

1. American actor (1918–1996).

2. Coral Browne, Vincent Price's wife.

3. Roddy McDowall (1928–1998), actor, photographer; starred in Ford's *How Green Was My Valley* (1941).

and marched her off to the bathroom. 'You're behaving disgracefully,' he told her. 'Pull yourself together and behave in a proper way or go home . . . You should be ashamed of yourself.' The transformation was total. Bette changed her manner, was pleasant, courteous . . . insisted Coral and Vinny came in for a drink on their way home, suggested they get an apartment in the same block as her . . .

'And did you?'

'Not on your nelly!'

Back to the Regency for Francis Lederer.[1] At 4.30 he phones, unable to find the Hotel . . . I go out to meet him, excellently preserved, rather waxen-cheeked, very much all there in his big, beautiful car. We talk most enjoyably, of Elizabeth Bergner.[2]

25 August 1986

Bette's costume parade: Mike, Jocelyn and I take off with apprehension, for the discreetly swanky Lowell Hotel. We arrive a quarter of an hour early. The hotel bar is closed; the little bar-restaurant across the road is empty and echoing with taped music . . . We retreat to the lobby of the hotel, where two cool young men are building luxurious floral displays . . . I feel more than ever stifled by the omnipresent materialism and display of New York.

Julie Weiss comes in – a very fat lady in a mackintosh. She puts on grimacy smiles as she greets us . . . goes up: we continue to wait in the lobby. At 12 Mike calls up and we are permitted to take the elevator. Jocelyn has of course left her portfolio at the desk: I finger my tape recorder in my jacket pocket.

In the apartment we are greeted by Caroline, the devoted young Frenchwoman who has protected and supported Bette through years of illness. Throughout the ensuing dress parade she sits at a desk in the living room, discreetly hostile, 'working' busily on a script, smart and irritating in her humourless Parisian elegance.

Bette is in the bedroom, with Rudi in attendance. Rudi heard about but never seen, turns out to be surprisingly young, blonde, with curly hair, passably pretty in a hard American way. Julie Weiss, shapeless in black, makes the presentations – directing me to the sofa, where I sit next to Jocelyn.

(How exactly was Bette dressed when she marshalled us to our seats? – I think I was so keyed up for the situation – so determined not betray possible disapproval of *anything* – that I didn't really notice what she was wearing).

The parade began. In a makeshift wig provided by Paul Huntley, Bette marches in (limping slightly) erect and self-consciously aggressive. She finds it necessary to explain that though we 'probably think this is my wig' it is in fact a scratch article, provided for

---

1. (1899–2000). An international star after Pabst's *Pandora's Box* (1928).
2. Lederer played Romeo to Bergner's Juliet in Max Reinhardt's 1922 production .

the occasion. She states (rather than explains) the function of each costume in an abrupt manner which manages to imply our stupidity – and also the irrelevance of any comment we might feel called upon to make.

Since we have already decided to accept the costumes, provided they are halfway decent, without criticism, there is not much discussion. My personal feeling is that, though the ideas are quite real, the materials suitably aged and faded, the general style is rather *neat*, a little skimpy and untheatrical . . . I would have preferred a rather more full-blooded style. Is Bette anxious to suggest she is younger than she is? She is certainly adept, I'd say, at suiting the character she's playing to her personal whims and image. Probably unconsciously.

Having invited Jocelyn to attend, she continues to be consistently and unattractively rude to her. Jocelyn's approval of the costumes is ignored. When she makes the mistake of saying anything, she is snubbed. Like – do you have slippers?

'Of course I have slippers. If you'd been looking, you'd have noticed I was wearing them with my first costume.' And on the next entrance Bette brings in a pair of knitted slippers, which she throws down contemptuously on the coffee table in front of the sofa: '*These* are my slippers!'

But a certain skittishness makes itself evident. One of her dresses had a small gold stud at the neck. I suggested something more important. After some thought, Bette produced a cameo brooch – certainly better. She kissed it gratefully. There was some talk about a locket which was inside the dress. 'Would you like to see it?' asks Bette flirtatiously. 'I think the director should get it out'. I respond without hesitation, though I am not at all sure what is expected of me. 'How do I do it?' I ask, tentatively approaching the tightly fastened neck of Bette's dress – and certainly not anxious to put my hand down her bosom . . . Amid laughter, fortunately Julie Weiss fishes it out.

28 August 1986

When I take Bette Davis the revised script, she has executed a complete about-face. Conciliatory, complimentary, positive. I explain that I will be rewriting the last scenes – 'You're a good editor I know – You'll be the first talented director I've had for years . . .' I demur in a modest, British way . . . Then we had our chat (that *on the floor* I must insist on professional respect and discipline), and I was careful not to strain my luck . . . Leaving I said, quite spontaneously, 'Perhaps we'll even have a good time.'

'Oh we will,' said Bette, 'We'll have a ball.'

5 September 1986

They said Bette Davis was coming out from Portland in a yacht. In the event it was a white cabin-cruiser cutting impressively through the water. As it drew in to the jetty I went down with Mike Fash, Marc followed with the camera.

As the cruiser drew in, there appeared about us – it being low tide – this tense, unsteady yet firm little figure, mostly in black, a jaunty pillbox on her abundant hair, haggard and big-eyed. Bette was talking, but it was impossible to hear what she was saying. The steps were positioned on the landing stage and proved ludicrously short. Bette was assisted forward to stand above the steps, but far short of them. She would have to be lifted down, but everyone was nervous, having heard that she didn't like to be touched, steered or helped.

I called up something cheery. It was still impossible to make out exactly what Bette was saying. Her legs were terribly thin in their smoky-silk stockings. 'You'll have to lift her down,' I called. A bulky fellow up on the deck moved forward to help her. I pushed Broderick forward: he stretched out his arms; courageously Bette let herself be lowered down, spindle legs dangling, and Broderick grasped her and lowered her gently to the stage.

I moved forward, uttering some banalities about the journey. Bette was grasping the rail of the stage now, never for an instant relaxing her fierce tense control. She asked Broderick who he was. 'I'm Broderick Miller, Miss Davis, First Assistant Director. Welcome to Cliff Island.'

'I hope you feel like that at the end of the picture,' she said.

There was a wheelchair on the landing stage, but Bette did not feel inclined to take it. She would walk up the long gangway to the jetty.

'You sure you can manage it?'

'Oh, I can manage it. Don't worry.'

She marched steadily and determinedly up the gangway.

26 September 1986

End of the third week of shooting – our first two-day weekend off, and just in time . . . Bette Davis has been so destructive this week, so fatiguing to everyone, that we desperately need a break, and a recharging of batteries.

It all started on Monday, with a clear sunny morning and the 'Hairbrushing Scene' on the patio. Bette at her worst. (I suddenly find myself overcome with fatigue and boredom in writing about the wretched, crazy woman: perhaps I'll take it up tomorrow.)

Letter to Mike Fash (extract)

27 November 1986

How long is it, it seems a long time ago, since you sailed off in pursuit of *Whales*? I heard how it went: Mike Kaplan turned up late that evening, to the supper we were supposed to be having with Lillian and Bette . . . He looked utterly exhausted . . . To be met, poor fellow, by a tirade from Bette, who went on and on and on about the wrap party, and how it had been utterly spoiled by the presence of Islanders . . . Poor

Bette, I'm sure she started off with the best of resolutions, to be a well-behaved guest at Lillian's gracious table. But of course she can't keep that up long.

But I've called Bette since, at her New York hotel (the Ritz Carlton) and found her friendly and even nostalgic. I think she looks on the whole experience now with affection and even a certain regret.

It was a great experience, Mike, and I'm immensely and eternally grateful to you for your help, not only in your own terrific contribution, but for the splendid unit you provided.

30 November 1986
I have been looking forward to today: a day off; take no calls; make no calls . . . except I would like to call Lester and Sumitra in Sri Lanka – are they all right? And Mary and Malcolm . . . *Holiday*[1] looms ahead . . . And Jill – is she all right? Yesterday I shopped in Waitrose . . . took the bedsheets to Sketchley and collected the laundry . . . Took a mini in to the cutting room – found that Nick [Gaster] had been unable to cut Tisha's 'berrying' sequence (of three shots) satisfactorily and *certainly* had not tidied up the last reel . . . So we plunged in and worked through to about 4.15. (I have to recognise the essential lack of flair of Nick as an editor, and be thankful for his neatness, willingness and adeptness – while groaning at my fate never – well hardly ever – to strike lucky in this matter of collaborators. 'The fault, dear Brutus is not in our stars . . .')

1 January 1987
How old Freddie Ayer[2] looked last night when I briefly greeted him as I left Alan Bates's party, urging Malcolm and Mary away . . . Eyes dimmed and somehow withdrawn . . . I remembered the vivacious, active figure in Wadham Quad. I was only ten or fifteen minutes at Alan's party, having come from Mu's, and there was Anna Massey, now playing Goneril at the National to Tony [Hopkins]'s Lear, and T. S. Eliot's widow, blonde and sizeable with a gold-and-black jacket . . . I fleetingly saw Ron Eyre, and Jocelyn Rickards and Clive Donner and some smart young men; Alan giggling and hiding his neck, though I'm always glad to see him. Brian Cox had left.

I was glad to get back and have a cup of tea, and a modest glass of champagne to welcome the new year with Malcolm and Mary and Frank and Ginette and David [Grimes] – now such a good-looking and charmingly-mannered young man.

Tomorrow is the Thursday of our third week of rehearsals for *Holiday*. It is *so far* a smooth and agreeable experience, excellently cast and we are all mostly enjoying it . . .

---

1. L.A.'s production, starring Malcolm McDowell and Mary Steenburgen, designed by Michael Pavelka, opened at the Old Vic on 14 January 1987.
2. A. J. Ayer (1910–1989). Oxford philosopher, whose best-selling *Language, Truth and Logic* was published when he was twenty-five.

Frank disconcerted me yesterday, after demonstrating beautifully his rightness for the role of Ned, by suddenly finding my direction 'shallow', losing all the humour of the part, and playing the run-through of Act II with sort-of gruff bad temper . . . We must hope this is a temporary aberration . . . Mary [Steenbergen] is coming up steadily, and Malcolm settling very well – Cherie Lunghi[2] is excellent, highly intelligent and expert, and with exactly the right mixture of attractiveness and conventionalness for Julia. Geoffrey Burnidge not exactly right for the (impossible?) Nick, but with admirable *brio*.

19 January 1987

The snow is still here and we've now done five previews of *Holiday*. One more tonight (Monday) then the opening tomorrow evening. It's funny how we cling to this idea of an 'opening', which only means that the performance will be attended by large numbers of those ignorant, self-important but alas influential creatures – the critics. Apart from that, everybody looks as scruffy as usual. On this occasion, however, I've decided I'd better wear a dinner jacket, as a tribute to the elegance of the piece – and also to confound those who write me off as perpetually leather-jacketed and radically avant-garde.

20 January 1987

The morning after the opening. The show went very well last night – apparently. But of course with all those friends and sympathisers being so friendly and sympathetic, one can't have a very objective view of the occasion. I thought I would pay compliment to the shade of Philip Barry by putting on my dinner jacket, only to find that I couldn't get into the trousers. I *did*; but it meant that I had to carry my programme carefully to conceal the ill-fit. *Holiday* is a really charming play, and the actors did it beautifully. Mary Steenburgen, who hasn't been on the stage for about ten years did brilliantly. She really is a remarkable actress and personality. Malcolm hasn't exactly got Cary Grant's charm, but he has truthfulness and skill and proper sincerity.

May 1987

Cannes [for the world premiere of *The Whales of August*] was really no fun at all. Not only has the Festival surrendered completely to commerce, publicity and the media, but the conglomeration of smiling personnel from Alive/Embassy/Nelson Entertainments ensured that I spent the few days in a state of frustrated fury. Lillian was flown from New York by Concorde, together with Jim and his boyfriend; at London into a private plane and flown on down to Nice. I'll freely admit that I was wrong to say it would all be too much for Lillian: she rationed her appearances firmly (at the Gala Performance

---

1. Made her London debut at the Court in David Hare's *Teeth and Smiles* (September 1975).

and at a press conference the next day), behaved splendidly and looked marvellous. What was sad though, as well as disgraceful, was the fact that the Festival quite plainly didn't give a damn whether she was there or not. No pride and precious little respect. I had to go into my famous shouting act to ensure that Lillian appeared on the stage after the screening of *Whales*, to be presented with some kind of idiotic trophy. (The Festival were so intimidated and pulverised by the presence of Prince Charles and Princess Diana that they wanted to keep Lillian firmly in her seat, where she could not be seen).

Carolyn Pfeiffer [co-producer] and I had to sit in the 'Royal Box' (more like a Royal Enclosure at the back of the theatre, where it couldn't be seen by two-thirds of the audience). Carolyn was next to Charles and dutifully answered his inane questions during the first half of the picture. I was next to Diana, who took off her left earring after about a third of the film, and spent the rest of the time fiddling with it in her lap, never managing to glance at the screen. She seems a really naive girl without style and rather unhappy in her position, and certainly unhappy in her marriage.

The press show went well, though, and many of the hardened critics emerged with tears in their eyes. Afterwards there was a drinks party attended by a large number of Britishers, none of whom spoke to me except Charles Dance. However, Lillian met the Royal Couple, which I think pleased her.

Although Lillian Gish would win the National Board of Review Award for Actress of the year, and Ann Sothern would win an Oscar nomination for her supporting role, The Whales of August *failed to win any of the major prizes at Cannes. Still smarting from this, Anderson had the misfortune to run into Alan Bridges in London, whose film* The Hireling *won the top prize at Cannes in the year* O Lucky Man! *went unrewarded.*

Letter to Alan Bates (extract)

4 *June 1987*

You'd be surprised I'm sure – and I hope gratified – by the number of times I've reproached myself for not getting in touch with you. Because, as I am sure you felt, you were certainly owed an apology for that distressing/comic incident in which we were involved – when was it? It must have been months ago – about which I've felt sorry and guilty for ages.

I think in the first place I must plead the excuse – though not justification – of drunkenness. Clive [Donner] and Jocelyn [Rickards] really did lace us with champagne (which reminds me – I've not written to *them* to thank them for their hospitality!), which inevitably led to irresponsible high spirits and runaway tongues. And of course

I was not at all expecting such a high-powered gathering – particularly the presence of John [Schlesinger] and Noel [Davis], which inevitably created (to someone of my prickly and defensive sensibility) something of an insider/outsider atmosphere.

So, naughtiness stimulated by alcohol, then, as I say, defensive-aggressiveness exacerbated by that strong element of successful satisfaction by which I felt myself surrounded. Of course you will feel it unjust that *you* should have been identified with any such element, and of course you weren't really – except by the accident of your friendly professional relationship with Alan Bridges[1] . . . It's only another aspect of the comedy that I should be so scornfully outraged by Bridges congratulating me at the first night of *Holiday* on a 'first-class professional job', and that I should have it in for the aforesaid Bridges for having been awarded the Cannes Grand Prix (a share of, anyway) for a film I despised – in the year when we (I'm including Malcolm in this) had (unsuccessfully) offered *O Lucky Man!* . . . It's comic too, I suppose, that Bridges' tasteful, passionless respectability (I'm talking subjectively) should somehow come briefly to symbolise the kind of art that could only arouse my contempt.

The word 'bourgeois' can always be relied on to inflame any discussion. I'm not sure – I didn't clearly hear – how poor dear Fiz used it: I'm sure inaccurately. She would have done much better to have kept out of the by now lacerating crossfire – Jocelyn, I seem to remember, was going great guns. Anyway, you put an end to the nonsense by your abrupt and understandable and probably *wise* departure . . .

I'm sure that we – the smart, destructively-tongued, malicious party – seemed to be in the ascendant – the party of the stronger. The only thing I would like you to understand is that what you were experiencing was the defensive (and of course unavailing) anger of dissidents in a complacently conforming world.

19 June 1987
Down to the National Theatre to see Ingmar Bergman's production of *Hamlet* from the Royal Theatre in Stockholm. An appalling evening, as it turned out, with the kind of gimmicks one would expect from a bright and silly young director in his undergraduate days: half-in and half-out of modern dress, with a Hamlet in leather jacket and shades, and Gertrude struggling violently on the floor in mimed sex orgies with Claudius . . . I have always suspected that Bergman had no sense of humour. Now I know.

2 September 1987
TWA 755 Heathrow–Philadelphia (Philadelphia–St Louis, St Louis–Denver).

I take up my pen . . . (On the airplane screen, Michael J. Fox? is that his name? is scampering around in *The Secret of My Success* . . . I reflect on the hygienic,

---

1. Who directed him in *The Return of the Soldier* (1982).

pre-packaged style of this characteristic today-movie . . . as personalityless (Herbert Ross) as a . . . what? . . . TV commercial? So shallow and predictable. Is this really an industry I can consider myself a part of? Or conversely. Why am I so incapable of the *action* necessary to produce the work of which I know myself to be capable. What is the block? If I am to surmount it, I'd certainly better hurry . . . Nearly halfway through my sixty-fifth year now. And what the hell am I doing with it?)

I got back from Italy two weeks ago. It was a good holiday at Sperlonga – how long must it have been since I last saw Lorenza? Was it after *This Sporting Life*? No, the Festival of Free Cinema at Porretta Terme? God knows![1] Anyway, it surely says something that after many years – twenty at least – we met as if it were yesterday. Lorenza remains the charming little survivor – exploiter of yore . . . She loves to talk Communist intrigue and she worked hard and generously on my behalf, with those endless telephone calls to Medusa and friends at *Repubblica* and *Corriere della Sera*, and finally we had our showing [of *The Whales of August*] at Technicolor, and our mini-press conference afterwards. Lorenza maintains her whimsicality, her sophisticated childishness, so you can never be exactly sure how *serious* she is, and yet she is not unserious. Her taste in films clashed radically with mine: she spoke warmly of *The Big Chill*[2] . . . and she hadn't liked *Britannia Hospital* because of the blood . . . She enjoyed meeting Karel (and enjoyed *The French Lieutenant's Woman*). I was several times moved to call her *bourgeois*: the taste of a *Guardian* reader!

Approaching Denver – I know very little about the Telluride Film Festival, except that people speak well of it. Non-competitive, a festival for enthusiasts, connoisseurs. Mike will be there for the showing of *Whales* . . . It would be nice if Ben Johnson was there also . . . Will the idea of my introducing *They Were Expendable* materialise?

Most of the flight I occupied myself with reading *My Mother's Keeper*, the book about Bette by her daughter, B. D. Hayman. I was foolish not to have read it before we started work on *Whales*. I would have been better prepared for the compulsive hostility – negativity – destructiveness that is her strongest characteristic. Once again, I wonder that people still try to search for rational explanations for behaviour that is plainly irrational: you can describe Bette much more easily than you can explain her. Perhaps her grandson came nearest. 'She's loony-toons' was how he put it.

22 October 1987

Chateau Marmont. Last night at the Budapest Restaurant on Fairfax, [I was] asked several times how I'd passed my day . . . and this spurs me to put at least something on paper about this visit to publicise *The Whales of August*. How had I spent the day?

---

1. It was June 1966.
2. Touchy-feely American film by Lawrence Kasdan (1983).

In the morning I was visited by a TV crew from CNN – Cable News Network, Ted Turner's outfit – and interviewed by Sandy Kenyon: fair-haired, young, plumping and a real enthusiast and more knowledgeable than I expected. Indeed from Charterhouse and – Oxford? His genuine enthusiasm loosened my tongue.

Letter to Bette Davis (extract)

22 October 1987

I was sorry you were not there, even though the occasion was no more pleasurable than these functions habitually are.[1] I thought of calling you from New York, but did not because I was pretty sure you wouldn't welcome it, and I really hate having the telephone put down on me before a conversation is finished, as is your wont (of course it signifies that *you* have finished, but conversation is a two-way collaboration – n'est ce pas?!)

I have often wanted to talk with you – having often enjoyed our chats on Cliff Island, on and off the set. I realise that probably we won't talk again, and I'm sorry . . . I have no idea why you evidently feel such resentment at the very idea of *The Whales of August* – and I think it is especially regrettable since you gave such a magnificent performance in it, one which shows that your talent has in no way diminished, and if anything has deepened. If *I* were to give you any advice it would be to *use* this work – the film I mean, of which we all can be and should be proud – and above all not to allow yourself to be exploited and manipulated by the media. I hate it when they insist on calling you 'feisty', and I wish you wouldn't give them reason to.

I don't mind in the least that you insist now that I am a theatre – not a film – director: but you really shouldn't, because it only makes you look ignorant – or ungracious. If I were bold enough to give you a note on your present performance, I think it would be 'Noblesse Oblige'. After all, you are a great actress as well as a great star, and you do belong to the aristocracy of our profession. Generosity, you know, is a very *attractive* characteristic. Also, it's good to surprise your audience – not always to give them what they expect, and what they've seen before. Well, Bette – hail and farewell! I shall always think of you with affection as well as respect. And I'm truly sorry our friendly relationship did not flourish. We did well up there on Cliff Island, you know, and I suppose that's the most important thing . . .

---

1. The New York premiere of *The Whales of August*. Bette Davis boycotted it because it coincided with Lillian Gish's birthday.

On 25 September 1987, Mary Astor died. Anderson wrote a tribute to her that was
published in autumn 1990, in the last edition of Sight and Sound *edited by his old*
friend, Penelope Houston.

30 December 1987

9 Stirling Mansions. A strange time. I am alone now in the flat. I am supposed to relish
having the flat to myself, but the solitary life is somewhat pointless . . . On January 9th
I go to Warsaw. In my present mood the prospect of a 'Retrospective' is depressing, and
I know that I shall be faced with the request to do *King Lear* with Tadeusz.[1] I should say
yes, I suppose, but I find I have no idea how to approach it – or anything.

16 March 1988

It must be just over a week since the script of *Sister Ruth*[2] arrived via my Hollywood
agent, Ronda Gomez – a six-part TV series to be made by producer Bonny Dore in
conjunction with Orion Television and Home Box Office.

The aim apparently is to start shooting at the beginning of May in order to finish by
the end of June, a three-hour movie in eight weeks, to satisfy some mysterious requirements, which also means shooting in Canada.

The script struck me by its satirical sharpness – unusually frank in its language, its
disrespectful attitude to religion, its openness about sex and drugs. A vital element in
it is the Rock performance of serio-comic rock ballads by the raunchy, coarse-spoken,
witty and (of course) finally soft-hearted principal character – a Janis Joplin-style
singer who would seem to me to call for a Bette Midler.

The script arrived only a few days after I had rejected Duncan Weldon's terms for
directing *The Admirable Crichton*, an enterprise which had some things to commend it
(Rex Harrison and Edward Fox, a pleasant, old-fashioned text, almost certain success)
yet which somehow seemed like a defeat. Duncan refused even a nominal payment for
a casting director – a £5,000 fee for the job and no percentage on tour – then 3 per cent
at the Haymarket, rising to 4 per cent after the production was paid *plus* £100,000 –
lowered by Maggie to £50,000 . . . All the squabbling over terms, the repeated telephone
calls from Maggie, further put me off. I could raise no enthusiasm for it.

No enthusiasm anywhere, in fact . . . The Haymarket Leicester? Lee Menzies and his
Agatha Christie mirage? Nick Salmon, who sees Helen Mirren in *The Letter*? I suppose
it's partly on a rebound from all this that I suddenly find myself thinking – why not? A

---

1. L.A. visited Poland, but declined the offer.
2. L.A. changed the title to *Glory! Glory!* A tele-evangelistic church uses rock singer Ruth to raise
ratings and gets a 'divine' windfall when she is blessed with the gift of healing.

last chance to do a highly paid American job to which I am *not* personally committed. Fantasy or commonsense? I have no idea.

And Maggie is off again, deal-making with fury, pushing Ronda to go higher (the $150,000 which was originally offered – with Maggie pressure it has been upped to $275,000![1] Fairy gold . . . plus expenses of $1,500 a week). None of all this seems very real, though I have called Mike Fash, who would be available, and *he* might make it real.

23 March 1988
Each time I come to Hollywood now I find the place more depressing, more shabby under the expensive surfaces, more soulless – or rather with its soul more conclusively sold to the most crass kind of materialism.

As reported to me by Bonny Dore, my pleasant, 'respectful' specious producer, a tall, leggy girl with glasses, the HBO Executive, so well-mannered to meet, called her to insist that when Sister Ruth is really flying in her act, 'The men in the audience want to cream in their pants' . . . and, 'In the first scene, Bobby Joe is torn between wanting to fuck her or to hire her' . . . This is not, in my judgement, exactly the jovial or savage vulgarity of the old-style tycoon: it betrays more the insecurity of the TV Executive scared for his job and with no real confidence in his ability or his sense of audience, just parroting the clichés of the business. But of course it betrays also a shallowness, an opportunism, a cheapness of sensibility which only makes more nightmarish the well-carpeted, luxuriously appointed pseudo-'tasteful' huge glass-and-concrete palaces in which the Devil's work is conducted.

The key word is 'superficiality': everything is surface, of the instant, designed for seductive effect – whether of luxury, sensuality or violence. I am reminded of my oft-repeated definition of Americanism – 'energy without depth'. I was supplied with a tape of a current successful film of intrigue, *No Way Out*, to see the performance of a young actress (Sean Young) of high-voltage personality, attractive and (I'd guess) ruthless. Early in the film there is a scene of intercourse in the back of a limousine between this girl, beautiful, beautifully groomed and hot for sex, and a good-looking naval officer, also greedy for it, who has just met her for the first time . . . To describe such a scene, in today's climate, as disgusting would be astonishing to most people. Yet it *is* disgusting: not for its open display, but for the absolute lack of view, of comment on the part of the film-makers, who show the scene not nakedly but with gloss, the amused satisfaction of sensual abandonment designed to create envy and fantasised complicity in the viewer. The sleek surface of an advertisement for perfume, hairspray or a luxury hotel.

---

1. This compares well, for example, with the $100,000 he was paid to direct *The Whales of August*.

This superficiality explains the lack of any kind of concentration or thought beyond the moment. The use of catchphrases which can be used to evade criticism or commitment. 'They're working on it': which means, 'That's an awkward question they (or we) would rather not face.' 'They want you over Tuesday at the latest' (*not* 'Would you be able to come over on Tuesday'). 'They loved you' (meaningless).

Nobody thinks; nobody knows anything; everyone is too busy keeping afloat on their little area of the surface. Friendly relationships are extremely rare: most exist only in terms of current success or possible use. At my first meeting with Bonny Dore and her associate Leslie Greif and scriptwriter Stan Daniels,[1] we were visited by a smiling Mike Medavoy . . . friendly Mike, whom I first met so many years ago as Karel's agent, who gave me my development deal with Orion (absurdly abortive), with whom I had supper last time I was here . . . Big smile and warm embrace, but no 'How long are you here for?','You must come over for a meal', or 'Let's meet'. Big smile, warm embrace, joke – and he disappears. Everyone mightily impressed though. 'Mike thinks you're great – he doesn't often do that'.

I arrived in LA a week ago. I've talked with, or 'auditioned', four actresses – Annie Potts, Carrie Fisher,[2] Ellen Green and Sean Young . . . In truth none of these is probably exactly right. Annie Potts a good little actress, but rather affected – sticking it on. Carrie Fisher a competent, intelligent actress, and agreeable, intelligent person, but just not of the required temperament or voltage. Ellen Green authentic and probably of good potential, though I guess lacking in sensuality and perhaps *size*. Sean Young perhaps the most likely *star*, but too young and beautiful to be quite rightly cast: certainly not lacking in size (monstrosity?) . . . I was exhausted after talking with her.

Well, after the sexual and sensational anxieties of HBO ('How are we going to sell it'). A conference call was arranged, to be shared between Brigitte Potter, the other HBO representative whose name I've not even tried to learn, Bonny Dore, Stan Daniels and myself. Of course the language used in my intimidating presence was much less coarse than that used to Bonny . . . In fact, though the cowardly part of me couldn't help hoping we would meet with intransigence and final refusal, it was quite easy to offer the needed reassurance. I don't exactly remember what I said, except to suggest that the 'respectable' audience should find themselves 'outraged – but *envious*', which seemed to fit the bill . . . In fact all that is wanted from these occasions is reassurance, since what one is faced with is simply the insecurity of the backers. Not what one says, but how one says it . . . (NB: thinking back – how foolishly I played that meeting many years ago, at which Mike Medavoy kicked off in relation to *In a Lonely Place* with the question 'Who're we rootin' for?' How easy to have replied with glib, even half-truthful,

---

1. As a Rhodes Scholar at Oxford, Daniels devised and presented a revue in which Alan Bennett took part.

2. Princess Leia in the *Star Wars* films.

reassurance, on the lines of: 'It may seem paradoxical, but I think we are rootin' for the villain – or the victim . . . of course we know that Dix is a murderer, but we also know that he is the victim of his compulsions: we share his fear, his anxiety, we can't help hoping he'll escape, even as we (and he) feel the net closing around him . . . It's essentially a subjective story – which is why they couldn't make it properly the first time. They were forced to stand the story and the characters on their heads. It's a brilliant part for Jon Voight . . .' I would even have been able to win Jon Voight over, I think).

In the afternoon, I visited K-Mart with Broderick, and in the evening we went to John Waters's *Hairspray* at the Beverly Centre – jolly good, nice fun.

30 March 1988
Ellen Green has been signed.

That means I am 'pay or play'.

I lead this vacation-style existence at the Regency (my old room). I wake at 6.30 . . . I potter about, exercise on the smooth astro-grass, swim, have my breakfast, glance at the paper, guiltily watch TV . . . and somehow manage *not* to write my diary, read or write any of the several assignments I should be working on, or 'lay hold on life . . .'

Think of the money,

think of the money,

think of the money . . .

Two quite long, quite exhausting sessions last week with Bonny, Stan and the engaging Leslie . . . We are in the strange situation of needing to examine the script, but of being unable frankly to rewrite since Stan is 'on strike' . . . However, he can attend to 'structure' – particularly by putting on his producer's hat . . . The discussions are quite boring, especially since I can't take it all as seriously as they do: Benny and Stan tend to get locked into long discussions about motivation which tend to lose me rapidly. I look at Leslie, sitting alongside me on the sofa, and mouth softly: 'Do they always go on like this?' He nods, smiling.

5 April 1988
Bonny drops me off at the Four Seasons, that 'elegant' whorehouse of modern style where we lunched the LA critics for the opening of *Whales* . . . Realistic dummy figures sit on benches in chairs, unpleasantly somehow . . . I stroll around and encounter Ian Rakoff, hugging a canvas satchel, fresh from work. We drink a whisky each in the lounge bar . . . Hugh Hudson appears, looking very well and sunburned. We walk down the street to an Italian restaurant where (as almost always) the food is inferior to the decor. Predictable, featureless conversation. A bit of Puttnam dirt – he stole a subject from Hugh and gave it to Roland Joffe: we both lay into him . . . I am conscious with Hugh of having to 'feed' him, though he couldn't be more agreeable.

Bullying, I make Ian drop me off at the Regency – though he lives in quite the other direction.

I see Bette in a David Letterman rerun. She looks painfully grotesque in a huge, crown-like hat with large medallions of different colours stuck round it, and a big tinsel heart on her little black dress: wizened, gaunt, like an old witch. Letterman fawning skillfully. A brief allusion to *Whales* – 'And there isn't a whale in it . . .' – Not a mention of Lillian of course.

Letter to Richard Harris

14 April 1988

My dear Richard – Sorry to have been away when your letter came – I think my secretary phoned to explain.

I'm sorry too, that you weren't tempted by *Long Day's Journey*. I honestly don't think that the Lemmon–Miller production was sufficiently notable, or sufficiently well received to present an obstacle. The play is, after all, a classic – and Tyrone is certainly a part you'd play magnificently. I also thought the opportunity to do it at a good, well-subsidised provincial theatre was quite providential. But of course, if you're thinking primarily of the West End, that's another matter.

Quite by chance, when I heard you weren't interested in O'Neill, I received a script from California, for a miniseries for HBO – something I've never attempted before. I went out to investigate and find (though I can't quite believe it) that I am now committed to shooting the series in Toronto (for all the usual, complicated tax reasons), starting in June. This means I'll be exiled, shooting and finishing off the thing, until the autumn. My last chance, I keep telling myself, to Sell Out.

I hope that *Maigret* went well and that you've shaken off the bronchitis. And that when I get back to London, you'll be on the boards again. Anouilh isn't one of my favourite authors – but I know that if you do a *Beckett*, you'll make it a memorable occasion.

All best, as ever,

Lindsay.

23 May 1988

Toronto. Two weeks served now of my fifteen-week sentence . . . kicked off with a pricey dinner at Le Bistingo in Queen Street West – Bonny arriving late and smart in a black hat and what seemed to be a black cloak . . .

One of those friendly 'jokey' occasions, with nothing serious or practical being discussed, wine flowing freely and also the chatter. As usual on these occasions, I find myself forced into being 'controversial', 'outspoken' etc., occasioning mirth by my apparent intransigence and categorical opinions.

27 May 1988

Mike Fash has gone home for the weekend after making a universally approved start this week. We have inspected some principal locations. The sketchy work by the art department has become very apparent. The costume designer, the desperately neurotically insecure Kathy, has resigned – after an abortive costume meeting on Wednesday at which she steadfastly refused to be in any way influenced by my ideas.

8 June 1988

Yesterday the whole thing *almost* fell through. After a full-scale production meeting in the afternoon, driven through with great energy and precision by Jamie, our First Assistant Director, Jamie felt obliged to make it absolutely clear that the extremely packed thirty-five day schedule could not possibly be executed with a star actress who was clearly – in fact who had announced herself – to be unreliable, hysterical and anything but 'part of the team'. We had rehearsed in the morning, and Ellen had arrived in large dark glasses. She came up to me with some kind of whine or complaint which I tried to deflect with a joke. She was temperamental, however, and turned away with a moan of self-pity. I followed her and within a few moments she was in tears. I walked her up and down the corridor outside our rehearsal room and listened to a flow of emotional, silly complaints. I can't remember clearly what she was talking about, except complaining about Bonny, about her make-up man, her hairdresser, etc. I devoted all my attention to reassuring her, telling her not to be silly, bringing her back to the idea of work. After about ten minutes of this, we went back into the rehearsal room and found Richard Thomas[1] (calm, professional, friendly and intelligent) already there, looking through a scene and perfectly oblivious to the suppressed hysteria outside. In fact, rehearsal went surprisingly well. Ellen is erratic, talks too much, uses phrases like 'rounded' and 'pointed' in a way that doesn't make much sense to anyone but herself, is inclined to throw her lines away and speak too fast. She talks quite a lot about 'comedy', but is really too self-obsessed to have much sense of humour, which is certainly a loss in trying to play Ruth. She wants quite a lot of cuts and changes – none of which are really significant, but all need to be explained at length and in a generally incomprehensible way. I realise it's more the *act* of objecting and changing that she needs, not the changes themselves. She displays an unexpected prudery about language, refuses to use the word 'turd' and is very nervous of nudity.

I'm not quite sure what has been decided – nobody, of course, tells me, but Bonny announces with her big smile that she has 'got me out of it'. In other words, whoever is going to read the Riot Act to Ellen Green, it doesn't have to be me.

---

1. American actor (1951–), known for *The Waltons* (1973–1976).

12 June 1988

4.30 a.m. First day over. The scenes: Lester's office. The location: the Sunquest Head-quarters, 30 Marton Street. The first-floor office well transformed by the Art Department. It's a beautiful day outside and everyone is in good humour. The shooting starts with James Whitmore and Richard Thomas: both first-class artists. Firm in their characterisations and pretty good (Richard perfect) on their lines. We start with Lester's explanation to Bobby Joe of the tax manipulation by which he has managed to guide the fortunes of the church. Then a couple of short scenes for them both. And finally the more complicated scene of Lester's confrontation with the tapes of Vincent's confession.

The last scene is my Waterloo. Quite complicated to stage – the arrival of three visitors in Lester's office – then long talks, with reaction shots, etc. We arrive at the top of the scene at 4, but it is 5.30 before the whole thing is worked out, run through, lit and we start shooting. By 7.30 (we have to be out of the place by 8) we have done the body of the scene, but we haven't finished our 360-degree turn-round, and about five 'reaction' setups. Everybody very pleased with the day's work, but I am unhappily conscious that we haven't got through the schedule, and I realise with greater force than ever that 'instant' staging is absolutely *not* my forte. I have never been able to find instant solutions to where people should sit and move – nor am I able to accept an absolutely uninventive, dull, static positioning of characters, with the kind of concentration on dialogue which I suppose is necessary for this kind of shooting. It is like solving a crossword puzzle at speed – and I've never been any good at crossword puzzles whether at speed or not. All the other things about direction – the characterisation, the working with actors, the overall conception, the rhythm, etc., I can manage more or less well. But give me a sheet of dialogue, especially one featuring three or more characters, and I have the greatest difficulty is visualising it, in saying where everyone should be and what the camera has to do. It takes me back to that day of rehearsing *Andorra* at the National Theatre when I was confessing to the assembled company that I hadn't the slightest idea how to stage the Jew Detection scene, and I looked round and saw Larry standing inexpressive at the door. Of course I got it sorted out in the end, but it took a bit of time. And here we have no time. Probably this is why I wake at 4 a.m., panicking at the thought of our second day in the Office.

14 June 1988

There's nothing like a set of bad – or technically inadequate, or inadequately presented – rushes to remove the glow of self-congratulation after a day, or even three days of good shooting. By which I mean, of course, *speedy* shooting.

Ruth Foster, charming, pregnant, who is our editor, said that the material was excellent, but the hour and a half we spent viewing the stuff they'd transferred was a disappointing and frustrating experience. The scenes heavily contrasted, not very easy to 'read' and a monitor which gave us the full 'academy' image, without TV framing (with the result that everything looked a bit too loose, a bit too far away and lacking in impact). At times during the projection I had to close my eyes and repeat to myself the magic words: 'Two hundred and seventy-five thousand dollars . . . Two hundred and seventy-five thousand dollars . . .'

16 June 1988

Plenty of lip-service is paid to me, particularly on the subject of getting through the first five days on schedule and without overtime. Bonny frequently reiterates how she feels it to be her function to make things easy for me on the floor, but there is very little evidence of this in fact. Tuesday, for instance, we were shooting in the boardroom, in the large all-glass Prudential Building, and on Wednesday we moved upstairs to shoot the office of Leonard Everett, the President of the TV Network in Los Angeles. In spite of there being a full complement of six producers, hanging around and getting excited about such important matters as Ellen's wardrobe and the necessity for Bonny to change it and the difficulty of so doing, and Bonny's contractual *right* to inspect the costumes and HBO's similar contractual *right* to approve said costumes – it occurred to no one to go up to the sixteenth floor to inspect our set for tomorrow. And Mike and I, slaving away at breakneck speed to get through the boardroom schedule, certainly didn't have any time to do so . . . As a result, when we did get up there after shooting, we found a room which seemed to have no dressing for the particular function we were to film the next morning. When I queried this, I was mysteriously informed that I had been reported (by whom? to whom?) as saying that the Chief Executive, whose office this was, should be a completely anonymous man without interest and without family . . . When I explain the situation to Bonny at rushes, she evinces alarm and goes off to make a phone call. Later she tells me that 'they' will be coming in at 6.30 in the morning to 'work on' the set. The next day I find this simply meant that the Art Department had come in to supervise the positioning of the furniture. I do some shouting and hasten around and find a couple of suitable pictures, belonging to the Prudential, and we also manage to scrape up a few trendy, eccentric art-objects. The Art Department sends one of their team back to the studio to pick up some flags, but two hours later he has not returned. Bonny shows up about half an hour after the call, and explains that she has come in early to see that all is properly prepared. She then vanishes and I see nothing more of her until the end of the day.

17 June 1988

Whatever the 'ultimate' value of the Tyrells' score, they have certainly done a splendid job in following the requirements of the script, and producing numbers which really do satisfy its dramatic demands. The music is not exactly raunchy, more middle-of-the-road, but that is probably a good thing. How 'good' is the music? Really, I've no idea. It certainly sounds like rock and roll to my untutored ear, and round the table people are jerking their heads and bodies in the customary way as they listen to it. Mike isn't jerking, though, and neither am I: our eyes meet occasionally across the table, with a look of covert amusement.

There is a great deal of discussion about the prerecording of 'Shall We Gather at the River?', the revivalist hymn with which our picture starts. Also, of course, by happy coincidence, a favourite John Ford theme, memorable from *Tobacco Road* and *My Darling Clementine*. Steve Tyrell has had his guys prerecord this in his Los Angeles studio: the result is a spiritless trudge, certainly not evoking what I describe as 'The Springtime of Faith'. For some reason, everyone gets very alarmed when I say we will record the number ourselves on location, using our choir and the organist they will bring with them – an insufficiently technological solution to our problem, I guess. Bonny is particularly anxious that this recording should be 'conducted' by Steve Tyrell. Steve, thank God, proves eminently sensible, agrees with me about the Los Angeles recording and remarks that since I know the tempo I want, I can surely conduct it myself. This kind of commonsense is rare.

19 June 1988

Arriving at our church location, I survey the crowd of vehicles, the hordes of technicians and extras with a certain dismay. Another little world to create – another load of humanity and material to drag into use (of course sometimes the load itself charges and propels us). I survey the church moodily. In fact it's an excellent location, but I take time to acclimatise myself: at first it looks too small, with the elements disposed not quite as I'd imagined. But the dressers and electricians get to work and I gradually become reconciled. The extras are another matter. No one, apparently, has read the script, which calls for 'farmers and working-class' types. Instead I am confronted by a tremendously respectable, middle-class crowd – rather like the parents at a private school speech day. Ages are spent removing pearl necklaces and earrings and white gloves; the men remove their coats and one or two overalls and working shirts are dug up from somewhere. Small very bourgeois hats are removed.

Our choir – which is a real choir – are excellent and before anything starts we record 'Shall We Gather at the River'. This takes about five minutes – even though the Anglican Hymnal with which everyone has been provided doesn't, of course, contain the hymn. I sing it to the organist, who picks it up immediately. The choir seems to know it.

25 June 1988

The Bar, with Ellen's first number ('In Johnnie's Arms') and a big Toronto crowd, dressed up in check shirts and cowboy hats, playing Texans, went surprisingly well.

Ellen had (inevitably?) quarrelled with her choreographer and the engaging Otis spent the day hovering at the back . . . Ellen starts a bit tentatively at first, but soon works into a full-energy, properly sensuous-aggressive rendering of the song. I should also add that there's considerable discussion about Ellen's costume, which we finally succeed in adapting so that she doesn't appear in solid red from neck to knee. Mike, with all his authority as lighting man, is much better on these occasions than I am, and almost always gets his way. I will always remember how he persuaded Bette Davis not to play her entire role in *The Whales of August* wearing large black glasses.

After Ellen's number we turn around and shoot Bobby Joe, isolated among the crowd, fascinated both by Ruth's performance and by the crowd's reaction. Once again I admire Richard's concentration, precision and *energy*. For it is this intense internal energy which enables him to turn apparently passive into active: he is always working internally towards his objective. Indeed, by the end, when Ruth appears to have succumbed to a belief in God, I'm sure we shall achieve for Bobby Joe the true passion of Power. Whether this is exactly what the script is aiming for, I'm not sure. But it is what *I* am aiming for.

28 June 1988

An interesting little clash on the floor in the morning. I notice that the stills cameraman, a chap I've been told is good and certainly has a good opinion of himself, seems to have the air of a visitor to the set rather than a part of our unit. On enquiry I found that he is indeed engaged for only ten days of our schedule. Who, I wonder and ask, has selected the days on which the stillsman will appear and what exactly is he shooting? The answer seems to be that our friends, the unidentified 'they', have decided what they need for publicity. The attitude of unquestioning complacency on the part of all concerned gets my goat, and I speak sharply to the stillsman (who couldn't care less) and decide to send a memo, complaining about the situation, the lack of consultation – and suggesting that I would be interested myself to see the results of the stillsman's work. I soon discover that my memo has exceedingly displeased Bonny, who obviously senses unwarranted criticism and interference. I caution myself severely *not* to get uselessly involved. 'Think of the money.'

30 June 1988

. . . but of course it's impossible not to get involved. The work itself is involving, the people one is working with are involving, the continuing challenge of the schedule is involving. So when the maddening irresponsibilities of HBO and Orion, down there in New York and LA in their luxuriously appointed boxes of glass and steel and concrete, begin to upset things with their ignorant interference, it is almost impossible to remain unaffected. In addition there is the American love of hysteria (Canadian too?) which can be relied on to make the most of any difficulty or criticism, which will blow up the mildest reservation or enquiry into a violent objection. We have been suffering this week from reported objections from HBO in Los Angeles – and note that it's always the menacing, anonymous 'HBO' and never an identifiable individual – as to our standard of focus, with four shots pronounced 'soft', and also with criticisms of the style and the execution of our interior Night Scene. Unfortunately Mike was off for the weekend when the rushes came through, and were pronounced 'too dark' by Bonny. (I was working with the editor and didn't see them myself). When they had been reprinted, they were pronounced 'too light'. When Mike finally saw them he pronounced himself quite satisfied. Everyone apart from the anonymous critic at HBO also seems quite happy about our standard of focus – though this didn't prevent Sean (Production Manager) and Jonathan (Line Producer) coming onto the set with a list of shots and directly challenging the wretched focus-puller, trying to press on with the day's work. All evidence of the love of a dramatic scene – and a complete lack of professionalism in not coming to talk quietly either with Mike or myself – preferably both. As a result Marvin, our focus-puller, who is a sensitive, capable and conscientious fellow, is nervously upset. The editor, however, says there's absolutely nothing wrong with the shots – nor has anybody here complained about them (and this includes myself) when they were seen on rushes . . . I then have to take a meeting with Bonny, who explains that HBO have 'rejected' the Night Scene on both 'technical and creative grounds'. 'They' find the scene – uncut, of course, and ungraded – 'unreal', and want us to go out and shoot it on a night exterior. When? Well, they have noted that on Sunday, we have exterior shooting at York University (for the Citadel exteriors): couldn't we just stay on and do the scene during the night? Of course my response to all this mocking and uncooperative – particularly when I hear that HBO are not volunteering to pay for any of this.

2 July 1988

A complicated, concentrated scene to shoot – Bobby Joe and Lester come to confront Chet in Ruth's bedroom with the taped evidence of his affair with her . . . I'm apprehensive of the scene, which I know has to get a lot of dramatic and character points across, besides the essential improbability of this confrontation taking place in Ruth's bedroom – a location chosen more for convenience of schedule and shooting. Richard, in fact, draws my attention to it, and we could easily have got bogged down in a lot of discussion if I hadn't come clean and made it clear that there's a certain level of *improbability* and jiggery-pokery which we'd better accept, or we might find the whole structure of the piece come tumbling down . . . Happily, Richard is professional enough and sensible enough to understand what I'm saying and get on with it. We agree that the only way to play this kind of stuff is to play the *emotion*, the truth of the moment, rather than the actual words, often threadbare, which one has to say.

As we work, I find myself thinking often about John Ford ('Old Master, Old Artificer'). I find myself recognising, or feeling that I recognise, the conditions under which he did so much of his work – his work in the twenties and thirties, anyway, when he was what he liked to call a 'traffic cop' at Fox – and doing some of his finest work on subjects assigned to him by Zanuck. On such assignments, always supposing the subjects have been well prepared and well chosen, there is a certain freedom: the director is not burdened by absolute and final responsibility, but can work with the kind of committed detachment that sometimes produces the very best results. It used to seem extraordinary that Ford would claim that he never saw his rushes. Now I don't find it extraordinary at all (without necessarily believing the claim was always absolutely true). Nor have I got a great desire or impatience to see our rushes: with this schedule there is no question of retakes – unless our results are disastrous – and indeed I do know more or less what we've got. Ford, of course, knew even more clearly what he'd got, and was surely happy to go home at the end of the day and leave the rushes to Zanuck and to the editor.

(Such were the benefits of working in a studio system. Particularly if one's was the kind of talent that fitted into the traditional, popular style of entertainment which the studios existed to produce). *Sister Ruth* has many of the characteristics of intelligent, popular entertainment, with much of the script obeying the popular conventions. Only we don't have the benefit of Zanuck, or producers who really know anything about the business of shooting and completing a movie.

24 July 1988

Ronda Gomez is in Toronto visiting her friend Howard Zieff, who is directing a full-scale feature here.[1] (His star, Michael Keaton, is in the two million dollar bracket now, it appears.) After supper with Rhonda, we go down to Queen Street – Toronto's Greenwich Village – to visit Howard at work. He is setting up a long tracking shot down the sidewalk, with Michael Keaton. The usual huge caravan of trucks, etc., lamps and cables . . . The cameraman is an affable Pole,[2] who tells me we last met when I visited the Lodz Film School in the late sixties, and addressed the students there. I remember the visit very well: the students staged the last scene of *If . . . .* when we arrived, 'firing' from the rooftops, and I flung myself into the snow . . . Our cameraman friend remembers it vividly too.

25 July 1988

Strains and cracks and fissures appear in the good ship *Sister Ruth* (or *Amazing Grace*, or *Glory! Glory!*) which makes me wonder if we are a vessel steaming proudly into port, or one on the verge of coming apart and sinking . . . Arguments proceed, spasmodic

---

1. *The Dream Team.*
2. Adam Holeander. His first film was *Midnight Cowboy.*

and inconclusive, about the exact composition of the cast for the finale. At lunchtime I am told that half the actors I have asked for are not available. No one (which I should have anticipated) has made any effort to see that all the necessary people are available – or not until this morning, when the third assistant was charged (by somebody) to phone the agents and find out their clients' availability. Stan and Jonathan propose that we should try to get Reverend Dan [played by Barry Morse], which surprises me after all the discussions of psychological probability, since he, of course, is dead: which is a more Brechtian effect than even I was anticipating . . . Of course I say, 'Get him if you can.'

Can we make up the line with extras, dressed in recognisable Citadel costumes? At first I'm told we can, and that the extras can open their mouths in the song, as long as they don't *sing*. A couple of hours later, I'm told that this is an error. The extras can *sway*, but if they *sing* they become 'actors', with a corresponding huge increase in payment. I don't know exactly how this discussion ended, because we were deflected by Ellen's near-hysteria when she heard that she was expected to perform her song and her breakdown speech without crowd extras to play to. This followed Ellen's production of the new speech on which she and Sharon (her intimate female attendant) have laboured over night after night (we are told). The speech doesn't seem to me so different from the one in the script, except for a silly and self-pleasuring vain of self-justification. Stan and I decide that the best thing is to accept the speech without argument, Ellen having already stated that if it is not accepted she will refuse to do the scene, and neither of us can at this stage face the fighting, hysteria, etc. We both, of course, think immediately in terms of the cuts we can make in editing, and cunning old Stan produces a line which he persuades Ellen to put into her speech which will make it easy to cut a couple of her worst paragraphs.

The kindest word for Ellen, when one has got over the temptation to strangle her, is, I suppose, 'unstable'. Hysteria is never far away, particularly when she feels threatened by the necessity to *perform*. One can only envy her absolute and all-excluding egotism, which can see the world simply and solely in terms of her own emotions, her own sensibility, her own being. It is *her* achievement that we are still on schedule, so how can she be denied a few extras to perform in front of? *She* is exhausted: *she* is breaking under the strain. Her voice goes tense, the eyes fill with tears – hysteria is just around the corner. At such moments, the overriding concern is to get the patient to the operating table without catastrophe. '*Get the fucking extras, and subtract them from Wednesday's call,*' I hiss to Jamie – and leave the field to Bonny.

27 July 1988

The fifty extras she had demanded the night before gave her a kick at the start of shooting, but by lunchtime she got tired of them and they were dismissed. The 'confessional' speech over which she had laboured long and indulgently started sentimentally and with a self-justifying whine. I managed, however, to work it up into something harder and more declamatory – more *theatrical* in fact, as was necessary if the whole style of the film was to mount to our very theatrical and non-naturalistic finale. I was pleased with the result. Richard and James had to mount rapidly to the style with their self-abasing speeches to the audience, which they managed beautifully, ending with a trio of redeemed souls that reminded me of the final group at the end of Joe Orton's *What the Butler Saw*. Barry [Morse] who had, like the great trouper he is, delayed his flight to London so that Reverend Dan could rise from the grave, provided a fine note of ambiguity.

30 July 1988

Shooting completed. Thirty-five days: on schedule. We finished, in fact, yesterday morning at 3.50 a.m. exactly, after a night shoot at Global Television. Something of an anticlimax after shooting the grand finale of the picture on Wednesday with a rich selection of characters – some specified in the script and some not – together in a line-up giving out to the world with repeated choruses of 'Look at Yourself' – halfway between a curtain call and a full-blooded set piece of showbiz religion – a poetic round-up in the manner of *O Lucky Man!*

14 August 1988

A week ago I made my usual mistake, of endeavouring to act honourably as well as professionally. As we started editing it became immediately clear that three weeks would be inadequate to get the whole picture together. I thought it would be wise to make this clear from the start. Indeed, I had already, but HBO and Bonny Dore had come up with a 'No.' So I called Elaine Spurber, our 'Production Coordinator' at HBO, who had always expressed herself so strongly on the side of our creative effort, to warn her that it was very unlikely we would be able to meet our delivery date for the director's cut. I thought we could discuss the question and she could advise me on the best tactic. But her reception of my news was – as I should have known it would be – one of immediate resistance and panic. Couldn't I just get through it as best as I could, without worrying too much about getting everything right – in order to fulfil the all-important schedule. She professed herself amazed that my request for an extra week had been turned down, but after that there was nothing to be said.

Well, I countered, if the cut just isn't finished, what is anyone going to do about it?

'They'll send in an editor to finish it.'

But where, I reasonably ask, is this editor to come from? And where are they going to find an editor to work the Editmix system (which keeps breaking down)? And don't they know that my editor will certainly not cooperate and is the only one who will be able to understand the work we have already done? But questions like this are much too rational for an organisation person in a state of panic. I realise that just as HBO as an entity wields power without responsibility, so the wretched minions of HBO are given responsibility without power. So I have resolved to stop communicating with anybody, and to press on with the work as well and as speedily as we can. The only possible tactic is to wait until the finishing date of the director's cut arrives in a couple of weeks' time, then to explain that we're not 'quite finished yet' – and to proceed. It is *us* who have got *them* by the short hairs.

And meanwhile, sequence by sequence, line by line, moment by moment, the picture is coming together. I begin now to be really curious to see what it's all like when we have it accurately assembled. I really don't know what the overall effect is likely to be, but I begin to feel it will be *something*.

19 September 1988

Fame is not the spur, but what is? As I walk down the busy, everyday streets from 65th to 55th Street, I can't help wondering – what is this obsession that drives us on – Ruth and me, so that we cannot leave any foot of this material weaker than it should be, less rhythmically and expressively *right* than it can be? Nobody else shares this obsession: very few, if any, are even aware of the felicity of style we are working to achieve. 'Perfection is not an aim', we announced among our Free Cinema principles all those years ago. And yet as one works on and on at a film, it becomes increasingly an aim. Not *the* aim: all that the film is trying to express cannot be summed up in the word 'style'. But we strive for clarity and accuracy and (above all perhaps) rhythm, not just as carriers of meaning, but as the nearest we can get to perfect expression of it.

It is a fantastic stroke of luck for the enterprise – and for me – that Ruth is as obsessive as I am about this expressive detailing. When I, careless of synchronisation of continuity would let something pass with a shrug, she insists on labouring on and achieving polish. But when she would accept a rhythm which I feel to be false, she needs no persuasion to 'try it my way'. This is the irrational dedication of the artist.

What on earth are we creating? Of course the limitations of the work, and its qualities, will be the limitations and qualities of the script. An original idea, worked out with a lot of invention and ambition, yet limited by TV 'situation comedy' influences, and finally a lack of rigour and logic in conception. Mostly the acting is very good – with the exception, of course, of the leading actress. I am too conscious of the falsities and weaknesses which we are labouring to cover up.

21 September 1988

Yesterday afternoon at three o'clock we showed our cut of *Glory! Glory!* to our two 'producers' and also Bridget Potter from HBO. When the film ended, I was extremely

grateful to Bridget, who declared herself satisfied, immediately and without qualific-
ation. She appreciated the ambiguity of the film, the reality of the characters and their
emotions. She was favourable to Ellen's performance, which relieved me a lot. In fact,
I don't remember a great deal of the spasmodic, friendly, appreciative conversation
that ensued. It really just seemed that the entire film was accepted with enthusiasm.

25 September 1988
Back home. Back in low-voltage Britain. Not exactly less provincial in atmosphere
than Toronto and New York – but more settled in its complacency, less vital in its push
for success. Martin Scorsese's *Last Temptation of Christ* has been passed by the censor
as fit to be seen by anyone over the age of eighteen, though various bishops are still
protesting against its emphasis on blood and violence, and Mary Whitehouse is
encouraging local councils to continue the fight for suppression. The coffee shop on
the corner of Finchley Road and Goldhurst Gardens has disappeared, replaced by a fast-
service photographic printer, the facade repainted in violent yellow.

3 October 1988
I called Ruth, seemingly in good spirits and good health. I was not at all amazed –
though I must admit to being a little shocked – to hear that Bonny Dore was in the
cutting room the day I left, seeking to amend shots of problematic synchronisation . . .
She alarmed me more when she told me that Seaton Maclean had suggested the insertion of a close shot of our three leading stars at the end of the film, which would, if
such a shot existed (which it doesn't) effectively destroy the pulling away from the garish
spectacle of the TV show, and make nonsense of the final dissolve back to the (relatively) innocent days of faith with which we began the film. My response to the idea
was explosive, whereupon Ruth assured me that she would not attempt to implement it.

13 November 1988
Today I should be back in Toronto, to supervise the dub (sound and music mix) of
Glory! Glory! I am not – after a couple of days of revelations, explosions and recriminations. In short, it has become rapidly clear that my departure all those weeks ago,
after completing the edit of the film, and receiving enthusiastic clearance, was the signal for Bonny Dore to move into the cutting room, accompanied by a pained Seaton,
to exercise her right of 'producer's cut', and leave her foolish little signature scribbled
across various passages of carefully timed, edited and considered work.

Most idiotically, the scene after Bobby Joe's interview with Chet, in which Bobby
Joe starts packing his suitcases then gets calmed out of his tantrum by Ruth's promise
to marry him (never again referred to in the picture) – all this has been reinstated.
Together with numerous other 'minor' alterations and cuts, all testifying to Bonny

Dore's absolute lack of humour, sense of rhythm or construction – televisual insensibility ... For instance, the guard's statement that Sister Ruth is conducting her 'choir practice', when in fact she is rehearsing her fake cripples for the phony healing, has been cut 'because it wasn't true'. The take of Everett making his enthusiastic call to Lester on his exercise bicycle, supervised by an unexpectedly frumpish secretary has been omitted, with the one take we did *without* the secretary in its place. This was the demand, apparently of Rosenblum of Orion – the only change he insisted on – because he regarded it as unthinkable that a highly placed executive would not have a 'sexy' secretary ... The magnificently sustained performance of the elderly gentleman extra listening to Bobby Joe's 'confession' in the final sequence, sobbing and wiping his eyes, has been crassly chopped in half, reducing it to a proper 'telly' close-up, etc., etc.

The only alteration which makes any sense are a couple of changes to bring Ellen back into synch in her 'Healing' number.

Of course no one who has ever worked in television will be surprised by this turn of events. Nor should I be surprised, having entered into this whole project with such realism and determination to accept the limitations of the exercise. But, once again, I have to admit the absurdity of any such idea. The only way, I suppose, I could have escaped unscathed, would have been to quit Toronto immediately we had finished shooting. Or to do my allotted three weeks of editing, then dump the whole thing in 'their' lap, take the money and run (or limp) ... But imagine what *Amazing Grace* ('their' favoured title) would have turned out like: interesting and unusual, maybe, but essentially just another Bonny Dore fuck-up. Mike, with his humorous realism, has the right idea. But, as I tell Seaton, if I didn't share with Browning the conviction that 'a man's reach should exceed his grasp, or what's a heaven for', we probably would never have even got through the shooting. Anyway, I'm just not made like that, and that's why I haven't a longer record of filmic achievement behind me ... I have come very far from that initial resolution, so easily assumed, to do the work with detached professionalism – to take the money, and run. No, it doesn't work like that.

So my fury, even if 'unreasonable', was inevitable and I had to have an explosion somewhere.

Glory! Glory! *was screened without fanfare on BBC2 in two parts from 4 August 1990. Earlier in the year, Broadway producer, Gladys Nederlander, negotiated the rights to stage it as a musical with Cher.*

7 February 1989

I saw Malcolm in London the other day, on his way to Stuttgart, where he is shooting a film[1] with Charles Aznavour, I believe. Then he is going to Italy for another of those strange Italian pictures he makes.

23 March 1989

Great news from Japan! A clipping from Barry Spikings – which numbered *Whales* among the three or four biggest grossers in Japan, together with *Full Metal Jacket* and a couple of others ... It would certainly be a good thing to re-release the picture.[2]

---

1. *Il Maestro*, directed by Marion Hänsel.
2. Curiously, by the end of 1988, and before its Japanese release, *The Whales of August* had earned more than twice as much money on video ($2,703,215) than on its theatrical release ($1,004,845).

16

Scattering Ashes

The March on Russia – Is That All There Is?
Remembering If . . . .

'Today the sun is shining and I shall be bathing in the placid lake.'
(Postcard from Anderson to Vladimir Pucholt, 30 August 1994)

18 May 1989
David Hare's *Secret Rapture* had the most fantastic reviews, but I found it a load of pretentious bollocks. Not that I saw it all, forty-five minutes was enough for me. I've also seen about half an hour of the Richard Eyre–Daniel Day-Lewis *Hamlet*, which I thought extremely dull and cold, without humour or passion. I saw about twenty-five minutes of *Bartholomew Fair*,[1] of which I hardly understood a word: a great deal of 'acting' going on. I went to a preview of *Ghetto*[2] with Jocelyn and suffered a great deal. Elaborate, expressionist decor, showy (and accomplished) staging. But really it isn't possible for English actors to dress up in rags and impersonate Jewish victims of the concentration camps – however sincere and earnest their efforts. Poor old Brecht, he must be whirring round in his grave, whimpering 'I lived in vain.'

Laurence Olivier died on 11 July 1989. Anderson attended the memorial service at Westminster Abbey and reported on it to Jocelyn Herbert:

I went along, and to the celebratory buffet at the National Theatre afterwards (to which we were invited by 'the Lady Olivier') and it was all exactly as you would have imagined it, only a bit more pretentious and even more vulgar, with its 'staging' by

---

1. Richard Eyre's National Theatre production of the play by Ben Jonson.
2. Adapted/translated by David Lan.

Patrick Garland. The chief feature of this was an initial procession of stars up to the altar, bearing such relics as Larry's OM (carried by Douglas Fairbanks Jnr, on a velvet cushion), silver models of the National and Chichester, the script of the film of *Hamlet*, a couple of crowns worn in some production or other, and Edmund Kean's sword, which John Gielgud had given Larry some years back ... These were transported by a po-faced procession of notables, such as Scofield, Derek Jacobi, Michael Caine, Maggie Smith (unrecognisable behind dark glasses and a large hat), Dorothy Tutin, Peter O'Toole, with Frank Finlay bringing up the rear with the Sword. Really awful, but a shabby-successful coup de théâtre, I suppose ... As always, I felt completely alienated from the whole business, and indeed the society it represented. Like intruding into a club of which I am not, and don't want to be, a member. Albert Finney read one of the lessons, very badly, in a plummy upper-crust 'Shakespearean' manner; John Mills followed, barking out 'Faith, Hope and Charity ...', but at least not hamming it up; Peggy Ashcroft recited from 'Lycidas' with gallant clarity, and John Gielgud read a Donne sonnet with his habitual grace and feeling. He really is the best, which made all the glib encomia from the officiating clergy – sanctifying Larry as our 'greatest' actor, etc. – all the more offensive ... Alec Guinness delivered the address, with his usual tact and style, with hints of irony – an excellent performance.

I walked from the Abbey to the National, accompanied (unfortunately) by Peter McEnery and Kathleen Tynan – joined en route by Peter O'Toole and Dorothy Tutin ... Which made me feel more 'European' and less 'English' than ever ... Looking round on the NT balcony, at all that mediocre crowd scoffing their champagne and eating cold salmon, I really thought how awful they all are ... But I was glad to see Joan, who carried the whole thing off extremely well, looked fine and so did her children. Jill was there, feeling rather neurotic – and [there were] a couple of human beings like Joyce Redman and Geraldine McEwan, whom I don't really know but find pleasant and ready to be amused. Isn't it odd how immediately and gratefully one recognises a human quality amongst so much pretension and shallowness?

Anderson reunited Constance Chapman and Bill Owen as the Pasmores, in David Storey's play The March on Russia *and noted that 'If anything, they are even better than they were in* In Celebration. *It's good to think that maturity confers some benefits!' (30 June 1989). The set was designed by Jocelyn Herbert; Alan Price composed the music. It opened at the Lyttelton Theatre on 6 April 1989 and toured the country the following year under the better title,* Jubilee: *'Travelling round the English provinces is a depressing business. Such devitalised provincialism and such ugliness everywhere. York has been mostly preserved from the developers, but at the price of turning the entire centre of the city into one enormous souvenir shop.*

I was amused to see that next week, following us at the Theatre Royal, is Richard Harris in Pirandello's Henry IV. They've just had their fourth director-replacement and the leading lady (Sarah Miles) has walked out. I'm tempted to feel sorry for Duncan Weldon, but any producer who embarks on a production with Richard Harris really deserves all he gets' (21 April 1990).

June 1989

I saw half of the Peter Hall–Dustin Hoffman *Merchant of Venice* – the first half. The production is typically 'polished' – everyone speaking in that emotionless, artificial way which people seem to think is the way to play Shakespeare. Hall is an unfeeling director, and now that he has done so much opera, he 'stages' rather than directs. Hoffman had a good try, but is simply not experienced enough and without sufficient technique to bring off a role like that – particularly in this kind of shop-window production. It is a sell-out, of course.

21 September 1989

Bill [Gaskill]'s production of the Pirandello *Man, Beast and Virtue* has just opened at the Cottesloe and been quite well received. I saw him briefly in the NT Green Room the other evening, looking extremely benign and happy about the place and the production. He's off to New York to do something or other.

In the last four years of his life, Anderson all but abandoned his diary, recording events mostly in notebook jottings and copies of letters dictated to his secretary, Kathy Burke. On 10 January 1990, responding to an American fan's letter asking him to list the best performances he had ever seen, he compiled the following list:

Henry Fonda in *My Darling Clementine* and Robert Montgomery in *They Were Expendable*. Edna May Oliver in *Drums Along the Mohawk*, or as Betsy Trotwood in *David Copperfield*. Garbo in pretty well anything, but especially in *Grand Hotel*.

Margaret Dumont in *Duck Soup*, 'Alfalfa' Switzer in the *Our Gang* comedies. John Garfield in *Force of Evil*.

Wendy Hiller in *Pygmalion* and *Major Barbara*. Edith Evans in the *theatre* production of *The Importance of Being Earnest* (the film was not so good). Likewise Laurence Olivier in his *theatre* performance of *Richard III*.

Arletty in *Les Enfants du Paradis*. Cherkassov in *Ivan the Terrible*.

Theatre again: Innokentii Smoktunovsky as Dostoyevsky's *The Idiot*, John Gielgud and Dandy Nichols in my production of David Storey's *Home*. And two Hamlets, Serge Reggiani and Frank Grimes.

Mary Astor in practically everything – *The Maltese Falcon, Meet Me at St Louis, The Great Lie* . . . Bette Davis in *The Letter* (or *The Little Foxes*). The little boy (Enzo Staiola) in *The Bicycle Thieves*.

Malcolm McDowell in *A Clockwork Orange* – a film I dislike, but a marvellous performance.

Anderson spent much of the year working with David Sherwin on two new scripts: When the Garden Gnomes Began to Bleed *and* The Private Death of Joe Stalin. *The following year, in August, he was the president of the jury at the Karlovy Vary Film Festival. In October, he spent a week in Russia with Malcolm McDowell who was filming* Assassin of the Tsar.

August 1990

It was very hot in Karlovy Vary. I was very happy to have Miroslav Ondricek, on the jury with me, and to meet Vaclav Havel, who visited the Festival one day and proved to be a man of immense dynamic and optimism. And I attended a discussion about the future of the Czech cinema. I was extremely pleased to meet Shirley Temple (!) who is serving as American Ambassador in Prague, and doing, as far as I can make out, an excellent job. We watched the American entry, *Glory*, together and she talked very affectionately about John Ford[1] . . . Unfortunately, about halfway through the Festival I fell victim to a sudden attack of sickness and giddiness – was transported in an ambulance to hospital, where they gave me the kind of treatment which at least seemed to be effective – they were blessedly free from the 'nanny-like' attitude of English doctors and nurses . . .

Jill Bennett committed suicide on 5 October 1990 . Her last film was Bernardo Bertolucci's The Sheltering Sky, *which is dedicated to her.*

---

1. Who directed her in *Wee Willie Winkie* (1937).

Letter to Alexander Walker (extract)

31 October 1990

Thank you so much for writing. In fact, I had just got back from Russia when I heard the news about Jill. And you know how one blames oneself always, feeling one should *immediately* have telephoned and perhaps one could have done some good . . . But the truth is, I know, that there was nothing to be done. Jill had made her decision and for someone who was often unsure of herself, she had an extraordinarily firm will. I did try, tremendously hard, to get her to end a relationship which obviously was not going to succeed. No question of blame, I think, to either her or Thomas: they just weren't temperamentally suited, and Thomas could never understand just what an actress is and must be. And, with all her qualities, Jill would always be an actress. Well, she has the peace she wanted now, and the loss is ours.

Letter to Stephen Daldry (extract)

28 November 1990

Russia was pretty sad . . . The real reason of the piece I wrote for the *Independent* (severly cut) was to lament that their freedom could only have been bought at the price of disillusion and a false idea of the glories of capitalism. It's difficult to look back, I think, on the years when socialism was an alternative ideal for the labouring masses. The disabused cynicism and the ambitious materialism of, say, *Time Out* is not much of a replacement. Is this the way the non-attached, European policy of the Gate [Theatre] has been such a success?

Way back in 1956, the Court at least had a quite well-positioned establishment to declare itself against. Of course the classic English Stage Company, under George Devine and Tony Richardson, was never really 'socialist', although generally labelled as such. It was inevitably anti-Conservative but essentially humanistic in its allegiance. Which is why it never espoused the cause of Pinter. It's interesting that George Devine never liked Pinter's work, although he was a terrific supporter of Beckett. In fact, Jocelyn Herbert remained a great friend of Beckett's until the end and was recently in Paris putting up her set of *Krapp* which was taken there from Leicester.

If you have any days off, give me a call and perhaps we can have dinner.

Letter to Jon Voight (extract)

30 January 1991

Well, well indeed! I don't know when you wrote that card (a picture by David Hockney) which I was very glad to get. You say you'll be speaking in Oxford in mid-October, so I suppose that was last year. I don't know where I was, but I'm sorry to have missed you.

I'm glad Anthony [Page] said he liked my script [*When the Garden Gnomes Began to Bleed*], which I wrote in collaboration with my old friend David Sherwin – whom you'll remember from our chequered past . . . The script was about David's altercation with the Department of Health and Social Security, trying to get a grant out of them as an unemployed writer. Well, anyway, the BBC turned it down – and so have twenty other producers (although I think it's good and would certainly create a stir). But we're living in strange times, aren't we? and above all conformist times.

It was really good to hear your voice, speaking with such vigour and positiveness on your card. I'm awaiting the arrival of Menahem Golan, who says he has made a 'deal' with Lenfilm for the production of *The Cherry Orchard*.[1] What exactly this involves I don't know, and it hardly seems as though this is quite the moment to be setting out for Russia with a company of actors.

If all these plans come to nothing, I might well come over to LA. If I do get over there, I'll certainly look forward to seeing you and talking about everything. It really has been much too long.

22 May 1991

I shall be appearing in the new picture by Ken Russell for Home Box Office – *Prisoner of Honor* . . . Not a big part, I'm glad to say, but there seem to be an awful lot of lines. It's not at all a typical Ken Russell picture but a characteristic HBO feature, mostly dialogue. Interesting though, about the Dreyfuss case. I can't imagine exactly why Ken Russell asked for me – but I was delighted to take part. Not that it is 'fun' exactly. Ken Russell, though a nice chap, breezy and unpretentious, isn't one of those directors with a very strong feeling for actors: one would get to run-through the scene for camera (Ken himself operating), then the dreaded voice would be heard: 'Okay, let's try one . . .' So there wasn't much chance to develop a characterisation and one left in the end just to pray that one would get through all the dialogue . . . Still it was interesting (if a bit nerve-racking) to play opposite Oliver Reed, and Richard Dreyfuss himself – who seemed a nice fellow. I don't think he got on marvellously with Ken Russell.[2] My driver remarked to me as he ferried me up to Luton Hoo, the great country house which was our location: 'The boys told me that you used to be some kind of director . . . Is that true?'

---

1. To star Malcolm McDowell, Gary Oldman and Maggie Smith.
2. Indeed he didn't. Dreyfuss, wearing the producer's hat, botched the film while recutting and partially reshooting it, behind Russell's back.

Anderson directed Frank Grimes in The Fishing Trip, *a play written by Grimes about the run-up to a repertory season in Cleveland. It opened at the Warehouse Theatre, Croydon on 20 June and ran for five weeks. The cast included Ian Hogg, Stuart Milligan and Paul Birchard:*

PAUL BIRCHARD

In style, *The Fishing Trip* was hyper-real. There was a stunning and completely practical log cabin set created by Michael Pavelka. My character, Chuck, had to fillet a fish where everyone could watch. Real beer was drunk (though real marijuana wasn't smoked).

While Lindsay was grateful to Ted Craig, Artistic Director of the Warehouse, for providing a home for *The Fishing Trip*, Lindsay had no illusions about where we then figured in the perceived pecking order for our profession. More than once during rehearsals, he would preface his remarks with the clause: 'Working – as we are – in the *underbelly* of the British theatre . . .' But Lindsay believed in *The Fishing Trip*. One never felt he was doing it as a fill-in between other assignments. He championed it to West End producers and worked hard to get a transfer, but the economy was slipping into recession.

Letter to Malcolm McDowell (extract)

3 July 1991

I've continued to run away, in a cowardly and indecisive fashion, from the dreaded *Hay Fever* [by Noël Coward]. The money has still not been raised, although the producer [Roger Peters] still talks about shooting in August. Maggie Smith is still supposed to be playing the lead, though I only discovered that she has a stop date for the middle of October, when she has to do a film for the BBC. Sean Connery was offered the part of the husband (without my knowledge) and of course politely 'passed'. Jeremy Irons (I'm glad to say) has turned down the part of the diplomat . . . The only other parts seem to be cast are Sigourney Weaver (who is very nice but is hoping to have a baby) and Rosemary Harris as the Cook . . . Dustin Hoffman loaded Maggie Smith with questions about *The Cherry Orchard* when they were shooting *Hook* [for Steven Spielberg]; but although I wrote to him personally, I got no answer – and have even been told that he never got the letter. Perhaps . . . When I did speak to John Burnham, he asked me if I would have any objection to Dustin Hoffman bringing in a writer of his own choice! Naturally I exploded.

The Fishing Trip has opened and has been running a couple of weeks. The usual tremendously uneven notices – one or two very enthusiastic, one or two picking holes in a typical 'liberal intellectual' way and one or two scornful. On the whole, audiences enjoy the play very much indeed and it's tremendously well acted. The fast-talking Helen Montagu has sent me a play written by John Osborne a couple of years ago which she says Peter O'Toole is willing to do. Need, of course, for 'considerable cutting and reworking'.

Last week I went down with Jocelyn to visit John [Gielgud] . . . I'm afraid John has begun to look distinctly frail, and of course the recent sad death of Peggy Ashcroft has hit him hard. A service last week for Bernard Miles at the crematorium off the Great North Road . . . It's not so very long ago since we had the Memorial Show for Bernard at the Mermaid, which he attended, sadly in his wheelchair. I liked him, though he was certainly very naughty.

In September, Anderson spent three weeks in America to attend a retrospective of his films in Cincinnati and to fly on to Evansville to visit Miroslav Ondricek, who was filming Madonna in Penny Marshall's film, A League of Their Own: *'It was hot and not awfully stimulating. Madonna looked unpretentious and hardworking' (from a letter to Paul Birchard, 1 October 1991).*

20 November 1991

A BBC team is arriving here this morning to record a contribution from me for *The Late Show* about Tony Richardson [who has died] . . . I really don't want to do it, having turned decisively against the media, but Karel thought that one or other of us should take part – and he didn't want to! It's curiously catastrophic for us this disappearance of Tony's, in spite of all the criticisms we've made in the past. So much a part of our lives – well, my life anyway – both in theatre and film. Tony could be awfully wicked, and I certainly couldn't call him close, but his determined individuality made him a figure always unique.

Letter to Stephen Daldry (extract)

4 December 1991

Just to thank you again for a fine theatrical experience with *Damned for Despair* (I wonder if *Damned by Despair* would put the meaning across better in English?) All the terrific ingenuity necessary to put a play like that across in such a confined space – and I thought you did it clearly and powerfully. I was shocked afterwards (not during) to remember that Lorcan Cranitch had come in to read when we were casting Frank Grimes's *The Fishing Trip* and had read very interestingly. He's an excellent actor, even if he sometimes joins in the general error of shouting to indicate power. This seems to happen quite often on the Fringe. Is there a tendency to underestimate the intimacy which a comparatively small space can give? Or is there a tendency to mistake volume for sincerity?

Tadeusz Lomnicki died on 22 February 1992, a week before the premiere of his
long-cherished production of King Lear, *which Anderson had turned down:*
'I never felt sure enough of myself to feel that I would be able to do something that
came up to Tadeusz's own high standards and expectations. Of course life has not
been easy these past years – life and/or career. This also has made it very difficult –
impossible, in fact – for me to leave Britain and go to Poland for the length of time
it would take to do a serious Shakespeare production. So the dream, alas, never
came true . . . This has been one of the most cherished friendships and relation-
ships in my life' (from Anderson's letter to Maria Bojarska, 29 April 1992).

4 March 1992

Malcolm is now off to Munich, making another of what he calls these 'Europuddings',
which will take him off to Venice shortly.[1] He seems to have made a lot of these
European pictures which nobody ever sees, but at least he gets paid for them. He has
an incandescent personality, on and off the screen. What a pity Warners and that idiot
Brian de Palma cast Bruce Willis [instead] as the British journalist in *Bonfire of the
Vanities*. I've just reviewed the book (*The Devil's Candy*) about the making of that big
flop.

20 March 1992

Is it more likely that depression, or fatigue, or whatever you call it, is the result of a
career that seems to have drawn to a close? Maybe it all started, most obviously, with
the precipitate rejection of *When the Garden Gnomes Began to Bleed* by Mark Shivas –
never a friend since those early days of *Movie*, and now in command of films for BBC
Television (who had originally commissioned the script from David Sherwin).

Then also *The Private Death of Joe Stalin*,[2] supposedly in the hands of the producing duo of Daniele Senatore and the infirm Joe Janni . . . But the contract negotiated
with a great deal of talk by Maggie Parker and Sandy Lieberson – to no effect of course.
Then much time wasted – entirely my fault – on [the proposed film of] *Hay Fever*, still
apparently being 'pushed forward' by Roger Peters at the Savoy. Who has now engaged
Charlie Crichton as his financeable director.

The failure of the film of *The Cherry Orchard*, precipitated by my (surely correct)
refusal to work with Menahem Golan. Maggie buying back the rights of the script, but
of course with no possible idea of setting it up elsewhere. And since then the assiduous
but vain attempts of Trevor Ingman.

---

1. *Night Train to Venice*, costarring Hugh Grant.
2. 'A grotesque and melodramatic black comedy.'

And most recently *The Monster Butler*.[1] My removal from Maggie to David Watson – with an attempt by the way (rejected) to remove to Jenny Caseroto . . . Rather against my instincts. David Sherwin and I worked on a draft script, which has now been passed to David Watson, who remains firm in his attachment to Tim Bevan and Working Title – about which I am sceptical – but also to Michael Winner.[2]

There remains – of course – David Storey. The only writer it seems Richard Eyre will invite me to direct. His *Stages* is now scheduled for October, which is the date by which Alan Bates will be free . . . Alan in the meantime has gone to New Mexico to work with Sam Shepard on a film which he has written, and will direct – Alan's costar, he says, being Richard Harris! Jocelyn has done a set. Alan Price has agreed to do the music.

20 May 1992

I was diagnosed shortly before Christmas as 'suffering' (though I hardly noticed it) from an uneven heartbeat. Had a few days at the Royal Free, which was quite pleasant, and since then have been taking pills every morning, which seem to have restored me to 'sinus rhythm' (which is what the medical profession term okay). But I think pills always have side effects, which in my case seems to be to make one perpetually rather tired and liable to yawn a lot.

Later in the month, Anderson went up to Manchester to do a 'cameo' role for Silvio Narizzano's Ngaio Marsh series, The Alleyn Mysteries. *'My part consisted simply of delivering a speech at an anarchist meeting – but Silvio got carried away with the shots of the audience and they never got round to me at all. I shall ring my agent this morning and hope I can get out of the whole thing. I thought it was rottenly organised and I thought very little of the BBC unit who were responsible – nowhere for the artists to sit during the hours they were waiting to be used.'*
In September, Anderson agreed to direct Michael York in a production of Kieran Tunney's play, Moon on the Run, *but the finance was not forthcoming. In October, he made a* Day in the Life Of *film for BBC Scotland. Taking its title from an old Peggy Lee song, 'Is That All There Is?', the film climaxed with Anderson and fifty friends aboard a river boat called* The Connaught, *scattering the ashes of Jill Bennett and Rachel Roberts.*

---

1. From the book by Norman Lucas and Philip Davies. A butler murders his way through high society.
2. Popular British film-maker, who once employed David Sherwin as an office boy.

Notebook record

Friends: we are here today, as you all know, to say goodbye to two good friends –
friends to each other and friends to us. Not a memorial, but a celebration, of a kind
I am sure they both would like. Rachel and Jill – Jill and Rachel – were two of a rare
kind. They were Celts. They were spirited and independent and funny. They were
both fine actresses, and they left us too soon. Life is not the same without them. Both
of them, I am sure, would have enjoyed and approved of this party. Perhaps, for all
we know, they are enjoying it now. I am also quite sure they would have enjoyed the
cameras that are recording it. They were both joyful and full of zest. And they both
had a lot of humour. They enjoyed a laugh. And it is with laughter, surely, that they
would want to be remembered.

Letter to Lois Smith, formerly Sutcliffe (extract)

18 November 1992

I don't know about being creative – but I know I've been busy . . . The play, which
is called *Stages*, has its press night tomorrow, having been previewing since last
Thursday. It's gone pretty well. It doesn't really matter very much what the critics say,
since I believe the first booking period is already sold out. Alan Bates leaves in the
middle of February, I believe, so it isn't at the Cottesloe for very long. And I certainly
don't want to try to put anyone else into it!

And next Monday we dub *Is That All There Is?* whose titles are being shot
tomorrow. I'll be awfully glad to see it completed. The BBC Scotland producer [John
Archer] wants to send it to Florence, where there's a documentary festival, at which
I was jury president two or three years ago (so I know that the whole thing amounts
to very little). Anyway, I've promised to do a commentary for Kevin Brownlow, who's
been working very hard on a series of films about D. W. Griffith. So I won't be able to
get to Florence.

I know very well what you mean about diminished vitality and I only hope your
house is nice and warm. I feel exactly the same and was rather appalled this morning
to hear from my agent the suggestion that I undertake the direction of *Quartermaine's
Terms*, a play by Simon Gray which I think I saw on television. To start rehearsing the
week after Christmas. I really don't think I can take it on – I've been looking forward
to having some time off for a bit. We need it at our age.

JOCELYN HERBERT

Stages, with Alan Bates, was a love story in a way, but Lindsay just didn't seem to be
able to get his way round it. I thought, 'He really doesn't understand this play.' He
was always saying to me: 'What's it all *about*?' The design was very very simple.
It only had a chair and a table and practically no other furniture. At the rehearsal

I got some things in which I thought were slightly suitable, not necessarily the things we would use, but Alan Bates fell in love with the chair. They were just stand-ins and Lindsay just accepted them as that. Then finally, one day, Lindsay said: 'When are you going to get the real stuff?'

Alan said: 'What do you mean?'

'Well, these are just stand-ins.'

And Alan said: 'Oh no, I like this chair. I want to keep it.'

So we kept that particular chair. There was a question of a carpet or not a carpet and always these terrible discussions and rows. Just really to wind me up, I suppose.

10 March 1993

I was happy to read in the press recently that *If . . . .* was one of the favourite films of President Clinton. *That*, you might think, might make it easy to set up a sequel.

17 April 1993

My seventieth birthday, a tea party thrown by the girls from *Stages* in a church hall and attended by numerous friends from theatre, film and the past . . . It was much better, I think, than the usual kind of drinks celebration, with people talking at the tops of their voices and drinking their way into the small hours. A tea party is much better, and one realises how *everybody* really enjoys eating sandwiches and cake and scones with cream and jam.[1]

August 1993

I was in Italy on a ten-day holiday, on an island called Ponza which is a two-hour boat ride from Rome, but refreshing as far as it went . . . On the way back, the British Airways plane broke down and we got back to London Airport twenty-four hours late. Then, on my way up to Edinburgh, to deliver the BAFTA–Scotland Lecture,[2] I got left behind on the Darlington platform as a result of the electronic operation of the doors on British Rail's new Intercity Express. Which put an end to the refreshment of my holiday.

Notes for Edinburgh Film Festival lecture (brief extract)

When I was invited to give this address I was rather flattered, then rather intimidated, then I thought I should accept. Then I realised that the time was a bit short – obviously someone had dropped out. Who, I wondered, could this be? I was told, Martin Scorsese. Ah yes, I said, of course. For Martin Scorsese, besides being one of the most

---

1. A wonderful account of the party is given by Alan Bennett in his book *Writing Home*.
2. 'The Britishness of British Cinema.'

famous as well as one of the most successful directors in the world today, is also an American. And I realised that if any film-maker was going to be invited to make a speech at a British film festival today, he would have to be an American. For the Americans – as anyone who tries to make a British picture today will soon find out – have certainly won: artistically, financially and in their effortless domination of the media ... So when I heard that I would be replacing Martin Scorsese at Edinburgh, I knew that I would have to apologise – for not being American ... I'm sorry I haven't time to deplore the present triumph of the media – and the surrender of the media to the values of Hollywood: the Oscars; the American faces on the cover of the *Radio Times*; the vital importance of American names. Let me remind you that not a single one of those British renaissance films [made by Tony Richardson, Karel Reisz and myself] featured an American. Today *Tom Jones* would have to be played by Tom Cruise. I wanted to finish this address with the last sequence of *If....* and to ask you with whom you identify. But no print of *If....* is available from the National Film Archive. Need I say more?

By 1994, Anderson's health was failing him. Although the doctors had assured him that his heart was back to normal after the scare in Czechoslovakia in 1990, he was still taking pills to combat tiredness and to alleviate the symptoms of depression brought on by the rejection of his film projects.

Letter to Ridley Scott (*extract*)

2 *February 1994*

I think it's quite possible that I didn't make clear my attitude towards Roy Fontaine, the principal character of *The Monster Butler*.[1] I agree that he is an entirely reprehensible character, but I think it's important that he should be presented also as comically outrageous. I suppose it may come as a surprise for me to say that I think *The Monster Butler* is essentially a comedy – even if a *violent* comedy. After all, if we consider the hero of *Kind Hearts and Coronets* solely in terms of his actions, he would seem pretty monstrous too. But this would be to disregard the elements of style and satire which surely characterise that film and make it one of the most individual and justly famous films ever made in this country. I suppose that Roy Fontaine is a more purely wicked character than the one played by Dennis Price in *Kind Hearts* – but

---

1. The film, to star McDowell, Joan Plowright and Graham Crowden, was rejected by Ridley Scott, the new co-owner of Shepperton Studios, who was fronting a scheme, partly financed by the government, to reinvigorate the British Film Industry. Scott chose instead to produce *Monkey Trouble*, an American film about a girl's pickpocketting pet monkey, and a remake of Rattigan's *The Browning Version*, starring Albert Finney and Ben Silverstone.

I do think it's important that he should be seen and should be presented in comic terms. And that's why I've always seen it as a splendid part for Malcolm, whose comic gift is very characteristic.

I didn't quite gather from Julie Payne whether you had 'passed' on *The Garden Gnomes*, or whether you'd passed it on . . . It's a very English story, I suppose, but one which surely speaks quite clearly (unfortunately) about English philistinism. I suppose that's one reason why I'd very much like to make it. Perhaps it's also a reason why it was so rapidly and decisively turned down by Mark Shivas and the BBC and Channel 4 etc. It certainly isn't a characteristically middle-class story, nor conventionally working-class. I shall be very sorry not to have made it.

Letter to Lionel Miskin[1] (extract)

16 March 1994

I was foolish enough the other day to write a letter to the Royal Free, complaining of the doctor from the Cardiac Unit who had seen me and told me, rather brusquely, that I'd been 'taken off the list'. Not, as I tried to make plain, that I'm a hypochondriac, but I do think they should talk to one as though one was an adult. Of course, I only got back one of those letters that said how the doctor in question was a first-class chap and that nobody had ever complained about him before. Served me right! . . . They fixed it up that on my next visit I would see the specialist who is head of the unit, and whom I've never met. That was nice, except that (of course) he never turned up! I had an apologising telephone call offering me another appointment but I told them not to bother. The NHS here is in an awful mess, with hospitals being closed right and left by the ineffable Virginia Bottomley.

Letter to Malcolm McDowell (extract)

5 May 1994

Interest has been shown in *If* (2). . . . by Ileen Maisel, who was in charge of Paramount over here before. She's a fast talker and persuader, but I can't tell how good she'll turn out to be. She is close with Mary Selway, and got Mary to produce the disastrous *Wuthering Heights*, on which they made every mistake you can imagine. Including [hiring] the French actress, Juliette Binoche, as Cathy. Whether it was as a result of this that Ileen Maisel lost her position with Paramount, I've no idea.

I went a week ago to see *Rope*, which I'm happy to say Richard Warwick[2] had a part in. I saw an advertisement in the *Evening Standard*, which quoted a number of excellent reviews, all completely nonsensical since I'm afraid Keith Baxter had done

---

1. Artist, then resident in Australia.
2. Played Wallace in *If* . . . .

a quite bad production, absolutely without the necessary conviction of the play. Afterwards I went with Richard to dinner at the Ivy ... Richard seemed in good form, amiable and humorous as ever – and quite aware of the shortcomings of the evening. It was, as always, good to see him again.

Letter to Robin Askwith (extract)

9 June 1994

Good to hear from you and to know where you are. I'm sure that Panto with Ian Botham[1] was good fun, even if not advancing your 'quality' career. Still, how one does that in this 'classless' (to quote from John Major) society, I really don't know.

Funnily enough I went to Wimbledon this last Christmas to see *Jack and the Beanstalk,* in which my friend Kevin Lloyd appeared – an excellent actor with whom I worked in *What the Butler Saw.* He's been slaving away in *The Bill* for ages, which has at least made him rich (also very fat now). I took Frank Grimes's little girl and a friend of hers, both of whom enjoyed it enormously. I wrote a sequel to *If . . . .* recently with David Sherwin, having been commissioned by Paramount to do a first draft for 'minimum dollars'. It has a good part for you, of course.

Letter to Vladimir Pucholt (extract)

6 July 1994

I'm very glad that I was at home, sitting by the telephone, when you rang the other day from Toronto. Do you remember Pani [Eileen] O'Casey, as Miriam Brickman and I always used to call her? I went up to see her yesterday, at Denville Hall, which is the very pleasant retirement home where many old professionals of theatre and cinema end their days. Eileen O'Casey is now there, having gone from her flat to an old people's home, when she suffered from a stroke in her flat, and for a time was quite incapacitated. Now her daughter has got her a room at Denville Hall, and she is enormously improved. Mostly in a wheelchair, of course, but very lively, mentally at least. She likes to talk of the past and remembers Prague and you and *Bedtime Story* at the Cinoherni Klub very well. She reminded me of how you used to go for long walks together, by the river, and told me to be sure to remember her to you with love when I wrote. So here it is. More memories from the past came to me when I got Milos's autobiography *Turnaround,* which was sent to me by my friend Robert Benton in New York. Milos writes with great admiration of you and *Loves of a Blonde.* I quote: 'I never considered anyone but Vladimir Pucholt for our piano player. This great actor, who had tremendous artistic intuition, completely distrusted his talent. I think this was because he had a very rationalist disposition and could

---

1. One of English cricket's greatest ever all-rounders, instrumental in the 1981 defeat of Australia.

never see, much less measure, the results of his acting. It took him only a few years to become one of the biggest film stars in Czechoslovakia, until suddenly in 1967 he defected to England . . .' Well, that's handsomely said, don't you think?

Thinking back on the heyday of the Czech cinema, so integral to the making of If . . . . , he was stirred into writing an angry riposte when, in the Headmaster's Conference journal, David Ashcroft, ex-Headmaster of Cheltenham College, published his account of the making of If . . . . Full of wild inaccuracies, it called the film 'a can of worms' and included the paragraph: 'We saw little of Roddy McDowell and his associates off the set (and of course none of their indoor scenes which we knew would be filmed in mock-ups elsewhere). Nor did we see much of the three gymnastic youths; they by the law of course had to have their daily lessons: I shared the general consensus that they were spoilt brats.' Anderson wrote a reply to the editor, C. J. Driver:

26 July 1994

I read with considerable interest David Ashcroft's reminiscences of the shooting of *If . . . .* at Cheltenham College twenty-five years ago. I found its inaccuracies remarkable, though not perhaps tremendously surprising. I always felt that the world of cinema was remote from the awareness of College, and I must admit that I was disappointed that the whole experience of shooting a film at Cheltenham seemed to arouse so little interest among either staff or boys. The inaccuracy of David Ashcroft's recollections convey only too clearly the unimportance with which he regarded our venture.

Memorial Films, which produced *If . . . .* , was a company which had been formed by Albert Finney, out of his considerable earnings from *Tom Jones*. He invited his friend and colleague Michael Medwin to be the Executive Producer of Memorial's undertakings. It was certainly not a 'small experimental company'. Nor was I a founding partner in it. When David Sherwin and I finished the script of *Crusaders*, which was based on an original which David and his friend John Howlett had written out of their experiences together at Tonbridge School, we showed it to Michael Medwin, who understood and enjoyed it and accepted it for production . . . Michael Medwin, I should add, was never a 'handsome, smiley young lead in several Ealing Studio comedies'. He had, in fact, been a regular in the enormously successful TV series *The Army Game* and had only made one film at Ealing. (This was *Another Shore*, not one of the most successful Ealing comedies.) I myself was certainly an 'Old Cheltonian', but I was not particularly known as a director of 'avant-garde "shorts",' which is a very misleading description of the Free Cinema shows which I helped to mount at the National Film Theatre. I had done several productions at the Royal Court Theatre, which included *The Long and the Short and the Tall* and *Serjeant Musgrave's Dance* and (in the West End) *Billy Liar*. My first feature film, of which David Ashcroft had apparently never heard, was *This Sporting Life*, which certainly had been on general release.

If . . . . was not designed as a film about my schooldays at Cheltenham. In fact it was probably more influenced by David Sherwin's and John Howlett's days together at Tonbridge. We had not at first intended to shoot at Cheltenham but, when Charterhouse proved uncooperative, we (David and I) visited my old school and were happy to be received with courtesy and the offer to help. The buildings and location generally seemed ideal – though a number of scenes for the film were shot at Aldenham, including the 'Sweat Room', the House Dining Hall and the Gym. Of course there was never any suggestion that the Housemaster, played (brilliantly) by Arthur Lowe, bore any resemblance to my own Housemaster, Dick Juckes.

Michael Medwin and I met David Ashcroft at the Headmaster's house in Cheltenham; neither of us has any recollection of the hotel in Cheltenham where we were alleged to have met to discuss the possibility of shooting 'some film sequences' at College. I don't know who the Head of English was, described as 'a keen drama man and a reliable mixture of prudence and enthusiability'. Neither Michael nor I have any recollection of him and he certainly made no contact later, as shooting proceeded. As I have said, I did my best to make the boys who acted in the film – all of whom performed extremely well, when they were not worrying about the money they were being paid, or not being paid for appearing – feel part of the project and know what was going on. I'm very glad that David Ashcroft at least got the feeling that I was keen to make the experience 'instructive and enjoyable'. I was very happy that my friend Miroslav Ondricek from Prague was able to shoot the picture – though I've no idea where David Ashcroft got the impression that I had largely to communicate with him 'through his wife' (who was not with us).

I've no idea who were the 'three gymnastic youths' . . . Was the general consensus really that they were 'spoilt brats'? The patronising, not to say snobbish tone of this comment is surely as regrettable as it is untrue. The leader of the rebels was of course played by Malcolm (not Roddy) McDowell, who began with this film a particularly fine career both in cinema and in theatre. I wonder if David Ashcroft has ever heard of *O Lucky Man!* or *Britannia Hospital* – or if he was proud to think that they were made by an Old Cheltonian, with the lead in both films being played by the actor who once took part in *If . . . .* at College?

There are too many mistakes in David Ashcroft's article for me to correct them all. I think it is important, though, for me to stress my disappointment that the making of our film clearly meant so little to the ex-Headmaster of Cheltenham, and that he remembers it so mistakenly. I suppose his attitude is quite symptomatic of the difficulty we had in making the film at all, and of the fact that we were quite unable to get any British backing for the film, and that it is prefaced by the shot of the Paramount Mountain, which shows that it was American-financed. I think that we who made it are proud to this day that so many people saw it, especially when young, and that the film meant and still means so much to them. Not bad for a 'can' of 'worms'.

Sincerely

Lindsay Anderson'

Despite protestations from Mr Ashcroft, permission was granted for Lindsay Anderson to film the sequel to If . . . . on location at Cheltenham College.

With David Sherwin back at work on the script, Anderson took up an offer of a holiday at Lois Smith's summer house in the South of France. They spent most evenings swimming and picnicking at a lake fed by the River Dronne. On Tuesday 30 August, while dressing after a swim, Lindsay Anderson had a heart attack, fell back into the water, and died. He was seventy-one years old.

Chronology

1923
Born Bangalore, South India, 17 April.

1926
Arrives in England.

1936–1941
Pupil at Cheltenham College; Head of Cheltondale House, 1941.

1942
Studies Classics at Wadham College, Oxford.

1943–1945
Commissioned into the 60th King's Royal Rifles and then attached to the Intelligence
    Corps; works on cryptology in India.

1946–1947
Returns to Oxford to take a degree in English.

1947–1952
Publishes and co-edits the film journal *Sequence*.

1948
Makes his first documentary film *Meet the Pioneers* (33 mins).

1949
Idlers That Work (17 mins).

1951
Writes the book *Making a Film: the Story of 'Secret People'*.

1952
Produces and acts in James Broughton's film *The Pleasure Garden*.
Three Installations (28 mins).
Wakefield Express (33 mins).

1953
Thursday's Children (20 mins).
O Dreamland (12 mins).

1954
Trunk Conveyor (38 mins).
Hired to assist Serge Reggiani on *Hamlet* (in French) in Paris.
Plays an extra in Tony Richardson's production of *The Changeling* at Wyndhams (May).

1955
Thursday's Children wins the Oscar for Best Documentary Short.
Green and Pleasant Land (4 mins).
Henry (5 mins).
The Children Upstairs (4 mins).
A Hundred Thousand Children (4 mins).
£20 a Ton (5 mins).
Energy First (5 mins).
Foot and Mouth (20 mins).
Organises a John Ford retrospective at the National Film Theatre.

1955–1956
Television series: *The Adventures of Robin Hood*. Epsiodes – Secret Mission, The Imposters, Ambush, The Haunted Mill, Isabella (25 mins each), with Richard Greene and Donald Pleasence.

1956
Organises the first programme of Free Cinema films at the National Film Theatre (February).
Essay: 'Stand Up! Stand Up!' published in *Sight and Sound* (Autumn 1956).

1957
Everyday Except Christmas (40 mins) wins the Grand Prix for Documentary at the Venice Film Festival.
Play: *The Waiting of Lester Abbs* by Kathleen Sully at the Royal Court Theatre (30 June), with Ian Bannen and Robert Stephens.
Essay: 'Get Out and Push!' published in *Declaration*.

1959
Play: *The Long and the Short and the Tall* by Willis Hall at the Royal Court Theatre (7 January), transfers to the New Theatre (8 April), with Peter O'Toole and Robert Shaw.
Play (world premiere): *Progress to the Park* by Alun Owen at the Royal Court Theatre (8 February), with Harry H. Corbett and Tom Bell.
Play (world premiere): *The Trial of Cob and Leach* and *Jazzetry* by Christopher Logue at the Royal Court Theatre (26 April), with Peter O'Toole.
Play (world premiere): *Serjeant Musgrave's Dance* by John Arden at the Royal Court Theatre (22 October), with Ian Bannen, Frank Finlay and Stratford Johns.

1960
Play (world premiere): *The Lily White Boys* by Harry Cookson, with songs by Christopher Logue, at the Royal Court Theatre (27 January), with Albert Finney and Shirley Ann Field.
Play (world premiere): *Billy Liar* by Keith Waterhouse and Willis Hall at the Cambridge Theatre (13 September), with Albert Finney (later Tom Courtenay) and Mona Washbourne.

Play (world premiere): *Trials by Logue*, two one-act plays (*Antigone* and *Cob and Leach*) by Christopher Logue at the Royal Court Theatre (23 November), with George Rose and Mary Ure.

1961

Play: *The Fire Raisers* by Max Frisch at the Royal Court Theatre (21 December), with Alfred Marks and Ann Beach.

1963

This Sporting Life (134 mins), starring Richard Harris and Rachel Roberts.
Play: *The Diary of a Madman*, adapted by Lindsay Anderson and Richard Harris from the story by Gogol, at the Royal Court Theatre (7 March).

1964

Play: *Andorra* by Max Frisch at the National Theatre (28 January), with Tom Courtenay, Robert Stephens and Derek Jacobi.
Play: *Julius Caesar* by William Shakespeare at the Royal Court Theatre (26 November), with Ian Bannen, Graham Crowden and Anthony Hopkins.

1965

Acts in Donald Howarth's production of David Cregan's play *Miniatures* (25 April), with Nicol Williamson, George Devine and Graham Crowden.

1966

Play: *The Cherry Orchard* by Anton Chekhov at the Chichester Theatre (19 July), with Celia Johnson, Tom Courtenay and Ben Kingsley.
The White Bus (46 mins), starring Patricia Healey and Arthur Lowe.
Play: *Inadmissible Evidence* by John Osborne, at the Contemporary Theatre, Warsaw (in Polish), with Tadeusz Lomnicki.

1967

Raz Dwa Trzy (*The Singing Lesson*, 20 mins).

1968

If . . . . (112 mins), starring Malcolm McDowell.
Plays a Barrister in Anthony Page's film of John Osborne's *Inadmissible Evidence.*

1969

Play (world premiere): *In Celebration* by David Storey at the Royal Court Theatre (22 April), with Alan Bates, Bill Owen, Brian Cox, Constance Chapman and James Bolam.
Plays the Gestapo Lawyer in Anthony Page's television production of David Mercer's *The Parachute* (August).

If . . . . wins the Palme d'Or at the Cannes Film Festival.
Play (world premiere): *The Contractor* by David Storey at the Royal Court Theatre (20 October), transfers to the Fortune Theatre (6 April 1970), with Constance Chapman and Bill Owen.

1970

Play (world premiere): *Home* by David Storey at the Royal Court Theatre (17 June),
    tranfers to the Apollo (29 July) and to the Morosco in New York (17 November),
    with John Gielgud and Ralph Richardson.

1971

Play (world premiere): *The Changing Room* by David Storey at the Royal Court Theatre
    (9 November); transfers to the Globe (15 December), with Warren Clarke and
    Brian Glover.
Films *Home* (86 mins) for television.

1973

O Lucky Man! (177 mins), starring Malcolm McDowell, Rachel Roberts, Alan Price,
    Ralph Richardson, Arthur Lowe.
Play (world premiere): *The Farm* by David Storey at the Royal Court Theatre
    (26 September); transfers to the Mayfair (1 November), with Frank Grimes, Patricia
    Healey, Bernard Lee.

1974

Films *In Celebration* (130 mins) for American Film Theatre; restages it at the Royal Court
    Theatre (13 October).
Play (world premiere): *Life Class* by David Storey at the Royal Court Theatre (9 April),
    transfers to the Duke of York's in June, with Alan Bates.
Play: *What the Butler Saw* by Joe Orton at the Royal Court Theatre (16 July), transfers
    to the Whitehall (19 August), with Michael Medwin, Valentine Dyall and Brian Glover.

1975

Play: *The Seagull* by Anton Chekhov at the Lyric (28 October), with Joan Plowright and
    Helen Mirren.
Play (world premiere): *The Bed Before Yesterday* by Ben Travers at the Lyric (9 December).

1976

Play: *The Bed Before Yesterday*, American production with Carol Channing tours the
    East Coast.

1977

Lindsay Anderson exhibition, *The Thirty Years War*, at the National Film Theatre.
Play (world premiere): *The Kingfisher* by William Douglas Home at the Lyric (4 May),
    with Ralph Richardson and Celia Johnson.

1978

The Old Crowd by Alan Bennett, with Rachel Roberts, Jill Bennett and Frank Grimes.
Play: *The Kingfisher* by William Douglas Home at the Biltmore (New York, 6 December),
    with Rex Harrison and Claudette Colbert.

1979

Play: *The Bed Before Yesterday* by Ben Travers (Australian production, January), with
    Rachel Roberts.

In Hollywood on a two-picture deal with Orion, and development deals with Twentieth Century Fox.

Organises a Marek Piwowski retrospective at the National Film Theatre.

1980

Acts with John Gielgud in Hugh Hudson's film *Chariots of Fire*.

Play (world premiere): *Early Days* by David Storey at the National Theatre (17 April), with Ralph Richardson.

Films Ted Craig's New York production of *Look Back in Anger* (101 mins), starring Malcolm McDowell.

1981

Play: *Hamlet* by William Shakespeare at the Theatre Royal, Stratford East (15 May), with Frank Grimes.

Book: *About John Ford* published.

1982

Britannia Hospital (116 mins), with Malcolm McDowell, Graham Crowden and Leonard Rossiter.

Play: *The Holly and the Ivy* by Wynward Browne at the Roundhouse Theatre, New York (21 September).

1983

Play: *The Cherry Orchard* by Chekhov at the Haymarket Theatre (12 September), with Joan Plowright, Frank Grimes and Leslie Phillips.

1984

Play: *The Playboy of the Western World* by J. M. Synge at the Oxford Playhouse, with Frank Grimes.

Play: *In Celebration* by David Storey at the Manhattan Theatre Club (28 October), with Malcolm McDowell.

1985

Play: *Hamlet* by William Shakespeare at the Folger Theatre, Washington D.C. (21 February), with Frank Grimes.

If You Were There (*WHAM! In China*, 80 mins), unreleased, with George Michael.

Free Cinema TV documentary.

1987

The Whales of August (91 mins), starring Lillian Gish, Bette Davis and Vincent Price.

Play: *Holiday* by Philip Barry at the Old Vic (14 January), with Malcolm McDowell and Mary Steenburgen.

1988

Glory! Glory! (205 mins), starring Richard Thomas, James Whitmore, Ellen Greene.

1989

Play (world premiere): *The March on Russia* by David Storey at the National Theatre (6 April), with Constance Chapman and Bill Owen.

1990

Play: *Jubilee* (*The March on Russia*) by David Storey, UK tour.
Writes and presents the TV documentary *John Ford*.

1991

Acts in Ken Russell's HBO feature *Prisoner of Honor.*
Play (world premiere): *The Fishing Trip* by Frank Grimes at the Warehouse Theatre,
   Croydon (20 June).

1992

Is That All There Is? (52 mins).
Play (world premiere): *Stages* by David Storey at the National Theatre (17 November),
   with Alan Bates.

1994

Dies by a lakeside near Angoulême in the South of France (30 August).

Key Figures

For ease of reference, a brief snapshot of some of the key figures mentioned in the diaries is provided below.

Alan Bates   Had a supporting role in the world premiere of *Look Back in Anger*, became a world star wrestling Oliver Reed in Ken Russell's *Women in Love*. Starred in *In Celebration*, *Life Class* and *Stages*. Cameos in *Britannia Hospital*.

Jill Bennett   British Actress married to Willis Hall (1962–65) and John Osborne (1970–77), worked with Anderson on *The Old Crowd* and *Britannia Hospital*. Committed suicide in 1990.

Brian Cox   Scottish theatrical actor greatly prized by the leading lights of American independent cinema. Worked with Anderson on *In Celebration*.

Bette Davis   Top female box-office star during Hollywood's Golden Age. Nominated for ten Academy Awards, winning the Best Actress prize twice. Co-starred with Lillian Gish in Anderson's 1987 film *The Whales of August*.

George Devine   Hired by Tony Richardson to play the central role in a 1955 BBC adaptation of Chekhov's *The Actor's End*, and joined forces with Richardson to form the English Stage Company at the Royal Court Theatre. He was the artistic director from the first season (1956) until 1964, when Anthony Page temporarily assumed the directorship until 1965.

Albert Finney   Anderson directed him to theatrical stardom in *The Lily White Boys* and *Billy Liar*. Reisz and Richardson directed him to film stardom in *Saturday Night and Sunday Morning* and *Tom Jones*. It was through Finney's own production company, Memorial Pictures, that Anderson made *If . . .* .

Milos Forman   Czech film director who became the toast of Hollywood; won Oscars for *One Flew Over the Cuckoo's Nest* and *Amadeus*.

Robin Fox   Theatrical agent; succeeded Neville Blond as Chairman of the English Stage Company (shared with Oscar Lewenstein) in 1970, but died six months later (21 January 1971). Father of actors James and Edward Fox.

William (Bill) Gaskill   Appointed artistic director of the Royal Court Theatre in 1965, and part of the directorial triumvirate with Lindsay Anderson and Anthony Page from 1969; established Edward Bond and Christopher Hampton as major playwrights; associate director of the Olivier Theatre from 1978; world-renowed director of Brecht.

John Gielgud   Great stage and screen actor who played his first Hamlet in 1930. Starred with Ralph Richardson in Anderson's production of David Storey's *Home* (1970). Played a Cambridge don with Anderson in *Chariots of Fire;* acted with Malcolm McDowell in *Caligula.*

Lillian Gish   D. W. Griffith discovery who appeared in his most famous films, including *Birth of a Nation* (1915), *Intolerance* and *Broken Blossoms.* She was more than ninety years old when she starred in Anderson's *The Whales of August* (1987).

Brian Glover   A schoolteacher and wrestler who turned actor for Ken Loach's *Kes*, and who worked with Anderson on *The Changing Room, O Lucky Man!, Life Class, What the Butler Saw* (1975) and *Britannia Hospital.*

Frank Grimes   Irish actor who came to notice winning a 1970 Tony nomination for *Borstal Boy.* First worked with Anderson on *The Farm* (1973) and thereafter was a featured player in much of his film and theatre work. He wrote *The Fishing Trip*, which Anderson directed at The Warehouse, Croydon, in 1991.

Richard Harris   Powerful Irish actor, replaced Peter O'Toole in the film version of *The Long and the Short and the Tall* (1961), caught the eye in a one-scene role in *The Guns of Navarone* (1961), played alongside Brando in *Mutiny on the Bounty* (1962) and won his first Academy Award nomination for *This Sporting Life.* Anderson also directed him in a one-man show of Gogol's *The Diary of a Madman* (1963). He walked out of Anderson's 1964 theatrical production of *Julius Caesar* and 1966 production of *Dylan.* Plans for Anderson and Harris to film *Wuthering Heights* and *Dylan* came to nothing.

Rex Harrison   A film star in Britain from the 1930s (under contract to Alexander Korda). World famous after stealing *Cleopatra* from Elizabeth Taylor (1962) and for his Oscar-winning performance as Henry Higgins in *My Fair Lady* (1964). He had six wives including Rachel Roberts and Elizabeth Harris (Richard's ex-wife). Anderson directed him on Broadway in *The Kingfisher* (1978).

Jocelyn Herbert   Hugely influential theatre designer noted for her work with Samuel Beckett, Tony Harrison, Tony Richardson, John Dexter and Lindsay Anderson. First worked with Anderson on the seminal production of *Serjeant Musgrave's Dance* (1959) and thereafter was always his first choice. She designed his productions of *Julius Caesar, Inadmissible Evidence, Home, The Changing Room, Life Class, What the Butler Saw, Hamlet* (1979), *Early Days* and *Stages*; and the films *If . . . , O Lucky Man!* and *The Whales of August.*

Oscar Lewenstein   Impresario. General Manager of the Royal Court Theatre from 1952; artistic director from 1972 to 1975. Associate producer of Tony Richardson's *Tom Jones*, Richard Lester's *The Knack* and Anderson's *The White Bus.*

Sandy Lieberson   Agent, whose clients included Anderson, Sergio Leone and The Rolling Stones, who became President in Charge of Production at Twentieth Century Fox.

Tadeusz Lomnicki   Legend of the Polish theatre, appeared in films by Andrzej Wajda and Krzysztof Kieslowski. Anderson directed him in Warsaw in *Inadmissible Evidence* (1966).

Arthur Lowe   A household name from playing Captain Mainwaring in TV's *Dad's Army*, worked with Anderson on *This Sporting Life, The White Bus, If . . . . , O Lucky Man!* (for which he won a BAFTA award) and *Britannia Hospital.*

Malcolm McDowell   Popular British actor who made his film debut in *If . . . .* , starred in Kubrick's *A Clockwork Orange*, killed Captain Kirk in *Star Trek Generations* and excelled in Robert Altman's *The Company.* Worked with Anderson on the Mick Travis trilogy (*If . . . . , O Lucky Man!* and *Britannia Hospital*) and in the theatre in *In Celebration* (1984) and *Holiday* (1987). Anderson directed him in a 1980 American TV production of *Look Back in Anger*, and cast him in the lead role of the unrealised film of *The Monster Butler.*

Michael Medwin   British actor turned film producer, who oversaw *If . . . .* and *O Lucky Man!* (in which he also acted). In the theatre Anderson cast him as Dr Prentice in *What the Butler Saw* (1975).

Miroslav Ondricek (Mirek)   Czech cinematographer responsible for the 'look' of the films of the Czech New Wave. Worked with Anderson on *The White Bus, If . . . .* and *O Lucky Man!.* Won Academy Award Nominations for Milos Forman's *Ragtime* (1981) and *Amadeus* (1984).

Joan Plowright   Theatrical star who married Laurence Olivier in 1960. Worked with Anderson in the theatre on *The Seagull* (1975), *The Bed Before Yesterday* (1975) and *The Cherry Orchard* (1983), on the film of *Britannia Hospital,* and was cast in the unrealised film of *The Monster Butler.*

Alan Price   Musician. Internationally famous for his work with The Animals, Bob Dylan and Georgie Fame. First worked with Anderson on *Home*, and was thereafter his first choice composer. Won a BAFTA award for *O Lucky Man!.*

Vladimir Pucholt   Star of several of Milos Forman's early films including *Konkurs* (1963) and *A Blonde in Love* (1965). With Anderson's help fled from communist Czecholslovakia to train as a doctor in England. Emigrated to Canada. Returned to the screen in 1999 in *Return to Paradise Lost*, directed by Vojtech Jasny.

Serge Reggiane   Italian-born actor/singer who lived in France until his death in 2001. Anderson helped him to stage *Hamlet* in Paris in 1954.

Karel Reisz   Czech-born British film-maker whose short film *We Are the Lambeth Boys* was shown in the final Free Cinema programme. His feature films include *Saturday Night and Sunday Morning* (1960), *The Gambler* (1974) and *The French Lieutenant's Woman* (1981). He produced *This Sporting Life.* Married to actress Betsy Blair (from 1963 until his death in 2002).

Ralph Richardson   One of the great theatrical 'knights', on stage from 1921. Worked with Anderson on *Home* (with John Gielgud), *The Kingfisher, Early Days*, and *O Lucky Man!.*

Tony Richardson   With George Devine, founded the English Stage Company at the Royal Court Theatre and, in the first season, directed the world premiere of *Look Back in Anger.*

Anderson showcased his short film *Momma Don't Allow* (1956) in the first Free Cinema programme. Richardson returned the favour by inviting Anderson to direct at the Royal Court. He won an Oscar for *Tom Jones* (1963). Married to Vanessa Redgrave from 1962 to 1967.

Rachel Roberts Welsh actress, worked with Anderson on *This Sporting Life, O Lucky Man!* and *The Old Crowd*, and on stage in *The Bed Before Yesterday*. Won BAFTA awards for *Saturday Night and Sunday Morning, This Sporting Life* and *Yanks*. Married to Rex Harrison from 1962 to 1971. Committed suicide in 1980.

Robert Shaw English actor best remembered as Quint in Spielberg's *Jaws*. Anderson directed him in the 1959 Royal Court production of *The Long and the Short and the Tall*. He played the Sheriff of Nottingham to Sean Connery's Robin Hood and Richard Harris's King Richard in *Robin and Marian* (1975), one of many 'Shaw' projects that Anderson turned down.

David Sherwin Screenwriter of *If....*, *O Lucky Man!* and *Britannia Hospital*, and author of *Going Mad in Hollywood*, which chronicles his work with Anderson.

David Storey Wrote the novel and the subsequent screenplay of *This Sporting Life*, the unrealised screenplay of *Wuthering Heights*, and the film of *In Celebration*. In the theatre, Anderson directed the world premieres of Storey's *In Celebration* (1969), *The Contractor, Home, The Changing Room, The Farm, Life Class, Early Days, The March on Russia* and *Stages* (1992).

Acknowledgements

Lindsay Anderson's diaries form part of the Lindsay Anderson Collection – an inexhaustible wonderland of manuscripts and memorabilia, including the core of his library, his photographs and his leather jacket – housed at Stirling University. My thanks go to the staff of the University Library, in particular the porters, Gordon Willis, Robin Davis, Peter Kemp and the Collection's brilliant archivist, Karl Magee.

At Methuen, I'm indebted to Elizabeth Ingrams, who commissioned the book, to Peter Tummons, and to my editor, Mark Dudgeon, surely unique within his profession in that he put more in than he took out.

Special thanks to Lindsay's brother, Murray Anderson, and to Monty White, Lindsay's accountant.

Thank you John Arden, Alan Bennett, Paul Birchard, Kevin Brownlow, Kathy Burke, Brian Cox, Stephen Frears, William Gaskill, Richard Gere, John Haynes, the late Jocelyn Herbert, Anthony Hopkins, Hugh Hudson, Robbie Lantz, Sylvia Myles, Brian Pettifer, the great Ken Russell, David Sherwin, Lois Smith, Rupert Webster.

Many thanks to Aryan Argi, Steve Guillon, Ben Halligan, Richard Marquis-Hirsch, Joanna Ney.

Mum and Dad.

And thank you, Malcolm McDowell, whose global championing of Lindsay's name and works redefines what it means to be a star.

For permission to use photographs, acknowledgements to: The Lindsay Anderson Collection, University of Stirling: 1, 2, 3; Murray Anderson: 4, 9; George Courtenay Ward / Rank Organisation: 6, 7; Lewis Morley: 5; Nick Hale: 11, 12; Brian Pettifer: 13, 14; Leo Mirkine: 15; John Haynes: 16, 17, 23; Memorial Productions: 18, 30; Warner Brothers: 19; David Montgomery: 21; Reg Wilson: 22; Frank Connor: 26, 27; Alive Productions: 28; Christopher Terry: 29.

Index

Films are listed in the index under their titles; plays are listed under their titles followed by the authors' names; books are listed under the names of their authors.

References that occur only in the footnotes are indicated by the page numbers in brackets.

Page numbers in **bold type** indicate main entries in the 'Key Figures' section. The contents of that section, and of the Chronology, are not otherwise indexed.

Abbreviations used in the index are: LA for Lindsay Anderson; NT for the National Theatre; RCT for the Royal Court Theatre.